Computer law

Fourth edition

Colin Tapper

Longman
London and New York

Longman Group UK Limited,
Longman House, Burnt Mill, Harlow,
Essex CM20 2JE, England
and Associated Companies throughout the world.

First published 1978
Second edition 1982
Third edition (first paperback edition) 1983
Second impression 1986

ISBN 0-582-02481-1 PPR
ISBN 0-582-05932-1 CSD

Printed and Bound in Great Britain
at the Bath Press, Avon

Contents

Part 3   Procedure   **363**

Table of cases

Table of Cases

Table of Cases

Table of Legislation

(c) *Other legislation*

Table of abbreviations

A *Atlantic Reporter (First series)*
A.2d *Atlantic Reporter (Second series)*
A.C. *Appeal Cases*
A.C.C.L. *Applied Computer and Communications Law*
A.C.T. *Australian Capital Territory*
A.D. *Appellate Division*
ADAPSO *Association of Data Processing Services*
Alb. L.R. *Albany Law Review*
A.L.J. *Australian Law Journal*
All E.R. *All England Reports*
A.L.R. *Australian Law Report*
A.L.R. Ann. *American Law Reports Annotation*
A.L.R. Fed. *American Law Reports Federal*
Ariz. St.L.J. *Arizona State Law Journal*
Auckland U.L.R. *Auckland University Law Review*

Beav. *Beavon*
B.C.C.A. *British Columbia Court of Appeal*
Boston U.L.R. *Boston University Law Review*
Buff. L.R. *Buffalo Law Review*
Burr. *Burrows*
Bus. L *Business Lawyer*
C.A. *Court of Appeal*
Cal. App. *California Appeals*
Cal. Rptr. *California Reporter*
Cal. L.R. *California Law Review*
C.B. *Common Bench*
C.C.A *Court of Criminal Appeal*
C.C.C. *Canadian Criminal Cases*
C.C.C.R. *Court for Crown Case Reserved*
C.C.P.A. *Court of Claims and Patent Appeals*
C.F.R. *Code of Federal Regulations*
Ch. *Chancery*
Cir. *Circuit*
C.J. *Chief Justice*
C.L.R. *Commonwealth Law Reports*
C.L. & Prac. *Computer Law and Practice*
C.L.S.R. *Computer Law Service Reporter*
Cm. *Command Paper*
Cmnd *Command Paper*

C.M.L.R.   *Common Market Law Report*
Col. L.R.   *Columbia Law Review*
Comp. Gen.   *Comptroller General's Decisions*
Comp. L.J.   *Computer Law Journal*
CONTU   *President's Commission on New Technological Uses*
Corn. L.Q.   *Cornell Law Quarterly*
Cour de Cass.   *Court of Cassation*
Cox C.C.   *Cox's Criminal Cases*
C.P.D.   *Cape Provincial Division*
C.P.R.   *Canadian Patent Reports*
C.R.   *Criminal Reports*
Cr. App. R.   *Criminal Appeal Reports*
Cr. App. R(S.)   *Criminal Appeal Reports of Sentencing Cases*
Cr.Ct.   *Crown Court*
Crim. L.J.   *Criminal Law Journal*
Crim. L.R.   *Criminal Law Review*
Crim. L.Q.   *Criminal Law Quarterly*

D.L.R.   *Dominion Law Reports*
De G. & S.   *De Gex and Smale*
Duke L.J.   *Duke Law Journal*
E. & B.   *Ellis and Blackburn*

E.C.   *European Court*
E.E.C.   *European Economic Community*
E.H.R.R.   *European Human Rights Reports*
E.I.P.R.   *European Intellectual Property Review*
Emory L.J.   *Emory Law Journal*
Exch   *Exchequer*

F.   *Federal Reporter (First Series)*
F.2d   *Federal Reporter (Second Series)*
F.C.A.   *Federal Court of Australia*
F.C.C.   *Fedearl Court of Canada*
F.D.C.L.J. *Federal Drugs and Consumer Law Journal*
F.L.R.   *Family Law Reports*
F.R.D.   *Federal Rules Decisions*
F.S.R.   *Fleet Street Reports*
F.Supp   *Federal Supplement*

Ga. L.R.   *Georgia Law Review*
Geo. Wash. L.R.   *George Washington Law Review*
G.S.A.   *General Services Administration*

H. & C.   *Hurlstone and Coltman*
Harv. J. of Leg.   *Harvard Journal of Legislation*
Harv. L.R.   *Harvard Law Review*
H.C.A.   *High Court of Australia*
H.L.   *House of Lords*
H.L.C.   *House of Lords Cases*

I.C.R.   *Industrial Cases Reports*
I.I.C.   *International Review of Industrial Property and Copyright Law*
I.R.L.R.   *Industrial Relations Law Reports*
Iowa L.R.   *Iowa Law Review*

J. of Bus. L.   *Journal of Business Law*
J.L.I.S. *Journal of Law and Information Science*
J. Pat. Off. S.   *Journal of the Patent Office Society*
J. Pub. L   *Journal of Public Law*

Jur. Jo.   *Jurimetrics Journal*

Kansas L.R.   *Kansas Law Review*
K.B.   *King's Bench*
K.B.D.   *King's Bench Division*

Law Soc. Gaz.   *Law Society's Gazette*
L.C.   *Lord Chancellor*
L.C.J.   *Lord Chief Justice*
L.J. Ch.   *Law Journal Chancery*
Ll.R.   *Lloyd's Reports*
L.Q.R.   *Law Quarterly Review*
Law Com.   *Law Commission*
Loy. L.R.   *Loyola Law Review*
L.R.R.M.   *Labor Relations Reference Manual*

M.C.C.   *MacGillivray's Copyright Cases*
Man. C.A.   *Manitoba Court of Appeal*
Mich. L.R.   *Michigan Law Review*
Minn. L.R.   *Minnsota Law Review*
Mo. L.R.   *Missouri Law Review*
Mon. L.R.   *Monash Law Review*
M.R.   *Master of the Rolls*
M.U.L.L.   *Modern Uses of Logic in Law*

N.E.   *Northeastern Reporter (First series)*
N.E.2d   *Northeastern Reporter (Second series)*
N.P.   *Nisi Prius*
New L.J.   *New Law Journal*
Notre Dame L.R.   *Notre Dame Law Review*
N.S.S.C   *Nova Scotia Supreme Court*
N.S.W.L.R.   *New South Wales Law Reports*
N.S.W.U.L.R. *New South Wales University Law Review*
N.T.,   *Northestern Reporter (First series)*
N.W.2d   *Northwestern Reporter (Second series)*
N.Y.S.   *New York Supplement (Second series)*
N.Y.S.2d   *New York Supplement (Second series)*
N.Y.U.L.R.   *New York University Law Review*
N.Z.L.J.   *New Zealand Law Journal*
N.Z.L.R.   *New Zealand Law Reports*

O.J.L.S.   *Oxford Journal of Legal Studies*
Ok. L.R.   *Oklahoma Law Review*
Ont. H.C.   *Ontario High Court*
Ott. L.R.   *Ottawa Law Review*

P.   *Pacific Reporter (First series)*
P.2d   *Pacific Reporter (Second series)*
P.A.T.   *Patent Appeal Tribunal*
Pat. Off   *Patent Office*
Pat. Trademark and Copy. J   *Patent, Trademark and Copyright Journal*
P.C.   *Privy Council*
P.D.A   *Probate, Divorce and Admiralty*
P.L.   *Public Law*

Q.B.   *Queen's Bench*
Q.B.D.   *Queen's Bench Division*
Qd. R.   *Queensland Reports*
Q.W.N.   *Queensland Weekly Notes*

R. & R.   *Russell and Ryan*
R.P.C.   *Reports of Patent Cases*
R.T.R.   *Road Traffic Reports*
Rutg. L. & C. T. L. J..   *Rutgers Law and Computer Technology Law Journal*
S.A.   *South Africa*
San Diego L.R.   *San Diego Law Review*
Santa Clara L.R.   *Santa Clare Law Review*
Santa Clara C. & H.T.L.J.   *Santa Clare Computer and High Technology Law Journal*
S.A.S.R.   *South Australian State Reports*
S.C.C.   *Supreme Court of Canada*
S.C.C.R.   *Scottish Criminal Case Reports*
S.C.F.C.   *Full Supreme Court*
S.C.R.   *Supreme Court Reports*
S.Ct.R.   *Supreme Court Reporter*
S.E.   *Southeastern Reporter (First series)*
S.E.2d   *Southeastern Reporter (Second series)*
S.I.   *Statutory Instrument*
S.L.C.   *Scottish Law Commission*
So.   *Southern Reporter (First series)*
So.2d   *Southern Reporter (Second series)*
S.R.I.   *Stanford Research Institute*
Stan. L.R.   *Stanford Law Review*
Stark   *Starkie*
S.W.   *Southwestern Reporter (First series)*
S.W.2d   *Southwestern Reporter (Second series)*

Tas. S.R.   *Tasmania State Reports*
T.C.   *Tax Cases*
Tex. S.U.L.R.   *Texas Southern University Law Review*

U.C.C.   *Uniform Commercial Code*
U.C.C.R   *Uniform Commercial Code Reporter*
U. Chi. L. R.   *University of Chicago Law Review*
U. Pa. L. R.   *University of Pennsylvania Law Review*
U. Pitt. L.R.   *University of Pittsburgh Law Review*
U.S.   *United States*
U.S.C.   *United States Code*
U.S.C.C.N.   *United States Code and Congressional News*
U.S.P.Q.   *United States Patent Quarterly*
U. Tor. L.J.   *University of Toronto Law Journal*
U. Wash. L.Q.   *University of Washington Law Quarterly*

V.C.   *Vice Chancellor*
V.R.   *Victoria Reports*
VDU   *Video Display Unit*

Wash. and Lee L.R.   *Washington and Lee Law Review*
W.P.   *Working Paper*

Yale L.J.   *Yale Law Journal*

Preface

This is the fourth edition of *Computer Law*. Or is it? The first edition was published in 1978, and as the first monograph in its field attempted to introduce the subject of the law as it applied to computers. That edition was deliberately and squarely based upon the relatively few decided cases and enacted pieces of legislation dealing specifically and explicitly with computers. Most of the secondary literature was perused, and much of it summarised. The second and third editions which appeared in 1982 and 1983 amounted to reprints of the original text of the 1978 edition, supplemented by a new last chapter which attempted to draw attention to further developments. On this occasion the opportunity has been taken to re-write and to re-organise the entire text. In so doing the number of chapters has been increased, as has the total length of the book.

It is always desirable to take a fresh look at a subject, and in this case two closely linked factors contributed to the decision. The first relates to the basic subject matter of the book. It is concerned with computers as we all understand them. No attempt is made to define computers, nor does the book contain any account of their operations. While this was, perhaps, a bold step to take in 1978, by 1988 it could more readily be justified on account of the vastly increased penetration of computers into everyday life. Most schoolchildren are today introduced to computers at school, many homes now number them among the appliances they contain, few small businesses do without them, and virtually all large ones are totally dependent upon them. Microprocessors are increasingly built into everyday pieces of machinery such as cars and domestic gadgetry. Databases are available through teletext services, and transmitted through a network of public and private communication systems by means of modems, facsimile machines and personal computers to remote individual users. Such basic tasks as writing, calculating and storing information have been transformed by the application to them of computer technology. This penetration has been facilitated by the ever-increasing power and decreasing cost of computing. The power of large computer installations has been increasing at a similar rate to that of small, thus vastly extending the range of applications penetrated by the technology at the top as well as at the bottom end of the market. Ordinary production machines can already perform 4 thousand million floating point operations per second. The most significant developments in the law have responded to this expansion and shift of focus. From this point of view the most significant features are the increase in the consumer market for computers, and the more widespread use of databases. The implications for the law permeate every part of the book. On the property side it means that in a mass-market greater weight has to be placed upon intellectual property concepts to combat infringement than upon contractual restraints since the lengthening of the chains of supply has divorced users from contractual relations with producers. There is also greater pressure to work to uniform standards so as to facilitate data transmission between applications. In the liability area the diffusion of facilities and data has increased vulnerability to crime and intrusion upon personal privacy, while the increased market penetration has emphasised a new consumer-based dimension to the problems of contract and tort. Finally, in the area of procedure the very ubiquity of computer operations means that to an ever-increasing extent evidence needs to be sought from computers for the conduct of an increased volume of computer-related litigation.

This increased strain upon legal provision is reflected in an even more dramatic expansion in the law's response. In 1978 when the first edition of this work appeared it was the only general monograph on the subject in English. That edition attempted to consider all of the specifically computer-related primary source material in the United Kingdom and a large part of that in the United States. Most secondary legal commentary in English specifically related to computers was taken into account, and much of it summarised. A series of searches on LEXIS gives some indication of the expansion of primary materials. The searches were conducted for references to the word 'computer' in items in existence in 1977, just before the first edition, and then for similar references in 1987. In the United States there were, in 1977, 291 federal cases and 246 state cases in which the word appeared; by 1987 these figures had increased to 963 federal cases and 873 state cases, an increase of some 330 and 354 per cent respectively. In the United Kingdom it was also possible to take into account references in statutory materials. Similar searches revealed that references in cases had increased from only 20 cases up to 1977 to 102 by 1987, a 510 per cent increase, while in terms of statutory sections the increase was from 28 up to 1977 to 97 by 1987, an increase of 346 per cent. Such huge increases have however been far out-stripped by the expansion of commentary. In many small parts of the subject there is already a vast literature comprising encyclopaedias, monographs and specialist journals. Bibliographies in some areas number their pages in hundreds. It has been impossible even to attempt to peruse all of the available material. Paradoxically this vast increase in the amount of material which renders the task of presenting a summary so much more difficult makes the need for such a work even more acute.

In the introduction to the first edition I justified devoting a book denominated by its non-legal subject-matter upon the basis that computers operate in so different a way that they justify separate treatment. That view is now widely accepted. Indeed, it can be argued that it has been taken too far, and that some commentators have concentrated so exclusively upon the specific problems of the computer as to ignore the need to integrate the treatment of computers into that of surrounding and interlocking areas of the law. One of the worst examples of such tunnel-vision is exhibited in relation to the law of evidence in the United Kingdom where special rules are proposed to handle the admissibility of computer output different from those applying to other business documents, apparently quite oblivious of the arbitrary results of having different regimes for the output of word processors and electric typewriters, for example. From a commentator's point of view the need to explain the interaction of ordinary rules and special rules relating to computers imposes a need to indicate in a very short space the basic principles of almost the whole range of legal subjects. The commentator must range from intellectual property to evidence, from competition law to privacy, and from contract to crime. No one can be a master of all. I do not pretend to be. Every legal reader will know more about at least some of the topics dealt with. A possible answer to this problem is to have a team of authors. The disadvantage may then lie in coordination and coherence of approach. If there is a need for a short unified summary of the law, it is felt that there is no real substitute for the single author. At least everyone will know who to blame for any deficiencies.

This edition seeks to accomplish the same task as its predecessors, and it employs the same basic philosophy. It is intended to provide an introduction to the subject for a newcomer, or for a lay reader, but at the same time to provide some discussion and some leads of interest to the more expert legal reader. This last category, it may be remarked, is now much greater than it was ten years ago. There are now many more practitioners with substantial expertise in the field, and many firms have special departments or individual partners who are expert in the law of high technology. Such practitioners have unique opportunities for insight into the working practices of the computer industry, manifested in the drafting of agreements which never give rise to serious disputes, the negotiation of disputes which never give rise to litigation, and the settlement of litigation which never comes to court. Many of the same experts also work behind the scenes advising and lobbying in the preliminary stages of legislation. While only occasionally acting in such a role, the author gratefully acknowledges the opportunities to meet such experts, and to secure the benefit of their wisdom, by way of informal contact, and especially through the work of the London Computer Group supported by IBC Legal Studies and Services Ltd.

It is still the case that the United States provides the greatest repository of materials in English on the subject matter of this book. In many areas there is no United Kingdom case or statute to illustrate or govern explicitly the application of general legal principle to computers. The technique of including copious reference to the law of the United States for the purposes of illustration and comparison has been retained. It is a practice which has been widely adopted by courts both in the United Kingdom and in other Commonwealth jurisdictions. The author is well aware of the hazards of expounding a system of law different from his own, but if the subject is to be presented adequately there seems no alternative. However, it is stressed that the exposition is for the purposes of illustration and comparison; reference should be made to the principal domestic United States sources for fuller treatment of particular topics.

Although the general approach has been retained from previous editions, the organisation of the material has been changed. The whole of the law is now expressed in the main body of the text of this edition, so there is no longer the need, as in its two predecessors, to consult both main text and supplementary chapter. The book has now been divided into more chapters, and they are grouped together into three somewhat uneven parts, dealing respectively with property, liability and procedure. The first part, on 'property', covers the topics previously dealt with in the first chapter. There has been so much development that it has been necessary to devote separate chapters to the law of patent, copyright and trade secrets or confidence. It has also been possible to add further coverage of other aspects of the law of trade competition, such as misappropriation, unfair competition, passing off and trade marks. The part entitled 'liability' merely groups together the four chapters in the previous edition dealing respectively with the law of contract, tort, crime and privacy. The final part on procedure has divided discussion between the law of evidence and that of procedure. The bibliography is still offered merely as an abbreviated introduction to the available literature, but has necessarily expanded to reflect in part the expansion of commentary in this area.

Within each chapter there has been considerable development in the period since the first edition. Some of it has been driven by the passage of major pieces of legislation. In the United Kingdom this period has seen the completely new Copyright, Designs and Patents Act 1988. Many provisions of this legislation affect the law relating to computers, and many are at present submerged in obscurity which only their being brought into force and litigated can illuminate. A wholly new type of intellectual property has been created to deal with chip topographies, in the United States by legislation and in the United Kingdom by regulations. There has also been major legislation in the field of privacy in the shape of the Data Protection Act 1984. It is possible that major legislation may be forthcoming in relation to the law of crime and breach of confidence where there have been considerable preliminary stirrings in the shape of reports and discussion documents. More minor legislation in the shape of the Criminal Justice Act 1988 has affected the relevant parts of the law of evidence. In the United States, as mentioned above, there have been extensive modifications to the United States Code so far as it relates to copyright both to accommodate semiconductor chips and to adjust to computer technology more generally. There has been considerable legislation both at federal and state level in such fields as crime, trade secret misappropriation and privacy. More minor legislation has been addressed to contractual and tortious issues, especially in the field of consumer protection and bankruptcy.

I have attempted to state the law as it was at 31 December 1988, though looking forward to the provisions enacted at that time, but not by then brought into force. 1 am conscious of having had to treat some subjects more cursorily than 1 would have wished in the interest of limiting the inevitable increase in the length of the book, and the time taken to produce it. 1 appreciate that for this, and other reasons, errors may be found. 1 shall be grateful to be told of them.

It is customary at this point to offer thanks to one's secretary. Mine are due to XyWrite III Plus without whose inestimable assistance 1 could not have hoped to produce this text.

Part 1

Property

The computer can be considered as bearing a similar relationship to the human mind as most other machines bear to the human body. It enables tasks to be performed without the expenditure, at least at the time of performing them, of quite so much human effort. It has achieved its great success largely because of its speed and versatility. Because it works so fast it can, by the aggregation of vast numbers of simple basic operations, capable of being performed conditionally upon the performance of others, perform very complex tasks. Because these operations are so basic they can be assembled in any number of different ways to perform an almost infinite range of different tasks. It may be compared to the way in which a strictly limited number of letters of the alphabet can be combined together to create all the words of a language. Similarly groups or modules of instructions can be combined and permuted so as to complete virtually any intellectual task just as the words of a language can be so used as to express virtually any thought.

Computers pose special problems for the law of intellectual property because they are not, like other machines, merely the product of human intellect, but in addition mimic its functions. These effects are achieved against a background of rapid technological and commercial change. In the primeval world of the first edition of this work the landscape was dominated by vast dinosaurs of computers, the exclusive preserve of a few large users, more often than not financially secure, trustworthy, competently manned, and enjoying a close relationship with their supplier, often in those days combining the rôles of designer, manufacturer, programmer and vendor. That world has gone for ever. The dinosaur has not yet become quite extinct, but no longer dominates the landscape. It is now largely populated by a wide variety of smaller machines, some general and some special purpose, whose users and owners cover the whole spectrum of wealth, competence and integrity. The supply industry has become correspondingly fragmented into colonies of designers, manufacturers, assemblers, programmers, distributors, dealers and retailers. Because so many of the ultimate users possess such limited computing skills, partly because their main expertise lies elsewhere, a wholly new software industry has developed to deliver to such customers products which they can use without needing to modify or even to understand them. It is further necessary that such products be capable of running on the widest possible variety of machine, and in combination with the widest possible range of other products. Such compatibility is unobtainable except by detailed reference to the points of interaction, or interfaces. In the age of the dinosaur it was just about possible to survive in a legal sense on a basic staple of contractual relations, supplemented to a limited extent, in the case of systems delivered to customers, by a leavening from the laws of patent, copyright and trade marks; and in the case of those that were not delivered, by the law of trade secrets and confidentiality. The diversification of parties at both ends of an ever-lengthening chain has reduced the utility of the law of contract, and the law of intellectual property has had to take more of the strain in an increasingly complicated situation. A major complicating factor is the increased importance of software in the market place which creates serious conceptual problems for the two major planks of the law of intellectual property, patent and copyright. In brief and crude terms the law of patent has traditionally protected the inventor by granting him a limited monopoly over the exploitation of his invention; and the law of copyright has traditionally protected the writer, by granting him an exclusive right to reproduce his work. In each case the idea, whether of invention or work, was protected only to the extent that it had progressed to the stage of physical implementation, typically as machine or writing. The problem becomes acute when the new step consists of the use of the computer to automate a mental process. It is exacerbated when it is understood that such automation may either take the form of a physical arrangement of tangible elements, or that of a set of instructions which can replicate the same result when fed into a highly versatile standard machine. On the one hand the law of patent may be said to be inappropriate to protect such sets of instructions which seem in principle more akin to literary works; and on the other the law of copyright may be said to be inappropriate to cater for the means of controlling machines. The first two chapters in this part will examine the strains imposed upon the traditional areas of patent and copyright, and the nature of their response. The last two chapters will consider other areas of intellectual property, such as trade secrets, unfair competition, trade marks and passing off, and various suggestions for new and unique regimes specially designed to meet the peculiar problems presented by computer technology.

Chapter 1

Patent

The law of patent has its origin in the attempts of the early Stuart kings of England to secure sources of revenue free from parliamentary control. The royal prerogative was invoked to license, for a fee, the use of new inventions. In its modern form the law is more conventionally regarded as a method of encouraging inventors by granting a monopoly of its exploitation for a limited period. These considerations determine the basic structure of the law, namely that it is limited to what is demonstrably an invention, and for a limited period prevents any incursion into a specific area. Thus in order to secure a patent a method of new manufacture must be specified, and a particular area of application claimed. At the end of the period such specification can then be used by others as a springboard for further development, and so to advance the relevant art.

The law has to strike a careful balance between the need not to reduce the encouragement it offers to inventors to make their inventions known by allowing them to be too strictly confined during the limited period of monopoly, and on the other of inhibiting the enterprise of others too much by granting too wide a monopoly. It is in an effort to achieve the second of these aims that the law insists upon the invention having progressed to the area of practical application. To permit the discovery of natural phenomena or mere ideas to be monopolised would be to go too far.

There are differences between both the statutory regimes and their application in the United Kingdom and in the United States. In particular the question of the patentability of software has, in the United States, repeatedly engaged the attention of the Supreme Court, while in the United Kingdom it has been rarely ventilated, even in the lower courts. It is proposed first to compare the statutory framework in the two jurisdictions, very much in outline, and then to examine the way in which it has been applied to the area of computers by the courts, ending with an assessment of the rôle best played in this area by this branch of the law.

A. Statutory framework

In both jurisdictions patent is a creature of statute, and in the United States is supported by the express authorisation of the Constitution.[1] In both jurisdictions also the main body of legislation is of relatively recent origin, in the United States contained in title 35 of the United States Code,[2] and in the United Kingdom expressed in the Patents Act 1977.[3]

1. Patentable subject matter

The Patents Act 1977 provides in section 1 that,

(1) A patent may be granted only for an invention[4] in respect of which the following conditions are satisfied, that is to say-
(a) the invention is new;
(b) it involves an inventive step;
(c) it is capable of industrial application;
(d) the grant of a patent for it is not excluded by subsections (2) and (3) below[5]

while in the United States the conditions are encapsulated in section 101 of title 35 of the United States Code,

Whoever invents or discovers any new and useful process, machine, manufacture, or composition of matter, or any new and useful improvement thereof, may obtain a patent therefor, subject to the conditions and requirements of this title.

Although these provisions are different in form, they involve basically similar requirements which are further defined in subsequent provisions. Thus the Patents Act 1977 so elaborates the concepts of novelty,[6] an inventive step,[7] and industrial application,[8] while the United States Code defines those of novelty,[9] and that of non-obvious subject-matter.[10] A different approach is, however, adopted to classes of excluded subject-matter which are statutorily listed in section 1 of the Patents Act 1977 in the United Kingdom, but in the United States left to judicial exegesis of section 101.

2. Application

In both jurisdictions patents have to be applied for,[11] and it is a condition of grant that the applicant describe his invention sufficiently fully for a person skilled in the relevant art to reproduce it, and that the applicant claim protection in a well-defined area.[12] The purpose of these requirements is partly to enable the examiner to determine whether the alleged invention is truly novel and inventive, and partly so as to ensure that the monopoly will

---

1. Constitution of the United States Art. 1 sect. 8 cl.8.
2. Largely revised in 1972.
3. To some extent supplemented by the Copyright, Designs and Patents Act 1988
4. An invention may be either a product or a process, see sect. 60(1).
5. These sub-sections specify a number of exceptions, see below p. 6
6. Sect. 2.
7. Sect. 3.
8. Sect. 4.
9. 35 U.S.C. sect. 102.
10. 35 U.S.C. sect. 103, as amended by P.L. 98–622 of 1984.
11. And a fee paid.
12. Patents Act 1977 sect. 14(2)(b); 35 U.S.C. sect. 112.

not be granted too broadly, or without securing the public benefit of bringing the invention within the domain of eventual competitive exploitation.

3. Grant and term

If upon such an application the relevant conditions are found to be satisfied the office makes a grant which entitles the applicant to the exclusive right to exploit his invention as claimed in his application for, in the United Kingdom, a period of 20 years,[13] or, in the United States, of 17 years.[14]

4. Ownership

There is a clear difference between the two jurisdictions in their approach to inventions made by employees. Under the modern law of the United Kingdom, inventions made by employees are vested in their employers if either the invention was made in the course of general or specially assigned duties in such circumstances that an invention might reasonably be expected, or if because of the particular circumstances the employee could be regarded as under a special obligation to further the interests of his employer.[15] In the United States an invention normally inheres in the inventor, even though an employee,[16] subject only to express assignment, though such an assignment may be contractually required without violation of the Constitution,[17] and a term to such effect will be implied if an employee is employed specifically to make a particular invention.[18]

5. Infringement and remedies

In the United Kingdom the Patents Act 1977 distinguishes between the infringement of a product and of a process, in the former case prohibiting manufacture, use, disposal, offer, import, or even possession of the product, and in the latter case going beyond use of the process to prohibit use, disposal, offer, import or possession of a product obtained directly by use of the process.[19] The available remedies include injunction, delivery up or destruction, damages or an account of profits, and a declaration of the invalidity of the patent.[20] In the United States the manufacture, use or sale of a patented invention or active inducement of infringement constitutes

---

13. Patents Act 1977 sect. 25(1).
14. 35 U.S.C. sect. 154.
15. Patents Act 1977 sect. 39. Subject to compensation for the employee where the patent has resulted in outstanding benefit to the employer, sect. 40.
16. *Blum* v. *Commissioner of Internal Revenue* 183 F.2d 281 (3rd Cir., 1950).
17. *Hapgood* v. *Hewitt* 119 U.S. 226 (1886).
18. *Hebbard* v. *American Zinc and Lead Smelting Co.* 66 F. Supp. 113 (D.C.Mo., 1946)(aff. 161 F.2d 339) (8th Cir., 1947).
19. Sect. 60.
20. Sect. 61.

infringement.[21] The remedies include injunction,[22] damages,[23] and the award of attorney's fees.[24]

B. Application to computers

Computer hardware alone, like any other sort of machine, is clearly patentable upon satisfaction of the required conditions, and requires no further consideration here. Much more difficult questions relate to the extent to which inventive programs can be protected by patent law. The development of the law in this area has been so different in nature, pace and volume between the United Kingdom and the United States that it is best to consider the two jurisdictions separately.

1. United Kingdom

It might be thought to be a closed question in the United Kingdom whether or not programs can be protected by the law of patent since the Patents Act 1977, in its attempt to conform to the general provisions of the European Patent Convention 1973, provides in section 1 that,

(2) It is hereby declared that the following (among other things) are not inventions for the purpose of this Act, that is to say, anything which consists of-
(a) a discovery, scientific theory or mathematical method;
(b) a literary, dramatic, musical or artistic work or any other aesthetic creation whatsoever;
(c) a scheme, rule or method for performing a mental act, playing a game or doing business, or a program for a computer;
(d) the presentation of information
but the foregoing provision shall prevent anything from being treated as an invention for the purposes of this Act only to the extent that a patent or application for a patent relates to that thing as such.

It should also be noted that sub-section 5 empowers the Secretary of State by order[25] to vary the list of exclusions in sub-section 2 for the purpose of maintaining them in conformity with developments in science and technology.

The scheme of exclusions apparently reveals a comprehensive intention to preclude the protection of ideas as such. Computer programs might, quite apart from sub-section 2(c), be disqualified in appropriate cases as scientific theories, mathematical methods, methods of doing business, the presentation of information, or even as aesthetic creations thanks to the width of 'whatsoever'.[26] Doubts are raised however by the inclusion and terminology

---

21. 35 U.S.C. sect. 271.
22. 35 U.S.C. sect. 283, including both preliminary and final injunctions.
23. 35 U.S.C. sect. 284, defined to include an account of profits, and allowing for treble damages in cases of bad faith.
24. 35 U.S.C. sect. 285. In the United States, unlike the United Kingdom, costs do not normally follow the event.
25. Subject to approval by resolution of both Houses of Parliament.
26. Though the practical effect of the exclusion may be open to doubt since those most inclined to credit programs with aesthetic quality are also likely to be those most anxious to secure protection for them, namely their authors.

of the enigmatic qualification. It can be best understood, first by considering the previous law; then the guidelines suggested for its interpretation by the European Patent Office, which was originally responsible for its inclusion; and finally by examining the latest United Kingdom case law on the question.

(a) The old law

Before the passage of the Patents Act 1977 controversy had arisen in the United Kingdom whether a computer program was patentable as a 'manner of new manufacture' as required under the old law. This notion extended to processes of manufacture, but by general consent did not cover purely mental functions, for example ideas as such, or methods of calculation. One test was whether or not a 'vendible product' had been created. In reliance upon this doctrine the practice of the British Patent Office was expressed in a note issued by the Office in February 1969 to be that,

Patents are not granted for computer programmes expressed as such. No objection is, however, raised in respect of inventions for novel methods of programming computers to operate in a specified way, or for computers so programmed, or for tape etc. having recorded on it a novel programme to control a computer to operate in a stated way. Nor, in general, is objection taken to inventions involving new uses of computers in controlling manufacturing processes or to methods of testing, involving novel programmes, for computers under manufacture.

That attitude seemed to enshrine the views first expressed by a superintending examiner in *Slee and Harris's Application*.[27] As no case had, by 1970, come before the Court the Banks Committee felt unable to express a firm view of the then state of the law, though some doubt was cast upon the validity of the distinction between claims drafted so as to relate to a piece of machinery, or to a computer controlled process, and claims drafted so as to relate to programs or methods for operating a computer as such.[28] The whole question of the patentability of computer programs was subsequently re-ventilated by the Patent Appeal Tribunal in *Burroughs Corporation (Perkins') Application*.[29] The claims in question there were for a method of transmitting data between a central computer and remote terminals. The superintending examiner disallowed the claim on the basis that the reasoning of the decision in *Slee and Harris's Application*[30] operated to bar claims for the simple processing of information. It was further decided that the practice of the Patent Office was to rely upon that decision to refuse patents claimed as methods of transmitting data or for controlling a computer, but to allow them for computers programmed in a particular way, or for programs embodied in a physical form,[31] and for methods of programming a computer. The Court rejected as unrealistic the purported distinction between methods of controlling and methods of programming a computer. It further overruled

27. [1966] R.P.C. 194, Pat. Off.
28. Cmnd. 4407 para. 474 (1970).
29. [1974] R.P.C. 147, P.A.T.
30. [1966] R.P.C. 194, Pat. Off.
31. Following the decision in *Gever's Application* [1970] R.P.C. 91, P.A.T.

Slee and Harris's Application[32] so far as it countenanced the old 'vendible product' test. Instead the Court argued that,[33]

If the bare method or idea is also clothed by the patentee in his application with a practical garment in the shape of apparatus enabling that method or idea to be realised in practice, it should no longer be regarded as a naked conception, for it has found a practical embodiment in the apparatus.

It is conceded that a mere plan not embodied in a physical modification of apparatus would not be patentable. It is thus dubious whether a program written on a standard programmer's pad would qualify. On the other hand the Court clearly believed that computer programs should be capable of being patented,[34]

in our view computer programmes which have the effect of controlling computers to operate in a particular way, where such programmes are embodied in physical form are proper subject matter for letters patent.

The Court went on to stress the desirability of achieving some internationally consistent solution to the problem, adverting to the then forthcoming review of patent legislation in the United Kingdom.

The last case relating to computer programs to be decided in the United Kingdom under the old law was *International Business Corporation's Application*.[35] It approved the reasoning in *Burroughs Corporation (Perkins') Application*[36] in deciding that the crucial question was whether or not the claim related to the computer as programmed, and did not explicitly extend either to a standard computer as such, or to a scheme for doing business. The software in the case was a program designed to calculate automatically the selling price of stock or shares by comparing a set of buying and selling orders. Although it was accepted that the scheme was not itself novel, and that a completely standard computer could be programmed to perform it, the Court still upheld the claim as,

a method involving operating or controlling a computer in which, so far as the contested claims are concerned, the computer is programmed in a particular way or programmed in physical form to control a computer so that it will operate in accordance with his method. The method is embodied in the programme and in the apparatus in physical form and in our view the superintending examiner was right.

Much the same process of development took place in Canada, where guidelines[37] issued by the Patent Office making the same basic distinction as that expressed in the British Patent Office note of February 1969 were mirrored in a decision of the Patent Office Appeal Board[38] eroding the 'vendible product' doctrine there also. There too the decision was taken

---

32. [1966] R.P.C. 194, Pat. Off.
33. At 158.
34. At 161.
35. [1980] F.S.R. 564, Pat.
36. [1974] R.P.C. 147, P.A.T.
37. Canadian Patent Office Record 28 Dec. 1971 p. viii.
38. *Waldbaum's Application* Canadian Patent Office Record 18 Jan. 1972 p. vii though this case was influenced by the USPCA decision in *Benson* subsequently reversed by the Supreme Court in *Gosschalk v. Benson* 409 U.S. 63 (1972).

against a background of Committee recommendations hostile to the patentability of computer programs.[39]

(b) European Patent Office guidelines

It is somewhat ironic that the original impetus behind a strong movement to limit, or even to eliminate, the patenting of computer programs came from the United States in the report of the President's Commission in 1966.[40] This view, largely inspired by practical considerations, was speedily echoed in France where it was implemented in new legislation explicitly excluding computer programs from patentable subject matter,[41] a provision widely construed by the Courts.[42] This same approach seeped into international provisions by way of the Patent Co-operation Treaty 1970 which provided in rules 39 and 67 that computer programs were not required to be the subject of search by the appropriate international searching agency to the extent that such bodies were not equipped to search the prior art.[43] These definitions were then repeated in a slightly modified form as article 52 of the European Patent Convention, a form in all relevant respects identical to that enacted as Patents Act 1977 sect. 1(2).[44] The European Patent Office published guidelines for the interpretation of these provisions. The function of these guidelines is partly to mould the practice of the relevant officials in the European Patent Office, and partly to inform the public of the approach which they will adopt. However, the guidelines are not binding upon the ultimate interpreters of the European Patent Convention, namely the Boards of Appeal. So, if and when, these Boards become apprised of a case involving the patentability of computer programs some revision of the guidelines may become necessary. The guidelines were quite explicit about the treatment of computer programs,

A computer program may take various forms, e.g. an algorithm, a flow chart or a series of coded instructions which can be recorded on a tape or other machine-readable record medium, and can be regarded as a particular case of either a mathematical method or a presentation of information. If the contribution to the known art resides solely in a computer program, then the subject matter is not claimable in whatever manner it may be presented in the claims. For example, a claim to a computer characterised by having the particular program stored in its memory or to a process for operating a computer under control of the program would be as objectionable as a claim to the program *per se* or the program when recorded on magnetic tape.

These guidelines suggest a more restrictive interpretation than that accorded by the then existing law of the United Kingdom. Thus it could hardly be maintained as stated in the 1969 guidelines issued by the British Patent Office that programs recorded on tape would be patentable.[45] It was also

---

39. Economic Council of Canada 'Report on Intellectual and Industrial Property' (1971) at p. 103.
40. 'To promote the Useful Arts' (1966) S.Doc. No.5 90th Congress Ist session (1967).
41. Patent Act 1968 Art. 7 para. 2(3)
42. *Re Mobil Oil Corp.* [1973] **PIBD** 111 197.
43. This reflects not only the recommendation but also the reasoning of the President's Commission.
44. See p. 6 above.
45. See p. 7 above.

more restrictive than the position which developed in the United States in the aftermath of *Diamond* v. *Diehr*.[46] New, and expanded, guidelines were accordingly published in 1985,

A computer program claimed by itself or as a record on a carrier, is unpatentable irrespective of its content. The situation is not normally changed when the computer program is loaded into a known computer. If however the subject matter as claimed makes a technical contribution to the known art, patentability should not be denied merely on the ground that a computer program is involved in its implementation. This means, for example, that program-controlled machines and program controlled manufacturing and control processes should normally be regarded as patentable subject matter. It follows also that, where the claimed subject matter is concerned only with the program-controlled internal working of a known computer, the subject matter could be patentable if it provides a technical effect. As an example consider the case of a known data-processing system with a small fast working memory and a larger but slower further memory. Suppose that the two memories are organised, under program control, in such a way that a process which needs more address space than the capacity of the fast working memory can be executed at substantially the same speed as if the process data were loaded entirely in that fast memory. The effect of the program in virtually extending the working memory is of a technical character that might therefore support patentability.

Where patentability depends on a technical effect the claim must be so drafted as to include all the technical features of the invention which are essential for the technical effect.

Where patentability is admitted then, generally speaking, product, process and use claims would be allowable.

In an explanation of these guidelines the Director of Legal Affairs at the European Patent Office has claimed[47] that article 52 was never intended to do more than restate the generally accepted position that ideas and methods before being translated into a particular application could not be patented. This may seem to ignore the real motivation which was the practical problems for examiners as a matter of history, but may nevertheless represent the current attitude as a matter of practice. He also argues that it is immaterial that the only novel element in an invention is the computer program if the invention as a whole is not excluded from being patentable. Thus if it exhibits a technical result an invention passes the first test, whether or not it includes a computer program. The invention, *as a whole*, is then to be considered from the point of view and novelty and not being obvious, so it does not matter at that stage that these characteristics derive exclusively from the program.

This view seems to have been vindicated by the Technical Board of Appeal of the European Patent Office in *Vicom Systems Inc.'s Application*.[48] In that case the Board overruled the view of the Examining Division that a new method of processing signals in a computer was an unpatentable mathematical method. Instead, it held on the apparatus claim that,[49]

---

46. 450 U.S. 175 (1981).
47. Gall, 'European Patent Office Guidelines 1985 on the protection of inventions relating to computer programs' 2 *Computer Law and Practice* 2 (1985).
48. Decision T208/84 [1987] Off. J. EPO 14.
49. Para. 15.

Generally claims which can be considered as being directed to a computer set up to operate in accordance with a specified program (whether by means of hardware or software) for controlling or carrying out a technical process cannot be regarded as relating to a computer program as such and thus are not objectionable under Article 52(2)(c) and (3) EPC.

(c) *The new law*

Few cases involving patents for computer-related subject matter were reported in the immediate aftermath of the Patents Act 1977, and none considered the effect of the qualification to section 1(2). It was however the central focus of the recent decision in *Merrill Lynch Inc.'s Application.*[50] The applicant sought to patent an automated securities trading system which would use a computer to assist market makers dealing in securities. The system as specified envisaged performance on an indefinite, but very wide, class of computers; and could be implemented in virtually any computer language.

The first point established in this connection was that the Patents Act 1977 was not to be construed as a mere re-enactment of the old law, and in particular that 'an invention' could not simply be equated with 'a manner of new manufacture' under the old law. This had been relied upon in this context since, on account of the ability to perform any given program by the construction of hardware, it had been argued that a 'means' claim could never be unpatentable in relation to the use of such a program. The Court took the view that the change of language prevented any such automatic endorsement of programs.

It might nevertheless be argued that even if programs are not automatically patentable, once the claim related to the program actually running on a given computer, that is 'the computer as programmed type of claim', then the claim necessarily related to patentable subject matter. In the examiner's view this was not automatic, but rather depended upon the nature of the function being performed, and unless the whole function of the system was to produce a new effect, it could not be argued that the requirement of novelty had been fulfilled.[51]

It remained to reconcile this conclusion with the language of section 1(2), and in particular with the qualification. It was argued for the applicant that the words 'as such' indicated that so long as the claim was not expressed in terms to be for 'a program', it was not excluded by section 1(2). The Court felt that so literal an approach, making all turn on the applicant's use of language could not have been intended by Parliament.[52] It was pointed out that so to construe the qualification distorted the words '*only to the extent that* a patent . . . relates to that thing [i.e. the program] as such', by equating their meaning to 'only if'. The construction adopted by the examiner, and upheld by the Court, was that while the qualification indeed implied that inventions are not automatically unpatentable just because they incorporate programs, it does not imply that all applications which do include new

---

50. [1988] R.P.C. 1, Pat.
51. At 4.
52. At 12.

programs are patentable so long only as they somehow avoid claiming the program in so many words. It is first necessary to consider whether the claim, taken as a whole, achieves a new effect. If it does, then it is not disqualified merely by the fact that the only novel element is the computer program. If it does not, and the only novel element is the program, then it is immaterial that it is the system as a whole, and not merely the program, which is claimed. The Court explained that,[53]

the wording 'only to the extent that' means that there cannot be a patentable invention in so far as the invention reads on the computer program itself, but if some practical (i.e. technical) effect is achieved by the computer or machine operating according to the instructions contained in the program, and such effect is novel and inventive (i.e. not obvious) a claim limited to that practical effect will be patentable, notwithstanding it is defined by that computer program.

By such a construction the Court was able to avoid the charge that it was running together the tests of patentability and novelty. In this case the only effect was a method of doing business, and this was unpatentable, however novel it might be. This does not however exclude cases where the effect is internal to the computer, but will apply only where such an effect is the intended final effect. Thus the decision can be reconciled with *Vicom System Inc.'s Application* [54] where a computer program had been involved and the intended effect had been simply to improve the performance of the internal operations of the computer. The United Kingdom Court would equally accept this as a technical effect. It should be noted that it was accepted that the European Patent Office guidelines would be persuasive in a United Kingdom Court on any question of the interpretation of cognate provisions of the Patents Act 1977,[55] and that judicial notice could be taken of decisions of the Board of Appeals of the European Patent Office.

Leave to appeal was refused, but as some claims were amended to specify a possibly novel combination of hardware the saga may not yet be complete. It seems however, that it has had the effect of interpreting the new law so as to reduce the latitude of the old, especially in eliminating the idea that it would always be possible to succeed on a claim for a computer 'as programmed'. Such claims prostituted reality to form; the innovation consisted of a new program, not of a new computer. However, it cannot be claimed that the new approach will always be easy to apply. The concept of 'technical effect' is not self-evident.[56] It may also be felt, despite the attempt of the Court to distinguish *Vicom Systems Inc.'s Application*,[57] that its tenor, and that of the 1985 guidelines to the European Patent Office Convention,[58] is now rather more generous than that prevailing in the United Kingdom.

53. At 12.
54. Decision T208/84 [1987] Off. J. EPO 14; see also a similarly expansive decision in the
.   Netherlands [1987] B.I.E. Nr. 42, 174 ([1987] 10 E.I.P.R. D-205)
55. See Patents Act 1977 sect. 130(7).
56. See von Hellfield, 'Protection of Inventions Comprising Computer Programs by the European and German Patent Offices', 2 *Computer Law and Practice* 182 (1986).
57. Decision T208/84 [1987] Off. J. EPO 14.
58. Certainly as understood by the organisation's own Director-General, see above p.10

It seems that the position in Canada is similar to that in the United Kingdom, comparing *Schlumberger* v. *Commissioner of Patents*[59] where a claim for a new method of processing oilwell data was refused with subsequent applications including more obvious effects, such as modulating tests of jet engines,[60] which have been allowed notwithstanding their inclusion of a novel computer program to help achieve the desired effect.[61] In Australia a more negative approach appears still to prevail.[62]

2. United States

The first cases to reach the courts in the United States adopted a liberal view towards the patentability of computer programs. It was first indicated in *Re Prater*[63] that a claim limited to particular mechanical apparatus as programmed might succeed, an indication consummated in *Re Bernhart*[64] where such a process claim was allowed. It was thus hardly surprising that the Court of Customs and Patent Appeals unanimously upheld an appeal from the Board of Appeals in *Re Benson*,[65] and decided that claims to a method for converting binary coded decimal notation to pure binary were patentable, even though not specifying any particular piece of equipment upon which the process was to be executed. References in one of the claims to a 're-entrant shift register' were conceded by the applicants not to relate to any particular apparatus. The result was achieved on the basis of the practical argument that the process became valuable only if performed upon a digital computer, though it could, as claimed, be performed perfectly accurately, though extremely tediously, by the use of no more than pencil and paper. *Benson* went to the Supreme Court, and was followed by no fewer than four further patent cases involving computers within ten years.

The first such case was thus *Gottschalk* v. *Benson*.[66] Justice Douglas handed down the opinion of a unanimous Court[67] disallowing the claim under section 101 of the Code as not amounting to patentable subject matter. The claim was, in the opinion of the Court, tantamount to a claim to patent an idea. The claim was cast as one for a process, and the Court, at one point, appeared to endorse the doctrine, previously enunciated in *Cochrane* v. *Deener*,[68] that transformation and reduction of an article 'to a different state or thing' is the clue to the patentability of a process claim that does not involve particular machines.[69] The statutory definition of a process as meaning 'a process, art or method and includ[ing] a new use of a known

---

59. 56 C.P.R. (2d) 204 (F.C.A., 1981).
60. E.g. *McDonald's Application* (1983) 7 E.I.P.R. D-17 (1985)
61. See also Hoffman, Grossman, Keane and Westley 'Protection for Computer Software: An International Overview Pt. 11' [1989] 1 E.I.P.R. 7 at 12, 13.
62. See e.g. *Telefon A/B L.M. Ericsson's Application* [1975] F.S.R. 49, A.P.O.
63. 415 F.2d 1393 (C.C.P.A., 1969).
64. 417 F.2d 1395 (C.C.P.A., 1969).
65. 441 F.2d 682 (C.C.P.A., 1971).
66. 409 U.S. 63 (1972).
67. Though Justices Stewart, Blackmun and Powell took no part.
68. 94 U.S. 780 (1876).
69. At 70.

process, machine, manufacture, composition of matter or material'[70] is not very illuminating. In *Gottschalk* v. *Benson* no article was to be so transformed or reduced and no particular machine was specified. The Court also seemed to be exercised by the fact that the only practical use of the algorithm was in connection with a digital computer, though it could, as noted above, have been performed using only pencil and paper. The Court thus felt that given the essential unspecificity and indeterminacy of potential computer applications, to have allowed the claim would indeed have pre-empted use of the algorithm, and have amounted to allowing an idea to be patented. Yet, as remarked above, the Court explicitly refrained from making any general pronouncement about the patentability of computer programs,[71]

It is argued that a process patent must either be tied to a particular machine or apparatus or must operate to change articles or materials to a 'different state or thing'. We do not hold that no process patent could ever qualify if it did not meet the requirements of our prior precedents. It is said that the decision precludes a patent for any program servicing a computer. We do not so hold.[71]

It is hardly surprising that this opinion was found to be rather opaque, and not only failed to reduce the volume of claims for the protection of computer programs, but contrived to confuse examiners and lower courts quite intolerably.

Among the rash of consequently split decisions in the Court of Customs and Patent Appeals was one relating to an application for a machine system for the automatic record keeping of bank cheques and deposits.[72] The claimant in that case had taken care to express some of his claims as being for a specific piece of apparatus, namely a computer in the IBM 1400 series, as programmed according to the specifications in the claim. It was for that reason that the majority of the Court felt able to distinguish the decision in *Gottschalk* v. *Benson*,[73]

the instant claims, in *apparatus*[74] form, do not claim or encompass a law of nature, a mathematical formula, or an algorithm. For these reasons, we do not find the holding of Benson to be applicable to claims of the type now before us.

Judge Rich had been the author of the Court's opinion in *Re Benson*[75] which had been subsequently overturned by the Supreme Court. In a loyal effort to follow that decision he felt impelled to dissent from his colleagues.[76] He pointed out that an apparatus claim which defined only broad means for embodying particular programs was really no different from a claim for a process constituted by the use of those programs. He felt that the fact that the claimant was seeking to sell programs, rather than machines, indicated where the essence of the claim lay. In view of more recent decisions of the

---

70. 35 U.S.C. sect. 100(b).
71. At 71.
72. *Re Johnston* 502 F.2d 765 (C.C.P.A., 1971).
73. 409 U.S. 63 (1972).
74. Original emphasis.
75. 441 F.2d 682 (C.C.P.A., 1971).
76. Baldwin, Lane and Miller JJ. Markey C.J. also dissented, but on different grounds.

Supreme Court it is helpful to quote the key passage from his judgment in full:[77]

I am quite familiar with the legal doctrine that a new program makes an old general purpose computer into a new and different machine. This court has been through that many times and I am not denying the validity of this principle – which partakes of the nature of a legal fiction when it comes to drafting claims. My problem is that, knowing the *invention*[78] to be a new program, I must decide whether it is patentable in any claimed form in view of *Benson*, whether claimed as a machine, a 'machine-system' or otherwise. I am probably as much – if not more – confused by the wording of the *Benson* opinion as many others. What the court *did*[79] in its *decision*[80] reversing the holding of this court that Benson's and Tabbot's method claims were patentable subject matter under section 101 contains a message that is loud and clear. If these claims are not to be patentable subject matter, neither, in my view are the claims here, regardless of difference in form. Benson et al. had a program invention too and they could have cast their claims in machine-system form just as appellant did. Every competent patent draftsman knows how to do that.

To the surprise of most commentators, and of counsel who had argued the point at some length in their briefs, the Supreme Court decided *Dann* v. *Johnston*[81] not on section 101 grounds, but by applying section 103 and rejecting the claim as obvious. On this point the Court unanimously[82] endorsed the view of the patent examiner, the Board of Appeals and Markey C.J. in the Court below. Once again the decision was inconclusive and cryptic. It is possible, however, with the benefit of hindsight, to see in the opinion an implicit affirmation of Rich J.'s rejection of the distinction between an apparatus and a process claim. In *Dann* v. *Johnston* the claim was expressed to be for apparatus as programmed. It is really not at all plausible to assert that this particular arrangement of charges and signals was obvious to anyone. All that was obvious was the use of data processing equipment, including the IBM 1400 series, to prepare accounts for customers of banks in this sort of way. In other words the *process* was obvious. This could be fatal to the success of a claim drafted as one for apparatus alone, if the distinction between an apparatus claim and a process claim were rejected, as Rich J. had rejected it in the Court below.

This view was endorsed by the Patent Office as indicated in its arguments in a number of subsequent cases,[83] and in an official pronouncement.[84] The majority of the judges in the Court of Customs and Patent Appeals took a

---

77. At 773.
78. Original emphasis.
79. Original emphasis.
80. Original emphasis.
81. 425 U.S. 219 (1976).
82. Justice Marshall delivered the opinion of the Court with Justices Blackmun and Stevens playing no part.
83. *Re Noll* 545 F.2d 141 (C.C.P.A., 1976); *Re Chatfield* 545 F.2d 152 (C.C.P.A., 1976); *Re Flook* 559 F.2d 21 (C.C.P.A., 1977); *Re Waldbaum* 559 F.2d 611 (C.C.P.A., 1977); *Re Warmus* 561 F.2d 816 (C.C.P.A., 1977); *Re de Castelet* 562 F.2d 1236 (C.C.P.A., 1977); *Re Richman* 563 F.2d 1026 (C.C.P.A., 1977), and *Re Freeman* 573 F.2d 1237 (C.C.P.A., 1978).
84. 954 O.G. 550 (1976) reported at 77 F.R.D. 104 (1978)

different view, and continued to read *Gottschalk* v. *Benson*[85] extremely narrowly. Judge Rich remained a frequent dissenter. Such a split between the Patent Office and the Court of Customs and Patent Appeals, between the majority of the judges in the Court and the judge who had himself helped to redraft the Patent Act on this very point,[86] and, at least in the result, between the Supreme Court and the Court of Customs and Patent Appeals was clearly unsatisfactory. Almost any of the cases could have been taken to the Supreme Court in order to resolve the issue.[87] *Re Flook*[88] was the final choice. It was, in some ways, an odd one. The claim was for a method of up-dating alarm limits in a catalytic hydrocarbon process. The method depended upon the use of an algorithm intended to be used in a computer to adjust the alarm limits automatically as the operation progressed. Argument concentrated upon whether or not the addition of steps in the process, that is the adjustment of the alarm limits, after, and consequential upon, the solution of the algorithm, was, by itself, sufficient to remove the case from the proscription of *Gottschalk* v. *Benson*[89] upon patenting a mathematical formula. The Court, including Judge Rich, held unanimously in a brief opinion that it was sufficient. Perhaps it was the very simplicity of the facts, involving no more than one easily comprehended claim, which induced the Supreme Court to grant *certiorari*. Or perhaps it was the Court's perception that the issue of whether or not the claim concerned statutory subject matter for the purpose of section 101 was unsullied by considerations of novelty and obviousness which raised issues under section 102 or section 103, as *Dann* v. *Johnston*[90] had been. In any case the whole profession held its collective breath, and hoped, in view of the chaos and confusion created by the earlier cases, that this time the guidance provided by the Supreme Court would be clear.[91]

The opinion of the Court[92] was handed down by Justice Stevens[93] with whom Justices Brennan, White, Marshall, Blackmun and Powell joined. A dissenting opinion was delivered by Justice Stewart, in which Chief Justice Burger and Justice Rehnquist joined. Thus for the first time all nine Justices of the Supreme Court participated in one of these decisions, and for the first time the Court was openly split.

The majority categorised the issue much as the Court below had done, namely whether or not the post-solution steps were sufficient to remove the case from the ambit of *Gottschalk* v. *Benson*.[94] It was argued that the claim

---

85. 409 U.S. 63 (1972).
86. See his dissent in *Re Chatfield* 545 F.2d 152 at 159 n.1 (C.C.P.A., 1976).
87. In fact, in both *Re Noll* 545 F.2d 141 (C.C.P.A., 1976) and in *Re Chatfield* 545 F.2d 152 (C.C.P.A., 1976) review was sought by the Patent and Trademark Office, but in both the papers were served just one day too late.
88. 559 F.2d 21 (C.C.P.A., 1977).
89. 409 U.S. 63 (1972).
90. 425 U.S. 219 (1976).
91. In his dissent in *Re Johnston* 502 F.2d 765 at 774 (C.C.P.A., 1971) Judge Rich had concluded by quoting the words of John W. Davis that, 'The first requirement of any judicial opinion is utter clarity.'
92. *Parker* v. *Flook* 437 U.S. 584 (1978).
93. Neither Stevens J. nor Blackmun J. had been party to either of the two previous decisions.
94. 409 U.S. 63 (1972).

covered a very wide range of applications of the relevant algorithm, but by no means all. The majority, perhaps somewhat reluctantly, conceded that it was too late in the day to limit process claims to those resulting in the transformation of materials.[95] It was further conceded that a process claim was not unpatentable simply because it incorporated a mathematical algorithm. On the other hand it is quite clear that ideas or algorithms cannot be patented as such. Here the Court of Customs and Patent Appeals had acceded to the claimant's contention that the specification of post-solution steps was sufficient to transform an unpatentable principle into a patentable process. The Supreme Court disagreed. It felt such an approach to be excessively technical and formalistic. In language reminiscent of Judge Rich's dissent in *Re Johnston*,[96] it held:

The notion that post-solution activity, no matter how conventional or obvious in itself, can transform an unpatentable principle into a patentable process exalts form over substance. A competent draftsman could attach some form of post-solution activity to almost any mathematical formula, the Pythagorean Theorem would not have been patentable, or partially patentable, because a patent application contained a final step indicating that the formula, when solved, could be usefully applied to existing surveying techniques.[97]

The question then becomes one of just how the distinction is to be drawn, if not upon formal criteria such as whether the claim is for process or apparatus, or whether post-solution steps are, or are not, specified. The answer of the majority was to refer back to the essence of the patent system as being for the protection of inventions and not of natural phenomena, whether known or unknown, which have forever been available to mankind free of legal constraint. In this case the only 'invention' was the algorithm for calculating the new alarm limits, and, on the approach of the majority, that had to be considered as if it were well-known. The Court dealt with two possible objections to such an approach. The first was that it pre-empted the tests of novelty and obviousness provided by sections 102 and 103, thus compressing all three tests into one composite test of whether the subject matter is statutory under section 101. The Court answered this by pointing out that these tests were by no means pre-empted, since they would still apply to subject matter passing the section 101 test. In other words the test of statutory subject matter is still logically prior to tests of novelty and obviousness, but not, for that reason, necessarily precluded from using similar, but not identical, criteria in determining the sorts of things which the system exists to protect. The second objection was one based upon a number of decisions of the Court of Customs and Patent Appeals[98] that a claim is not to be dissected into its component parts, and if any one of them can be shown in isolation to be non-statutory subject-matter the claim disallowed for that reason. The Court accepted that principle, and its application to section 101, but argued that here the process looked at as a

---

95. At 588.
96. 502 F.2d 765 at 773 (C.C.P.A., 1971) See extract quoted above p.15
97. At 590.
98. *Re Chatfield* 545 F.2d 152 at 158 (C.C.P.A., 1976) is cited, but the governing decision is really *Re Bernhart* 417 F.2d 1395 at 1399, 1400 (C.C.P.A., 1969).

whole still disclosed no inventive concept since every part was in fact well-known, or in the case of the novel method of calculation, should be presumed to be well-known.

Even so, the Court felt, like its predecessors, that its decision should not be regarded as an absolute denial of any possibility of protecting computer programs by patent:

The youth of the [computer programming] industry may explain the complete absence of precedent supporting patentability. Neither the dearth of precedents nor this decision, should therefore be interpreted as reflecting a judgment that patent protection of certain novel and useful computer programs will not promote the progress of science and the useful arts, or that such protection is undesirable as a matter of policy. Difficult questions of policy concerning the kinds of program that may be appropriate for patent protection and the form and duration of such protection can be answered by Congress on the basis of current empirical data not equally available to this tribunal.[99]

The view of the minority of the Supreme Court was essentially that of the Court below.

The burning question was what effect the decision would have on the basic attitude towards the general topic of patent protection for computer programs. Dissenting judgments sometimes obscure the law, but more often they clarify it by sharpening the outline of the decision of the majority. That is the case here. The close identification of the dissent with the decision of the Court below, which was itself in line with that Court's majority decision in the other cases decided since 1976, clearly eliminated any such line of reasoning for the future. It was made particularly clear that the purely formal dressing up of program claims as apparatus claims would not suffice.[100] The plea for legislative investigation and response has, so far, proved even more unproductive in the United States than in the United Kingdom. The Court of Customs and Patent Appeals was not at all diffident in making its views clear. It tended to differ radically from the examiners, and from the Office, in denying categorically any suggestion that a simple rule of thumb could be applied to reject all claims involving the implementation of algorithms, even when that was the only way of implementing them.[101] *Gottschalk* v. *Benson*[102] and *Parker* v. *Flook*[103] were distinguished on the basis that they proscribed only mathematical algorithms and methods of calculation *stricto sensu*. In *Re Freeman* the Court propounded a two-step approach to the question. The first question was to ask whether or not the claim directly or indirectly recited a forbidden algorithm. Only if this were answered affirmatively should the Court then go on to ask itself a second

---

99. At 595.
100. *Re Freeman* 573 F.2d 1237 (C.C.P.A., 1978) and *Re Maucorps* 609 F.2d 481 (C.C.P.A., 1979). It should be noted that this was very far from the case in a contemporaneously decided case in the United Kingdom, *International Business Corporation's Application* [1980] F.S.R. 564, Pat.
101. *Re Freeman* 573 F.2d 1237 (C.C.P.A., 1978); *Re Bradley* 600 F.2d 809 (C.C.P.A., 1979); *Re Diehr* 602 F.2d 982 (C.C.P.A., 1979); *Re Sherwood* 613 F.2d 809 (C.C.P.A., 1980); and *Re Walter* 618 F.2d 758 (C.C.P.A., 1980).
102. 409 U.S. 63 (1972).
103. 437 U.S. 584 (1978).

question as to whether or not the claim, looked at in its entirety, wholly pre-empted the algorithm. The claim in *Re Freeman* in respect of an algorithm to improve computerised typesetting was upheld because no forbidden algorithm was recited. The Court was inclined to stress the necessity of examining each claim minutely to discern the answer to these questions, and hinted quite broadly that the Office had been inclined to take a strict and simple view, not so much out of respect for the decisions of the Supreme Court as out of a desire to reduce its burden of work in this area. The result which the Court sought to achieve by this elaboration of the criteria for patentability was summarised in *Re Johnson*:

> Very simply our decision today recognises that modern technology has fostered a class of inventions which are most accurately described as computer-implemented processes. Such processes are encompassed within 35 U.S.C. 101 under the same principles as other machine-implemented processes, subject to judicially determined exceptions, inter alia, mathematical formulae, methods of calculation and mere ideas. The overbroad analysis of the Patent and Trademark Office errs in failing to distinguish between a computer program, i.e. a set of instructions within a computer, and computer-implemented processes wherein a computer or other automated machine performs one or more recited process steps. The distinction must not be overlooked because there is no reason for treating a computer differently from any other apparatus employed to perform a recited process step.[104]

The views expressed in these cases finally won the approval of a majority of the Supreme Court of the United States in the leading case of *Diamond* v. *Diehr*.[105] The claim was for a method of curing rubber, the novel element in which was the constant recalculation of the time required to complete the process obtained by continuing remeasurement of the temperature inside the moulding press. The judgment of the Court was delivered by Justice Rehnquist,[106] and the majority was achieved as a result of the defection from the majority in *Parker* v. *Flook* of Justices White and Powell. Justice Stevens, who had spoken for the majority in *Parker* v. *Flook* now spoke for the minority, and spoke with some acerbity. In essence the majority upheld the general approach of the Court of Customs and Patent Appeals in the post-*Flook* cases, and explained the decisions in *Gottschalk* v. *Benson* and *Parker* v. *Flook* as simply rejections of an attempt to patent a mathematical algorithm, albeit thinly disguised in *Flook* by the admixture of some insignificant post-solution activity.

> When a claim recites a mathematical formula (or a scientific principle or a phenomenon of nature), an inquiry must be made into whether the claim is seeking patent protection for that formula in the abstract. A mathematical formula as such is not accorded the protection of our patent laws, *Gottschalk* v. *Benson*, and this principle cannot be circumvented by attempting to limit the use of the formula to a particular technological environment, *Parker* v. *Flook*. Similarly, insignificant post-solution activity will not transform an unpatentable principle into a patentable process, *ibid*. To hold otherwise would allow a competent draftsman to evade the recognised

---

104. 589 F.2d 1070 at 1081 n.12 (C.C.P.A., 1979).
105. 450 U.S. 175 (1981).
106. Despite the presence among the majority of Justice Stewart, who had delivered the essentially similar dissenting opinion in *Parker* v. *Flook*.

limitations on the type of subject matter eligible for patent protection. On the other hand, when a claim containing a mathematical formula implements or applies that formula in a structure or process which, when considered as a whole, is performing a function which the patent laws were designed to protect (e.g. transforming or reducing an article to a different state or thing), then the claim satisfies the requirements of section 101.

This view has been welcomed by the Court for Customs and Patent Appeals, and indeed invoked to justify some modification of the second limb of the test propounded in *Re Freeman*. This modification was advanced by Judge Rich in the case of *Re Walter*[107] in the context of an invention relating to the interpretation of seismic data. He noted that the decision in *Parker* v. *Flook* while not endorsing a point of novelty approach, nevertheless took the view that total pre-emption of the algorithm need not be proved. It showed that the essential task was to determine whether or not the claim, taken as a whole, amounted to an attempt to patent a phenomenon of nature. Thus the decision in *Flook* suggested an alteration to the second limb of the *Freeman* test as follows:

If it appears that the mathematical algorithm is implemented in a specific manner to define structural relationships between the physical elements of the claim (in apparatus claims) or to refine or limit claim steps (in process claims) the claim being otherwise statutory, the claim passes muster under section 101. If however, the mathematical algorithm is merely presented and solved by the claimed invention, as was the case in *Benson* and *Flook*, and is not applied in any manner to physical elements or process steps, no amount of post-solution activity will render the claim statutory; nor is it saved by a preamble merely reciting the field of use of the mathematical algorithm.[108]

Although this test was not explicitly approved by the majority[109] in *Diamond* v. *Diehr*, the Court of Customs and Patent Appeals clearly has no doubt but that it is quite consistent with the reasoning of the majority.[110] The test was further refined in *Re Abele*[111] so as to require,

no more than that the algorithm be 'applied in any manner to physical elements or process steps' provided that its application is circumscribed by more than a field of use limitation or non-essential post-solution activity.

In the light of that view an algorithm designed to re-order steps in a computer program in the course of compiling code has been held to be statutory subject matter,[112] as has a further claim relating to seismic analysis processes.[113] In both of these cases the Court was able to go on to consider whether or not the invention was obvious within the purview of section 103.

---

107. 618 F.2d 758 (C.C.P.A., 1980).
108. At 767.
109. Nor specifically rejected by the minority.
110. The same view was also adopted in the new guidelines for examiners issued by the United States Patent and Trademark Office in the aftermath of *Diamond* v. *Diehr*, 'Manual of Patentable Subject Matter sect. 2110: Patentable Subject Matter – Mathematical Algorithms or Computer Programs', 538-38.3 (October 1981).
111. 684 F.2d 902 (C.C.P.A., 1982).
112. *Re Pardo* 684 F.2d 902 (C.C.P.A., 1982).
113. *Re Taner* 681 F.2d 787 (C.C.P.A., 1982).

For these purposes the test adopted in *Re Pardo* was the three-pronged one laid down by the Supreme Court in *Graham* v. *John Deere & Co.*[114] requiring the Court to determine the scope and content of the prior art, to determine the difference between the prior art and the claimed invention, and to ascertain the level of ordinary skill in the art at the time the invention was claimed.

The limits of the new approach have still to be defined, but one case falling foul of them was *Re Meyer and Weissman*[115] which decided that a claim for a system designed to provide a diagnostic aid to a physician was non-statutory on the basis that it merely replicated the mental steps that a physician might take without producing any more tangible an end-product than a sharpened awareness of the nature of the disease in question.

It remains to be seen how far these decisions will be regarded as having opened the floodgates. It seems that by early 1980, and even before the decision in *Diamond* v. *Diehr*, the Patent and Trademark Office had some three thousand claims for programs pending, of which 40 per cent were mathematical.[116] Much may depend upon the stringency with which the standards of novelty and non-obviousness are applied. An indication may have been provided by the decision of the District Court in *Paine, Webber, Jackson, Curtis Inc.* v. *Merrill Lynch, Pierce, Fenner, Smith Inc.*[117] The defendants had devised a computerised package linking together investment in securities, investment in money funds, and a credit card. The idea was to invest any spare cash from the securities fund in the money funds, and to use such investments as security for credit, and to make payments on the credit card from the most liquid source, and by automating these transactions thus to optimise the use of the customer's financial resources. A claim for a patent on this package was initially rejected by the Examiner as being obvious, but after amendment a patent was subsequently issued by the Patent and Trademark Office. The plaintiffs, and other interested parties, sought revocation of the grant upon the basis that the claim did not relate to patentable subject matter, since it was for a method of doing business. The Court was disinclined to attach any weight to the consideration that the claim failed to specify any particular apparatus,[118] but instead concentrated on what it regarded as the essence of the claim. In so doing it restricted the first leg of the *Re Freeman*[119] test by construing 'algorithm' to refer only to its strictly mathematical, and not broader computational, meaning. It was found that the claim in this case did not recite any such mathematical algorithm. It also regarded any objection to the claim as being merely for a method of doing business as concentrating unduly upon the intended result, rather than upon the means of reaching it. This seems to be an extraordinarily lax interpretation of the existing law, given that no specific apparatus

---

114. 383 U.S. 1 (1966).
115. 688 F.2d 789 (C.C.P.A., 1982).
116. Brief by the Patent and Trademark Office to the Supreme Court in *Diamond* v. *Bradley* 450 U.S. 381 (1981).
117. 564 F. Supp. 1358 (D.Del., 1983).
118. Following *Re Maucorps* 609 F.2d 481 (C.C.P.A., 1979). See above p.15
119. 573 F.2d 1237 (C.C.P.A., 1978).

was specified. It suggests that any new computer program, capable of commercial use, will be patentable, provided only that it avoid reciting a strictly mathematical algorithm. It should be noted that it was actually conceded[120] in *Merrill Lynch* that the system was obvious, and that a manual implementation would not have been patentable. The result thus seems to contradict the dominant strain in the reasoning of the Supreme Court in *Diamond* v. *Diehr* to the effect that attention should be directed not to the nature of the means, but to the function of the invention looked at as a whole.

The fifth case to reach the Supreme Court was *Diamond* v. *Bradley*[121] in which the claim related to an improved operating system for a computer. Unfortunately, in the absence of the Chief Justice, the remaining judges split four to four, no doubt dividing for and against patentability as they had in *Diamond* v. *Diehr* with the result that the decision of the Court of Customs and Patent Appeals to allow patentability was upheld. An interesting feature of this case was that the software had been embodied in microcode and installed in a silicon chip. The Court of Customs and Patent Appeals considered the claim as a whole, in accordance with its usual practice, and expressly declined to rule on whether the claim would have been upheld if it had related to nothing more than the software on the chip, or the chip itself. The Court was, however, most dismissive of an attempt by the Examiner, and the Board, to hold the system unpatentable because the operations in the computer, while not spelled out in mathematical terms, were essentially mathematical because that is the way computers work. The Court observed, quite rightly, that such an approach would lead to the automatic rejection of any computer-based system, just because all computers necessarily work in such a fashion. The Court insisted that the ends of the application must be considered, and that the claim must not be reduced to the means of attaining those ends.

A claim in respect of a chip did however succeed in *Magnavox* v. *Sanders and Mattel*.[122] In that case the original patent for a video game was based on analog technology, and the question was whether the same patent applied to prevent the achievement of the same results by the use of digital technology employing a microprocessor. The Court described the case as the first to involve the resolution of such a question, and held in favour of the patentee, in so doing applying the law as stated in *Reeve & Co.* v. *International Harvester*.

Except where form is of the essence of the invention, one device is an infringement of another if it performs substantially the same way to achieve the same results, so that if two devices do the same work, in substantially the same way, and accomplish substantially the same result, they are the same, even though they differ in name, form or shape, and when one has achieved something new involving invention, it is infringed when someone does the same thing in substantially the same way and thereby produces the same result.[123]

---

120. At 1369.
121. 450 U.S. 175 (1981).
122. Unreported, decided 24 September 1982 (N.D. Ill., 1982).
123. 658 F.2d 1137 at 1142 (7th Cir., 1981).

C. Suitability

The final concern to be examined here relates to the suitability of the law of patent for the protection of computer technology. This question can be considered both at a theoretical and at a practical level. They will be discussed in turn.

1. Theoretical considerations

The essence of the theoretical debate is whether or not the provision of a monopoly for a limited period in order to secure the ultimate advance of human knowledge is really beneficial to society. It is, of course, arguable whether such a system ever is beneficial in any context, but even assuming that still broader question to be answered in favour of the patent system,[124] a question still remains as to whether or not it should embrace computer technology in the same way as other subject matter. If the patent system is to continue to apply anywhere, it must surely continue to apply to computers themselves, as pieces of hardware. Machines lie at the very core of the potential application of the patent system. In the early days of computers, before the development of the notion of stored programs, different functions were achieved only by physical alteration to the wiring patterns. Nowadays similar effects can be achieved by programming, sometimes in the shape of microcode permanently embedded in silicon chips, though such chips may not themselves be permanent features of a given machine. They may also, and more commonly the higher the level of the program, take the shape of transient programs temporarily inhabiting the ephemeral memory of the machine at a given time. Such software is as versatile as it is volatile, and already programs exist which can make a general purpose machine of one architecture and design behave exactly as if it were of a quite different architecture and design.

It is a characteristic of the law of patent that it protects an invention, not only against competing devices of exactly the same form, but also against those that achieve identical effects by equivalent means. This suggests that any attempt to exclude programs in principle from patent protection would lead to serious and unacceptable anomaly. If this argument leads to the conclusion that it would be contrary to principle to exclude *all* programs from protection, it still leaves open the question of whether *any* programs should be so excluded. Questions may also be raised as to whether the conditions for securing protection, or the means of protection, are suitable in this area.

It may be argued that while some programs are designed to duplicate the functions of hardware, not all are of such a character, but many are intended rather to secure a given intellectual purpose, such as the solution of an equation or the playing of a game. While it may be true that such programs duplicate the functions of physical devices such as calculators or game-playing machines, they do so only incidentally, and not as an intended

---

124. Since it seems highly unlikely that the whole system of patent will be imminently abolished, however powerful the arguments against it, it seems sensible to make this assumption.

result. The current approach to the patentability of computer programs, certainly in the United States, and probably in the United Kingdom and Europe, seems to follow such a distinction. It remains to be seen whether there is any good reason to protect programs designed to produce mechanical or physical results, and not those which are designed to satisfy less material ends. At this point it may be necessary to look back at the history of the law of patent, and forward to the practical considerations to be discussed in the next section. It may well be considerations of practicality which have historically restricted the law of patent to the confines of a finite physical universe, and restrained it from excursion into the infinitely variable world of intellectual creativity.

So far as conditions are concerned, the law of patent affords protection only to the inventive, novel and non-obvious. If something is already in existence, just awaiting discovery, or is already available to all, or easily made available, then it is hard to see that the process of exploiting such a thing justifies the price of granting a monopoly, even for a limited period, upon its exploiter. In such a case the basic object of the advancement of human knowledge has not been sufficiently furthered. In the case of computer programs, and of programming techniques, some special considerations apply. Computer programs are composed of combinations of extremely simple steps and processes. It is their combination, and multiplication, which enables complex tasks to be completed. Many of the steps involved in creating such systems involve more meticulous and detailed tracing of the implications of different possible steps than inspiration in choosing between available alternatives. These are exactly the qualities possessed in greatest measure by computers themselves, and sure enough increasingly large amounts of the process, especially the generation of code, are now consigned to machines. Automation is inexorably ascending the ladder of system design. This seems to supply a satisfactory way of delimiting the area of possible patentability. It can exclude those parts performed by computers themselves. If, however, the relevant system still requires the involvement of human beings, it will at least be eligible for further consideration, which may involve the question of obviousness. If a new method is commercially viable, and has not so far been developed, there should be a presumption, though a weak one, that it is not obvious. It is, of course, possible that some new advance in technology was required for commercial exploitation to become feasible, but that once the advance had been made, then the application was obvious; in such a case the presumption would be rebutted.

The final question to be considered here is how appropriate it is to grant a monopoly on the exploitation of the invention for as long as twenty, or even seventeen, years. It should be remembered that the requirement of novelty casts a shadow before it, strictly limiting the exposure to which new ideas can be put in their development stage. It should also be remembered how fast modern technology changes, and changes in hardware technology inevitably enforce changes in software to allow the new hardware to be exploited. It is generally reckoned that the time lag in the development of software is already unduly long. All of these considerations suggest that the life of a program after a patent has been issued is likely to be relatively short, and that the periods are not too short. If a program has already lived its useful life long before its patent expires, the damage would appear to be slight, and it hardly seems justified to disrupt the general rules applying to other subject matter by going to the trouble of providing a specially curtailed period.

2. Practical considerations

The initial impetus to the special treatment of computer programs, and the continuing debate and conflict, particularly that between the Patent Office and the Court of Customs and Patent Appeals in the United States, was inspired by much more practical concerns. In 1966 the President's Commission explained that the extension of protection by the law of patent to computer programs would result only in undermining the foundations of that branch of the law of intellectual property.[125]

The Patent Office now cannot examine applications for programs because of the lack of a classification technique and the requisite search files. Even if these were available, reliable searches would not be feasible or economic because of the tremendous volume of prior art being generated. Without this search, the patenting of programs would be tantamount to mere registration and the presumption of validity would be all but nonexistent.[125]

The essence of the patent system is that a judgment is required before issuing the patent that the claimed invention is novel and not obvious. Given the volume of programming activity, the complete absence of any universal approach to classification or indexing, and the impenetrability of the code on its face, the task of the examiners becomes quite impossible. It is indicative of the difficulty of dealing with programs that professional and commercial programming houses complain when the industry leader, International Business Machines Ltd, is prepared to release its products only in object code versions. If professionals in the same narrow field find it difficult to follow object code it is unreasonable to expect generalists in the Patent Offices of the world to be able to do so. This concern is clearly universal, and the reasoning of the President's Commission in the United States was echoed in the United Kingdom by the Banks Committee.[126]

This basic administrative problem finds expression in the length of time, and difficulty of moving to the stage at which a patent is issued. Because of the technical requirements of drafting patent applications, and making adequate disclosure, in all serious applications it is necessary to hire specialist advisers. These come neither speedy nor cheap. They must negotiate with the Patent Office itself, and the result, in the United States, is that several thousand dollars will have been spent and on average between two and three years will have passed before the patent will issue. Before that time it is extremely difficult to secure preliminary relief, and in its absence permanent relief will be granted only for the period after the patent has issued. Further problems are created by the potential fallibility of the whole process. The claim may be inadequately drafted with the result that while

---

125. Report of the President's Commission on the Patent System (1966) ch. IV para. 3.
126. Cmnd. 4407 ch. 17 para. 483 (1970).

the method is disclosed to potential competitors, effective relief is not secured. Even if the claim is properly drafted the examiners may err and issue a patent when they should not. If such a patent is then successfully challenged in the Courts, or if it is simply disregarded by competitors, the claimant has once again sacrificed his position. It might be argued that if the reason for invalidity is that the program is not sufficiently novel, no harm has been done because the program had already been anticipated in the prior art. In practice, however, the publication of the patent is much more likely to bring the attention of competitors to the program than is its mere unheralded existence among the billions of lines of code nestling anonymously somewhere in the public domain. In these circumstances it is easy to understand that small software houses designing essentially ephemeral products might think the patent system inappropriate as a means of protecting their interests.

It must also be understood that even after a patent has been issued there is need for constant vigilance, and expense, to ensure that it is not infringed. Once again it is much more difficult to determine whether or not a patent on a program has been infringed than a patent on a machine. It will be particularly difficult to detect infringement where a program is used as part of a privately owned system used to manufacture products for the public, rather than sold directly.

These costs, and perhaps particularly those of litigation, do however make patent protection popular in some quarters of the computer industry. Those firms which manufacture hardware, seek a competitive edge by combining hardware and software exploitation, and have sufficient resources both to claim and to police their patents, are put into an extremely powerful position to squeeze out competition. There is now some evidence that the very largest firms are turning increasingly to the law of patent to lay the foundations of their strategy to secure protection for their products, and to seek to monopolise not just the underlying hardware, but the software markets which feed upon it.

Chapter 2

Copyright

Copyright is the second main bastion of the law of intellectual property, and probably the one most commonly relied upon to protect software, especially that part marketed through retailers. It is first necessary to explain its basis, and in particular its relationship to the law of patent. The law is complicated because it applies to a number of different types of entity, and it is best to consider each of these separately, not least because some have generated new and unique legislative provision. The chapter will conclude with the examination of a number of more general problems, relating to ownership, infringement and remedies in general.

A. The basis for protection

Like patent, the law of copyright is overwhelmingly based upon statutory provision. In the United Kingdom the first statute was enacted in 1709, and the most recent, and most comprehensive, in 1988. In the United States the law is underpinned by clause 8 of section 8 of Article 1 of the Constitution of the United States which endowed Congress with the power,

> To promote the Progress of Science and useful Arts, by securing for limited terms to Authors and Inventors the exclusive Rights to their respective Writings and Discoveries.

This power has often been exercised, and the most recent general revision took place in 1976, effectively concentrating the law upon a federal and statutory basis. The 1976 legislation has itself already been supplemented in relation to computers by the Computer Software Copyright Act 1980 and by the Semiconductor Chip Protection Act 1984.

Exactly the same reasoning as that exhibited in the provision quoted above was enunciated at about the same time in the United Kingdom by Lord Mansfield:

> We must take care to guard against two extremes, equally prejudicial, the one, that men of ability, who have employed their time for the service of the community, may not be deprived of their just merits, and the reward of their ingenuity and labour; the

other that the world may not be deprived of improvements, nor the progress of the arts be retarded.[1]

It is worth noting that these objects are best achieved by different means in the cases of patent and copyright. In the former case progress is promoted largely by encouraging inventors to disclose their inventions so that others may improve upon them and so benefit society materially; in the latter by encouraging authors to publish as much and as widely as possible to satisfy society aesthetically and intellectually.[2] It is for this reason that patent requires high threshold standards of novelty and protects quite comprehensively for short periods, while copyright requires lower standards of originality and provides shallow protection for much longer periods. Such discrimination contrasts the paradigmatic case of utilitarian and scientific invention with that of creative and literary writing. This was never very realistic, even in the earliest period, when copyright was already invoked to protect a wide variety of utilitarian works such as non-fictional writings, directories and maps.[3] Still less is it appropriate in the world of modern technology which has vastly expanded the range and form of commercially valuable subject-matter. Quite apart from the problems caused by new types of work such as computer programs, or new forms of communication such as by audio-visual display, it should not be overlooked that the classical subject-matter of copyright, even creative literary works, may become the data for a computer application. Nevertheless the basic distinction between patent and copyright has been invoked to deny protection by copyright to many of these innovations.

Arguments against extending protection into the sphere of computers, and especially to programs, are both conceptual and pragmatic. Conceptual arguments deny that computer programs are the proper subject-matter of copyright; pragmatic arguments deny that progress will be promoted by extending copyright protection to them.

1. Conceptual arguments

Two principal conceptual arguments have been advanced; first that computer-readable materials are not 'writings', and second that computer programs, and some other materials, are strictly utilitarian, and protectible, if at all, by other branches of the law, such as that of patent, unfair competition or contract.

(a) Not writings
Both in the United States and in the United Kingdom copyright legislation habitually refers to 'writing', and at one time objections were made to copyright protection of computer-readable materials because they were not readable or visible. In both jurisdictions such arguments received short shrift

---

1. *Sayre* v. *Moore* 1 East 361 (1785).
2. See Goldstein, 'Infringement of Copyright in Computer Programs', *47 U. Pitt. L.R.* 1119 (1986).
3. The preamble to the 1707 Act refers to 'useful books'.

from the courts, and the matter has now been put beyond any doubt at all by the modern legislation which in the United States refers to,

any original works of authorship fixed in any tangible means of expression, now known or later developed, from which they can be perceived, reproduced or otherwise enunciated, either directly or with the aid of a machine or device.[4]

and in the United Kingdom 'writing' is defined to include,

any form of notation or code, whether by hand or otherwise and regardless of the method by which, or medium in or on which, it is recorded . . .[5]

This accords with the common linguistic practice in the computer industry of referring to materials as being 'written' or 'read', both by human beings and by machines. Nor should the secondary terminology of computer 'languages', complete with 'dialects', of 'copying', of 'interpreting', of 'files', and of 'documents' be overlooked in ascertaining the perceived functions and roles of computers.

(b) Too utilitarian

The second argument, that copyright is fundamentally an inappropriate form for the protection of utilitarian works, is weakened by the long-established tradition of protecting quite utilitarian literary works such as maps or recipe books. It is nevertheless an objection which is raised to some forms of computer-readable materials, and especially against programs the function of which is to activate machine reactions directly without the intervention of human beings, typically operating systems. These arguments have been more widely accepted and deserve further consideration. They rest on the basic distinctions between the laws of patent and copyright mentioned above,[6] and were articulated in the leading United States authority of *Baker* v. *Selden*,[7]

To give to the author of the book an exclusive property in the art described therein . . . is the preserve of letters patent, not of copyright.

In that case the Supreme Court refused to protect the forms used as examples to implement the new system of accounting set out in the plaintiff's book against publication by the defendant of another set of forms which could also be used to implement the plaintiff's system of accounting. The Court feared that otherwise the law of patent would be undermined since the plaintiff would in effect receive a monopoly on the practice of his system without first having to satisfy the more stringent threshold conditions imposed by the law of patent. Much the same point was made in the United Kingdom case of *Hollinrake* v. *Truswell* where copyright was claimed for a cardboard pattern with writing and scales inscribed upon it and used for making sleeves of garments. Here too the Court refused protection because the work was intended,

not for the purpose of giving information or pleasure, but for practical use . . .. The

---

4. 17 U.S.C. 102(a).
5. Copyright, Designs and Patents Act 1988 sect. 178.
6. See p. 59.
7. *Baker* v. *Selden* 101 U.S. 99 (1879) at 103.

fallacy of the . . . argument seems to me to lie in a failure to distinguish between literary copyright and the right to protect an invention.[8]

Here the Court was most concerned about the grant of the extended period offered to copyright given the lower threshold conditions.

These lines of argument were adopted by Commissioner John Hersey in his dissenting opinion on this point in the investigation into the question of the copyrightability of computer programs conducted in 1978 by the President's Commission on New Technological Uses (CONTU),

the program itself in its mature and usable form, is a machine control element, a mechanical device, which on constitutional grounds and for reasons of social policy ought not to be copyrighted.[9]

The same reasoning permeates one of the leading authorities to deny copyright protection to computer programs, *Computer Edge Pty. Ltd* v. *Apple Computer Inc.* where Deane J., after citing *Baker* v. *Selden* compared[10] the function of the program in coded form to a book of instructions in relation to the generation of a pattern of charges in a computer's read-only memory chip, which was claimed to infringe copyright in the earlier forms.

A closely related aspect of the distinction between the law of patent and that of copyright is that while neither protects underlying ideas, copyright may protect its expression and patent its implementation. The distinction between uncopyrightable ideas and copyrightable expression is fundamental to the law of copyright, and finds explicit expression in sub-section 102(b) of the United States Copyright Act which, as a corollary to sub-section 102(a)'s list of categories of protected works, provides that,

In no case does copyright protection for an original work of authorship extend to any idea, procedure, process, system, method of operation, concept, principle, or discovery, regardless of the form in which it is described, explained, illustrated or embodied in such work.[11]

However, it is clear that while the general principle that copyright protects expression rather than ideas may be sound, it cannot be pressed too far. It is well established that copyright extends beyond the exact form of a work to protect against, for example, a translation or adaptation of it.[12] It is obvious that in such cases where the form may be completely different the identification of the alleged infringing copy with the original can be accomplished only by reference to the underlying content or, in some sense, idea. Thus in the case of an adaptation of a copyright screenplay it has been said that:

---

8. *Hollinrake* v. *Truswell* [1894] Ch 420, C.A. per Davey L.J. at 428, explicitly approving *Baker* v. *Selden*.
9. CONTU Final Report (1979) at 27. It should be noted that Commissioner Hersey was prepared to accept copyright in flow charts and source code versions of computer programs because they were directed at human beings.
10. *Computer Edge Pty. Ltd* v. *Apple Computer Inc.* 65 A.L.R. 33 (H.C.A., 1986) at 62, although Deane J. found it unnecessary to decide whether the source and object code versions were themselves capable of being protected by copyright.
11. 17 U.S.C. sect. 102(b).
12. See Copyright, Designs and Patents Act 1988 sect. 21(3).

Upon any work, especially upon a play, a great number of patterns of increasing generality will fit equally well, as more and more of the incident is left out. The last may perhaps be no more than the most general statement of what the play is about and at times may consist of only its title, but there is a point in this series of abstractions where they are no longer protected since otherwise the playwright could protect the use of his ideas to which apart from their expression his property is never extended.[13]

These sentiments are applicable to computers where systems are expressed as groups of modules in a specification, or where there is a progression from flow chart to detailed coding. Much of the current litigation on infringement turns on the exact place at which this line can be drawn. In broad and general terms it may be said that the more utilitarian and uncreative the work, the less inclined will the Court be to protect against variations upon the form of the original. This is, however, a matter best discussed below in relation to particular categories of work.

2. Pragmatic arguments

These arguments are concerned with the complementary questions about the advantage to society of using copyright to provide protection in the computer environment. The basic argument in its favour is that authors will publish only if they are guaranteed a certain level of reward by the conferment of a limited monopoly. The argument is often thought to be particularly strong in the computer area where the costs of development are very high and the costs of reproduction very low. It has however been questioned first whether providing protection for computer programs really does promote publication in the sense of disclosure to the public, and second whether it is necessary to provide copyright protection in order to encourage such publication. These arguments will be addressed separately.

(a) Disclosure[14]

The argument here is that while publication of a literary work in conventional form automatically makes it available for public scrutiny, this is not true of computer programs which, if made available only as object code, are quite unintelligible. It is certainly the case that many programs are made available only in such a form, and it is probably true that part of the motivation for this practice is to prevent making the programming techniques too readily apparent to potential competitors. So common is the practice of publishing computer programs only in a machine-readable form that special provision has been made for the deposit of such materials in the United States by the Code of Federal Regulations.[15] The basic requirement

---

13. *Nichols* v. *Universal Pictures Co.* 45 F.2d 119 (2nd Cir., 1930) at 121 per Learned Hand J.
14. The best, and fullest, deployment of these arguments is to be found in Samuelson 'CONTU Revisited: The Case Against Copyright Protection for Computer Programs in Machine-Readable Form', 1984 Duke L.J. 663, at pp. 705–27. See, in reply, Raskind, 'The Uncertain Case for Special Legislation Protecting Computer Software', 47 U. Pitt. L.R. 1131 (1986), at pp. 1139–1143.
15. 37 C.F.R. sect. 202–20.

is that, in addition to simple identifying information, only the first and last twenty-five pages of the work[16] need be deposited. Given the ease of manipulating the coding of programs, this need be no more informative than the depositor chooses it to be. Once it is accepted that no true disclosure is made in such cases the balance between copyright and other forms of intellectual property such as the law of patents and trade secrets may become distorted.

It is, however, necessary to distinguish between the concern of the Copyright Regulations with the form of deposit, irrespective of the clarity of the subject-matter once processed by machine, and the class of programs opaque not only because in machine-readable form, but also because they are designed to activate machines directly without the intervention of human beings, typically programs in object code. It may well be true that they are disclosed to potential users less fully than novels are disclosed to readers by being published. It is, however, arguable that this reflects merely the different ways in which society benefits from their being made available. Society cannot benefit from an undecipherable copy of a novel, but can benefit from the use of a program which it cannot decipher so long as the program will run satisfactorily. The argument becomes convincing only when the relevant work is regarded not as something to use, but rather as something to improve and exploit. The strength of the argument thus rests upon the policies underpinning different types of work. The argument from distortion is susceptible to similar analysis. In respect of some classes of work there is no real danger of distortion, in the case of others there may be, but then it will be a matter of assessing how far other branches of the law afford protection, and whether the existing balance can be defended.

(b) Economic need

The general economic argument for copyright has come under some attack, more particularly in relation to copyright in computer programs in one well-known article.[17] That particular article was written in very different circumstances from those which prevail in the computer industry today, and it is noteworthy that the author himself conceded that the focus of concern would centre upon a situation in which an independent software house sold general purpose software by retail in large quantities at low prices. Such circumstances now exist. Nevertheless there is still considerable validity in Breyer's general argument that the author of computer software is protected by his lead time, by his control of documentation in conventional form, and by his ability to market secondary products and services in the form of maintenance, up-grades and troubleshooting. It is arguable that these factors will suffice to secure a sufficient market for the original product, and some support may be found for such an argument in the increasing tendency of software suppliers to abandon physical restraints upon copying their products. The validity of the economic case for copyright protection is very difficult to demonstrate. The United States Copyright Office accepted

---

16. Or their equivalent.
17. Notably by Breyer, 'The Uneasy Case for Copyright: A Study of Copyright in Books, Photocopies, and Computer Programs', *84 Harvard L.R.* 281 (1970).

programs for registration upon a provisional basis from 1964 onwards, but in the period from 1964 to 1977 no more than 1205 programs out of an estimated 13 million were registered, two-thirds of these not by software houses but by two major computer manufacturers.[18] Yet that coincided with a period of rapid growth in the American software industry, which has continued to flourish to the extent that by 1986 there were more than 21 000 different software products on sale in the United States from 2900 different suppliers. It is, of course, possible that more effective copyright protection would have induced still more progress, but this must remain a matter for speculation.[19]

B. Range of application

Many of the legal problems generated by computers may be traced to their versatility. It is because computers can be used for so many different purposes that legal rules, perfectly adequate when applied to one particular use, prove defective when applied to another. The law of copyright is a good example of this tendency. There are innumerable points of the existing law to which computers are relevant, but it is by no means obvious that all should be treated alike. For example, from the point of view of computers there is no distinction between programs and data, yet they clearly raise quite different problems. Even within the area of programs it is necessary to distinguish between programs which affect only the internal working of the machine, and those which have a visible manifestation to the user in the form of an audio-visual display. Similarly in the area of data it is helpful to distinguish between the law as it relates to input formats and as it applies to the content of databases.

1. Programs

Computer programs are prepared and implemented in a myriad of different ways, some of which have attracted particular legislative responses. Programs may also pass through various stages, and some arguments turn upon the difference between programs in their source code version, which usually implies that they are written in a high-level language, and in their object code form which is a machine-usable version derived from the source code. Such high-level source code is sufficiently close to ordinary human language to be readily comprehensible to programmers, especially when interlarded with comments in ordinary free prose. It is also sufficiently structured to be capable of being transformed automatically by a compiler into an executable set of machine instructions in object code. At a lower level such instructions are implemented within the machine by the operation of still more basic programs which utilise the special functions provided by particular microprocessors. These instructions are written in microcode, and may either be

---

18. See CONTU Final Report per Commissioner Hersey.
19. Industry estimates of the extent and economic consequences of software 'piracy' are inherently unreliable, and unconvincing in their tendency to equate pirated programs with lost sales.

held in software as microprograms, or built into the physical circuitry of a semi-conductor chip.[20] Since the latter has been accorded special protection, it is necessary to consider it separately.

(a) Source

It is apparent from the description above that programs in source code are closest to the traditional subject matter of copyright. They are often written by human beings using pencil and paper, they sometimes include passages of ordinary prose, and they both are, and are intended to be, comprehensible to other human beings familiar with the relevant language.[21] It is perhaps significant that there has never been much attempt to deny copyright protection to programs in this form. The issue has never reached the Supreme Court of the United States, and has never been fought out at trial in the High Court in the United Kingdom. Despite doubts aired by Whitford J.,[22] the Chairman of the Committee on Copyright and Designs Law,[23] in one of a number of interlocutory applications, the uniform provisional view taken in such applications was that programs were potentially copyrightable. This view accorded with that taken by law reformers,[24] by commentators,[25] and by overseas authorities.[26] Any remaining doubts were dispelled by express provision in modern legislation in the United States,[27] in the United Kingdom,[28] and elsewhere.[29]

Once it is conceded that programs in source code are susceptible to protection by the law of copyright, the question of infringement arises. In broad terms such protection confers exclusive rights upon the author to copy, issue, perform, broadcast or adapt the relevant work.[30] Underlying ideas are not, in principle, protected, and infringement occurs only when a substantial

---

20. For a full description, including helpful diagrams, see Sternberg, 'NEC v INTEL: The Battle over Copyright Protection for Microcode', *27 Jur. Jo.* 173 (1987) at 176–80, and Appendices.
21. Sometimes even this level of coding is generated automatically from still higher level input by the use of a source code generator program.
22. Expressed in *Wilkins* v. *Prime* (unreported, 29 April 1981).
23. Cmnd. 6732 (1977).
24. *Ibid.* para. 479.
25. For example, see in the United States, *Nimmer on Copyright* (1963–87) and in the United Kingdom, Laddie, Prescott and Vitoria, '*The Modern Law of Copyright* (1980).
26. *Northern Office Micro Computers* v. *Rosenstein* 1981 (4) SA 123 at 130, citing this work.
27. The Computer Software Copyright Act 1980 in amending 17 U.S.C. sect. 101 by adding a definition of a computer program and by inserting a new sect. 117 to regulate programs was said in *Williams Electronics Inc.* v. *Artic International Inc.* 685 F.2d 870 (3rd Cir., 1982) at 875 to have established firmly the copyrightability of computer programs.
28. The Copyright, Designs and Patents Act 1988 sect. 3(1)(b) explicitly subsumes computer programs within the category of literary works.
29. For example in Australia where the courts had been stickiest in the Copyright Amendment Act 1984 (Cth), see Stern 'Computer Software Protection after the 1984 Copyright Statutory Amendments' 60 A.L.J. 333 (1986).
30. This is the terminology of Copyright, Designs and Patents Act 1988 sect. 16(1); in the United States 17 U. S. C. sect. 106 employs 'reproduce', 'distribute', 'perform', 'display', and 'prepare derivative work'.

part[31] of the original is the subject of one of the prohibited acts. The application of these principles has proved to be highly controversial in the United States where the bulk of recent litigation has been concerned with such issues. Given the rate of development of the industry and its highly competitive nature, it is hardly surprising to find innovators seeking to adapt programs successful on one generation or brand of machines, so as to run on the next generation or a competitive brand.

Thus in the leading case of *Whelan Associates* v. *Jaslow Dental Laboratory*[32] the dispute was precipitated by the defendant's attempt to adapt programs written for him by the plaintiff so as to run on a newer and more popular model. Because the machines were different, and because a different programming language was used, the actual coding was completely different, but the organisation and structure of the program was identical. In a careful analysis of the process of programming the Court noted that most of the effort[33] goes into organisation and structure, and much less into writing the code. It was argued by the defendants that they had used nothing but the ideas in the original programs, and that their expression of those ideas was completely different in form. This issue raises quite squarely the fundamental problem of abstraction often discussed elsewhere in the copyright context.[34] At a high level the 'idea' of these programs was to provide a service for administering a dental laboratory, at an intermediate level it was the arrangement of tasks so as to accomplish this, and at the lowest level it was the coding of programs to drive a given computer to implement such arrangement. There was no question but that the two programs were designed to provide the same administrative service, and none that the coding was different. The Court found that at the crucial intermediate level the organisation and structure[35] of the plaintiff's programs had been copied, and ascribed such organisation and structure to the realm of expression rather than idea, on the basis that 'everything that is not necessary to that purpose or function would be part of the expression of the idea'.[36] All turns on the precise abstraction of the purpose of the program. Once it was restricted to the high level of administering a dental laboratory, it became undeniable that any number of concatenations of programming modules could serve that purpose.[37] The high level of abstraction so articulated may be attributed to the fact that the litigation concerned a high level application program, and the result might vary significantly when applied to operating systems programs where there is much less scope for variation. It should also be noted that in this case a subsisting relationship between the parties had

---

31. Substance is determined qualitatively rather than quantitatively and in *SAS Institute Inc.* v. *S & H Computer Systems Inc.* 605 F.Supp. 816 (M.D. Tenn., 1985) infringement was held to occur when it could be shown that less than 0.1 per cent of the lines of code in the original had been reproduced in the copy.
32. 797 F.2d 1222 (3rd Cir., 1986).
33. Estimated at about 80 per cent.
34. See below p. 47.
35. More often referred to as 'look and feel'.
36. At 1236.
37. There were indeed a number of quite different and unconnected packages selling into the dental laboratory market.

broken down, and there was plenty of evidence of copying, so it was not necessary to rely heavily upon substantial similarity for that purpose. The basic finding of infringement upon reproduction of the structure and organisation of the program, despite differentiation of coding, has been duplicated in a number of lower courts.[38] A different approach was however adopted by the Fifth Circuit in *Plains Cotton Co-Operative* v. *Good-pasture Computer Services*[39] when in the context of a dispute relating to computer systems developed for the marketing of cotton, the Court refused to reverse a lower court decision that the defendant's system, developed by the same programmers as that of the plaintiff, did not infringe by 'organisational' copying. It had been suggested by the plaintiffs that the lower court's decision had been predicated only upon the absence of evidence of direct copying of the plaintiff's coding. The Court adopted a conservative view,[40] and was clearly inclined to restrict the ambit of 'organisational' copying which in the context it felt to be determined by the 'externalities of the cotton market' or, in other words, by the nature of the application. This decision may mark a swing of the pendulum away from the protection of computer programs against non-literal copying as a result of discerning the social value of securing improvements in existing programs, and of reducing costs by reducing the monopoly enjoyed by the first entrant into a particular area. A similar result may be achieved by market forces alone since there was evidence in *Plains Cotton* that so far as application programs are concerned it may be easier for an experienced programmer with knowledge of a particular market to write a completely new program, rather than to modify one previously developed. In *Whelan* the prime mover on the defendant's side had little programming expertise and needed to start from an existing program. In *Plains Cotton* the dispute was as to whether copying had taken place, and there was no question but that the defendant programmer was perfectly capable of writing a new program. Different considerations apply in the case of object code as will be seen in the next section. It should finally be noted in this connection that in *Digital Communications Associates* v. *Softklone Inc.*[41] the District Court was not prepared to find copyright in a program infringed simply by the defendant's use of a similar screen display. The Court was uncertain whether a single screen display could qualify as an audio-visual work,[42] but took the view that the substantially reproduced screen display was too far removed from the program generating the original for it to be infringed by the copied display.

---

38. In *SAS Institute Inc.* v. *S & H Computer Systems Inc.* 605 F. Supp 816 (M. D. Tenn., 1985) (statistical analysis programs for a different brand of computer); *Q-Co Industries Inc.* v. *Hoffman* 625 F.Supp. 608 (S.D. N.Y., 1985) (teleprompting programs for different brand of computer); *Broderbund Software Inc.* v. *Unison World Inc.* 648 F.Supp. 1127 (N.D. Cal., 1986) (personal printing displays for different brand of computer). *Broderbund* has been criticised for its failure to distinguish adequately between programs and screen displays, see case note by MacKay 13 Rutgers Law and Computer Tech. L.J. 105 (1987).
39. 807 F.2d 1256 (5th Cir., 1987).
40. Induced to some extent by the procedural posture appropriate to the issue of overturning a lower court on an interlocutory finding.
41. 659 F.Supp. 449 (N.D. Ga., 1987).
42. See below p. 46.

However, the plaintiff succeeded on the basis of a separate copyright in the screen display as a compilation of the textual elements which it comprised. The Court took the view that the communications package in question could be represented by any number of different screen displays, and hence that the display was separable from the idea.

It is interesting that the most recent case law addresses the underlying economic problems quite explicitly. In both *Whelan* and *Softklone* the Court adverted to the importance of achieving standardisation in the computer industry, but then deliberately held protection more likely to advance society's interest. In the case of systems programming rather than applications the argument might not be nearly so persuasive.

(b) Object[43]

Even though copyright protection may be conceded for source code, doubts have remained in relation to object code, just because it is implemented by machines without human intervention. Such doubts were endorsed at first instance in *Apple Computer Inc.* v. *Franklin Computer Corp.*,[44] but authoritatively rejected by the Third Circuit on appeal.[45] The situation there illustrated a common context within which the question arises. The computer industry is highly competitive both in hardware and software. Hardware succeeds to the extent that the largest range of popular software will run on it, and software to the extent that it will run on the greatest range of hardware. This creates considerable pressure towards standardisation, or at least compatibility, of operating systems. So each competitor in the hardware business needs to use an operating system which will run the most popular software, and to do this must reproduce on his machine the same results that the software achieves on the market leader. Given the complexity of modern software, and especially of operating systems,[46] this is a formidable and expensive operation. There must inevitably be a high degree of coincidence between the programs if they are to produce identical effects across a whole range of conditions, and equally inevitably this result cannot be achieved without access to the code being mimicked. It is plainly cheapest, fastest and, at least technically, safest, to copy the original code completely. Any change is fraught with danger. Here Apple had established its machine as the market leader in its own sector, and so potential competitors such as Franklin had to work to the Apple operating system. Franklin argued that operating systems were not copyrightable because they worked directly on machines and were akin to a machine part, and in the alternative that idea and expression merged because the exigencies of emulating an operating system eliminated

---

43. See Note 'Copyright Protection of Computer Program Object Code', 96 Harv. L.R. 1723 (1983).
44. *Apple Computer Inc.* v. *Franklin Computer Corp.* 545 F.Supp, 812 (e.D. Pa., 1982).
45. *Apple Computer Inc.* v. *Franklin Computer Corp.* 714 F.2d 1240 (3rd Cir., 1983)
46. The Court explained such systems clearly and simply at 1243, 'Computer programs can be categorised by function as either application programs or operating system programs. Application systems usually perform a specific task for the computer user, such as word processing, check book balancing, or playing a game. In contrast, operating system programs generally manage the mechanical functions of the computer or facilitate use of computer programs.'

any possibility of deviating from Apple's code. The Court found the answer to the first argument in the drafting of the definition of a computer program in section 101 as 'sets of statements or instructions to be used *directly* or *indirectly*[47] in a computer in order to bring about a certain result', which it took to be an implicit incorporation of both object and source code, an interpretation supported by its awareness that this very point had been taken in Commissioner Hersey's dissent from the majority CONTU decision which had been adopted as the basis for the new legislation. It should also be noted that the wholesale rejection of object code from protection by copyright would destroy the value of any protection for source code. In most cases programs are copied so as to be run, and for this purpose an object-code version is sufficient. Even if the copier is seeking to copy so as to improve the program, and requires source code for that purpose, it is possible to generate a primitive version of source code from object code by using a disassembly program.[48]

In the United Kingdom no attempt has been made to distinguish between the protection afforded to source or object code versions of programs, either in the vestigial case law,[49] or in the Copyright, Designs and Patents Act 1988 which contains special provision[50] relating to literary works[51] which are computer-generated, and object code programs appear to fall neatly and comprehensively into this category. The protection of programs whether in source or object code has been determined differently under the differently worded provisions of different parts of the Commonwealth.[52]

(c) *Microcode*[53]

The development of microprocessors as the efficient agents in modern computers led to the emergence of a still lower level of coding than that represented by object code. Microprocessors can interpret a large number of basic machine instructions by breaking them down into sequences of very primitive steps indeed.[54] The precise nature of these primitive operations

---

47. Emphasis in the Court's quotation.
48. In such a case it would be difficult to establish that such independently generated source code amounted to an infringing copy of the original source code. This very issue has been litigated in Japan, see Karjala, 'The First Case on Protection of Operating Systems and Reverse Engineering of Programs in Japan' [1988] 6 E.I.P.R. 172.
49. See *M.S. Associates Ltd.* v. *Power* [1988] F.S.R. 242, Ch. where some account was taken of the structure, as well as the coding, of the relevant programs on an interlocutory application.
50. Copyright, Designs and Patents Act 1988 sect. 9(3).
51. Defined to include computer programs by sect. 3(1)(b).
52. Compare the decisions of the High Court of Australia in *Computer Edge Pty. Ltd.* v. *Apple Computer Inc.* 65 A.L.R. 33 (H.C.A., 1986) with that of the Canadian Federal Court of Appeal in *Apple Computer Inc.* v. *Mackintosh Computers Ltd.* 44 D.L.R. 4th 74 (F.C.A., 1987)
53. See Sternberg, 'NEC v. INTEL: The Battle over Copyright Protection for Microcode', 27 Jur. Jo. 173 (1968); Laurie and Everett, 'The Copyrightability of Microcode: Is it Software or Hardware or Both?' *The Computer Lawyer*, March 1985 p. 1; Sandison, 'NEC Corp. v. Intel Corp.' [1987] 1 E.I.P.R. 25.
54. Thus to exchange the information in the registers A and B which might be regarded as one instruction, four sub-steps are required: (1) remove data from A to a temporary location (temp. A); (2) remove data from B to another temporary location (temp. B); (3) remove data from temp A to B; and (4) remove data from temp B to A.

depends entirely upon the architecture of the relevant microprocessor. If the manufacturer of a new microprocessor wants to compete with one already in the market, his new chip must be able to accept the same machine instructions as the original, and achieve identical results. In *NEC Corp* v. *Intel Corp.*[55] this was what occurred. NEC sought to market a new family of microprocessors or chips to compete with Intel's established family. They were designed to accept all of the same instructions as those accepted by the Intel chips,[56] and to produce the same results; but because of a different architecture they were able to work faster. The innovation was to duplicate the bus or channel used to transfer data.[57] This entailed using more bits for each instruction, but meant that the instructions could be performed faster. NEC sought a declaration that the microprogramming of their new chip did not infringe Intel's registered copyright in its microprogram. It was first litigated upon an interim basis whether or not microcode was in principle copyrightable. The Court held it to fall squarely within the definition of a computer program in section 101 of the United States Copyright provision,[58] to exhibit creativity,[59] and merely by being stored in a read-only memory not thereby to become a machine part.[60] The question of infringement was not however decided at that stage, and it may be argued that microcode does differ fundamentally from source and object code in being governed quite decisively by the design of a particular microprocessor and the functions which it seeks to perform. It may not, in such a case, be at all possible to separate, for example, the idea of exchanging information between two locations from its expression in removing data from each into temporary locations and then restoring them to the appropriate new locations. If so, the slightest difference in the microcoding used to accomplish such an operation might be sufficient to defeat a claim of infringement. It is certainly the case that if such primitive architecture-determined operations are protected, that in effect an unpatented microprocessor will achieve a considerable degree of protection, probably enough to prevent emulation. It is submitted that such questions are better determined on the question of whether the defendant has acted unfairly. In that context the economic and moral questions can be addressed unencumbered by technicalities primarily directed at a set of quite different problems.

(d) Chip design[61]
Although in the United States the new Semiconductor Chip Protection Act

---

55. 645 F.Supp. 590 (N.D. Cal., 1986).
56. And a few more of their own as well.
57. Thus in the example given above the time required to exchange data is almost halved, since two transfers can take place simultaneously. It is not quite halved, because the duplicating feature requires a slightly longer word length.
58. Para. 16, Conclusion 3 of the Court's opinion.
59. Para. 18, Conclusion 3.
60. Para. 23, Conclusion 5.
61. See Stern, *Semiconductor Chip Protection* (1986) and the special number of the *Minnesota Law Review* in December 1985 devoted to the Semiconductor Chip Protection Act 1984. For a comparison of the situation in the United States and Europe, see Hart, 'Semiconductor topography: Protection in the UK contrasted with the US Semiconductor Chip Protection Act and the EEC Directive on Topographies' *4 Computer Law and Practice* 151 (1988).

1984 was enacted as the culmination of moves to amend the Copyright Act,[62] appears in Title 17 of the United States Code,[63] and is administered by the Copyright Office, it actually provides a unique new form of protection.[64] It is nevertheless convenient to consider it here, since it was inspired by the deficiencies of copyright, and can apply to the physical embodiment of microcode, thus representing one end of the programming spectrum.[65] It is also significant that in the United Kingdom it was claimed that the ordinary law of copyright was capable of protecting chip designs.[66]

The underlying technology is developing very fast, but essentially consists of the concentration of electronic circuitry in very small components for the performance of given tasks. This is achieved by designing patterns of circuitry on very thin wafers of silicon, and then stacking differently laid out wafers in layers to achieve a three dimensional array of circuitry of very great complexity. The layout of the circuitry in the layered wafers is what the Semiconductor Chip Protection Act 1984 was seeking to protect. The design of such layouts is highly sophisticated, and nowadays assisted to a considerable extent by the use of computer-aided design techniques. Similarly, the production process for such chips requires the very highest standards of precision, and can be attained only by the most extensive use of automated procedures. The design is thus usually incorporated into a digital map held in a computer as an intermediate stage in the manufacturing process.[67]

The government of the United Kingdom argued in its claim for protection under the United States legislation that chip designs were already protected in the United Kingdom on the basis that a three-dimensional reproduction of a two-dimensional design amounted to an infringement of it.[68] This seems rather disingenuous in omitting all reference to section 9(8) of the Copyright Act 1956 which excluded from this category cases where the similarity was not obvious to a non-expert.[69] Copyright is now governed however by the completely new regime of the Copyright, Designs and Patents Act 1988. The aim of this legislation was to create a new unregistered design right, and concomitantly to exclude ordinary copyright protection for drawings of

---

62. See Kastenmeier and Remington, 'The Semiconductor Chip Protection Act of 1984: A Swamp or Firm Ground?,' 70 *Minn. L.R.* 417 (1985).
63. Otherwise concerned exclusively with copyright.
64. 17 U.S.C. sect. 912(b) insulates its provisions from the rest of Title 17.
65. Before programming was invented the earliest computers were themselves in a sense the physical embodiments of programs since their wiring was designed to accomplish a given task.
66. It was on this basis that the United Kingdom was granted protection for its works under the United States legislation by way of a Presidential proclamation under the provisions of section 902(a)(1)(C).
67. The process has become akin to writing a program so that there are now silicon compilers which translate functional designs into detailed layouts.
68. See *Dorling* v. *Honnor Marine Ltd.* [1965] Ch.1, *LB (Plastics) Ltd.* v. *Swish Products Ltd.* [1979] R.P.C. 551, H.L. and *British Leyland Motor Corp. Ltd.* v. *Armstong Patents Co. Ltd.* [1986] A.C. 577, H.L.
69. Though it is arguable that this provision could have been circumvented, see *Lerose Ltd.* v. *Hawick Jersey International Ltd.* [1974] R.P.C. 42, Ch. and *Hart* v. *Edwards Hot Water Systems* 61 A.L.R. 251 (H.C.A., 1985).

purely functional objects. It is not completely clear how the new legislation would have affected the question of the protection of the design of semiconductor chips. The provisions are not free from difficulty of interpretation in this context, but it appears that both the chip design and any chip made to it would amount to an 'artistic work' as defined by section 4.[70] In that case the provision[71] excluding three-dimensional infringement of a functional design would not apply. In such a case, given industrial exploitation, the period of protection would be reduced to twenty five years.[72] Even before the enactment of this legislation however special protection was accorded to semiconductor chip products by regulations[73] implementing a directive of the European Economic Communities. These regulations expressly exclude copyright protection for the topography of semiconductor chips,[74] and in accordance with a directive of the Council of the European Communities[75] adopt a common pattern of protection, different from established forms of intellectual property, effectively dictated by, and modelled upon, the United States legislation.

It is thus logical to examine that legislation first. As noted above much of the difficulty lay in the perceived inability of existing United States law to provide protection for the mask works customarily used in the manufacture of semiconductor chips.[76] Copyright seemed to be the most eligible branch of the law to provide protection, but it was well-established in the United States, first that the chips themselves as merely utilitarian objects could not be the subject matter of copyright protection as three-dimensional objects;[77] and second that even if the mask itself were to be regarded as apt for protection as a drawing, then section 113(b) would operate to prevent the reproduction of objects incorporating the circuits so depicted from amounting to an infringement.[78] The practical possibilities of securing protection in the United States for such works were explored in a dispute between Intel Corporation, a leading manufacturer of semiconductor chip products, and the United States Copyright Office. Intel secured the registration of copyright on nine layout sheets used in the manufacture of one of its chips. It then sought to deposit copies of the manufactured chips as the first published form of the drawings. The Copyright Office rejected this as an inappropriate form of deposit, and Intel commenced litigation to compel the Office to do

---

70. As 'graphic works' defined by section 4(2).
71. Sect. 51.
72. Sect. 52.
73. Semiconductor Products (Protection of Topography) Regulations 1987 (S.I. 1497), though only in relation to topographies created after 7 November 1987.
74. Para. 9(1) relating to the Copyright Act 1956; doubtless the exclusion will be extended to the Copyright, Designs and Patents Act 1988 in due course.
75. 87/54/EEC (OJ No. L 24/36) of 27 January 1987.
76. See Oxman, 'Intellectual Property Protection and Integrated Circuit Masks' *20 Jur. J.* 405 (1980); this article gives an excellent account of the stage of technological advance which dictated the passage of the Semiconductor Chip Protection Act 1984.
77. 17 U.S.C. sect. 101 in its definition of 'pictorial, graphic and sculptural works' which constitute the appropriate class in sect. 102(a)(5).
78. See *Esquire Inc.* v. *Ringer* 591 F.2d 796 (D.C. Cir., 1978); though a different result is achieved where a program is incorporated into a pirate chip, *Apple Computer Inc.* v. *Franklin Computer Corp.* 714 F.2d 1240 (3rd Cir., 1983)

so. However the dispute arose just as the 1976 copyright legislation was being enacted, and a compromise was achieved whereby Intel withdrew its litigation upon the understanding that the Office would conduct hearings into the whole question of the protection by copyright of semiconductor chip products. These hearings were in their turn preempted by the tabling of amendments to the Copyright Act to extend protection to such products quite explicitly. Problems emerged over the drafting of the amendment,[79] over the extent to which it commanded industry support,[80] and over the desirability of distorting the basic principle of copyright law in the United States that it does not protect purely utilitarian objects. The problem was then reconsidered by subsequent Congresses until in 1983[81] the version which was finally enacted opted for a new form of protection.[82]

It applies to semiconductor chip products defined sufficiently broadly to avoid freezing either the definition of the subject-matter,[83] or the form of reproduction,[84] in its current stage of development. The system resembles United States copyright law in requiring registration with the Copyright Office, but unlike copyright which requires only origination by the author, or patent which requires novelty by the inventor, this legislation adopts an intermediate position,

(b) Protection under this chapter shall not be available for a mask work that –
(i) is not original; or
(ii) consists of designs that are staple, commonplace, or familiar in the semiconductor industry, or variations of such designs, combined in a way that, considered as a whole, is not original.
(c) In no case does protection under this chapter for a mask work extend to any idea, procedure, process, system, method of operation, concept, principle, or discovery, regardless of the form in which it is described, explained, illustrated, or embodied in such work.[85]

It had been felt that mask work was rarely of such striking innovation as to amount to patentable subject matter, but that progress would be stultified if designers could not draw upon less strikingly innovative designs originated by others.[86] This standard is probably closer to that of copyright than to that of patent, and it is made clear that the only innovative feature may reside in the precise concatenation of standard modules.[87] If these requirements are

---

79. The definition was thought too rigid to cater for a rapidly moving technology.
80. Of four major semiconductor manufacturers represented at the hearings on the amendment, two supported and two opposed the amendment. A particular point of contention was the extent to which reverse engineering should be permitted.
81. For an account of the legislative history see Kastenmeier and Remington 'The Semiconductor Chip Protection Act 1984; Swamp or Firm Ground?', *70 Minn. L.R.* 233 (1985). The authors were respectively Chairman of and Counsel to the relevant House Committee.
82. The original Senate draft had retained a basis in copyright.
83. Sect. 901(a).
84. Sect. 905.
85. Sect. 902.
86. Since chips are usually combined together in finished devices, and since different designs are combined together in the same chip, some degree of convergence of design is inevitable. It is even common for manufacturers to hold individual design modules in cell libraries.
87. See Stern, 'Determining Liability for Infringement of Mask Work Rights Under the Semiconductor Chip Protection Act 1984' *70 Minn. L.R.* 271, at 317–322 (1985).

satisfied, the proprietor of the mask work is granted[88] for a period of ten years[89] exclusive rights to,

. . . do or authorise any of the following:
(1) to reproduce the work by optical, electronic or any other means;
(2) to import or distribute a semiconductor chip product in which the mask work is embodied; and
(3) to induce or knowingly to cause another person to do any of the acts described in paragraphs (1) and (2).[90]

This clearly covers all forms of reproduction of the mask work in the manufacture of chips, and even extends to taking a photograph of a commercially available chip. The legislation was, however, determined to legitimise the general industry practice of 'reverse engineering' whereby existing chips were improved upon enough to constitute original new designs. This is achieved by imposing[91] specific limitations upon these otherwise exclusive rights in the case of reverse engineering,[92] and by excluding restrictions upon the further distribution, but not reproduction, of a chip once it has been sold.[93] It is not quite clear what standard of originality is required for the purposes of this provision, but it is submitted that it will probably be held to extend beyond origination to the full standard required by section 902. It remains the case that there may be great difficulty in distinguishing in practice between the illegitimate reproduction of a chip under an elaborate disguise of reverse engineering, and genuine reverse engineering given the enormous economic benefits of plagiarisation.[94]

Because it was generally accepted that United States law did not protect such works by means of the law of copyright there was no need to exclude overlapping protection by such means when the new legislation was introduced. However, to the extent that a chip is sufficiently innovative it may still be protected by the law of patent,[95] and this is preserved.[96] One of the reasons for choosing a new form of protection was desire to avoid the compulsory reciprocity imposed by international copyright law under the Universal Copyright Convention to which the United States is party, which would have meant that the United States would have had to extend protection to foreign chips upon the same basis as for its own. By choosing a new method it felt free[97] to offer protection to foreign chips only when similar protection was offered in such jurisdiction to United States chips.[98]

---

88. Sect. 904.
89. Running from the earliest to occur of first registration or commercial exploitation, thus giving a shorter period of protection than either the law of copyright or that of patent.
90. Sect. 905.
91. Sect. 906.
92. For a full account, see Raskind, 'Reverse engineering, unfair competition and fair use under the Semiconductor Chip Protection Act 1984' *70 Minn. L.R.* 385 (1985).
93. So called 'first-sale' rights.
94. In 1987 world sales of semiconductor chips amounted to $36.6bn, projected to increase to $44.3bn in 1988.
95. See Stern *op. cit.* at n. 122 for such a case.
96. Sect. 912(a).
97. Though it can be argued that this legislation is caught by the Paris Convention of 1883 on Industrial Property.
98. Sect. 914.

Many governments sought and secured such protection soon after the passage of the Act including, as noted above, the United Kingdom.[99] In general the response of the international community has been to follow the lead of the United States by enacting similar new forms of protection, urged on to do so by recommendations from international[100] and supranational[101] bodies alike.[102]

The Commission directive has been implemented in the United Kingdom by regulations.[103] Both directive and regulations are closely modelled upon the United States provisions, though with some differences in terminology which could conceivably become significant.[104] All provisions clearly intend to apply to the same subject-matter, and provide similar forms of protection, for the same reduced term of ten years.[105] The basic qualification for protection is the same in both directive and regulations, and shows improvement over the United States terminology by eliminating ambiguity[106] over the use of the term 'original'. Where the United States draft requires both originality and that the mask-work be more than standard within the industry, the United Kingdom form *defines* originality as a combination of the creator's own efforts and their having resulted in something more than the merely commonplace.[107] The exclusive rights conferred are the same as those conferred by the United States legislation, and there is a similar reservation for 'reverse engineering'. Although the European directive contains provisions permitting member states to impose registration requirements,[108] these have not been implemented in the United Kingdom which has never required registration for copyright purposes either.

2. Audio-visual displays

One of the principal means for human beings to communicate with

---

99. See p. 40.
100. See WIPO Draft Treaty on the Protection of Intellectual Property in respect of (Semiconductor) Integrated Circuits (IPIC/CE/11/2)(17 March 1986)
101. Council Directive on the legal protection of topographies of semiconductor products (87/54/EEC)(OJ No. L 24/36)(27 January 1987)
102. Though this strategy has been criticised, see Jehoram 'The European Commission Pressurized into a Dis-harmonising Directive on Chip Protection' [1987] E.I.P.R. 35.
103. Semiconductor Products (Protection of Topography) Regulations 1987 (S.I. 1497).
104. Thus both the United States and European provisions refer to the pattern as being 'encoded or fixed' while the United Kingdom regulations refer to it as being 'fixed or intended to be fixed'. The position is further complicated by the fact that to the extent of any conflict between them the terms of the United Kingdom regulations will be construed so as to accord with the terms of the directive.
105. Subject in the case of the United Kingdom regulations to the time starting to run from a slightly different point owing to there being no registration provision in the United Kingdom.
106. The ambiguity arises because it seems that when 'original' recurs in sect. 905 it must embrace both of the conditions specified in sect. 902.
107. Para. 3(3). It is made equally clear that a new combination of known elements may satisfy this condition.
108. Though rather foolishly providing for the use of a different symbol to signify satisfaction of the formalities: 'T' for topography being substituted in the European provision for 'M' for mask-work in the United States.

computers is by the use of a keyboard or other device to transmit, and by perusal of a visual display to receive, instructions and information. In applications where continuing human interaction is important the design of such visual displays achieves great importance, its apogee being reached in the case of computer games which derive most of their attraction and commercial value from the nature of the display. It is there used first to attract customers to play the game, and thereafter becomes essential to the play. Both in the United Kingdom[109] and in the United States,[110] screen displays may be the subject of copyright separate from their status as literary works. Some attempt was at first made in the United States to deny the copyrightability of computer games as audio-visual works on the basis that the display was not original to the author of the game, nor fixed, since the sequence displayed on the screen during the playing of the game was partly determined by the actions of the player. However, these arguments were rejected upon the basis that there was sufficient originality and fixation in the choice of the appearance and sounds of the images and noises to be manipulated during play, and in *Midway Manufacturing Co* v. *Artic International Inc.*[111] this was declared to be the universal view in the federal courts.

The relationship between the protection of displays as such and the programs which generate them, on the one hand, and the elements of which they are composed, on the other, have been most extensively considered in the United States. It should be noted, however, that in the United Kingdom it is arguable that the definition of a film in terms of movement may prevent some static[112] screen displays from attracting protection as anything other than a literary work. It was early established in the United States that since the underlying programs and the displays were separately registrable in different categories they required separate consideration.[113] In *Midway Manufacturing Co* v. *Strohan*[114] the plaintiffs had registered their copyright both in the display of a very popular[115] computer game as an audio-visual work, and in the underlying program as a literary work. It was held that the defendants had changed the appearance of the display sufficiently to avoid infringement of the copyrighted display. Nevertheless, so much[116] of the underlying

---

109. Copyright, Designs and Patents Act 1988 sect. 1(1)(b) as 'films' themselves defined by sect. 5(1) to mean 'a recording of visual images, in any medium, from which a moving picture may by any means be produced'.
110. 17 U.S.C. sect. 102 (a)(6) as 'audiovisual works' defined in sect. 101 as 'works that consist of a series of related images which are intrinsically intended to be shown by the use of a machine or devices such as projectors, viewers or electronic equipment, together with accompanying sounds, if any, regardless of the nature of the material objects, such as films or tapes, in which the works are embodied.'
111. 704 F.2d 1009 (7th Cir., 1983) at 1012.
112. Screen displays are never really static but rather continuously renewed or 'repainted'.
113. Though the United States Copyright Office has persisted in a policy of requiring a single registration for display and underlying program, see Notice of Registration Decision, 3 June 1988; for criticism see Stern, 'The Copyright Office's Response to the *Softklone* decision: Not Serendipitous' [1988] 9 E.I.P.R. 255.
114. 564 F.Supp. 741 (N.D. Ill., 1983).
115. 96 000 games were sold at $2500 each in little more than a year, thus grossing some $240 million.
116. 97 per cent of the sequencing instructions controlling the playing of the game, and 84 per cent in all.

program had been copied as to infringe its copyright as a literary work. Sometimes copyright in display and program may even be held by different parties.[117] By the time of litigation in that case, however, the plaintiff had both forms. The Fourth Circuit held there that the changes to the display were merely trivial, and that although separately registrable, copyright in the audio-visual display carried with it the exclusive right to copy that part of the underlying program by which it was generated. The position is that while a given display can be generated by any number of different underlying programs,[118] a given underlying program cannot generate any number of different displays.[119] This view was confirmed in *Digital Communications Associates* v. *Softklone Distributing Corporation*[120] where the court explicitly held that while copyright in a display might be infringed by copying the underlying program, copyright in the underlying program was not infringed by copying the display.[121] In that case however the relevant screen was the subject of a separate copyright as a literary work, being a compilation of the textual elements of which it was composed, and it was held that such copyright had been infringed.

The question of infringement of copyright in an audio-visual work may be just as difficult to decide as that of the infringement of copyright in programs, and for similar reasons. It is especially difficult in the case of applications programs where a human being needs to communicate continuously with a program. As computers are increasingly used by non-specialists and non-typists, so there has been an increasing tendency to by-pass words as the primary medium for such communication. Options are now often displayed to the user in graphic form,[122] and his responses conveyed by manipulation of pointing and firing devices.[123] The success of such programs is highly dependent upon the design of the screen displays. Different families of personal computers achieve these results in very different ways owing to fundamental differences in their chip architectures and their operating systems. There is thus considerable pressure to adapt programs which have succeeded on one family of machines so as to be able to run on another. The problem is analogous to that in relation to copying operating systems.[124] A potential competitor is there constrained by his need to cause the same hardware to respond in the same way to applications programs as does the operating system being emulated. Here a competing applications program is constrained by the need to communicate with its human user in the manner to which he has become accustomed. This can be achieved only

---

117. As at one stage in *M. Kramer Manufacturing Co. Ltd.* v. *Andrews* 783 F.2d 421 (4th Cir., 1986).
118. *Stern Electronics Inc.* v. *Kaufmann* 669 F.2d 852 (2nd. Cir., 1982).
119. *M. Kramer Manufacturing Co. Ltd* v. *Andrews* 783 F.2d 421 (4th Cir., 1986) at 441, 442.
120. 659 F.Supp. 449 (N.D.Ga., 1987).
121. Disapproving any suggestion to the contrary in *Broderbund Software Inc.* v. *Unison Wolrd Inc.* 648 F.Supp. 1127 (N.D.Ca., 1986).
122. For example, as 'icons' (stylised pictures of the operation in question).
123. For example, by 'mice' (devices which can be moved on the surface of a desk to generate movement of the cursor or pointer on the screen, and equipped with buttons, depression of combinations of which generate certain functions within the programs).
124. See p. 37 above.

by providing and accepting information and instructions in the form of the program being emulated.

The question is thus one of how far the emulator can go in duplicating the original display before he infringes its copyright. In *Broderbund Software Inc.* v. *Unison World Inc.*[125] the plaintiffs owned copyright as an audiovisual work in the screen display of a printing program for use on personal computers. The defendants sought to reproduce this program so as to run on a different family of machines. They first agreed to co-operate with the plaintiffs in a joint venture to this end, but relations soured and, after they had already prepared parts of the program as an exact emulation, the defendants subsequently finished off the project by going their own way and attempting to improve on the plaintiffs' original. For reasons of time and expense they did not re-write the parts exactly emulating the plaintiffs' program. Discussion centred on the structure, sequencing and arrangement of the menu screens which guided the user through the process of designing the finished product. The evidence showed that there was considerable scope for variation in all of these areas, so it could not be established that idea and expression merged.[126] Nor was the court prepared to accept that these screens fell within the exclusion from protection of rules and instructions. No monopoly in the idea of using personal computers to compose printed graphic output by the use of personal computers was being conferred directly or indirectly. It was further held that the copyright notice need not explicitly refer to its nature as an audio-visual work protecting the menu screen displays.[127] In order to determine the question of substantial similarity in order to ascertain whether copying had taken place, the Court adopted the two-tier approach operated by the Ninth Circuit.[128] This comprises an 'extrinsic' test of the underlying idea, and an 'intrinsic' test of the 'total concept and feel' of the expression of the idea. In *Digital Communications Associates* v. *Softklone Distributing Corporation*,[129] some of this reasoning was rejected, at least in a case where copying was not denied, in holding that copyright in the underlying program did not protect the screen displays so generated. However, the status screen display had been registered there not as an audio-visual, but as a literary, work comprising a compilation of the terms it used. In that regard the Court also rejected arguments relying upon the reasoning in *Baker* v. *Selden*[130] that idea and expression were indistinguishable, and that the status screen display was the equivalent of the blank accounting forms in that case. The Court recognised that this cast the whole weight of the decision upon the characterisation of the 'idea' of the status

---

125. 648 F.Supp. 1127 (N.D. Ca., 1986).
126. Cp. *Synercom Technology Inc.* v. *University Computer Co.* 462 F.Supp 1003 (N.D. Tex., 1978) p. 49 below.
127. At 1135. Nor is it necessary that the copyright notice appear on every protected screen, so long as it appears on the first ('boot-up') screen which is regarded as analogous to the title page of a book, see *Digital Communications Associates* v. *Softklone Distributing Corporation* 659 F.Supp. 449 (N.D. Ga., 1987) at 464.
128. *Sid and Marty Krofft Television Products Inc.* v. *McDonald's Corporation Inc.* 562 F.2d 1157 (9th Cir., 1977) at 1162. See also *Arnstein* v. *Porter* 154 F.2d 464 (2nd Cir., 1946).
129. 659 F.Supp. 449 (N.D. Ga., 1987).
130. 101 U.S. 99 (1879).

screen. It felt that while the use of a command screen to convey instructions to, and to monitor the status of, the system could indeed be regarded as an idea, and could not be protected for fear of granting a monopoly, it was nevertheless an infringement of the expression of that idea to copy the detail of the commands and patterns used to accomplish these ends.

Case law in the United Kingdom is so far much less well-developed in this area,[131] though it should be noted that copyright was explicitly claimed for screen displays associated with a video game as an artistic work and as a film in addition to a claim for the underlying program under the provisions of the Copyright Act 1956 in *Sega Enterprises Ltd.* v. *Richards*.[132]

3. Formats

There is some analogy between the relationship of programs and audio-visual displays in the area of programs, and that between formats and databases in the area of data. In much the same way as the program determines the appearance of the display, so the format determines the organisation of the database. It so happened that one of the most influential of the early cases, *Synercom Technology Inc.* v. *University Computer Co.*[133] concerned this very problem. It arose in the familiar context of an attempt by a newcomer to break into an established market, in this case for civil engineering analysis programs. There was the usual complex and volatile mixture of personal and human relationships, but in essence the plaintiffs developed a leading position in the market for conducting structural analysis by computer. The program, like many others of the period, operated on a bureau basis, the customer preparing data to be run on the vendor's computer. To operate successfully, the vendor had to ensure that the customers all prepared their data in the same form. By training and by the publication of manuals persuading customers to adopt a common format, this task was accomplished, and the system achieved market dominance. In order to be profitable the service had to recoup in charges the large sums expended[134] in developing the market. This created an opportunity for anyone able to develop a competing program which could use the same data, since it would be easy to persuade existing users to subscribe to a new system if they could use their existing data, and secure exactly the same results at lower cost. The lower cost reflected only the expense of writing the new programs, but not that of creating and developing the market. The plaintiffs had published a format, in which they had been granted copyright, according to which customers were required to prepare the punched cards used as input data. The defendants simply re-arranged these formats, and then wrote a pre-processing program to produce the required results from cards prepared in the plaintiffs' format.

---

131. For the position in Australia, see Greenleaf, 'Screens, studies and ideas on the boundary of copyright' 62 A.L.J. 630 (1988).
132. *Sega Enterprises Ltd.* v. *Richards* [1983] F.S.R. 73, Ch. It was, however, unnecessary for the Court to consider these claims since it was satisfied that a sufficient case had been shown of infringement in the underlying program.
133. 462 F.Supp. 1003 (N.D. Tex., 1978).
134. About half a million dollars.

It was argued that in so doing the defendants had infringed the plaintiffs' copyright in its formats. Although it accepted that forms can amount to expression if they convey original information,[135] the court found it impossible to separate idea from expression in relation to the sequence and order of elements[136] in the format:

If sequencing and ordering are expression, what separable idea is expressed?[137]

The court drew an analogy with the pattern of relationships of gears in the shift mechanism of a car, arguing that even though one manufacturer might originally have developed an 'H' pattern, other manufacturers would be free to adopt it in their own cars. It was suggested that otherwise it would be an infringement to write a computer program to implement a series of steps described in ordinary prose.[138] It should be noted that the court was able to provide relief for the plaintiff without undue difficulty on the basis of infringement of its manuals.

The holding on formats has, however, been criticised in subsequent cases upon the ground that idea and expression merge no more inevitably in the computer field than in any other, and that the line between idea and expression should be drawn in a different place, at least where more complex program modules are being considered.[139] It may be conceded that *Synercom* does display some internal inconsistency on the question of how far the formats were dictated by the nature of the function to be performed, and that the Court may have been unduly severe in its view of the 'idea' being implemented by the formats. However, the decision has been accepted in the most recent authorities. In particular, it was emphasised in *Digital Communications Associates* v. *Softklone Distributing Corporation*[140] that in *Synercom* the defendants had not copied the formats as such, but had merely written a pre-processing program capable of accepting data prepared in that format. In *Plains Cotton Co-Operative* v. *Goodpasture Computer Services*[141] the Fifth Circuit re-affirmed *Synercom* in noting that it prevents the monopolisation of methods of programming dictated by the externalities of the relevant market.

It seems that here once more the real issue is one relating to the propriety of the form of competition adopted by the defendant, and it is not without significance that in *Synercom* itself the element of relief in respect of formats was subsequently held to have pre-empted relief in a basis of misappropriation or as an unfair trade practice.[142] Furthermore, the efficacy of such an

---

135. Following *Harcourt Brace & World Inc.* v. *Graphic Controls Corp.* 329 F.Supp. 517 (S.D.N.Y., 1971) at 524.
136. Despite finding on p. 1007 that hundreds of programs were available for statistical analysis, fifteen of them directly competitive with the plaintiffs' program, yet of these fifteen only that of the defendant used the same input format.
137. At 1013.
138. It may be noted that this very phenomenon *was* regarded as an infringement in *Williams* v. *Arndt* 626 F.Supp. 571 (D.Mass., 1985).
139. *Whelan Associates* v. *Jaslow Dental Laboratory* 797 F.2d 1222 (3rd Cir., 1986) at 1239, 1240. Followed on this point in *Broderbund Software Inc.* v. *Unison World Inc.* 648 F.Supp. 1127 (N.D. Cal., 1986) at 1132, 1133 in relation to the appearance of the audio-visual display.
140. 659 F.Supp. 449 (N.D. Ga., 1987) at 460.
141. 807 F.2d 1256 (5th Cir., 1987).
142. *Synercom Technology Inc.* v. *University Computer Co.* 474 F.Supp 37 (N.D. Tex., 1979).

approach is illustrated by *Dickerman Associates Inc.* v. *Tiverton Bottled Gas Co.*[143] where use by the defendant of a similar pattern of menu screens to be used for the entry of information in the course of running a program to perform the administrative functions involved in retailing oil was considered exclusively within the context of trade secrets. The Court was there uninhibited by considerations of novelty or originality, and was able to consider the underlying policies much more directly. It is significant that it adopted an approach very reminiscent of the cases discussed above in its determination that the organisation of the screens in this program was not wholly dictated by the necessity of providing certain information in a common form, but instead represented a free choice from among a number of possible alternatives.

4. Databases

A further problematic area concerns the extent to which copyright may attach to the data which are the subject of computer application. In some ways the problem is most acute in this context. In most database applications the cost of creating, storing and up-dating the database is much greater than the costs of programming the system. What is more, the form of the data is much less volatile than the form of the programs which manipulate it. It is also inherent in the nature of a database application that the data are readily available to the users in an easily usable form. This means that database proprietors are in a particularly vulnerable position. Their stock-in-trade is expensive to create, and the market for information notoriously difficult to cultivate. Yet when this has been done it is extremely cheap and simple for a competitor to copy the database and sell into the existing market at a discount as a result of the saving of such start-up and development costs.

(a) Varieties

The database proprietor will be protected by copyright only to the extent that the materials in his database or the database as such is protected. If an original literary work like a novel is protected in its conventional form, that protection will extend to any form of reproduction including transcription into a computer-readable form.[144] It is also possible that if an anthology is prepared consisting of extracts from a number of different copyright works, then that anthology may attract separate copyright protection. Even if the individual items are not protected, perhaps because they have come into the public domain, there may still be copyright protection for the new anthology. More difficult questions arise in relation to the storage of such works in a computer in a different form such as a summary, an index or an inverted file.[145]

---

143. 222 U.S.P.Q. (BNA) 529 (D.Mass., 1984).
144. In the United Kingdom this has been made quite explicit by the Copyright, Designs and Patents Act 1988 sect. 17(2).
145. It has been held in France that summaries of newspaper articles held in machine-readable form do not infringe copyright in the articles themselves, *Société Microfor* v. *Sàrl 'Le Monde'* [1988] F.S.R. 519 (Pl. Cour de Cass., 1987).

Different questions may arise in relation to works of non-fiction which tend to have a more utilitarian purpose. Such works themselves exhibit wide variety and include textbooks, reports, maps, items of news, lists, directories, rules, instructions, programmes of events, advertisements and many others. The use of all of these may benefit from the application of the computer.[146] Some such works may collect together copyright items in the same way as an anthology, but more often their individual components will not attract copyright, perhaps because they are no more than facts, perhaps because they are in the public domain, or perhaps because too little originality has been expended in their expression. In many cases such factual works have a dual role. They can be used to guide or assist an ultimate user directly, or they can be used by a developer as the foundation for further improvement in the quality of such guidance. Thus a map can be used either to guide a user to his destination, or as the basis for the production of another more useful map. It is in relation to such works that the conflict between the dual aims of copyright to protect the author and to encourage progress is most apparent. While it is clear that simple reproduction of such a work achieves little or no advance, it becomes much more problematic when the new work is something more. In many cases value can be added to a work merely by representing it in a different form. To the extent that copyright protects expression rather than idea it might be thought that no problem would arise. However, it is clear that protection extends beyond identical reproduction of the whole copyright work. It is enough to perform an infringing act in relation to a substantial part of the work,[147] or to make an adaptation of the work.[148]

(b) Originality[148]

Both the Copyright, Designs and Patents Act 1988 in the United Kingdom[150] and the copyright legislation in the United States[151] explicitly require originality in the work to be protected by copyright. This has traditionally been regarded as a minimal requirement in both the United Kingdom,

the Act does not require that the expression must be in an original or novel form, but that the work must not be copied from another work – that it should originate from the author.[152]

and in the United States,

Originality in this context 'means little more than a prohibition of actual copying'.[153]

In both jurisdictions this seems to have represented an extrapolation of the

---

146. Cuadra in his 1986 *Directory of On-line Databases* listed 3169 as being then available in the United States through 486 different services. EPS consultants in 1988 estimated the United Kingdom market as being worth £546.5 million, through over 800 services.
147. Copyright, Designs and Patents Act 1988 sect. 16(3)(a).
148. Copyright, Designs and Patents Act 1988 sect. 21.
149. See generally Olson, 'Copyright Originality' *48 Mo. L.R.* 29 (1983).
150. Sect. 1(1)(a).
151. 17 U.S.C. sect. 102(a).
152. *University of London Press* v. *University Tutorial Press* [1916] 2 Ch. 601 at 608, C.A.
153. *Alfred Bell & Co.* v. *Catalda Fine Arts Inc.* 191 F.2d 99 at 102 (2nd Cir., 1951).

notion of being an author. While such a minimal requirement is likely to
cause little difficulty in relation to creative or artistic works, it is more
problematic in relation to purely utilitarian works. It is well-established that
copyright cannot inhere in facts themselves.[154] This position would be
defeated unless copyright should also be denied to short and simple
statements of such facts. Thus in *Rose* v. *Information Systems Ltd.*[155] Hoffman J.
refused copyright in the title of a book which merely characterised its
contents in an obvious way on the grounds that it was not 'a literary work of
originality', and pointed out that to ascribe copyright to it would invest the
plaintiff with a monopoly of the use of part of the English language. In the
United States it has similarly been held that obvious combinations of
commonplace elements may be 'too simple to be copyrightable'.[156]

Similar considerations apply to obvious, but more extensive, arrangements
of such elements so as to deny copyright in such a compilation. Thus a list of
the counties of England or the states of the United States in alphabetical
order would be denied sufficient originality of arrangement to qualify as a
compilation or list.[157] Here too a *de minimis* requirement applies both in the
United Kingdom,

> commonplace matter put together or arranged without the exercise of more than
> negligible work, labour and skill in making the selection will not be entitled to
> copyright[158]

and in the United States,

> in some cases, where are involved labor, talent, judgment, the classification and
> disposition of subjects in a book entitle it to copyright ... but the arrangement of
> cases and the paging of volumes is a labor inconsiderable in itself[159]

This result is justified in a number of different ways, sometimes that the
form of expression is dictated by the function being performed,[160] sometimes
that too little effort has been expended,[161] or sometimes that too little
creativity has been involved.[162] Any of these may militate against copyright
in a given database, though it is obvious that they are capable of yielding
different results on occasion, for example if a complicated function dictates a

---

154. *Elanco Products Ltd.* v. *Mandops Ltd.* [1980] R.P.C. 213, C.A. at 226; *Harper & Row Publishers Inc.* v. *Nation Enterprises Inc.* 471 U.S. 539 (1985) at 556.
155. In England it seems that a single created word is also disqualified even though shown to be the product of creative effort, *Exxon Corp.* v. *Exxon Insurance Co.* [1981] 3 All E.R. 241, C.A.
156. *Smith* v. *George E. Muechelbach Brewing Co.* 140 F.Supp 729 (W.D. Mo., 1956) (a combination of two musical notes to mimic the sound of the tick of a clock).
157. *Purefoy Engineering Co Ltd.* v. *Sykes Boxall & Co Ltd* (1955) 72 R.P.C. 89, C.A.; *Cooling Systems & Flexibles Inc.* v. *Stuart Radiators Inc.* 777 F.2d 485 (9th Cir., 1985).
158. *Ladbroke (Football) Ltd* v. *William Hill (Football) Ltd.* [1964] 1 All E.R. 465 at 475, H.L.
159. *Myers* v. *Callaghan* 128 US 617 at 662 (1888), quoting *Myers* v. *Callaghan* 20 F 441 at 442 (Circ.Ct., N.D.Ill., 1883]).
160. *Morrissey* v. *Proctor & Gamble Inc.* 379 F.2d 675 (1st Cir., 1967) (rules for a simple lottery).
161. *Leslie* v. *Young & Son* [1984] A.C. 335, H.L. (Sc.) (compilation of a local railway timetable form a non-copyright national timetable).
162. *Donald* v. *Zack Meyer's T.V. Sales and Service* 426 F.2d 1027 (5th Cir., 1970) (a combination of a number of legal forms in the standard jargon).

form of expression which takes effort and ingenuity to draft.[163] There is some divergence between the prevailing view in the United Kingdom that a sufficient expenditure of even uncreative effort may suffice to satisfy the minimal requirement of originality,[164] and that of some influential United States Circuits which require at least a modicum of creativity, except perhaps in the case of wholesale appropriation.[165] The argument in these United States cases reflects the views expressed in *Nimmer on Copyright*[166] that to protect mere effort in this context is to place too much basic knowledge beyond the useful reach of subsequent workers in the same field. The position in the United Kingdom seems to square better with the opposite view in distinguishing between the expression of one person's name and telephone number which would fail to meet the minimal requirement to justify copyright protection, and the expression of the names and telephone numbers of everyone in the district which certainly would be protected, but which represents an increase in the expenditure of effort rather than of creativity. It also squares better with the results achieved in those cases where the re-ordering of such a list has been held an infringement of copyright. The strength of Nimmer's view is that in such cases, where neither the selection nor the arrangement of materials is reproduced in the allegedly infringing work, argument is likely to turn on the issue of the commercial and competitive propriety of permitting such subsequent use of someone else's prior efforts. It is eminently arguable that the law of unfair competition provides a preferable forum for the resolution of such disputes, and that to attempt to do so within that of copyright may lead to distortion.[167] The argument is important because it is nowadays very easy to re-arrange information by the use of a computer. It would require little effort to select the items for a particular place from a general timetable,[168] or to re-arrange a telephone directory so as to list by arithmetic order of subscriber's number rather than by alphabetic order of subscriber's name.[169] A particular problem is that without holding an exact copy of either the selection or arrangement of an existing copyright compilation, it has become possible for a user to re-create the desired selection or arrangement without difficulty and so to undercut the market for the works as originally selected or arranged.

The whole question of the changes wrought by the introduction of computers into the field of databases is very well illustrated by the recent

---

163. Thus the rules of a complicated game will attract protection, *Caley & Sons Ltd.* v. *Garnett & Sons Lts.* [1936–45] M.C.C. 99 (Ch., 1936); *Whist Club* v. *Foster* 42 F.2d 782 (S.D.N.Y., 1929).
164. See, for example, *Football League Ltd.* v. *Littlewoods Pools Ltd.* [1959] Ch. 637 at 656, C. and *Express Newspapers P.L.C.* v. *Liverpool Daily Post and Echo* [1985] F.S.R. 306 at 309, Ch
165. See *Financial Information Inc.* v. *Moody's Investors Services Inc.* 808 F.2d 204 at 207 (2nd Cir., 1986).
166. Para. 3.04 at 3–20
167. Though this view is contested by those who like Denicola in 'Copyright in Collections of Facts' 81 Col. L.R. 576 (1981) argue that these issues are already present within the law of copyright, and may be resolved by the application of fair use or fair dealing rationales.
168. See note 17 above
169. As in *Leon* v. *Pacific Tel. & Tel. Co.* 91 F.2d 484 (9th Cir., 1937)

American case of *West Publishing Co* v. *Mead Data Control Inc.*[170] This case
concerned the rights of Mead Data Central the proprietors of the LEXIS
legal information retrieval system, to interpolate into their representations of
certain public domain federal court opinions an indication of the page breaks
and numbering of the representation of the same cases in the conventional
and copyright West Publishing Co. volume of law reports. It is well settled
in the United States[171] that while the judgments of the courts are in the
public domain,[172] copyright is capable of existing in additional matter added
by the reporter.[173] West has accordingly secured copyright registration for its
volumes as compilations 'of previously published case reports including but
not limited to opinions, synopses, syllabi or case law paragraphs, key
number classifications, tables and index digest with revisions and
additions.'[174] It should be noted that no explicit reference is made to
pagination or to arrangement, though the list is expressed not to be
exclusive. Mead collected the judgments within its system quite independently of West, omitted all of the features explicitly mentioned in West's
copyright registration, and did not copy any of the editorial changes to the
text of the opinions made by West. Mead did however include as a reference
at the beginning of its representation of the opinion citations to all other
published representations of the case. For many federal cases the only such
citation was to the West reporter volume in which the case appeared. This
practice was conceded by West to be a fair use. West nevertheless objected
to Mead's proposal to include in the text of the cases displayed on the
LEXIS terminal an indication of all of the pagination and numeration of the
West text. The practice of including such an indication of the pagination and
numeration of competing series of law reports had been common in the
United States for more than a century.[175] Moreover, it had, in relation to
conventional publication, survived attack as being in breach of copyright in
Banks Law Publishers Inc. v. *Lawyer's Co-Operative Publishing Co.,*[176] and in that
medium survives today, not least in a number of West's own publications.
The question thus raised in this litigation was whether the fact that the same
device was now being used in a computer database was sufficient to make a
difference. It seems clear that the object of including the 'star pagination'[177]
feature in LEXIS was no different from its object in conventional book
publishing, namely to assist cross-reference, and hence communication,
between users of different sources of the basic public domain materials. It

---

170. 799 F.2d 1219 (8th Cir., 1986).
171. In England the position is less clear, though it is submitted that the better view is that the
judgments of the courts are also in the public domain, see Tapper 'Genius and Janus' *11
Monash Law Review* 75 (1985), though these arguments may to some extent have been
undermined by the passage of the Copyright, Designs and Patents Act 1988 sect. 163
which redefines the scope of Crown Copyright
172. *Wheaton* v. *Peters* 33 U.S. 591 (1834).
173. *Callaghan* v. *Myers* 128 U.S. 617 (1888).
174. There was some slight variation between different forms of claim, but this seems to be the
most extensive.
175. It was used in volume 1 of Curtis's American Reports published in Boston in 1854.
176. 169 F. 386 (2nd. Cir., 1909).
177. The name of this feature reflects the original typographical representation on a conventional page.

seems that the only difference is that the computer database is sufficiently flexible to enable a user to reproduce more easily the database materials corresponding to those in the copyright volume in the order in which they appear in that volume. It was this capability to which West objected on the basis that Mead was infringing its copyright in the arrangement of material in its volume, and that the pagination and numeration was an intrinsic part of that arrangement. Mead's answer was that West was, in effect, seeking to protect the purely mechanical task of dissecting its book into pages. Its position was that West could not plausibly claim that the page numbers were an original work of authorship. The Court of Appeals disagreed and upheld West's arguments on this point:

> The key to this case, then, is not whether numbers are copyrightable, but whether the copyright on the books as a whole is infringed by the unauthorised appropriation of these particular numbers.[178]

and that:

> West's case arrangements, an important part of which is internal page citations, are original works of authorship entitled to copyright protection.

The Court had examined the process by which West channels the deluge of opinions showering down upon it so as to make up different volumes of different series of reports, concluding that it was the result of 'considerable labor, talent and judgment' and easily sufficient to meet the minimal standard of originality required for copyright purposes. This result can be achieved only by assimilating the tasks of assembling the opinions in the desired order together with that of dividing them into pages numbered consecutively in arabic numerals. The question of how far back preliminary work is to be taken into account is a perennial source of dispute in relation to database and compilation cases. It is interesting to note that outside the computer context, English courts[179] have arrived at the same conclusion, at least when ultimate publication has been envisaged, namely that the enterprise is to be considered as a whole rather than to be divided into preliminary and executory portions so as to assess originality. Even granting such an approach, it remains arguable whether it really was legitimate for the Court to consider the labour involved in applying the arrangement of the whole West system when copyright was claimed only for individual volumes. Within each volume the ordering of the material has no significance to the user, and requires the application of only the most straightforward criteria which might be thought too little in the case of a database to surmount even the most modest requirement of originality.[180] If, as *West* holds, a copyright arrangement is infringed by the reproduction of page-breaks in a different rendering of material derived from a common source, it remains to be seen if

---

178. At 1227.
179. See especially *Football League Ltd* v. *Littlewoods Pools Ltd*. [1959] Ch. 637, Ch. and *Ladbroke Ltd* v. *William Hill Ltd*. [1964] 1 All E.R. 465, H.L.
180. Thus in *Financial Information Inc.* v. *Moody's Investors Services Inc.* 808 F.2d 204 (2nd Cir., 1986) the scanning of called bond advertisements in newspapers and the extraction from them of five categories of information to be placed on a card was held to be too simple a clerical task to pass the test.

this applies only when the competing rendering is held on a computer. The Court of Appeals in *West* purported to distinguish the contrary finding for conventional competition in the *Banks* case on three grounds: first, that the case involved an official reporter whose duties left no discretion in relation to selection or arrangement, second that at that time in the United States the relevant legislation made no explicit provision for compilations, and third that the requirements of originality have since then become less stringent. These arguments are unconvincing. *Callaghan* v. *Myers* expressly refuted the suggestion that an official reporter might be in a worse situation than a private reporter:

Even though a reporter may be a sworn public officer . . . in the absence of any restriction forbidding him to take a copyright for that which is the lawful subject of copyright in him . . . he is not to be deprived of the privilege of taking out a copyright which would otherwise exist.[181]

In other words, if any reporter can claim copyright in pagination and arrangement, an official reporter can equally well do so, in the absence of any explicit contrary legislation, and none was present in *Banks*. The Supreme Court in *Callaghan* regarded pagination and arrangement as too insubstantial a feature of law reporting to secure protection, and where, as in *Banks*, nothing else had been copied the Circuit Court of Appeal accordingly refused to intervene. Whatever the wording of the Copyright Act these cases, and their predecessors stretching back for decades, had all proceeded on the basis that compilations were, in principle, entitled to copyright protection. There are no subsequent cases protecting pagination alone, while in *Eggers* v. *Sun Sales Corporation*,[182] where the defendants had used the plaintiff's pagination of a public domain document in their incorporation of it into a very similar souvenir item, the Court remarked that:

It is possible that the defendant's printers set up the official report from a copy of plaintiff's book: identity of pagination leads to that suspicion; but legally that is not of sufficient importance to constitute breach of copyright.[183]

Similarly a numbering scheme *per se* was held not to merit copyright protection in *Toro Company* v. *R. R. Products*;[184] nor was a simple alphabetic arrangement of names thought protectable in *Cooling Systems & Flexibles Inc.* v. *Stuart Radiators Inc.*[185] It should be further noted that in a very recent pronouncement the Second Circuit has indicated that in the case of databases the Court is less well-disposed to find copyrightable subject-matter, just because the danger of stultifying progress by prohibiting use of such material is there greatest.[186]

It remains to be discussed whether any special rules apply to the

---

181. 128 U.S. 617 (1888) at 647.
182. 263 F. 373 (2nd Cir., 1920).
183. At 375.
184. 787 F.2d 1208 (8th Cir., 1986). In England a similar view was taken in relation to race cards assigning trap numbers to greyhounds, *Greyhound Racing Association* v. *Shallis* [1923–31] M.C.C. 370 (1928, Ch.).
185. 777 F.2d 485 at 492 (9th Cir., 1985).
186. *Financial Information Inc.* v. *Moody's Investors Services Inc.* 808 F.2d 204 at 206 (2nd Cir., 1986).

originality requirements in relation to the creation of computer databases. In most cases there will be little difficulty since the content of the database will either consist of copyright material, will have been compiled upon some sufficiently original principle of selection, will have been arranged in an original way or, if it is sufficient, will reflect the expenditure of sufficient effort. The only doubt may be as to those where none of the material is itself copyright, a complete field of resource is tapped quite automatically, and the material is held without any further arrangement in the computer. Suppose a database is compiled by simply subscribing to every known on-line source of public domain material, downloading it to create a single composite database. Each piece of material is held in its original form, and all of the originality of the service lies in the software to manipulate information held in different forms in response to user requests. Would such a database attract copyright protection sufficient to prevent a competitor from simply downloading the whole database to supply his own service based on quite different retrieval software? It is far from clear that copyright would in these circumstances attach, at least in the United States, and it might well be preferable to resolve the matter by recourse to the law of unfair competition. In the United Kingdom the effort of the original compiler would be more likely to be rewarded by the recognition of copyright. It is interesting to speculate whether this is an effect or a cause of the less developed state of the law on unfair competition.

(c) *Fixation and registration*

It is a requirement both in the United Kingdom[187] and in the United States[188] that copyright attaches only to works which are 'recorded' or 'fixed'.[189] Although registration is no longer a condition for the ascription of copyright in the United States, it remains a condition for bringing an infringement suit.[190] These requirements present special problems in relation to databases held on computers. There is as previously noted[191] no particular problem over 'recording' or 'fixation' just because a work is held in machine-readable form. More difficulty resides in relation to the identity of the work which is the subject of copyright, especially in the case of a typical database which is constantly being added to, subtracted from, and rearranged. The central case of copyright is the publication of a single discrete work. Automated databases are neither 'published' in the conventional sense, nor as a corollary made available as a single discrete work. At present the United States Copyright Office has power to permit a single registration for a group of related works such as those represented in a database,[192] and special regulations have been made to specify the material to be deposited in support of such registration.[193] The proprietor is required to register the

---

187. Copyright, Designs and Patents Act 1988 sect. 3(2).
188. 17 U.S.C. sect. 102(a).
189. See above p. 29.
190. 17 U.S.C. sect. 411.
191. See above p. 29.
192. 17 U.S.C. sect. 408(c)(i).
193. 37 C.F.R. sect. 202–20(c)(2)(vii)(B).

database either as a single file, if it relates to a single subject, or as multiple files, if it does not. A statement describing the database must also be supplied to include such matters as its title, subject matter, origin, approximate number of records, and the manner and frequency of display of any copyright notice. All of these rules, together with the deposit requirements which also apply somewhat unhappily to databases, have recently been revised, but it is far from clear that all criticisms of the old rules have been answered.[194]

The United Kingdom does not require registration, nor hence deposit, as a condition for the ascription of copyright; nor is it necessary even for the limited purposes for which it is now required in the United States. Some evidential advantages may however accrue from voluntary registration,[195] or from use of the copyright symbol.[196] In the United Kingdom it seems that copyright accrues to the database as a whole each time it is up-dated:

> A book which consists of a specification of the conditions at the present moment of a constantly changing subject-matter is a new work even though some of the particulars given may not have altered from what they were, and were stated to be, at some prior date, perhaps years before.[197]

While it is true that these words were uttered of a hard copy publication, it is hard to see why exactly the same reasoning should not apply to databases held in a computer once it is accepted that such databases are subject to copyright protection. Indeed, unless this were the case a database continuously changed by minute accretions and deletions, perhaps entirely, would by the effluxion of time become quite unprotectable. Commercially the greatest value of such a database often resides in its most recent adjustments, and they thus provide its most substantial qualitative part from the point of view of infringement.

(d) Infringement

Infringement resides in the unauthorised exercise by another of the rights invested by the law of copyright exclusively in an author. In both the United Kingdom and the United States these rights are similar in character, and in outline comprise exclusive rights to copy, publish, perform or adapt the work in which copyright subsists. These rights do not encompass exclusive use of the copyright work. Nor are such rights absolute. They are subject to a number of limitations, of which the most important in the case of databases is that of fair dealing[198] or use.[199]

In the Copyright, Designs and Patents Act 1988 the exclusive right to

---

194. For criticism of the old rules see Horwitz, 'Proposed Changes in the Regulations concerning Deposits of Computer Programs with the Copyright Office' *26 Jur. Jo.* 305 (1986).
195. As a result of the Civil Evidence Act 1968 sect. 4 or the Criminal Justice Act 1988 sect. 24.
196. See *J. Whitaker & Son* v. *Publisher's Circular* [1946-47] McG. C.C. 10 at 14, Ch.
197. *Blacklock* v. *Pearson* [1915] 2 Ch 376, Ch.
198. Copyright, Designs and Patents Act 1988 sects. 28–29, and see other related limitations in Chapter 3.
199. 17 U.S.C. sect. 107, and see other related limitations in sects. 108–112, and in the case of computer systems, sect. 117.

copy is bestowed by sub-section 16(1)(a), and elaborated by section 17 as follows:

(2) Copying in relation to a literary, dramatic, musical or artistic work means reproducing the work in any material form. This includes storing the work in any medium by electronic means.

(6) Copying in relation to any description of work includes the making of copies which are transient or are incidental to some other use of the work.

In the United States it has been left to the courts to elaborate untramelled the exclusive statutory right to 'reproduce' the work.[200]

It is clear that in both jurisdictions reproduction of the whole database in a material form will amount to infringement of it. Other situations may be less obvious. It seems that it is not an infringement to publish an independent index to a copyright work, even though some words and phrases are necessarily borrowed from the original text.[201] The same view has been taken of the reproduction of a complete sub-set of index terms, though without their accompanying references. In *New York Times* v. *Rothbury Data Interface Inc.*[202] the plaintiffs not only published their daily newspaper, but also published each year an annual index, about half[203] of the entries of which were proper names. The defendants decided to publish a single volume index to the names which appeared in these annual indexes. The plaintiffs' annual index related the name to the place in the newspaper where it was mentioned; the defendant's index related the name to the place in the annual indexes where it appeared. Thus a researcher would need to use the defendant's volume, and both the plaintiffs' annual indexes and its newspapers in order to trace relevant materials. By using the defendant's volume, the researcher would simply be able to focus upon relevant annual indexes with less difficulty. It was obviously a necessary condition for the effectiveness of this enterprise that all of the names appearing in the plaintiffs' index volumes should be reproduced in the defendant's volume. The court indicated that this did not amount to infringement of the plaintiff's copyright since only the names had been copied, not the references; and the defendant's work differed in form, arrangement and function. It is not easy to segregate from the question of infringement that of fair use, where the court applied[204] the four factors listed in section 107 of the United States copyright legislation, namely:

(1) the purpose and character of the use;
(2) the nature of the copyrighted work;
(3) the amount and substantiality of the portion used in relation to the copyright work as a whole; and

---

200. 17 U.S.C. 106(1).

201. *Kipling* v. *G.P. Putnam & Sons* 120 F. 631 ar 635 (2nd Cir., 1903). See also *Societeté Microfor* v. *Sarl Le Monde* [1988] F.S.R. 519 (Pl. Cour de Cass., 1987).

202. 434 F.Supp. 217 (D.N.J., 1977) (though in the context only of an application for a preliminary injunction).

203. Though representing no more than 10 per cent of the total text of the book.

204. Though only as guidelines, since the new Copyright Act, now 17 U.S.C. sect. 107, had not become effective by the time of the opinion; and in any case it has been decided that the section is never more than indicative, *Universal City Studios* v. *Sony Corporation of America* 464 U.S. 417 (1984).

(4) the effect of the use upon the potential market for or value of the copyrighted work

In this connection the matters which weighed most with the court were that the defendant's index would serve the public interest in the dissemination of information; that in the case of a compilation, as opposed to a more creative work, fair use licensed the reproduction of larger amounts of the original material; that the use of the names was mandated by the purpose of the application, and that nothing more than was so necessary had been copied; and that in the result the market for the plaintiffs' works was not diminished since use of the defendant's work required access to the plaintiffs' works.[205] Much the same considerations arose even more squarely in the computer context in *West Publishing Co.* v. *Mead Data Central Inc.*,[206] once again in the context of an application for a preliminary injunction. It was explicitly argued in the District Court[207] that the pagination of the West volume of the law reports constituted an index to West's arrangement of cases. If a full-text database is to be regarded as self-indexing then it seems that it must be upon the basis that the words of the text are the equivalent of the index terms, and the citation is the reference. If so, the alleged infringement seems to be the converse of that alleged in the *New York Times* case. There the terms were copied but the references were not; here the references were copied, but the terms were not.[208] Similarly the copying of the references in the *New York Times* case and of the references in the *West* case were equally mandated by the nature of the enterprise; in both cases to facilitate reference to the relevant copyright work.[209] Notwithstanding these similarities the result was different, and the injunction granted. This result may be attributed to the court's acceptance of the argument that here Mead's work would undercut West's market if it inserted West's pagination into its own text. It seems that Mead failed to pursue its claim of fair use upon appeal.[210] It must certainly be conceded that it was much more probable in the *Mead* case that the market for the copyright work would be affected. However, it is hard to understand why this should be attributed to infringement of copyright in the West arrangement of its individual volumes, rather than to the enhanced communicability of public domain material by using the *de facto* standard of reference. The key to the result appears to lie in the assimilation of West's arrangement of its volumes with the overall scheme of reference to the relevant reports. It should, however, be noted that West neither claimed for, nor could consistently with copyright principle receive, copyright in the arrangement of its series; and that West conceded the use

---

205. For some unexplained reason the plaintiff made no formal claim in respect of infringement of its computer databank comprising a subject index to the indexes for the years after 1969, and including some 350 000 names.
206. 799 F.2d 1219 (8th Cir., 1986).
207. 616 F.Supp 1571 at 1578 (D.C. Minn., 1985).
208. Because the text of the opinions was in the public domain, was independently collected by Mead, and did not correspond exactly to the West version.
209. Cp. *Dow Jones & Co* v. *Board of Trade of the City of Chicago* 546 F. Supp. 113 at 120 (S.D.N.Y., 1982) where this factor was held to justify literal reproduction of a complete and exact copy of the copyright compilation.
210. See p. 1228 n.3.

by Mead of the first page references to individual law reports as a fair use. Yet that conceded fair use was itself sufficient to permit any user of the Mead version to reproduce the arrangement of any given West volume without recourse to star-pagination at all.[211]

C. Ownership and third party rights

Unlike some other more traditional literary works, programs are rarely written by lonely authors on a purely speculative basis, to be hawked around different software houses by an agent. They are more often the product of the joint enterprise of a team of programmers, commissioned by a software house, working to improve an existing product. These factors may create difficulty in identifying the holder of the rights granted by the law of copyright.

The general rule for literary works in the United Kingdom under the Copyright, Designs and Patents Act 1988 applies to computer programs without any special adaptation, except in the case of computer-generated works. The rights inhere in the author of the program who is defined as its creator,[212] except that in the case of an employee any program which he writes in the course of such employment is owned by his employer, subject to any agreement to the contrary.[213] The Act also provides for joint authorship where two or more authors collaborate,[214] and for works of unknown authorship where it is not possible to discover the identity of the author by reasonable inquiry.[215] In the case of computer-generated works, after some preliminary disarray,[216] the Act has adopted the solution previously applied to films,[217] of ascribing authorship to the 'person by whom the arrangements necessary for the creation of the work were undertaken'.[218] No satisfactory adaptation of these provisions to ownership of databases held on computers has been made. In principle, the regime for computer-generated works would seem the most desirable option, and will indeed apply to the extent that such databases are in fact created by downloading from other such databases. The general position in the United States is similar except that rights in 'works made for hire' also accrue to the hirer, and this phrase clearly covers a wider range of situations than is indicated by the concept of employment in the United Kingdom[219] in extending to specially commissioned works, falling

---

211. By using no more than the standard substitution utility. Thus a search on LEXIS for 'CITE (616 pre/3 15**)' retrieves references to all of the reports in 616 F.Supp. with first page numbers between 1500 and 1599. It is then a trivial matter of using the browsing facilities to display the text of the opinions in the same order as they appear in West's volume.
212. Copyright, Designs and Patents Act 1988 sect. 9(1).
213. Copyright, Designs and Patents Act 1988 sect. 11(2).
214. *Ibid.* sect. 10(1).
215. *Ibid.* sects. 9(4), 9(5).
216. See Whitford Committee Report (Cmnd. 6732) paras. 513–517 and Green paper (Cmnd. 8302) Ch. 8 para. 7.
217. Copyright Act 1956 sect. 13(10).
218. Copyright, Designs and Patents Act 1988 sect. 9(3).
219 The Copyright, Designs and Patents Act 1988 actually reduces the extent to which copyright inheres in the commissioner of a work.

into certain limited categories,[220] subject to the written agreement of the parties, to such designation.[221]

The precise issue of the ownership of computer programs rarely seems to have been the main focus of a decision in the British courts.[222] It should, however, be noted that it has been held in South Africa that even if for some reason or another copyright does rest in an employee, it may be negated in practice if nevertheless the program is held to be a trade secret of the employer, the use of which he may enjoin.[223] In the United States, however the matter was canvassed by the District Court in *Whelan Associates* v. *Jaslow Dental Laboratory*.[224] The defendant, the proprietor of a dental laboratory, attempted to write computer programs to automate his business. Upon failing to do so successfully, he contracted with the predecessors of the plaintiff upon the basis that they would design and create a system to his specifications. This they did, upon terms that they retained ownership of the system so designed, but also upon payment of a royalty to the defendant in respect of sales to third parties.[225] The plaintiff registered copyright in the relevant programs. These programs were designed to run on a machine rapidly becoming obsolete, and the defendant then attempted once more to write a program capable of running on newer and more popular machines. He failed once again, and had to employ another programmer to perform this feat. In the meantime he had renounced his agreement with the plaintiff, and asserted ownership in the system. His claims rested on his contribution to the original; to his having commissioned the creation of the original package; and to the recital in the supplementary agreement of his ownership. The Court held that his original contribution was too trivial to entitle him to be regarded even as a joint author; that the conditions of the Copyright Act under the 'works for hire' doctrine had been unfulfilled so as to vest ownership in the commissioner;[226] and that the reference to ownership in the revised agreement was to be considered as relating to a copy of the package rather than as to copyright in its intellectual property.

D. Contributory infringement

Even though a party may not himself infringe copyright in a work or

---

220. Which include, among others, contributions to collective works, translations, supplementary works and compilations.
221. It should be noted that in the United States, unlike the United Kingdom, any agreement defeasing ascription of copyright must be in writing, 17 U.S.C. sect. 201(b).
222. Although in *Leisure Data* v. *Bell* [1988] F.S.R. 367, C.A. such a dispute was the subject matter of an application for a mandatory injunction.
223. *Northern Office Micro Computers* v. *Rosenstein* 1981 (4) S.A. 123, C.P.D. No attempt was made to argue that copyright rested in the employer.
224. 609 F.Supp. 1307 (D.C.Pa., 1985) aff. 797 F.2d 1222 (3rd Cir., 1986) but without any appeal on this point having been lodged.
225. The original agreement was supplemented by a subsequent marketing agreement increasing the royalty, and reciting ownership in the 'Dentalab Package' in the defendants, but as designed and developed by the plaintiff.
226. There was no written agreement in relation to the package as required by 17 U.S.C. sect. 101's definition of 'works for hire' (2). See also *B. P. I. Systems Inc.* v. *Leith* 532 F.Supp. 208 (W.D. Tex., 1981) where this consideration was alone held decisive in a software case.

authorise another to do so, he may be sufficiently involved in the process of infringement as to become the subject of legal liability. In the case of computer programs attention has been focused upon those who facilitate the infringement of copyright by others, for example by the production of either hardware or software which enables infringement to take place.

It is quite clear that any explicit authorisation of infringement of copyright will, both in the United Kingdom,

Copyright in a work is infringed by a person who without the licence of the copyright owner does, *or authorises another to do*, any of the acts restricted by the copyright.[227]

and in the United States,

'Anyone who violates any of the exclusive rights of the copyright owner,' anyone who trespasses into his exclusive domain by using *or authorizing the use of the copyrighted work* in one of the five ways set forth in the statute, 'is an infringer of the copyright'.[228]

amount to a primary act of infringement of copyright.

A more difficult question arises if the secondary infringer cannot be shown to have given any explicit authorisation to infringement, but has nevertheless facilitated it in some way. The British legislation is more explicit in this regard, providing in the Copyright, Designs and Patents Act 1988, under the rubric 'Secondary Infringement of Copyright' that:

Copyright in a work is infringed by a person who, without the licence of the copyright owner–
(a) makes,
(b) imports into the United Kingdom,
(c) possesses in the course of business, or
(d) sells or lets for hire, or offers or exposes for sale or hire, an article specifically designed or adapted for making copies of that work, knowing or having reason to believe that it is to be used to make infringing copies.[229]

It seems that much may depend upon the interpretation of the phrase 'specifically designed or adapted'. Before the passage of the Act the question was ventilated in *Amstrad Consumer Electronics PLC* v. *The British Phonographic Industry Ltd.*[230] in the context of the sale of dual deck cassette recorders capable of copying cassettes from one deck to the other at high speeds.[231] The plaintiffs manufactured and marketed these machines, and sought a declaration that their so doing was lawful. Their labelling and advertising incorporated warnings to users against infringement of copyright, but in so muted a way that the trial judge held them not intended to be taken seriously.[232] It was held not unlawful for the plaintiffs to have supplied a machine which was to their knowledge capable of being, or likely to be, used

---

227. Copyright, Designs and Patents Act 1988 sect. 16(2), emphasis supplied.
228. *Universal City Studios* v. *Sony Corporation of America* 464 U.S. 417 (1984) at 433, emphasis supplied, interpreting 17 U.S.C. sect. 501(1).
229. Sect. 24.
230. (1986) 12 F.S.R. 159, C.A.
231. Although the case considered explicitly only the copying of musical cassettes, it applies equally to the copying of computer programs which at the bottom end of the games playing market are indeed encoded on cassettes capable of being copied on the very machines in question.
232. At 185, a finding explicitly accepted in the Court of Appeal by Slade L.J. at 215.

to infringe copyright.[233] The reason for this is that the rights guaranteed by the Copyright Acts[234] are *prima facie* in restraint of trade, and to be construed strictly. It would be necessary to show more active involvement in the infringement, such as incitement or encouragement. In this case the machines were not retained by the alleged infringer,[235] and were not sold directly by the plaintiff to the public. The Court found any common law action for negligence to be pre-empted by the statutory provision. It was still not prepared, however, to make the declaration sought, since it was not satisfied that the plaintiff's advertising campaign might not on further consideration in an appropriate case be shown to amount to criminal conduct in breach of sub-section 21(3) of the Copyright Act 1956. It certainly seems that if an article is manufactured which can be used only for the commission of an infringing act, then that act is incited by the manufacturer.[236] Similarly it has been held in Canada to amount to an incitement to infringe to sell a blank chip, directing the purchaser to a different establishment where an infringing program could be burned on to it.[237] While the interpretation of the new provision is as yet unclear, there is nothing in its phraseology to suggest that the existing law cannot apply.

In the United States the leading authority[238] also deals with the marketing of recording devices, in this case video-recorders. It is clear that video-recorders can be used to infringe copyright in films and television programmes, but it was held that there is also a substantial non-infringing use in the form of recording non-copyright material, or merely using the recorders for 'time-shifting'.[239] By a bare majority the Supreme Court held this to be the decisive factor, and that the sale of such devices would amount to contributory infringement only if there were no significant non-infringing use. This view was applied to software in *Vault Corp.* v. *Quaid Software Ltd.*[240] where the plaintiff sold specially encoded disks upon which programs could be written, but which would not run without the original disk being present in the computer. Manufacturers who did not wish their proprietary programs to be run from copies were encouraged to market their products on such 'copy-protected' disks. Many manufacturers, at one time, considered this a much more effective way of fighting small-scale domestic piracy than by engaging in legal proceedings. The defendants marketed software which enabled users to evade the protection on such disks, and to make usable copies of the programs encoded upon them, thus defeating the purpose for which such disks were sold. The plaintiffs argued that in so doing the defendants were

---

233. Following *Dunlop Pneumatic Tyre Co Ltd.* v. *Moseley & Sons Ltd.* (1904) 21 R.P.C. 274, C.A. *A fortiori* if they lacked knowledge, and were merely the dupe of an international infringer, *Paterson Zochonis & Co Ltd.* v. *Merfarken Packaging Ltd.* [1983] F.S.R. 273, C.A.
234. And the Patent Acts.
235. By contrast with the University in *Moorhouse* v. *University of New South Wales* [1976] R.P.C. 151, H.C.A. where the photocopier in question was installed on the University's premises.
236. Cp. *R.* v. *Hollinshead* [1985] A.C. 975, H.L.
237. *Apple Computer Co.* v. *Mackintosh Computers Ltd.*
238. *Universal City Studios* v. *Sony Corporation of America* 464 U.S. 417 (1984).
239. Recording a program temporarily so as to be able to see it at a more convenient time. Many copyright holders have no objection to such recording, and it was in any case found to be a fair use within 17 U.S.C. sect. 107.
240. 655 F. Supp. 750 (E.D.La., 1987).

guilty of infringement of their copyright in the copy protection programs, were contributory infringers of the programs recorded on the protected disks, and were in breach of the Louisiana Software License Enforcement Act.[241] The first point was easily disposed of by the Court's finding of fact that no part of the plaintiff's program was reproduced by the defendant's current[242] version of its program,[243] and this was held to prevent its being regarded even as a derivative work.[244] On the question of contributory infringement the Court held that the plaintiff lacked standing since it was not the proprietor of the programs protected by the disks. This is dubious since the defendant's program has the effect of copying the protecting code onto the disks as well as the application program.[245] This was however irrelevant to the result since the Court went on to hold that there were here significant non-infringing uses of the defendant's programs; for making copies explicitly authorised by the Copyright Act,[246] for making particularly accurate copies of unprotected programs, and for disk analysis. The local law was in part relied upon to show that because of breach of the contractual terms which the statute validated, it was an infringement even to load the plaintiff's program for a use unauthorised by the plaintiff. It was held that so far as this statute trenched upon the area of copyright, it was pre-empted by federal law. Either its provisions were in accordance with the federal legislation, in which case they were ineffective; or they were inconsistent with it, in which case they were invalid. It was held that by providing for contractual terms, in effect giving perpetual protection, for works not necessarily shown to be original, and in flat contradiction of the explicit federal authorisation to make archival copies, the legislation did trench upon the area of copyright, was inconsistent with federal law, and was hence invalid as being unconstitutional.

In the United Kingdom this situation has now been addressed by a specific provision introduced into the Copyright, Designs and Patents Act 1988 at a late stage. Section 296 invests the owner of a copy-protected copyright work with special rights against the promoters of devices for evading such protection,

(2) The person issuing the copies to the public has the same rights against a person who, knowing or having reason to believe that it will be used to make infringing copies –
(a) makes, imports, sells or lets for hire, offers or exposes for sale or hire, or advertises for sale or hire, any device or means specially designed or adapted to circumvent the form of copy-protection employed, or
(b) publishes information intended to enable or assist persons to circumvent that

---

241. LSA-RS 51:1431–51.
242. Both systems had undergone changes as measure was met by counter-measure.
243. And only 1/80th by amount in the pre-1984 version.
244. Within 17 U.S.C. sect. 106(2).
245. Disks copies using the defendant's program cannot themselves be further copied in a usable form without the use of the defendant's program. Thus the benefit of protection is, in effect, transferred to the defendant, and it is interesting to note that it has itself sued for infringement of its copying program.
246. 17 U.S.C. sect. 117(2).

form of copy-protection, as a copyright owner has in respect of infringement of copyright.

(4) References in this section to copy-protection include any device or means intended to prevent or restrict copying of a work or to impair the quality of copies made.

This seems adequate to deal with the perceived problem, though there may be some difficulty in proving specific design or adaptation, or the intent to circumvent.

E. Remedies and proof

The remedial aspects of copyright are concerned with the range of remedies available, the procedure for pursuing them and the evidence necessary to justify their imposition. These topics will be addressed in turn.

1. Range of remedies

Copyright is a form of intellectual property regulated by statute. Because it is proprietary in nature, it attracts proprietary remedies, and because it is statutory, these remedies are defined by the relevant statutory provisions. It was, indeed, just because of the requirement for a statutory foundation that where remedies were found to be deficient in the United Kingdom, in particular in relation to the piracy of musical and audio-visual works, and in relation to computers, it was, before the passage of the Copyright, Designs and Patents Act 1988, necessary to fill the gaps with a piecemeal statutory patchwork.[247]

The remedies now provided by the Copyright, Designs and Patents Act 1988 are variously, civil, criminal and administrative, and those that are civil are generally available only to the copyright owner or to an exclusive licensee. The principal civil remedy is an action for damages for infringement which may include 'additional' damages.[248] Under the previous legislation there was a further possibility of securing conversion damages, but this was felt to be inequitable[249] and has now been removed. By way of partial compensation some of the restrictions upon obtaining 'additional'[250] damages have been ameliorated. Such damages have regard especially to the flagrancy of the infringement, and benefit the defendant.[251] Another way of tapping the defendant's profit is to secure an account of profits, an equitable remedy explicitly preserved by the Copyright, Designs and Patents Act 1988.[252] Damages may not be awarded against a defendant ignorant of his infringement, though no such restriction applies to securing an account of profits.[253]

---

247. Composed of the Copyright (Amendment) Act 1982, the Copyright (Amendment) Act 1983 and the Copyright (Computer Software) Amendment Act 1985, all of them now repealed by the Copyright, Designs and Patents Act 1988 Sch. 8.
248. Copyright, Designs and Patents Act 1988 sect. 96.
249. Whitford Committee Report (Cmnd. 6732) paras. 700–706, Green Paper (Cmnd. 8302) Ch. 14 para. 3.
250. Said in *Beloff* v. *Pressdam* [1973] 1 All E.R. 241, Ch at 265 to mean aggravated rather than exemplary damages.
251. Copyright, Designs and Patents Act 1988 sect. 97(2).
252. Sect. 96(2).
253. Copyright, Designs and Patents Act 1988 sect. 97(1). The corresponding provision in the old law was always very strictly construed.

The plaintiff is also entitled to delivery up of infringing copies, or of articles specifically designed or adapted to make them,[254] though only if damages would not be an adequate remedy.[255]

In many cases however, the plaintiff is more concerned to secure specific relief by terminating the defendant's infringement, or by preventing it from taking place, and for this purpose injunctive relief is available,[256] often on an interlocutory application. Such prohibitive[257] injunctions are governed by the general rules established in *American Cyanamid Co.* v. *Ethicon*, [258] the rough effect of which is that if the plaintiff has an arguable case then the issue of the injunction will depend upon the adequacy as a remedy of damages at the trial; if that is uncertain, upon the balance of inconvenience; and if that fails to give a clear indication, then the *status quo* will be preferred, though at that stage the result may be swayed by the court's assessment of the relative strength of the parties' cases. In a number of cases involving computers, relief has been obtained upon such a basis.[259]

Criminal remedies have been available under copyright legislation in the United Kingdom for many years, but prosecutions were few.[260] This was ascribed in part to difficulty of proof, in part to the inadequacy of the penalties, and in part to the reluctance of the police to take an active role in the prosecution of what might be regarded as essentially commercial disputes. The rapid growth of large-scale infringement of sound recordings, films and computer programs led to pressure for change. As noted above,[261] such change was introduced piecemeal by a series of amending acts. The computer industry also combined together for enforcement purposes setting up a special organisation, the Federation Against Software Theft (FAST), to pursue its interests. This body has secured a number of convictions under the new legislation.[262] The Copyright, Designs and Patents Act 1988 has now consolidated the statutory law relating to criminal remedies. The principal criminal offences cover the intentional making, importation, possession or distribution of infringing articles or, in the course of business, the selling, letting, offering, exhibiting or distributing of such articles.[263] The legislation provides for sentences of up to two years' imprisonment[264] and, in the case of infringement by a corporate body, of proceedings against corporate officers personally.[265] As a subsidiary remedy the Court may also order forfeiture, destruction or delivery up of infringing articles or things specifically designed

---

254. Copyright, Designs and Patents Act 1988 sect. 99.
255. *Ibid.* sect. 114(2).
256. *Ibid.* sect. 96(2).
257. Different principles apply in the case of mandatory injunctions, see *Leisure Data.* v. *Bell* [1988] F.S.R. 367, C.A.
258. [1975] A.C. 396, H.L.
259. See, for example, *Gates* v. *Swift* [1982] R.P.C. 339, Ch.
260. In *Rank Film Distributors Ltd.* v. *Video Information Centre* [1982] A.C. 380, H.L. Lord Wilberforce was aware of no more than one prosecution since 1911.
261. P. 137.
262. The first sentence of imprisonment for such offences in the United Kingdom was awarded early in 1988, see *Computer Weekly*, 14 January 1988, p. 1.
263. Copyright, Designs and Patents Act 1988 sect. 107.
264. *Ibid.* sect. 107(4)(b).
265. *Ibid.* sect. 110(1).

or adapted to produce them.[266] It should be noted that these remedies do not exhaust the possible range of criminal offences in this connection, since here the specifically statutory remedies do not pre-empt the application of the common law of crime, and there may well be grounds for charging such offences as theft, conspiracy to defraud, forgery or false accounting. Indeed, in *Rank Film Distributors Ltd.* v. *Video Information Centre*,[267] where the House of Lords would have denied a remedy upon the basis that the specific statutory offences were so rarely charged, it was nevertheless prepared to grant it upon the basis that a charge of conspiracy to defraud was a distinct possibility and that, in fact, one of those involved had been so charged.

The administrative remedy bestowed by the Copyright, Designs and Patents Act 1988 enables a copyright owner to give notice to the Commissioners of Customs and Excise requesting them to treat infringing copies of his work as goods prohibited from import into the United Kingdom.[268]

Very much the same range of statutory remedies is available in the United States.[269] The principal remedy is also the action for damages for infringement of copyright, but there the relevant statutory provision[270] offers an election to the plaintiff. He is required to choose between claiming such actual damages as he is able to prove, and a special statutory award within the discretion of the Court, but subject to an upper limit of $10 000. The notion of actual damages here incorporates also the remedy, separate in the United Kingdom, of an account of profits,[271] thus in *Whelan Associates* v. *Jaslow Dental Laboratory*[272] the system designer was awarded the net profit on the sales by the infringer of the relevant system. The plaintiff need prove only the gross return from infringing material, leaving the defendant to prove any costs which should be set off against it. In software cases, margins may be very high.[273] It is also possible for a Court to award punitive damages, or to make a penal award of attorney's costs.[274] However, it has been held[275] that punitive measures are most appropriately awarded as a disincentive to further infringement, and are thus unsuitable for application in a case where an injunction has been issued against such further infringement. Because, in many cases, it is hard to prove either loss of profits by the plaintiff or their attainment by the defendant, special provision is made for the award of statutory damages.[276] The nominal maximum of $10 000 may be increased to $50 000 in the case of wilful infringement; or, alternatively, if the infringer can prove that he was not aware of his infringement and had no reason to be

---

266. *Ibid.* sect. 108.
267. [1982] A.C. 380, H.L.
268. Copyright, Designs and Patents Act 1988 sect. 111.
269. See Kenfield, 'Remedies in Software Copyright Cases' 6 *Comp. L. J.* 1 (1985).
270. 17 U.S.C. sect. 504.
271. *Ibid.* sect. 504(b).
272. 609 F.Supp. 1307 (D.C. Pa., 1985).
273. In *Whelan Associates* v. *Jaslow Dental Laboratory* the profit amounted to more than 92 per cent of the total return.
274. 17 U.S.C. sect. 505. In the United States costs do not generally follow the event as they do in the United Kingdom.
275. In *Whelan Associates* v. *Jaslow Dental Laboratory* 609 F.Supp. 1307 at 1323 (D.C.Pa., 1985).
276. 17 U.S.C. sect. 504(c).

so aware, then the statutory award can be reduced below the normal minimum of $250 to as little as $100.[277] An important limitation both upon this remedy of statutory damages, and of the penal award of costs designed to encourage early registration of a work for copyright, is that they can apply only in cases where the infringement occurs *after* registration.[278] This can sometimes lead to difficulty and dispute in relation to the identification of the first infringing act.

As in the United Kingdom the Court may also order infringing materials, or the means of producing them, to be impounded, delivered up or destroyed as it thinks best.[279] In theory, this could apply to the defendant's whole computer system, but as yet this seems not have been ordered.

Injunction is just as popular a remedy in this area in the United States as in the United Kingdom, both as a temporary, and as a final, remedy.[280] At the preliminary stage its availability turns upon four factors:[281] probability of success on the merits; threat of irreparable harm to the plaintiff if denied; the balance between such harm and that to the defendant if granted; and the public interest. Once infringement has been held likely to be established, even in so arguable a case as *West Publishing Co.* v. *Mead Data Central Inc.*,[282] a presumption of irreparable harm is normally[283] applied. There is also traditional reluctance to attach very much importance to the harm to be suffered by the infringer if the injunction is issued, since if that were to be regarded as decisive 'a knowing infringer would be permitted to construct its business around its infringement'.[284] Nor, despite some suggestion to the contrary in *Universal City Studios* v. *Sony Corporation of America*[285] that care should be taken in granting such injunctions not to impair public access to materials, do the Courts in cases involving computers seem to have attached any greater importance to the public interest factor. In the case of final injunctions the principal problem may be to draft the prohibition in appropriate terms so as not to sanction easy evasion by simple manipulation of the infringing code into a different form nor, on the other hand, chilling a whole field of activity into frozen infertility. The solution to this lies partly in careful discrimination between idea and expression,[286] and partly in willing-ness to attach innovative conditions to such injunctions, such as a require-ment that any new program be submitted to an independent assessor for appraisal, and pending the result requiring payment of a small royalty on

---

277. The provision contains provision to regulate the computation of the number of infringe-ments on any given state of facts.
278. 17 U.S.C. sect. 412.
279. 17 U.S.C. sect. 503.
280. *Ibid.* sect. 502(a).
281. See e.g. *Dataphase Systems Inc.* v. *CL Systems Inc.* 640 F2d 109 at 113 (8th Cir., 1981) (en banc).
282. 799 F.2d 1219 at 1229 *8th Cir., 1986), applying *Apple Computer Inc.* v. *Franklin Computer Corp.* 714 F.2d 1240 at 1254 (3rd Cir., 1983) (a program case).
283. Though not invariably, for a counter-example see *Plains Cotton Co-Operative* v. *Goodpasture Computer Services* 807 F.2d 1256 at 1261 (5th Cir., 1987) where it was held that damages at the trial would suffice.
284. *Apple Computer Inc.* v. *Franklin Computer Corp.* 714 F.2d 1240 ar 1255 (3rd Cir., 1983).
285. 464 U.S. 417 (1984)
286. See above p. 30.

any sales into an escrow account.[287]

Criminal remedies are also provided in the United States copyright legislation,[288] and there too subsequent legislation was felt necessary to raise penalty levels.[289] The basic requirement is that the prosecutor must show wilful and knowing infringement of copyright for profit.[290] In addition, there are further offences relating to the fraudulent imposition[291] or removal[292] of copyright notices, and of securing registration by means of fraudulent representations.[293] As a subsidiary remedy the Court may order the forfeiture or destruction of infringing materials, or the means of producing them, though here neither does any attempt seem to have been made to invoke the power against the accused's whole computer system. An administrative system similar to that prevailing in the United Kingdom applies in the United States to permit the prohibition of the importation of infringing materials.[294]

2. Procedure

Modern technology has made the copying of most formats in which works subject to copyright exist much easier than it used to be. It is no longer necessary to set up expensive factories filled with cumbersome machines. Transportable devices can be set up in private or temporary premises without undue difficulty. In order to prevent damaging infringement by the use of such devices it is often necessary to be able to move fast, to detect, to secure evidence of, and to prevent further infringement. Since much infringement involves the commission of criminal offences, it might be thought that the most appropriate procedural device would be a search warrant. Provision was indeed made for such warrants as early as the Musical Copyright Act of 1906, but was then repealed in 1956, and the Whitford Committee saw no reason to restore the situation.[295] It soon became apparent that the scale of the problem, especially in the sound recording and audio-visual area, required reconsideration, and in 1983 an appropriate amendment was made to the Copyright Act 1956 authorising the issue of such warrants.[296] Similar provisions were subsequently applied to infringing copies of computer programs by the Copyright (Computer Software) Amendment Act 1985.[297] These provisions have now been consolidated into section 100 of the Copyright, Designs and Patents Act 1988.

---

287. See e.g. *Yale University Press* v. *Row, Peters & Co.* 40 F.2d 290 (S.D.N.Y., 1930); *Columbia Broadcasting System Inc.* v. *ASCAP* 167 U.S.P.Q. 754 (S.D.N.Y., 1970).
288. 17 U.S.C. sect. 506.
289. 17 U.S.C. sect. 506(a) as amended by the Piracy and Counterfeiting Amendment act 1982 (P.L. 97–180).
290. *U.S.* v. *Atherton* 561 F.2d 747 (9th Cir., 1977).
291. 17 U.S.C. sect. 506(c).
292. *Ibid.* sect. 50d(d).
293. *Ibid.* sect. 506(e).
294. *Ibid.* sect. 603, 19 C.F.R. 133.41–133.46.
295. Cmnd. 6732 para. 718.
296. Copyright (Amendment) Act 1983 inserting a new sect. 21A in the 1956 Act.
297. Copyright (Computer Software) Amendment Act 1985 sect. 3 inserting a new sect. 21B into the 1956 Act.

It nevertheless remains the case that the police may have higher priorities than the assistance of possible victims of the infringement of copyright. For this reason the Courts themselves created a new remedy designed for those situations in which it is desirable for a party to act more swiftly, and more surreptitiously, than by the normal process of discovery, for example, where there are good grounds for suspecting that the party in possession of the relevant material will destroy or tamper with it as soon as he learns that it has come to the knowledge of his opponent. This is, of course, a particularly acute danger in the case of information held on computers, which can be destroyed or altered without trace, literally at the touch of a button. Indeed the very first case, *Anton Piller KG* v. *Manufacturing Processes Ltd.*,[298] to come to the Court of Appeal to test the validity of a new extraordinary process to counter this difficulty involved a computer, though in that instance, it must be conceded, hardware and plans, rather than software and data.

The essence of this procedure which was devised by the High Court in pursuance of its own original jurisdiction is that a party may apply *ex parte* for an order authorising inspection of premises and materials thereon with a view to securing information, including originals and copies of documents. The procedure achieves its effect by operating *in personam* upon the party upon whom the order to admit the other is served, by rendering him in contempt of court if he should refuse to accede. This is clearly a drastic incursion into the privacy or, if refused, even liberty, of the subject, and some safeguards have accordingly been built into the procedure. For example the applicant should normally be accompanied on to the premises by an officer of the court; and most often the applicant's solicitor acts in this capacity. The subject of the order must also be given an opportunity to apply for the discharge of the order. This might seem to go too far in the other direction by destroying the utility of the procedure were it not for the fact that the court has power to draw inferences adverse to a party who refuses entry to an applicant. It was also decided by the House of Lords that such an order could not override the privilege against self-incrimination,[299] though this has now been remedied by statute in cases concerned with questions of intellectual property.[300] There is no doubt that the procedure applies to documents which are not themselves in issue, but which will provide evidence of the matters in issue.[301] In such a case, however the applicant must show that the documents are essential to his case, and that there is a strong possibility that unless the order is granted they will be altered or destroyed.[302]

The application of this procedure to computer software was upheld in *Gates* v. *Swift*.[303] This case related to an allegation of infringement of

---

298. [1976] Ch 55, C.A.

299. *Rank Film Distributors Ltd.* v. *Video Information Centre* [1982] A.C. 380, H.L.; but see *Thorne EMI Video Programs Ltd.* v. *Kitching and Busby* [1984] F.S.R. 342, N.Z.C.A., for a different view of the common law in New Zealand.

300. Supreme Court Act 1981 sect. 72.

301. *Centi-Spray Corp.* v. *Cera International Ltd.* [1979] F.S.R. 175, Ch.

302. *Yousif* v. *Slama* [1980] 3 all E. R. 405, C.A.

303. [1981] F.S.R. 57, Ch. (order only); [1982] R.P.C. 339, Ch. (also including headnote and argument of counsel).

copyright in both application programs and in system utilities. Once the question of the possibility of infringement of copyright in computer programs had been disposed of, the court raised no objection to a provision in the order relating to the procedure for securing information from the relevant computer in the following terms:

the defendants ... disclose ... all the documents and articles ... which are in the power possession custody or control of the defendants on the same premises or elsewhere or are being held on their behalf by any other person and do for that purpose cause to be displayed or printed out by a computer or computers any such documents as are in computer-readable form.[304]

It will be noted that this order contains no explicit reference to the expenses of running such programs, but it is normal for an applicant to be required to give an undertaking to pay any damages caused by the order should it be discharged, and any application is made at peril as to costs, which will include the costs of complying with any part of the order as to the running of programs and the compiling of printouts. The order will be discharged if it has been obtained without full disclosure by the applicant, and may be so discharged even after it has been fully executed.[305] It must be stressed that this remedy always has been, and still is, regarded as quite extraordinary because:

Where the production and delivery up of documents is in question, the courts have always proceeded, justifiably, on the basis that the overwhelming majority of people in this country will comply with the court's order, and deliver up documents without it becoming necessary to empower the plaintiff's solicitors to search the defendant's premises.[306]

A still more summary procedure has been introduced by the Copyright, Designs and Patents Act 1988 in certain cases of infringement of copyright.[307] This provides that where a person has in his possession by way of business an infringing copy of a copyright work, defined to include a computer program,[308] then the copyright owner may himself seize such infringing copy from a public place without any prior judicial authorisation whatsoever so long as no force is used. Even after such seizure the owner is not obliged to seek ratification of his actions by a court, though in the case of a genuine dispute the person deprived of the copy would no doubt take legal steps to seek its return.

The new copyright legislation in the United States, as noted above,[309] retains the remedy of impounding infringing material.[310] Under that legislation the remedy may be sought at any time during which the action is pending.[311] Under the Rules of Practice adopted to facilitate the operation of

---

304. At 341
305. *Booker McConnell P.L.C.* v. *Plascow* [1985] R.P.C. 425, C.A.
306. At 441.
307. Sect. 100.
308. Sect. 3(1)(b).
309. P. 70.
310. 17 U.S.C. sect. 503.
311. *Ibid.* sect. 503(a).

the remedy under the Copyright Act 1909, provision was made[312] for the plaintiff to file an affidavit and lodge a bond[313] with the Court, whereupon the defendant might be required to deliver up allegedly infringing material to a United States marshal, or become liable to its seizure by him. The defendant might then either object to the value of the bond or the sufficiency of the required sureties, or subsequently seek a hearing for the return of the materials. It should be noted that the plaintiff is not required to make an initial formal showing of likelihood of success on the merits. So secretively, speedily and easily obtainable a remedy authorising so drastic an invasion of another's property and privacy raises, in the United States, obvious and serious constitutional questions, involving the possible invocation of the First,[314] Fourth,[315] and Fifth Amendments[316] to the Constitution.[317] Nevertheless the Rules have in the past resisted such constitutional challenge in the courts,[318] and were not invalidated when the new copyright legislation was introduced.[319] The lack of specificity required by these Rules may be contrasted with the meticulous scrutiny made of the grounds for issuing search warrants in criminal cases, including those for offences against the copyright legislation.[320] It is possible that the Court will take a similar line to that taken in respect of contributory infringement in *Universal City Studios* v. *Sony Corporation of America*,[321] and hold the remedy unconstitutional[322] only when the materials to be impounded are capable of a significant non-infringing use.[323]

3. Evidence

Evidential problems in copyright cases tend usually to be factual rather than legal. It is more often a case of finding any means of showing that infringement has taken place than defending the legitimacy of such means. In the United Kingdom there has been some discussion of the allocation of the burden of proof. The Whitford Committee felt it right to assist the plaintiff by providing a presumption of title in interlocutory proceedings,[324] and, where innocence is raised as a defence to a charge of indirect infringement, to place the burden of so proving upon the defendant,[325] even

---

312. Copyright Rules 3–13.
313. For at least twice the value of the allegedly infringing materials.
314. Protecting freedom of speech.
315. Prohibiting unreasonable searches and seizures.
316. Prohibiting seizure of property without due process of law.
317. See Owens 'Impoundment Procedures Under the Copyright Act; The Constitutional Infirmities' *14 Hofstra L.R.* 211 (1985).
318. See *Jondora Music Publishing Co* v. *Melody Recording Inc.* 362 F.Supp. 494 (D.C.N.J., 1973) (vacated on other grounds 506 F.2d 392 (3rd Cir., 1975)).
319. Though they were said by the Rules Committee to be of dubious validity and to be subject to continuing review.
320. See *U.S.* v. *Klein* 565 F.2d 183 (Ist Cir., 1977).
321. 464 U.S. 417 (1984).
322. For an indication of this, see *Duchess Music Corp.* v. *Stein* 458 F.2d 1305 (9th Cir., 1972).
323. See above p. 64.
324. Cmnd 6732 para. 730.
325. *Ibid.* para. 738.

in the case of a criminal prosecution.[326] A number of presumptions, largely accepting these recommendations, are provided by the Copyright, Designs and Patents Act 1988.[327] The only one[328] specifically related to computers presumes that statements as to the owner and date of publication on copies issued to the public are correct, subject to proof of the contrary. The main departure from the recommendations of the Whitford Committee was a refusal to place the burden of proving innocence upon the accused in a criminal prosecution, even for a copyright offence,[329] though the presumptions do apply in forfeiture proceedings.[330] In the United States the existence of the registration procedure facilitates the use of such presumptions.[331] Thus a valid certificate of registration entitles its holder to a *prima facie* presumption of ownership, originality, copyrightability and compliance with all statutory formalities.[332]

One of the factual questions least susceptible of direct evidence is whether or not the defendant did copy the plaintiff's work.[333] This is thus usually proved by circumstantial evidence of the defendant's access to the plaintiff's work, and its substantial similarity to it. In the case of computer programs of any complexity, comparison of the coding can be decisive. In a number of cases the program has been written in such a way as to provide appropriate evidence. Thus in *Apple Computer Inc.* v. *Computer Edge Pty*.[334] it was revealed that the original programmer had inserted his initials in an unobtrusive way into the program with the result that they appeared in the defendant's version. Similarly, in *SAS Institute Inc.* v. *S & H Computer Systems Inc*.[335] a vestigial, and quite redundant remnant of a previous version of the program which had been inadvertently retained by the plaintiff constituted virtually irrefutable evidence of copying when found to be reproduced in the defendant's work. It has been remarked that the most compelling evidence of copying is often to be found in a transparent effort to disguise similarities between different works.[336]

There is a clear role for the use of expert witnesses in computer copyright cases, at least to establish the existence of substantial similarity between two works which may, on their face, appear to have little in common with each other. In the United States it is generally accepted that an expert may testify freely on the question of the 'extrinsic' test of the similarity of the functions of the relevant programs,[337] and similarly experts have been allowed to

---

326. *Ibid* para. 711.
327. Sects. 104–6.
328. Sect. 105(3).
329. Copyright, Designs and Patents Act 1988 sect. 107(6), foreshadowed by the Green paper Cmnd. 8302 Ch. 14 para. 12.
330. Copyright, Designs and Patents Act 1988 sect. 99.
331. 17 U.S.C. sect. 410(c).
332. *Telex Corp.* v. *International Business Machines Corp* 367 F.Supp. 258 (N.D.Ok., 1973) (reversed on other grounds 510 F.2d 894 (10th Cir., 1975)).
333. Though it is sometimes, see *Broderbund Software Inc.* v. *Unison World Inc.* 648 F.Supp 1127 (N.D. Cal., 1986).
334. 53 A.L.R. 225 at 274 (F.C.A. 1984).
335. 605 F.Supp 816 (M.D. Tenn., 1985)
336. *Atari Inc.* v. *North American Philips Consumer Electronics Corp.* 672 F.2d 607 at 618 (7th Cir., 1982).
337. *Broderbund Software Inc.* v. *Unison World Inc.* 648 F.Supp. 1127 (N.D. Cal., 1986).

testify in the growing number of cases where a composite test is applied.[338] It is uncertain whether such testimony would be permissible on the purely 'intrinsic' test of whether or not the expression is sufficiently similar since this is, in theory, determined by the impression of a layman.

---

338. *Whelan Associates* v. *Jaslow Dental Laboratory* 797 F.2d 1222 (3rd Cir., 1986).

Chapter 3

Trade secrets and unfair competition

The very title of this chapter signifies a slight shift in focus compared with its two predecessors. They principally dealt with two distinct forms of intellectual property, patent and copyright, and the remedies associated with them. Here the title indicates a certain duality of approach. There is a proprietary element in the notion of trade secrets, but unfair competition is plainly not proprietary in character. It is focused not so much on the property interest of the plaintiff, as on the delictual conduct of the defendant. A further difference from the two previous chapters is that whereas they dealt with areas wholly regulated by statute, legislation plays here a more muted role.[1] Although this might suggest greater uniformity between the law of the United Kingdom and the United States in this area, such is not really the case. This body of law is much more maturely developed in the United States, and is affected by the constitutional requirements of a federal system in a way unknown in the United Kingdom. It is further the situation that much more of the relevant case law has, in the United States, involved the computer industry. Nevertheless there is still enough basic similarity to make comparison rewarding, and to give a possible indication of future developments.

It is particularly important to examine the relationship between this branch of the law and its surrounding areas, because it cannot be denied that the law in the United Kingdom has suffered from conceptual confusion. As one critic has said of one part of the subject:

A cursory study of the cases, where the plaintiff's confidence has been breached, reveals great conceptual confusion. Property, contract, bailment, trust, fiduciary relationship, good faith, unjust enrichment, have all been claimed, at one time or another, as the basis of judicial intervention. Indeed some judges have indiscrimin-

---

1. Though this may change if in the United Kingdom the draft bill proposed by the Law Commission in *Law Com.* 110, 'Breach of Confidence', Cmnd. 8388 (1981) App. A were to be enacted; or in the United States as more states enact the model Uniform Trade Secrets Act approved in 1979 by the National Conference of Commissioners on Unfair Competition Laws.

ately intermingled all these concepts. The result is that the answer to many fundamental questions remains speculative.[2]

There is no agreement whether the law is derived from right or remedy, or whether the remedies are legal or equitable, real or personal. After this problem has been ventilated, the remainder of the chapter will deal in turn with the type of interest of the plaintiff which is to be protected, the sort of conduct of the defendant which should be proscribed, and finally the range of remedies which are available.

A. Relation to other areas

This section will first consider the conceptual overlapping with other areas of the law, and then the special problem in the United States created by the doctrine of pre-emption, whereby state law is restrained from encroaching upon the exclusive territory of federal regulation. Here the relevant potential encroachment is principally that of the state law of trade secrets and unfair competition upon the federal law of intellectual property, especially that of patent and copyright.

1. Conceptual overlapping

As noted above, the basic tension is between a proprietary and a personal approach. This is, in part, due to the wide range of situations which need to be considered here. There is much less coherence than in the purely statutory domains of patent and copyright. Some parts of the topic, for example, the idea of a novel algorithm or a list of customers for software, have a clearly proprietary stamp about them, and in some manifestations can indeed become subject to those purely proprietary forms of intellectual property, for example as hard wired programs or as written lists of customers. In such cases a reproducer of the program may infringe a patent, or a copier of the list its owner's copyright. But what if the idea of the algorithm is taken before it has been incorporated into a hard-wired program, or the names of the customers are merely memorised and a selection of them solicited, without any copy of the list ever being made? In these situations it is possible that the law of trade secrets may provide a remedy under certain conditions. But at some point the proprietary basis for a remedy dwindles away, and attention is directed instead at the conduct of the defendant who may have competed unfairly, for example by deliberately adopting programming techniques compatible with those of the plaintiff, who has developed a market for the purpose of exploiting it, or one who deliberately seduces key programming staff away from a competitor so as to be able to construct a competing system so much more cheaply, quickly and easily. Here there is little trace of a proprietary element. It may be felt that these two extremes have no more in common than an element of unfairness.

---

2. Gareth Jones, 'Restitution of Benefits Obtained in Breach of Another's Confidence', *86 L.Q.R.* 463 (1970)

It is just because there is no statutory bedrock exclusively and exhaustively defining its ambit that this branch of the law is so confusing. Its proprietary elements are strongest in the law relating to trade secrets, and weakest in the area relating to unfair competition. The common element of unfairness has led to some stress upon the equitable character of many of the remedies. The defendant is presumed to have behaved in an unconscionable manner, and in equity should be enjoined from so acting, or prevailed upon to make restitution of things or profits thereby unfairly obtained. The contrast can be seen between the law of trade secrets where it is the character of the information as secret which is determinative, and that of breach of confidence where it is the character of the relationship between plaintiff and defendant which is more important. The two need to be distinguished. Certain key programs may be trade secrets. Obligations of confidence may arise from the commissioning of turnkey programming services. The proprietor of the key programs, which are trade secrets, will have a remedy whether or not he has entered into a confidential relationship with one who has misappropriated it. Conversely the confidant in the turnkey programming case will be bound to respect the confidence, whether or not it has the necessary characteristics to amount to a trade secret.[3] However, the interaction is complicated by the fact that a trade secret may change its character, and hence its special protection, just because it is communicated to another in a way which negates the notion of any confidence.[4] Conversely a situation may arise in which a third party acquires information from one party to a confidence, either improperly or even innocently, and a question may then arise as to whether even though not himself party to the original confidence he should be bound to respect it. One of the problems in this area is that information does not always carry with it the indicia of whether it constitutes a secret or a confidence or neither. It must also be remembered that while most physical objects are subject to proprietary rights, most information is not. This is partly related to the protean character of information, as opposed to physical objects. Many people can possess the same piece of information without knowing that any of the others also possesses it. Even in a case where a piece of information is known exclusively, and known to be so known, it is often impossible to be able to detect when that exclusivity has ended, since its physical manifestation may exhibit no signs of violation.

For all of these reasons the law in this area defies simple conceptual characterisation. It cannot be explained or understood solely in terms of contract, property or confidence, but all have their part to play in the inter-relation of liabilities and remedies. It can indeed be argued that it is this diversity which particularly fits this area for a flexible and innovative role in dealing with a new technology which cannot easily be pigeon-holed into an established area of intellectual property, or characterised by a historic theory of liability.

---

3. For a particularly clear expression of this distinction, see *Nucor Corp* v. *Tennessee Forging Steel Service Inc.* 476 F.2d 386 (8th Cir., 1973).
4. See *Coco* v. *A.N. Clark (Engineers) Ltd.* [1969] R.P.C. 41, Ch. at 47.

2. Pre-emption[5]

In the United States, controversy first arose over the validity of the application of trade secret and confidentiality law to this area. The source of the difficulty was the explicit provision in the Constitution[6] authorising federal patent and copyright law, and its consequent enactment. In two leading cases in 1964[7] the Supreme Court was unanimous in holding that the supremacy of federal law implied that state law could not by-pass the restricted ambit of federal patent or copyright protection under the guise of providing remedies of a different conceptual character:

Just as a state cannot encroach upon the federal patent laws directly, it cannot, under some other law such as that forbidding unfair competition, give protection of a kind that clashes with the objectives of the federal patent laws.[8]

It could thus be argued that assuming the case law to establish the object of federal patent law to be to deny protection to computer programs as purely mental processes,[9] and another as being to deny any such protection to a program which is obvious,[10] it would amount to just such a clash to protect purely mental processes or obvious programs for an indefinite period on a basis of trade secrets or unfair competition. In *Sears* the plaintiff had failed to secure a design patent on a lamp which the defendant had copied, and in *Compco* a design patent which had been copied by the defendants was held by the District Court to be invalid. In both cases claims based on an Illinois unfair competition law were upheld by the federal District Court, but reversed by the Supreme Court. It should be noted that in neither case was the patent denied on the ground that the subject matter was non-statutory, that is outside the class of patentable design, in neither case was there any element of breach of confidence, nor was there any clash with trade secret law since both products were on public display, and plainly exhibited the features to which the claims related. For these reasons trade secret law and confidentiality appeared to be unaffected by the decisions. This view predominated both in the courts,[11] and among commentators,[12] until 1969. Then in *Lear* v. *Adkins*[13] the issue came before the Supreme Court,

At the core of this case, then, is the difficult question whether federal patent policy bars a State from enforcing a contract regulating access to an unpatented secret idea.

---

5. See Bender, 'Protection of Computer Programs: The Copyright/Trade Secret Interface', *47 U.Pitt. L.R.* 907 (1986)
6. Constitution of the United States art. 1 sect. 8 ch. 8
7. *Sears Roebuck & Co.* v. *Stiffel Co.* 376 U.S. 225 (1964); *Compco Co* v. *Daybright Lighting Co.* 376 U.S. 234 (1964), hereafter referred to as *Sears* and *Compco.*
8. *Sears* at p. 231.
9. See above Ch. 1 at p. 11.
10. See above Ch. 1 at p. 14.
11. See, for example, *Sears Corp. of America* v. *General Electric Co.* 337 F.2d 716 (4th Cir., 1964); *Dekar Industries Inc.* v. *Bisset-Berman* 434 F.2d 1304 (9th Cir., 1970); and *Water Services Inc.* v. *Tesco Chemicals Inc.* 410 F.2d 163 (3rd Cir., 1969).
12. See, for example, Milgrim, 'Trade Secrets' (1968) pp. 7–68; Callman, 'Unfair Competition, Trademarks and Monopolies, 3rd ed. (1969) and Turner, 'Law of Trade Secrets' (Supp. 1968) following Preface; but cp. Adelman, 'Trade Secrets and Federal Preemption: The Aftermath of Sears and Compco', *49 J Pat. Off. S.* 713 (1967).
13. 395 U.S. 653 (a969), at 672.

The issue was whether or not the licensor of a new process could enforce royalty payments from his licensee in the absence of any authoritative ruling that the process was the subject of a valid patent. The licence preceded the grant which still awaited adjudication since the doctrine of licence estoppel had been applied in the lower courts. The court was thus confronted by claims in respect of three separate periods, that before the grant, that between the grant and the adjudication, and that after the adjudication. It took the view that where the patent precedes the licence this doctrine of estoppel does not apply, and that the same conclusion should apply to both of the other post-patent situations. But none of this was directed to the trade secret area, since the grant of a patent inevitably disclosed the process, and prevented it from remaining secret. The pre-grant period which raised the issue expressly was remitted, by a majority, for the state court to decide and so, in effect, deferred for further consideration by the Supreme Court. But a minority[14] of the Court took the view that the 1964 decisions governed,

> no state has a right to authorize any kind of monopoly on what is deemed to be a new invention, except when a patent has been obtained from the Patent Office under the existing standards of the patent laws. One who makes a discovery may, of course, keep it secret if he wishes, but private arrangements under which self-styled 'inventors' do not keep their discoveries secret, but rather disclose them, in return for contractual payments, run counter to the plan of our patent laws, which rightly regulate the kind of inventions that may be protected and the manner in which they may be protected. The national policy expressed in the patent laws, favoring free competition and narrowly limiting monopoly, cannot be frustrated by private agreements among individuals, with or without the approval of the state.[15]

Justice White took the view that the trade secret question was not raised at all. Such nibbling around what the court had itself proclaimed to be the core of the problem threw the initiative back to the lower courts. It was hardly surprising to find that they differed among themselves.[16] The chaos which might well have ensued was first stemmed by the Supreme Court in *Goldstein* v. *California*[17] which held, though only by five to four,[18] that Californian legislation purporting to prohibit 'private' re-recording of original sound recordings and tapes was not pre-empted by federal copyright laws.[19] It might still have been possible to distinguish between copyright and patent pre-emption, but such an argument was scotched by the Supreme Court in *Kewanee Oil Co.* v. *Bicron Corp.*[20] In that case the majority[21] trenchantly

---

14. Chief Justice Warren and Justices Black and Douglas.
15. At p. 677.
16. In *Painton & Co.* v. *Bourns Inc.* 442 F.2d 216 (2nd Cir., 1971) the 2nd Circuit held there to be no pre-emption in respect of unpatented secrets, while in *Kewanee Oil Co.* v. *Bicron Corp.* 478 F.2d 1074 (6th Cir., 1973) the 6th Circuit held that Ohio legislation on trade secrets was pre-empted in respect of products sold to the public for more than a year, and so unpatentable under federal patent law.
17. 412 U.S. 551 (1973).
18. Justices Douglas, Brennan, Marshall and Powell dissented.
19. It is interesting to note that the Court deliberately adopted a very wide definition of 'writings' as 'any physical recording of the fruits of intellectual or aesthetic labor', a formulation manifestly wide enough to encompass computer programs.
20. 416 U.S. 470 (1974).
21. Justices Douglas and Brennan dissented, Justice Marshall concurred on slightly different grounds, and Justice Powell was absent.

upheld Ohio trade secret law against pre-emption by federal patent law. Although the 1964 cases were upheld it was decided that there was no essential conflict between trade secret and patent law. Nor did the majority see in trade secret law any threat to the policy of patent law that that which is in the public domain should stay there, since *ex hypothesi* such material has not been kept secret. Nor would the abolition of protection by way of trade secrets encourage greater disclosure in respect of non-statutory subject matter for which federal law provides no protection at present. The proprietor of such material would still stand to benefit from keeping it secret, not because to do so would give him legal protection, but because as a matter of fact it would preserve the material from his competitors. This leaves three categories of material, that which is clearly unpatentable, that which is doubtfully patentable, and that which is clearly patentable. The argument in respect of the first does not differ from that relating to non-statutory material set out above; in the case of the second category it was felt that the strain on the Patent Office would be increased and that doubtful patents would proliferate if trade secret protection were to be eliminated; and as to the third the majority felt that trade secret law offered such slight benefits compared to those bestowed by patent that the prospect of extensive reliance upon it in preference to patent was remote.[22] The last reason is unconvincing, and a more pragmatic explanation may be that if pre-emption were to be limited to this category, chaos would ensue in the state courts where the test would have to be, not the sufficiently difficult one of whether or not a device were patentable, but instead whether or not a reasonable inventor[23] would consider it clearly unpatentable, with the bizarre twist that the inventor seeking protection would have to argue for the obvious unpatentability of his own invention so as to avoid pre-emption, while the misappropriator would have to argue in favour of patentability so as to attract pre-emption of state trade secret protection.

No sooner had this head of the Hydra been struck off than another emerged as a result of the passage by Congress of explicit pre-emption by the Copyright Act 1976 of

all legal or equitable rights that are equivalent to any of the exclusive rights within the general scope of copyright . . . no person is entitled to any such right or equivalent right in any such work under the common law or statutes of any state.[24]

though it was also made explicit that matters falling outside the reach of the Copyright Act were not the subject of such pre-emption.[25] The danger of this provision, given the Supreme Court's reliance in *Kewanee Oil Co.* v. *Bicron Corp.*[26] upon *Goldstein* v. *California*,[27] was that it would re-open the pre-emption issue in relation to patent as well as copyright.

The threat was serious since the matter had previously been considered in relation to computer-related matters in *Synercom Technology Inc.* v. *University*

---

22. At pp. 489, 490.
23. An unlikely enough concept in itself.
24. 17 U.S.C. sect. 301(a).
25. *Ibid.* sect. 301(b).
26. 416 U.S. 470 (1974).
27. 412 U.S. 551 (1973).

Computing Co.[28] There the defendant without any breach of contract or confidence, and without any theft of trade secrets, had copied the plaintiff's input formats for data, so as to supplant his product in the market which he had expended time, effort and money to develop. The Court there held that state law had been pre-empted. The input formats were within the broad class of matters regulated by copyright, but had been deliberately excluded from protection on the basis that, as ideas, they should be freely available.[29] In those circumstances it was held that to grant a state remedy would be to nullify this exercise of federal copyright policy. That decision was followed in another computer case, *Videotronics Inc.* v. *Bend Electronics*,[30] where once again the state cause of action was misappropriation of the plaintiff's idea, rather than that of a trade secret. The programs in question there had been distributed widely, without being registered for copyright, and could have been copied by any purchaser. Here again, once the Court had determined that copyright protection was available for computer programs, it determined that the policy of the Act would be undermined by allowing a state claim for misappropriation. It will be noted that in neither case did the question of secrecy arise. In one there was no copyright because it was not copyrightable subject matter, and in the other because it had not been so registered. Of these the width of reasoning in the former case is the more threatening, since many trade secrets can be categorised as 'ideas', and are, for that reason, not capable of being registered for copyright.

Neither of these cases relied upon the specific provision of section 301, and it was not directly applicable[31] in *M. Bryce Associates Inc.* v. *Gladstone*[32] where it was claimed that as a potential customer for a computer-based management information system the defendant had received copies of a series of manuals, but had then gone on to reject the system, and instead write his own very similar system, on the basis of the trade secrets thereby revealed to him. The court used section 301 of the 1976 Act to illustrate the pre-emption problem which had not been addressed explicitly in its 1909 predecessor. The Court analysed the somewhat convoluted legislative history of section 301[33] before concluding[34] that state law in the area of secrets embodied in computer software was not intended to be pre-empted. This view was further fortified by the Court's perception that the demarcation between copyright and trade secrets permitted recovery under the latter on these facts, but not on the former; and also by the position ultimately arrived at in the patent cases in the Supreme Court.[35] The most recent decisions to address section 301 directly in the context of computers[36] have come to the same

---

28. 474 F.Supp. 37 (N:D.Tex., 1979). See above p. 49 for copyright proceedings in respect of the same subject-matter.
29. Despite the fact that in this case idea and expression had merged, so that it was impossible to use the idea without also using its expression.
30. 564 F.Supp. 1471 (D. Nev., 1983).
31. Because the facts arose before the Act came into force in 1978.
32. 319 N.W.2d 906 (Wisc., 1982).
33. Which at one point had contained an explicit reference to the pre-emption of misappropriation law.
34. After referring to the legislative history of the Computer Software Act 1980 which amended the 1976 Act in other respects relating to computers.
35. Above p. 19.

conclusion[37] in the case of secret programs revealed only on a basis of confidence to customers.[38] It should be noted that in *Warrington* the disclosure was not to the competitor, but to a third party customer with whom the competitor was alleged to have conspired. It was also the case that there was no explicit requirement of confidence, but the court was prepared to take into account the practice within the software industry of not revealing secret programs, except upon a basis of confidence. It should also be noted that *Warrington* explicitly disavows the limitation suggested in respect of mere ideas in *Synercom Technology Inc.* v. *University Computing Co.*[39] instead taking the view that it was one of the distinguishing features of trade secret law to offer protection for ideas which prevented it from being regarded as providing equivalent remedies to those offered by the law of copyright.

It cannot be regarded as yet completely settled how far section 301 will pre-empt state law in the area of computers. It seems that if the subject matter is capable of being registered for copyright, and the plaintiff is simply trying to avoid the consequences of not having done so, state law will be pre-empted. The current tendency, however, is to allow state law to protect vendors against unscrupulous conduct by customers, and potential customers, when a limited publication is made to them in the form of sales aids such as manuals, brochures and demonstration copies of programs.

Whatever the quality of reasoning in this area it seems that the most serious objections to the use of state trade secret law have now been removed. Such protection might be sought for a number of reasons. The most compelling are that it is cheaper, quicker, and generally more convenient to secure protection in this way. No application need be filed with any government agency, no claim need be drafted or vetted, and nothing is disclosed to any competitor. If the secret can be kept, it can be maintained indefinitely upon any conditions which may be desired. Not least of the advantages is the avoidance of any uncertanty attaching to the dubious applicability of patent, or the avoidance of any uncertainty attaching to the dubious applicability of patent, or copyright law. No distinction need be drawn between programs, chips, screen displays, object, source or micro code, and any accompanying documentation since all are equally eligible for this form of protection. So too, no difficulty of interpreting such contentious words as 'copy', 'writing', 'author', 'obvious', 'novel', 'original', 'look and feel', or 'process' which plague the law of patent and copyright arise in this context. The price for this immunity is in the notion of secrecy to be considered in the next section of this chapter.

---

36. But not in the context of news gathering, *Peckarsky* v. *American Broadcasting Co.* 603 F.Supp. 688 (D.D.C., 1984) at 695; nor of non-original compilations, *Financial Information Inc.* v. *Moodys Investors' Service Inc.* 808 F.2d (2nd Cir., 1986) where the court rejected the idea of a general exemption from pre-emption in cases of 'commercial immorality' as suggested in *Nimmer on Copyright* (1986) sect. 1.01[B] 1 at 1–20, 1–21.

37. Although in *B.P.I. Systems Inc.* v. *Leith* 532 F.Supp 208 (N.D. Tex., 1981) upon the patently insufficient ground that the material in question *had* not been registered for copyright.

38. *Warrington Associates Inc.* v. *Real-Time Engineering Systems Inc.* 522 F.Supp. 367 (N.D. Ill, 1981); *Southern Mississippi Planning and Development District Inc.* v. *Robertson* 660 F.Supp. 1057 (S.D.Miss., 1986).

39. 474 F.Supp. 37 (N.D. Tex., 1979).

Before doing so it should be noted that if the law of trade secrets has the advantages mentioned above, and if it is not pre-empted by copyright,[40] why should not both remedies co-exist? It certainly seems that affixing a copyright notice does not necessarily vitiate secrecy so as to prevent a claim under state trade secret law from arising.[41] It is also unlikely that claiming state protection for a trade secret would preclude a federal copyright claim, the hypothesis of a conflict between the secrecy sought to be protected by state trade secret law and the free publication objective of copyright not so far having been made explicit.[42] Some commentators have hence recommended that copyright protection should normally be sought for material containing trade scerets so as to maximise protection.[43]

B. Interest of plaintiff

The law of the United Kingdom has always been more catholic than that of the United States in this area in seeking to accommodate information of very different types and degree of confidentiality. Indeed, in one of the founding cases for the jurisdiction in England, *Abernethy* v. *Hutchinson*,[44] the information in question, a series of lectures, seems to have contained nothing new, and was presumably heard by all who attended. Since then it has become established that in order to be protected, information must possess a number of characteristics, of which the first of three stated in *Coco* v. *A.N. Clark (Engineers) Ltd.*[45] was that the information must have the necessary quality of confidence about it.[46] At this point Megarry J. was quoting from the earlier decision in *Saltman Engineering Co. Ltd.* v. *Campbell Engineering Co. Ltd.*[47] where Lord Greene M.R. went on to equate this with the information not being in the public domain and public knowledge. Although there has been a recent attempt to distinguish between being a matter of public knowledge and being in the public domain,[48] this seems rather unorthodox, subject to an argument, which will be addressed later, as to the relevance of the means by

---

40. The question does not arise so readily in the case of patent because it is of the essence of a patent application that it reveal the method, but copyright can be claimed in some aspects of a secret, or for limited purposes, while effectively maintaining secrecy for key elements, especially in the case of computer programs and databases, given the attenuated disclosure required under the system of registration, see above Ch. 2 pp. 32 and 58.
41. See *Technicon Medical Information Systems Corp.* v. *Green Bay Packaging Corp.* 657 F.2d 1032 (7th Cir., 1982); *M. Bryce Associates Inc.* v. *Gladstone* 319 N.W.2d 906 (Wisc., 1982); *Management Science America Inc.* v. *Cyborg Systems Inc.* 6 C.L.R.S. 921 (N.D. Ill., 1978).
42. Though *Synercom Technology Inc.* v. *University Computing Co.* 474 F.Supp 37 (N.D. Tex., 1979) comes close, and the question is considered, but only to be rejected, by Bender, 'Protection of Computer Programs: The Copyright/Trade Secret Interface', *47 U. Pitt. L.R.* 907 (1986) at pp. 953–8.
43. See Solomon, 'The Copyrightability of Computer Software Containing Trade Secrets', *63 U. Wash. L.Q.* 131 (1985).
44. (1825) 3 L.J. Ch. 209, Ch.
45. [1969] R.P.C. 41, Ch. at 47.
46. This was accepted as axiomatic for the purposes of granting equitable relief by the High Court of Australia in *Moorgate Tobacco Co. Ltd.* v. *Philip Morris Ltd.* 56 A.L.R. 193 (H.C.A., 1984) at 208.
47. (1948) 65 R.P.C. 203, C.A.
48. By Lord Donaldson M.R. in the Court of Appeal in *Att.-Gen.* v. *Guardian Newspapers Ltd.* [1987] 3 All E.R. 316, H.L. at 337.

which the information becomes known.

In some contexts, especially that of the validity of contractual restrictions placed upon employees and ex-employees, the law of the United Kingdom does distinguish between trade secrets to which more extensive restrictions are allowed, and mere confidences which enjoy less protection. This distinction was considered by Neill L.J. in *Faccenda Chicken Ltd.* v. *Fowler*[49] where he seems to have accepted that the criteria were unclear:

It is clearly impossible to provide a list of matters which will qualify as trade secrets or their equivalent. Secret processes of manufacture provide obvious examples, but innumerable other pieces of information are *capable* of being trade secrets, though the secrecy of some information may be only short-lived. In addition, the fact that the circulation of certain information is restricted to a limited number of individuals may throw light on the status of the information and its degree of confidentiality . . . though an employer cannot prevent the use or disclosure *merely* by telling the employee the information is confidential, the attitude of the employer towards the information provides evidence which may assist in determining whether or not the information can properly be regarded as a trade secret.

Even in the lesser category of confidential information there are some limitations. There can, for example, be no confidence in a totally useless piece of information,[50] nor in 'trivial tittle-tattle.'[51] Nor can there be any confidence in what was once styled an iniquity,[52] but which was then broadened into a defence[53] to an action on the basis that there exists a public interest in disclosure.[54]

The principal consideration, however, is that the information should not have become sufficiently public to have lost its right to be protected. This is a complicated issue, since it is not completely clear whether such publicity is to be regarded as a formal matter subject to a technical definition of becoming public, or whether it is a matter of realistic judgment in each case. In many cases this will be closely connected with the extent to which a matter has been made public, both in terms of how fully and to how many people. The better view seems to be that the matter is not, at least now, a matter of formal technicality. As Cross J. put it in *Franchi* v. *Franchi*[55] it may be sufficient if relative secrecy remains, stressing that the determination must be a matter of degree depending upon the facts of each particular case. Similarly, it was said in *Mustad (O) & Son* v. *S. Allcock & Co. Ltd. and Dosen*[56] that a remedy would be denied only because the whole of the relevant information had become public, and there was no part of the process which had remained unrevealed.

It also seems that information will not necessarily be regarded as being in

---

49. [1987] Ch. 117, C.A.
50. *McNichol* v. *Sportsman's Book Stores* [1928–1935] MacG. C.C. 116, Ch.
51. *Coco* v. *A.N. Clark (Engineers) Ltd.* [1969] R.P.C. 41, Ch. at 48.
52. *Gartside* v. *Outram* (1856) 26 L.J. Ch. 113, Ch.
53. In the case of government secrets there is a positive duty upon the plaintiff to show that there is a balance of public interest against disclosure, see *Att.-Gen.* v. *Guardian Newspapers Ltd. (No.2)* [1988] 3 All E.R. 545, H.L.
54. See, for example, Lord Denning M.R. in *Fraser* v. *Evans* [1969] 1 Q.B. 349, C.A. at 405
55. [1967] R.P.C. 149, Ch. at 152, 153.
56. [1963] 3 All E.R. 416, H.L. (1928).

the public domain if some effort would still be required from the defendant to assemble it. Thus in *Ackroyds (London) Ltd.* v. *Islington Plastics Ltd.*[57] it was said that,

the mere publication of an article by manufacturing it and placing it upon the market, whether by means of work done in it or calculation or measurement which would enable information to be gained, is not necessarily sufficient to make such information available to the public. The question in each case is: Is such information available to the public? It is not, in my view, if work would have to be done upon it to make it available.

This is highly relevant to the software industry since it would seem to prevent any challenge to the confidentiality of programs released to customers in object code form, as some effort is required to decompile so as to reconstruct the source code. On the other hand. if a program were released in source code the minimal amount of effort required to copy it in such a form would certainly not have such an effect. A similar view was taken in *Schering Chemicals Ltd.* v. *Falkman Ltd.*[58] where information was imparted in confidence, but was also available in widely diffused public sources. It was held that such availability did not entitle the confidence to be disregarded. It is not, however, clear how much of that decision has survived the decision in *Att.-Gen.* v. *Guardian Newspapers Ltd. (No.2)*.[59] This too is of great interest in the context of computers, here in relation to computerised databases. A similar strain of reasoning may underlie the decision in *Under-Water Welders and Repairers Ltd.* v. *Street & Longthorne*[60] where the process was a simple one, and all of the elements were commonplace, but so long as the defendant had not acted independently of the confidence in reconstructing the process, he was bound by it.

A further controversial point in this connection is the extent to which it is relevant to consider how the information got into the public domain, for example whether it were put there by confider, confidant or a third party. The clearest case is that of publication by the confider, typically in a patent application. This arose in *Mustad (O) & Son* v. *S. Allcock & Co Ltd. and Dosen*[61] where the appellants were the successors in title of a defunct Norwegian company, the respondents were an English company and Dosen was one of their employees who had learned the relevant secret while in the employ of the Norwegian firm. It had been made an express condition of Dosen's contract with his Norwegian employers that he would neither use, nor make any use of, any trade secret.[62] Dosen was advised that upon the

---

57. [1962] R.P.C. 399, Ch. at 104.
58. [1982] Q.B. 1, C.A.
59. [1988] 3 All E.R. 545, H.L., where its authority was explicitly doubted by Bingham L.J. in the Court of Appeal at p. 626, and implicitly by Lord Goff in the House of Lords in his general endorsement of the approach of the Law Commission in this area, which was extremely critical of the decision, see *Law Com.* 110, 'Breach of Confidence' Cmnd. 8388 (1981) para. 6.67.
60. [1968] R.P.C. 498, Ch.
61. [1963] 3 All E.R. 416, H.L. (1928).
62. As appears from the judgment of Atkin L.J. in the Court of Appeal as extracted in *Cranleigh Precision Engineering Ltd.* v. *Bryant* [1966] R.P.C. 81, Ch., at 94, though the speech of Lord Buckmaster in the House of Lords as reported at [1963] 3 All E.R. 417 suggests a much less precise formulation.

liquidation of his erstwhile employers he was no longer bound by this term, and he accordingly imparted it to the respondents who started to use it. After proceedings had commenced, and upon the advice of counsel, the appellants applied for a patent, accepting that by so doing they had made the information public. It was held that once the information had been made public the appellants were not entitled to an injunction restraining Dosen from disclosing the information. It is unfortunate that the case is so sparsely reported[63] as a number of interesting questions were, as a result, left either obscure or unresolved. Thus the precise contractual term is not quoted although its construction must have been crucial to the case against the corporate defendants, nor is it made clear whether the respondents were regarded as *bona fide* purchasers for value of the information, nor how the associated claim for damages was resolved. It is submitted that only if Dosen's contract of employment explicitly restrained the use or disclosure of trade secrets could the injunction to restrain use by the corporate defendants have been justified, and perhaps only then after they had notice both of such term, and of its breach.

This case should be compared with *Cranleigh Precision Engineering Ltd.* v. *Bryant*[64] which also concerned information in a patent specification. The defendant had been employed as the managing director of the plaintiffs, and in that capacity had invented a swimming pool, which they marketed. On applying for a patent for that pool he was made aware of the existence of a patent for a basically similar pool, lacking only a couple of features of the one which he had invented. Bryant withheld knowledge of this patent from the plaintiffs, and after leaving their employment acquired the rights to the other patented pool for a company which he proceeded to establish. Roskill J. held that the plaintiffs were entitled to an injunction to restrain use of secrets relating to the two features not present in the patented pool, and also to restrain use of confidential information about the previous patent. Although it was not strictly necessary for him to decide the point, Roskill J. also held that the defendant could be enjoined against the use of information about the previous patent despite its publication. He distinguished *Mustad* on the basis that there disclosure had been by the plaintiff himself, whereas here it had been by the previous patentee. It is not clear why this should, by itself, have been decisive. A number of other distinctions might have been made. Thus in *Mustad* it seems that there had been no witting breach of confidence whereas in *Cranleigh* the facts reeked of bad faith on behalf of the defendant, who owed especially strong fiduciary duties for having been a director as well as for having been an employee. A more fruitful approach might have been to argue in terms of causation. In other words it was not so much the publicity of the information as the opportunity to discover and exploit it which the position of the defendant afforded him.[65] As noted above, if effort is still required to extract the information, then the secret may be upheld. It is suggested that it would not be much of an extension to hold the necessity to abuse a position of confidence to be similar. It is also noteworthy

---

63. It was reported for the first time no less than thirty-five years after being decided.
64. [1966] R.P.C. 81, Ch.
65. Cp. *Shellmar Products Co.* v. *Allen & Quayling Co.* F.2d 104 (7th Cir., 1937).

that in *Mustad* itself it was felt that if there had been evidence of further secrets beyond those disclosed in the patent, then the result might have been different. So too in other cases where the final result is achieved by a combination of public information and by something derived from an abuse of confidence the latter may be sufficient to provide some remedy, even though not extending so far as the full proprietary protection of trade secrets in the strict sense.

The third situation is that in which it is the confidant who makes the information public. Once again a relevant case involved a patent application. In *Speed Seal Products Ltd.* v. *Paddington*[66] the defendant resisted an application for an injunction[67] to restrain him from using information confided to him by the plaintiff on the basis that it had become public knowledge as a result of his patent application. The Court of Appeal took the view that since in *Cranleigh* the Court had distinguished *Mustad* on the basis that publication was there by a third party rather than by the confider, it would be odd if the defendant were to be better off if he published himself. This reasoning was re-examined by the House of Lords in *Att.-Gen.* v. *Guardian Newspapers Ltd. (No.2)*[68] where the confidence had also been breached by the defendant himself. That case did not involve commercial secrets, and many of the judges reversed their position, but Lord Goff, who did examine it in some detail, reached the same conclusion as that of the Law Commission.[69] His view, which it is submitted has a sound logical basis, is that it ought not to be material how information comes to be in the public domain. Once it is no longer secret or confidential there ought not outside the law of contract[70] to be an obligation to keep secret or confidential that which has lost such quality. It is, of course, quite another matter whether there should be remedial consequences such as an action for damages, or even an account of profits in relation to any wrongful conduct of the defendant in breaking such an obligation while it was in existence.

However, one further qualification is needed. If the defendant, as a result of his wrongful action, has secured a temporal advantage over those who have had to wait for the information to be made public, then he might be restrained for such a temporary period as is necessary to allow them an opportunity to catch up. Such a doctrine seems first to have been enunciated in the United Kingdom by Roxburgh J. in *Terrapin Ltd.* v. *Builder's Supply Co. (Hayes) Ltd.*,

the essence of this branch of the law, whatever the origin of it may be, is that a person who has obtained information in confidence is not allowed to use it as a spring-board for activities detrimental to the person who made the confidential communication, and spring-board it remains even when all the features have been published or can be ascertained by actual inspection by members of the public.[71]

---

66. [1986] 1 All E.R. 91, C.A.
67. It seems clear that he would have been liable in damages.
68. [1988] 3 All E.R. 545, H.L.
69. *Law Com.* 110, 'Breach of Confidence', Cmnd. 8388 (1981) para. 4.30.
70. And perhaps not even there.
71. [1960] R.P.C. 128, C.A. (the appeal did not deal with this point).

It is arguable that *Cranleigh* is no more than a further example of the operation of this doctrine.[72] It also seems clearer now that despite the wide language at the end of the quotation above there is a limit upon the period of time during which such an injunction will be available. This doctrine is once again of particular importance in the context of the computer industry. The industry contains many highly talented but undercapitalised innovators. They are often naive in business, and unable or unwilling to employ legal advisers. The result is that in their attempts to secure financial support, or marketing arrangements, they may easily disclose the secrets of their latest device or program. It would be wrong to allow those to whom such information becomes known to secure an advantage over others who might learn of the details only by an expensive process of reverse engineering or decompiling.

It should finally be noted in relation to the type of thing that can be protected by invoking this branch of the law that one of its main advantages is that it can supplement patent and copyright by protecting ideas, and know-how.

In the United States there has been more development of this branch of the law.[73] Most states recognised a tort consisting of the misappropriation of a trade secret, and and it was formerly included in the Restatement of Torts.[74] The Restatement defined a trade secret as,

any formula, pattern, device or compilation of information which is used in one's business, and which gives him an opportunity ,to obtain an advantage over competitors who do not know or use it.

As this branch of the law became more significant it attracted the attention of the Uniform Law Commissioners, and in 1979 a Uniform Trade Secrets Act was approved which redefined trade secrets to mean,

information, including a formula, pattern, compilation, program, device, method, technique or process, that:
(i) derives independent economic value, actual or potential, from not being generally known to, and not being readily ascertainable by proper means by, other persons who can obtain economic value from its disclosure or use, and
(ii) is the subject of efforts that are reasonable under the circumstances to maintain its secrecy.

The Model Act has been adopted in some ten states,[75] but like all such model acts it is liable to be enacted in a modified form. The most significant

---

72. Others include *Peter Pan Manufacturing Corp.* v. *Corsets Silhouette Ltd.* [1963] R.P.C. 45, Ch.; *Seager* v. *Copydex Ltd.* [1967] R.P.C. 349, C.A.; *Potters-Ballotini* v. *Weston-Baker* [1977] R.P.C. 202, C.A.; *Harrison* v. *Project and Design Co. (Redcar) Ltd.* [1978] F.S.R. 81, Ch.; *Bullivant (Roger)* v. *Ellis* [1987] I.C.R. 464, C.A.

73. For a general treatise see Milgrim 'Trade Secrets', and in the computer context see the seminal article of Bender 'Trade Secret Protection of Software' 38 Geo. Washington L.R. 909 (1970).

74. (1939) para. 757. The topic was omitted from the Second Restatement of Torts in 1979 on the basis that it had become part of the law of unfair competition and trade regulation, see 4 Restatement of Torts 2nd (1979) para. 1–2

75. California, Connecticut, Delaware, Indiana, Kansas, Louisiana, Minnesota, Montana, North Dakota and Washington.

state in this context to have adopted it so far is California,[76] and a significant alteration there has been the elimination from (i) of the reference to 'not being readily ascertainable by proper means'.[77] It seems likely that the phrase was included to allow for reverse engineering, but while accepting that, California took the view that the words could have a wider effect, and preclude protection when a secret had in fact been taken from the plaintiff if there were anywhere in the world someone who could have worked it out.

The requirements of a trade secret are usually characterised as being value, novelty and secrecy. The element of value is rarely significant in this context, since it is usually satisfied simply by a showing of the time and expense devoted to developing the relevant system. It is also implicitly recognised in the equivalent doctrine in the United States[78] to the spring-board doctrine in the United Kingdom. The Model Act thus allows for an injunction even after an erstwhile secret has lost that property:

> Upon application to the court, an injunction shall be terminated when a trade secret has ceased to exist, but the injunction may be continued for an additional reasonable period of time in order to eliminate the commercial advantage that otherwise would be derived from the misappropriation.

There are a number of examples of the operation of this doctrine in the context of computers.[80]

Nor does novelty usually present much of a problem since it is as well established in the United States as in the United Kingdom that it is enough to assemble commonplace ingredients in a new way, or to perform a given function in a different way. Thus in *Telex Corp.* v. *International Business Machines Inc.*[81] it was said that such items even though not 'new, novel, secret or innovative' in themselves could in combination constitute a trade secret. So too in *Cybertek Computer Products Inc.* v. *Whitfield*[82] it was not enough that the general functions of a program for the insurance industry were well-known when the program in question was sufficiently complicated for it to reflect a combination of a number of unique programming decisions.

The most commonly fought issue, however, relates to the quality of secrecy. This is essentially a question of fact, and the relevant considerations in deciding this question were conveniently summarised in *Forest Laboratories Inc.* v. *Formulations Inc.*,[83]

1. the extent to which the information is known outside the business;
2. the extent to which it is known by employees and others involved in the business;

---

76. See Burns, 'Litigating Computer Trade Secrets in California' 6 *Comp. L. J.* 485 (1986)
77. Civil Code sect. 3426.1(d)1.
78. See *Winston Research Corp.* v. *Minnesota Mining & Manufacturing Co.* 350 F.2d 134 (9th Cir., 1965) at 142.
79. Uniform Trade Secrets Act sect. 2(a).
80. For example, *Sperry-Rand Corp.* v. *A-T-O Inc.* 447 F.2d 1387 (4th Cir., 1971); *Data General Corp.* v. *Digital Computer Controls Inc.* 297 A.2d 433 (Del., 1972); *Analogic Corp.* v. *Data Translation Inc.* 358 N.E.2d 804 (Mass., 1976).
81. 367 F.Supp. 258 (N.D. Ok., 1973).
82. 203 U.S.P.Q. (B.N.A.) 1020 (Cal., 1977).
83. 299 F.Supp. 202 (E.D. Wisc., 1969), following the notes to the Restatement.

3. the extent of the measures taken to guard the secrecy of the information;
4. the value of the information to the business and to its competitors;
5. the amount of effort or money expended in developing the information; and
6. the ease or difficulty with which the information could be properly acquired or duplicated by others.

The first, third and last of these considerations are particularly relevant to the important question of how far trade secrets law can be relied upon to protect mass-marketed software.[84] It seems clear that limited disclosure to customers will, provided that reasonable efforts are taken to avoid further dissemination, not necessarily constitute an insurmountable obstacle.[85] The court will accept industry practice in this regard, and limited distribution qualified by a proprietary notice may be sufficient without any explicit requirement of secrecy.[86] Similarly in *M. Bryce Associates Inc.* v. *Gladstone*[87] where a confidentiality agreement was circulated at a meeting, and signed by some, but not by all, of those who continued to be present, it was held that sufficient had been done to retain secrecy. The court may also take into account the nature of the employees and the work they do in determining how explicit efforts to protect secrecy need be. Some sorts of work done by some sorts of employee are so obviously secret that 'heavy-handed measures' are unnecessary.[88] On the other hand if the alleged secret has been revealed generally without any reasonable effort to secure secrecy, then there will, applying these principles, be nothing left to protect.[89] A court may some-times take the view that putting a product on to the market without taking any explicit steps to preserve confidentiality, as in a sale of software, or taking inadequate steps, such as using shrink-wrap licence agreements in a mail-order business, may nevertheless not disable recovery, provided that it is sufficiently difficult to discover the secret from what has been freely made available. In such a case, however, the court may be inclined to apply the springboard doctrine so as to limit the period of any injunction taking into account the time expected to be necessary for such reverse engineering.[90]

The second principle is particularly relevant to the questions relating to the validity of restrictions in employment contracts to be discussed in the next section. In many high technology corporations, especially on the hardware side of the industry, there is often obsessive concern with security, and certainly enough for these purposes. The full panoply of such protection

---

84. See Gilburne and Johnstone, 'Trade Secret Protection for Software Generally and in the Mass Market', *3 Comp. L.J.* 211 (1982); McNeil, 'Trade Secret Protection for Mass Market Software', *51 Alb. L.R.* 293 (1987).

85. In *Management Science America Inc.* v. *Cyborg Systems Inc.* 6 C.L.R.S. 921 (N.D. Ill., 1978) 600 copies of the program had been distributed, but it was still regarded as secret.

86. *Warrington Associates Inc.* v. *Real-Time Engineering Systems Inc.* 522 F.Supp 367 (N.D. Ill, 1981).

87. 319 N.W.2d 906 (Wisc., 1982).

88. *Structural Dynamics Research Corp.* v. *Engineering Mechanics Research Corp.* 401 F.Supp. 1102 (E.D. Mich., 1975) at 1117.

89. See, for example. *Republic Systems amd Programming Inc.* v. *Computer Assistance Inc.* 322 F.Supp. 619 (D.Conn., 1970) at 628 where a list of customers was published in an advertising brochure.

90. See *Analogic Corp.* v. *Data Translation Inc.* 358 N.E.2d 804 (Mass., 1976) at 808.

was invoked by the defendant in *Telex Corp.* v. *International Business Machines Inc.*[91] who not only secured written agreements from employees to keep information secret, and re-emphasised the continuing nature of the restriction prior to an employee leaving, but within the premises used magnetic locks, security guards, dogs, specially controlled access routines, and any number of other measures to keep information secure. It is interesting to note that part of the cost of such measures was actually awarded as damages since the peculiar stringency had been dictated by the plaintiff's efforts to secure secret information. This may be contrasted with *Defiance Button Machine Co.* v. *C. & C. Metal Products Corp.*[92] where the plaintiff left a list of customers on a hard disk in a computer which it was selling, to which the defendant secured access by using an ex-employee of the plaintiff to operate the computer. The operator was able to print out the list by use of a book containing the relevant codeword which had been left lying in the computer room. The Court of Appeals refused to interfere with the trial court's finding that this was not sufficient to protect the secrecy of the list. In *Amoco Production Co.* v. *Lindley*[93] the plaintiff failed largely on account of the disdain with which it treated the defendant's efforts to develop a program. It forbade him to develop his idea during company time, then reluctantly required him to merge his efforts into a company production, made no special efforts to protect any of the materials exclusively relating to his program, but then when his program proved vastly superior to theirs sought to enjoin him. It seems fitting that they should have failed.

There was formally some disagreement in the United States on the question of whether or not revelation of a secret by a third party led to the elimination of liability.[94] This controversy seems now to have been decided in favour of the view that such disclosure does destroy the secret, even though some limited injunctive relief might be available in respect of any advantage gained by the defendant's own improper conduct.[95] This seems to accord with the dominant view in the United Kingdom.[96] In general it seems that in the United States there is now much less exclusive concentration upon the interest of the plaintiff, perhaps echoing Justice Holmes' eloquent refutation of such a basis for relief in *E. I. du Pont de Nemours* v. *Masland*,

'property' as applied to trade-marks and trade secrets is an unanalyzed expression of certain secondary consequences of the primary fact that the law makes some rudimentary requirements of good faith. Whether the plaintiffs have any valuable secret or not the defendant knows the facts, whatever they are, through a special confidence that he accepted. The property may be denied but the confidence cannot be. Therefore the starting point for the present matter is not property or due process of law, but that the defendant stood in confidential relations with the plaintiffs, or one

---

91. 367 F.Supp. 258 (N.D.Ok., 1973).
92. 759 F.2d 1053 (2nd Cir., 1985).
93. 609 P.2d 733 (Ok., 1980).
94. It was held not do to so in *Shellmar Products Co.* v. *Allen & Qualling Co.* 87 F.2d 104 (7th Cir., 1937), but to do so in *Conmar Products Corp.* v. *Universal Slide Fastener Co. Inc.* 172 F.2d 150 (2nd Cir., 1949).
95. See *Aronson* v. *Quick Point Pencil Co.* 440 U.S. 257 (1979).
96. See above p. 87.

of them. These have given place to hostility, and the first thing to be made sure of is that the defendant shall not fraudulently abuse the trust reposed in him.[97]

Although some would not accept so categorical a rejection of the notion of property, or the interest of the plaintiff,[98] it does seem to be the case that both in the United Kingdom and in the United States greater attention is now directed to the conduct of the defendant, and with it the emphasis shifts a little from the notion of trade secrets to that of unfair competition.

C. Conduct of Defendant

The different forms of misconduct on the part of the defendant which might give rise to liability reflect the same broad categories of wrong to be found in any branch of the law, running from breach of contract, to betrayal of trust, to delictual liability, tortious or criminal. Although it is not unknown for other forms of contractual liability to be involved in the context of computers, for example under a program licence or a contract for services, by far the most common situation relates to a contract for employment. Liability would be too narrowly confined if it were so restricted, failing to meet such situations as abuse of a pre-contractual confidence, perhaps in the case of a projected business merger. To meet this, equity supplemented the law with the notion of abuse of confidence. Finally, there are cases where there is involved breach of neither contract nor confidence, but nevertheless the conduct of the defendant is so heinous that it requires restraint. A typical situation is the misappropriation of the trade secrets or information of another. These three different types of misconduct will be considered in turn.

1. Contract[99]

The general advantages of reliance upon contractual remedies apply just as much here as elsewhere. The parties can determine the terms of their obligation, liability for breach is strict, and so both parties need be under no illusions as to their position. The disadvantages apply also, remedies are strictly limited by the doctrine of privity of contract, subject only to the availability of parasitic remedies such as inducement of breach of contract, or conspiracy to injure by such breach. Here also, however, certainty may be undermined both by the invalidity of some express terms agreed between the parties, for example on grounds of public policy, and the implication of some terms not expressly agreed between the parties.

These points are all illustrated in the context of contracts of employment within the computer industry. It is a business in which technology changes fast, and the first business to market a new product is likely to establish a highly profitable position.[100] It is thus particularly necessary both to develop

---

97. 244 U.S. 100 (1917) at 102.
98. See, for example, Callman, *Unfair Competition, Trademarks and Monopolies* (3rd edn, 1973) at Vol. 2 sect. 51.1.
99. See also Ch. 5 sect. 5 below.
100. In *Bell Telephone Laboratories* v. *General Instrument Corp.* 8 C.L.S.R. 297 (Pa., 1983) where such a covenant was litigated it was said to be 'worth millions' to be among the first in the relevant market.

new products and to keep them secret from competitors. Innovation is still predominantly the preserve of human beings, so innovative human beings with the necessary computing skills are in great demand. This makes for a highly volatile employment situation. An employer will want his employees to develop new products, to preserve knowledge of them from his competitors, certainly during the period of their employment, and perhaps afterwards, and he will not want his employees to work for his competitors. His competitors will seek exactly the converse. They will want to gather information upon the plans of competitors, and may see a need to leapfrog any new development by engaging employees with a proven record of successful innovation for a competitor whose product they seek to surpass. The court will be pressed on the one hand by the need to encourage investment in innovation by offering protection, and on the other by the need not to hamper the cross-fertilisation which will be optimised by the exchange of information, and the mobility of those able to exploit it. The question is how far the original employer can attain his objectives by contractual stipulation, and how far an employee or a competitor can go in furthering a competitive product. Analysis is clarified by making two distinctions, first between terms which forbid an employee to disclose his master's secrets, and those which forbid him to work for a competitor; and second between those terms which operate during the period of employment, and those which operate after its termination. These two distinctions yield four possible situations to examine.

(a) Competition during employment

There seems to be no question but that an employee is bound not to work for a competitor while employed under a contract of service. This might be the subject of an express term binding the employee to work exclusively for his employer, but even if it is not, it will be implied, even extending to work done in the employee's spare time.[101] It may also be the case that an employee is bound to obey lawful and reasonable instructions within the scope of his employment, and there can be no doubt that an express instruction not to work for a competitor while remaining employed would bind the employee. It has, however, been held in the United States that using an employer's computer for personal business, in the absence of proof of a direct order not to do so, and for non-competitive purposes, is not necessarily in breach of contract.[102] It has, nevertheless, been held in the United Kingdom that there is an implied term in commercial contracts not to act so as to frustrate the commercial object of the contract,

in the case of a contract of a commercial character the wilful act of one party which, although not, maybe, departing from the literal letter of the agreement, nevertheless defeats the commercial intention of the parties in entering into the contract, constitutes a breach of an implied term of the contract to perform the contract in such a way as not to frustrate that commercial objective.[103]

---

101. *Hivac Ltd.* v. *Park Royal Scientific Instruments Ltd.* [1946] Ch. 169, Ch.
102. *Gliss* v. *Sumrall* 409 S.2d 1227 (La., 1981).
103. *Secretary of State* v. *ASLEF (No.2)* [1972] 2 Q.B. 455, C.A., by Buckley L.J. at 498.

This goes beyond not engaging in competitive activities, and applies to misuse of confidential information by way of preparing to do so after leaving. Thus in *Faccenda Chicken Ltd.* v. *Fowler*[104] it was held that an employee was not entitled to copy or even to memorise confidential information, such as a list of customers, to facilitate competition after leaving employment. Similarly in California it was held in *Computer Sciences Corp.* v. *Ferguson*[105] that the employee was not in breach by engaging in discussions about starting up a competitive company, and even drawing up its articles of association while still employed, so long as no use was made of confidential information. It may also be held to violate such a duty of fidelity to an employer to solicit customers while still employed, or to prepare and put in competitive bids.[106] In the United States it has even been held justified to dismiss the spouse of a competitor in the computer industry because of the high interest in secrecy, though the court may have been influenced by the fact that the competing spouse had been an employee of the plaintiff, and was dismissed for setting up that very business while still employed.[107]

(b) Disclosure during employment

Here again the law seems clear both in the United Kingdom and in the United States. It should be noted that disclosure is taken to include use by the employee himself for his own competitive purposes, whether such use occurs during or after employment. The range of information to which this obligation applies is wider than that which applies after the termination of employment. There seems no theoretical reason why a contract of employment should not forbid the disclosure of any information, however trivial, and however easily discoverable from accessible sources, though it is also unlikely that any such obligation could be enforced directly, or even indirectly by dismissal.[108]

The duty of fidelity discussed in the previous section would clearly extend to disclosure of confidential information or trade secrets. It is thus, in such a case, not necessary that there be an express term relating to such materials. As Cross J. put it in *Printers and Finishers Ltd.* v. *Holloway*,

> not all information which is given to a servant in confidence and which it would be a breach of his duty for him to disclose to another person during his employment is a trade secret which he can be prevented from using for his own advantage after the employment is over, even though he has entered no express covenant with regard to the matter in hand.[109]

Exactly the same situation prevails in the United States. In *Jostens Inc.* v. *National Computer Systems Inc.*[110] it was said that 'employees have a common law duty not to wrongfully use confidential information *or*[111] trade secrets

---

104. [1987] Ch. 117, C.A.
105. 74 Cal. Rptr. 86 (Cal., 1968).
106. *C-E-I-R Inc.* v. *Computer Dynamics Corp.* 183 A.2d 374 (Md., 1962).
107. *Moore* v. *Honeywell Information Systems Inc.* 558 F.Supp 1229 (D.Haw., 1983).
108. Dismissal for such a reason would be manifestly unfair.
109. [1964] 3 All E.R. 731, Ch. at 738n. See also *Faccenda Chicken Ltd.* v. *Fowler* [1987] Ch. 117, C.A.
110. 318 N.W.2d 691 (Minn., 1982) at 701.
111. Emphasis supplied.

obtained from an employer'. The difference was stressed in another computer industry case in relation to an express contractual term: 'The express contracts in issue apply not only to trade secrets but also to privileged, proprietary and confidential information.'[112]

It was indeed said that such an expanded concept was particularly appropriate in 'an area of knowledge and rapid technological change such as the computer field'. It is, however prudent not to rely upon such an implication into the ordinary contract of employment but to draft express terms as in the latter case. Quite apart from the direct efficacy of such clauses, they are useful in promoting a more coherent approach to the security of information on the part of the employer, and a greater awareness on the part of the employee of the existence and extension of any such obligation. Indeed, the direct efficacy of such terms is often questionable, especially where there is an attempt to impose them upon the employee during the course of his employment. In such a case, in order for the obligation to become legally binding as a matter of contract some further consideration must be shown. It was accepted in *Jostens* that 'greater wages or a promotion or access to technical or operational parts . . . that non-signing employees did not have' might be sufficient. However, it was not enough that the employee was not dismissed, at least in the light of failure to dismiss other non-signing employees. It was also accepted that such an agreement might merely memorialise an agreement for which consideration had been given.[113]

(c) Competition after employment

The relevant consideration both in this respect and in that of disclosure is that any restriction which is held to be in restraint of trade will be void. The law is concerned that no one shall be prevented from earning a living. On the other hand, it accepts that an employer needs some protection even after an employee has left his employment. It is acceptable for the law to enforce some degree of disincentive to employees to leave so as to compete with their ex-employer. In the United Kingdom the line is drawn between competition and disclosure or use of highly confidential information or trade secrets. Not only will the law strike down a simple agreement not to compete, but it will also permit the employee to use the general skills which he has acquired, and his knowledge of the broad means of conducting the relevant business:

> To acquire the knowledge of the reasonable mode of general organization and management of a business of this kind, and to make use of such knowledge, cannot be regarded as a breach of confidence in revealing anything acquired by reason of a person having been in any particular service, although the person may have learnt it in the course of being taught his trade; but it would be a breach of confidence to reveal trade secrets such as prices, etc. or any secret process or things of a nature which the man was not entitled to reveal.[114]

In the United States, quite apart from problems created by the possible

---

112. *Structural Dynamics Research Corp.* v. *Engineering Mechanics Research Corp.* 401 F.Supp. 1105 (E.D. Mich., 1975) at 1114.
113. *Cybertek Computer Products Inc.* v. *Whitfield* 203 U.S.P.Q. (B.N.A.) 1020 (Cal., 1977)
114. *Herbert Morris Ltd.* v. *Saxelby* [1916] 1 A.C. 688, at 705

application of anti-trust law, the position is more confused. A number of states[115] have specific legislative provisions prohibiting simple non-competition agreements, though these do not extend to restrictions on disclosure of secrets, after employment has terminated. In *Structural Dynamics Research Corp.* v. *Engineering Mechanics Research Corp.*[116] this gave rise to a problem in the Conflict of Laws since Ohio where the agreement was executed, allowed such clauses if reasonable, while Michigan, where it was to be executed, operated a total ban. In fact the court was able to avoid the problem since it concentrated on the disclosure aspect. It seems, however, that it would have invalidated the restriction on competition so far as it applied to competition in Michigan.[117]

There are a number of variants upon such covenants. Sometimes it is simply against competition, but it may sometimes be against taking employment with a customer, or soliciting customers. It may be limited either by the geographical area in which it applies, or by the nature of the work to which it relates. The governing principle is that it should be reasonable to protect the relevant interest of the covenantee. In the computer industry, which is international in coverage and can be operated in remote locations by telecommunication techniques, it is not *prima facie* unreasonable to impose a restriction with appropriate world-wide application. Such a restriction was indeed upheld in *Business Intelligence Services Inc.* v. *Hudson*.[118] It was made more palatable because it was limited in time to one year, and because there were plenty of alternative opportunities open to the employee in less closely competing employments. These factors are also likely to be relevant in other cases in the computer industry. Because the pace of change is so fast, information quickly loses its value so long periods of restraint will be unacceptable. The industry is also sufficiently diverse for the type of competing work to be narrowly defined. Skills can extend over a very wide range of applications, so many types of employment will offer no truly competitive threat. It needs to be noted that in general[119] courts will not simply strike down an over-broad covenant, but will instead seek to write it down to a reasonable level. In more technical language the express term will not prevent the implication of a narrower term relating to the same subject-matter.[120] Sometimes, however, the covenant is so vague that it offers little possibility of redemption in this way.

The whole point of invalidating such clauses is to protect employees from exploitation. Such covenants are generally enforceable in agreements for the sale of a business, and perhaps also where the relation, though having some elements of employment, is more akin to the sale of a business, for example

---

115. Including Alabama, California, Colorado, Florida, Hawaii, Louisiana, Michigan, Montana, North Dakota, Oklahoma, South Dakota and Wisconsin.

116. 401 F.Supp. 1105 (F.D. Mich., 1975).

117. Since this is a rule of public policy it is likely to prevail even against an explicit choice of law clause, see below p. 223

118. 580 F.Supp. 1068 (S.D.N.Y., 1984).

119. A few states in the United States take a different view, see, for example *White* v. *Fletcher-Mayo Ass.* 303 S.E.2d 746 (Ga., 1983).

120. See *Triplex Safety Glass Ltd.* v. *Scorah* [1938] Ch. 211. C.A.

the contract of a director,[121] or a partner, there is most chance of such a covenant being upheld.[122] A further consequence of such a rationale is that the restriction may be enforced if the contract contains some other method of insulating the employee from harm. Thus in *Modern Controls Inc.* v. *Andreadakis*[123] the contract provided for the employee to be paid a sum equivalent to his base salary for the continuance of the covenant if its existence was the cause of his not securing employment. The efficacy of this clause was unaffected by the fact that the covenantee had an option to release the covenantor from the restriction in lieu of making such payment. A more dubious technique was upheld in *J & K Computer Systems Inc.* v. *Parrish*[124] whereby the employee contracted to pay a liquidated[125] sum to the employer, in the event of his working for a competitor or customer, expressed to represent the agreed value of training. In the United Kingdom it seems unlikely that such a term would be upheld, but that it would be regarded as an unconscionable attempt to restrain trade.[126]

(d) Disclosure after employment

In neither the United Kingdom nor the United States is it necessarily in restraint of trade to restrict disclosure of information learned or developed during a period of employment. Express terms restricting the disclosure or use of such information will be enforced, at least to the extent that they are reasonable for the purpose of protecting the employer. In the United Kingdom it seems that a covenant not to disclose will be enforceable only if it relates to matters which are at least confidential.[127] In the absence of an express covenant restriction will be imposed only upon the disclosure of trade secrets,[128] or possibly upon the sale, rather than use, of merely confidential information.[129] Courts in the United States similarly distinguish between those matters to which an implied term applies and those which can be restricted by an express term.[130] In *Structural Dynamics Research Corp.* v. *Engineering Mechanics Research Corp.*[131] the information had not been learned by the employee but created by him during his employment. It was held that while the implied term would not extend to such information it was possible to restrict its disclosure by an express covenant.

It will often be difficult to detect whether information has, or has not, been disclosed to a competitor for whom the employee is now working. In practice it is to meet this problem that the courts tend to impose limited

---

121. *M. & S. Drapers* v. *Reynolds* [1975] 1 W.L.R. 9, C.A.
122. *Kerr* v. *Morris* [1987] Ch. 90, C.A.
123. 578 F2d 1264 (8th Cir., 1978).
124. 642 P.2d 732 (Ut., 1982).
125. Crudely scaled to reflect the duration of employment.
126. See *Electronic Data Systems Ltd.* v. *Hubble* 4 A.C.C.L. 6 (Feb. 1988), C.A. where the Court of Appeal was hostile to such a term, given the large sum and its disproportion to the value of the training actually received.
127. *The Littlewoods Organisation Ltd.* v. *Harris* [1978] 1 All E.R. 1026, C.A.; *Faccenda Chicken Ltd.* v. *Fowler* [1987] Ch. 117, C.A.
128. *Printers and Finishers Ltd.* v. *Holloway* [1964] 3 All E.R. 731, Ch.
129. See *Faccenda Chicken Ltd.* v. *Fowler* [1987] Ch. 117, C.A. at 139.
130. See, for example, *Ungar Electric Tools* v. *Sid Ungar Co.* 13 Cal. Rptr. 268 (Cal., 1961).
131. 401 F.Supp. 1105 (E.D. Mich., 1975) at 1111.

bans on taking such competing employment.[132] The time regarded as reasonable for the covenant not to compete will relate directly to the realistic effective life of the information.

A closely related type of covenant requires the return of physical equipment, and any materials containing or representing relevant information, together with a prohibition on making further copies. In the United Kingdom it is probably necessary that such a term be made expressly.[133] In the United States a clause requiring such return was applied in *Sperry Rand Corp. v. Pentronix*.[134] It should not, however, be supposed that such a clause excludes obligations in relation to the memorisation of information contained in such documents, nor that if employees depart doing no more than carrying what they have learned in their minds that they are thereby immune from liability.[135]

2. Confidence

It can be argued that a number of the situations considered above ought really to be subsumed under this heading, namely those where the contractual obligation was not explicit, but implicit. It seems however a matter of indifference in such cases how they should be labelled. It is nevertheless necessary to have some further category which can apply in the absence of any binding contract between the relevant parties. A very common situation in the computer industry is that ideas must be disclosed to potential financiers, partners, distributors or customers in anticipation of a contract, but before it comes into existence. If there is no contract into which to imply a term it will be necessary to rely, instead, upon some notion of breach of confidence. It may also be useful where there are contracts in existence, but not between the relevant parties. In such a chain the confidence may be reposed by the first party in a second, and by the second in a third. If it is the third who, knowing of the confidence placed by the first, proposes to reveal the information, there is no contract between first and third parties into which to imply a term. Once again breach of confidence may be an appropriate concept. A further situation may be one in which an apparent contractual situation is not to be one for some purely technical reason, perhaps that the parties to the contract have changed owing to a reorganisation without the appropriate formalities of assignment having been observed. In some situations there is overlap with the third category to be discussed in the next part of this section, namely misappropriation. Although it is recognised that no rigid distinction can be drawn, it is proposed to reserve situations in which an element of misappropriation is very strong to the next section.

In the United Kingdom a broad approach was suggested by Megarry J. in *Coco v. A.N. Clark (Engineers) Ltd.*:

---

132. But see *SI Handling Systems Inc. v. Heisley* 753 F.2d 1244 (3rd Cir., 1985) where the court was reluctant to repair the omission to impose a non-competition covenant by taking an extensive view of trade secret protection.
133. See *Regina Glass Fibre Ltd. v. Schuller* [1972] R.P.C. 229, C.A.
134. 311 F.Supp. 910 (E.D. Pa., 1970).
135. See *Bell Telephone Laboratories v. General Instrument Corp.* 9 C.L.S.R. 297 (Pa., 1983).

It seems to me that if the circumstances are such that any reasonable man standing in the shoes of the recipient of the information would have realised that upon reasonable grounds the information was being given to him in confidence, then this should suffice to impose upon him the equitable obligation of confidence. In particular, where information of commercial or industrial value is given on a business-like basis and with some avowed common object in mind, such as a joint venture or the manufacture of articles by one party for the other, I would regard the recipient as carrying a heavy burden if he seeks to repel a contention that he was bound by an obligation of confidence.[136]

This approach concentrates upon the attitude of the confider, and it has been argued that it goes too far in a commercial context by enabling such a person to impose an obligation upon others by his own unilateral action. It seems that this is a real commercial problem, and that elaborate steps are, in fact, taken by businessmen to avoid such obligations arising as a result of the receipt of unsolicited confidential communications.[137] The problem is exacerbated by the holding in *Seager* v. *Copydex Ltd.*[138] that in such a case the unsolicited confidence is abused, even though the information is used unconsciously rather than consciously in the design of a new product.

The Law Commission compared this wide view with a more restricted view under which a confidence would come into being only when it was either expressly, or by inference, accepted by the recipient. It pointed out that in many cases these views would coincide, but that while on the wider view an unsolicited piece of information sent on a confidential basis, say to a prospective financier, might well give rise to a confidence; yet on the narrower view if the recipient immediately upon receipt expressly rejected the confidence, that might be enough to prevent a confidence from arising. In other words there will not always be identity between the attitude of a reasonable man in the position of the recipient, and that of the recipient himself. The Commission preferred the narrower view, upon the basis that a businessman should not be compelled to adopt elaborate precautions to avoid obligations of confidence from being thrust upon him.[139] However, it was prepared to accept that in the case of the unsolicited communication, if the recipient should profit by exploiting the information, then there would be room for a restitutionary remedy.[140]

Some of the cases discussed earlier[141] involved this sort of situation in the United States, but it was explored more fully in *Burten* v. *Milton Bradley Co.*[142] The defendant, a publisher of games, had devised a form under which any confider was required to waive any claim as a condition of the defendant considering the material submitted. Although the defendant succeeded at first instance upon the basis of the form, the appellate court took a different view. It found that the disclosure form was ambiguous, and set out the

---

136. [1969] R.P.C. 41, Ch. at 48.
137. See *Law Com.* 110, 'Breach of Confidence', Cmnd. 8388 (1981) para. 5.3
138. [1967] R.P.C. 349, C.A.
139. *Law Com.* 110, 'Breach of Confidence', Cmnd. 8388 (1981) para. 6.10.
140. *Ibid.* para. 6.11, citing in support a note to the United States Restatement on Torts para. 757 in which a restitutionary remedy is proposed for a case in which confidential information is received by an innocent third party.
141. For example, *M. Bryce Associates Inc.* v. *Gladstone* 319 N.W.2d 906 (Wisc., 1982).
142. 763 F.2d 461 (1st Cir., 1985).

arguments of policy which justified taking a strict view:

The underlying goal of the law which protects trade secrets, like that which protects copyrights and patents, is to encourage the formulation and promulgation of ideas by ensuring that creators of ideas benefit from their creations ... Massachusetts encourages the protection of trade secrets not only because the public has a manifest interest in commercial innovation and development, but also because it has an interest in the maintenance of standards of commercial ethics ... Fundamental to this, we believe, is the expectation by the parties that, absent an explicit waiver, the exchange of ideas will take place in trust and confidence.[143]

Another situation in which confidential information may be disclosed in the expectation that it will be kept in confidence in this field occurs when bids are being solicited for a secret project from potential sub-contractors.[144]

An example in the United States in the computer context of the situation where an obligation of confidence was necessary because of the lack of privity at the ends of a contractual chain arose in *Data General Corp.* v. *Digital Computer Controls Inc.*[145] where manuals supplied on a confidential basis to customers were disclosed to a competitor.

3. Misappropriation

The degree of protection offered under this rubric is both vague and controversial. Its investigation constituted the second main focus for the report of the Law Commission in the United Kingdom.[146] It is largely inspired by the perception that it is much clearer that information obtained in breach of contract or confidence is subject to protection than it is that information obtained by more heinous means such as theft or intimidation is protected. It is true that in the United Kingdom there are dicta in early cases[147] which suggest the possibility of such protection, but they have not yet generated a substantial or coherent body of case law. Such conduct is clearly reprehensible, but in *Malone* v. *Metropolitan Police Commissioner*,[148] a case involving the acquisition of information by telephone tapping, the court distinguished sharply between moral obligation and legal remedy:

I do not see why someone who has overheard some secret in such a way should be exposed to legal proceedings if he uses or divulges what he has heard. No doubt an honourable man would give some warning when he realises that what he is hearing is not intended for his ears: but I have to concern myself with the law, and not with moral standards.

These remarks were, however, made *obiter*, in a case where it had been held

---

143. At p. 467.
144. As in *Electronic Data Systems Corp.* v. *Sigma Systems Corp.* 500 F.2d 241 (5th Cir., 1974).
145. 297 A.2d 437 (Del., 1972).
146. *Law Com.* 110, 'Breach of Confidence', Cmnd. 8388 (1981), although not reflected in the title of its report.
147. In *Miller* v. *Taylor* (1769) 4 Burr. 2303, K.B., at 2330 (an injunction will lie to prevent 'surreptitiously or treacherously publishing what the owner has never made public at all, nor consented to the publication of'); *Ashburton* v. *Pape* [1913] 2 Ch. 469, C.A. at 475 (a power exists in the court to restrain publication of information 'improperly or surreptitiously obtained').
148. [1979] Ch. 344, Ch. at 376.

that the acquisition of the information had been lawful, and in a later case where similar acquisition was clearly unlawful the Court of Appeal distinguished these remarks, at least to the extent of recognising that in such a case there was an arguable issue to be tried.[149]

The whole notion of a separate tort of misappropriation of information or of unfair competition was lambasted by Deane J. speaking for a unanimous High Court of Australia in *Moorgate Tobacco Co. Ltd.* v. *Philip Morris Ltd.*[150] He rejected the reasoning of the majority in the United States case of *International News Service* v. *Associated Press*,[151] accepting instead the contrary views expressed by the House of Lords in *Warnink B.V.* v. *Townend J. & Sons (Hull)*[152] in declining to extend the tort of passing off into a more general wrong of unfair competition, and those expressed by the High Court of Australia in *Victoria Park Racing and Recreation Grounds Co. Ltd.* v. *Taylor*[153] where he quoted Dixon J.'s grounds for distinguishing the British from the American position with some approval,

courts of equity have not in British jurisdictions thrown the protection of an injunction around all the intangible elements of value, that is, value in exchange, which may flow from the exercise by an individual of his powers or resources whether in the organization of a business or undertaking or the use of ingenuity, knowledge, skill or labour. This is sufficiently evidenced by the history of the law of copyright and by the fact that the exclusive right to inventions, trade marks, designs, trade name and reputation are dealt with in English law as general heads of protected interests and not under a wide generalization.

Such a policy of restricting the causes of action was not intended by Deane J. to be necessarily inflexible, but rather as more consistent with the proper distribution of powers in a democratic state,

The rejection of a general action for 'unfair competition' involves no more than a recognition of the fact that the existence of such an action is inconsistent with the established limits of the traditional and statutory causes of action which are available to a trader in respect of damage caused or threatened by a competitor. These limits, which define the boundary between the areas of untrammelled competition, increasingly reflect what the responsible Parliament or Parliaments have determined to be the appropriate balance between competing claims and policies. Neither legal principle nor social utility requires or warrants the obliteration of that boundary by the importation of a cause of action whose main characteristic is the scope it allows, under high sounding generalizations, for judicial indulgence of idiosyncratic notions of what is fair in the market place.

The Law Commission had nevertheless regarded the absence of some new remedy for the misappropriation of information as a 'glaring inadequacy' in the scheme of available protection.[154] It should, however, be noted that in a

---

149. *Francome* v. *Mirror Group Newspapers Ltd.* [1984] 2 All E.R. 408, C.A.
150. 56 A.L.R. 193 (H.C.A., 1984).
151. 248 U.S. 215 (1918). He preferred the reasoning of Justices Brandeis and Holmes, and the criticism of the doctrine by Learned Hand J. in the later case of *Chenet Bros.* v. *Doris Silk Corp.* 35 F.2d 279 (2nd Cir., 1929).
152. [1979] A.C. 731, H.L.
153. 58 C.L.R. 479 (H.C.A., 1937) at 508, 509.
154. *Law Com.* 110, 'Breach of Confidence', Cmnd. 8388 (1981) para. 5.5. See also Gurry, 'Breach of Confidence' (1984) pp. 55–6.

number of cases there may be a possibility of recovering damages under different branches of established law. Thus if the misappropriation is accomplished by means of trespass to land or goods, or by the conversion of a tangible object, or by inducing breach of contract, or more generally by conspiracy to damage a competitor by the use of unlawful means there may well be a remedy in damages, and even occasionally by injunction.

So far attention in this part of this section has been concentrated upon situations in which no obligation of contract or confidence exists at all, but the situation in which such an obligation exists, but not so as to bind plaintiff and defendant, is clearly analogous. A third party may acquire information which has been imparted to another in breach of contract or confidence. He may, or may not, know of this at the time of acquisition, and even if he does not know at such time, perhaps he ought to have known. The question arises of how far he is to be bound not to use or disclose the information, and whether he should be liable to the plaintiff for past use. It seems to be well-established that a third party is bound by the confidence if he knew of it at the time of acquisition. Thus it was said in the House of Lords in *Att. Gen.* v. *Guardian Newspapers Ltd. (No.2)*:

In a case of commercial secrets with which the development of the law of confidence has been mostly concerned, a third party who knowingly receives the confidential information directly from the confidant, which is the usual case, is tainted and identified with the confidant's breach of duty and will be restrained from making use of the information.[155]

Although this passage refers to direct receipt, it would probably regard as direct any receipt with knowledge of the original confidence, irrespective of the number of intermediate transactions. It is, however, necessary that the information remain confidential,[156] and the greater the number of intermediate transactions the less the chance of its so remaining.[157] The position of the unwitting recipient is less clear. It seems likely that on general principles if the third party ought to have known of the confidence, or if he deliberately shut his eyes to it, and may be regarded as having constructive knowledge of it, then he will be bound. The most difficult case is the wholly, and justifiably, ignorant third party, and especially such a third party who is a *bona fide* purchaser for value, or one who has altered his position upon the basis of the information innocently received so that he will suffer loss if he should be bound. There are conflicting indications upon these matters. In the old case of *Morison* v. *Moat*[158] there are dicta to the effect that a *bona fide* purchaser for value would not be bound, but in *Stevenson, Jordan & Harrison Ltd.* v. *MacDonald & Evans*[159] the trial judge rejected such a defence, though the appellate court expressly withheld its view on the point, deciding the case on the basis that no confidence had ever existed in the relevant matter.

In the United States this part of the law is better developed. As long ago

---

155. [1988] 3 All E.R. 545, H.L. at 652.
156. See above p. 88.
157. See *Sun Printers Ltd.* v. *Westminster Press Ltd* [1982] I.R.L.R. 292, C.A.
158. (1851) 9 Hare 241, Ch. This also seems to be the position in Canada, see *International Tools Ltd.* v. *Kollar* 67 D.L.R. 2d 386 (Ont. C.A., 1968) at 391.
159. 68 R.P.C. 190 (1951), Ch.

as 1918 the Supreme Court held that even in the absence of breach of contract or confidence, and without infringing trade secrets, a remedy was available for misappropriation of information. In *International News Service* v. *Associated Press*[160] a competitor was thus enjoined from taking news items published by a competitor[161] and using them for his own purposes.[162] In *Synercom Technology Inc.* v. *University Computing Co.*[163] an attempt was made to argue that the then new approach to pre-emption had overtaken this decision, but as was noted earlier pre-emption has now been reined back.[164] Although in *Synercom* the doctrine was limited to cases where the required restraint was merely to be temporary, it is by no means certain that it will be so restricted in cases where there is no real issue of pre-emption. Thus in *University Computer Co.* v. *Lykes Youngstown Corp.*[165] where the defendant deliberately decided to subvert an employee of its competitor so as to use its programs, the principle of providing a remedy for such misappropriation went unchallenged. The law is materially assisted in this regard in the United States by the readier provision of protection of trade secrets by legislation in both the criminal and tortious realm. Thus the Uniform Trade Secrets Act makes it clear that circumstances may be such that otherwise lawful conduct can amount to misappropriation, and in the notes to the relevant clause the Commissioners refer to aerial reconnaissance.[166] There seems to be no reason why a similar approach should not be taken to, for example, electronic eavesdropping on computer operations.

Such legislation has also been of assistance on the difficult question of the extent of the obligation. The Restatement on Torts conferred absolute immunity upon *bona fide* purchasers for value, but this view has been rejected in the new Model Act. It defines misappropriation to mean:

(i) acquisition of a trade secret of another by a person who knows or has reason to know that the trade secret was acquired by improper means; or
(ii) disclosure or use of a trade secret of another without express or implied consent by a person who
(A) used improper means to acquire knowledge of the trade secret;
(B) at the time of disclosure or use knew or had reason to know that his knowledge of the trade secret was
(I) derived from or through a person who had used improper means to acquire it;
(II) acquired under circumstances giving rise to a duty to maintain its secrecy or limit its use; or
(III) derived from or through a person who owned a duty to the person seeking relief to maintain its secrecy or limit its use; or
(C) before a material change of his [or her] position, knew or had reason to know that it was a trade secret and that knowledge of it had been acquired by accident or mistake.[167]

---

160. 248 U.S. 215 (1918).
161. In such a form as not to infringe copyright.
162. Although this case has been frequently attacked, it has also been ably defended, see Baird, 'Common Law Intellectual Property and the Legacy of *International News Service* v. *Associated Press*', 50 U. of Chi. L.R. 411 (1982).
163. 474 F.Supp. 37 (N.D. Tex., 1979).
164. Above p. 83.
165. 504 F.2d 518 (5th Cir., 1974).
166. Citing *E.I. du Pont de Nemours & Co.* v. *Christopher* 431 F.2d 1012 (5th Cir., 1970).
167. Uniform Trade Secrets Act sect. 1(2).

It is thus clear that having reason to know is assimilated to knowing, and that such knowledge takes effect at the moment of disclosure or use, rather than at that of acquisition in the case of third party acquisition. The whole position so far as third parties is concerned is clarified by the contrast between (B) which deals with improper acquisition and (C) which deals with accidental acquisition. In the latter case prior material change of circumstance is taken into account, but not in the former. It is also worth noting that courts in the United States have generally taken a strict view of what amounts to disclosure of trade secrets, and of their acquisition by another. Thus in *Micromanipulator Co. Inc* v. *Bough*[168] the court held that a confidential customer list had been disclosed to a competitor when a salesman to whom the list had been confided solicited customers on the competitor's behalf, and notified him of the names of purchasers. Similarly in *Nalley's Inc.* v. *Corona Processed Foods*[169] it was held that the defendant had acquired knowledge of a similar list as soon as two ex-employees of the plaintiff began soliciting customers on the list. They have also taken a correspondingly narrow view of the 'value' provided for an acquisition of information sufficient to justify continued use after discovery of a misappropriation. In *Computer Print Systems Inc.* v. *Lewis*[170] neither the continuation of an account with the plaintiffs, nor payments on the account at a high rate for a substantial period, were regarded as the conferment of such value, even though they might have exceeded the costs of developing the programs in question. The court took the view that these charges merely compensated the plaintiff for the risk it took in developing programs without exacting any long term commitment to their use, and were quite unrelated to the acquisition of any rights of the plaintiff in the programs themselves.

In the United Kingdom the Law Commission was originally attracted to the position on third parties contained in the Restatement, but resiled in the face of hostile comment, and ended up by adopting a flexible approach imposing general liability upon third parties once they acquired knowledge, and leaving discretion in the court to adjust and mitigate remedies in appropriate cases.[171]

D. Remedies

As mentioned earlier, this branch of the law has drawn upon concepts of property, trust, contract, tort and confidence. Such diversity of rationale is reflected by, or perhaps reflects, the diversity of remedies which is available. In the United Kingdom there is some doubt as to the inter-relation of remedies at law and in equity. Equitable remedies, and in particular injunctions, which can be interlocutory[172] or final, will often be especially appropriate in this context, if the secret or confidence can still be kept. If it cannot, then damages may be the only recourse. In addition, there is a miscellaneous group of remedies of which an account of profits, restitution of

---

168. 779 F.2d 255 (5th Cir., 1985).
169. 50 Cal. Rptr. 173 (Cal., 1966).
170. 422 A.2d 148 (Pa., 1980).
171. *Law Com.* 110, 'Breach of Confidence', Cmnd. 8388 (1981) paras. 6.52–6.55.
172. 'Temporary Restraining Orders' prior to a preliminary injunction in the United States.

unjust enrichment and an order for delivery up are the most important. The Restatement asserted the same assortment in the United States, and explicitly provided for the award of any combination of them in the same action.[173]

1. Injunction

Injunction is an equitable remedy designed to secure specific relief, and in this context usually by restraining the defendant from disclosure of information. Because it was in origin an equitable remedy it is always within the discretion of the court. It is designed for urgent use, and it is possible to secure an injunction at an early interlocutory stage, even without the issue of a writ, and *ex parte*, without giving notice to an opponent. The principles upon which such a preliminary injunction could be issued were reconsidered by the House of Lords in *American Cyanamid Co.* v. *Ethicon Ltd.*[174] The plaintiff must first show that there is a serious case to be tried and that damages will not be an adequate remedy; then, on the hypothesis that damages would not be adequate to compensate the defendant if the injunction should not have been granted, it will be necessary to consider the balance of inconvenience; this should be assessed largely upon the basis of the comparative adequacy of damages, but in a close case might be swayed by a gross disproportion in the likelihood of success upon the merits; and finally, if the balance is still even, the court should act to preserve the *status quo*. In assessing the balance of convenience a court may pay attention to such factors as the size of the relevant market,[175] the predominance of the plaintiff in that market,[176] whether the information relates to a product which has already reached the market or not,[177] and whether the question relates to disclosure or merely use by the defendant. In the United States the Federal Rules of Civil Procedure[178] provide for a temporary restraining order as a first step in an appropriate case. It seems that in the United States more stress is put upon the likelihood of success on the merits, at least at the first stage of a temporary restraining order. It should be noted that a court will be slow to find a danger of irreparable injury in respect of a program which is still in the development stage.[179]

At the stage of a final injunction the balance is inevitably struck on the different basis of the strength of the cases made by the parties, but even there, since the remedy is equitable, it may be tempered by the court. One way of so tempering it is by the award of damages in lieu of the injunction, and this has been allowed since the passage of Lord Cairns' Act in 1858.[180] Such a course is most likely to be taken if the defendant has acted innocently, and has altered his position to his detriment, for example by

---

173. Comment (e) to para. 757.
174. [1975] A.C. 396, H.L.
175. *Collins (Engineers) Ltd.* v. *Roberts & Co Ltd* [1965] R.P.C. 429, Ch.
176. *United Sterling Corporation Ltd.* v. *Felton and Mannion* [1974] R.P.C. 162, Ch.
177. *Coco* v. *A.N. Clark (Engineers) Ltd.* [1969] R.P.C. 41, Ch. at 54.
178. Rule 65(b).
179. *Q-Co. Industries Inc.* v. *Hoffman* 625 F.Supp. 608 (S.D.N.Y., 1985) at 618.
180. Chancery Amendment Act 1858.

having already marketed a product based upon the confidential information used in ignorance of its confidentiality.

2. Damages

If damages are to be awarded in lieu of an injunction the result is a form of compulsory licensing. In *Seager* v. *Copydex Ltd.*[181] the defendants quite honestly, though probably unreasonably, used secret information passed on to them by the plaintiffs in the course of unsuccessful negotiations for a contract, and were not enjoined, no reason being vouchsafed. The explanation may, however, have been that as all of the negotiations had sounded in terms of pecuniary compensation, a remedy in the same terms seemed appropriate. This was certainly the view of Megarry J. in *Coco* v. *A.N. Clark (Engineers) Ltd.*[182] where he said, 'the essence of the duty seems more likely to be that of not using without paying than that of not using at all'. If this came to be adopted as a general rule it would have the incidental advantage of strengthening the patent system, so far as the information were patentable, by reducing the protection awarded for simple breach of confidence below that provided by the patent system.[183]

It is not absolutely clear that damages can be awarded on a strictly equitable claim apart from this situation. Although the trial judge seems to have contemplated such a claim in *Nicrotherm Electrical Co. Ltd.* v. *Perry*[184] the Court of Appeal left the point open. There have been conflicting dicta in subsequent cases, with Lord Denning M.R. seeming to accept the possibility of damages alone in *Seager* v. *Copydex Ltd.*:

It may not be a case for injunction or even for an account, but only for damages, depending on the worth of the confidential information to him [the recipient of the confidential information] in saving him time and trouble.[185]

While in *Malone* v. *Metropolitan Police Commissioner*[186] Megarry J. expressed the tentative view that:

Under Lord Cairns' Act 1858 damages may be granted in substitution for an injunction: yet if there is no case for the grant of an injunction, as when the disclosure has already been made, the unsatisfactory result seems to be that no damages can be awarded under this head: see *Proctor* v. *Bailey* (1889) 42 Ch.D. 390. In such a case, where there is no breach of contract or other orthodox foundation for damages at common law, it seems doubtful whether there is any right to damages as distinct from an account of profits.

It remains dubious, therefore, in the United Kingdom whether or not damages can be awarded in respect of past transgression. In the United States this is expressly allowed both under the Restatement and under the Uniform Trade Secrets Act.[187]

---

181. [1967] R.P.C. 349, C.A.
182. [1969] R.P.C. 41, Ch. at 49.
183. See Cornish, 'The Protection of Confidential Information in English Law', 6 *I.I.C.* 43 (1975) at p. 55.
184. [1957] R.P.C. 207, C.A.
185. [1967] R.P.C. 349, C.A. at 368.
186. [1979] Ch. 344, Ch. at 360.
187. Sect. 3(a).

The correct approach to the assessment of damages was considered in *Seager* v. *Copydex Ltd. (No.2)*.[188] Lord Denning M.R. distinguished between information of a mundane and of an inventive quality. In the former case he took the view that damages should be assessed on the basis of a reasonable fee for consultancy services calculated to create such information. In the latter case he took the view that they should be assessed on the basis of a contract between a willing seller and buyer of the novel development, essentially on the basis of a capitalised royalty. Exactly the same approach has, on occasion, been adopted in the United States in relation to a computer program where there was neither gain to the defendant nor loss to the plaintiff as a result of the misappropriation.[189] He also felt that any special factors, such as the impact upon other comparable products marketed by the confider, should be taken into account in their assessment. This gives the court a certain amount of flexibility since the duration and extent of the, in effect, compulsory licence can be determined, and the compensation varied accordingly. In the case of programming this seems quite satisfactory since programs are sometimes sold and sometimes licensed. A further possibility is to assess the damages by reference to the development cost of the information. This will be particularly suitable when there is no market either for sale or licence, and the defendant has made no profit. Here again the Uniform Trade Secrets Act 1979 makes the position clear in the United States by providing that 'damages caused by misappropriation may be measured by imposition of liability for a reasonable royalty for a misappropriator's unauthorized disclosure or use of a trade secret'.[190] This was applied in *Aries Information Systems Inc.* v. *Pacific Management Systems Corp.*[191] to permit recovery, not only of all of the revenues derived by the defendants from use of the misappropriated program, but in addition what was described as a standard industry royalty fee of 33 per cent in addition. It is not necessarily a matter of diminution of damages that the plaintiff has retained the use of his own information despite a misappropriation, since the capital value of the information is reduced once it is no longer exclusive to the plaintiff. In such a situation the information might become unmarketable, and in any case would command only a small fraction of its value when exclusive.[192]

As in other areas the United Kingdom is reluctant to go beyond awarding compensatory damages in civil litigation to which trade secret cases are no exception.[193] This is not the case in the United States, and the Uniform Trade Secrets Act makes specific provision for double damages in cases of wilful or malicious misappropriation.[194]

---

188. [1969] R.P.C. 250, C.A.
189. *University Computer Co.* v. *Lykes Youngstown Corp.* 504 F.2d 518 (5th Cir., 1974).
190. Uniform Trade Secrets Act 1979 sect. 3(a). For a comprehensive survey of the principles applied in the United States to the assessment of damages in trade secret cases, see 11 A.L.R. 4th 12 (1982).
191. 366 N.W.2d 366 (Minn., 1985).
192. *Computer Print Systems Inc.* v. *Lewis* 422 A.2d 148 (Pa., 1980) at 157.
193. See *Rookes* v. *Barnard* [1964] A.C. 1129, H.L. at 1225. 'Additional' damages may, however, be awarded for infringement of copyright, see Copyright, Designs and Patents Act 1988 sect. 97(2).
194. Sect. 3(b).

3. Account

Equity also devised the idea of ordering an account of profits made by the defendant's use of the material as an additional restitutionary remedy. However, it is proverbially clumsy and unsatisfactory, largely because of the difficulty of apportioning the profit between the different elements which have contributed to the final product.[195] It is nevertheless sometimes appropriate where it can be demonstrated that without the plaintiff's information there would have been no product at all.[196] In the context of programming it will hardly ever be possible to demonstrate any such thing, since the advantage of one program over another almost invariably lies merely in achieving greater efficiency. This remedy does have one theoretical advantage in that it avoids questions of whether the availability of the remedy against a third party depends upon whether he has altered his position to his disadvantage, since, even if he has, this can be taken into account in establishing the profit balance.

An account of profits can be combined with an injunction, but not with an award of damages. The difference between an account of profits and damages was succinctly explained in *Colbeam Palmer Ltd.* v. *Stock Affiliates Pty. Ltd.*:

The distinction between an account of profits and damages is that by the former the infringer is required to give up his ill-gotten gains to the party whose rights he has infringed: by the latter he is required to compensate the party wronged for the loss he has suffered. The two computations can obviously yield different results, for a plaintiff's loss is not to be measured by the defendant's gain, nor a defendant's gain by the plaintiff's loss.[197]

It is however possible to combine an injunction with an order for delivery up, and both either with an award of damages,[198] or with an account of profits.[199]

4. Delivery up

The court has the power to reinforce the effect of an injunction not to disclose or use confidential information by ordering the defendant to deliver up any confidential materials in his possession. In the case of information, this will apply to tangible objects containing the information, for example discs containing copies of confidential programs. To the extent that the information has been included in products made by the defendant he may be ordered either to remove the offending parts or, if they are irremovable, to destroy those products which contain them. In one striking Australian case where the information related to a new strain of plant, the defendants were ordered to destroy all the progeny of the misappropriated plants.[200]

---

195. See the remarks of Lindley L.J. in *Siddall* v. *Vickers* 9 R.P.C. 152 (1892) C.A. at 163.
196. *Peter Pan Manufacturing Corp.* v. *Corsets Silhouette Ltd.* [1963] R.P.C. 45, Ch.
197. 122 C.L.R. 25 (H.C.A., 1968) at 34.
198. *Industrial Furnaces Ltd.* v. *Reaves* [1970] R.P.C. 605, Ch.
199. *Peter Pan Manufacturing Corp.* v. *Corsets Silhouette Ltd.* [1963] R.P.C. 45, Ch.
200. *Franklin* v. *Giddins* [1978] Qd. R. 72, S.C.

Chapter 4

Alternative approaches

This chapter completes the proprietary part of the book by first mentioning some of the other weapons which the law can deploy to preserve the delicate balance between competitors in a fundamentally free market for computer systems. It will then go on to consider a few suggestions for more innovative approaches which have been inspired by a perception that existing régimes are based upon concepts not wholly appropriate to computer systems. The dangers are, on the one hand, of providing protection which is inadequate, just because it has not been designed to cope with the special features of computer systems and, on the other, of distorting the existing remedies by attempting to stretch their coverage to take in the unusual features of computers with the result that their protection of traditional subject-matter is adversely affected.

It should be noted that the first three parts of this chapter which deal with different aspects of and approaches to the regulation of competition are treated in less detail than the three major branches of the law of intellectual property considered so far. In the case of passing off and trade marks this simply reflects the smaller amount of activity specifically related to computer systems in those areas, even in the United States, while in the case of monopolies and anti-trust this is a vast and highly specialised field, and one peculiar to each individual jurisdiction, to which a book of this nature can do no more than provide the very briefest of introductions. All three of these parts are concerned to secure the appropriate balance between the activities of competitors, the first two by providing means of quelling unacceptable forms of strife between competitors, and the third with preventing the elimination of competition by the imposition of an unacceptable form of peace.

A. Passing-off[1]

The law of the United Kingdom has responded to increasingly fierce competition between traders in a number of different ways, partly at

---

1. More often 'palming off' in the United States.

common law and partly by statute. The tort of passing-off represents the current state of development of the common law in this area. Although it has experienced some input from the action for damages caused by the tort of deceit as expounded by the courts of common law, it probably owes more to the use by courts of equity of the weapon of injunction. The essence of the wrong is the creation of the false impression that the goods of one trader are those of another, whose goods have attracted a high reputation, with the result that such reputation is, or is likely to be, damaged. Given such a nature it was clearly desirable to be able to act as soon as possible to restrain the defendant, and so the injunction was the most obviously appropriate remedy.

Although in the United States, as in the United Kingdom, the common law remedy of passing off co-exists with statutory remedies under the relevant legislation,[2] in the United States the common law has to a much greater extent been overtaken by the wide provisions of federal legislation.[3] Common law claims are normally no more than appended to federal claims, and discussion of the position in the United States is accordingly postponed to the next section of this chapter.

It has been recognised by the House of Lords[4] that the modern form of the tort has extended its classic ambit. As the tort developed in the last century, driven on by the pressure of mass-production, brand name marketing and widespread advertising, it was designed to protect the goodwill which a trader had acquired in the product of his business, whether goods or services. Such goodwill could be threatened by express representations that the defendant's products in question were those of the plaintiff, for example by using the same, or a confusingly similar, trade name, mark, or packaging. In its classical form the action consists of three elements, the goodwill enjoyed by the plaintiff; the representation of similarity by the defendant; and the threat of damage so caused. These elements will first be explained, and then the extended form of the tort will be described.

1. Interest of plaintiff

Although there has been some vacillation, it is generally accepted that the action exists to protect the goodwill or reputation which the plaintiff has built up in his goods or services. It is thus necessary that such goods and services are being actively traded by the plaintiff. In some circumstances this may be a disadvantage in so volatile a marketplace as that for computer systems and products. It may be very difficult to protect start-up products in this way, thus in *Compatibility Research* v *Computer Psyche Co.*[5] it was held that a logo for a newly established computer-based dating system could not be so protected. At the other end of the spectrum it is also necessary that trading

---

2. In the United Kingdom the Trade Marks Act 1938, the Trade Marks (Amendment) Act 1984, and the Patents, Designs and Marks Act 1986; in the federal law of the United States the Lanham Act 1945, codified as 15 U.S.C. sect. 1051 *et seq.*, there is also a substantial body of state legislation.
3. Especially 15 U.S.C. sect. 1125(a).
4. In *Warnink B.V.* v. *Townend J. & Sons (Hull)* [1979] a.C. 731, H.L. at 739.
5. [1967] R.P.C. 201, Ch.

of the relevant product has not so long ceased as to dissipate any reputation which might once have been enjoyed.

This reputation must have found expression in some distinguishing feature of the relevant product. This will usually be its trade name or logo, but can be its 'get-up' or appearance, and it need not incorporate any specific reference to the name, or identity, of the plaintiff in person, so long as the outward manifestation is peculiar to, and identifies the goods. In some situations the reputation may be contained in a product name consisting of ordinary descriptive words, but in order to justify protection in such a case the court will require a showing of a special secondary meaning of the words which has become attached to them so as to cause them to be regarded as identifying the plaintiff's product.[6] However, the court will require very strong proof of such a secondary meaning so as to avoid crippling restrictions upon the use of ordinary descriptive language. Even if such a secondary meaning can be established, it will not necessarily prevent the same wording being used on a competitive product, provided that there is some other satisfactory means of avoiding confusion with the plaintiff's product. It should also be noted for the purposes of so international a business as that relating to computers that the relevant reputation may have been predominantly established in a foreign market.

2. Conduct of defendant

At least so far as the issue of an injunction is concerned, it is immaterial that the defendant was acting innocently, though it seems to be unsettled whether or not damages can be awarded in such circumstances. In most cases, however, the intention of the defendant will not be in doubt. In most cases the critical question here is likely to be whether or not the representation was sufficiently close to the distinguishing characteristic of the plaintiff's product. Much may, however, depend upon the intention of the defendant in resolving the question. If the whole course of conduct was designed to deceive purchasers into believing that the product was the plaintiff's, a court will be slow to find similarity of representation insufficient. As Lindley L. J. once put it, 'Why should we be astute to say that [the defendant] cannot succeed in doing that which he is straining every nerve to do?'[7] In doubtful cases the court is prepared to admit evidence of surveys conducted by the parties, though these require careful scrutiny in view of their provenance. It is also possible to commit the tort by less direct means. For example, it may be sufficient if orders for the plaintiff's product are met by the supply of the defendant's, or even by imitating the defendant's advertising campaign.[8] Still more subtly it is also possible to pass off the plaintiff's own goods, if his goods of an inferior quality are sold in such a way as to mislead purchasers into thinking that they are getting goods of his superior quality.[9]

The essence of the offending conduct is the creation of confusion with the

---

6. *Reddaway* v. *Banham* [1896] A.C. 199, H.L.
7. *Slazenger* v. *Feltham* 6 R.P.C. 531, C.A. (1889), at 538.
8. *Cadbury Schweppes Pty, Ltd.* v. *Pub Squash Co. Pty. Ltd.* [1981] 1 All E.R. 213, P.C.
9. *Spalding & Bros.* v. *Gamage (A.W.) Ltd.* 84 L.J. Ch. 449 (1915), H.L.

plaintiff's product, and the court is entitled to take into account in determining this all the circumstances of the case. Relevant factors will include the nature of the product, the opportunity and likelihood of careful examination, and the sophistication of the purchaser. It is, in these respects, becoming more likely that causes of action will be maintained in respect of computer-based products. When computers were very expensive, and software was purchased only by programmers, it was unlikely that much confusion would occur. The situation has changed dramatically now that computers have become accessible to the lay public. It is exacerbated by the heavy use of magazine advertising and mail-order selling. There is every indication that purchasers, and even vendors, do become confused. It is also the case that the possibility of making cheap copies of expensive original items generates a real risk of passing-off in its most classical form.

3. Damage

As noted above the essence of the tort in the United Kingdom is damage to the goodwill of a business. In the ordinary case of passing-off there is likely to be direct evidence of damage in the shape of the diversion of customers from plaintiff to defendant. Sometimes, however, it may be necessary to rely instead upon more speculative damage to goodwill. If the plaintiff and defendant are not direct competitors the complaint may be that the general reputation of the plaintiff is damaged by misleading association with the defendant's product. In the computer industry some hardware manufacturers have good reputations for reliability and quality of service, yet may not sell applications software. If a vendor of such products seeks to associate such a manufacturer with his software so as to take advantage of that reputation he may well be liable to them. Indeed if, as is sometimes the case, they have in fact allowed some approved software vendors to associate their products with the relevant hardware, those who falsely represent such approval may also be liable to the approved vendors on the more direct basis.

4. Extension

In its classical form the tort protected a particular product of a particular trader from a misleading appropriation of the goodwill associated with it. In its extended form it prevents not simply the misleading appropriation of the goodwill associated with a particular product, but rather regulates misleading claims which might damage goodwill in a market segment as a whole without spotlighting any particular product. In this generalised form, Lord Diplock listed five elements which needed to be satisfied:

(1) a misrepresentation (2) made by a trader in the course of trade, (3) to prospective customers of his or ultimate consumers of goods or services supplied by him, (4) which is calculated to injure the business or goodwill of another trader (in the sense that this is a reasonably foreseeable consequence) and (5) which causes actual damage to a business or goodwill of the trader by whom the action is brought or (in a *quia timet* action) will probably do so.[10]

---

10. *Warnink B.V.* v. *Townend J. & Sons (Hull)* [1979] A.C. 731, H.L. at 742.

Although his Lordship noted that these were necessary and not sufficient[11] conditions for liability, and that exaggerated claims for a product could not be restrained, nevertheless his speech signalled a willingness to extend the boundaries of the tort, partly under the influence of parliament's lead,

the increasing recognition by Parliament of the need for more rigorous standards of commercial honesty is a factor which should not be overlooked by a judge confronted by the choice whether or not to extend by analogy to circumstances in which it has not previously been applied a principle which has been applied in previous cases where the circumstances although different had some features in common with those of the case which he has to decide. Where over a period of years there can be discerned a steady trend in legislation which reflects the view of successive Parliaments as to what the public interest demands in a particular field of law, development of the common law in that part of the same field which has been left to it ought to proceed on a parallel rather than a diverging course.[12]

His lordship seems to have had in mind the Merchandise Marks, Trade Description and Fair Trading legislation designed to protect the consumer by imposing criminal liability upon deceptive traders. The closest legislation to the tort of passing-off, and that which was largely inspired by defects which traders found in the protection and facilities bestowed by it, is to be found in the statutory law of trade marks to be discussed in the next section.

B. Trade marks[13]

In the United Kingdom the first trade mark legislation[14] was passed to remedy defects in the common law of passing-off, and to provide a better basis for international protection. The principal defects of the common law were that it was cumbersome to have to prove the relevant goodwill afresh every time infringement occurred, and there was no way of knowing in advance whether a new name could be adopted without risk of infringing another's rights. Internationally a system of registration seemed desirable so as to secure reciprocal treatment from those, mainly European countries, which had already[15] adopted registration systems.[16] This legislation underwent refinement in a series of further statutes which culminated in the enactment of the Trade Marks Act 1938. All of these statutes were confined to the registration of marks for goods, but following the recommendation of the Mathys Committee in 1974[17] coverage has been extended to service marks by the enactment of the Trade Marks (Amendment) Act 1984.[18]

---

11. Though capable of being defeated only by an 'exceptional feature' on grounds of public policy.
12. *Ibid.* at 743.
13. See Vines, 'Consumer meets Computer: An Argument for Liberal Trademark Protection of Computer Hardware Configurations under Section 43(a) of the Lanham Trademark Act', 44 Wash. & Lee L.R. 283 (1987).
14. Trade Marks Registration Act 1875.
15. The French had legislated to establish such a system in 1857.
16. It also provides a firm basis for control by customs authorities, see E.E.C. Directive 3842/86.
17. Cmnd. 5061 (1974) paras. 65–70.
18. Itself amended by the Patents, Designs and Marks Act 1986.

In the course of this development a number of further advantages over the common law of passing-off accrued. It is worth mentioning in this context that the terminology of the legislation now makes it quite clear that a trade mark can be registered in respect of a prospective product, as well as an existing one.[19] So a company contemplating the launch of a new computer product can assure its name against imitation in advance of its appearance. The legislation also divorces the transfer of a mark from transfer of goodwill in the business in which the mark is used.[20] In this way it is possible to set up a system of franchising. Other points include the possibility of making a 'defensive' registration in respect of goods which are not traded so as to prevent dilution of a mark by its use for different products;[21] the prevention of comparative advertising;[22] and the registration of marks of certification.[23]

It is a distinctive feature of the registration process in the United Kingdom that careful prior vetting is conducted by the Registrar, and that objections by opponents of registration are admitted, and considered. The Registrar is required to satisfy himself that the mark satisfies the relevant basic criteria, though he may register a mark subject to certain conditions, limitations and waivers, thus enabling some objections to be surmounted.

The basic criteria are that the mark be distinctive;[24] that it not be deceptive;[25] and that it not be scandalous or immoral.[26] In addition the Registrar has a wide discretion to refuse to register a mark,[27] but although no positive guidelines are laid down to govern the exercise of this discretion it must be capable of being articulated on a rational basis.[28] The register is divided into two parts, A and B, giving differing degrees of protection, and requiring different standards of distinctiveness. The Act provides both for devices and for words to be used as marks, and for combinations of the two.[29] Words must, in order to be registered in Part A, which has the higher requirements, be both inherently distinctive, and distinctive in fact.[30] Perhaps the best course, and one readily adopted within the computer industry, is to use invented words as marks. So far as deception is concerned, the mark must neither be too similar to any other mark[31] nor liable to create a misleading impression of the products sold under the mark, for example 'bug free' in respect of programs.

A mark may be opposed before registration.[32] Once registered however, it

---

19. Trade Marks Act 1938 sects. 9(2), 10(1).
20. Trade Marks Act 1938 sects. 22–25.
21. Trade Marks Act 1938 sect. 27; it should be noted that registration is in principle permitted only for the goods in which a proprietor trades, or goods of the same description.
22. Trade Marks Act 1938 sect. 4(1)(b).
23. *Ibid.* sect. 37; usually by trade associations, and certainly not by traders in goods of the relevant type.
24. *Ibid.* sects. 9 and 10.
25. *Ibid.* sect. 11.
26. *Ibid.*
27. *Ibid.* sect. 17(1).
28. *Ibid.* sect. 17(4).
29. *Ibid.* sects. 9 and 10.
30. *Ibid.* sect. 9. To satisfy the requirements for Part B they need only be *capable* of distinguishing the product, once again inherently and in fact, *Ibid.* sect. 10.
31. *Ibid.* sect. 12(1); subject to exception in favour of honest concurrent use, *Ibid.* sect. 12(2).
32. *Ibid.* sect. 18.

is presumed to be valid, and in the case of Part A marks after a seven-year period the presumption is very strong.[33] It is nevertheless possible to secure the removal of a mark from the register by showing non-use,[34] that it is no longer distinctive, or that it has become deceptive.[35] Non-use may be established either because there never was any *bona fide* intent to use the mark in trade, or because it has not been used for a five-year period. These requirements help to prevent a stock-pile from being established. Use by a licensee registered as a user is sufficient.[36] In the case of deception, it is only deception which is somehow blameworthy that will justify expunging a mark from the register.[37]

Infringement is defined by section 4 of the Trade Marks Act 1938, in a section judicially described as being one of 'fulginous obscurity',[38] to comprehend two different types of act. The older form of infringement involved unauthorised use of the plaintiff's trade mark as a mark for the defendant's goods. This is closest to the common law tort of passing off, but differs from it in that the plaintiff need show only registration of the mark, and is not required to show already accrued goodwill associated with the mark. Although it is necessary to show that infringement occurs within the same description under which the plaintiff's mark has been registered, this seems unlikely to cause undue difficulty in this context. In principle, it is not an infringement for third parties to deal in marked goods unless the registered proprietor or user has imposed special conditions.[39] A defendant is not liable if he can show a genuine belief in the absence of any possibility of confusion.

The second form of infringement, introduced into the law of the United Kingdom for the first time in 1938, was designed to prevent the importation of a spurious reference to the plaintiff's mark in the promotion of the defendant's products. The courts have not shown much enthusiasm for this form of infringement, and its limits are not yet clearly defined. It is, however, of potentially significant impact upon the current state of the computer industry. A special defence is provided by the Trade Marks Act 1938[40] for reasonably necessary reference to another's mark for products which are adapted to form part of, or be accessory to, other products. It has been suggested[41] that this will not apply to cases where the defendant seeks to state only that the products can be used together or, in the jargon of the computer industry, are compatible. This seems a remarkably fine line to draw, but one which is crucially important in an industry where the ability of one product to work with another is a prime selling point.

The federal law in the United States is in many respects similar to that in the United Kingdom, even, for example, to the extent of having a divided

---

33. *Ibid.* sect. 13.
34. *Ibid.* sect. 26.
35. *Ibid.* sect. 32.
36. *Ibid.* sect. 28(2).
37. *General Electric Co.* v. *The General Electric Co. Ltd.* [1972] 2 All E.R. 507, H.L.
38. By Mackinnon L.J. in *Bismag* v. *Amblins* 57 R.P.C. 209 (1940) C.A. at 237.
39. Trade Marks Act 1938 sect. 6 regulates these matters.
40. Sect. 4(1)(b).
41. By Kerly, 'On Trade Marks' (1986) sect. 14–35.

register.[42] It employs both broadly similar principles to the determination of what may be registered[43] and to the procedure for registration. Here, as elsewhere, the law of trade marks has been more frequently illustrated by cases involving the use of computers, and in respect of false advertising or marking the law goes far beyond the limits imposed in the United Kingdom by allowing a remedy in the absence either of the imitation of a competitor's goods or the infringement of his mark.[44]

The fundamental principle is that the mark must be used to identify the relevant goods or service. In *United States Golf Association* v. *St. Andrews Systems Data-Max Inc.*[45] the defendants used the plaintiff's algorithm to provide a computerised service for calculating golf handicaps. It was held that the algorithm had a basically functional purpose and that such use, even though reference was made to the fact that it was that used by the plaintiff, could not be regarded as an infringement of the plaintiff's use of its trade name. It will not necessarily be fatal to the success of a claim for infringement that the relevant trade mark has not been copied exactly, provided that there is a sufficient possibility of confusion. In the computer area it is not uncommon for such a claim to be coupled with a claim for infringement of copyright in the underlying programs. Thus in *Apple Computer Inc.* v. *Formula International Inc.*[46] the plaintiffs claimed both on the basis of copying their operating system, and to restrain the defendants from using the name 'Pineapple' for their kit emulations of one of the plaintiff's range of fully assembled personal computers. A preliminary injunction was being sought, and it was held to be unnecessary for the Court to consider all of the factors which would be appropriate at a trial on the merits. It was held not to be an abuse of his discretion for the judge to take the view that the names were confusing when applied to the same line of products,[47] and further that a purchaser might, on the basis of the name, have believed even the kits to represent a new venture of the plaintiff.

It is more difficult to succeed when a genuine name is used. This can occur in the area, common in the computer industry, of parallel importing. In *NEC Electronics* v. *Cal Circuit Abco*[48] the plaintiff licensed the use of its mark on an exclusive basis to its American subsidiary. The defendant purchased the plaintiff's chips outside the United States, but sold them within the United States using the plaintiff's name to designate them. In rare circumstances in the United States, just as noted above in relation to the United Kingdom,[49] it is possible to maintain an action in respect of goods of the origin genuinely indicated by the mark.[50] Such authority was distinguished on the basis that there the mark had been given up irrevocably

---

42. With Tables A and B replicated by a Principal and Supplemental Register.
43. Though service marks were capable of registration in the United States long before they were made registrable in the United Kingdom.
44. 15 U.S.C. sect. 1125(a).
45. 749 F.2d 1028 (3rd Cir., 1984).
46. 725 F.2d 521 (9th Cir., 1984).
47. There was evidence that the defendants were contemplating the sale of fully assembled machines.
48. 810 F.2d 1506 (9th Cir., 1987).
49. See above p. 112.
50. See in the United States *A. Bourjois & Co.* v. *Katzel* 260 U.S. 689 (1923).

for use in the United States, and the purchaser would have been deprived of its bargain if the defendant had been able to continue selling its products through third parties. The plaintiff was also there a manufacturer of goods to which it could attach the licensed name in the United States, and hence the goods it manufactured in the United States might acquire quite a different reputation from goods bearing the same mark manufactured elsewhere, thus creating a real risk of confusion as to the comparative quality of different goods bearing the same mark. In the *NEC* case, however, since the plaintiff could use its controlling power over its United States subsidiary to secure acceptance by the subsidiary whether consistent with any prior agreement between parent and subsidiary or not, it could hardly be said that the subsidiary had been deprived of the benefit of any bargain, and since by the same token the parent could control the quality of any goods produced by the subsidiary, there could be no real danger of any confusion.

One of the functions of the process of registration is to reveal potential confusion. There are a number of examples of this in relation to the computer industry. It is particularly likely that manufactured names will seek to emphasise a link to some technological feature of the industry, and so names are inclined to resemble each other quite innocently. An early example is provided by litigation brought by *Digicom Inc.* against *Digicon Inc.*,[51] the former name being a contraction of digital communications and the latter of digital consultants. The two firms had started business quite independently in different parts of the United States, and it was only when one sought registration of the name under which it was trading that the other felt impelled to object. The court had no difficulty in determining that the names were confusingly similar, and allowed registration only to the company which it decided had first started trading under the disputed designation. Sometimes in such a situation the two parties will agree between themselves to continue to use the similar designations, but under the conditions they themselves think adapted to avoid confusion. This occurred in *Computer Associates International Inc.* v. *Computer Automation Inc.*[52] where the defendants learned that both they and the plaintiffs had been using their initial letters[53] as an unregistered trade mark only when seeking to register. They agreed between themselves that registration by the defendants would go unopposed by the plaintiffs upon the basis that the defendants would not sue for infringement by the plaintiffs in respect of continuance of their existing usage. The dispute arose on account of an alleged breach of this agreement. The defendants believed that the plaintiffs were extending their use of the mark beyond the limits agreed, and accordingly proposed to take infringement proceedings unless such extended use ceased. The plaintiffs regarded their use as authorised by the agreement, and the threat to sue as being in breach of the agreement, and in itself an infringement of the extended protection provided for a mark under United States law. The Court felt that the alleged infringement, being part of the preliminary proceedings,

---

51. *Digicon Inc.* v. *Digicom Inc.* 328 F.Supp. 631 (S.D. Tex., 1971).
52. 678 F.Supp. 424 (S.D.N.Y., 1987).
53. Though differently represented.

could not be held to have occurred in the course of trade, and hence that the issue remained a strictly contractual one.

The extended ambit of trade mark protection sought to be relied upon was based upon section 1125(a) of title 15 of the United States Code which provides that:

Any person who shall . . . use in connection with any goods or services . . . any false description or representation . . . and shall cause such goods or services to enter into commerce . . . shall be liable to a civil action . . . by any person who believes that he is or is likely to be damaged by the use of any such false description or representation.

This goes far beyond the false description of origin to which the extended provisions are appended. It has, however, been given a somewhat restrictive interpretation in relation to computers, and was held not to be applicable to the functional algorithm in *United States Golf Association* v. *St. Andrews Systems Data-Max Inc.*,[54] or where there was no use in trade as in *Computer Associates International Inc.* v. *Computer Automation Inc.*[55] Of perhaps greater significance is the fact that in litigation brought by Digital Equipment Corporation against C. Itoh, a Japanese manufacturer of terminals which emulated Digital's products, it was held not to protect the general shape of the plaintiff's VT220 terminal against the defendant's substitute, its CIT-220+. The court applied three tests: of functionality; of secondary meaning; and of likelihood of confusion. In respect of functionality the court was concerned to protect competition in the 'after-market' for computer products, and so found that there was a functional need to reproduce the shape, features and general layout of the emulated terminal. This was dictated by the view, expressed in *United States Golf Association* v. *St. Andrews Systems Data-Max Inc.*,[56] that industry standards should be available to all,

the standard gauge of railroad track allows a locomotive of one company to run on the track of another. Allowing one provider to obtain exclusive rights in such a standard would enable it to exclude competitors desiring to provide the same product or service, particularly if the original provider, . . ., starts with a virtual monopoly. To allow a monopoly over such a standard would defeat the policy of fostering competition that underlies the functionality doctrine.

This view finds further support in the consideration that trade mark protection is potentially infinite in point of time, whereas for an inventive patentable feature the maximum length of monopoly is, in the United States, seventeen years. It is not clear why trade marks of a perhaps lesser status should enjoy so much longer a possible period of protection.

The second element is secondary meaning, and here the court concluded that the shape and configuration had not acquired the secondary meaning of signifying that the equipment was manufactured by Digital, though in so finding it disregarded evidence of a survey of ninety-seven respondents, forty-four of whom, when shown the terminals in question, had said that they believed them to be Digital's. In particular, the court required an

---

54. 749F.2d 1028 (3rd Cir., 1984).
55. 678 F.Supp. 424 (S.D.N.Y., 1987).
56. 749 F.2d 1028 (3rd Cir., 1984 at 1034).

already established secondary meaning, rather than the mere capacity for one to develop, which might well inhibit the utility of the doctrine in so volatile an industry as that relating to computers.

The final consideration is the degree of confusion likely to be engendered. Here the court paid particular attention to the clear labelling of the products as C-Itoh's, the expense of the products, the sophistication of the purchasers, and the sales campaign of the defendant which aimed to differentiate the products by claiming them to be much more cost-effective than those produced by Digital. The court also intimated that Digital would have done better to have spent a tiny fraction of the amount devoted to advertising to the registration for trade mark purposes of the distinctive features of the terminals.[57]

It may finally be noted that trade marks may sometimes be used to justify otherwise anti-competitive measures. Thus in *Will* v. *Comprehensive Accounting Corp.*[58] it was held that tying arrangements can in some circumstances amount to the least restrictive means of upholding standards under a trade mark. That raises the more general question of how far anti-competitive practices in the shape of monopolies, and other techniques, can be prevented.

C. Monopoly and anti-trust

These topics are nowadays among the most difficult and highly contested areas of law, involving the consideration of highly complex modern statutes, in the United Kingdom involving interaction with the competition law of the European Economic Communities and in the United States with federal anti-trust law. Although the computer industry, and especially the hardware segment, where International Business Machines has so commanding a position, is necessarily at the heart of the area, it is far too recondite a topic to be treated at any length in an introductory work of this nature. The very briefest of indications will be given of the nature of the regulative efforts in the United Kingdom and in the United States.

1. United Kingdom

Legal regulation takes three forms in the United Kingdom. Common law laid the foundation in its regulation of contracts by the doctrine of restraint of trade, though this became increasingly ineffective under the doctrines of *laissez-faire* which strengthened during the nineteenth century. It was only in the twentieth that concern once more became manifest, and was reflected both in domestic regulatory legislation and, after accession to the European

---

57. It should be noted that no such registration would be permitted in the United Kingdom on the basis that 'A rival manufacturer must be free to sell any container or article of similar shape provided that the container or article is labelled or packaged in a manner which avoids confusion as to the origin of the goods in the container or the origin of the article' per Lord Templeman in *Re Coca-Cola's Application* [1986] 2 All E.R. 274, H.L. at 276 (in rejecting an application to register the shape of a Coca-Cola bottle).
58. 776 F.2d 665 (7th Cir., 1985).

Communities, in the provisions for regulating trade within the Communities. It is worth glancing at each in turn.

(a) Common law

In the United Kingdom the common law prohibiting contractual provisions in restraint of trade once occupied the whole field. It required any contract in restraint of trade to be justified in terms both of the interest of the parties to the agreement to be protected, and that of the public at large. It was never very clear what sort of interest justified restraint but, at least in some cases, it seems to have been sufficient to seek to protect a trading interest against competition.[59] Even if such an agreement were contrary to the public interest, it was not obvious how it could be attacked otherwise than by one of the parties to it.[60] It should be noted that the common law rules accepted price maintenance agreements as not necessarily being in restraint of trade.[61] Another much litigated aspect of the doctrine of restraint of trade relates to tying agreements whereby one party is required to trade exclusively with another. In the computer industry such agreements are not unknown in the field of dealerships or maintenance contracts. To the extent that such agreements have become commonplace in a particular industry, they may fall outside the doctrine of restraint of trade altogether, but this is far from an automatic conclusion even in the case of standard form contracts.[62] Contracts within the scope of the restraint of trade doctrine may still be upheld to the extent that they are reasonable in all the circumstances of the case. In particular, the court will pay attention to the adequacy of the consideration. It will scrutinise such agreements with special care when made between parties of unequal bargaining strength.

(b) Statutory provision

As noted above, one of the defects of the common law doctrine of restraint of trade is the difficulty within it of upholding the public interest when it runs counter to the interests of the parties to the relevant agreement. This problem has been addressed in the United Kingdom in an interlocking network of statutory provisions. A central feature is provided by the rôle of the Director General of Fair Trading who has oversight of restrictive agreements, both in respect of goods and of services, under the Restrictive Trade Practices Act 1976.[63] Any such agreements have to be notified to the Director General, and brought by him for validation before the Restrictive Trade Practices Court. It is then for the parties to show that it is beneficial in one of the ways defined in the Act, and that such benefit is not outweighed by detriment to the public at large. It should also be noted that the Director General has similar powers in respect of 'information agreements' which might otherwise have served as a means of undermining the

---

59. See, for example, *English Hop Growers* v. *Dering* [1928] 2 K.B. 174, C.A.
60. Though it is possible that an aggrieved third party might be able to obtain a declaration of its illegality, as in *Eastham* v. *Newcastle United Football Club Ltd.* [1964] Ch. 413, Ch.
61. Nor is price maintenance in respect of services subject to the modern statutory restrictions under the Resale Prices Act 1976.
62. See *A. Schroeder Music Publishing Co. Ltd.* v. *Macaulay* [1974] 3 All E.R. 616, H.L.
63. As amended, principally by the Competition Act 1980.

basic thrust of the legislation. A recent government green paper[64] has proposed that this part of the law of the United Kingdom should be brought more into line with the approach adopted by the European Economic Communities, to be discussed below.

A second role of the Director General of Fair Trading is that of reference to the Monopolies and Mergers Commission of monopoly situations in relation to the supply of goods or services,[65] or of mergers involving more than a quarter of a given market,[66] or of other anti-competitive practices having the effect of restricting, distorting or preventing competition in the production, supply or acquisition of goods or services.[67]

(c) *International obligations*[68]

Articles 85 and 86 of the Treaty of Rome prohibit respectively agreements between undertakings which have as their objective or effect the prevention, restriction or distortion of competition within the Common Market, and those which amount to an abuse of a dominant position within the Common Market or a substantial portion of it, in so far as such agreements or abuse affect trade between member states. As a result of section 2 of the European Communities Act 1972, the Treaty of Rome is part of English law. This means that not only can proceedings under these articles be pursued in the European Court, but English courts are bound to give them direct effect. Thus in *Cutsforth* v. *Mansfield Inns Ltd.*[69] an injunction was granted to restrain the defendants from acting upon a policy of restricting supplies to their licensees to a restricted list of suppliers, and in particular from excluding the defendants from that restricted list.

Selective distribution agreements are not necessarily in breach of article 85, and in the case of computer products have been the subject of investigation[70] by the European Commission in relation to the system of distribution set up in Europe by International Business Machines Ltd. The Commission upheld the selective distribution agreement upon the basis that it was necessary for the benefit of consumers that dealers should have undergone adequate training, and be of sufficient financial and technical stature to ensure continuing support for the product line. The Commission gave its clearance, however, only upon the satisfaction of further conditions such as that the dealer should have complete freedom over pricing, be entitled to deal in competing products, and be obliged to carry out warranty work even when the goods had been sold by a different dealer. The Commission has also published regulations for a block exemption for exclusive dealing arrangements.[71] While these regulations permit such arrangements to be made with dealers, they are not allowed between

---

64. 'Review of Restrictive Trade Practices: A Consultative Paper', Cmnd. 331 (1987).
65. Fair Trading Act 1980 Pt. IV.
66. Fair Trading Act 1980 Pt. V, or involving assets of more than £30 million as fixed in 1984, but a figure subject to periodic review.
67. Competition Act 1980.
68. See further Frazer, 'Competition law: mapping the minefield', *3 C.L. & Prac.* 199 (1987).
69. [1986] 1 All E.R. 577, Q.B.
70. Commission Dec. 84/223/EEC.
71. 1983 Off. Jo. L173/1.

manufacturers so as to partition the market between different products. Block exemptions have also been offered in relation to joint research and development projects,[72] notwithstanding some anticompetitive effects, and for specialisation agreements between small producers.[73] In the absence of any block exemption, parties who anticipate difficulty under these articles should notify the Commission of the situation, which will at least prevent fines from accruing if the practice is eventually found to be in breach of the Treaty. It should also be noted that there is a procedure for negative clearance with the Commission, rather like that operated within the United Kingdom by the Director General for Fair Trading.

2. United States[74]

The United States was the first major nation to impose a statutory framework in this area. Public disquiet at the domination of whole areas of business by the aggregation of businesses into large trusts led to the passage in 1890 of 'anti-trust' legislation in the shape of the Sherman Acts which provided quite bluntly that:

'1. Every contract, combination in the form of trust or otherwise, or conspiracy in restraint of trade or commerce among the several states, or with foreign nations is declared to be illegal . . . .
2. Every person who shall monopolize, or attempt to monopolize, or combine or conspire with any other person or persons, to monopolize any part of the trade or commerce among the several States, or with foreign nations shall be deemed guilty of a felony . . . .'[75]

As may be noted, the provisions of this legislation were primarily criminal in nature, but in 1914 the Clayton Act added a civil dimension by permitting recovery of treble damages and attorney's fees to competitors damaged by anti-trust infringement,[76] and imposed its own explicit ban on price fixing and tying arrangements.[77] Later still the Robinson Patman Act in 1982 added discriminatory pricing arrangements to the list of forbidden practices.[78] It should be noted that the Federal Trade Commission has also been endowed with powers to prohibit 'unfair methods of competition in or affecting commerce, and unfair or deceptive acts or practices in or affecting commerce'.[79] It should further be noted that these federal measures have in many states been buttressed by the enactment of state anti-trust legislation of a similar character.

    This legislation has created one of the most distinctive, and difficult, areas

---

72. 1985 Off. Jo. L53/5. For comparable relaxation in this context in the United States, see 15 U.S.C. sect. 4301 *et seq*.
73. 1985 Off. Jo. L53/1.
74. See further Lavey, 'Antitrust Issues Critical to Structuring Vertical Channels of Distribution for Computer Businesses', 4 Comp. L.J. 525 (1984); Helein, 'Software Lock-in and Antitrust Tying Arrangements; The Lessons of Data General', *5 Comp. L.J.* 329 (1985).
75. 15 U.S.C. sect. 1 *et seq*.
76. *Ibid.* sect. 15.
77. *Ibid.* sect. 14.
78. *Ibid.* sect. 13.
79. *Ibid.* sect. 45(a)(1).

of United States law which cannot be considered at any length in a work of this sort. It has generated its own terminology, and has attracted considerable economic analysis. Despite the apparently peremptory tone of the legislation, it was early decided that although some types of agreement, such as price-fixing arrangements, were *per se* illegal, in many cases it was only unreasonable arrangements that fell foul of the rules, and in the terminology adopted such cases were to be decided according to a rule of reason. In applying such a rule a distinction is often made between restraints which operate 'vertically', that is between different links in a common chain of supply between producer and ultimate consumer, and those which operate 'horizontally', that is between equivalent positions in chains relating to different products, for example between competing manufacturers, distributors or retailers.

There has been a substantial number of cases in the United States applying these principles to the computer industry. This is hardly surprising given the unbalanced structure of the industry, both as between different hardware manufacturers, and as between hardware and software sectors as a whole. It is also fiercely competitive and highly volatile. Some of the issues are demonstrated in *Digidyne Corporation* v. *Data General Corporation*[80] which was itself the culmination of a number of suits and crosssuits after a process of litigation lasting some nine years. Indeed, the issues raised were sufficiently momentous to lead some of the Justices of the Supreme Court of the United States to dissent from refusal to grant *certiorari:*

> At stake is more than the resolution of this single controversy or even the clarification of what may seem at times to be a collection of arcane legal distinctions. In the highly competitive, multi-billion dollar a year computer industry, bundling of software and hardware, or of operating systems and central processing units, is somewhat common, and any differentiated product is especially attractive to some buyers. The reach of the decision in this case is potentially enormous . . ..[81]

The basic issue was whether Data General were in breach of the anti-trust rules in refusing to sell their copyright operating systems for mini-computers separately from the sale of a minimum amount of their own hardware. The plaintiffs claimed that this constituted an illegal tying arrangement with the operating system as the tying product and the hardware as the tied. In order to succeed, the plaintiffs had to show first that operating system and hardware were separate products. Since it was possible to obtain alternative hardware to run the software, which was indeed the nub of the complaint, it was difficult to argue that there were not two separate products. It is much harder when they are traditionally sold together, and in at least one previous case this had been held to be true of operating system and hardware.[82] It has also been held to exist as regards a franchise for a time-sharing service and the computer on which the time was to be shared,[83] as regards a disc drive and head assembly,[84] as regards additional memory and control

---

80. 734 F.2d 1336 (9th Cir., 1984).
81. 473 U.S. 908 (1985) at 909.
82. *United Software Corp.* v. *Sperry Rand Corp.* 5 C.L.R.S. 1492 (E.D. Pa., 1974) at 1497.
83. *Response of Carolina Inc.* v. *Leasco Response Inc.* 537 F.2d 1307 (5th Cir., 1976) at 1350.
84. *Memorex Corp.* v. *International Business Machines Corp.* 636 F.2d 1128 (9th Cir., 1980).

functions in a central processing unit,[85] and as between up-grade parts and the labour costs of installing them.[86] The second requirement is that the defendant must exert some degree of coercion[87] and this will usually require the presence of the third condition, sufficient economic power in the market for the tying product to affect the market for the tied product. There the court was heavily influenced by the fact that the operating system was defendant's copyright. The general importance attached to this feature has now declined, and *Digidyne* criticised for the emphasis placed upon it.[88] It is not quite so simple, however. After all, the operating system was not the only operating system on the mini-computer market taken as a whole. The definition of the relevant market is likely to be the key factor. In this case the defendant's sales were predominantly to its own existing customers, and it was those who, it was claimed, were tied. Nor were they tied simply by the relationship of operating system and hardware. They were also tied to the operating system by their own investment in applications software which could not economically be re-written to run with a different operating system. The court was inclined by these factors to take a restrictive view of the relevant market and, accordingly, found that the defendant did have sufficient economic power in that market. Questions relating to the relevant market frequently give rise to the most complex economic arguments concerned with such matters as possible product substitution.[89] This approach was taken in *A. I. Root Co.* v. *Computer/Dynamics Inc.*[90] where the plaintiff sought to limit the relevant market to owners of a particular operating system, but the court held that systems using this operating system did not constitute a market separate from that for mini-computer systems in general. As the defendants held less than 5 per cent of that larger market, it was held that their economic power was insufficient.[91] *Digidyne* was distinguished upon the basis that there was evidence of a special attraction attaching to the combination of operating system and hardware which could not be shown in the instant case. The court in *Root* further accepted the argument that it was necessary for the tie to operate at the time of the sale of the tying product, and that it was not sufficient that it was designed to operate in the future, when further products were needed. The final element is that the amount of business involved should not be insubstantial.

---

85. *Telex Corp.* v. *International Business Machines Corp.* 367 F.Supp. 258 (N.D. Ok., 1973) at 347, reversed on other grounds 510 F.2d 894 (10th Cir., 1975).
86. *Allen-Myland Inc.* v. *International Business Machines Corp.* 693 F.Supp. 262 (E.D. Pa., 1988).
87. Another computer industry claim failed because no coercion could be shown, *MDC Data Centres Inc.* v. *International Business Machines Corp.* 342 F.Supp. 502 (E.D. Pa., 1972) at 504. Coercion will normally be implied when the tying arrangement is contained in a binding written contract.
88. See *A.I. Root Co.* v. *Computer/Dynamics Inc.* 806 F.2d 673 (6th Cir., 1986) at 677; *3 P.M. Inc.* v. *Basic Four Corp.* 591 F.Supp. 1350 (E.D. Mich., 1984).
89. See the elaborate discussion of the possibilities of substituting smaller systems, peripheral equipment and even software for large main-frame computers in seeking to define the relevant market in *Allen-Myland Inc.* v. *International Business Machines Corp.* 693 F.Supp. 262 (E.D. Pa., 1988) at 269–83.
90. 806 F.2d 673 (6th Cir., 1986).
91. The court took 30 per cent as a rule of thumb measure, see *Jefferson Parish Hospital District No. 2* v. *Hyde* 466 U.S. 2 (1984) at 26.

D. Bespoke régimes

Various legal approaches to the protection of property in computer-related products have been outlined in the book so far. A gradual consensus has emerged that copyright is probably the régime best adapted to the protection of computer programs and databases. This has most recently been endorsed by such legislation as the Copyright Act in the United States[92] and the Copyright, Designs and Patents Act 1988 in the United Kingdom. At an international level, similar recognition has been accorded in the recent Directive of the Council of the European Economic Communities.[93] Despite such popularity, there has always been a body of opinion in favour of the creation of a new bespoke régime for computer-related products in recognition of their unique characteristics. As early as 1968, Mooers had suggested trade mark as a more eligible approach,[94] and in the same year International Business Machines Corporation suggested a registration system for programs to the United States Patent Office. Behind such suggestions, and providing much of the motivation for them, was a deep suspicion that copyright was unsuitable as vehicle for protection,[95] and that it would be harmed by being shoe-horned into providing the means for providing protection.[96] It may also be significant that when it was decided to provide protection for mask-works and semiconductor chips, neither patent nor copyright law was applied as such, but a new régime was devised, and consequently a need to find a new means of providing international protection. These doubts have recently resurfaced in a number of thoughtful commentaries.[97] Needless to say they have also been subjected to principled riposte from the copyright school.[98] The special problems must first be identified, and then the recommended solutions examined.

---

92. 17 U.S.C. sect. 101 *et seq.*
93. Off. Jo. 1989
94. Mooers, 'Accommodating Standards and Identification of Programming Languages', 4 C.L.S. sect. 4–5.
95. For a masterly exposition of this view, see Breyer 'The Uneasy Case for Copyright: A Study of Copyright in Books, Photocopies, and Computer Programs', *84 Harvard L.R.* 281 (1970).
96. Such a view inspired Commissioner Hersey's dissent from the majority view of the President's Commission on New Technological Uses (CONTU) (1979).
97. See, for example, Davidson, 'Protecting Computer Software: A Comprehensive Analysis', *23 Jur. Jo.* 337 (1983); Samuelson, 'CONTU Revisited: The Case Against Copyright Protection for Computer Programs in Machine-Readable Form', *1984 Duke L.J.* 663; Comment 'Softright: A Legislative Solution to the Problem of Users' and Producers' Rights in Computer Software', *44 Loy. L.R.* 1413 (1984); Samuelson, 'Creating a New Kind of Intellectual Property: Applying the Lessons of the Chip Law to Computer Programs', *70 Minn. L.R.* 471 (1985); Kidwell, 'Software and Semi-Conductors: Why Are We Confused?' *70 Minn. L.R.* 533 (1985); Brown, 'Eligibility for Software Protection: A Search for Principled Standards' *70 Minn. L.R.* 579 (1985); Higashima and Ushiku, 'A New Means of International Protection of Computer Programs Through the Paris Convention – A New Concept of Utility Model', *7 Comp. L.J.* 1 (1986); Stern, 'The Bundle of Rights Suited to New Technology', *47 U. Pitt. L.R.* 1229 (1986); and Menell, 'Tailoring Legal Protection for Computer Software', *39 Stan. L.R.* 1329 (1987).
98. See Raskind 'The Uncertain Case for Special Legislation Protecting Computer Software', *47 U. Pitt. L.R.* 1131 (1986).

1. Special problems

The difficulty of applying the conventional concepts of the law of intellectual property to computer-related products is caused partly by the peculiar nature of the computer industry, and partly by uncertainty about questions of policy.

The special characteristics of the industry are well-known. It is at the leading edge of technological development. Vast resources are needed to develop new products, with no guarantee of commercial success, and even when marketed successfully, with a relatively short period of dominance in an unimproved form. Products are easily copied, and it is difficult to preserve secrecy in an area where mobility of labour is high, and where freely accessible academic research is common. The problem is compounded by the international nature of the industry, and the huge economic and industrial, and hence political and social, impact of the products of the industry.

From the point of view of the law of intellectual property, it is extremely difficult to cater for a situation in which products can be presented either as hard-wired pieces of machinery or as intangible programs, and where programs and data cannot sensibly be distinguished from each other. The protean nature of the applications of these products is also disconcerting. They range from the purely functional and utilitarian, to the most highly aesthetic and hedonistic.

At the policy level there is continuous tension between the need to encourage innovation and to nurture competition. On the one hand, it is argued that unless the market is regulated so as to confer rights and rewards upon producers no innovation will be undertaken; while on the other it is felt that if competition is inhibited by such regulation then there will be no incentive to improve existing products and to widen the market by reducing their price.

It has been noted[99] that the market for computer related products, and especially for software, is distorted by two endemic features, the problems of public goods and of network externalities. The public goods problem arises because of the ease of copying. This makes it difficult to exclude non-purchasers from products brought to market, and enables demand to be satisfied without depleting the supply. If a key program can be copied at minimal cost and without any possibility of detection, there will be a very small market, and hence no great spur to incur research and development costs. It is to remedy this problem that higher degrees of proprietary protection and enforcement are proposed. It is suggested, however, that this fails to grasp the fact that innovation takes place, not only in developing a new program, but in improving and refining programs which have already appeared. Here, however, the argument runs in the opposite direction, away from restricted proprietary rights and rigid enforcement.

A further distorting factor is to be found in the role of network externalities in the computer industry. The value of a product depends, not only upon its own intrinsic merits, but on the extent to which it benefits

---

99. By Menell, 'Tailoring Legal Protection for Computer Software', *39 Stan. L.R.* 1329 (1987).

from interaction with other products. The analogy of the telephone or railway system is apposite. The more users who can communicate easily with each other the greater the benefit to the group as a whole. This need for communication applies not only to different users at a given moment of time, but even to a single user over a period of time. In other words, not only should as many devices and programs as possible be able to operate with each other now, but they should also be able to operate with those of the preceding and succeeding generations so as to permit a smooth path of development. This seems to suggest that standards for such inter-communication should be established, and that they should be free of proprietary control. It is to the benefit of all that no one is locked out of the path of development, and that by insistence on proprietary protection innovation is confined to successful subversion of existing standards. It can, however, also be argued that an advantage of providing protection is that competitors will be forced to develop radically new alternatives, and the industry will be less likely to be locked into an out-dated and eventually inappropriate standard. While these considerations are especially important in the realm of hardware and operating systems, they also exist in relation to applications programs which are increasingly required to interact with each other, and with common data.[100]

2. Suggested solutions

It is not possible to do justice to the many ingenious solutions proposed in a work of this nature. No more than a few illustrative examples can be mentioned. Proposals vary from small amendments to existing régimes, such as the proposal to amend United Kingdom patent law so as to allow abbreviated search, shorter periods of protection, and lower charges, rejected in 1977 by the Banks Committee,[101] or the modification of copyright law proposed by the World Intellectual Property Organisation in 1978,[102] to the replacement of traditional intellectual property concepts in this area by completely new systems.

(a) *Registration system proposed by International Business Machines corporation* (1968)[103]

One of the most comprehensive early alternatives to have been proposed is contained in a report submitted by International Business Machines Corporation to the United States Patent Office in 1968 which advocates a system of registration. The aim of this proposal was to supplement the existing law, especially in providing protection for programs which were too obvious to be patentable. In outline the applicant would be required to register both a copy of the program, together, if so desired, with a detailed

---

100. As, for example, in *Synercom Technology Inc.* v. *University Computing Co.* 462 F.Supp. 1003 (N.D. Tex., 1978).
101. Cmnd. 4407 (1970) Ch. 18 para. 491.
102. Reproduced in Niblett, 'Legal Protection of Computer Progams' (1980) App. IV.
103. Galbi, 'Proposal for New Legislation to Protect Computer Programming', 17 *Bull. Copyright Soc.* 280 (1970), reproduced 3 C.L.S.R. 1168.

description of it, and a description of the concepts employed in it. The registrar would keep the program and its detailed description secret until the expiration of a period of protection of ten years, but would publish the description of concepts immediately. The system envisaged no examination of the prior art, but instead a simple check that the format of the description of concepts was in proper form, and the payment of a small[104] fee. It was thought that such registration would be invoked to protect only long and complex sequences of instructions. These would be protected against unauthorised reproduction, translation, use or transfer. However, no protection would be offered against the use of the published conceptual description to create independently a similar, or even identical, program to that registered. The scheme also contained provision for the marking of registered programs, and for protection to be given for a year preceding registration upon insertion of a notice of intention to register.

Although such a scheme would have added to the protection enjoyed under existing law either in the United States or in the United Kingdom, it was doubted whether it was right to give protection for so long to 'obvious' programs, and difficulty seemed inherent in the question of whether programs were sufficiently long and complex as to be entitled to such protection, and whether particular sequences of instructions had been copied from registered programs or developed truly independently. The proposal was not accepted by CONTU, and appears to have lapsed, though a number of its features[105] seem to be reproduced in the new régime applying to semiconductor chips.

(b) Japanese proposals[106]

Japan has become a major force in the computer industry, and dominates large sections of it, especially in relation to basic components, such as chip production. Its growing power has led to clashes in the international arena with other major powers such as the United States and the European Economic Communities. It has sometimes been felt that Japanese growth has been assisted by lax protection afforded to computer products in Japan, and consequent plagiarisation of ideas developed elsewhere. In an effort to improve protection, various initiatives have been taken by Japan's Ministry of International Trade and Industry (MITI). One such initiative was the preparation of a comprehensive Program Right Law. The underlying theme was that the law of copyright is inappropriate for computer-related products, partly because it is based upon consideration of form rather than function, and accordingly affords protection for far too long, and not in respect of the most damaging type of infringement, namely use. Although MITI was itself overruled in favour of a counter proposal put forward by the Ministry of

---

104. $100 was originally suggested.
105. Such as the ten-year period, intermediate standard of originality, and provision permitting reverse engineering.
106. MITI interim proposal, 'A Registration and Certification Type of System to Protect Computer Programs' reproduced in 5 C.L.S. sect. 9-4 art. 3; see also Higashima and Ushiku, 'A New Means of International Protection of Computer Programs Through the Paris Convention – A New Concept of Utility Model', 7 *Comp. L.J.* 1 (1986); Karjala, 'Lessons from the Computer Software Debate in Japan', *1984 Ariz. St. L.J.* 53.

Education to tailor protection to the demands of the Berne Convention, that is, to a copyright model, some Japanese commentators have proposed a different approach, derived from the MITl idea of a *sui generis* scheme.

They have accordingly sought to bring computer programs explicitly beneath the broad umbrella of a 'utility right', and so within the ambit of the Paris Convention for the Protection of Industrial Property.[107] This Convention offers protection to,

patents, utility models, industrial designs and models, trade marks, commercial names and indications of origin, or applications of origin, as well as the repression of unfair competition.[108]

The system of protection proposed for computer programs owes much to the utility model of continental Europe, or the petty patent of Australia, and to régimes for the protection of design rights.[109] It is designed to cater for programs which are not sufficiently novel to be patented, but too utilitarian for copyright to be truly appropriate.

The essential proposals are for an unexamined system of registration, but for disclosure so that a third party can understand the basic concepts of the program. It is envisaged that an application should contain the proprietor's name and address, the program name, a listing, a claim for protection and a brief description of the program. Of these only the listing would not be published. A significant feature is the proposal for a claim for protection. This was included so as to allow the proprietor to claim protection only for some routines in a program. The proposal also allows for selective withholding of some claims from disclosure. As it is envisaged that the system would complement not only the patent system, but examined registration systems, the term of protection is also conceived as being complementary, that is, shorter. The major advantage to be gained would be the prohibition of use by a third party, giving a patent-like monopoly to the proprietor for the limited period of protection. It is stressed that the system differs from patent in that it is the program itself, rather than the process it embodies, which is protected. A further perceived difficulty with the system of copyright which it is hoped to eliminate is that of gaining protection for improved versions of the program. A system of supplementary applications is proposed to accomplish this. It is finally thought that international protection can be achieved under the Paris Convention.

It seems unlikely that this system will commend itself to the United Kingdom or the United States which have always been sceptical of petty patents, and more fundamentally of the protection of unoriginal functional artifacts. To the extent that any such suggestion might be relied upon to diminish the protection afforded to computer programs by copyright, it was criticised by the government of the United States[110] and, partly as result of such pressure, Japan was induced to introduce its own copyright protection

---

107. As revised in 1967.
108. Art. 1(2).
109. Not extended to functional articles in the United Kingdom, see *Amp Inc.* v. *Utilux Pty. Ltd.* [1972] R.P.C. 103, H.L.
110. See 'U.S. Opposes Japanese Proposal for Limited Software Protection', 27 *Pat., Trademark and Copyright J.* (BNA) 309 (2 Feb. 1984), 424 (1 March 1984).

for computer software in January 1986.[111] Despite its reservations it has also agreed to the primacy of protection by copyright,[112] and to co-operate in eliminating piracy of programs.[113]

(c) Use of the semiconductor chip precedent

It is significant that, when confronted by the problem of protecting semiconductor chips, the United States chose not to expand copyright protection,[114] but to enact a new and unique form of protection. It is even more significant that the rest of the nations of the developed world fell over themselves to emulate it for fear of incurring the penalty of being left unprotected in the United States market. It is arguable that this scenario illustrates realisation of the limitations and inappropriate nature of copyright protection, and an efficient means of providing protection both domestically and internationally. Professor Samuelson is the most eloquent and energetic proponent of such a view.[115] It derives strong support from the legislative history of the Semiconductor Chip Act[116] in the United States. The Senate had been attracted to providing protection by means of extending the law of copyright, accepting the arguments of Professor Miller, who had chaired the relevant subcommittee of CONTU, that there was close analogy between the protection of computer programs, especially in object code, and chip designs, because they both performed a purely utilitarian function. This view was opposed in the House of Representatives on the basis that to protect chips by copyright law would violate basic principles of copyright law, blur its distinction from patent, and erode the recognition implicit in that distinction of the public value of permitting some forms of copying:

> The prohibition against copyright in useful articles is a fundamental principle of our copyright laws, adhered to for the nearly 200 years of their existence. In philosophical terms, the prohibition rests on the distinction between protection for expression and nonprotection for ideas under copyright, and on the differences in scope, standards, term, and purpose of the patent and copyright systems. In pragmatic terms, the nonprotection of useful articles that do not meet patent standards of novelty and invention represents a societal judgment that the public benefits from relatively unhampered copying of non-novel useful articles . . ..[117]

Given the force of Miller's analogy, the acceptance of this argument in relation to maskwork on chips suggests doubts about the wisdom of having extended copyright protection to programs, at least when in machine-readable form.

The argument against so treating computer software has a number of

---

111. Law 62, passed 7 June 1985 and coming into effect 1 January 1986; see Karjala, 'Protection of Computer Programs Under Japanese Copyright Law' [1986] 4 E.I.P.R. 105.
112. At a conference on 2 June 1987 in Munich organised by the European Computing Services Organisation, though only on the basis of a further study into the nature of programming, *Computer Weekly* 9 July 1987.
113. At a meeting in Oslo in October 1987 also organised by the European Computing Services Organisation, *Computer Weekly* 15 October 1987.
114. See above p. 43.
115. See her articles cited above at p. 126
116. 17 U.S.C. sect. 901.
117. House Report, 1984 U.S. Code and Congress. News 5757.

facets. One is simply that of confusion. It is suggested that the basic distinction between patent law which conveys extensive rights for a short period in respect of novel processes, and copyright which conveys narrow rights for long periods in respect of original forms of expression will be destroyed if some programs are both patentable and copyrightable. It will be necesary to devise some form of election of remedies.[118] Ugly indications of the problems of overlapping have been signalled by the problems in the law of the United Kingdom in the area of the overlap of design registration and copyright.[119]

Nor does the reluctance of the computer industry to abandon trade secret protection,[120] or to eschew the bespoke protection provided by licensing agreements,[121] suggest that copyright is regarded, even by the industry itself, as ideally suited to its needs. A further argument against extension of copyright law lies in the broad sweep of the notion of a derivative work in United States law, and the problems that this might create for programs which have a generative capacity.[122] Here the case for a new approach is simply that effective protection of computer programs requires provisions not normally associated with copyright. It may be reasonable to protect against unauthorised use of the program for example, while on the other hand it may be desirable to permit other types of conduct, such as reverse engineering, customarily antithetical to copyright law.

It may, however, be argued that the use of such a model for the protection of computer-related products is apposite only when similar conditions exist, namely a discrete and easily defined product, and unanimity in the industry that such a new form of protection is appropriate.[123] It has already been noted that the products of the computer industry cross the entire spectrum from machine parts to creative works and, given the clear overlaps with patentable inventions and copyright literature, it is far from obvious that the scope of a new area could easily, exclusively and exhaustively be defined. Still less is it clear that all participants in the industry, consumers and producers alike, would be likely to agree on one new form of protection to supplant existing forms. Despite its practical success in the chip context there is also likely to be strong opposition to international imposition of any new régime by unilateral action seeking reciprocal treatment under threat of trade sanctions.[124] It has accordingly been proposed[125] that the

---

118. See Kline, 'Requiring an Election of Protection for Patentable/Copyrightable Computer Programs', 6 Comp. L.J. 607 (1986).
119. See British Leyland Motor Corp. Ltd. v. Armstrong Patents Co. Ltd. [1986] A.C. 577, H.L., and the extensive legislative solution in Parts 1, 111 and IV of the Copyright, Designs and Patents Act 1988.
120. See above p. 83.
121. See below p. 180.
122. In the United Kingdom this problem is addressed by explicit provision in the Copyright, Designs and Patents Act 1988 sect. 9(3).
123. See further Raskind, 'The Uncertain Case for Special Legislation Protecting Computer Software', 47 U. Pitt. L.R. 1131 (1986) at 1148–1158 arguing that the conditions proposed by Kastenmeier and Remington in 'The Semiconductor Chip Act of 1984: Swamp or Firm Ground?', 70 Minn. L.R. 417 (1985) cannot be satisfied in this context.
124. See Cornish, 'The Canker of Reciprocity' [1988] 4 E.I.P.R. 99, and the difficulties being experienced by the United States in the General Agreement on Tariffs and Trade where it is being accused of discriminatory action against foreigners.
125. By Raskind at p. 1183.

application of current copyright legislation to computer software be re-examined by the legislature with a view, either to making copyright legislation more appropriate or to identifying the features which a successful new régime should incorporate.

(d) A dual régime[126]

Professor Menell, in consequence of his penetrative economic analysis, distinguishes quite sharply between the protection required for operating system software and that required for applications programs. He discriminates further between operating systems according to the category of computer and size of the relevant market, concluding that the problem of protection is most acute in the area of operating systems for machines at the low end of the market, that is, for small personal computers, where development costs and research costs tend to be low.[127] In this situation he recommends a patent-based solution, partly because of the easier interchangeability of software and hardware in relation to operating systems, and partly because patent comes much closer than copyright to protecting ideas. He generally favours making protection difficult to acquire, which fits the patent model, and of short duration. The latter argument suggests departure from patent towards a new form of protection, but he feels that it is necessary to require a high threshold before protection is provided in order to minimise the danger of locking-up an industry standard. It would not be quite so high as that required by the patent system at present, but to qualify for protection a system would still have to be shown to be novel, not obvious and useful. However, he is in favour of a system of speedier examination than at present, which he feels will be even more necessary if the period of protection is to be reduced. He advocates provision for reverse engineering and permitted modification upon the lines of the régime for chip protection. To avoid the difficulty over network externalities, he rejects injunctive remedies in favour of a system of compulsory licensing. The fee for such licensing should permit a reasonable return to the innovator, augmenting the figure to take account of the high risk of failure in new technological enterprises.

The analysis for applications programs also starts from his basic economic analysis. Here too he feels that there is little problem in relation to the sort of contract programming used for very large commercial applications. In that area the individual negotiation of contracts gives ample scope for the provision of appropriate levels of protection. He sees the main problem once again lying in relation to applications for smaller personal computers where the software developers rely upon high-volume initial sales to recover their investment. Here he recognises that no system of protection is likely to be effective against small-scale domestic copying, but is likely to be limited in its effect to commercial infringement. The problem with providing such

---

126. See further Menell, 'Tailoring Legal Protection for Computer Software', *39 Stan. L.R.* 1329 (1987).
127. He showed that the average development cost was less than one dollar for each operating system sold for the Apple 11 computer, and much less again for each copy of PC-DOS used in the IBM PC.

protection is, however, that it inhibits development of existing products, for example by making it easier to integrate them with other applications programs. Here, however, by contrast with operating systems, there is not the same necessity to use identical coding. The proposed solution here is a modification of existing copyright law, once again adjusted to reduce the period of protection, which is grossly excessive in relation to the likely useful life of the programs. Here too he favours the permission of reverse engineering and compulsory licensing, though perhaps only after a delay to permit recovery of investment, rather along the lines of the 'springboard doctrine' of trade secret law.[128]

(e) Maximisation of flexibility[129]

The whole of this section has been devoted to attempts to escape the shackles of the established law of intellectual property in relation to computer-related areas. To that extent all of the approaches have demanded an increased dimension of flexibility. In most cases, however, it has been suggested that a single new régime, or in the final suggestion, two new régimes, should govern. The distinctive feature of Stern's contribution to the debate is not simply his analysis of the problems and solutions, but his suggestion that it may be necessary to provide a new institutional process of constantly reviewing and renewing the rules upon a moving basis.

He does, it is true, also suggest the dimensions of a new régime, based loosely upon a registration system, and specially adapted to non-code aspects of software, such as instructions sets, icons and algorithms. He is aware that there is a need for flexibility on such matters as the term of protection, the definition of infringement, and the remedies to be made available. He is, moreover, aware that other technologies than that of computing may be affected by similar factors exposing the innovator to piracy and inhibiting the utility of patent or copyright as suitable means of protection. It is this sense of the variety of new technologies requiring protection which leads him to suggest a switch from legislative rule-making to administrative rule-making.[130] He believes that the legislature cannot easily be stirred into action to create a régime for every new technology which needs one, or often enough in respect of any one to maintain the current applicability of the regulatory framework. The solution proposed, though without conspicuous hope of its adoption, is that the legislature should lay down broad principles for the establishment, or alteration, of any regulatory framework, and delegate the implementation of such measures to an arm of the executive, perhaps the Department of Commerce. This framework would specify the outlines of the recommended régime including a ten-year term of protection, registration but not initial examination, the requisite standard of advance, the exclusive rights granted, the definition of and remedies for infringement. He envisages that in relation to each technology this regulatory body should take the initiative to consult the various interests affected and to negotiate

---

128. See above p. 88.
129. See Stern, 'The Bundle of Rights Suited to New Technology', *47 U. Pitt. L.R.* 1229 (1986).
130. The discussion is conducted exclusively within the context of the constitutional position in the United States.

the necessary compromises between them. In order to validate such regulations he envisages either a system of legislative vetoing, or the enactment of automatic 'sunsetting', whereby the regulations automatically pass out of force at a given date, but subject to a prior report to the legislature a couple of years in advance of that date so that the regulations can be extended or revised. It is felt that such a scheme would promote greater flexibility and increased co-operation between executive and legislative arms of government, and in particular allocate to legislature and executive that part of the process most appropriate to each.

As noted above, even the author seems doubtful of the political feasibility of this suggestion in the context of the United States. This may be echoed from the viewpoint of the United Kingdom. However jaded a legislative body may be when faced with the demands of understanding the requirements of new technology, nothing is more likely to stimulate it than the prospect of its power being delegated to an administrative agency. There may also be some loss to the community in general, especially in the United Kingdom, to the extent that the process of bargaining is removed from the public forum of debate in the legislature so as to take place in private behind closed bureaucratic doors.

Part 2

Liability

This part of the book covers three basic types of legal liability to be found in all common law systems. These are contractual, tortious and criminal liability. These forms of liability go back to the origins of the common law system, and were first moulded by the judiciary. They have, however, become the subject of considerable statutory intervention, most in the case of criminal, and least in that of tortious liability. The same act may, of course, give rise to all three types of liability. For example, one company could contract with another to conduct its computer business so as not to cause damage to the business of the first. If it then subsequently offered bribes to government customers of the first company to transfer their business to the second, it would be perfectly feasible to find that the second company was not only in breach of the contract, but was guilty of criminal offences of corruption and in tort for inducing breaches of contract. The broad aims of the three types of liability are, however, distinct. The law of contract seeks to provide a remedy for breaches of agreement; the law of tort to compensate those who have suffered damage as a result of the wrongful acts of others; and the law of crime to punish those who have committed acts sufficiently contrary to the public interest. In practice, the law of contract and the law of tort are concerned with the redress of private injury, and the law of crime with that of public wrong. Criminal liability is most easily segregated from the other forms, and will be dealt with in the third chapter of this part. It is much harder to distinguish between the two forms of civil liability. As mentioned above the most obvious distinguishing feature is that in order for there to be liability in contract there must be a binding agreement between the parties, whereas this is not essential to liability in tort. The two major areas of difficulty are first those cases where there is an overlap because there is not only an agreement between the parties but also a tortious act, perhaps deriving from breach of a duty imposed by the agreement; and second those cases where the law has imposed contractual-like liabilities in the absence of any binding agreement between the parties, as in some modern consumer protection legislation where liability is imposed upon a manufacturer to a consumer who is in contractual relations only with a retailer. The difficulty is exacerbated in the case of a work encompassing both the law of the United States and that of the United Kingdom because the two jurisdictions vary in their willingness to conflate the two forms of liability. There are enough distinctive differences to justify division into two separate chapters, and the principle adopted here is that most of the law relating to the overlapping will be considered in the chapter of tortious liability, while that on contract will generally be confined to cases where no, or little consideration was given to alternative claims in tort. There will, inevitably, be some places where it is not possible to apply such a principle. All three forms are capable of applying in the area of privacy discussed in the fourth chapter of this part of the book. It might, however, be more realistic to characterise the law's intervention there as more administrative or constitutional.

Chapter 5

Contract

The contract is the most common legal institution in everyday life. We all make contracts with the same facility, frequency and unawareness as that with which M. Jourdain talked prose. No modern society could function without the institution of contract, and social life itself could barely exist. Now, in a world in which computers and computer-based services and products play so large, and so fast enlarging a part, many of these contracts relate to computers directly, or indirectly. Because contracts are so ubiquitous, and the world of computers so diverse, the variety both of types of subject matter and of legal provision is far too wide to be capable of complete coverage here. Already multi-volume encyclopaedic works are devoted to this topic.[1] As in other areas there is considerable disparity between the volume of reported litigation dealing with computer contracts in the United Kingdom and in the United States. In both jurisdictions the case law is supported on a central statutory spine, in the United Kingdom the legislation regulating the Sale of Goods and Services, and in the United States, the Uniform Commercial Code.[2]

This chapter will first consider some general problems in applying the law of contract to the special case of computers, and will then go on to considerations applying to particular sorts of subject matter in the area of computers, such as hardware, software, maintenance, personnel, and bureau services. The choice between alternative frameworks for supply, such as sale, lease and licence will then serve as an introduction to contentious issues in relation to such contracts for supply, such as the terms of such supply, remedies for breach of such supply, and alternative means of resolving these issues.

A. Nature of problem

It is helpful to start by making two pairs of distinctions, one relating to the

---

1. See Bigelow, 'Computer Contracts Negotiating and Drafting Aids' (1987).
2. Adopted in every state except Louisiana, though often with local variations. Even in Louisiana the Uniform Commercial Code is often applied by analogy, see, for example, *Southern Hardware Co.* v. *Honeywell Information Systems Inc.* 373 So.2d 738 (La., 1979).

subject matter of computer contracts, and the other to the very nature of a contract. It must first be stressed that there is in commercial, and consequently in legal, terms a distinction to be drawn between business and consumer transactions. In the former the law is inclined to stand back and to let the parties reach the agreement which they themselves consider best meets their needs. In the case of the latter, the law is more interventionist because it recognises frequent inequality of knowledge, means, and acumen which prompts it to offer a minimum safety net of protection to the consumer. The development of a strong consumer market for computers, and for computer-based products and services, is a phenomenon which has developed since the first edition of this work was prepared. The second distinction relates to two different functions served by the institution of contract. On the one hand it is *operative* and signifies that the parties have come to an agreement intended to be binding. It is necessary and sufficient to enable performance by one party to take place in advance of performance by the other, so as to provide some degree of assurance that the other will then either perform, or be held liable for failing to do so. This function predominates in most of our unarticulated, and almost unconscious, simple contracts of purchase and for services. Such contracts may be oral, or even made by a gesture such as shaking hands or presenting a selected article to a salesperson. It is far from uncommon for consumer contracts to be signified in such an informal manner. A second function of the institution is more *definitive*. A contract may also, and even primarily, have the function of defining the terms by which the parties are bound. It is in this light that lay opinion tends to refer to contracts. Where such a function predominates, the contract is more likely to be written than oral, and to have been agreed only after some lengthy process of negotiation between the parties where their bargaining positions are roughly comparable, or by acceptance of a carefully premeditated and prepared set of terms presented by one of the parties where they are not. It should be noted that comparability of bargaining position is not intended to denote merely comparative economic strength, but also allows for comparability of knowledge and experience in the type of transaction in question.

It might have been expected that to the extent that consumer contracts are under consideration there would be little in the way of detailed negotiation, but rather reliance upon mass advertisement, representations by retailers, and adherence to standard terms. What has been surprising in the past has been the degree of informality in the commercial area. Given that computers are generally expensive[3] and durable items of equipment, and that their use tends to be addictive in the sense that very few business operations, once mechanised, can ever again revert, at least permanently, to manual methods,[4] it might be expected that the latter of the two functions mentioned above would predominate, that contracts relating to computers would always be drafted with care in the light of expert advice, and would be negotiated fiercely and competitively between the parties. While this may

---

3. And in real terms used to be far more costly.
4. It has been estimated that a bank deprived of computer services would nowadays have to cease business within two days.

have been true of a few large corporations and government departments, it seems not to have been true of the majority of such contracts. Many reported cases illustrated this phenomenon.[5] It was also documented dramatically by a survey conducted in the community of Palo Alto in California.[6] Palo Alto is a suburban town situated some thirty-five miles south of San Francisco. It abuts Stanford University and the Stanford Research Institute, and is situated in an area so thick with computer-related firms and industries as to be dubbed 'Silicon Valley'. Average educational attainment and per capita income is probably as high as in any community in the world, and technological awareness rather greater. Nevertheless, of the ninety-six local businesses surveyed in the 1970s which had contracts relating to computers or computer-based work less than a third of the parties had taken any form of advice before entering into them, and if the computer firms themselves are excluded from the sample, then less than a fifth of the customers secured such advice. Still more surprising, over a third of the customers had no written contract of any sort, and many of those who did had no more than a purchase slip, or an exchange of loosely drafted letters. By contrast, nine-tenths of the computer firms had at least that much protection. What was the explanation? As with any question worth asking, there is no clear or obvious answer. A number of factors probably contributed. One was that a large number of computer contracts was being made between parties of whom one had never before entered into such a contract. This meant that no institutional form could be referred to, nor traditional practice invoked. It is still not unusual for a small business to start its computing career by mechanising its billing or payroll procedures. The personnel responsible for these procedures were unlikely to be familiar with computers, and were also unlikely to be skilled in negotiations with outside bodies, since in the past such services were always likely to have been provided within the firm using only such bought-in items as typewriters and printed forms. Such persons were likely to accept the assurances of a computer salesman with little real understanding, and to be prepared to use a standard form as evidence of the agreement. Even at more sophisticated levels of management there was unlikely to be either the technical expertise necessary to ensure that the contractual terms really would accomplish the manager's intentions, and still less accomplish those things which he would have intended if he had understood the position more thoroughly. One common refuge from such a situation may be to choose to deal only with a 'reputable' supplier. Unfortunately this may be translated into the firm which is best known because of its commercial success in the relevant market. Yet it is not self-evident that dominance in a highly competitive market is necessarily achieved by contracting with customers on the terms most favourable to them.

---

5. See *Associated Tabulating Services Inc.* v. *Olympia Life Insurance Corp.* 414 F.2d 1306 (5th Cir., 1969) (no contract ever drafted); *National Cash Register Co.* v. *IMC Inc.* 491 P.2d 211 (Or., 1971) (contract signed with blank in key clause); *Lovely* v. *Burroughs Corp.* 527 P.2d 557 (Mont., 1974) (purchase form used for lease without either alteration or execution); *Badger Bearing Co.* v. *Burroughs Corp.* 444 F.Supp 919 (E.D.Wis., 1977) (seller never signed contract).
6. Reported in Douglas, 'Some Ideas on the Computer and the Law', *2 Tex. S.U.L.R.* 20 (1973).

In the field of commercial contracts, much of this has now changed. Firms have become aware of the importance of conducting preliminary research before entering into negotiations, of negotiating thoroughly, and of taking legal advice at an early stage. An interesting phenomenon has been the growth, not only of computer departments in most large firms of lawyers both in the United States and in the United Kingdom, but alongside them of firms specialising in contracting work in the computer field.[7] There are also highly practical guides to prospective purchasers,[8] and even specialised newsletters.[9] Nevertheless there are still many smaller businesses to which the older situation remains applicable. Thus in one recent case[10] the old scenario was re-enacted on a smaller stage. A doctor wanted to computerise his practice, and delegated the task to his book-keeper. She had no experience of computers, and went to an establishment from whom she had in the past bought a copying machine. The contract negotiations, such as they were, found no reflection in the standard forms. It was left to the court to extricate the parties from the disastrous consequences of their insouciance. The parties too often bring to such negotiations too dissimilar a background of competence and experience. Computers are complicated devices, and are still little understood. The average small businessman regards them much as the early Greeks regarded their Gods, as beings with inscrutable wills of their own, and quite unaccountably benevolent or malevolent in their interference in human affairs. Such an attitude is partly explained by the technology involved. Few non-scientists can penetrate the electronic mysteries of core architecture or channel specifications, or assess the advantages of one given operating system or programming language over another. But these are really secondary considerations. After all, few small businessmen in the early years of the century had much understanding of the working of the internal combustion engine, but this did not prevent them from replacing their horses by petrol-driven machines without undue legal difficulty. The real problem is not with the computer as such, but in the difference between the way in which it operates, and in which human beings operate. A lorry may, in replacing physical effort, quite plausibly be regarded as a more powerful team of horses; a computer, in replacing mental effort, cannot plausibly be regarded as a more powerful brain. It is significant that the power of engines was for years measured in horse-power, but that of computers has never been measured in brain-power. It is because computers operate in so alien a fashion from the human beings whose efforts they are destined to replace that their application presents such a challenge to understanding. The old procedures of a business have to be dissected and examined in much more minute detail than those conducting them have ever been previously required to contemplate. New procedures must then be

---

7 See, for example, services offered in the United Kingdom by 'The Computer Law and Contracts Consultancy' in *Computing* 2 January 1986 and in the United States by 'International Computer Negotiations Inc.' in *Computerworld* 22 October 1975.

8. For example, Auer and Harris, *Computer Contract Negotiations* (1981); Kutten, *The Computer Buyer's Protection Guide* (1985).

9. For example, *Computer Negotiations Report* and *Computer Contract Resource Service*.

10. *Neilson Business Equipment Center Inc.* v. *Montelone* 524 A.2d 1172 (Del., 1987).

devised geared to the computer's way of operating. This deconstruction and reconstruction are best conducted by those most familiar with the process, namely those employed by computer companies as systems analysts. In other words the result is that the seller has to formulate the buyer's requirements for him, and the danger is that in all innocence the analyst's training and experience may tend to warp these requirements more towards the machines he is accustomed to work with and which his company sells, than to what the buyer really needs. It must also be confessed that not all computer salesmen and analysts are completely impartial in their appraisal of their own and their competitors' products. Even if a first-time buyer is inclined to seek unbiased technical assistance, he may have difficulty in appraising the credentials of those who are offering it, and may also under-estimate the extent to which apparently independent advice is distorted towards some particular supplier. He may also then be at a loss to resolve any conflict which arises between the advice he receives from different sources.

In a large business setting there are likely to be sufficient resources, and perhaps sufficient leverage, to make thorough research and negotiation a practicable proposition. In the case of smaller businesses there is likely to be no such scope, except perhaps on questions of price. At the end of the scale is the private purchaser of packaged software from a retailer who may have scope for negotiation neither on price nor terms. He is likely to find the terms in the box only after acquiring it. It is worth a brief glance at these two very different situations.

1. Negotiated purchase.[11]

It cannot be over-emphasised that the more thoroughly an acquisition can be considered in advance, negotiated and the contract anticipated, the better the result is likely to be for both parties. Perhaps the first step is for the prospective acquirer to determine exactly what he hopes the computer will be able to provide, and why it is preferable to any other solution. It must be accepted that there is an inevitable circularity in this procedure. Unless the acquirer knows what facilities are available, he will not know whether he wants them. There is, however, no harm in securing informal general advice about computer capabilities in general in order to formulate a more detailed approach to prospective suppliers. If the acquirer is satisfied that the computer offers the best solution to his needs, the next step is to formulate his requirements in the most minute detail he can manage. It should, of course, be recognised that requirements are likely to change with changed circumstances, so it will be essential not only to analyse present, but also future, requirements. Once this has been completed the prospective acquirer is in a position to approach prospective suppliers in a formal way. This is commonly done by providing an invitation to tender or request for proposals. In preparing this document it is wise to involve expert assistance, of a technical, business and legal character. The technical assistance is required to ensure that the invitation provides sufficient information to permit potential suppliers to draft an acceptable tender, and the business assistance

---

11. For a fuller, incisive account, see Edwards, *Understanding Computer Contracts* (1983) ch. 2.

to ensure that the needs of the business really are set out fully and accurately. Legal assistance is desirable, even at this early stage, to ensure that the document is drafted in such a way as to provide the maximum possible help in any subsequent dispute, and to avoid possible legal pitfalls, such as its being capable of being construed as an offer. The invitation should be a document setting out not only the detailed requirements mentioned above, but the procedures to be followed at each step of the negotiations, and the conceptual basis of the proposed contract, for example whether the contract is to be for the supply of ascertained equipment and systems, or for the satisfaction of defined functions. Such a document has the further merit of forcing prospective suppliers to tender in comparable terms, thus easing the process of evaluation. Some indication of the financial parameters of the proposed transaction is also desirable for much the same purposes. In relation to a business of any complexity the invitation to tender is likely to result in a series of requests for amplification and explanation. It is sensible to retain copies of any, and all, such communications, as they may become invaluable if a dispute should eventuate. When tenders are received they must be evaluated, and it is usual to establish a short list of possible suppliers. The same assistance secured in connection with drafting the invitation to tender should again be enlisted for the purpose of evaluation. It is quite likely that those on the short list will have been asked to nominate reference sites and to conduct demonstrations. It is important to note everything that transpires on any such occasion since it may be relevant to any subsequent dispute. Once preference is accorded to a particular tender detailed negotiations can take place as to the precise terms of any contract. Some purchasers may have their own standard terms, and some, such as government departments, are even so powerful as to be able to insist upon their being adopted, at least as a starting point. Some organisations such as the Institute of Purchasing and Supply in the United Kingdom can provide contractual forms drafted from a prospective purchaser's point of view from which to start. In most cases, however, it will be the supplier who takes the initiative with his own standard form, from which he will not easily be deflected. One such contract was described as 'the best job of boiler-plating since the building of the Monitor'.[12] Further discussion of particular contractual terms typical in the context of computers appears below.[13]

2. Unnegotiated purchase

In some contexts there is no realistic possibility of negotiating, especially at the private consumer's end of the spectrum. It is often as unrealistic to think of bargaining for a software package as for a tin of beans. This would not be particularly serious if the legal incidents of such a contract were as well-known and as well regulated as those for a tin of beans. The problem arises because suppliers attempt to impose quite complicated and sometimes draconian terms upon acquirers without allowing any possibility of negotiation. One of the most extreme and controversial methods of doing this is by

---

12. By Bertelsman J., *Horning* v. *Sycom* 556 F.Supp. 819 (E.D. Ky., 1983) at 821.
13. At p. 183 below.

way of 'shrink-wrap' contracts. This is a system whereby a program, usually an applications program, is provided on a disk or disks, and these are packaged together with a set of manuals, often in a stout cardboard box. The whole is encased in a sealed transparent container. Such a package is typically purchased, either in a retail shop or by mail order. Although there is some variation in practice, the idea is that the purchaser should be able to see through the packing to read a notice attached to the outside of the box setting out the terms of a licence, and warning him that by opening the packing he will be taken to have accepted the terms of the licence. The licence usually contains a provision requiring the licensee to return a reply-paid form confirming his acceptance of the terms of the licence, and at the same time registering as a licensed user, entitling him to some further benefits, such as supply of new versions of the program on preferential terms, or providing free telephonic assistance. There seems little doubt that in a clear case where the user knowingly performs these steps, such a procedure is enough to create a contract on the terms of the licence. Equally clearly there is unlikely to be any difficulty if the package is returned unopened. The problem lies in situations falling between these two extremes. What if the customer intends to purchase the package, does not notice or read the licence, opens the package and uses the program, never bothers to send off the slip signifying acceptance, and fails to register as a licensed user? There is a well-established principle of the law of contract both in the United Kingdom[14] and in the United States[15] that a contract may not be imposed upon another by construing silence as acceptance of an offer. In order for such an argument to prevail however it must be clear that the supplier is the offeror in these circumstances, and that the user is being bound merely by silence, and not for example by conduct, and does not fall within the narrow class of exceptions to the general rule. It would be possible to argue that the user is the offeror either at the point of presenting the package to the retailer together with his payment, or shortly after the time of opening the package by his conduct, inconsistent with the terms of the licence.[16] Even if it is possible to find a valid offer and acceptance in principle, there remains a difficulty if one party intends and believes that the contract is one of sale, while the other intends and believes that it is one of licence. In this case an alternative analysis nullifying any contract on the basis of a mistake as to its fundamental terms might be available. It can further be argued that, despite the shrink-wrapping, the supplier has acted in such a way as to induce in the customer a reasonable belief that the transaction was one of sale, and that a sale was thus consummated. A slightly different approach would suggest that despite the supplier's explicit reference to a licence, the terms themselves which require full payment in advance, and allow use for an unlimited

---

14. *Felthouse* v. *Bindley* (1862) 11 C.B. (N.S.) 869, C.B.
15. See Restatement (Second) of Contracts para. 89 (1979).
16. The first approach to the salesman would amount to an offer, the licence in the package to the first counter-offer, but the inconsistent conduct to a further counter-offer. Cf. *Rust* v. *Abbey Life Insurance Co.* [1979] 2 Ll. R. 355, C.A. where the recipient of such a documentary first counter-offer was bound, but had performed no positive act in relation to the subject matter of the contract.

period, really suggest a sale.[17] It is very tentatively suggested that a court would be reluctant to hold that there was no contract at all, so the choice is between construing the contract as a licence or as a sale. It seems more likely that sale will be preferred, at least so far as the user believes and intends a purchase.[18] In the United States this will have the further advantage of bringing the provisions of the Uniform Commercial Code more directly to bear on the transaction. Some support for this interpretation might be derived from the fact that a few states in the United States have felt that the only way to make all of the terms of such agreements binding is to legislate to that effect,[19] though even then such legislation is of dubious effect since it might be regarded as being inconsistent with federal copyright[20] or anti-trust legislation. Nor does it seem that the situation would be affected by the provision of further wrapping around the program discs inside the package, even though it might then be physically impossible to unwrap them without seeing the warning. By that time the contract would have been completed, and any further attempt to impose the terms of the licence would be regarded as a unilateral attempt to vary the existing terms of the contract. The whole arrangement is reminiscent of attempts in the United Kingdom to impose contractual obligations to maintain retail prices by similar means which were uniformly rejected by the courts as contrary to the basic principles of the law of contract.[21]

B. Hardware contracts

Hardware has been defined in the United Kingdom as 'the physical parts of the computer and ancillary equipment'[22] in the United States as 'the computer itself and its mechanical appurtenances'.[23] Few users would ever wish to contract exclusively for such mechanical devices, except for scrap metal. The contention that they might was ridiculed by Judge Edenfield in his dissent in *Lovable Corp.* v. *Honeywell Inc.*:

The contention of Honeywell, adopted by the majority, is that it was to do little more than to furnish certain naked pieces of equipment. It did imply that the machine would run, since it was to furnish maintenance, but its contention is that it did not promise that it would accomplish any result whatsoever or even print a single line. Like the Mona Lisa of the ballad, its computer, as far as guaranteed results were

---

17. Examination of purported licences to discover whether they are disguised sales is common in the United States, see *Straus* v. *Victor Talking Machine Co.* 243 U.S. 490 (1917); *U.S.* v. *Masonite Corp.* 316 U.S. 265 (1942). In the United Kingdom support for such a view may be derived from *Eurodynamic Systems plc* v. *General Automation Ltd.* 5 A.C.C.L. January 1989 5, Q.B. (1988) where the substance prevailed over form even in the case of a negotiated contract.
18. Though this might be difficult to establish in the case of a regular buyer of packaged programs who would be likely to become aware that there was invariably a licence to be found in the box.
19. See, for example, Louisiana's Software License Enforcement Act 1984 L.R.S. 51:1951–6.
20. See *Vault Corp.* v. *Quaid Software Ltd.* 655 F.Supp 750 (E.D.La., 1987) discussed above at p. 64.
21. See, for example, *Taddy* v. *Sterious* [1904] Ch. 354, C.A.
22. By Savill J. in *DPCE* v. *ICL Ltd.* LEXIS report 31 July 1985, Q.B.
23. By Asa Herzog, Referee, in *Law Research Services Inc.* 5 C.L.S.R. 220 (S.D.N.Y., 1972) at 222.

concerned, was just a cold and lovely work of art. I simply cannot conceive of two capable businessmen negotiating for the sale or lease of a computer except on the basis of what it would do.[24]

It would now be accepted that a working operating system is necessarily implied in such a sale. Nevertheless, any contract for a computer must contain some provisions relating to hardware. Such provisions are indeed now likely to be a separate, or at least severable, part of the contract since litigation[25] in the United States compelled suppliers to 'unbundle' their systems. Prior to this the general practice in the industry had been for suppliers to quote a global price for a complete computer system including such associated services as systems design, programming assistance, training customers' own staff, pre-installation testing, provision of back-up facilities in case of machine failure and routine maintenance. Such services are now, in the business area, more likely to be priced separately. However, it is not uncommon for a similar array of associated services, though on a much smaller scale, to be offered at the consumer end of the market, as an incentive to purchase.

The computer industry is one in which the technology changes very rapidly, and so far such changes have been most rapid in the area of hardware. This often means that to maintain a competitive position a manufacturer must continually offer enhancements to his product. It is also a capital intensive industry in which enormous sums are required for research into, and development of, such new products. Nor is the transition from prototype to production either easy or inexpensive. It is extremely important that in any contract for hardware the buyer should so far as possible guard himself against the dangers associated with these features. It is not unknown for a manufacturer to offer a machine for delivery which has never been constructed,[26] or which, when constructed, is not as efficient as was hoped, or promised.[27] The obvious way to do this is to specify the hardware as precisely as possible, both by description and prescription. The description should descend to minute particularity in terms of model and part number.[28] The prescription should require specified levels of performance by reference to an objective standard, and should specify an acceptable form of testing for its satisfaction. The design of any such scheme of testing is complex and requires technical knowledge. There is a danger that in the euphoria of selecting a particular supplier, the customer will be tempted to leave the matter of testing in the supplier's hands. In some reported cases this has been done by an explicit reference to certification by the supplier that the machine was 'installed and available for use'. In one such case the supplier

---

24. 431 F.2d 668 (5th Cir., 1970) at 677.

25. *Control Data Corp.* v. *International Business Machines Inc.* settled in 1973 on terms reported in 3 C.L.S.R. 862.

26. In *U.S.* v. *Wegematic Corp.* 360 F.2d 674 (2nd Cir., 1966) the machine never was constructed.

27. In *Consolidated Data Terminals Inc.* v. *Applied Digital Data Systems Inc.* 708 F.2d 385 (9th Cir., 1983) the defendants promised that their new terminal would operate at 19,200 characters per second when it was capable only of about a tenth of that speed.

28. Though even this will not invariably attain its object since manufacturers have been known to forge false part numbers, see *Glovatorium Inc.* v. *National Cash Register Corp.* 684 F.2d 658 (9th Cir., 1982).

so certified although data for the relevant operations had not been converted, and some of the peripheral equipment had not so much as been delivered.[29] Even where a more objective test is planned, its design may require so much expertise that its specification is left to the supplier. Once again this may prove to be unwise since the supplier will be tempted to devise tests similar to those used during the manufacturing process which he knows the machine can pass, but which may sound more impressive than they really are when divorced from the user's actual requirements. Any such tests should apply both to performance and reliability, and should relate to the user's requirements and environment. It has accordingly been suggested that testing should be considered in multiple stages.[30] The first stage would perhaps take place on the supplier's premises, and would consist in the satisfaction of the advertised specifications of the relevant components. A second stage might then involve repetition of these tests on the customer's premises, and using the customer's working environment. A final stage might ultimately involve a test simulating, or even using, the customer's data, deadlines and workload. The scoring of such tests is itself a complex matter, weighing performance of different components of the system against each other. For example, if reliability is to be measured in mean-time between failures, it is no good if failure can be averted by reducing performance in terms of speed of access, or the number of simultaneous users or of jobs running concurrently. So complicated has the task of evaluation become that proprietary packages are now available to assist with it.[31] In order to ensure compliance with such a programme of testing it is sensible to arrange for payments to be staged. Most suppliers' standard forms of contract require payment upon installation of the computer. The usual object is to accelerate payment, and the supplier's sales staff are likely to support this policy enthusiastically since commission payments, which traditionally constitute a high proportion of total remuneration in the sales area of the computer industry, are likely to be geared to installation.[32]

The supplier is more likely to be concerned about securing payment from his customer. In many cases a leasing arrangement is preferred to a sale, at least in part so as to accomplish such early payment.[33] However in the case of an outright sale it is prudent to make some specific provision postponing the passing of property until payment has been made in full. Such a provision is effective as between the contracting parties,[34] but is less likely to be effective against third parties.[35] If such a provision is included in a

29. *National Cash Register Co.* v. *Marshall Savings and Loans Assoc.* 415 F.2d 1131 (7th Cir., 1969).
30. By Harris, 'Complex Contract Issues in the Acquisition of Hardware and Software', *4 Comp. L.J.* 77 (1983).
31. See Hart, 'User's Guide to Evaluation Products', *Datamation* 15 December 1970 p. 55.
32. See *LTV* v. *Commissioner of Internal Revenue* 63 T.C. 39 (U.S. Tax Ct., 1974) where a manufacturer's records showed installation long before payment from the customer had even been demanded, although under the contract payment was geared to installation.
33. See further below p. 180.
34. Under sect. 17 of the Sale of Goods Act 1979 property in goods passes when it is intended to pass, and this may be determined by a specific contractual provision retaining title in the vendor, *Aluminium Industrie Vassen BV* v. *Romalpa Aluminium Ltd.* [1976] 2 All E.R. 552, C.A.
35. See *Hendy Lennox (Industrial Engines) Ltd* v. *Grahame Puttick Ltd.* [1984] 2 All E.R. 152, Q.B.

contract for hardware which is delivered in advance of payment, the supplier should make separate provision for risk to pass to the buyer upon delivery, and should probably contract to insure as agent for the buyer, just to make absolutely sure that cover is provided.

A further point for consideration is the compatibility of any new hardware with hardware which is already in place, or which is to be supplied by another supplier, and most importantly of all with future enhancements planned by the supplier. It is highly unlikely that the requirements of the customer, or the products of the supplier, will remain the same after the decision to go ahead has been taken. It is not uncommon for the originally agreed hardware to contain a substantial amount of spare capacity, so some business growth can usually be accommodated without specific contractual provision for enhancement. In fact such provision is normally necessary, not to secure enhancement since the supplier will be only too ready to provide it, but to regulate the price and compatibility of such enhancement. It may even be the supplier who seeks a provision entitling him to substitute different equipment for that contracted to be provided. Although this is not unreasonable in a fast-moving industry, it is certainly advisable to agree upon the degree of deviation from original specification and price in advance, if at all possible. A prudent customer will also do well to seek compatibility with some other similar machine in his vicinity to which he can have recourse in case of some calamity which puts his own machine out of commission.

As can now be appreciated, the acquisition of a large computer system is so complex and demanding that a customer very quickly becomes tied in to a particular supplier. This applies even before a contract has been concluded, since the option of breaking off negotiations and starting again from scratch will be extremely expensive in money and manpower and, most obviously of all, in time. It is rare for a customer not to be in a hurry once the decision to acquire has been taken in principle. Although dependence upon a supplier may promote compatibility, it has few other advantages for a customer. It is wise to reduce it so far as possible. One approach is to negotiate for rights to enhance the system from other sources. This can save very large sums of money.[36] It is also useful to try to contract on a modular basis, paying separately for individual components of the complete system, though this more naturally applies to a total system procurement contract consisting of applications software as well as hardware. A customer should also ensure that he preserves options to move to different, and less expensive, hardware, so that if advances in inexpensive machines are more rapid than the expansion of his work he can switch to such equipment without penalty. This is likely to be easier now that the mainframe suppliers are also in the business of supplying smaller machines and have adopted software capable of allowing jobs to be more easily transferred from one family of machines to another.

It should also be noted that in very large procurements it may make sense

---

36. As long ago as 1971 a customer in the United States was able to save $20 000 a week by changing to a different brand of tape drives and discs, see letter to *Storage Technology Corp.* 18 August 1971, 3 C.L.S.R. 407.

to divide the order between different suppliers. This will lead to much greater complication, especially when the equipment of different suppliers has to communicate and harmonise. Performance testing can become a nightmare in such a situation, since there will always be a tendency for each supplier to blame the other for any difficulty. One solution to this type of problem is for the customer to nominate one of the suppliers as the lead contractor, and to leave him to sub-contract with the others. It is interesting that this is a common practice in the construction industry, where it is also necessary to cater for comparably large and complex co-ordination of many different suppliers.

There are so many separate factors to consider and to contract for that an increasing practice in the area of government procurement in particular is to create a scoring algorithm the function of which is to evaluate one bid against another, taking into account such factors as delivery date, perform-ance, reliability, compatibility, flexibility and cost in the proportions appropriate to the particular application.[37] There is no reason why private customers who can afford to devise such methods should not adopt similar techniques to guide their path through the negotiating maze, and then to make sure that such indicators are given full contractual effect whether by keying payment to them, or otherwise.

C. Software contracts

It is necessary to be especially careful about terminology in this section. 'Software' is not a term of art, and can be used to refer to different things. At times it is restricted to programming as such both in the United Kingdom, 'the instructions to the hardware to perform particular functions or sets of functions for use with . . . computers'[38] and in the United States, '"Software" refers to the programming part of data processing'.[39] At others it is extended to include the whole range of services necessary to support the hardware:

'Software' denotes the information loaded into the machine and the directions given to the machine (usually by card or teleprompter) as to what it is to do and upon what material. 'Software' is also frequently used to include 'support' – that is, advice, assistance, counselling and sometimes even expert engineering help furnished by the vendor in loading the machine for a certain programme such as inventory control or preparation of payroll.[40]

The latter, and broader, view may be taken as a provisional definition, subject to reconsideration in the light of any particular contract, which should preferably be drafted in much more specific terms. Whatever the extent of the term, it clearly includes a number of quite different types of situation. It is helpful to distinguish first between systems and applications programs:

---

37. See letters to *Computer Network Corp.* 28 September 1970, 50 Comp. Gen. 222; *Storage Technology Corp.* 19 June 1972, 4 C.L.S.R. 871.
38. *DPCE* v. *ICL Ltd.* LEXIS report 31 July 1985, Q.B.
39. *Honeywell Inc.* 1 C.L.S.R. 810 (1971) at 812 by the Board of Contract Appeals of the General Services Administration.
40. *Honeywell Inc.* v. *Lithonia Lighting Inc.* 317 F.Supp. 406 (N.D., 1970) at 408.

A 'systems programme' is a computer programme designed solely to help someone else programme or use a computer. An 'applications' programme is a computer programme which is designed to solve a particular problem; for example, to maintain personal files or to handle a company's payroll. It is generally any computer programme which is not a systems programme.[41]

1. Systems programs

In general, systems programming is developed and offered by hardware manufacturers. It comprises the basic operating system, compilers which translate or interpret particular programming languages, and often the communications interface which is that part of the programming which enables the user to get his data and programs into the computer, and his results out of it. This is especially complicated and important when the system is being operated on an interactive basis with large numbers of users simultaneously connected to the central processor. Since such services are not, at least in the case of mainframe computers, offered otherwise than by hardware manufacturers their separation from the hardware under the general practice of unbundling makes little sense. Thus in *Lovable Corp.* v. *Honeywell Inc.*[42] provision by the manufacturer of such software was regarded as so fundamental that it was made a prerequisite of the contract, and failure to develop such a program was held to invalidate all claims for payment under the contract, even though the machine was otherwise installed satisfactorily and, indeed, used by the customer as a stand-alone device. It has become increasingly common for basic systems programming to be provided in microcode on a chip, and the distinction from hardware has become still more exiguous. Even so, a substantial third party market has developed in systems programming of all types.[43] This development has been stimulated in the United States by the decision in *Digidyne Corp.* v. *Data General Corp.*[44] that any attempt to tie hardware users in by refusing to license a popular proprietary operating system to run on other computers is illegal under the United States anti-trust legislation. An important consideration was the impracticality of re-writing applications programs so as to run on a different operating system. There has also been some regulatory activity in the European Economic Communities to help secure adequate levels of competition by requiring large systems procurements to adopt some standard features into the operating software.[45] To the same end there has been pressure on hardware suppliers to provide advance information about new developments to facilitate such provision as, for example, in proceedings brought against IBM in the European Economic Communities, and subsequently settled upon terms providing for such advance disclosure.[46] So keen

---

41. *Computer Sciences Corp.* v. *Commissioner of Internal Revenue* 63 T.C. 327 (U.S. Tax Ct., 1974) at 330.
42. Above p. 146.
43. The industry leader, Computer Associates Inc., is expected to gross $1 billion in 1989, *Computerworld* 29 August 1988 p. 1.
44. 734 F.2d 1336 (9th Cir., 1984). See above p. 124.
45. Thus all public procurement contracts in the United Kingdom for systems costing in excess of £70 000 must specify open systems interconnection, see *Computer Weekly* 30 July 1987 p. 6.
46. *The Community* v. *International Business Machines Corp.* [1984] 3 C.M.L.R. 147.

is the Commission of the European Economic Communities to encourage such moves that it has provisionally approved an agreement between leading software developers to provide a common application environment for programs to run on Unix, subject only to oversight to ensure that the agreement is not used to lock some potential suppliers out of the market.[47] Similar development has taken place at the personal computing end of the spectrum, where operating systems are frequently provided on a competitive basis by third party suppliers.

The same general considerations which apply to the acquisition of hardware apply also to the acquisition of systems software. In particular, the customer should specify in detail what operating system is to be supplied, what peripheral devices are to be accommodated, what programming languages and data formats supported, and what performance in terms of response times and throughput required. It must be remembered that operating systems typically undergo a continuing process of minor, and sometimes major, improvements. Minor improvements are often expressed in small alterations or patches to the main code, and major improvements in new releases of the whole program so as to incorporate the new developments.[48] Compatibility with existing programs and data is extremely important, and often causes considerable trouble.[49] In one case it took a highly experienced software house over three months to convert a legal information retrieval package which was running quite happily on IBM equipment so as to run on a different machine.[50] In another, the buyer had some 450 programs to run, but the prospective contractor was willing to convert only 117 of them, apparently on the basis that this was equivalent to the 200 hours of computer time and six months of onsite programming and data conversion specified in the request for proposals.[51] It is equally important where the customer needs to achieve compatibility with a reserve or back-up computer, or if he intends to expand the capacity of his system in the future. Both of these factors were present in the requirements of the United States army for a numerical control system for installation in an arsenal.[52] The system had both to be as compatible as possible in its programming language with a much larger computer which it was intended to use for back-up purposes, and to be capable of being up-graded to handle direct numerical control. Although twenty different languages could accomplish the immediate task, only one met the compatibility requirement.

2. Applications programs

From the point of view of the user, systems programs are merely the necessary background to the provision of applications programs which

---

47. *The X/Open Group* [1986] 3 C.M.L.R. 373, European Commission Notice.
48. In fact it is often a three stage process with a two part number indicating the upper levels, such as MS DOS 3.4, and patches operating beneath that level.
49. See Fakes, 'Mainframe Computer Conversions: Buyer and Seller Beware', 6 *Comp. L.J.* 469 (1985).
50. *McDonnell Automation Co.* 49 Comp. Gen. 124 (1969).
51. *Xerox Corp.* 5 C.L.S.R. 734 (1974).
52. *Manufacturing Data Systems Inc.* 5 C.L.S.R. 723 (1974)

actually perform the functions for which he acquired the computer in the first place. From this point of view such programs are every bit as essential as systems programming, and in *Carl Beasley Ford Inc. v. Burroughs Corp.*[53] were even equated with the hardware itself:

There was testimony at trial that the E-4000 machine was virtually worthless without proper programming . . . although two separate agreements were used, one in writing for the physical equipment, and the other oral to cover the programming of the equipment, the two were virtually inseparable insofar as the utility of the equipment was concerned.

There are roughly four ways to secure a 'package' of applications programs sufficient to achieve the results that the customer requires, and which he should have specified in his initial analysis prior to deciding upon acquiring a computer at all. First, the customer can develop the programs himself. If he already has well-trained staff, and the job is within their compass, then this may be the best approach. It is today assisted by the widespread availability of program generators designed to make the writing of programs relatively easy. It is however necessary to be absolutely sure that these conditions are satisfied, because if they are not, this is invariably the worst approach.[54] It is, in any event, usually impractical for the first-time user. Even if such a user is prepared to employ programming staff to conduct the work, he may well find that the absence, and often irrelevance, of formal and agreed standards for the education and qualifications of programmers makes such employment well-nigh impossible and certainly inadvisable. The second alternative is to hire outside labour to write the programs. If this is to be on a simple time basis, it is subject to difficulties similar to those outlined above. The problems attendant upon such contracts of service will be considered in more detail in a following section. The remaining two alternatives involve dealing with a 'software house', a firm which deals in programming. Exceptionally, and more especially before the general adoption of the practice of 'unbundling', it was possible to contract for such programming to be carried out by the hardware supplier, though such suppliers often sought to avoid explicit reference to any such promise of assistance in their formal contracts.[55] If a contract is to be made with a software house, then it is necessary to make a further distinction between the acquisition of a proprietary package, like a suit off the peg, and the acquisition of a set of specially written programs, like a bespoke suit.[56] In fact the distinction is often rather blurred since a specially written set of programs may well contain some standard modules, and a proprietary package may be modified in some small respects to fit the customer's particular requirements.

If the customer merely wishes a well-defined function to be performed and

53. 361 F.Supp. 325 (E.D. Pa., 1973) at 334.
54. For an example of the problems created for a small first-time user by attempting to program for itself, see *Whelan Associates* v. *Jaslow Dental Laboratory* 797 F.2d 1222 (3rd Cir., 1986).
55. See, for example, *Carl Beasley Ford Inc.* v. *Burroughs Corp.* 361 F.Supp. 325 (E.D.Pa., 1973); *International Business Machines Corp.* v. *Catamore Enterprises Inc.* 548 F.2d 1066 (D.R.I., 1976)
56. This distinction may also be important for some tax purposes, see *Computer Sciences Corp.* v. *Commissioner of Internal revenue* 63 T.C. 327 (U.S. Tax Ct., 1974).

is sure that a proprietary package will be able to perform the function without any significant modification or adaptation, he may wish to acquire it. He may be able to buy it, but it will be much more common for a licence to be made available, for the reasons to be explained in a later section.[57] In essence, such a licensor seeks to retain greater control over the use of the program. In particular, he will be anxious not to allow any use which might prejudice future revenue accruing from use of the program. Thus the customer will usually be restricted to using it for his own purposes, often on only one machine, and with even more explicit restrictions upon disposal. The supplier will also often seek to protect his position by supplying the program only in the relatively opaque object code version so as to preserve secrecy and to prevent reverse engineering.[58] If this course is adopted, and the customer may have no alternative, then he will be well advised to specify in the most minute detail possible the computer environment in which the package must work, and its performance specification, wherever possible keying the completion of the contract, or at least payments made under it, to their satisfaction.

The final alternative is for the customer to contract for a set of programs to be written by the software house so as to perform a set of operations explicitly specified by the customer. If the customer is unable to do this, he should first contract for the supply of such a specification, preferably by a firm not intended as the ultimate supplier of the package.[59] Even after the drawing up of such a specification there are likely to be at least two further stages in the programming, first a detailed systems design, typically delimiting the modules into which the program is to be broken down, and the relationships between them, and then the actual coding in the chosen source code.[60] One of the problems is that this form of software contract will most often be adopted when the customer knows least about computing. There is a significant danger of misunderstanding between customer and supplier. Thus in *Catamore*, although the supplier referred to systems design, the lay customer believed that final coding was encompassed. Such initial misunderstanding may have cumulative ill effects. The customer may not have understood enough about computers to have foreseen exactly which parts of his business would benefit, so he may want to add further features as he gains more understanding, and the supplier may not have been made aware enough of the nature of the customer's business to see immediately which approach to the systems design and programming would yield the best results. It is the danger of such altered specifications and implementations which makes the estimation of the cost of programming so problematical. The best that can be done is to specify as precisely as possible what needs to be accomplished in the invitation to tender, and to refine it in the outline

---

57. See below p. 180.
58. In *Com-share Inc.* v. *Computer Complex Inc.* 338 F.Supp. 1229 (E.D. Mich., 1971) a package in such a form was held still to be a proprietary trade secret despite installation at the sites of numerous customers.
59. *McArdle* v. *Board of Estimates of the City of Mount Vernon* 347 N.Y.S.2d 349 (N.Y., 1973) for a case illustrating the dangers of ignoring such a precaution.
60. See *International Business Machines Corp.* v. *Catamore Enterprises Inc.* 548 F.2d 1066 (D.R.I., 1976) at 1068.

system design. Unfortunately, even the largest and most knowledgeable contractors are not immune from slipshod specification. Two particularly glaring examples concerned contracts for law oriented packages in which lawyers might have been expected to be involved in drawing the specifications. Thus in one the National Labour Relations Board was prevented from awarding a contract for the design and implementation of a legal retrieval and typesetting system,[61] while in another the County of Los Angeles was advised that it could not sue for the allegedly defective performance of a court information system,[62] in both cases because the specifications were so vague and ambiguous. The casual and ignorant attitude of some smaller customers is well illustrated by *Rossi Quality Foods Inc.* v. *Friden Inc.*[63] In that case the customer, a frozen pizza wholesaler, wished to automate his office procedures. No care was taken over the job specification despite every effort by the supplier, including submission of the ultimate specifications for scrutiny and signature by the customer. The system had to be continually reprogrammed to meet subsequent changes in specification. When it was finally ready the customer refused to inspect its performance before installation on his premises, and declined the supplier's suggestion that he should run his old system in parallel for a time to ensure that the new installation was working properly. Finally, despite elaborate training programmes conducted by the experienced supplier, the customer's employees used the system with almost incredible ignorance and ineptitude by, for example, annotating one punched paper tape with instructions in ink, and even cutting and splicing it back together with sticky tape. It is not surprising both that the customer's defence of defective performance to an action for the price was rejected, and that he subsequently and speedily became bankrupt.

Once a satisfactory specification of the requirements has been defined it may be possible to construct the contract so as to key acceptance and payments to successive stages of development. The development of satisfactory testing procedures may itself provide useful information in the light of which specifications may be revised. If at all possible, it is desirable to construct the contract so that payments are staged and keyed to the satisfaction of the relevant tests and, wherever possible, actual delivery of the program module. These techniques assist both parties. The tests may enable the customer to prove breach or the supplier to prove satisfactory performance much more easily than if the contract is left vague.[64] It should be noted that however carefully designed they may be, it is impossible for any set of tests to be completely comprehensive, in the sense of testing every aspect of the program under all possible conditions. It is usually most satisfactory for the testing to take place on the premises of the customer, and in the course of his normal operations. It is not clear that evidence of tests done on the manufacturer's prototype will even be admissible as relevant to the perform-

---

61. *National Labour Relations Board* 51 Comp. Gen. 635 (1972).
62. See advice of City Counsel dated 10 August 1973 as reported in 4 C.L.S.R. 912.
63. 4 C.L.S.R. 912 (N.D. Ill., 1973).
64. In *California Computer Products Inc.* 4 C.L.S.R. 1449 (1972) the prospective supplier complained that a request for proposals by the Navy had not provided for such performance test of the software required.

ance of production models in the field.[65] Nor will any such acceptance tests necessarily indicate satsifactory performance. In *Sha-1 Corp.* v. *City and County of San Francisco*[66] the acceptance tests were carefully devised and satisfactorily completed, but nevertheless performance was soon afterwards regarded as so unsatisfactory that the defendant refused to make even the first payment under the relevant contract. However, he was held liable for failing to do so, so the moral is that such tests *must* fully reflect operational conditions. It is partly for this reason that attempts are being made to devise methods of mathematical analysis capable of much more comprehensive coverage of programs. Although such techniques are still under development, they are beginning to be adopted by some large concerns in the computer industry.[67]

The software industry contains many talented, but small and undercapitalised firms. In these circumstances the parties walk a financial tightrope. It helps the software house if it can receive staged payments in advance, and it provides security to the customer to receive something that he can use for the payments that he makes. It is not always possible to achieve a perfect solution to the problem by staged and keyed payments in this way, however, since the heaviest requirement is likely to be at the development stage when the tangible results are slightest, and even when modules are delivered they may not be easily used if their supplier goes out of business, and has to be replaced by another who will inevitably adopt a somewhat different approach to the problem.

3. Security provisions[68]

The least glamorous, but a most useful, aspect of programming is its documentation. Any contract for software should seek to provide for the fullest documentation which the supplier can be induced to provide. This documentation should contain an explanation of the general principles of the supplier's approach to the problem, the detailed system design, operating instructions and, wherever possible, copies of source code. If the supplier disappears from the scene for whatever reason, the provision of such documentation is likely to minimise, though it will not remove, the difficulties of another supplier upon taking over the project. Although their provision is unpopular there should be little trouble in securing all of the above forms of documentation, except the source code. Software suppliers rightly regard their source coding as their most valuable resource, and fear that if it is supplied to their customers it will somehow or another become available to further users, otherwise than by payment to them or, worse still, will become the basis upon which someone else markets an improved

---

65. See *Renfro Hosiery Mills Co.* v. *National Cash Register Co.* 552 F.2d 1061 (4th Cir., 1977).
66. 612 F.2d 1215 (9th Cir., 1980).
67. For example, by International Business Machines in the design of one of its operating systems, see *Computer Weekly* 29 September 1988 p. 17. The two most common languages are Z developed at Oxford University and VDM developed by IBM Vienna.
68. For a full account of the position in the United States, see Hemnes and Montgomery, 'The Bankruptcy Code, The Copyright Act and Transactions in Computer Software', *7 Comp. L.J.* 327 (1987). See, in addition, the Intellectual Property Bankruptcy Protection Act 1988 which is designed to ameliorate the worst effects of the previous position.

product. As so many software houses seem to be successful with only one product, this is an understandable fear. On the other hand, customers fear that if they do not have access to the source code they will be unable to keep their system updated, or replaced in case of catastrophic accident, if the supplier disappears. The usual compromise is to contract for the deposit of the source code with an independent third party upon condition that it will be released only in certain specified eventualities, such as the supplier going out of business.

It is common, both in the United States[69] and in the United Kingdom,[70] to refer to the deposit of source code for security purposes as an escrow agreement. Such a deposit may also be used for other reasons, such as the establishment of an archive recording changes made to programs, or so as to provide a means of recourse in case of physical disaster to programs held at a computer installation. It is apparent that the form of deposit may need to be different according to the purpose which it is designed to serve. When it is to be used as a means of providing access to the source code in case the supplier fails to maintain the program, either because he has gone out of business or for some other reason, the question arises of how far such an arrangement is likely to be effective. This will depend upon the precise nature of the contract for the supply of the software, and of the laws of bankruptcy and intellectual property in computer programs of the jurisdiction in question.[71] It is possible to do no more here than to indicate the nature of the difficulties which may arise. It may be accepted that the usual contract for the supply of software gives to the customer only a licence to use the program, and typically restricts copying, beyond that necessary to support the customer's own use, and deliberately withholds source code in order to preserve secrecy, and to preserve any rights to trade secrets. By such means the supplier retains some rights under the law of intellectual property in the programs. He often binds himself to perform some services, such as the supply of revised versions or corrections, or the provision of advice, free or on favourable terms, partly in order to keep himself informed of the location of his program, and partly to provide evidence in case of any dispute as to the terms upon which the program was supplied. The user may be prepared to accept supply on those terms so long as the supplier is able and willing to provide the relevant services. However, as a business can rapidly become completely dependent upon its key software, it needs to have any errors corrected, to have it kept current so that it will run with subsequently developed software and machines, and to have it modified as business conditions and needs change. Such a customer may feel that this can be accomplished only if he has access to the source code of the program if conditions should change, and the supplier becomes unable or unwilling to provide these services. It should perhaps be noted that source code alone is

---

69. See, for example, Nycum, Kenfield and Keenan 'Debugging Software Escrow: Will It Work When You Need It?', *4 Comp. L.J.* 441 (1984).
70. See, for example, Morris, 'What Sort of Protection Can Users Expect?' *Computer Weekly* 9 July 1987 p. 10.
71. The position in the United States is much complicated by its requirement that copyright be registered before it can be enforced, a requirement from which the United Kingdom is mercifully free. See above p. 57.

unlikely to be sufficient for most of these purposes and, at a minimum, full documentation of the program should also be made accessible. A common technique is to seek to have these materials deposited with a third party on terms that they will be released to the customer upon the satisfaction of certain conditions, such as that the supplier goes out of business, or that he fails to provide the relevant services upon demand. The difficulty is that the eventuality thought most likely to occur is that the software house may cease trading because of financial difficulty. In such a case, however, its assets, legal and equitable, may become vested in a liquidator[72] or a trustee in bankruptcy.[73] These assets are expressly defined to include intangible property. If this is the case, the escrow agreement would then appear to be ineffective, since the customer will fail to gain just those rights to copy and use trade secrets for which he secured deposit with a third party in the first place. The liquidator or trustee also has the power in the United Kingdom to disclaim any onerous property,[74] and in the United States 'any executory contract or unexpired lease of the debtor'.[75] In the United States it was decided in *Lubrizol Enterprises Inc.* v. *Richmond Metal Finishers Inc.*[76] that a trustee could so repudiate a technology licence, so long as it were non-exclusive.[77] The effect of such rejection is to convert the customer's right to performance of the supplier's obligations into an unsecured right to damages for non-performance. Even in the case of an exclusive licence it would be essential for the initial deposit to have been arranged early enough to avoid any suggestion of fraudulent preference. This decision was severely detrimental to the whole concept of licensing agreements in respect of intellectual property since it meant that licensees were liable to be divested of their rights to use the subject matter of a licence upon the happening of the highly uncertain future event of the licensor's insolvency, without being able to secure any adequate specific remedy. This situation has now been reformed by the passage of the Intellectual Property Licenses and Bankruptcy Act 1988[78] which permits the licensee to elect to continue the licence, or to retrieve the source code from escrow, subject only to continuing to make royalty payments. The licensee cannot, however, require any positive act, such as continuation of efforts to enhance the licensed product. Nor does the Act affect the law relating to trade marks. The broad analogy is to the protection of lessees of real property, though here in the case of intellectual property licences protection applies even before the licence term has started to run. It is, of course, of the essence of any such arrangement that the escrow agent be completely independent of both customer and supplier.[79] In

---

72. In the United Kingdom under the provisions of the Insolvency Act 1986 sect. 145.

73. In the United States under 11 U.S.C. sect. 541.

74. Insolvency Act 1986 sect. 178. Defined by sub-sect. 3 as '(a) any unprofitable contract, and (b) any other property of the company which is unsaleable or not readily saleable or is such that it may give rise to a liability to pay money or perform any other onerous act'.

75. 11 U.S.C. sect. 365.

76. 756 F.2d 1043 (4th Cir., 1985).

77. If it were exclusive then it might still not avail the user unless the transfer of copyright were registered under the copyright legislation.

78. P.L. 100–506. Operating by way of amendment of 11 U.S.C. sect. 365.

79. In practice there is no difficulty in finding public bodies such as the National Computing Centre in the United Kingdom, or specialist companies, to act in this capacity. There is usually scope for negotiation over how the fee is divided between customer and supplier.

any case, where a number of different copies of a program have been licensed it is conceivable that an escrow arrangement will be set up in such a fashion that licensees are given an option to join in such a scheme. If this is the case, then it will be necessary for the option to have been exercised before any insolvency arises.

Quite apart from such complications in the case of insolvency, this type of escrow agreement can present problems. It is effective only if the supplier does in fact deposit the code[80] and then regularly keeps it up to date and well-documented, but the whole aim of the process is to prevent the customer having access to the program before the occurrence of the relevant conditions. How then is the customer to know that such deposit and regular up-dating has taken place? The best answer may be to incorporate well-defined notice requirements, supported by a requirement for demonstration of the operation of the deposited program. A further difficulty, because of the dependence of customers upon their software, is the need to move very rapidly when the conditions for release of the program are claimed to have been satisfied. This may often be contentious, so it is as well to include some, preferably self-executing, provision for speedy arbitration of this limited question.

D. Maintenance contracts[81]

It is quite common for contracts of acquisition relating to both hardware and software to contain provisions relating to their maintenance after the expiration of a usually short warranty period. It is, however, generally more satisfactory for maintenance contracts to be separate from the main agreement since quite different considerations apply, and it is nowadays becoming increasingly common for maintenance to be provided otherwise than from the original supplier.[82] This is especially true at the bottom end of the market, where the very variety of different types of machine makes third-party maintenance attractive in limiting the number of contracts and so reducing all the associated administrative problems. It is convenient to distinguish between the maintenance of hardware and software since the notion of maintenance is rather different in the two cases. These will accordingly be considered separately, and then a final section will deal with special considerations relating to third-party maintenance.

1. Hardware maintenance

The apparent advantage of having equipment maintained by its manufacturer is that he is likely to understand the equipment best so as to be most able to diagnose faults, have the readiest access to spare parts so as to be best able to repair, or more likely replace, them fastest. These advantages are,

---

80. For a case where the software house appears to have failed to make an agreed deposit, see *Patriot General Life Insurance Co.* v. *CFC Investment Co.* 420 N.E.2d 918 (Mass., 1981).
81. See Martin and Deasy, 'Licensing of Intellectual Property Rights Needed for Software Support: A Life Cycle Approach' *28 Jur. J.* 223 (1988).
82. Third-party suppliers had some 10 per cent of the United Kingdom market of £1.6 billion in 1988, see *Financial Times* 26 January 1989 p. 21.

however, somewhat illusory. Although the hardware supplier may understand the hardware very well, he will not necessarily understand so well other hardware forming part of the system or the software running on it, especially the applications software. Since he is not responsible for such other hardware or software, in cases where the precise cause of the failure is uncertain, he may be inclined to blame the other manufacturer's equipment[83] or the software.[84] It may also be the case that the manufacturer's charges for replacement equipment are higher than those offered by third-party suppliers. In some cases manufacturers rely upon the steady flow of revenue from maintenance contracts to keep the prices for their hardware at a competitive level. In such circumstances it is important from the customer's point of view to negotiate the maintenance contract at the same time as the contract for the acquisition of the hardware. It is quite common for maintenance charges to be fixed as a percentage of the cost of the hardware. If a vendor is extolling the reliability of his hardware it becomes difficult for him, at the same time, to press for a high fixed price for maintenance. The manufacturer may also seek to tie the provision of maintenance to the exclusive use of the manufacturer's hardware. The trend has run against such restrictive practices both in the United States[85] and in Europe.[86] Perhaps as a result of these developments the latest trend seems to have been in the opposite direction with manufacturers increasingly being prepared not only to maintain their own equipment despite the addition of third party components, but even entering the business of maintaining equipment wholly provided by other manufacturers.[87]

A further advantage of contracting for hardware maintenance so far as the manufacturer is concerned is that it keeps him in touch with his market. He can get earlier intelligence of a change in the business environment of the customer which might induce him to enhance or upgrade his equipment, or of any proposal to change suppliers. Such information will, however, be acquired only by regular on-site visits, and these are most likely to be necessary whenever the maintenance agreement contains a preventive element. Such an element should specify the number of such visits to be conducted, though with the advent of more sophisticated communications and maintenance programs much more can nowadays be conducted on a remote basis. In the case of hardware in particular the most urgent aspect of maintenance is likely to be remedial maintenance. Some businesses have a computer at their heart, and are as dependent upon its continued operation as their human analog. It is vital to provide, so far as possible, for guaranteed working and, so far as it is not possible, for guaranteed repair or replacement times. It has become possible for suppliers to offer machines,

---

83. See, for example, *Strand* v. *Librascope Inc.* 197 F.Supp. 744 (E.D. Mich., 1961).
84. See, for example, *Bruffey* v. *Burroughs Corp.* 522 F.Supp. 769 (D. Md., 1981) at 774.
85. *Digidyne Corp.* v. *Data General Corp.* 734 F.2d 1336 (9th Cir., 1984).
86. It may, for example, amount to a restraint of trade at common law in the United Kingdom, or constitute a referable monopoly practice under the Fair Trading Act 1973 sect. 7, or may be in breach of Art. 86 of the Treaty of Rome as an abuse of a dominant trading position.
87. Thus Control Data Corp. has announced a programme to maintain IBM equipment, see *Computerworld* 5 September 1988 p. 10.

which by parallel working can guarantee continuous operation, though this is expensive and can be justified only in the most sensitive environments. In other situations it is more common for the contract to specify an overall minimum of time out of commission, or down-time. However, the negotiation of such terms is complicated by the modular nature of most systems, and by differences between the sensitivity of different businesses to failure in particular components or at particular times. If there are such critical differences an overall guaranteed percentage of operating efficiency on a temporal basis, or an average mean time between failures is unlikely to be satisfactory, even if 'down-time' or 'failure' can be satisfactorily defined, and the application of the definitions agreed. Another common provision in terms regulating remedial maintenance is a guaranteed response time. This too requires careful definition, and should be supplemented by a guaranteed repair or replacement time. The enforcement of such agreements is also problematical. The customer is in a weak position. Litigation in respect of defective maintenance is unlikely to be worthwhile, and the mere withholding of payments is unlikely to be effective. The best guarantee of satisfactory performance is probably the development of a thriving third-party maintenance sector. The best contractual course may be to set up a system of credits and debits, whereby payments under the contract are reduced by failures to honour the contractual prescriptions, and credits are allowed for superior performance. In negotiating such terms it is important to realise that the value of performance to the customer may not be linear, in the sense that he gets much less benefit from a 1 per cent improvement in 'down-time' than the damage he suffers by a 1 per cent deterioration in it.

2. Software maintenance

From this point of view the most important difference between hardware and software is that software is currently marketed, and known to be marketed, in a state in which it has not been tested in all of the situations in which it will be used. Although formal specification and testing may one day reduce this problem, they will not eliminate it. It is fair to say that all software undergoes a continuing process of development from its first conception until its final abandonment. Because the perceived utility of computers derives from running applications software, it has to respond to every change in business conditions, and in the computer environment in which it operates. Applications software must respond both to increased demands and to enhanced opportunities. Because it does not have the same bedrock of physical science it has been difficult to devise consistent and communicable standards for software. It is one thing to specify input and output voltages, or pin placements for enhancements to hardware; it is quite another to ensure compatibility of one program with another. As a last resort every element of a hardware configuration is susceptible of physical examination, but it would be impossible to observe the operation of every possible permutation of the operations of any complex program, and the operation of all business or personal computers involves the operation of at least one highly complex program, its operating system.

Software maintenance has been analysed into three components,[88] corrective, perfective and adaptive maintenance. Corrective maintenance is essentially the correction of errors which become apparent during the operation of the program, often preventing it from producing usable output. Perfective maintenance refers to the improvement of a program so as to make it operate more efficiently or more usefully. Adaptive maintenance is concerned with the adaptation of software so as to enable it to interact with newly developed hardware or software, both systems and applications software. It has been estimated that the bulk of program maintenance falls into the latter two categories. Such an analysis suggests that the closer analogy is to a software development contract than to a hardware maintenance contract. It makes much less sense in the case of software to negotiate in terms of 'down-time' and 'mean time between failures' than in terms of ability to interact with other nominated hardware, operating systems or applications programs. In the case of packaged software it is likely that the supplier will make periodic changes as a matter of course. It is as well to negotiate in advance for the provision of such improvements, any preferential pricing that might be available, and whether the use of the new version should be mandatory or optional. In the case of bespoke software there will be no automatic periodic enhancement unless it is negotiated in advance, but the cost is likely to be high, since the supplier will be putting in almost as much effort as in the original development, but will be recouping it from only one customer. In such a case, however, it is quite likely that the customer's own staff may acquire sufficient familiarity with the operation of the software to be able to enhance it, at least by adaptation to changed conditions. In order to accomplish this they will almost certainly require access to the source code, and this will require negotiation with the software supplier. Since much ostensibly custom-built software is, in fact, based upon a number of standard modules, it may be possible to negotiate upon the basis that the supplier is licensed to exploit the customer-provided enhancements in other applications, though it is, of course, necessary to establish title to such improvements quite definitively. In any case the very nature of software, and the strong analogy to development contracts, dictates the supreme importance of securing adequate documentation of any changes made to software in the course of its maintenance in any of these senses.

3. Third party maintenance

As noted above, third-party maintenance, particularly of hardware, is becoming increasingly popular with customers. It can operate only if the third party is in a position to supply equipment parts and software which will operate successfully in connection with the original hardware and software. In order to operate successfully it is also desirable for the third party to have access to diagnostic programs similar to those used by suppliers, and to the source code and documentation of any relevant programs. Some difficulties have been placed in the way of third party

---

88. In Martin and Deasy, 'Licensing of Intellectual Property Rights Needed for Software Support: A Life Cycle Approach', *28 Jur. J.* 223 (1988).

suppliers in these respects. As also noted above, such obstacles to third party maintenance have been frowned upon by legislators.[89] In the United Kingdom the House of Lords has even construed copyright law in such a way as to permit a market for third party supply of spare parts for machines to continue.[90] The courts have also been alert to avert other legal threats to third-party maintenance. Thus in one case[91] an Anton Piller order[92] in respect of maintenance testing programs which it was alleged the third party had misappropriated from the original manufacturer was discharged because action was taken only to stifle competitive maintenance. In another,[93] a third-party maintenance firm contracted to buy a computer complete with operating software from its manufacturer. Because it was aware that the purchaser was a third party maintainer, the manufacturer excluded from the operating system error logging and automatic diagnostic modules normally supplied in cases where the manufacturer also contracted to provide mainte- nance. It was held that these modules were included within the contractually defined operating system, and had to be supplied to the third party. In the United States it has been stated[94] that it is immaterial that the tying practice occurs only after the supply of the tying product, so the delivery of a computer system inoperable without a maintenance contract which it was then insisted should be supplied by the supplier would probably[95] infringe the Sherman Act.[96] As important as such tools are the qualifications of those who are to wield them. It is clearly important for third-party maintainers to employ maintenance engineers with sufficient knowledge and experience of maintaining the relevant equipment. Third-party maintainers are often prepared to go to considerable lengths to lure trained engineers from the manufacturers. The constraints upon such practices, and counters to them, will be considered more fully in the next section.

Hardware seems to have become increasingly reliable, probably as a result of better quality control during the manufacturing process. This may at times create a gap between the pessimistic expectations of users and current reality. If this is manifested in a readiness to pay an unjustifiably high price for maintenance, there may be a temptation for third parties to enter the market, not with a view to maintaining equipment themselves, but merely contracting to do so, and then sub-contracting on an *ad hoc* basis. It is arguable that in the United Kingdom any such activity would require a

---

89. As being monopolistic and subject to anti-trust, monopoly, restrictive practices, fair trading, and competition legislation.
90. *British Leyland Motor Corp.* v. *Armstrong Patents Co.* [1986] A.C. 577, H.L. It is interesting that features of configuration are expressly excluded from the new regime of design right instituted by the Copyright, Designs and Patents Act 1988 sect. 213(3)(b), and even though the new legislation modifies the general effect of the *British Leyland* case it is, in effect, preserved in any case where there is anti-competitive abuse by sect. 238 of the Copyright, Designs and Patents Act 1988.
91. *Burroughs Corp.* v. *Computer Investments Ltd.* LEXIS report 23 June 1986, Ch.
92. See above p. 71.
93. *DPCE* v. *ICL Ltd.* LEXIS report 31 July 1985, Q.B.
94. *MDC Data Centers Inc.* v. *International Business Machines Corp.* 342 F.Supp. 502 (E.D. Pa., 1972).
95. The statement was *obiter* because on the facts there was no evidence of any such insistence.
96. 15 U.S.C. sect. 1.

licence from the Department of Trade and Industry to carry on the business of insurance, given that in such a case the customer pays a sum of money, the maintenance fee, in return for compensation in money's worth, the repair or replacement of defective equipment, upon the occurrence of an uncertain event, the breakdown of the system.

E. Personnel contracts

These fall into many different categories. It has already been noted that one type of software development contract is upon the basis of the supply of services from an outside supplier. Such contracts slide by imperceptible stages into consultancy agreements, depending upon the degree of specificity of any programming tasks to be performed. In any case, except that of the one-man business, and sometimes even then, there will also be a contract of employment to be considered. These three scenarios will be considered separately, though there is a considerable degree of overlapping between them.

1. Programming services contracts

As explained in a previous section of this chapter, a supplier of programming services will prefer to contract on a temporal basis wherever he can, rather than commit himself to contracting for the completion of a task which may be difficult to gauge in advance, and which may be subject to continual need for adjustment. However, customers are inclined to baulk at such open-ended commitments. One technique to try to overcome such reservations is to provide an estimate of cost, perhaps accompanied by a right to terminate if the estimate is exceeded. None but the most naive and trusting of customers is likely to be gulled by such an arrangement. The option of termination is illusory once the customer has committed expense and the expiration of, often vital, time to the project. A more satisfactory option would be for the customer to seek to insert a clause permitting the conversion of the completion of the contract to a fixed fee basis upon the estimate being exceeded, subject to the fixing of an arbitrated amount if the parties are unable to agree. By the stage of excess over estimate it is more likely that a realistic estimate of further cost can be arrived at. Further protection is provided in such a situation, as previously explained, by staging payment to the delivery of usable modules and adequate documentation. Express provision for the customer to be able to terminate and to secure completion by another contractor may also be a useful accompaniment to such a payment provision. It may not, however, be possible to secure such a provision, either because of disparity of negotiating leverage, or simply because the nature of the job does not permit such dissection into modules.

Any such agreement should contain all provisions necessary to govern the accommodation of the supplier's services into the customer's working environment. Agreement should be reached upon where the work is to be performed, the numbers and quality of the personnel assigned to it, and their rate of remuneration. The question of such elements as overhead cost and employee benefits should be covered explicitly. It is sometimes desirable for the work to take place upon the premises of the supplier, for example, if the customer's computer has not been installed at the time that the software is being written. In such cases it is fair that some overhead costs should be allocated in the pricing. The contract should be quite explicit about the formulae for charging these, since suppliers engaged upon a mix of fixed and variable fee work will naturally seek to load such costs upon the variable fee work.[97] Any contingent liabilities of the customer to the supplier's employees if the contract is prematurely terminated should also be spelled out explicitly.[98]

2. Consultancy contracts

In any area of valuable arcane expertise there is a need for access to that expertise, and in the computer industry it is frequently provided by consultants, who may practise either as individuals or as employees of larger firms. Partly because the industry has developed so recently and so fast, and partly because the scope of computing applications is so vast, there has never been the same tight professional organisation as is to be found in such other areas of arcane expertise as law, medicine or accounting. It follows that the framework of the relationship needs to be prescribed to a much greater extent by the consultancy contract. Unfortunately such contracts are typically among the most informal to be found in this area.

Consultancy agreements can cover an almost unlimited range of activities from the most general advice to the provision of detailed remedial coding. Consultants may in some cases verge upon being employees, for example when paid a substantial annual retainer and required to work on an exclusive basis, or at the other end of the scale may verge upon being completely independent suppliers as, for example, when required for a fixed fee to produce a particular piece of code. However, more usually such contracts are on a time and materials basis, plus reimbursement of out-of-pocket expenses. In many cases a consultant is engaged just because the customer knows so little about computing, and in such circumstances there is no realistic possibility of defining the consultant's role with any great precision. However, it is necessary, so far as possible, to cater for the consultant's capacity, independence and reliability.

If the customer knows little about computing he may be in a weak position to appraise the consultant's capacity before engaging him. He should, of course, do what he can by way of examining formal qualifications, experience and references. However, in the computer industry these are perhaps less likely to be predictive of performance than in others. In such circumstances the only recourse is to ensure that any contract is terminable at short notice, and to seek regular means of checking performance whether by the submission of reports or the accomplishment of practical tasks. It should be noted that dismissal is the most effective remedy for defective performance. It is most unlikely that a consultant would be prepared to give

---

97. See *Wolf Research and Development Corporation* 1 C.L.S.R. 1074 (1969).
98. See *Telecomputing Services Inc.* 1 C.L.S.R. 953 (1968).

a warranty of effective performance sufficient to ground an action and, as will be explained further below, there is no established strict remedy for professional malpractice in the computer industry.[99] The customer will be thrown back upon a cause of action in negligence, and that may be very difficult to establish. An approach sometimes adopted in an attempt to ensure competence is to employ as a consultant in his spare time someone who is a full-time employee of another. This may sometimes be an indicator of competence, but it is not always an indicator of reliability. In such a case the customer would be wise to ensure that the consultancy is known to, and accepted by, the consultant's full-time employer.

Clearly the advice of a full-time employee of another firm, working as a consultant with his employer's permission, would be regarded with some scepticism so far as it related, directly or indirectly, to his full-time employer's interests. Unfortunately it is not always so clear that the advice of a consultant is not completely disinterested. In one particularly flagrant case a consultant was called in to advise a bank, which already had a computer, upon the design of its data-processing systems. He designed and programmed a system which could not be run on the bank's computer with the result that time had to be hired on his own firm's machine, yet it was established that any competent programmer could equally well have designed a system to accomplish the given objectives which would have run on the bank's computer.[100] In another case[101] a consultant spent four months investigating an exceedingly complex administrative structure with a view to automation. He conducted numerous feasibility tests and summarised his conclusions in a long report. That report was then used to solicit proposals for the supply of such a system giving prospective purchasers only five days to raise queries, and a further five in which to submit tenders. The feasibility studies were made available only to one firm, that of the consultant. It is hardly surprising that it turned out to be the sole bidder. In some cases, such results could be avoided by some form of restriction upon competitive activity or conflict of interest, though they might on occasion prove very difficult to draft efficiently and validly.

A related concern is the preservation of trade secrets and confidential information which either come into the hands of the consultant or are created during the course of the consultancy. Provision should certainly be made in the consultancy agreement for the preservation of such secrets and confidences, both during the course of the consultancy and after its termination. In some cases it may also be necessary to make express provision about the ownership of any intellectual property created during the course of the consultancy. Many of these matters are also relevant, and the law relating to them better developed in the rules relating to ordinary contracts of employment.

---

99. See *La Rossa* v. *Scientific Design Co.* 402 F.2d 937 (3rd Cir., 1968); *Chatlos Sysems Inc.* v. *NCR Corp.* 635 F.2d 1081 (3rd Cir., 1980).
100. *Trilog Associates Inc.* v. *Famularo* 314 A.2d 287 (Pa., 1974).
101. *McArdle* v. *Board of Estimates of the City of Mount Vernon* 347 N.Y.S.2d 349 (N.Y., 1973).

3. Contracts of employment[102]

Some parts of the computer industry are highly competitive. In particular, the demand for trained and experienced personnel has so far tended to outstrip the supply. The main reason for this is that in many areas the industry is so young and developing so fast that formal training is either non-existent or irrelevant, and there is no substitute for experience, but this is itself in limited supply. It is further the case that the costs of the independent development of programs are invariably greater than that of their reconstruction by someone familiar with the relevant area from having programmed it before.[103] Whatever the reason, competition is always fierce, and often unscrupulous. The law reports are littered with examples of raiding operations conducted by one firm upon another, ostensibly for people's innate talents, but really for the benefit of their experience. Therein lies the legal difficulty. If the raiding firm can show that it is interested only in the employee and his natural talent, quite divorced from the training, experience, contacts and information bestowed upon him by his former employer, then all is well. Thus in one case[104] it was held permissible for an employee, who had developed one of two existing programs upon which a new program to accomplish a particular task could be based, to leave, and go on to develop the other for his new employer. This is rare. In most cases there are several major sources of legal liability,[105] one in tort for the misappropriation of trade secrets or confidential information,[106] one in quasi-contract arising from betrayal of a relationship of trust, independent of contract, and one in contract for breach of express, or occasionally implied, terms requiring the preservation of secrecy, or restricting post-termination conduct. The rules relating to trade secrets and to misappropriation are dealt with more fully in other chapters.[107]

In a very few raiding situations there is no remedy under any of these theories. Thus in *Republic Systems and Programming Inc.* v. *Computer Assistance Inc.*[108] the employees had no formal contracts of employment, and were thus held entitled to terminate without notice or cause. The prime mover was a vice-president of the plaintiff company and the head of one of its three branch offices. He wrote his letter of resignation on a Friday, knowing that it would not be delivered until the following Monday. Previous customers of the plaintiff were then immediately solicited. This devious and damaging conduct was not actionable in contract since there was no applicable implied term, and not in quasi-contract or tort since no confidential or secret

---

102. For a full account, see Wheeler, 'Trade Secrets and the Skilled Employee in the Computer Industry', *61 U.Wash.* 823 (1983).
103. In *Computer Print Systems Inc.* v. *Lewis* 422 A.2d 148 (Pa., 1980) it was estimated that a program which would take four months to write without such assistance might have been done in ten days with it.
104. *Electronic Data Systems Corp.* v. *Kinder* 360 F.Supp. 1044 (N.D. Tex., 1973).
105. There may also be criminal liability for conspiracy, or in some jurisdictions for fraud or theft.
106. In appropriate circumstances there might also be tortious liability for conspiracy, inducement of breach of contract, interference with contract or passing-off.
107. See ch. 3 for trade secrets and ch. 7 for misappropriation.
108. 322 F.Supp. 619 (D. Conn., 1970), aff. 440 F.2d 996 (2nd Cir., 1971).

materials of the plaintiff were held to have been used.

However, generally there is a formal contract, and generally it does contain provisions relating to confidential materials, and to subsequent competitive employment. It should be noted, however, that in order to constitute a term of the contract the provision must be supported by consideration. It has been held that where an employer simply requires an existing employee to sign such a provision, without offering any material improvement in his contractual status,[109] such a provision lacks consideration and will not be enforced.[110] It might be otherwise if the formal contract were merely recording a prior oral contract. Nor would this doctrine affect the situation where as a matter of trust there was an obligation independent of any contract to maintain confidentiality, for example in the case of an unpaid non-executive director of a company. If there is such a provision in a valid contract it is likely to be construed fairly strictly, especially if it is a standard printed form. Thus in *Amoco Production Co.* v. *Lindley*[111] the contract explicitly imposed obligations to keep secret 'inventions and discoveries' made by the employee. The appellate court construed these terms narrowly, and found on the facts that the computer program in question had not been treated in such a way as to constitute a trade secret.

If there is a valid contractual term which applies to the particular computer programs in question, a two-stage test must be undertaken, first to discover whether there is any duty owed outside the contract, and then whether the contract imposes one. This is very clearly illustrated in *Structural Dynamics Research Corp.* v. *Engineering Mechanics Research Corp.*[112] So far as the non-contractual stage was concerned, the court distinguished between cases where the employer introduced his employee to an existing secret program, and those in which the employee developed the program himself during the course of his employment. The non-contractual obligation would be more likely to be found to exist in the former situation. Even in the latter it might still be found if the employee was assigned such development as a specific task, and given full support by his employer in its accomplishment.[113] It was found here that the circumstances under which the program was written vested no claim in the employer in tort or quasicontract, so it was necessary to examine the contractual terms. They had been freely entered into by the employees in question,[114] covered the programs in issue, and signally failed

109. In *Modern Controls Inc.* v. *Andreadakis* 578 F.2d 1264 (8th Cir., 1978) a promise either to release the employee from the obligation not to compete, or to pay him his salary for the two years of its duration was held to be good consideration.
110. *Jostens Inc.* v. *National Computer Systems Inc.* 318 N.W.2d 394 (Minn.,1982), but see *J & K Computer Systems Inc.* v. *Parrish* 642 P.2d 733 (Ut., 1982) where this point seems to have been overlooked. In *Aries Information Systems Inc.* v. *Pacific Management Systems Corp.* 366 N.W.2d 366 (Minn., 1985) the point was taken, and rejected, but apparently only on the basis that the attempt to impose the provision was evidence of the secret nature of the program to which it referred, and of the employer's efforts to maintain such secrecy.
111. 609 P.2d 735 (Ok., 1980).
112. 401 F.Supp. 1102 (E.D. Mich., 1975).
113. It would be hard to find a greater contrast to these conditions than those present in *Amoco Production Co.* v. *Lindley* 609 P.2d 733 (Ok., 1980) where the employer forbade the employee to work on the program even in his own time
114. In fact one of them had drafted his own terms.

to exclude any materials developed by the defendants themselves, thus having a wider ambit than that of the common law. The terms embodied an obligation not to compete for a year after termination of the contract of employment, and an obligation not to use or disclose confidential information, knowledge or technology gained during their employment. Here the defendants proposed to do precisely that immediately upon leaving their employment, and were held liable in damages for breach of contract.

Some jurisdictions in the United States invalidate all covenants not to compete on grounds of public policy; in most the question is whether the covenant is reasonable. This question has been examined in the United States in a number of cases involving the computer industry. The relevant policies were identified by the court in *Amoco Production Co.* v. *Lindley*[115] when summarising the reasoning in *Structural Dynamics Research Corp.* v. *Engineering Mechanics Research Corp.*:

> The Court then approached the concept of whether a process is a trade secret from the point of view of weighing the fact that in a highly technological society useful knowledge should be disclosed, against the fact that secrecy may favor and motivate inventiveness, with special consideration given to the genuine concern for the technically skilled worker whose job mobility may be diluted if knowledge he acquires is deemed to be a trade secret.[116]

In *Business Intelligence Services Inc.* v. *Hudson*[117] the plaintiff was in the business of providing computer systems for financial institutions. The defendant was employed upon terms of keeping information confidential and refraining from joining a competing firm for a period of one year after leaving the plaintiff. The defendant left the plaintiff in order to take up employment with a competitor, under the impression that she was not bound by the non-competition provision which she claimed had not originally been present in her contract. The defendant was employed as senior consultant, and in that capacity had considerable knowledge of the structure of the plaintiff's programs, of problems which had plagued them, and of the customer base. It was felt that such knowledge would inevitably percolate through to her new employer. Thus the plaintiff had a clearly protectable interest, and the question centred on whether or not a covenant not to compete anywhere in the world for a period of a year was reasonable. The court had no difficulty with the period of one year, relating it to the time during which the defendant's knowledge would retain its ability to harm the plaintiff if disclosed. It was influenced by the fact that the defendant was not precluded from continuing in the same employment with her old employer, or in taking up non-competing employment with another computer company. It also held, given the limited temporal restriction, that it was appropriate to impose a world-wide restriction since the business competition between the relevant firms extended throughout the world. This interdependence of the various covenants is important. In *Sperry Rand Corp.* v. *Pentronix Inc.*[118] a perpetual restriction was upheld, but only on the use of misappropriated trade secrets in a physical form.

---

115. 609 P.2d 733 (Ok., 1980) at 744.
116. 401 F.Supp. 1102 (E.D. Mich., 1975).
117. 580 F.Supp. 1068 (S.D.N.Y., 1984).
118. 311 F.Supp. 910 (E.D. Pa., 1970).

It is important to draft restrictive covenants of this type with some care. In most jurisdictions the contract will be read in such a way as to strike down only so much as is unreasonable and to leave in force whatever remains. Although this approach is most common in relation to geographical or temporal restrictions, it may also be applied to the substance of the obligation. Thus in *Electronic Data Systems Inc.* v. *Powell*[119] a general covenant not to compete was read down to proscribe only engaging in programming of the same type as had been practised with the old employer. It is thus desirable to draft in such a fashion as to facilitate such a possible construction. *Trilog Associates Inc.* v. *Famularo*[120] is instructive. In that case the contract contained two covenants, but one was without limitation as to place, while the other was unduly wide and vague in referring to taking employment with anyone associated with someone first contacted during the original employment. Neither could be reduced. It would have been better to have contracted in the alternative for different times and extent of limitation in the hope that some combination would be upheld. It is perhaps dubious whether a provision cast in such terms as 'such extent as the court deems reasonable' would suffice, since courts are not in the business of making the parties' contracts for them. Nor would it be in accord with public policy for them to do so, since it might encourage the cowing of employees by drafting unduly wide clauses relying upon judicial creativity to extricate some element of enforceability should a case ever come to court. It is also possible to fortify the possibilities of restrictions being upheld by such devices as an offer of payment in the event of the restriction preventing employment,[121] or by permitting the employee to purchase his discharge from the obligation.[122]

It should be noted that while it is advisable to contract so as to vest ownership of copyright in any programs made by the employee in his employer, it is not necessarily fatal if copyright vests in the employee. This is because the courts can distinguish copyright from trade secret, and find in the case of the same program that it is the employee's copyright, but the employer's trade secret. In such a case they may restrain its exploitation by the employee.[123] It was similarly regarded as irrelevant to the enforceability of a covenant not to compete in *Modern Controls Inc.* v. *Andreadakis*[124] that a contractual provision vesting rights to inventions in the contract was too widely drawn.

It is not necessarily a cause for dismissal that an employee has made preparations to join a competitor, or to set up in competition himself, at least in the absence of any restrictive provision and of any attempt to solicit other employees to leave,[125] or of existing customers to transfer their custom.[126]

---

119. 508 S.W.2d 137 (Tex., 1974).
120. 314 A.2d 287 (Pa., 1974).
121. As in *Modern Controls Inc.* v. *Andreadakis* 578 F.2d 1264 (8th Cir., 1978).
122. As in *J & K Computer Systems Inc.* v. *Parrish* 642 P.2d 733 (Ut., 1982).
123. See *Northern Office Micro Computers (Pty.) Ltd.* v. *Rosenstein* (1981) 4 S.A. 123, C.P.D. (South Africa), cp. *Computer Print Systems Inc.* v. *Lewis* 422 A.2d 148 (Pa., 1980) where a similar distinction is made between the general concept of the program and the detailed coding.
124. 578 F.2d 1264 (8th Cir., 1978).
125. Courting the plaintiff president's secretary with the result that she also chose to leave did not count as such solicitation.
126. *Computer Sciences Corp.* v. *Ferguson* 74 Cal.Rptr. 86 (Cal., 1968).

F. Bureau services contracts

So far, the primary situation considered has been that in which the customer has been doing his own computing, buying in the necessary equipment, programs or programming services. This section considers the different situation when the customer arranges access to a third party's computer, typically located off his own premises, and not subject to his own general control. Within this general pattern there a number of variations. At one time it was very common for small businesses which could not afford a computer of their own to contract for their computing to be conducted for them by a bureau.[127] This has become less common with the dramatic reduction in the cost of computing, the greater ease of use and availability of powerful but simple program packages, and the increased general understanding of computer operation. Nevertheless there are still some situations in which bureau services as traditionally established are appropriate, perhaps for highly specialised tasks or where the need to use a machine is only occasional. It is also possible for some users to make the transition into computing through the use, first, of a wholly remote bureau service,[128] and then to move on to a stage where terminal equipment is situated on the customer's premises to make contact with a remote bureau,[129] and then finally the whole operation is taken over by the customer. In the traditional bureau service the customer prepares the data according to a specification provided by the bureau, which then collects the data, runs it on its computer, and delivers the output to the customer. This frees the customer from all of the intellectual chores of computerisation, but at the cost of inflexibility and absence of any control.

A different, and nowadays much more common, form of remote computing takes the shape of subscription to a computerised information service. In this situation the customer does not himself prepare either data or programs. These are the province of the information provider. The information provider will typically sell a subscription to the service, and deliver it through terminal equipment installed on the customer's premises. At one time such terminals were normally provided as part of the service, and remained the property and responsibility of the information provider. Nowadays it is more common for the subscriber to use his own terminal equipment, sometimes mediated by his own in-house computer system which may relay the services of many different information providers to individual users. Such an arrangement is very typical of the financial services sector which subscribes to many different services for stock prices and dealing, exchange rates, commodity prices, interest rates and the like, and often combines them into one unique screen display.[130]

---

127. For a description of the industry at this stage of development, see *GTE Service Corp.* v. *Federal Communications Commission* 474 F.2d 724 (2nd cir., 1973).
128. Just such a transition is illustrated by the facts of *Samuel Black Co.* v. *Burroughs Corp.* 33 U.C.C. Rep. 954 (D. Mass., 1981).
129. See *Com-Share Inc.* v. *Computer Complex Inc.* 338 F.Supp. 1229 (E.D. Mich., 1971) where the dispute concerned just such bureau services.
130. See Sharrock and Staton 'Information Vendors and the Copyright, Designs and Patents Bill' 4 *Computer Law & Practice* 138 (1988).

Such contracts are essentially for the supply of services, and although the service may involve the delivery of tangible supplies such as paper with printing on it, this generally constitutes an insignificant part of the total service. Such a factor may be important in attempting to determine how the transaction will be taxed under local law,[131] and in order to decide whether the local rules relating to the sale of goods apply.[132] This, in turn, is relevant to the question of any warranties to be implied into the contract, to what extent oral representations will be incorporated, and how far express contractual provisions can exclude these possibilities. It is, however, clear that if the contract provides explicitly for separate payment for tangible supplies incidental to the service, the main contract is one for services, and does not then fall within provisions relating to the sale of goods.[133]

Perhaps because they are contracts for services rather than contracts of sale, there has seemed an even greater tendency here than elsewhere towards informal drafting, or occasionally for there to be no drafting at all. Thus in *Associated Tabulating Services Inc.* v. *Olympia Life Insurance Corp.*[134] despite the stature of the parties, and the length of negotiations between them, no contract was ever drafted, and the parties simply drifted into an arrangement whereby one party supplied forms and the other started processing them. Not surprisingly this made questions of the duration and termination of the contract extremely difficult to resolve. An even more serious problem arises in such situations in those jurisdictions in the United States which still retain statutory provisions derived from the Statute of Frauds.[135] It is remarkable that so twentieth century a device as the computer should still be regulated by the prescriptions of the seventeenth.

It is equally as important in these contracts as in any others that the parties should specify precisely what their mutual responsibilities and entitlements are to be in relation to the provision of facilities, services and data, and what is to happen in the event of failure to discharge or honour them. Thus one contract foundered largely because the bureau which was writing the programs failed to reveal a key characteristic to the customer who was preparing the data, with the result that it could not run.[136] A bureau will frequently offer reduced rates for regular use. In such cases it is advisable to set out explicitly and unambiguously how premature termination is to be handled. In one case[137] a contract provided for processing bank accounts, the fee to be calculated upon the number of items to be processed. The contract also provided for a minimum charge in case the number of items should not reach the corresponding level, and under the termination provisions six months' notice was to be given. As the bank's business grew, it decided to install its own computer. It did so, and gave notice of termination under the contract. The transaction seems to have been unusually efficiently accomplished with the result that the bank was ready to commence its own

---

131. See for example, *Accountant's Computer Services Inc.* v. *Kosydar* 298 N.E.2d 519 (Oh., 1973).
132. See further below p. 181.
133. See *Computer Servicenters Inc.* v. *Beacon Manufacturing Corp.* 328 F.Supp. 653 (D.S.C., 1970).
134. 414 F.2d 1306 (5th Cir., 1969).
135. For example South Carolina, see *Computer Servicenters Inc.* v. *Beacon Manufacturing Corp.* 328 F.Supp. 653 (D.S.C., 1970) above.
136. *Law Research Services Inc.* v. *Western Union Inc.* 1 C.L.S.R. 1002 (N.Y., 1968).
137. *Brown* v. *American Bank of Commerce* 441 P.2d 751 (N.M., 1968).

processing before the contractual period of notice had expired. It was held that for the remainder of the period the bank was nevertheless obliged to pay the full contractual price for services which were not needed or provided, and that the bank could not limit its liability to the minimum charge. Similarly it has been held[138] that where a minimum payment has been contracted for, the analogy of a contract for services prevails to the extent that it is for the customer to show any matter in reduction of damages, with the result that the contracted payment, in the absence of explicit agreement to the contrary, will not necessarily be reduced so as to reflect the lower cost of processing fewer materials. Customers should generally be very wary of agreeing to take bureau services for extended periods of time since conditions are prone to change. To the extent that such changes can be anticipated, they should be provided for, for example to secure the mutability of data, programming and services in case of need. To the extent that change cannot be anticipated in detail so as to make explicit provision, termination periods should be short, and the procedures specified in as much detail as possible to minimise dispute and acrimony.

Since the essence of bureau service is that the computer operation typically takes place outside the customer's premises and control, and in a business environment which is becoming increasingly hostile for bureaux, it is clear that the customer will be right to be concerned about the security of his data while it is off his premises, about securing the continuity of his operation should the bureau run into difficulty, and for the orderly termination or transfer of his bureau business whenever he should require either option.

There is always a danger of a breakdown in a computer system for one reason or another, though it is becoming less common as more reliable machines and parallel processing are being introduced. Nevertheless if a bureau is successful it may be handling a very large volume of business of some complexity, and it is only prudent for the customer to contract for the provision of adequate back-up facilities to be made available. It is unlikely to be sufficient for these to be left to the discretion of the bureau, given that the parties may fall out, or the bureau run into financial diifficulty.[139] In principle the customer should be responsible for any elements under his control, for example data and applications programs, and the bureau for the elements under its control, for example hardware and systems programs. Unfortunately, as the *Law Research Services* case[140] illustrates, it is not always so simple to apportion responsibility.

The customer will require his data and applications programs to be secure while they are in the custody of the bureau, and the bureau will want to keep any information about its own mode of operation confidential. Although the customer will be protected by the ordinary law of copyright there is every reason to fortify it by explicit contractual provision for confidentiality of any materials supplied to a bureau.[141] Any data should be labelled as

---

138. *Autotax Inc.* v. *Data Input Corp.* 220 S.E.2d 456 (Ga., 1975).
139. See *Data Probe Inc.* v. *575 Computer Services Inc.* 340 N.Y.S. 56 (N.Y., 1972).
140. Above p. 172.
141. See Lickson, 'Protection of the Privacy of Data Communications by Contract', *23 Bus. L.* 971 (1968).

being secret and supplied on a confidential basis, the bureau should be required to insert confidentiality provisions into its contracts with its own employees and to institute, enforce and report to the customer on its security procedures, to give the customer rights to make representations, and perhaps even to include limited arbitration provisions in the event of disagreement. Some price may be exacted in return for such provisions, but it is worth paying, and the adequacy of any such provision may be an important factor in deciding between different bureaux. By insisting on such provisions the customer will be most likely to preserve the status of his material as a trade secret, thus giving him remedies in tort in case of misappropriation by the bureau.[142] Since it is generally much more laborious to create and maintain accurate data than it is to write efficient programs, and often critical to the business of a customer that his data remain intact and inviolate, it is a matter of common prudence for the customer to retain a copy of any data transmitted to a bureau. In a case where the bureau performs incremental work which it is impossible to recreate only from the end product, the contract should ensure that the bureau's programs provide for periodic breaks so that in the event of a problem it is not necessary to go back to the beginning and start again.

There is sometimes a difficulty in relation to applications programs. Sometimes a bureau will develop such a program to handle the data to the precise specifications of the individual customer. Thus in the *National Surety Corp.* case above, the programming which had been of this type had taken over 470 man days of programming effort to complete. Bureau contracts are notoriously loosely drafted, and there is sometimes dispute as to the ownership of such programs. In *Computer Print Systems Inc.* v. *Lewis*[143] it was said that the two most common ways of providing for this situation are for the customer to pay for the development of the programs at the time, or for the bureau to recover the development costs by augmenting its processing charge. In either situation it would obviously be sensible to provide explicitly for ownership of both copies of, and copyright in, the program. In this case there was no such provision, and the second method had been adopted. It was held that the customer acquired no rights in the program, even after paying more than sufficient in processing charges to repay all development costs. The court took the view that such an arrangement was something of a gamble: if the customer terminated early, then the bureau would lose; but if he terminated late or not at all, then the bureau should gain, as otherwise it could not carry the costs of the cases in which it lost.

It is quite common for bureaux to adopt a policy of refusing customers access to programs, or even data, so as to tie them in to the bureau's services.[144] This is usually justified on the basis that release will reveal the bureau's trade secrets or confidential information relating to the organisation of its activities. Thus in *Smithsonian Institution* v. *Datatron Processing Inc.*[145] a

---

142. As in *National Surety Corp.* v. *Applied Systems Inc.* 418 So.2d 847 (Ala., 1982).
143. 422 A.2d 148 (Pa., 1980).
144. This was the whole substance of the dispute in *Computer Print Systems Inc.* v. *Lewis* 422 A.2d 148 (Pa., 1980).
145. 3 C.L.S.R. 393 (E.D.N.Y., 1971).

bureau which had been handling the distribution and billing documentation for a magazine refused to release the master tape containing the names and addresses of subscribers on the ground that this might involve revelation of the design of the bureau's system. Fortunately the contract was quite clear in relation to the supply of a copy of the master tape, and it was further held that nothing of significance relating to the design of the defendant's system would be revealed. In this case the bureau seems to have been acting simply out of pique. But suppose that instead the problems had arisen because the customer had consistently failed to pay his bills. Would the bureau then have been justified in withholding the data as a lien for the charges due under the contract?[146] No case seems to deal with this problem explicitly, and its correct resolution seems problematic whether considered under the common law or under particular statutory provisions.[147]

G. Sale, lease and licence[148]

As noted earlier,[149] in both the United Kingdom and the United States much of the case law relating to computer contracts, and especially that dealing with terms relating to quality and liability, is dictated by the statutory rules relating to the sale of goods. These rules have much in common, and are essentially distillations of the common law. However, as indicated in the preceding sections, it is common for both hardware and software to be acquired otherwise than by a contract of sale. Questions thus arise as to how far the statutory rules apply to leases of hardware, licences of software, or to contracts for data processing.

1. Hardware leases

At one time the main suppliers of computers and tabulating equipment offered them only on a rental basis. As a result of the settlement of a consequential antitrust suit in the United States in 1956,[150] such suppliers became obliged to offer their equipment for purchase upon terms not significantly less favourable to the customer than were being offered on a rental basis. Nevertheless in a situation in which the cost of the equipment was frequently very high and its rate of obsolescence very fast, the impetus towards some form of renting arrangement was very strong. This was illustrated by the facts of *LTV* v. *Commissioner of Internal Revenue*[151] where the purchase price of the computer was nearly 3 million dollars, yet its estimated value only five years later was no more than a tenth of that figure. Payments could be correspondingly high in the early years of an agreement. In that

---

146. See Wessel and Spalty, 'A Lien on Computer Tapes', *C.L.S.* sect. 3–5 art. 2.
147. For example, in the United States see the confusing circularity in the Uniform Commercial Code art. 9.
148. For extensive discussion of the position in the United States, see Annotation 37 A.L.R.4th 110 (1985).
149. At p. 139.
150. For the terms of the settlement, see *U.S.* v. *International Business Machines Corp.* 1 C.L.S.R. 41 (S.D.N.Y., 1956).
151. 63 T.C. 39 (U.S. Tax Ct., 1974).

case the payments during the first two and a half years ran at more than one million dollars a year. There the computer was leased from a third party.[152] Such leasing became common because it was devised to meet some of the features mentioned above. The original manufacturers tended to rent their equipment out at a very high monthly rent, reflecting the supposedly high risks of a situation in which agreements relating to such expensive and fast-ageing equipment could be terminated at any time. In fact the risks were never so high as they seemed in theory to be, simply because of the degree of dependence which computerisation established, not just upon the computerised process itself, but in relation to a particular type of equipment supplied and maintained by a particular manufacturer. Once the manufacturers were compelled to offer their equipment for sale on reasonable terms, this situation became ripe for exploitation by entrepreneurs who were prepared to assume these supposed risks at much more realistic rates. Thus the General Services Administration in the United States was able to cite cases where enormous savings could be achieved by leasing from a third party rather than from the original manufacturer. The Federal Bureau of Investigation, for example, was able to rent from a third party for $1450 a month, equipment which International Business Machines Corporation, its manufacturer, was offering at $3000 a month.[153] It was said as long ago as 1965 that on a conservative estimate[154] the adoption of such arrangements in half of the United States government computing establishments would save over one million dollars a month. Indeed, it was largely to take advantage of such opportunities that the General Services Administration was given sole jurisdiction over computer procurement pursuant to an amendment of the Federal Property and Administrative Services Act of 1949.[155] In his opinion the Comptroller-General was prepared to go further and to recommend that agencies give more serious consideration to purchasing, rather than any form of leasing, even from third parties. It is interesting that the current trend in the United Kingdom is just the opposite. Here the Central Computer and Telecommunications Agency which handles government procurement has recently relaxed its previous insistence upon outright purchase by government departments in favour of leasing and exchange arrangements.[156] Nor is the possibility of making such savings limited to government procurers. A private firm like Westinghouse Corporation has similarly estimated that it was able to save 3 million dollars in 1969 alone by renting from third parties rather than from the original manufacturer.[157] The typical strategy of such third parties was to buy a computer from the original manufacturer and then to lease it to a user for a longer term and at a lower price than the original

---

152. Said in *Chatlos Systems Inc.* v. *NCR Corp.* 635 F.2d 1081 (3rd Cir., 1980) at 1083 to be a common form of transaction.
153. *General Services Administration* 45 Comp. Gen. 527 (1966).
154. Of saving no more than 10 per cent per transaction.
155. 40 U.S.C. sect. 759. There has since been some trend towards a more decentralised approach, see *Computerworld* 19 January 1976 p. 42. A problem has been that really long leasing possibilities have not been readily available to annually funded agencies except through the inadequately financed revolving fund.
156. See *Computer Weekly* 6 October 1988 p. 3.
157. Burke, 'Third party leasing from a User's Viewpoint' *Datamation* November 1969, reproduced at 2 C.L.S. sect. 3–1 art. 1.

manufacturer would be prepared to offer. It is surprising that third parties are able to offer such competitive terms when it is appreciated that the purchase price of computing equipment can exceed its cost by some 500 per cent.[158] Some manufacturers adopted a practice of refusing to sell to third parties, but would sell only to existing lessees. This was ineffective, since it could be evaded by adding a few steps to the transaction, by which the lessee first leased, next exercised his option to purchase, then resold to the third party, and finally took a lease back.

In the case of peripheral hardware the economics of the situation tended to be different, but the end result the same. There the original suppliers were sometimes far too small, and working on far too tight a budget, to be able to carry the cash flow burden of leasing rather than selling. On the other hand, the cost of such equipment, while small for each item, could in bulk still be more than a small business customer would want to meet, and the rate of obsolescence was just as fast. The situation was thus one in which the manufacturer was anxious to sell and the customer anxious to hire. So once again there was a role for the third party lessor. Here he could intervene by purchasing equipment from the manufacturer together with an assignment of rental payments under existing leases. The equipment never left the premises of the customers, and the manufacturer received a lump sum.[159]

It is important to distinguish between two quite different sorts of lease since they have somewhat different consequences. The first are operating leases where the parties envisage that the payments made under the lease will not necessarily equate to the full purchase price of the equipment, and that at the end of the lease the equipment will revert to the lessor with further useful capacity so that it can be leased out again. An advantage of such a lease from the point of view of the customer is that a third party operating lessor will more rarely impose restrictions upon the periods of time within which the machine can be used, or provisions for additional payments should such prescribed periods be exceeded. Nor is a third party so likely to want to restrict the use of the computer to any one site. If more favourable terms are secured from a third party lessor in these respects, the customer should ensure that he is not paying for them indirectly in less favourable treatment so far as maintenance and service are concerned than he would secure if his contract were with the original supplier. In fact this will be rarely the case since it is most common for third-party lessors to contract with the original supplier, or a fourth party, for maintenance and service, since it is generally not feasible for them to provide such services themselves, though there is a distinct new breed of third parties who have progressed from offering simple maintenance or leasing to offering a combination of the two. The second sort of lease is essentially a financing lease where the full purchase price of the equipment is expected to be recovered together with interest during the period of the lease, and at the end of the lease the equipment will be retained by the customer or purchased for a nominal sum. Either of these types of lease may, under local tax law, become a vehicle for

---

158. See *Boothe Computer Corp.* v. *State Department of Assessment and Taxation* 5 C.L.R.S. 591 (Md., 1970).
159. *Alanthus Peripherals Inc.* 54 Comp. Gen. 80 (1974). See also Birnbaum 'Lease Financing for Fledgling Manufacturers of Computer Peripheral Equipment', *29 Business L.* 477 (1974).

special taxation privileges by way of investment credits.[160] The principal legal difference is that while there has been quite detailed intervention in the law of sale of goods, and hire purchase, there has been much less intervention in the law of leasing. It is sometimes to the advantage of one, and sometimes to that of the other party, to assert a sale or a lease. It is quite clear that the courts will look to the substance of the transaction rather than to the label which the parties attach to it to determine which it is.[161] Some courts prefer to import into leasing transactions some elements from the Uniform Commercial Code, but not all, being guided partly by the wording of particular provisions of Article 2 of the Uniform Commercial Code, and in particular whether there is an exclusive reference to a contract of sale, and partly by considerations of policy.[162] Some guidance as to its application is provided by the Uniform Commercial Code itself.[163] One of the most influential factors in making that determination is whether the lessee is able to cancel the lease without penalty.[164] Another important factor is the extent to which the whole value of the equipment is exhausted during the lease with the result that only a nominal payment is required to vest the equipment in the lessee upon its expiration.[165] A different approach to the same concept is to compare the total cost payable under the lease with the purchase price, a substantial excess of the former being indicative of a financing transaction.[166] Further problems may arise in deciding whether a terminal payment is or is not nominal.[167] A further indicator is whether or not default automatically accelerates payments due under the lease.[168] If the lease is held to be an operational lease it has in the United States fallen

---

160. Such rules are so parochial and so ephemeral as to defy coverage in a work of this sort, though they may well be crucial in practice to the financial viability of any proposed transaction.

161 *Burroughs Corp.* v. *Barry* 380 F.2d 427 (8th Cir., 1967); *Kalil Bottling Co.* v. *Burroughs Corp.* 619 P.2d 1055 (Az., 1980), 'It does not matter whether the parties all their contract a "security agreement or a spotted elephant".' For the same approach in the United Kingdom, see *Eurodynamic Systems plc* v. *General Automation Ltd.* 5 A.C.C.L. January 1989 5, Q.B. 1988).

162. See *Walter Heller & Co. Ltd* v. *Convalescent Home of the First Church of Deliverance 365* N.E.2d 1285 (Ill., 1977).

163. Sect. 1–201(37).

164. This was decisive in favour of an operational lease in *County of Sacramento* v. *Assessment Appeals Board* 108 Cal. Raptr. 434 (Cal., 1973) despite an option to purchase for a nominal sum at the end of the term. The absence of such an option was decisive against a true lease analysis in *Citicorp Leasing Inc.* v. *Allied Institutional Distributors Inc.* 454 F.Supp 511 (W.D.Ok., 1977).

165. This factor was stressed as indicative of a financing lease in *Leasco Data Processing Equipment Corp.* v. *Starline Overseas Corp.* 346 N.Y.S.2d 288 (N.Y., 1973), and its absence as indicative of an operational lease in *O.J. & C. Co.* v. *General Hospital Leasing Inc.* 578 S.W.2d 877 (Tex., 1979).

166. See *National Equipment Rental Ltd.* v. *Priority Electronics Corp.* 435 F.Supp. 236 (E.D.N.Y., 1977).

167. Compare *Burroughs Corp.* v. *Barry* 380 F.2d (8th Cir., 1967) where the fact that the option price roughly equated to the fair market value was regarded as indicative of an operational lease with *National Equipment Rental Ltd.* v. *Priority Electronics Corp.* 435 F.Supp. 236 (E.D.N.Y., 1977) where an explicit provision for the option to be at fair market value was disregarded, and the lease regarded as financing.

168. See *Computer Property Corp.* v. *Columbia Distributing Corp.* 5 C.L.S.R. 524 (D.S.C., 1973).

outside the provisions of the Uniform Commercial Code,[169] and in the United Kingdom outside those both of the Sale of Goods Act 1979[170] and of the Supply of Goods (Implied Terms) Act 1973. In the United States this may have meant that a shorter limitation period applied.[171] It has been held that such a form of leasing is not sufficiently analogous to banking business to be permissible under the strict restrictions imposed by the Federal Reserve Board.[172] It may determine whether repossession of the goods extinguishes liability for payments otherwise due under the lease,[173] and it may be relevant to whether the subject-matter is subject to distraint upon the lessee's insolvency.[174] If the lease is a financing lease it is in the United States subject to the Uniform Commercial Code,[175] and in the United Kingdom to the Supply of Goods (Implied Terms) Act 1973. Occasionally the manufacturer enters into a financing lease with the customer,[176] but more often the transaction involves a third party lessor. Questions may then arise as to the mutual obligations and responsibilities of the parties. The third-party lessor will not wish to be involved in any dispute between the supplier and the customer as to the quality of the goods supplied. For this reason it is common for such leases to contain clauses guaranteeing payments whatever calamity occurs, and in a number of cases third-party lessors have succeeded in enforcing payment against the lessee despite claims of highly defective performance.[177] Such a lessor cannot realistically be bound by any implied terms or held to the usual substituted remedies, so the question arises of how far the original manufacturer remains bound to the lessee. The strong tendency in the United States is to hold the manufacturer liable, since to do otherwise would distort the effect of the Uniform Commercial Code.[178] It is not uncommon for the third party lessor to secure from the lessee an acknowledgement of satisfaction with the equipment before finalising his part in the transaction,[179] nor for the benefit of any warranties in the contract of sale to the third-party lessor to be passed on by the lease to the lessee.[180] It is also common for the intended ultimate user to enter into a contract to

---

169. A new Art. 2A was introduced into the Uniform Commercial Code to cater for operational leases in 1987.

170. Though it would now come within the scope of the Supply of Goods and Services Act 1982.

171. See *Atlas Industries Inc.* v. *National Cash Register Co.* 531 P.2d 41 (Kan., 1975).

172. *Bankamerica Corp.* v. *Board of Governors of the Federal Reserve System* 491 F.2d 985 (9th Cir., 1974).

173. *National Equipment Rental Ltd.* v. *Priority Electronics Corp.* 435 F.Supp. 236 (E.D.N.Y., 1977).

174. *Computer Sciences Corp.* v. *Sci-Tek Inc.* 367 A.2d 658 (Del., 1976).

175. Art. 9.

176. The first lease in *W.R. Weaver Co.* v. *Burroughs Corp.* 580 S.W.2d 76 (Tex., 1979), and that in *Chatlos Systems Inc.* v. *NCR Corp.* 635 F.2d 1081 (3rd Cir., 1980), for example.

177. See *Acme Pump Co. Inc.* v. *National Cash Register Co.* 337 A.2d 672 (Conn., 1974); *Atlas Industries Inc.* v. *National Cash Register Co.* 531 P.2d 41 (Kan., 1975); and *Burroughs Corp.* v. *Century Steel Inc.* 664 P.2d 354 (Nev., 1983).

178. The application of the uniform commercial code between manufacturer and lessee was conceded in *Chatlos Systems Inc.* v. *NCR Corp.* 635 F.2d 1081 (3rd Cir, 1980) despite the intervention of a third-party financing lessor.

179. See *Citicorp Leasing Inc.* v. *Allied Institutional Distributors Inc.* 454 F.Supp. 511 (W.D. Ok., 1977).

180. As in *Atlas Industries Inc.* v. *National Cash Register Co.* 531 P.2d 41 (Kan., 1975).

order the equipment with the manufacturer. This technique was fully explored in *Earman Oil Co. Inc.* v. *Burroughs Corp.*[181] The customer signed an equipment sale contract before subsequently leasing the equipment from a third-party lessor who had purchased from the defendant. The equipment sale contract contained the defendant's standard terms excluding implied warranties and substituting a warranty limited to replacement of defective parts for a short period.[182] Thus it was in the customer's interest to claim that its only obligations were exclusively governed by the third-party lease. The court decided that it was immaterial for these purposes in the circumstances of this case whether the lease was a true lease or merely a financing transaction. If it were a true lease, then the customer was a third-party beneficiary of the warranties incorporated into the sale to the lessor by the stamping upon it of a reference to the terms of the equipment sale contract. Here the two agreements binding the supplier, the equipment sale contract with the customer and the sale to the third-party lessor, had to be considered as together setting out the terms of the bargain with the customer. If, on the other hand, the lease was regarded as no more than a financing transaction, then it is well established that, as between the supplier and the ultimate customer, the provisions of the Uniform Commercial Code apply as if it were a sale.[183] In the United Kingdom the same result has been achieved by legislation. Terms are implied into a true lease by the Supply of Goods and Services Act 1982, and into a financing transaction by the Supply of Goods (Implied Terms) Act 1973.[184] The extent to which any such terms can be excluded is governed by the provisions of the Unfair Contract Terms Act 1977. There is for this reason no case law in the United Kingdom comparable to that discussed above in relation to the position in the United States.

2. Software licences

It has become rare for computer programs to be formally the subject of sale. It is much more common to license the use of a copy of the program, though the copy itself is sold to the customer, usually on a chip, tape or disc. Part of the reason for so structuring the transaction is to maximise the market for copies of the program, given that programs, unlike books, can be easily and cheaply copied and then passed on. In such a situation it is arguable that the law of copyright provides inadequate protection for the supplier.[185] In any event, whether justified or not, it remains the case that programs are typically licensed rather than sold outright. The question then arises how far

---

181. 625 F.2d 1290 (5th Cir., 1980).
182. For the validity of such terms under the Uniform Commercial Code, see below p. 183.
183. See, for example, *Citicorp Leasing Inc.* v. *Allied Institutional Distributors Inc.* 454 F.Supp. 511 (W.D. Ok., 1977); *Chatlos Systems Inc.* v. *NCR Corp.* 635 F.2d 1081 (3rd Cir., 1980); and *Burroughs Corp.* v. *Century Steel Inc.* 664 P.2d 354 (Nev., 1983) rejecting at 357 n.2 dicta to the contrary in *Kalil Bottling Co.* v. *Burroughs Corp.* 619 P.2d 1055 (Az., 1980).
184. As amended by the Consumer Credit Act 1974 Sch. 4.
185. Though in practice it is dubious whether such small-scale operations provide much of a threat to the software industry, and the wholesale professional and commercial copying which does, is subject to adequate sanctions under the law of copyright.

such transactions are governed by the law of sale of goods, and in particular by the special statutory régimes incorporated in the Sale of Goods Act in the United Kingdom, and in the Uniform Commercial Code in the United States. Is a licence a sale? Is a computer program a good? Such questions have been the focus of some litigation, and much discussion,[186] in the United States. Article 2 of the Uniform Commercial Code is headed 'Sales', and applies in terms to 'transactions in goods'.[187] Goods are defined as 'all things (including specially manufactured goods) which are movable at the time of identification to the contract of sale'.[188] It is clearly arguable that a licence is not a sale, and a program, as opposed to a copy, is intangible, and hence not movable. It is sometimes argued that a program is not a 'good' because it is in origin an idea in someone's mind, and is not necessarily committed to a hard copy before transmission to the customer, for example if it is simply passed along a telephone line. These arguments are not very convincing. All human artifacts start as ideas in someone's mind, and it would be very odd to abstain from applying the régime adapted to the most common form of transaction, just because it is possible that it might not be obviously appropriate to a proportion of them. In almost all cases of transactions in programs, a number of physical objects will be delivered in the form of books, tapes or discs, boxes and plastic overlays. It is virtually inconceivable that a transaction would be consummated without any of these passing to the customer. It has, however, been held in the case of customised programming services that the essence of the contract is just that, the provision of services, and the mere fact that the service necessarily involves the delivery of disks or programs is irrelevant to its categorisation, and so it is governed by the common law and not by the Uniform Commercial Code.[189] In many cases the relevant transaction relates to a complete system consisting of hardware, software and maintenance or programming services. In such a case courts seem disinclined to dissect it into different parts, and to apply the provisions of the Uniform Commercial Code only to the hardware. The realistic view is that if the system is purchased as a whole the same legal analysis should apply to the whole.[190] In many such cases the hardware elements will predominate in the transaction and determine its categorisation.[191] In such a contract the fact that the supplier undertakes to provide incidental services makes no difference to such categorisation as a transaction in goods.[192] If a transaction relates only to software it may be argued that the value of the medium on which the program is inscribed is so insignificant compared with the value of the intellectual content of what is inscribed as to make it quite absurd to characterise the movable vehicle as

---

186. See Note, 'Computer Programs as Goods under the U.C.C.' *77 Mich. L.R.* 1149 (1979); Note, 'Computer Software as a Good under the Uniform Commercial Code; Taking a Byte out of the Intangibility Myth' *65 Boston U.L.R.* 129 (1985); Rodau, 'Computer Software: Does Article 2 of the Uniform Commercial Code Apply?' *35 Emory L.J.* 853 (1986).
187. Uniform Commercial Code art. 2–102.
188. *Ibid.* art. 2–105(1).
189. *Data Processing Services Inc.* v. *L.H. Smith Oil Corp.* 492 N.E.2d 314 (Ind., 1986).
190. *Neilson Business Equipment Center Inc.* v. *Monteleone* 524 A.2d 1172 (Del., 1987).
191. See *Triangle Underwriters Inc.* v. *Honeywell Inc.* 457 F.Supp. 765 (E.D.N.Y., 1978) at 769.
192. *Chatlos Systems Inc.* v. *NCR Corp.* 635 F.2d 1081 (3rd Cir., 1980).

the dominant element of the transaction. A similar view has occasionally prevailed in relation to the similar issue of the valuation of such a transaction for tax purposes.[193] However, this view is very difficult to reconcile with the treatment of such things as works of art or books. The most recent cases in a number of jurisdictions accept this analysis and value the transaction more realistically.[194] The same view has prevailed in relation to classification for the purposes of the application of Article 2. It no longer matters that the subject-matter is a program, nor whether it is a standard package,[195] or custom made.[196] It also seems to be immaterial that the supplier offers to perform quite substantial services in terms of installing, debugging and up-grading such software.[197] The resolution of whether or not a program licence amounts to a 'transaction in goods' has been just as easily resolved. In no case has a court found this to be an obstacle to its resolution of the dispute. In the one case where some doubt was expressed as to the application of the Uniform Commercial Code to a complex transaction for a complete system, the court thought it best to apply the Uniform Commercial Code either directly, or by way of analogy.[198] In another the same result was achieved at common law as under the Code.[199]

In the United Kingdom the most comparable legislation is the Sale of Goods Act 1979 which applies to contracts for the sale of goods.[200] Contracts of sale are those 'by which the seller transfers or agrees to transfer the property in goods to the buyer for a money consideration'.[201] Goods are defined to include 'all personal chattels other than things in action and money'.[202] There appear to be no fully reported English cases on the application of the Sale of Goods Act to computer programs.[203] Substantially the same provisions apply in Canada, however, and in two cases the Canadian courts seem to have entertained no doubts as to the application of the Sale of Goods Act to contracts involving both hardware and software, despite the intervention of a third-party lessor.[204] In Australia, which again has similar provisions, it was held after consideration of both United States

---

193. See, for example, *James* v. *Tres Computer System Inc.* 642 S.W.2d 347 (Mo., 1982) where a program costing £150 000 was valued at $50, the cost of the medium, for tax purposes.

194. See *Citizens and Southern Systems Inc.* v. *South Carolina Tax Commission* 311 S.E.2d 717 (S.C., 1984); *Chittendon Trust Co.* v. *King* 465 A.2d 1100 (Vt., 1983); and *Comptroller* v. *Equitable Trust Co.* 464 A.2d 248 (MD., 1983).

195. *Hollingsworth* v. *The Software House Inc.* 513 N.E.2d 1372 (Oh., 1986); *Harford Mutual Insurance Co.* v. *Seibels, Bruce & Co.* 579 F.Supp. 135 (D. Md., 1984).

196. *Schroders Inc.* v. *Hogan Systems Inc.* 4 U.C.C. Rep. 2d 1397 (N.Y., 1987); *Quad County Distributing Co. Inc.* v. *Burroughs Corp.* 385 N.E.2d 1108 (Ill., 1979).

197. *RRX Industries Inc.* v. *Lab-Con Inc.* 772 F.2d 543 (9th Cir., 1985).

198. *Samuel Black Co.* v. *Burroughs Corp.* 33 U.C.C. Rep. 954 (D. Mass., 1981).

199. *W.R. Weaver Co.* v. *Burroughs Corp.* 580 S.W.2d 76 (Tex., 1979) at 81.

200. Sect. 1(1).

201. Sale of Goods Act 1979 sect. 2(1).

202. *Ibid.* sect. 61(1).

203. The matter seems to have been decided in this sense, however, in *Eurodynamic Systems plc* v. *General Automation Ltd.* 5 A.C.C.L. January 1989 5, Q.B. (1988) where *Schroders Inc.* v. *Hogan Systems Inc.* 4 U.C.C. Rep. 2d 1397 (N.Y., 1987) was cited.

204. *Public Utilities Commission for the City of Waterloo* v. *Burroughs Business Machines Ltd.* 34 D.L.R.3d 320 (Ont.H.C., 1973); *Burroughs Business Machines Ltd.* v. *Feed-Rite Mills (1962) Ltd.* 42 D.L.R.3d 303 (Man.C.A., 1973).

and Canadian cases that where three items of hardware and two items of software were categorised as 'The Equipment' in a contract, it was one of sale. It was regarded as immaterial that the price was divided between hardware and software, and the court felt that it was significant that the package consisted entirely of mass-produced elements, none of which had been specially customised to the purchaser's requirements. The court reserved its position on whether a sale consisting entirely of software would be regarded as within the scope of the sale of goods legislation.[205] It should also be noted that in the United Kingdom special provision is made for the insertion of implied terms in licence agreements[206] by the Supply of Goods and Services Act 1982.[207]

3. Bureau services contracts

In most such contracts some movables are delivered to the customer, such as written reports, discs or tapes. Nevertheless, in such transactions it is most likely that the service element predominates, and in some such contracts there is even provision for separate payment for any goods which are supplied. In the United States it seems to be immaterial whether the contract is one performed wholly on the premises of the bureau, as in *Computer Servicenters Inc.* v. *Beacon Manufacturing Corp.*,[208] or one where some terminal equipment is installed on the premises of the customer, so long at least as such equipment remains the property of the bureau, and the customer acquires no option to purchase as an important part of the contract.[209] In neither case do the provisions of the Uniform Commercial Code apply directly. In the United Kingdom the relevant legislation is the Supply of Goods and Services Act 1982.

H. The terms of the contract

It is often surprisingly difficult to establish the terms of a contract, especially one relating to a computer. As noted above, the difficulty is sometimes one of excessive informality where no record exists of what, if anything, was agreed between the parties. More often nowadays, especially in large-scale contracts involving many different vendors, and perhaps governmental bodies and independent financing agencies, the difficulty is the converse one of establishing from the mass of forms, correspondence, telexes, proposals, specifications, drafts, amendments, minutes of meetings, and notes of telephone conversations, exactly which of many slightly different forms of words covering similar subject-matter was finally agreed. Nor is the establishment of the agreement of the parties necessarily the end of the matter, since in certain circumstances the law will incorporate further implied terms into the

---

205. *Toby Construction Products Pty. Ltd.* v. *Computer Bar Sales Pty. Ltd.* 50 A.L.R. 684 (S.C. N.S.W., 1983).
206. Categorised as 'contracts for the hire of goods'.
207. Sects. 6–11.
208. 328 F.Supp. 653 (D.S.C., 1970).
209. *Re Community Medical Center* 623 F.2d 864 (3rd Cir., 1980).

contract between the parties, and may also strike down some terms which have been agreed between them. This section will examine some of these problems, considering first the principles which govern the establishment of the terms of the contract, then the notion of express terms and implied terms. Particular attention will then be paid to the question of the exclusion of implied terms and the validity of terms purporting to limit contractual liability. Some terms relating to the assessment of damages and to the choice of law, which impinge upon the exclusion or limitation of liability, will be postponed until the last two sections of this chapter.

The computer industry was once dominated throughout the world by United States suppliers. Although Japanese suppliers have now challenged that dominance, English remains the language of computing, and United States models dominate the scene of legal contracting. It is not at all uncommon for United States suppliers to use in the United Kingdom standard forms originally devised in the United States. It is most important to note that, although similar, the law in the two jurisdictions is not identical, and statutory intervention has not been the same. Here, as elsewhere, litigation has proliferated in the United States. The factual background of such litigation provides an interesting source for reflection upon the interpretation of English law, but until more cases are reported on the interpretation of United Kingdom provisions in this area, the outcome of the litigation in the United States must be regarded, at best as merely persuasive, while in some areas it may be positively misleading.

1. Incorporation of terms

As stated above it is often difficult, and always vital, in the case of a contractual dispute to establish the terms to which the parties have agreed and by which they are bound. In the case of alleged oral terms the dispute may centre either upon whether anything, and if so, what, was said. In the case of alleged written terms it is more likely to centre upon whether the writing was intended to be considered as a term of the contract. In order to assist with the avoidance and resolution of such disputes, the law long ago developed two devices.

The first was a rule expressed in the Statute of Frauds 1677 that certain important contracts were not enforceable unless evidenced in writing, for example those by their terms not to be performed within a year. Although repealed in relation to sales of goods in the United Kingdom in 1954,[210] similar provisions remain in force in some states in the United States, are incorporated into the Uniform Commercial Code,[211] and on occasion have even been decisive in relation to computer contracts.[212] The Statute of

---

210. By the Law Reform (Enforcement of Contracts) Act 1954, though some contracts such as those involving the provision of credit still require certain written formalities before being fully enforceable, see for example, Consumer Credit Act 1974 sect. 15.
211. Art. 2–201.
212. See *Computer Servicenters Inc.* v. *Beacon Manufacturing Corp.* 328 F.Supp. 653 (D.S.C., 1970).

Frauds is, however, strictly construed, and in one case[213] where a computer system was to be delivered by a date over a year after the date on which the contract was signed, it was still held to fall outside the Statute since it would not have been inconsistent with such terms if the contract had been performed within the year, even though everyone knew that it would not be.[214]

The second device, in this case of common law origin, was the parol evidence rule. The classical statement of the rule is that:

Parol testimony cannot be received to contradict, vary, add to or subtract from the terms of a written contract or the terms in which the parties have deliberately agreed to record any part of their contract.[215]

It is reproduced in the United States in the Uniform Commercial Code:

A writing intended by the parties as a final expression of [their] agreement with respect to such terms as are included therein may not be contradicted by any evidence of any prior agreement or of a contemporaneous oral agreement . . ..[216]

Here too the object is to limit the means for dispute about the terms of the contract. Unfortunately the rule is not well-adapted to achieve its aim, and has never been very popular with the courts. It is premised upon the agreement of the parties to record the terms of their contract in the relevant writing, but this is precisely what is usually in dispute.[217] In practice the effect of the rule is to create a presumption that a written document which appears on its face to constitute a complete and definitive contract is what it appears to be,[218] and that the proponent of any attempt to vary it by reference to some other evidence must make out a very strong case for allowing in the extrinsic material.

Such an appearance is, in the context of computers, very frequently fortified by the inclusion of express terms designed to put the matter beyond doubt. Such clauses are usually described as 'integration'[219] clauses, and appear in standard forms both in the United Kingdom[220] and in the United

---

213. *International Business Machines Corp.* v. *Catamore Enterprises Inc.* 548 F.2d 1066 (1st Cir., 1976) at 1074 n.18.
214. Nor was it delivered by the contractual date.
215. *Bank of Australasia* v. *Palmer* [1897] A.C. 540, PC (Australia) at 545 by Lord Morris.
216. Art. 2–202.
217. For this reason the Law Commission was originally inclined to recommend its abolition, Law Commission Working Paper No. 76 (1976), and abandoned the proposal only on the basis that it was so ineffective as to do no harm, Law Commission No. 154 (1986). See also *Wang Laboratories Inc.* v. *Docktor Pet Centers Inc.* 422 N.E.2d 805 (Mass., 1981).
218. It is immaterial that some terms are printed and some typewritten, even when the typed terms do not expressly incorporate the printed terms, *Farris Engineering Corp.* v. *Service Bureau Corp.* 406 F.2d 519 (3rd Cir., 1969) at 521.
219. A term invented by Wigmore, a leading United States authority on the law of evidence.
220. In *DPCE* v. *ICL Ltd.* LEXIS report 31 July 1985, Q.B. the standard form of the United Kingdom supplier ICL specified that:

No agreement or document having as its purpose or effect the variation, extension or deletion of any of the printed terms and conditions of this contract will be binding unless annexed hereto and signed on behalf of ICL by an authorised signatory.

States.[221] They are usually accompanied by further clauses excluding warranties, substituting limited remedies, limiting the categories within which damages can be awarded, contracting the period within which a claim must be made, and nominating the law of the supplier's home jurisdiction to govern the contract.

Such contractual practices are highly unpopular both with customers and, more importantly, with the courts. Such agreements can be attacked upon the basis that there was no real intention to integrate the outcome of all of the prior negotiations into the final written form. In its most drastic manifestation it may be alleged that the written contract is no more than a sham, never intended to be acted upon.[222] In the absence of an integration clause, reference in the written contract to some other document will itself indicate that the written contract was not intended to embody all the terms of the agreement between the parties.[223] In some cases the omission of a vital term, such as the date of delivery of the system, has been held inconsistent with the application of the parol evidence rule, despite the inclusion of an integration clause, and the explicit exclusion of liability for any damage caused by delay in delivery.[224] In others it has been held that the omission of a delivery date from the written contract does not, despite an integration clause, preclude the implication of a term that the date of delivery should be at a reasonable time, nor resort to extrinsic evidence to determine what date was agreed between the parties, and so presumptively a reasonable one.[225] It may be argued that the written contract dealt only with a limited, and severable, part of the matters discussed between the parties. If there is no integration clause it is easier for the court to take the view that the omission from the written agreement for hardware of any reference to vital software itself indicates that it was not the intention of the parties that the writing comprehend the entire agreement between them.[226] Even if there is an integration clause it may not be effective in such circumstances. Thus in *Carl Beasley Ford Inc.* v. *Burroughs Corp.*[227] the written contract referred only to

---

221. For example in *Hi Neighbour Enterprises Inc.* v. *Burroughs Corp.* 492 F.Supp. 823 (N.D. Fla., 1980) the defendants, who figure very frequently indeed in litigation in this area, succeeded upon the basis of the following clause which was printed prominently on the front of the contractual form in large boldface uppercase characters:

Customer acknowledges by its signature that it has read this agreement, understands it and that it constitutes the entire agreement, understanding and representations, express or implied, between the customer and Burroughs with respect to the program products and services to be furnished hereunder and that this agreement supersedes all prior communications between the parties including all oral or written proposals. This agreement may be modified or amended only by a written instrument signed by the authorized representatives and Burroughs. The terms and conditions, including the warranty and limitation of liability, on the reverse side are part of this agreement.

222. Such a possibility was recognised in *Kilpatrick Bros.* v. *International Business Machines Inc.* 464 F.2d 1080 (10th Cir., 1972), though not there found to be the case.

223. *Computerized Radiological Services Inc.* v. *Syntex Corp.* 595 F.Supp. 1495 (E.D.N.Y., 1984) at 1505.

224. See *Southern Hardware Co.* v. *Honeywell Information Systems Inc.* 373 So.2d 738 (La., 1979).

225. *Samuel Black Co.* v. *Burroughs Corp.* 33 U.C.C. Rep. 954 (D. Mass., 1981).

226. See *Security Leasing Co.* v. *Flinco Inc.* 461 P.2d 460 (Ut., 1969).

227. 361 F.Supp. 325 (E.D.Pa., 1973). See also *Diversified Environments Inc.* v. *Olivetti Corp. of America* 461 F.Supp. 286 (M.D.Pa., 1978).

hardware, but it was orally agreed that thirteen applications programs would also be provided. It was conceded by the defendants that without the programs the hardware was virtually useless, and it emerged that the defendants had adopted a deliberate policy of instructing its salesmen to enter into only oral agreements to supply programs. In the light of these factors,[228] the court found,[229]

ample support for the conclusion that the writing did not encompass the entire agreement between the parties, and parol evidence was properly received to establish what the terms of the agreement were.

The court is entitled to look at all of the surrounding circumstances to determine whether the parties intended to integrate, and in one case[230] where months of negotiations were reflected in voluminous reassurances and where it was envisaged that development work on the untried equipment would continue after the contract had been signed, it was regarded as highly unlikely that the sparse terms of a standard hardware supply form could be regarded as containing the entire agreement of the parties, despite the presence of the usual integration clause. Where an agreement is written, but not signed, it is less likely to be regarded as embodying the final form of the parties' agreement.[231] The general rule in the United Kingdom, though not, as yet, illustrated by cases in the field of computers, is similarly prepared to contemplate a separate oral contract alongside a formal written contract.[232] The resolution of the question of whether the written agreement does represent an intent to integrate is in the law of some jurisdictions in the United States one for the court,[233] and in some for the jury.[234] In the United Kingdom, in the absence of juries, the point does not arise.

The parol evidence rule does not apply to prevent the establishment of a prior collateral contract to enter into the main contract upon certain terms. Thus in *National Computer Rental Ltd.* v. *Bergen Brunsweg Corp.*[235] where the written agreement was a lease[236] the court upheld the validity of a prior oral agreement that the execution of the lease was dependent upon the lessee having secured a particular contract for the use of the relevant computer hardware, a condition which was not, in the event, fulfilled. Similarly in *Wang Laboratories Inc.* v. *Docktor Pet Centers Inc.*[237] where the lease was silent on a number of matters allegedly negotiated, and in particular on any testing

---

228. Despite the fact that bundling of hardware and software was recognised by the court to be standard practice at that time.

229. At 333.

230. *Teamsters Security Fund of Northern California Inc.* v. *Sperry Rand Corp.* 6 C.L.S.R. 951 (N.D.Cal.,, 1977) at 967. See also *Garden State Food Distributors Inc.* v. *Sperry Rand Corp.* 512 F.Supp. 975 (D.N.J., 1981) where despite an integration clause representations in correspondence were accepted as being contractually binding.

231. *Badger Bearing Co.* v. *Burroughs Corp.* 444 F.Supp. 919 (E.D. Wis., 1977) at 923.

232. See, for example, *Mann* v. *Nunn* (1874) 30 L.T. 526, C.P.

233. For example, in California, see *APLications Inc.* v. *Hewlett Packard Co.* 501 F.Supp. 129 (S.D.N.Y., 1980) at 135 where California law was applied, and in Massachusetts, see *Wang Laboratories Inc.* v. *Docktor Pet Centers Inc.* 422, N.E.2d 805 (Mass., 1981) at 809.

234. For example in Pennsylvania, see *Carl Beasley Ford Inc.* v. *Burroughs Corp.* 361 F.Supp. 325 (E.D. Pa., 1973).

235. 130 Cal. Rptr. 360 (Cal., 1976).

236. Amending a previous lease.

237. 422 N.E.2d 805 (Mass., 1981).

or acceptance procedures before the payments became due, it was held that the court was justified in finding a prior collateral contract to enter into the lease only if the system successfully performed the negotiated two complete cycles of normal operation. The court was strengthened in this view by the failure of the supplier to call any of his negotiators to refute the allegation of such a prior condition. Exactly the same principle applies in the United Kingdom.[238] Nor does the rule exclude evidence of a posterior collateral contract to terminate a written contract. In *Chelsea Industries Inc.* v. *Accuracy Leasing Corp.*[239] the parties to a lease agreed in a side letter to terms upon which the lease might be terminated. It was held[240] that the letter could, despite the parol evidence rule, operate as a separate agreement. Here again the rule in the United Kingdom appears to be the same.[241] The parol evidence rule does not apply at all to evidence of a total failure of consideration which destroys the whole basis of the bargain between the parties.[242]

A court may also find that the written agreement was secured by fraud and for that reason disregard the parol evidence rule, so far as the evidence of fraud is concerned, though it has been held in the United States that such fraud must relate to the execution of the writing. so that the fraud must have led to the omission or misrepresentation of the relevant term of the contract, and that it is not enough to show that the representation itself was fraudulent.[243] It was argued that any less stringent view would destroy the parol evidence rule and defeat legitimate business expectations by permitting agreements to be reopened simply upon an allegation of fraud. Thus where the parties were seasoned commercial enterprises, and in the course of negotiations to repair previous shortcomings the supplier made an oral promise to allow a discount on future purchases, it was held that when the subsequent contractual letter of release failed to refer to the discount at all, and it was alleged that it had therefore been obtained by fraud, the court opined,

a party with the capacity and opportunity to read a written contract, who executes it not under any emergency, and whose signature was not obtained by trick or artifice cannot later claim fraud in the inducement.[244]

Nevertheless it is submitted that it will not generally be a matter of insuperable difficulty to persuade a court inclined to suspect fraud,[245] that

---

238. *Pym* v. *Campbell* (1856) 6 E. & B. 370, Q.B.

239. 699 F.2d 58 (1st Cir., 1983).

240. At 62.

241. *Morris* v. *Baron & Co.* [1918] A.C. 1, H.L.

242. *Nielson* v. *MFT Leasing Inc.* 656 P.2d 454 (Ut., 1982) at 456.

243. *National Cash Register Co.* v. *Modern Transfer Co. Inc.* 302 A.2d 486 (Pa., 1973) at 490. This strict interpretation may have been influenced by the fact that the court found the agreement to have been reached by two comparably competent parties, and by the fact that the standard form had been supplemented by a written agreement dealing specifically with many of the matters in issue.

244. *Management Assistance Inc.* v. *Computer Dimensions Inc.* 546 F.Supp. 666 (N.D. Ga., 1982) at 671, 672.

245. The matter is usually raised by a separate tortious claim based upon the fraud, see for example, *APLications Inc.* v. *Hewlett Packard Co.* 501 F.Supp. 129 (S.D.N.Y., 1980).

the final written agreement was not intended by the defrauded party to represent the entire and definitive agreement between the parties. In the United Kingdom there would clearly be tortious liability for any fraudulent misrepresentation inducing a contract,[246] and in such a case both rescission of the contract and damages for its breach can be obtained.[247] Nor will an integration clause defeat such claims since any exclusion clauses in the contract have been mitigated by the passage of section 3 of the Misrepresentation Act 1967[248] which provides:

If a contract contains a term which would exclude or restrict (a) any liability to which a party to a contract may be subject by reason of any misrepresentation made by him before the contract was made: or (b) any remedy available to another party to the contract by reason of such a misrepresentation, that term shall be of no effect except in so far as it satisfies the requirement of reasonableness as stated in section 11(1) of the Unfair Contract Terms Act 1977; and it is for those claiming that the term satisfies that requirement to show that it does.

Since the whole purpose of integration clauses is invariably to bring such exclusions into play, the effect of this section will be to defeat them, at least so far as they are unreasonable, and the mere fact that they were the subject of negotiation by equally skilled parties or industry standard forms will not necessarily show that they are reasonable.[249] Still less would their inclusion be likely to be held to be reasonable between parties of unequal bargaining power.[250]

The main practical problems which preference for a written contract is designed to solve are, first, prevention of the resurrection in litigation of points which were bargained away during pre-contractual negotiation; and second, hindrance of assignment, if the assignee of a written contract is to be held bound by further terms not apparent from the writing tendered by the assignor. It is not obvious, however, that the parol evidence rule is either sufficient or necessary to solve them. The rather peculiar facts of *ARB (American Research Bureau)* v. *E-Systems Inc.*[251] illustrate the former situation. The parties conducted lengthy negotiations in the course of which the plaintiffs deleted from the then current draft a clause requiring the defendant to bear the cost of reprocurement of the electronic equipment in question, if the contract were terminated on account of the defendant's default. Unfortunately no corresponding explicit amendment was made to the clause defining the assessment of damages. When the plaintiffs sought to recover these very reprocurement costs, the defendants were prevented by the parol evidence rule from proving that just such a claim had been bargained away. So in this situation the parol evidence rule achieved the exact converse of its normal justification. Nor is the rule necessary to assist assignment. In *Chelsea Industries Inc.* v. *Accuracy Leasing Corp.*[252] the parties to a lease agreed in a side

---

246. See, for example, *Doyle* v. *Olby (Ironmongers) Ltd.* [1969] 2 Q.B. 158, C.A.
247. *Archer* v. *Brown* [1985] Q.B. 401, C.A.
248. As amended by the Unfair Contract Terms Act 1977.
249. *Walker* v. *Boyle* [1982] 1 All E.R. 634, C.A.
250. *Howard Marine & Dredging Co. Ltd.* v. *A. Ogden & Sons (Excavations) Ltd.* [1978] Q.B. 574, C.A.
251. 663 F.2d 189 (D.C.Cir., 1980).
252. 699 F.2d 58 (1st Cir., 1983) at 62.

letter to terms upon which the lease might be terminated. It was held that the letter could, despite the parol evidence rule, operate as a separate agreement as between the parties to it, but that it would not necessarily bind an assignee. Precisely the same answer to this problem was proposed in the United Kingdom by the Law Commission in its study of the parol evidence rule.[253]

2. Express terms

It might be thought that few problems would arise in determining the express terms of a contract, for a computer as much as for anything else. The principles are indeed straightforward. The parties are bound by any terms, not inconsistent with public policy, to which they have agreed, or which they might reasonably be supposed to have manifested agreement. It is, subject to the previous section, immaterial that the term was expressed orally or informally. In oral dealings there is sometimes greater room for misunderstanding, leading in extreme cases to mutual mistakes of fact sufficient to prevent any contract from arising, as in *Konic International Corp.* v. *Spokane Computer Services Inc.*[254] where the statement of the price in dollars over the telephone was misunderstood by the buyer to refer to dollars and cents, thus leading to a discrepancy of a factor of a hundred. It is further necessary that there is some mutuality in the transaction, in the common law termed 'consideration'. Both parties must receive something in return for their promise, though it need not necessarily be very much. The general principle is that parties are free to make whatever agreement they choose, especially in a commercial context.

Given that terms can be expressed orally and informally, it is sometimes difficult to determine exactly which statements passing between the parties are to be regarded as terms of the contract, and which are not. In the United States, the Uniform Commercial Code offers some guidance in article 2-313 which provides that:

(1) Express warranties by the seller are created as follows:
(a) Any affirmation of fact or promise made by the seller to the buyer which relates to the goods and becomes part of the basis of the bargain creates an express warranty that the goods shall conform to the affirmation or promise;
(b) Any description of the goods which is made part of the basis of the bargain creates an express warranty that the goods shall conform to the description;
(c) Any sample or model which is made part of the basis of the bargain creates an express warranty that the whole of the goods shall conform to the sample or model;
(2) It is not necessary to the creation of an express warranty that the seller shall use formal words such as 'warrant or 'guarantee' or that he have a specific intention to make a warranty, but an affirmation merely of the value of the goods or a statement purporting to be merely the seller's opinion or commendation of the goods does not create a warranty.

In the computer field, questions may arise about claims for the performance of the equipment. It is not uncommon for a supplier to provide a potential

---

253. Law Com. 154 (Cmnd. 9700) (1986) at para. 2.43.
254. 708 P.2d 932 (Id., 1985).

customer with glossy brochures and sometimes custom-made proposals, setting out specifications of such performance. If the equipment fails to meet these specifications it will be necessary to determine whether or not they were contractually warranted standards of performance, failure to meet which amounts to breach. There is no intrinsic reason to reject statements made in brochures and advertisements.[255] In *The Cricket Alley Corp. v. Data Terminal Systems Inc.*[256] the warranty was construed from a mixture of advertisement, demonstration, oral assurance and system manual. It is, however, generally unlikely that claims made in such materials will be regarded as contractually binding, especially when the parties are on a comparable level of expertise. Thus in *APLications Inc. v. Hewlett Packard Co.*[257] claims for the number of terminals which could be accommodated without degradation of performance in such literature were disregarded in a contract between two commercial suppliers of computing equipment. The defendant in such situations is likely to claim that the statements in the brochures were merely 'puffing', or making clearly exaggerated, and often vague, claims, which no one could realistically suppose to be intended to bind. Another line of defence is to claim that the statements are not binding because they are no more than forecasts, or expressions of the opinion of the party making the claim. Given that the contract is for the performance of equipment, often itself in a developmental stage at the time of contracting, and in an unfamiliar environment, such claims often succeed.[258] As in that example, the situation may be clarified by an explicit statement in any pre-contractual dealings that any statements which may be made are not intended to bind, but are offered only as guidance, and will be subsumed in the terms of any final agreement. The question is, however, one of fact. In some cases the pre-contractual representations have been regarded as so fundamental as to have become terms of the contract. Thus in *Teamsters Security Fund of Northern California Inc. v. Sperry Rand Corp.*[259] correspondence passing between the parties and containing representations as to the performance of the equipment was incorporated as part of the contract. It is immaterial that, as there, the transaction is one of hire rather than sale, or even that the lessor is a third party,[260] though in the case of a retail sale by a dealer any express representations are likely to bind the dealer only.[261] Similarly where a number of documents relating to a transaction are executed simultaneously they may be construed as a whole. In one case[262] the plaintiff wisely stipulated that a sales contract and lease should be

---

255. They were accepted as creating express warranties in *Computerized Radiological Services Inc. v. Syntex Corp.* 595 F.Supp. 1495 (E.D.N.Y., 1984) at 1506.
256. 732 P.2d 719 (Kan., 1987).
257. 501 F.Supp. 129 (S.D.N.Y., 1980).
258. See, for example, *Westfield Chemical Corp. v. Burroughs Corp.* 21 U.C.C.R. 1293 (Mass., 1977). But not always, compare *Redmac Inc. v. Computerland of Peoria* 489 N.E.2d 380 (Ill., 1986), and *Iten Leasing Co. v. Burroughs Corp.* 684 F.2d 573 (8th Cir., 1982) where the court found the question very close.
259. 6 C.L.S.R. 951 (N.D. Cal., 1977).
260. See, for example, *Schatz v. Olivetti Corp. of America* 647 P.2d 820 (Kan., 1982).
261. *Gross v. Systems Engineering Corp.* 36 U.C.C.R. 42 (E.D.Pa., 1983).
262. *W.R. Weaver Co. v. Burroughs Corp.* 580 S.W.2d 76 (Tex., 1979).

supplemented by a statement of installation conditions. Because these conditions referred expressly to the design and installation of a working system adequate to meet the customer's needs, they were incorporated into the entire agreement between the parties. Although the sales contract and lease contained the usual integration and exclusion clauses, it was held that the express warranty in the installation conditions was inconsistent with the exclusion of all express warranties, and according to the normal principle of construing against the party creating the ambiguity, the express warranty survived. Such an approach has sometimes succeeded even in a commercial context, and even though the claim was made only in standard specifications for equipment. In *Consolidated Data Terminals Inc.* v. *Applied Digital Data Systems Inc.*[263] the plaintiff was a retailer of computer hardware and ordered large quantities of terminals from the defendant for resale, upon the basis of the performance specification of the terminals which claimed a speed of 19 200 baud and high reliability. In fact the terminals could not attain speeds of even 10 per cent of that claimed, and 25 per cent were inoperable upon delivery. Despite the presence of the usual exclusion of express warranties it was held that:

> Where a contract includes both specific warranty language and a general disclaimer of warranty liability, the former prevails over the latter where the two cannot be reasonably reconciled.[264]

Although no reported case in the United Kingdom has applied this principle in the case of contracts in the area of computing, there seems little doubt from the use of a similar approach elsewhere[265] that the result would be much the same. In fact, it will nowadays in the United Kingdom rarely be necessary to resort to such devices since the position of the purchaser has been vastly improved in the modern law. If he has been induced to contract on the basis of a false pre-contractual representation there is a special statutory form of recovery under the Misrepresentation Act 1967 section 2(1), unless the seller can prove that he believed in the truth of the representation and was reasonable in so doing, right up to the time of contracting.[266] This has been applied[267] in a situation of disparity of knowledge where a hirer represented the carrying capacity of some barges to be greater than it really was and, despite the absence of negligence, was held liable. Even at common law there is in the United Kingdom a tendency to regard statements of capacity not simply as representations of opinion, but as contractual promises that the statement has been made with care and skill, thus allowing a contractual cause of action, if no such care and skill were applied.[268]

It is very common for a supplier to make a limited warranty to repair or replace defective equipment in substitution for more generous warranties

---

263. 708 F.2d 385 (9th Cir., 1983).
264. At 391.
265. See, for example, *Couchman* v. *Hill* [1947] K.B. 554, C.A.
266. See further below p. 244.
267. In *Howard Marine & Dredging Co. Ltd.* v. *A. Ogden & Sons (Excavations) Ltd.* [1978] Q.B. 574, C.A.
268. *Esso Petroleum Co. Ltd.* v. *Mardon* [1976] Q.B. 801, C.A.

either implicit in extrinsic statements or capable of being implied by operation of law. In the United States such substitution is, in principle, allowed, but may be struck down if it is deemed unconscionable.[269] If such a clause survives, it is likely to constitute an effective way of limiting liability. Such limited warranties may be restricted to defects in workmanship or materials, and still further apply only to non-expendable parts. It seems that the courts will apply the sensible view that such a limitation does not implicitly render the warranty for expendable parts more generous than that for non-expendable parts.[270] It does seem, however, that the supplier's own extreme definition of 'expendable', as meaning those parts the nature of which dictates replacement rather than repair, may be accepted. Given the development in modern technology of ever-increasing miniaturisation and highly automated methods of production, very little hardware will qualify as anything other than expendable under such a definition, and virtually none that is likely to fail. It should be noted that it is for the plaintiff to show that his claim falls within the scope of any express warranty.

The most common difficulty relates to the incorporation of prior and informal representations into a subsequent written contract. In *Burnett* v. *Westminster Bank Ltd.*[271] the converse situation occurred. There the bank attempted the unilateral incorporation of a new term into an existing contract. The plaintiff was a customer of the bank, and although there was no written contract (and hence no scope for the parol evidence rule) the arrangement was clearly contractual in character, upon terms to be construed. When the bank introduced a new computerised accounting system, it used magnetic character recognition for its cheques. This made it very important that customers should not make manuscript alterations. Instructions to that effect were printed on the new cheque book issued to the plaintiff. He failed to notice them, and made a manuscript alteration to the address of the branch upon which a particular cheque was drawn. The bank processed the cheque automatically with the result that it was directed to the branch indicated by the magnetic ink coding. The plaintiff wished to stop payment on the cheque and addressed his stop order to the branch address which he had substituted. As a result the stop order never reached the original branch, and payment was not stopped. The plaintiff was held entitled to recover the full amount because the bank had not done enough to bring the changed terms of the contract, invalidating manuscript alterations, to the notice of the customer, or to secure his agreement to it. It should also be noted that in any case where a subsequent express term is to be added to a contract there must either be some entitlement to alter in the original contract, or separate consideration for the subsequent alteration.

3. Implied terms

Terms may be implied into a contract either upon the basis that as a matter of fact that parties may be taken to have contracted on the understanding

---

269. See below p. 198.
270. See *Bruffey* v. *Burroughs Corp.* 522 F.Supp. 769 (D. Md., 1981).
271. [1966] 1 Q.B. 742, C.A.

that a term so implied was a binding term of the contract, or upon the basis that as a matter of law the parties should be taken to have contracted upon a term implied by law, at least in the absence of a clear indication that they have deliberately excluded such a term from their contract, so far as they are free to do so.

(a) Implication of fact

Courts are reluctant to imply terms as a matter of fact, especially into commercial contracts, and even more especially into those resulting from detailed negotiation and professional drafting. At the other end of the spectrum the courts are sometimes faced with a situation in which there is no evidence of any agreement whatever. Thus in *Associated Tabulating Services* v. *Olympia Life Insurance Corp.*[272] the parties intended to contract with each other, but before signing, or even coming to a firm agreement as to terms, one party started supplying forms and the other began to process them. It was there necessary for the whole contract to be implied. In such a case the court will derive as much assistance as it can from the dealings between the parties, and will often incorporate any particular usage of a trade. Thus in *Gross* v. *Systems Engineering Corp.*[273] the court recognised a usage in the computer context of limiting warranties on hardware to sixty or ninety-day periods on the basis that faults would be most likely to emerge during such time. In order to be implied, any term must be obvious and necessary to give the contract business effect. It is not enough that it is reasonable.[274] The court will not act gratuitously to improve the terms upon which the parties have themselves contracted. It will be unwilling to imply a term which is inconsistent with any express term of the contract.[275] The court will, however, imply a term requiring good faith and fair dealing, and in one case a party who refused to supply all of the information necessary to the other's specification for custom-built software was held to be in breach of it, with the result that the obligation to supply the software lapsed.[276] Because a term will be implied only on the basis that the parties must have intended to include it in their agreement, any such term must be capable of being understood by both parties, and be within their willingness to agree to it. In the computer context the former consideration may disqualify many terms from implication into contracts with naïve users. In any context the latter consideration presents an obstacle since disputes about contracts occur only when the interests of the parties conflict in the light of the events which have occurred. It requires a very strong case to reconstruct a more harmonious prior contemplation of such events.

(b) Implication by operation of law

The terms most often implied by law into contracts for the sale of computing equipment which give rise to dispute are those relating to the merchantabil-

---

272. 414 F.2d 1306 (5th Cir., 1969).
273. 36 U.C.C.R. 42 (E.D. Pa., 1983).
274. *Liverpool City Council* v. *Irwin* [1977] A.C. 239, H.L.
275. *Duke of Westminster* v. *Guild* [1985] Q.B. 688, C.A.
276. *H.R. Stone Inc.* v. *Phoenix Business Systems Inc.* 660 F.Supp. 351 (S.D.N.Y., 1987) at 359.

ity of the equipment and its fitness for its purpose. Different terms are in the United Kingdom implied into contracts for the hiring of goods, and for the provision of services.

Merchantability

There is considerable similarity in the statutory expression of this implied term between that set out in the United Kingdom by section 14(2) of the Sale of Goods Act 1979,

Where the seller sells goods in the course of a business, there is an implied condition that the goods supplied under the contract are of merchantable quality, except that there is no such condition-
(a) as regards defects specifically drawn to the buyer's attention before the contract is made; or
(b) if the buyer examines the goods before the contract is made, as regards defects which that examination ought to reveal.

and that set out in the United States by section 2-314(1) of the Uniform Commercial Code,

Unless excluded or modified a warranty that the goods shall be merchantable is implied in a contract for their sale if the seller is a merchant with respect to goods of that kind . . ..

In the United States it is necessary to refer to this warranty explicitly in order to exclude it.[277] It seems that a computer which is so defective that it cannot carry out a simple function despite strenuous and competent efforts to program it to do so will be held to be unmerchantable.[278] It has further been held that the term is capable of applying to licensed software, even in the absence of the supply of any hardware whatever.[279]

In the United Kingdom the concept of merchantability is expanded to some extent by section 14(6) of the Sale of Goods Act 1979 which provides that:

Goods of any kind are of merchantable quality within the meaning of subsection (2) above if they are as fit for the purpose or purposes for which goods of that kind are commonly bought as it is reasonable to expect having regard to any description applied to them, the price (if relevant) and all the other relevant circumstances.

Although this definition was introduced into the law only in 1973[280] it has attracted some criticism, and was reviewed by the Law Commission.[281] It has been said that the very word 'merchantable' is archaic, and quite specifically that it is inappropriately applied to a modern computer system;[282] that the definition is vague; and, most significantly in the case of software, is consistent with the presence of defects in products where defects are customarily present, and further that no explicit reference is made to the

---

277. Uniform Commercial Code sect. 2–31(2). See *Jaskey Finance & Leasing Corp.* v. *Display Data Corp.* 564 F.Supp. 160 (E.D. Pa., 1983), applying Michigan law.
278. *Schatz* v. *Olivetti Corp. of America* 647 P.2d 820 (Kan., 1982).
279. *Schroders Inc.* v. *Hogan Systems Inc.* 4 U.C.C. Rep. 2d 1397 (N.Y., 1987).
280. In the Supply of Goods (Implied Terms) Act 1973 sect. 7(2).
281. Law Com. No. 160, 'Sale and Supply of Goods', Cm. 137 (1987).
282. *Ibid.* para. 2.10.

durability or safety of the goods. It should be noted that goods may be rendered unmerchantable by the instructions which accompany them, though since liability is statutory, rather than dependent upon negligence at common law, a court may be reluctant to find such unmerchantability unless the instructions, which might well comprise manuals, are not merely capable of being misunderstood, but very clearly wrong.[283]

In the United States the concept of merchantability is amplified in the latter parts of section 2-314 of the Uniform Commercial Code, those most closely relating to computers providing:

(2) Goods to be merchantable must be at least such as
(a) pass without objection in the trade under the contract description; and . . .
(c) are fit for the ordinary purposes for which such goods are used;

It should be stressed that neither of these is intended or to be taken as an exhaustive, or exclusive, definition of merchantability; they merely provide some guidance to the application of the term.

Fitness for purpose

Here too there is considerable congruence of provision in the United Kingdom and the United States. Thus in the United Kingdom the Sale of Goods Act 1979 provides in section 14(3) that:

Where the seller sells goods in the course of a business and the buyer, expressly or by implication, makes known-
(a) to the seller, or
(b) where the purchase price or any part of it is payable by instalments and the goods were previously sold by a credit broker to the seller, to that credit broker,
any particular purpose for which the goods are being bought, there is an implied condition that the goods supplied under the contract are reasonably fit for that purpose, whether or not that is a purpose for which such goods are commonly supplied, except where the circumstances show that the buyer does not rely, or that it is unreasonable for him to rely, on the skill or judgment of the seller or credit broker.

while in the United States section 2-315 of the Uniform Commercial Code provides:

Where the seller at the time of contracting has reason to know any particular purpose for which the goods are required and that the buyer is relying on the seller's skill or judgment to furnish suitable goods, there is unless excluded or modified under the next section an implied warranty that the goods shall be fit for such purpose.

The operation of this term in the United States is well illustrated by the early case of *Sperry Rand Corp.* v. *Industrial Supply Corp.*[284] The nature of the warranty as an implication of law, as opposed to one of fact, is emphasised by its being held unaffected by an integration clause in the written contract, and by its being governed by the law of the place of performance, rather than by that of the place of contracting. Perhaps the most remarkable feature, however, was that there was held to be an *express* warranty of fitness for purpose, made during pre-contractual negotiations, and that was held to have been validly excluded by the operation of the integration clause. The

---

283. *Wormell* v. *RHM Agriculture (East) Ltd.* [1987] 3 All E.R. 75, C.A.
284. 337 F.2d 363 (5th Cir., 1964).

court nevertheless found that the *implied* warranty of fitness for purpose survived because there was no explicit exclusion of implied warranties, and it was held not to be inconsistent with the limited express warranty to repair or replace contained in the written contract. The court took the general view that in order to succeed upon the basis of an implied warranty the buyer must show that the seller possessed superior knowledge of the type of goods in question, that the purpose for which the goods could be used was known to the seller, and that the buyer relied upon the seller's skill and judgment.[285] All of these conditions were found to have been satisfied. The defendants further sought to negate the effect of any such surviving implied warranty upon the basis that the buyer had had plenty of opportunity to inspect the goods and, having done so, failed to reject within a reasonable period, and in any event had contracted for specific goods, as designated in the contract by part numbers and trade names. The court was eloquent[286] in its rejection of the inspection argument:

Industrial Supply did not know and could not be expected to ascertain, except by use and experiment, the fundamental abilities and capacities of the electronic equipment, with its transistors, tubes and diodes, its varicolored maze of wiring, its buttons and switches, and the supplementing of machines and devices for the punching of cards and others for the sorting thereof. And of course, the personnel of Industrial Supply could not be expected to understand the processes by which a set of these modern miracle makers perform their tasks.[287]

Still less does the demonstration of software performing a different function from that required provide an opportunity of inspection sufficient to justify exclusion of the implied warranty.[288] So far as the reference to specific items of equipment was concerned, the court took the view that while such an argument might have validity in relation to any particular device, here the buyer was purchasing a combination of some ten different devices, and it was their integration which was unfit for his purpose. Even in the case of the sale of a single specific item, which may be a program, the warranty will not be excluded if there is disparity between the knowledge of the seller and of the buyer, and the seller represents that the item as specified will perform the function specified by the buyer.[289]

Although there seem to be no reported United Kingdom cases concerning the application of this implied term in the context of computers, the rather similar Canadian provisions have been twice so invoked, in *Burroughs Business Machines Ltd.* v. *Feed-Rite Mills (1962) Ltd.*[290] finding that the supplier was in the business of supplying accounting machines, that the user relied upon the

---

285. It is not necessary that the buyer make known his purpose, nor that he reveal his reliance upon the seller, if these facts can be inferred, as they have been in the case of the supply by a dealer of a bespoke software system, customised for the lay buyer's requirements, as in *Neilson Business Equipment Center Inc.* v. *Monteleone* 524 A.2d 1172 (Del., 1987) at 1175, 1176.
286. The technology now seems quaint, but the principle applies no less to the many times more powerful, complex and miniaturised systems of today.
287. At 370.
288. *Hollingsworth* v. *The Software House Inc.* 513 N.E.2d 1372 (Oh., 1986).
289. *Ibid.* at 1376.
290. 42 D.L.R.3d 303 (Man.C.A., 1973) (Canada).

seller's skill and judgment, and that the equipment was not reasonably fit for its purpose, and in *Public Utilities Commission for the City of Waterloo* v. *Burroughs Business Machines Ltd.*[291] finding that recovery was not barred by reference in the contract to specific pieces of hardware, when reliance was placed on the effect of the combination of items which were purchased. The United Kingdom Law Commission found general satisfaction with the terminology of this implied term,[292] though some anxiety was expressed about the need for the customer to make known a specific purpose where the goods, prototypically the case with computers, were intrinsically capable of a wide range of different uses.[293]

Terms implied in contracts for the supply of services

Many contracts relating to computers include the provision of services, and some, for example some maintenance, consultancy and data processing services, can be regarded as involving only the supply of services. In the United Kingdom terms to be implied in such contracts were first codified in Part II of the Supply of Goods and Services Act 1982. The two most likely to be applicable in the computer context are section 13 which relates to the quality, and section 14 which relates to the time, of performance. Section 13 provides that,

In a contract for the supply of a service where the supplier is acting in the course of a business, there is an implied term that the supplier will carry out the service with reasonable care and skill.

It seems that the principles to be described more fully in relation to the tort of negligence in the next chapter[294] will be applied to determine what is, or is not, reasonable. The flexibility of the term commended it to the United Kingdom Law Commission in a subsequent review of these provisions.[295] Section 14 deals with the time of performance and provides that:

(1) Where, under a contract for the supply of a service by a supplier acting in the course of a business, the time for the service to be carried out is not fixed in the contract, left to be fixed in a manner agreed by the contract or determined by the course of dealing between the parties, there is an implied term that the supplier will carry out the service within a reasonable time.
(2) What is a reasonable time is a question of fact.

Section 15, which is less likely to apply in the case of services relating to computers, provides similarly, where no charge is fixed, for the implication of a reasonable charge.

There are also some indications independent of express statutory provision that, at least in some cases, where a complex system is being designed, the designer will be liable to design a usable system, both in general,[296] and for

---

291. 34 D.L.R.3d 320 (Ont.H.C., 1973) (Canada).
292. Law Com. No. 160, 'Sale and Supply of Goods' Cm. 137 (1987) para. 2.19.
293. *Ibid.* para. 2.17.
294. See p. 251 below.
295. Law Com. No. 156, 'Contracts for the Supply of Services', Cmnd. 9773 (1986) para. 2.24.
296. *Basildon D.C.* v. *J.E. Leese (Properties) Ltd.* [1985] Q.B. 839, C.A. (that a building should be habitable); roughly corresponding to the implied term of merchantability.

the particular designated purposes of the customer.[297] In some Commonwealth jurisdictions such terms are occasionally implied by explicit statutory provision,[298] but in the United Kingdom the Law Commission, while not ruling out such a development, felt that more evidence should be acquired of the need for, and working of, such provisions.[299] In the United States it has been held that in a contract for the supply of programming services there is an implied term that the supplier possesses 'the skill and will exhibit the diligence ordinarily possessed by well-informed members of the trade or profession'.[300] It may also be implied that any such services will be provided in a workmanlike manner.

4. Exclusion clauses

The remaining two types of contractual term to be dealt with in this section are exclusion and limitation clauses. They tend to be closely connected with each other. It is extremely common in the field of computer contracts for a vendor to seek to minimise his liability both by reference to the types of loss for which he is to be responsible, and for the extent to which and procedure by which he is to be made liable. The line of demarcation between the definition of liability and its limitation is not always completely clear, and there is thus some overlap in the treatment of these two types of term. It is quite common to find contracts seeking to exclude first any terms not contained in the written contract, and second any terms implied by operation of law, and then finally going on to include in the written contract only a very limited express term. Since in the first case the vendor is seeking to exclude matters agreed with the other party, and in the second terms implied as a matter of public policy, it is hardly surprising that they are received unenthusiastically. This section will deal both with the exclusion of liability and the substitution of limited liability. The following section will deal with limitation to particular types of damage and the use of special procedures to minimise the incidence of successful claims. In many situations, particularly those of disparity of bargaining power, such practices are regarded as unfair, and have been curbed either as a matter of common law by the courts or by legislative intervention.

(a) Common law
The principal technique of the common law in this area is to adopt a very strict attitude towards the question of whether the relevant clause is indeed part of the contract, of the interpretation of such clauses, and of the question of proving that the facts of the case come within the interpretation so adopted. It should be noted that with the increased emphasis in modern

---

297. *Independent Broadcasting Authority* v. *E.M.I. (Electronics) Ltd.* (1980) Build. L.R. 1, C.A. (design of television mast); roughly corresponding to the implied term of fitness for purpose.
298. For example in Australia under the provisions of the Australian Trade Practices Act 1974 sect. 74(2), and in Victoria under the Goods (Sales and Leases) Act 1981 sect. 2(2).
299. Law Com. No. 156, 'Contracts for the Supply of Services', Cmnd. 9773 (1986) para. 2.45.
300. *Data Processing Services Inc.* v. *L.H. Smith Oil Corp.* 492 N.E.2d 314 (Ind., 1986) at 319.

times on legislative intervention the need for, and rigour of, these techniques has to some extent diminished.

It is first necessary to show that the relevant clause was part of the contract, and this will involve the question of bringing it adequately to the notice of the party to be bound by it before the completion of the contract. It will not be enough to proffer a document which looks more like a receipt than a contract, or to bring the term to the knowledge of the party only after he has made the contract. The former situation might apply to the use of a simple hardware supply contractual form after months of negotiation,[301] and the latter to an attempt to impose such exclusion under a shrink-wrap licence.[302]

The general rule of construction is that exclusion clauses will be interpreted strictly against the party proffering them in a standard form, or seeking to rely upon them. These attitudes were most appropriate to assist consumers, and to some extent have been overtaken by the legislative developments to be discussed below. It nevertheless remains the case that any ambiguity in the wording of an exclusion clause is likely to be construed against the interest of the party relying upon it. Thus in *Sperry Rand Corp.* v. *Industrial Supply Corp.*[303] a clause excluding liability for an express term that the goods would be fit for their purpose was construed so as not to apply to an implied term to exactly the same effect. Conversely in *Computerized Radiological Services Inc.* v. *Syntex Corp.*[304] it was held that a disclaimer referring only to implied terms was ineffective to disclaim express warranties. If a general form of words is capable of applying to distinctly different sets of circumstances it is likely to be construed as applying only to the least drastic, on the basis that the parties would be less likely to have agreed to exclude liability for anything more. In the United Kingdom this principle showed some signs of being pressed so far as to create ambiguity even in carefully worded exclusion clauses agreed between equal commercial parties, thus infringing general principles of freedom of contract, and generating uncertainty. Any such development was brought to a juddering halt in the leading case of *Photo Production Ltd.* v. *Securicor Transport Ltd*:

In commercial contracts negotiated between businessmen capable of looking after their own interests and of deciding how risks inherent in the performance of various kinds of contract can be most economically borne (generally by insurance), it is, in my view, wrong to place a strained construction on words in an exclusion clause which are clear and fairly susceptible of one meaning only even after allowance has been made for the presumption in favour of the implied primary and secondary obligations.[305]

---

301. See *Teamsters Security Fund of Northern California Inc.* v. *Sperry Rand Corp.* 6 C.L.S.R. 951 (N.D. Cal., 1977) at 967; *Burroughs Corp.* v. *Chesapeake Petroleum and Supply Co.* 384 A.2d 734 (Md., 1978) at 736. But see also *Kalil Bottling Co.* v. *Burroughs Corp.* 610 P.2d 1055 (Az., 1980).
302. See above p. 144.
303. 337 F.2d 363 (5th Cir., 1964).
304. 595 F.Supp. 1495 (E.D. N.Y., 1984) at 1507.
305. [1980] A.C. 827, H.L. by Lord Diplock at 851.

This decision was designed to emphasise that the role of the common law was limited to being one of construction, and to prevent its subversion by the introduction of a rule of law that provided a term, or breach, were sufficiently fundamental, then no exclusion clause, however carefully worded, could be effective. It remains the case, however, that the centrality of the obligation, or the seriousness of the breach, may be relevant to the question of construction. In the most extreme case to uphold the exclusion clause might negate the whole obligation of one party and effectively make his performance wholly optional. Thus in construing a facially comprehensive exclusion clause in a charterparty it was held that to accord it its full apparent effect would have the result that,

> the charter virtually ceases to be a contract for the letting of the vessel and the performance of services by the owners, their master, officers and crew in consideration of the payment of time charter hire and becomes no more than a statement of intent by the owners in return for which the charterers are obliged to pay large sums by way of hire, though if the owners fail to carry out their promises as to description or delivery they are entitled to nothing in lieu.[306]

Even in cases which have apparently applied the principle of construction most favourably towards the exclusion clauses there has been some indication of a minimum liability which cannot be excluded. Thus while in *George Mitchell (Chesterhall) Ltd.* v. *Finney Lock Seeds Ltd.*[307] the House of Lords was prepared to permit exclusion of liability for the catastrophic failure to supply cabbage seed as contracted but instead what was 'in a commercial sense no vegetable seed at all', still the House emphasised that it was not 'a peas and beans case' or, in other words, not a case of supplying something totally different from what was contracted for. In the computer context it is suggested that the delivery of a piece of hardware, totally useless without an operating system, would not be regarded as being capable of being protected by any general drafting of an exclusion clause in a contract for the supply of a computer system. Similarly in *Ailsa Craig Fishing Co. Ltd.* v. *Malvern Fishing Co. Ltd.*[308] where the limitation of liability for total failure to provide a service contracted for was upheld, it was intimated that a total exclusion of liability would not have been. Here again it may be supposed that an exclusion clause in a maintenance contract in respect of any breach would not bar liability when shortly after signing the agreement the prospective maintainer abandoned any intention to maintain the equipment, employed no staff to do so, and carried no stock.

If in such a case an exclusion clause is held not to be capable of applying to a particular type of liability, it will be for party seeking to exclude liability to bear the burden of showing that the circumstances which have occurred fall within those covered by the exclusion clause.

Quite apart from questions of construction some exclusion clauses would be contrary to public policy. Thus there seems to be no question but that a

---

306. *Tor Line AB* v. *Alltrans Group of Canada Ltd.* [1984] 1 All E.R. 103, H.L. by Lord Roskill at 112. Lord Diplock was among the unanimously concurring law Lords.
307. [1983] 2 A.C. 803, H.L.
308. [1983] 1 All E.R. 101, H.L.

clause purporting to exclude liability for a contracting party's own fraud would not be upheld.[309]

(b) Statutory provision

In the United Kingdom the validity of exclusion clauses will now most often be governed by explicit statutory provision. The principal enactment is the Unfair Contract Terms Act 1977. Although the Act generally refers to the exclusion or restriction of *liability*, it is made quite clear[310] that this form of words applies to terms which exclude or restrict the relevant *obligation or duty*, so that it applies both to the terms covered in this and in the next section. The Act in part differentiates between contracts where one party deals as a consumer and those where neither do so, and between contracts where one deals on the other's standard terms of business, and those where they do not. In all cases, however, the Act invalidates any term purporting to exclude or restrict liability for death or personal injury caused by negligence, and for any other loss or damage to the extent that the exclusion is unreasonable.[311] The one possible exception to the universality of this invalidation in domestic contracts[312] occurs in relation to a contract, such as a software licence, which is arguably excluded by the terms of Schedule 1 paragraph 1(c) to the Unfair Contract Terms Act 1977. This paragraph excludes any contract from the provisions of section 2 of the Act 'so far as it relates to the creation or transfer of a right or interest in any . . . intellectual property' or relates to its termination. While it is arguable that such contracts are totally excluded from the ambit of the Act, it is equally possible that the exemption extends only to the clauses which create or transfer the right or interest. This interpretation is assisted by the presence in paragraph 1(c) of the words 'so far as it relates to' which do not appear in other cases where a whole class of contracts are excluded.[313] Since there seems no special reason to treat software licences differently from other types of computer contract, especially as defects in them may well cause death or injury,[314] it is submitted that the latter view is to be preferred.

Although both the Sale of Goods Act 1979[315] and the Supply of Goods and Services Act 1982[316] permit the exclusion of the terms implied into the contracts governed by those Acts, any such exclusion is itself now subject to the limitations imposed by the Unfair Contract Terms Act 1977. In these cases a distinction is made between cases where one party deals as a

---

309. See in the United Kingdom, 10th Report of the Law Reform Committee (Innocent Misrepresentation), Cmnd. 1782 (1962) para. 23 in the surprising absence of more direct authority; and in the United States, see *Suntogs of Miami Inc.* v. *Burroughs Corp.* 433 So.2d 581 (Fla., 1983). The same view has been taken in Minnesota, despite the attenuated requirements for fraud required in that jurisdiction, *Clements Auto Corp.* v. *Service Bureau Corp.* 444 F.2d 169 (8th Cir., 1971) at 178.
310. In sect. 13(1).
311. Unfair Contract Terms Act 1977 sect. 2.
312. International contracts for the supply of goods are also excluded, see further below p. 222.
313. As in para. 2.
314. See below p. 228.
315. Sect. 55.
316. Sects. 11 and 16.

consumer where the exclusion of implied[317] terms is totally invalid against the consumer, and cases where neither party deals as a consumer, in which case the exclusion is valid only to the extent that it satisfies the statutory test of reasonableness.[318] The criteria of this test correspond closely to the concerns frequently expressed in the context of computer contracts, and take into account,

(a) the strength of the bargaining positions of the parties relative to each other, taking into account (among other things) alternative means by which the customer's requirements could have been met;
(b) whether the customer received an inducement to agree to the term, or in accepting it had an opportunity of entering into a similar contract with other persons, but without having to accept a similar term;
(c) whether the customer knew or ought reasonably to have known of the existence and extent of the term (having regard, among other things, to any custom of the trade and any previous course of dealing between the parties);
(d) where the term excludes or restricts any relevant liability if some condition is not complied with, whether it was reasonable at the time of the contract to expect that compliance with that condition would be practicable;
(e) whether the goods were manufactured, processed or adapted to the special order of the customer.[319]

It has been held that these criteria were not satisfied in *Mackenzie Patten & Co.* v. *British Olivetti Ltd.*[320] where a solicitor who knew nothing about computers, but who had called in a computer salesman because he wished to improve the procedure for maintaining his accounts, described his requirements, and was advised that the salesman's company could provide a machine which fitted his requirements exactly, that it represented the latest technology and was good value for money. None of these things was true. The report is, however, somewhat obscure as to the precise category of liability being considered, for example whether it was for breach of an express or implied term. It does, however, seem that only the strictly contractual claims were considered.[321] The case may be considered to apply in the field of computers the more general interpretation of the first of these criteria in *Howard Marine & Dredging Co. Ltd.* v. *A. Ogden & Sons (Excavations) Ltd.*[322] where the fact that the defendants were expert in shipping matters and the plaintiffs ignorant of them, indeed first-time users of barges, militated against the defendants in considering liability for inaccurate representations as to the capacity of the barges, basically induced by the plaintiffs having asked the wrong questions and misunderstood the answers. In other words, disparity of bargaining strength connotes disparity of knowledge as well as disparity of economic resources.

Since so much depends in this context upon the concept of dealing as a

---

317. In the case of the exclusion of express terms also if one party is dealing on the other's written standard terms as against that party, Unfair Contract Terms Act 1977 sect. 3.
318. *Ibid.* sect. 6(2).
319. *Ibid.* Sch. 2.
320. LEXIS report 11 January 1984, Q.B.
321. There were also claims under sect. 3 of the Misrepresentation Act 1967, and for negligence at common law.
322. [1978] Q.B. 574, C.A.

consumer, it is surprising that there has been so little direct litigation upon the topic. The Unfair Contract Terms Act 1977 provides in section 12(1) that:

A party to a contract 'deals as a consumer' in relation to another party if
(a) he neither makes the contract in the course of a business nor holds himself out as doing so; and
(b) the other party does make the contract in the course of a business; and
(c) in the case of a contract governed by the law of sale of goods or hire purchase, or by section 7 of this Act, the goods passing under or in pursuance of the contract are of a type ordinarily supplied for private use or consumption.

The burden of proof is also cast upon the party claiming that the other does not deal as a consumer.[323] The main guidance to the meaning of this important concept is currently derived from cases construing different legislation, concerned with trade description, which also employs that notion of dealing in the course of a trade or business. The House of Lords has held there that:

The expression 'in the course of a trade or business' in the context of an Act having consumer protection as its primary purpose conveys the concept of some degree of regularity. . ..[324]

In the context it was held immaterial that the goods in question were acquired and used almost exclusively in the course of a business, so long as the nature of the business did not itself involve trading in the articles in question. Such an interpretation might be quite devastating in the field of computers. Very few users of computers actually deal in them, and on this view, but for section 12(3), almost any transaction in the computer context would be categorised as a dealing as a consumer. Even section 12(3) is a somewhat weak instrument to avoid this conclusion since it depends upon whether or not such goods are 'of a type ordinarily supplied for private use or consumption'. Computers if thought of in sufficiently general terms could be considered such a type, and even if large main-frames and complicated business accounting packages might be excluded, the courts would have to become involved in minute examination, not of the actual use of a given machine or program, but of possible uses of classes of machine or program, without the benefit of any agreed classification, or reliable information as to actual practice. It is submitted that cases on the trade description legislation should not be regarded as a model. It imposes criminal penalties, and is construed in favour of the subject. It is not obvious that the Unfair Contract Terms Act 1977 should be approached in the same way, though it was so extended in *R & B Customs Brokers Co. Ltd.* v. *United Dominions Trust Ltd.*[325] but for no better reason than consistency with the Trade Description legislation. Despite this decision there still seems no convincing reason to abstain from the view that a computer is purchased in the course of a trade or business, when it is purchased predominantly for use in a trade or business, however irregularly such purchases are made, and however far the

---

323. Unfair Contract Terms Act 1977 sect. 12(3).
324. *Davies* v. *Sumner* [1984] 3 All E.R. 831, H.L. at 833.
325. [1988] 1 All E.R. 847, C.A.

business is from one dealing in computers.[326]

One of the features of the Unfair Contract Terms Act 1977 is its extensive coverage, and sophisticated and systematic revelation of the wide variety of devices used to exclude or limit liability. In this context it is odd to find that section 4, which imposes a condition of reasonableness only in the case of dealings as a consumer, apparently permits businessmen to contract for indemnification by the other, no matter how unreasonable, in respect of liabilities which they could otherwise limit or exclude only to the extent that they are reasonable. On the other hand, the legislature has been alert to the possible chilling effect of inserting into contracts exclusion terms, invalid under the provisions of the Unfair Contract Terms Act 1977. Given the lack of detailed legal knowledge of most of those dealing with computers, the presence of exclusion clauses in contracts might well induce them not to pursue claims which are apparently excluded. To try to help prevent any such effect, orders have been made[327] erecting the insertion of invalid exclusion clauses into consumer contracts a criminal offence. These provisions seem to be frequently overlooked by those seeking to market in the United Kingdom products emanating from the United States upon the basis of contracts drafted so as to satisfy not the law of the United Kingdom, but that of the United States. It should perhaps be emphasised that these criminal penalties apply to all relevant contracts made in the United Kingdom, irrespective of any clause choosing a foreign law or forum.

In the United States[328] the Uniform Commercial Code also permits the exclusion of liability, though in the case of express warranties found to constitute a part of the contract the warranty will prevail over an inconsistent disclaimer,[329] and words which have statutory power to exclude implied warranties may not exclude express ones.[330] Slightly different forms of exclusion are specified in respect of the warranties of merchantability and fitness for purpose. The former may be excluded orally, but specific reference must be made to 'merchantability';[331] the latter may be excluded only in writing, but any apt form of words will suffice.[332] The Code further provides that if the buyer has been given an adequate opportunity of inspection, then no warranty will be implied as to anything which might have been revealed

---

326. See also Brown 'Business and Consumer Contracts' [1988] *J. of Bus. Law* 386.
327. Consumer Transactions (Restrictions on Statements) Order 1976 (No. 1813) as amended by the Consumer Transactions (Restrictions on Statements) (Amendment) Order 1978 (No. 127) made under the Fair Trading Act 1973.
328. A number of states have, however, intervened to amend the law so as to provide a greater measure of protection for the consumer, though a highly publicised attempt to do so in California failed in 1986 in the face of intensive lobbying by the Association of Data Processing Service Organizations (ADAPSO), see *Computer Weekly* 4 August 1986 p. 102.
329. Uniform Commercial Code 2-316(1) as interpreted in *Consolidated Data Terminals Inc.* v. *Applied Digital Data Systems Inc.* 708 F.2d 385 (9th Cir., 1983) at 391. For a fuller discussion, see Chretien-Dar, 'Uniform Commercial Code – Disclaiming the Express Warranty in Computer Contracts – Taking the Byte out of the Uniform Commercial Code' *40 Ok. L.R.* 471 (1987).
330. *Walker Furniture Co.* v. *AKtion Associates* LEXIS 4277 (Oh., 1988).
331. An attempt to exclude it failed for this reason in *Jaskey Finance & Leasing Corp.* v. *Display Data Corp.* 564 F.Supp. 160 (E.D. Pa., 1983).
332. Uniform Commercial Code art. 2-316(2).

by such inspection,[333] and that trade custom or usage may also operate to exclude any implied warranty.[334] To be effective, any exclusion clause must be conspicuous,[335] defined as being 'so written that a reasonable person against whom it is to operate ought to have notice of it'.[336] It has been held that a disclaimer written in smaller type than the rest of the contract,[337] buried within the body of a paragraph[338] or, although italicised, in small type and printed on green paper, is not sufficiently conspicuous.[339] More usually such clauses are normally printed in a contrasting style, colour or size, headed or indented, close to the place where the buyer is required to sign. It has become rare in the United States for standard form contracts to fail to take effect for this reason. It should also be noted that even if such a clause fails to be conspicuous it may still be effective if the party bound by it was in fact aware of it.[340]

However, any such exclusion clause is, under the Uniform Commercial Code, subject to the requirement that it be not unconscionable as defined by section 2–302:

If the court as a matter of law finds the contract or any clause of the contract to have been unconscionable at the time it was made, the court may refuse to enforce the contract, or it may enforce the remainder of the contract without the unconscionable clause, or it may so limit the application of any unconscionable clause as to avoid any unconscionable result.

The application of the concept to exclusion and limitation clauses is more specifically addressed by section 2–719(3):

Consequential damages may be either limited or excluded unless the limitation or exclusion is unconscionable. Limitation of consequential damages for injury to the person in the case of consumer goods is prima facie unconscionable but limitation of damage where the loss is commercial is not.

The extent to which this concept is appropriate for the regulation of computer contracts has proved controversial in the United States.[341] It is argued on the one hand that the disparity of expertise and bargaining power in many computer contracts, the difficulty of securing significantly different terms from other suppliers, and the expense of cover all militate against the exclusion of all warranties. On the other it is suggested that expertise is available in the market-place and that the inevitable uncertainties in marketing such new and complex products, combined with the infinite

---

333. *Ibid.* art. 2-316(3)(b); but see *Sperry Rand Corp.* v. *Industrial Supply Corp.* 337 F.2d 363 (5th Cir., 1964) for the limitations upon this doctrine in computer cases.
334. Uniform Commercial Code sect. 2-316(3)(c).
335. *Atlas Industries Inc.* v. *National Cash Register Co.* 531 P.2d 41 (Kan., 1975).
336. Uniform Commercial Code sect. 2-201(10).
337. *Atlas Industries Inc.* v. *National Cash Register Co.* 531 P.2d 41 (Kan., 1975).
338. *Computerized Radiological Services Inc.* v. *Syntex Corp.* 595 F.Supp. 1495 (E.D.N.Y., 1984).
339. *Office Supply Inc.* v. *Basic/Four Corp.* 538 F.Supp. 776 (E.D. Wis., 1982).
340. *Ibid.*
341. See, for example, the very different views expressed in Plunkett 'Unconscionability and the Fundamental Breach Doctrine in Computer Contracts', *57 Notre Dame L.R.* 547 (1982) and Himelson 'Frankly Incredible: Unconscionability in Computer Contracts', *4 Comp. L.J.* 695 (1984).

variety of purposes and techniques which may be employed, make the allocation of risk to the purchaser quite acceptable, especially if a choice of different prices is offered to match a choice of allocation of risk.

It is common to distinguish between procedural and substantive unconscionability.[342] Given the express permission to exclude warranties bestowed by the Uniform Commercial Code, it is unlikely that courts will often contemplate substantive unconscionability in the sense that a provision excluding warranties will be regarded as *per se* unconscionable.[343] Similarly in *Consolidated Data Terminals Inc.* v. *Applied Digital Data Systems Inc.*[344] it was held that a limited remedy to repair defective hardware was not *per se* unconscionable. It can also be argued, even so far as procedural unconscionability is concerned, that exclusion clauses are governed exclusively by section 2-316 of the Uniform Commercial Code, and are left untouched by sect. 2-302 or 2-719. However, in *Earman Oil Co. Inc.* v. *Burroughs Corp.*[345] the concept seems to have been applied to the whole exculpatory basis of the contract without discriminating between exclusion and limitation clauses. The court enumerated[346] conditions of unconscionability,

(i) examination of the negotiation process as to length of time in dealing;
(ii) the length of time for deliberations;
(iii) the experience or astuteness of the parties;
(iv) whether counsel reviewed the contract;
(v) whether the buyer was a reluctant purchaser.[347]

It found on the facts that these conditions did not compel a finding of unconscionability, since two were completely absent, and the remainder far from decisive. It was said that,:

The procedural form of unconscionability alleged by Earman requires a showing of overreaching or sharp practices by the seller and ignorance or inexperience on the buyer's part, resulting in a lack of meaningful bargaining by the parties.[348]

In *Hunter* v. *Texas Instruments Inc.*[349] it was held enough to avoid unconscionability in the bargain that the purchaser, who knew little of computers, was college-educated, knew some commercial law and had shopped around for his system.

It seems that in order to get an unconscionability claim off the ground it must be specifically pleaded,[350] or raised by way of response to a motion for

---

342. See the quotation below from *Earman Oil Co. Inc.* v. *Burroughs Corp.* 625 F.2d 1290 (5th cir., 1980).
343. In a number of cases such total exclusion has been upheld, and unconscionability related only to limited alternative warranties: *Investor's Premium Corp.* v. *Burroughs Corp.* 389 F.Supp. 39 (D.S.C., 1974) at 45; *Bakal* v. *Burroughs Corp.* 343 N.Y.S. 2d 541 (N.Y., 1972); *Westfield Chemical Corp.* v. *Burroughs Corp.* 21 U.C.C.R. 1293 (Mass., 1977) at 1295.
344. 708 F.2d 385 (9th Cir., 1983) at 392 n.6.
345. 625 F.2d 1290 (5th Cir., 1980).
346. At 1299.
347. Taken from *Potomac Electric Co.* v. *Westinghouse Electric Corp.* 385 F.Supp. 572 (D.D.C., 1974) reversed on other grounds 527 F.2d 853 (D.C. Cir., 1975). The test was subsequently adopted also in *Office Supply Inc.* v. *Basic/Four Corp.* 538 F.Supp. 776 (E.D. Wis., 1982), another computer case.
348. At 1300.
349. 798 F.2d 299 (8th Cir., 1986).
350. *Badger Bearing Co.* v. *Burroughs Corp.* 444 F.Supp. 919 (E.D. Wis., 1977).

summary judgment,[351] since it savours of fraud, and the defendant must be given an opportunity to meet it.

In most computer contracts the exclusion of warranties is accompanied by the substitution of a limited express warranty. Here too the Uniform Commercial Code makes specific provision:

Where circumstances cause a limited remedy to fail of its essential purpose, remedy may be had as provided in this Act.[352]

This has occasionally provided a more effective method of attacking the defendant's scheme for excluding and limiting his liability. Thus in *Chatlos Systems Inc.* v. *NCR Corp.*[353] where there was a limited remedy, common in computer cases, to repair or replace defects, in this case within sixty days, it was held that from the buyer's point of view,

the repair remedy's aim is to provide goods that conform to the contract of sale and do so at an appropriate time.

Six programs had been promised for March 1975, but only one was installed on time, and by September 1976, at which time none of the others had still been provided, even that one was causing problems. It was held that a delay in remedying a defect could in some cases be as bad as a complete failure to deliver. The failure of this limited remedy operated to revive liability for breach of warranty. Similarly in *Consolidated Data Terminals Inc.* v. *Applied Digital Data Systems Inc.*[354] where there was never any prospect of the terminals coming up to the contracted specification so as to be capable of being sold, a limited remedy of repair was held to fail of its essential purpose. In *Chatlos* the contract also contained an explicit limitation of liability for consequential damages.[355] It was held that this remained valid, notwithstanding the failure of the limited remedy.[356] It may even be held that a limited remedy does not fail of its essential purpose if an adequate alternative to repair is also provided under the contract. In *Garden State Food Distributors Inc.* v. *Sperry Rand Corp.*[357] the alternative of securing the return of all monies paid under the contract was regarded as sufficient to prevent the limited warranty to repair from failing of its essential purpose, and thus to preserve the defendant's exclusion of any liability for breach of warranty. This case appears not to have been cited in *RRX Industries Inc.* v. *Lab-Con Inc.*[358] where failure to correct software was regarded as so fundamental a breach as to cause *both* the limited remedy *and* the limitation of damages to the contract price of the software to fail of their essential purpose, and thus to allow the recovery of consequential damages.[359]

---

351. *Ellmer* v. *Delaware Mini-Computer Systems Inc.* 665 S.W.2d 158 (Tex., 1983) at 160.
352. In sect. 2-719(2).
353. 479 F.Supp. 738 (D.N.J., 1979) affd. in part 635 F.2d 1081 (3rd Cir., 1980) (the District Court's decision was upheld in all respects except the computation of damages).
354. 708 F.2d 385 (9th Cir., 1983).
355. Of the type to be considered further in the next section.
356. See also *Computerized Radiological Services Inc.* v. *Syntex Corp.* 595 F.Supp. 1495 (E.D.N.Y., 1984).
357. 512 F.Supp. 975 (D.N.J., 1981).
358. 772 F.2d 543 (9th Cir., 1985).
359. Though this part of the judgment was subjected to a powerful dissent.

The occasion for a limited remedy to repair to operate must have arisen before it can be considered to have failed of its essential purpose. Thus where a plaintiff repudiated a contract for the supply of software before the extended time for final delivery had arisen, the court held that a limited remedy to provide remedial programming could not be said to have failed.[360] Similarly if nothing satisfying the contract is ever delivered, then the limited warranty to repair does not arise, let alone fail of its essential purpose.[361]

5. Limitation of liability

It will be recalled that this section is distinguished from its predecessor on the basis that here the relevant clauses do not concern the incidence of any of the primary, or even alternative, forms of liability in the contract, but are concerned with the limitation of remedies for an acknowledged breach of them. Perhaps the most commonly encountered form of such limitation in computer cases, certainly in the United States, is the exclusion from the computation of any consequential damage. There are, however, a number of other techniques which can be used to restrict liability. Sometimes a ceiling will be placed upon the amount of damages, or a fixed sum may be substituted for any computation at all, and this fixed sum may either be calculated as a total lump sum assessment or by reference to a particular element, such as per program not installed or per day late in installation, so that it may vary according to the degree of failure of performance. A different approach is to specify a particular procedure for launching a claim which may be in terms of the time allowed to claim, or the means by which the claim must be made. Some other techniques to be considered in the last section of this chapter, such as special dispute resolution procedures or choice of law clauses, may also be designed to secure a limiting effect.

The common law generally permits the parties to limit their liability as they choose. It is more concerned with the converse problem of the imposition of penalties for defective performance by way of agreement to pay fixed sums. It distinguishes between clauses providing for the payment of liquidated damages, and clauses providing for the payment of penalties. Various rules for the construction of such clauses were propounded in the United Kingdom in *Dunlop Pneumatic Tyre Co.* v. *New Garage & Motor Co.*[362] In order to avoid being accounted a penalty, the fixed sum should not be obviously disproportionate to the amount of damage likely to be caused by the breach, but the fact that a pre-estimate is difficult does not necessarily disqualify a case, provided that a reasonable attempt has been made to do so. Because computers are so versatile, such pre-estimation is particularly difficult, and hence the range of acceptable clauses is likely to be large.[363] It follows that where the fixed sum remains the same despite potential liability for a wide variety of different types of breach, likely to lead to equally wide variety in the amounts of damage, it is more likely that the clause will be

360. *Samuel Black Co.* v. *Burroughs Corp.* 33 U.C.C. Rep. 954 (D.Mass., 1981) at 964.
361. *Hawaiian Telephone Co.* v. *Microform Data Systems Inc.* 829 F.2d 919 (9th Cir., 1987).
362. [1915] A.C. 79, H.L.
363. *Computer Property Corp.* v. *Columbia Distributing Corp.* 5 C.L.S.R. 524 (D.S.C., 1973) at 530.

regarded as penal. It may also be regarded as penal when the acceleration of payments due under a licensing agreement upon early termination results in a gross disproportion between the benefit to the licensee and the sum so calculated.[364] On the other hand, if the pre-estimate is genuine, such as a fixed sum per day for delay, the mere aggregation of a large number of such sums in respect of a very long delay will not necessarily be regarded as penal.[365] The presence of such a term may, however, incline the court to take a more serious view of conduct by the other party which delays the relevant performance.[366] It should be noted, however, that the common law is concerned only with penally large sums. If the contract provides for maximum sums far lower than any genuine pre-estimate of loss, then the common law will not regard them as being penal,[367] though from the point of view of the party who has suffered greater loss and must bear the excess over the fixed sums, this may seem quite unsatisfactory.

It should also be noted that in the United Kingdom the strict rules which apply to the construction of terms purporting to exclude liability totally do not apply with the same rigour to clauses purporting merely to limit liability:

> There are . . . authorities which lay down very strict principles to be applied when considering the effect of clauses of exclusion or of indemnity . . . these principles are not applicable in their full rigour when considering the effect of conditions merely limiting liability. Such conditions will of course be read contra proferentem and must be clearly expressed, but there is no reason why they should be judged by the specially exacting standards which are applied to exclusion and indemnity clauses.[368]

Thus in *George Mitchell (Chesterhall) Ltd.* v. *Finney Lock Seeds Ltd.*[369] this reasoning was applied to prevent a general phrase from being construed so as to apply only to breaches of contract caused without negligence on the part of the party relying upon the clause to limit his liability.

Such a position at common law has led to statutory intervention in this area also. In the United Kingdom the principal vehicle is the Unfair Contract Terms Act 1977. The operation of the Act extends both to clauses which exclude, and to those which *restrict* liability. It thus applies to clauses falling within this section as much as to those falling within the last, and similar principles apply. It should be noted, however, that a fair liquidated damages clause which represents a genuine attempt at pre-estimation will not be covered, since it cannot be construed as an attempt to *restrict* liability. If it is genuine, it is just as likely to extend liability. On the other hand a clause deliberately underestimating the amount of damage for this purpose as in *Cellulose Acetate Silk Co. Ltd.* v. *Widnes Foundry (1925) Ltd.*[370] clearly would be subject to the provisions of the Act.

The Act is astute to detect attempts to evade it, attempts which are perhaps more likely in this context:

---

364. *Syncsort Inc.* v. *Indata Services* 541 A.2d 543 (Conn., 1988).
365. See, for example, *U.S.* v. *Wegematic Corp.* 360 F.2d 674 (2nd Cir., 1966).
366. *H.R. Stone Inc.* v. *Phoenix Business Systems Inc.* 660 F.Supp. 351 (S.D.N.Y., 1987) at 359.
367. *Cellulose Acetate Silk Co. Ltd.* v. *Widnes Foundry (1925) Ltd.* [1933] A.C. 20, H.L.
368. *Ailsa Craig Fishing Co. Ltd.* v. *Malvern Fishing Co. Ltd.* [1983] 1 All E.R. 101, H.L. at 105.
369. [1983] 2 A.C. 803, H.L.
370. [1933] A.C. 20, H.L.

To the extent that this Part of this Act prevents the exclusion or restriction of any liability it also prevents–
(a) making the liability or its enforcement subject to restrictive or onerous conditions;
(b) excluding or restricting any right or remedy in respect of liability, or subjecting a person to any prejudice in consequence of pursuing any such right or remedy;
(c) excluding or restricting rules of evidence or procedure;. . ..[371]

This means that any such clauses are either invalid or subject to the criteria of reasonableness, as indicated in the previous section.

Many of these points have been illustrated in the United States by cases in the area of computers. The limitation of liability to damage caused directly rather than consequentially is generally upheld and is not regarded in itself as being unconscionable.[372] Such a clause will not, however, be implied, if not expressed in the relevant contract.[373] Such clauses are also likely to receive a strict interpretation. In *Lovely* v. *Burroughs Corp.*[374] a clause excluding consequential damages caused by 'delay . . ., nor in any event for consequential damages' was held only to exclude damage consequential on delay, and failed to bar the recovery of damage consequential upon failure to deliver at all. So too in *Consolidated Data Terminals Inc.* v. *Applied Digital Data Systems Inc.*[375] where the damages consequential upon use or non-use of the terminals was excluded, it was held not to apply to a distributor's loss of goodwill. Clauses limiting the total amount recoverable to the contract price were upheld in *Garden State Food Distributors Inc.* v. *Sperry Rand Corp.*,[376] and even elsewhere to the amount paid under the relevant contract in the last six months,[377] or the total amount paid reduced by a reasonable rental for the machine during the time it was used.[378] As noted above,[379] a fixed daily rate of damage may be permitted, but its presence will not be construed as permitting the party bound by it to delay performance at will.[380] Although some onerous conditions precedent to recovery have been upheld,[381] these also tend to attract a strict construction. Thus in *Hawaiian Telephone Co.* v. *Microform Data Systems Inc.*[382] a requirement of written notice thirty days after

---

371. Unfair Contract Terms Act 1977 sect. 13(1).
372. See *Earman Oil Co. Inc.* v. *Burroughs Corp.* 625 F.2d 1290 (5th Cir., 1980); *Office Supply Inc.* v. *Basic/Four Corp.* 538 F.Supp. 776 (E.D. Wis., 1982); *Hi Neighbour Enterprises Inc.* v. *Burroughs Corp.* 492 F.Supp. 823 (N.D. Fla., 1980); *Investor's Premium Corp.* v. *Burroughs Corp.* 389 F.Supp. 39 (D.S.C., 1974).
373. It was thus not implied into an oral contract for programming even though present in the written contract for hardware in *Carl Beasley Ford Inc.* v. *Burroughs Corp.* 361 F.Supp. 325 (E.D. Pa., 1973), nor into a hardware contract from a parallel maintenance contract in *Huntington Beach Union High School District* v. *Continental Information Systems Corp.* 452 F.Supp. 538 (C.D. Cal., 1978) at 541.
374. 527 P.2d 557 (Mont., 1974).
375. 708 F.2d 385 (9th Cir., 1983).
376. 512 F.Supp. 975 (D.N.J., 1981); but not in *RRX Industries Inc.* v. *Lab-Con Inc.* 772 F.2d 543 (9th Cir., 1985).
377. *Farris Engineering Corp.* v. *Service Bureau Corp.* 276 F.Supp. 643 (D.N.J., 1967) affd. 406 F.2d 519 (3rd Cir., 1969), so far as repetitive services were concerned.
378. *Badger Bearing Co.* v. *Burroughs Corp.* 444 F.Supp. (E.D. Wis., 1977).
379. At p. 418.
380. *Hawaiian Telephone Co.* v. *Microform Data Systems Inc.* 829 F.2d 919 (9th Cir., 1987).
381. Such as the authorisation by the seller of the return of the system by the buyer in *Badger Bearing Co.* v. *Burroughs Corp.* 444 F.Supp. 919 (E.D. Wis., 1977).
382. 829 F.2d 919 (9th Cir., 1987).

formal notification of the complaint was construed so as to allow only one written notice to suffice. The Uniform Commercial Code expressly[383] permits parties to reduce the period within which action may be brought, and such reductions have been upheld in a number of cases involving computers.[384] Where a computer contract is not governed by the Uniform Commercial Code the parties may agree to even shorter periods of limitation, and where they do, they will be upheld.[385]

I. Remedies

Three principal options are available to a party faced by defective, or non-performance, of a contract involving computers. He may want the contract to be performed, and the law makes available in certain circumst- ances the remedy of specific performance to compel performance by the party in default.[386] At the other end of the spectrum a party may have become so disillusioned that he wants the position restored to what it would have been if no contract had ever been entered into. For this the law offers the remedy of rescission, and in case of rescission because of breach, this may be coupled with an award of damages. The most common situation, however, is that in case of breach a party seeks compensation in monetary terms from the other party to put him into the position he would have occupied had the breach not occurred. For this the law provides an action for damages. These will be considered in turn, but by far the greatest attention will have to be paid to the rules relating to damages, which in this context have been most often the subject of litigation.

1. Specific performance

This remedy is rarely appropriate in a computer context. It was in origin an equitable remedy, used where an action for damages at common law was, for some reason or another, inadequate. In cases where there is a contract for the supply of generic goods available from a number of different sources, there is usually no need to go beyond an action for damages.[387] If a party has contracted to be supplied with a computer system to replace the one he is currently using, there is no great harm in his purchasing an equivalent system from another supplier, so long as he is compensated for any additional expense which the need to switch suppliers causes to him. A situation in which the remedy would be appropriate would be where the goods were in some sense unique. If, for example, a system were custom-

---

383. Sect. 2-725.
384. *International Business Machines Corp.* v. *Catamore Enterprises Inc.* 548 F.2d 1066 (1st Cir., 1976), *Burroughs Corp.* v. *Suntogs of Miami Inc.* 472 So.2d 1166 (Fla., 1985) reversing *Suntogs of Miami Inc.* v. *Burroughs Corp..* 433 So.2d 581 (Fla., 1983) where a choice of law clause designed to shorten the limitation period had been held contrary to the public policy of Florida.
385. *International Business Machines Corp.* v. *Catamore Enterprises Inc.* 548 F.2d 1066 (1st Cir., 1976).
386. Or in certain situations, for example, contracts for exclusive services, an injunction to enforce compliance with a negative stipulation.
387. *Law Research Services Inc.* v. *Western Union Inc.* 1 C.L.S.R. 1002 (N.Y., 1968) at 1007.

built for a particular customer, and its constructor then died taking to the grave the principles upon which he had built the system, thus rendering it very difficult, and certainly expensive and time-consuming to manufacture another, a customer might well succeed in an action for specific performance, if the supplier were, say, contemplating breaking the contract and auctioning the system off to the competitors of the original customer. It is also suggested that the remedy might well be appropriate in the periodic situations of famine of components in the computer industry. If a supplier of computers has contracted for a supply of a particular type of chips, and the chip supplier in a time of shortage proposes to supply a competitor instead, once again specific performance might be regarded as more appropriate than to restrict the customer to a remedy in damages. Such a view would be fortified by the consideration that specific performance is traditionally regarded as more appropriate where the assessment of damages is particularly speculative, as it might well be in the marketing of computer systems where the loss of goodwill and market share can be, but is not necessarily, devastating.

The remedy is obviously inappropriate where performance is from a practical point of view impossible.[388] It may also be refused when both parties are at fault.[389]

A situation in which a party might most want specific performance is that where he has contracted for the services of a particular individual. Human beings are essentially unique, and in many contexts the services of one are an inadequate substitute for the services of another. So damages are an inadequate remedy for breach in this situation. Unfortunately specific performance is not available for contracts of personal service. Human autonomy has to come first. The law is not prepared directly to enforce such a contract because it smacks of slavery to force one person to work for another against his will. A more practical reason is that such a contract would be impossible to enforce satisfactorily. Levels of enthusiasm and performance can have a critical effect on how satisfactorily such a contract works. Given the premise that the work of the particular employee cannot adequately be replaced by the efforts of another, it is extremely unlikely that anyone would be in a position properly to monitor performance. The result is that in such a case the employer will probably be restricted to preventing the employee from breaking the terms of his contract of employment by working for a competitor, but even then only to the limited extent mentioned earlier.[390]

2. Rescission

A variety of similar terms such as revocation, rejection, repudiation, restitution and rescission is used for a variety of legal situations, the central feature of which is that a party disappointed by the result of his bargain wishes not to perform at all, or to recover his performance if it has already taken

---

388. *Syncsort Inc.* v. *Indata Services* 541 A.2d 543 (Conn., 1988).
389. *Law Research Services Inc.* v. *Western Union Inc.* 1 C.L.S.R. 1002 (N.Y., 1968) at 1007.
390. Above p. 168.

place.[391] Most typically a purchaser of a computer system is disappointed by it, and wishes to get rid of the system and to recover the price. He may find that the performance is not as promised, or that the system is delivered late, or not at all. Given the optimism of salesmen and suppliers, and the problems of designing novel systems, manufacturing innovative hardware and writing creative software, it is not surprising that such complaints are often justified. It must also be accepted that at a time of fast technological development and rapidly increasing cost-effectiveness, bargains which seemed excellent when made often seem disastrous when implemented, and customers are not averse to seizing upon any ground to avoid their old bargain in favour of better ones becoming available later. It should also be noted that these remedies will typically be sought only where a party is seeking to recover from what he now perceives to have been a bad bargain; if the bargain still seems to be good he will seek specific performance, or damages which will put him into the situation he would have occupied had the bargain been performed, rather than rescission which would put him back into the position he would have held had the bargain never been made. Repudiation has the further advantage of operating without necessary recourse to the courts, and avoids the problems and expense of quantifying and proving a claim for damages. This conflict of interest and policy is reflected in this branch of the law which has in the United Kingdom been described by the leading authority on the law of contract as 'complex and difficult'.[392] It is possible, in a work of this character, to give only the most cursory of outlines.

Many computer contracts will make explicit provision that performance by the supplier is a condition before payment by the customer becomes due. They may also provide explicitly for the quality and time of performance, for example that a particular benchmark must be achieved by a particular date. In a clear case it would then seem to follow that if the supplier failed to comply with such conditions, then the customer would be entitled to treat the contract as rescinded, and to decline to perform, or to accept some alternative performance tendered by the supplier. A corollary of this is that the customer is not so entitled if the supplier's failure has been induced by the customer's own acts,[393] or if the customer has repudiated before the supplier has become in breach, for example because the time for performance has not expired.[394] Even in this clear case it is still not obvious that if the relevant defect is trivial, or if the supplier is minimally late in performance, the customer should have an automatic right to repudiate the whole contract, upon which the supplier might have expended considerable amounts of time, effort and money.

---

391. The terminology remains confused in the United Kingdom despite Lord Diplock's criticism of the equation of 'repudiation' in *Photo Production Ltd.* v. *Securicor Transport Ltd.* [1980] A.C. 827, H.L. at 850; and in the United States, although the Uniform Commercial Code refers to revocation rather than rescission, the terms have been treated as functionally equivalent, see *Aubrey's RV Center Inc.* v. *Tandy Corp.* 731 P.2d 1124 (Wash., 1987) at 1128.
392. Treitel *The Law of Contract* 7th edn (1987) p. 576.
393. See, for example, *Triboro Quilt Manufacturing Corp.* v. *Nixdorf Computer Inc.* 387 N.Y.S. 2d 854 (N.Y., 1976) aff. 373 N.E. 2d 286 (N.Y., 1977); *H.R. Stone Inc.* v. *Phoenix Business Systems Inc.* 660 F.Supp. 351 (S.D.N.Y., 1987).
394. See. for example, *Samuel Black Co.* v. *Burroughs Corp.* 33 U.C.C. Rep. 954 (D.Mass., 1981).

Much of the law relating to this type of remedy is concerned with contracts of sale. In that area in the United Kingdom the buyer generally has a right to reject for breach of condition or for a serious breach of an innominate term, but not for breach of warranty, where he is instead confined to suing for damages. Most of the implied conditions likely to operate in the field of computers are classified in the Sale of Goods Act 1979 as conditions, and their breach gives an automatic right to reject.[395] However, this right is lost if the buyer has accepted the goods.[396] The buyer must be given an adequate opportunity to examine the goods before he can be deemed to have accepted them.[397] Subject to that, the buyer will be deemed to have accepted the goods if he intimates his acceptance to the seller, performs some act inconsistent with the seller's title, or retains the goods for an unreasonably long time after delivery without otherwise intimating acceptance of them.[398]

A special statutory regime governs rescission for misrepresentation. Section 2(2) of the Misrepresentation Act 1967 provides that:

Where a person has entered into a contract after a misrepresentation has been made to him otherwise than fraudulently, and he would be entitled, by reason of the misrepresentation, to rescind the contract, then, if it is claimed, in any proceedings arising out of the contract, that the contract ought to be, or has been rescinded, the court or arbitrator may declare the contract subsisting and award damages in lieu of rescission, if of opinion that it would be equitable to do so, having regard to the nature of the misrepresentation and the loss that would be caused by it if the contract were upheld, as well as to the loss that rescission would cause to the other party.

It should be noted first that this remedy does not apply automatically, but is completely within the discretion of the court, and second that it is offered in substitution for rescission, and not in addition to it. It is likely that where the misrepresentation is trivial the court will not exercise its discretion to permit rescission, but will affirm the contract and allow only a claim for damages. If the misrepresentation is not trivial and the court does allow rescission, while it may not be able to allow a claim for damages, the alternative of a claim for an additional indemnity in respect of some otherwise uncompensated expense is not barred by the legislation. It should finally be noted that this is without prejudice to the remedies for fraudulent or negligent misrepresentation to be discussed in the next chapter.[399]

Although once again there appear to be no reported cases in the United Kingdom on the application of these rules to the case of computers, there is a plethora of cases in the United States interpreting the broadly similar counterparts to the provisions of the Sale of Goods Act to be found in the Uniform Commercial Code.

To justify revocation under section 2-608 of the Uniform Commercial Code it is necessary that the non-conformity have substantially impaired the

---

395. Though in the case of non-consumer contracts the Law Commission has recommended that there should be no such automatic right to reject for trivial breaches, see Law Commission No. 160, 'Sale and Supply of Goods', Cm. 137 (1987) para. 4.21.
396. Sale of Goods Act 1979 sect. 11(4).
397. *Ibid.* sect. 34.
398. *Ibid.* sect. 35, and see also sect. 59.
399. Below pp. 240, 250.

value of the goods. This is a question of fact, but use of a computer in a commercial setting both before and after purported rejection will militate against a finding of such materiality,[400] though not if the prior use was simply an effort to make the system work, and the subsequent use an effort to transfer data to a substitute system.[401] It is immaterial that only a part of the goods is defective, or even that they satisfy the buyer's unarticulated subjective desires, if on an objective basis the impairment is substantial.[402] The right to revoke is determined as a question of fact, and five factors which have been listed[403] as influencing the decision are (i) what instructions for return of the goods were given by the seller; (ii) did the buyer's needs compel continued use; (iii) did the seller continue to promise cure; (iv) was the seller acting in good faith; and (v) was the seller prejudiced by continued use. Section 2-608 provides that a buyer is not barred from revocation if he has accepted the goods only upon an assurance by the seller that any defect will be seasonably cured.[404] It is extremely common in the computer context for such assurances to be offered, and it is often a matter of some nicety for a buyer to determine how long he should allow the seller to attempt to cure the defect.[405] In *Computerized Radiological Services Inc.* v. *Syntex Corp.*[406] the court was prepared to take into account such commercial considerations as the lead time for supplying alternative equipment, and the necessity for the plaintiff to preserve his market niche in its assessment of whether the equipment had been retained for an unreasonable length of time in this respect. In *Walker Furniture Co.* v. *AKtion Associates*[407] it was stressed that this is a question of fact, and there retention of the system for more than a year was held reasonable. It is further necessary that notice of revocation be given in a timely manner, and a purported rejection out of the blue three months after a telephone call indicating general satisfaction has been held not to comply with this requirement,[408] though no particular method of communication is required, and intention to revoke may be inferred circumstantially from complaints, and the general course of dealing between the parties.[409] If the buyer elects to return the equipment himself he should do so in a reasonable manner, but a court will be slow to invalidate a purported

---

400. *Iten Leasing Co.* v. *Burroughs Corp.* 684 F.2d 573 (8th cir., 1982) at 577.

401. *Walker Furniture Co.* v. *Action Associates* Lexis 4277 (Oh., 1988).

402. *Aubrey's RV Center Inc.* v. *Tandy Corp.* 731 P.2d 1124 (Wash., 1987) at 1128.

403. *Ibid*, at 1130 quoting *McCullough* v. *Bill Swad Chrysler-Plymouth Inc.* 449 N.E.2d 1289 (Oh., 1983) at 1292.

404. This possibility of cure is not available under the law of the United Kingdom, and a proposal to introduce it was rejected by the Law Commission in Law Com. No. 160, 'Sale and Supply of Goods', Cm. 137 (1987), para. 4.14 (consumer sales) and para. 4.17 (other sales).

405. See *Accusystems Inc.* v. *Honeywell Information Systems Inc.* 580 F.Supp. 474 (S.D. N.Y., 1982) where the buyer lost his right to revoke by continuing to attempt such a cure after the relevant defects had become conclusively established.

406. 595 F.Supp. 1495 (E.D.N.Y., 1984) at 1511. See also *Diversified Environments Inc.* v. *Olivetti Corp. of America* 461 F.Supp. 286 (M.D. Pa., 1978) at 291 where the plaintiff had continued to make payments only to preserve its credit rating.

407. Lexis 4277 (Oh., 1988).

408. *Iten Leasing Co.* v. *Burroughs Corp.* 684 F.2d 573 (8th Cir., 1982) at 577.

409. *Aubrey's RV Center Inc.* v. *Tandy Corp.* 731 P.2d 1124 (Wash., 1987) at 1129.

revocation for failure to do so. Thus in *Redmac Inc.* v. *Computerland of Peoria*[410] it was not enough that the equipment was angrily dropped on the floor of the supplier's premises, at least in the absence of evidence that the machine was damaged by such treatment.[411]

Revocation of acceptance under sect. 2-608 does not technically amount to rescission of the contract, and is without prejudice to an additional claim for damages, though in calculating any such damages the buyer must set off any benefit received from the use of the system,[412] but in many cases such benefit may not exceed additional costs incurred in attempting to cope with the defective equipment while attempts to cure it are being made.[413] It should be stressed that the object of damages in association with revocation is to ensure that the buyer has not been prejudiced by entering into the contract, and it is more appropriate to allow interest in this context, than in that where the contract continues and damages alone are awarded. Conversely the fact that tax credits must be repaid upon revocation cannot be regarded as an element of damages, since if the now rejected system had not been purchased and justified the credit, the tax would have had to have been paid.[414] In fact the purchaser has secured an advantage by delaying such payment. It will often be the case where a limited remedy fails of its esssential purpose that revocation is the only effective remedy.[415] In the United Kingdom also there is no doubt that a claim in respect of costs incurred in reliance upon the contract can be recovered in addition to any sums paid in anticipation of performance where subsequent breach justifies repudiation.

3. Damages

Damages may be combined as a remedy with either specific performance or rescission, at least in a loose sense, but it is often the sole remedy sought, or available, for example for breach of warranty. Whereas if the contract is repudiated damages will be used to ensure that a party is not damaged by his bad bargain, one of the reasons for suing in contract is often to secure the benefits of a good bargain. In the currently fashionable terminology, damages may be based upon the expectations of the disappointed party, as well as upon his reliance.

The basis of damages in contract at common law was settled in the leading case, at least as famous in the United States as in the United Kingdom, of *Hadley* v. *Baxendale*[416] where it was held that the plaintiff was entitled to recover all the damages which arose as the natural and probable result of the breach. In this phrase it was explained that 'natural' referred to

---

410. 489 N.E.2d 380 (Ill., 1986).

411. The risk will normally have passed to the buyer, and will remain with him until the goods are returned to the seller, see *Allstar Video Inc.* v. *Baeder* 730 P.2d 796 (Wy., 1986) where the goods were lost in the course of being returned to the seller.

412. *Sperry Rand Corp.* v. *Industrial Supply Corp.* 337 F.2d 363 (5th Cir., 1964).

413. *Alexander* v. *Burroughs Corp.* 350 So.2d 988 *La., 1977) at 993.

414. *Land & Marine Services Inc.* v. *Diablo Data Systems Inc. of Louisiana* 471 So.2d 792 (La., 1985) at 803, 804.

415. *National Cash Register Co.* v. *Adell Industries Inc.* 225 N.W.2d 785 (Mich., 1975) at 787.

416. (1854) 9 Exch. 341, Exch.

damages which would be incurred as a result of the normal course of events as anyone might foresee, while 'probable' referred to that which was probable given the knowledge of the parties of special factors in the particular case. In the case of computers the very versatility of the devices throws more emphasis upon the latter type of damage. This test has been held in the United Kingdom to go beyond the standard of reasonable foreseeability maintained in the law of tort, though the difference may often be obscured by the use of the same terminology.[417] The justification for the extension of liability in respect of such matters is that they will normally come into the contemplation of the parties by specific reference to them at the time of contracting. This gives an opportunity to make special provision for the allocation of such risk. Sometimes a party will choose to bear the risk, and adjust the price to reflect the cost of insuring against it; and sometimes a party will choose to hold the price, but to limit his liability. In the case of contracts involving computers, the latter is by far the more common strategy, and in the United States in particular it is common to employ the terminology of the exclusion of liability for 'consequential' damage.

In the case of the sale of goods which is governed by special statutory provisions in both jurisdictions, the statutory terminology expresses the basic common law rule. In the United Kingdom this is achieved, somewhat opaquely, by a combination of sections 51, 53 and 54 of the Sale of Goods Act 1979, and in the United States by sect. 2-715 of the Uniform Commercial Code.

Subject to any specific, and valid,[418] provision providing for a fixed, or liquidated, sum, damages are, both in the United Kingdom and in the United States, assessed in principle as amounting to the difference between the value of the performance actually provided and the value which would have been provided but for the breach. In the case of the sale of computing equipment, this may well comprise the two elements of the value of the equipment itself and the value of the use which could have been made of it. It is for the plaintiff to prove the damage which he has suffered, and in some cases plausible claims, such as that in *Burroughs Corp.* v. *Century Steel Inc.*[419] for the cost of storing a defective machine pending collection by the seller, was disallowed for this reason. Similarly in *Sperry Rand Corp.* v. *Industrial Supply Corp.*[420] the plaintiff was denied recovery in respect of the construction costs of a building built to house a defective computer system because no documented credit was given for its value to the plaintiff, nor for the salvage value of the equipment, such as air conditioning, installed in it. Conversely while a set-off may be allowed for the value of the use of the albeit defective equipment it will be for the defendant to prove such value.[421] Such proof need not, and indeed often cannot, amount to a precise and unchallengeable mathematical demonstration, though it has still been regarded as far too crude simply to pro-rate the price of a complete suite of six programs on the

---

417. *Koufos* v. *C.Czarnikow Ltd. (The Heron II)* [1969] 1 A.C. 350, H.L.
418. See above p. 209.
419. 664 P.2d 354 (Nev., 1983).
420. 337 F.2d 636 (5th Cir., 1964).
421. See *Computerized Radiological Services Inc.* v. *Syntex Corp.* 595 F.Supp.. 1495 (E.D.N.Y., 1984).

basis that only one of them had been provided, at least in the absence of any evidence as to the relative value of the programs.[422] This applies particularly to claims for loss of profits anticipated from the delivery of effective equipment. Sometimes the claim will depend simply upon direct loss in the ordinary course of events, and in such a case it has been said that:

It is not necessary that the *specific* injury or *amount* of harm be foreseen, but only that a reasonable person in Compugraphic's position would foresee that in the usual course of events, damages would follow from its breach.[423]

In the case of goods which are purchased for resale, an even greater amount of uncertainty is present, since such sales might not have been made, even if the contract had been performed. This will be especially true of individual large projects as opposed to high-volume low-price sales to many different customers. In this context, *National Controls Corp.* v. *National Semiconductor Corp.*[424] is a good example. The plaintiff was hopeful of securing a very large order to supply advanced telephones to a new supplier. The supplier established a program by which pilot experiments and trials would eventually culminate into full-scale marketing. The plaintiff was commissioned to supply telephones for the trial and the internal electronics for the pilot study. The defendant was commissioned to supply the relevant chips. They turned out to be defective, and although this did not prevent the plaintiff from securing the order for the pilot circuitry, it did not receive the order for which it had hoped for full-scale marketing.[425] The plaintiff was restricted to recovering damages for losses suffered as a result of the contracts which it had secured,[426] and could recover nothing in respect of its full-scale marketing, even though it had incurred expense in tooling up for the vast increase in production which it anticipated. Although this result may have been influenced by particularly restrictive local rules, the facts illustrate the problems which may arise.[427] Even in the case of high-volume sales, for example, by a retailer of terminals, any estimation of lost profits on the sale of terminals of a particular brand which are defective must allow a set-off for terminals sold in substitution which could not otherwise have been sold.[428]

Both at common law and under the statutory régimes for sales, the starting point for calculation is the value which the goods would have had, had they been as warranted, and in many cases the price under the contract will provide the best starting point for any such assessment.[429] This will not, however, be appropriate if the buyer has made a particularly good bargain, in which case the fair market value of the goods will be better, though it will be for the buyer to provide evidence of such deviation from the contract price.[430] In some cases it may also be appropriate to take financing charges

422. *Chatlos Systems Inc.* v. *NCR Corp.* 479 F.Supp. 738 (D.N.J., 1979).
423. *Barnard* v. *Compugraphic Corp.* 667 P.2d 117 (Wash., 1983) at 120, original emphasis.
424. 833 F.2d 491 (3rd Cir., 1987).
425. Which never in fact took place.
426. There was no evidence that it had suffered any damage in respect of these.
427. See also *Sha-I Corp.* v. *City and County of San Francisco* 612 F.2d 1215 (9th Cir., 1980).
428. *Consolidated Data Terminals Inc.* v. *Applied Digital Data Systems Inc.* 708 F.2d 385 (9th Cir., 1983) at 394.
429. *Schatz* v. *Olivetti Corp. of America* 647 P.2d 820 (Kan., 1982).
430. *Chatlos Systems Inc.* v. *NCR Corp.* 479 F.Supp. 738 (D.N.J., 1979).

into account, at least where the seller knew that such charges would be incurred.[431]

It is extremely common, especially in the United States, for a computer contract to contain an express exclusion of consequential damage.[432] Although the Uniform Commercial Code contains[433] partial definitions of 'incidental' and 'consequential' damage, it has still been said, in this context, that 'neither in Michigan or elsewhere does the term "consequential damages" have a clearly established meaning'.[434] However, it was decided that while general damages were those incurred in the usual course of business which anyone might anticipate, consequential damages corresponded to special damages, or those where special circumstances had been brought to the attention of the other contracting party, or of which he must have known as a result of the negotiations between the parties. In this case the buyer abandoned his existing equipment in favour of the defendant's. In order to do so he had to re-write all of his programs in a different programming language. When the new system proved to be defective the plaintiff incurred expense in respect of workers made idle, the placing of his work elsewhere, and the eventual removal of the defective equipment. All of these were regarded as direct, and thus not covered by a clause excluding liability for consequential losses. This was, however, held to cover the expense of converting all of the programs back to a different programming language, and the fact that it was now necessary to use a larger computer in the range of the original supplier than would have been required but for the attempt to change supplier.

Although no recovery was allowed for executive time devoted to attempting to remedy the problems caused by the delivery of a defective system in *Chatlos Systems Inc.* v. *NCR Corp.*[435] on the basis that executive time is paid for just in order to solve such problems in any event, the better view seems to be that taken in *Dunn Appraisal Co.* v. *Honeywell Information Systems Inc.*[436] where the claim was allowed on the basis that although the time would have been paid for anyway, the plaintiff had, on account of the defective performance by the defendant, lost the value of the time for which it was paying. Similarly in *Barnard* v. *Compugraphic Corp.*[437] where labour costs were a fixed expense, it was held that they need not be deducted from anticipated profit on further sales which could have been made without increasing labour costs, if the equipment had performed as promised.

The general rule both in the United Kingdom and in the United States is that it is wrong for a party, once the other is in breach, to wait supine while

---

431. *Carl Beasley Ford Inc.* v. *Burroughs Corp.* 361 F.Supp.325 (E.D. Pa., 1973) quoted in *Schatz* v. *Olivetti Corp. of America* 647 P.2d 820 (Kan., 1982); but see *Barnard* v. *Compugraphic Corp.* 667 P.2d 117 (Wash., 1983) where this view was rejected.
432. See above p. 211.
433. Sect. 2-715.
434. *Applied Data Processing Inc.* v. *Burroughs Corp.* 394 F.Supp. 504 (D. Conn., 1975) at 508.
435. 479 F.Supp. 738 (D.N.J., 1979).
436. 687 F.2d 877 (6th Cir., 1982), preferring the reasoning in *Clements Auto Corp.* v. *Service Bureau Corp.* 444 F/2d 169 (8th Cir., 1971) and *Convoy Co.* v. *Sperry Rand Corp.* 601 F.2d 385 (9th Cir., 1979).
437. 667 P.2d 117 (Wash., 1983).

losses, and potential damages, accumulate. He is rather under a duty to minimise, or mitigate, his loss. This may involve making a decision to use different equipment to accomplish the tasks for which that which was defective was intended. In the computer context such a party is liable to be put under pressure by his original supplier not to acquire such a substitute machine from a competitor, but to persist with the original one by supporting his efforts to cure the defects, and perhaps even to take further equipment from him to assist in doing so. It is often very difficult for the customer, who may understand little of the reasons for the defective performance, to know how far to accede to such pressure. A further factor is that even if the customer does decide to move to a competitor he may still need to use the original equipment in what might be a lengthy period of lead time and transition before the new system is delivered and ready for use. In many cases the customer will already have become completely dependent upon the automated, but defective system for which he contracted.[438] Once the system has been unequivocally and authoritatively shown to be deficient, however, the customer will be at risk in permitting his supplier to continue to attempt to cure it, though the burden of proving failure to mitigate remains upon the supplier.[439]

Where the supplier presses the customer to take further equipment to solve problems created by defective performance, the customer is quite justified in refusing to accept it. Once a party is in default it behoves the customer to be wary of acceding to further assurances from him.[440] In such a case the evidence that the additional equipment really would satisfy the deficiency will need to be very persuasive indeed, especially if, as is common, it is presented as part of a package in which the customer is required to release the supplier from any claims incurred up to that time.[441]

In the case of contracts relating to the provision of services, a provision is sometimes made for a minimum payment threshold irrespective of the use made of the service. If the service is then terminated by the customer in breach of contract the supplier may recover as damages no more than the accrued minimum payments for the remainder of the contract, and not his anticipated profits over that period, no matter how reasonable it might have been to have expected them.[442] No other solution is really available, since the customer could otherwise limit his liability by simply failing to terminate prematurely, but restraining his use of the service below the threshold.

In view of the complexity of many of the computational issues involving damages, and in order to reduce speculation and double counting, it has been suggested, in the United States where juries are still used in such cases, that charts and graphic representations of the evidence should be employed wherever possible.[443]

438. See, for example, *Clements Auto Corp.* v. *Service Bureau Corp.* 444 F.2d 169 (8th Cir., 1971).
439. *Carl Beasley Ford Inc.* v. *Burroughs Corp.* 361 F.Supp. 325 (E.D. Pa., 1973).
440. *Management Assistance Inc.* v. *Computer Dimensions Inc.* 546 F.Supp. 666 (N.D. Ga., 1982) at 675.
441. *Barnard* v. *Compugraphic Corp.* 667 P.2d 117 (Wash., 1983).
442. *Re Community Medical Center* 623 F.2d 864 (3rd Cir., 1980).
443. *International Business Machines Corp.* v. *Computer Enterprises Inc.* 548 F.2d 1066 (1st Cir., 1976) at 1076.

J. Dispute resolution

It is usually best for litigation to be conducted in the place most convenient to the parties and to be governed by the law of that place. It is not, however, always desirable, or desired, by the parties. It is sometimes suggested that some courts lack understanding or experience of the technical background to deal with contracts relating with computers, and that some systems of law are deficient in their legal provisions for doing so. If the parties subscribe to such views they may seek to provide in their contract for the system of law, place, or procedure for determining any disputes which arise under it. This section will accordingly consider attempts to choose a particular system of law, or to nominate a particular forum or, most radical of all, to provide for some extra-curial form of dispute resolution.

1. Choice of law

It might be thought that the choice of the law of a particular jurisdiction would do little to improve matters since such provisions will still have to be interpreted by local judges. However, it is widely felt that some jurisdictions have built up so much more precedential authority in computer matters as to be able to provide more authoritative guidance. It is also the case that given the wide jurisdictional spread of the activities of the larger companies in the computer field it is necessary from their planning and managerial point of view that there is some consistency in the legal consequences of common forms of agreement.[444]

In the United Kingdom the general rule is that the parties are free to nominate any system of law to govern their agreement, or even different systems of law to govern different parts of it. If they do not so nominate so as to indicate their intention, then the contract will be governed by the law which seems most appropriate taking all circumstances into account. This is, however, subject to considerations of public policy, though it is generally unlikely that such considerations would invalidate a choice of law provision in a contract relating to computers. It is also subject to statutory exception, and the provisions most likely to apply in this context are those of section 27(2) of the Unfair Contract Terms Act 1977 which invalidate any such choice of law clause if its main purpose is to evade the restrictions imposed by the Act, or if the contract is a consumer contract made in the United Kingdom in respect of a consumer habitually resident there. It should be noted, however, that the Act excludes from its ambit any contracts for the international supply of goods.[445]

The basic rule is the same in the United States subject to the qualification[446] that the system of law nominated in the contract bear a reasonable relation to the transaction. The operation of this qualification is exemplified in *Teamsters Security Fund of Northern California Inc.* v. *Sperry Rand*

---

444. *Triangle Underwriters Inc.* v. *Honeywell Inc.* 457 F.Supp. 765 (E.D.N.Y., 1978) at 768.
445. Unfair Contract Terms Act 1977 sect. 26. International contracts for the supply of services are not excluded from the ambit of the Supply of Goods and Services Act 1982.
446. Reproduced in Uniform Commercial Code sect. 1-105.

Corp.[447] where a contract, between a Californian and Delaware corporation with their principal places of business in California and Pennsylvania respectively, negotiated and to be performed in California, nevertheless nominated New York's as the governing law, and was held not to show such a reasonable relation.

Choice of a foreign system of law is, however, subject to a strongly contrary public policy of the forum, and in *Pan America Computer Corp.* v. *Data General Corp.*[448] the choice of New York law was disregarded because of such a policy in favour of the local law regulating dealerships. However, there are a number of examples of cases where a forum has applied the chosen law, and by so doing departed from the result dictated by its own law. Thus in *Burroughs Corp.* v. *Suntogs of Miami Inc.*[449] a choice of law clause was applied which effectively avoided Florida's statute prohibiting the contractual shortening of the limitation period.

Sometimes different aspects of the same dispute may be governed by different systems of law. Thus where there are separate contracts, either because of a leasing arrangement,[450] or for hardware and software,[451] it is by no means clear that the choice of law in one will be applied by implication in the other. The contract lacking the clause may well be governed by the system otherwise indicated by the conflict of laws rules of the forum. These may, as in *Sperry Rand Corp.* v. *Industrial Supply Corp.*[452] distinguish between the formation of the contract, governed by the law of the place of contracting, its performance, governed by the law of the place of performance, and the availability of remedies, governed by the law of the forum. Similar principles apply still more strongly to distinguish between the law governing contractual questions and that governing tortious causes of action arising from the same situation. In such a case an issue of, say, fraud, will be decided according to the proper[453] law of the tort, and not by the system nominated in a contract induced by that fraud.[454] It seems that the law of the United Kingdom would be the same.[455] It was however held in *Triangle Underwriters Inc.* v. *Honeywell Inc.*[456] that this would not apply where an allegation of fraud merely restated an essentially contractual claim. Nor will

---

447. 6 C.L.S.R. 951 (N.D. Cal., 1977) at 965.
448. 467 F.Supp. 969 (D.Pu.R., 1979); 562 F.Supp. 693 (D.Pu.R., 1983).
449. 472 So.2d 1166 (Fla., 1985) reversing the lower court, 433 So.2d 581 (Fla., 1983), on this point. See also *AMF Inc.* v. *Computer Automation Inc.* 573 F.Supp. 924 (S.D. Ph., 1983) (award of attorney's fees permitted under California, but not Ohio, law); *Hughes Associates Inc.* v. *Printed Circuit Corp.* 631 F.Supp. 851 (N.D. Ala., 1986) (noncompete clause valid under Massachusetts law, but not Alabama).
450. As in *Sperry Rand Corp.* v. *Industrial Supply Corp.* 337 F.2d 363 (5th Cir., 1964).
451. *Shapiro Budrow Associates Inc.* v. *Microdata Corp.* 8 C.L.S.R. 497 (S.D.N.Y., 1986).
452. 337 F/2d 363 (5th Cir., 1964). See also *Hughes Associates Inc.* v. *Printed Circuit Corp.* 631 F.Supp. 851 (N.D. Ala., 1986) at 855.
453. That with which it has the closest connection taking all of the circumstances into account.
454. *Accusystems Inc.* v. *Honeywell Information Systems Inc.* 580 F.Supp. 474 (S.D.N.Y., 1982); *Consolidated Data Terminals Inc.* v. *Applied Digital Data Systems Inc.* 708 F.2d 385 (9th Cir., 1983).
455. *Coupland* v. *Arabian Gulf Petroleum Co.* [1983] 3 All E.R. 226, C.A.
456. 457 F.Supp. 765 (E.D.N.Y., 1978).

a court be inclined to apply different systems of law to different elements of damages, for example to compensatory and to punitive claims.[457]

2. Choice of forum

Another technique is to nominate the courts of a particular jurisdiction in which action must be brought. Here too the ostensible aim is to ensure competence and consistency. It may also be designed to give a party 'home ground' advantage. In the absence of a choice of law clause, such a nomination may be presumed to imply the choice of the law of the nominated forum, though such presumption can be rebutted.[458] The converse inference from a choice of law clause to choice of forum seems much less strong,[459] and the normal rules for establishing jurisdiction are more likely to govern.

If such a clause is included it will, in principle, be applied both in the United Kingdom[460] and in the United States.[461] However, the Restatement explicitly excepts from the general rule cases where to bestow jurisdiction according to the prescription in the contract would be unfair or unreasonable, and in *Horning* v. *Sycom*[462] the relevant considerations were held to be: whether the clause was freely negotiated; whether the specified forum was convenient; whether its application would defeat a strong public policy of the forum from which transfer was sought; and whether that forum had more than a minimal connection with the transaction in question. It was there held that a small businessman was not bound by a clause nominating the courts of the state of the system's supplier when the contract was in a standard form, disparity of knowledge and experience made it close to unconscionable, and when it would be highly inconvenient for him to litigate in a remote part of the continent.

It should be noted that in the United States where suit can be brought in a federal court under diversity jurisdiction the federal statutory provision relating to transfer[463] applies, notwithstanding any policy of the state from which transfer is sought against such transfer pursuant to a choice of law clause.[464]

3. Arbitration

Perhaps the most radical remedy for the perceived incompetence of judge and jury in matters involving high technology is to contract so as to remove

457. *Computer Systems Engineering Inc.* v. *Quantel Corp.* 571 F.Supp. 1365 (D. Mass., 1983).
458. *Compagnie d'Armement Maritime S.A.* v. *Compagnie Tunisienne de Navigation S.A.* [1971] A.C. 572, H.L.
459. See *Data General Corp.* v. *Empire Telecommunications Inc.* 8 C.L.S.R. 228 (Mass., 1982); but see also *Sage Computer Technology* v. *P-Code Distributing Corp.* 576 F.Supp. 1194 (D. Nev., 1983).
460. Halsbury, *Laws of England* Vol. 8 para. 406.
461. Restatement 2d, 'Conflict of Laws', para. 80.
462. 556 F.Supp. 819 (E.D. Ky., 1983); but see also *Hoffman* v. *Burroughs Corp.* 571 F.Supp. 545 (N.D. Tex., 1982).
463. 28 U.S.C. sect. 1404(a).
464. *Stewart Organisation Inc.* v. *Ricoh Corp.* 108 S.Ct.Rptr. 2239 (1988).

such matters from them, and to place them in the hands of persons nominated by the parties. It should be noted, however, that there is statutory authorisation[465] for a judge to sit with expert assessors, though the power is hardly ever exercised. It is also possible for the court to appoint an expert witness to secure technical advice,[466] but this power is also somewhat rarely exercised, except in patent and admiralty proceedings.

At common law any agreement to oust the jurisdiction of the ordinary courts was regarded as contrary to public policy and, as such, invalid; though such clauses were valid, if they did no more than impose arbitration as the primary step in the legal process.[467] In the United Kingdom this was felt to be too restrictive a situation, and it was altered by the passage of the Arbitration Act 1979. Under that Act it is now possible to oust the jurisdiction of the court by specific agreement, but in the case of domestic[468] arbitration agreements only if the agreement were made in writing *after* the commencement of the relevant arbitration.[469] The Act also provides in other cases for an appeal to the High Court, but only on a question of law, and only with the consent of the parties or with the leave of the Court.[470] It seems that such leave will be granted only where such a decision will be likely to 'add significantly to the clarity and certainty of English commercial law'.[471] It was recognised that this might more often be the case where standard form contracts were involved, where the questions might relate to large classes of transaction where consistency was especially important. Many computer contracts will fall into this category.

A particular advantage of arbitration in cases involving parties from both the United Kingdom and the United States is that it may be easier to enforce an award by arbitrators than by the courts since the international enforcement of arbitration awards is governed by an international convention[472] to which both jurisdictions are party, whereas this is not the case with regard to the enforcement of judgments of the courts.[473]

In the United States arbitration is, at the federal level, governed by the provisions of the Federal Arbitration Act,[474] which will, in general, enforce arbitration clauses in much the same way as any other clause of a contract.[475] Although arbitration clauses are generally favoured, it has been held that the agreement to arbitrate must be binding under the general law of contract, and that at least in the case of contracts binding public bodies there are policy arguments in favour of public litigation. Thus in *El Camino*

---

465. Supreme Court Act 1981 sect. 70.
466. R.S.C. Order 40.
467. *Scott* v. *Avery* (1855) 5 H.L.C. 811, H.L.
468. Defined in sect. 3(7) to exclude arbitrations with a foreign element.
469. Sect. 3(6).
470. Sect. 1(3).
471. *Pioneer Shipping Ltd.* v. *BTP Tioxide Ltd. (The Nema)*]1982] A.C. 724, H.L.
472. New York Convention on the Recognition and Enforcement of Foreign Arbitral Awards 1958; for application in the United Kingdom, see S.I. 1984 No. 1168, and in the United States, see 9 U.S.C. sect. 201.
473. Part I of the Foreign Judgments (Reciprocal Enforcement) Act 1933 has never been extended to the United States.
474. Title 9 of the U.S. Code.
475. 9 U.S.C. sect. 2.

Community College v. *Superior Court*[476] where the relevant contract containing an arbitration clause had not been ratified, as required, by the plaintiff's Board of Trustees, a civil suit was not stayed. No appeal, as such, is provided against an arbitral award, though one may be vacated upon various procedural grounds, or if the arbitration is so imperfect as not to amount to a final and definite award at all. In diversity suits the provisions of section 2 prevail over any restrictions under the state law of the forum inhibiting arbitration.[477] It is also interesting to note that while only one of the three linked contracts in that case contained an arbitration clause, actions on the other two contracts were also stayed pending the arbitration of the third. In *International Ticket Group Inc.* v. *Copyright Management Inc.*[478] there was an oral contract for hardware consultancy, made naturally enough without any explicit reference to arbitration, and a written contract for software services which contained an arbitration clause extending to anything relating to the software. It was held that as the hardware and software operated as a single unit, so that defects in operation might arise from one or the other, it was appropriate to apply the arbitration provision so as to encompass disputes arising from both contracts, and not merely to limit it to those arising from the software contract.

Although it is possible for arbitration clauses to be limited to specific aspects of the agreement, courts will be inclined to interpret arbitration clauses generously, and in *Good (E) Business Systems Inc.* v. *Raytheon Co.*[479] applied one to both tortious and statutory claims arising out of the contract containing the arbitration clause.

It should be noted that some of the most important disputes to affect the computer industry are decided by arbitration, including the recent dispute between International Business Machines and Fujitsu over rights and access to vital proprietary information in basic operating systems. This dispute involved claims running into hundreds of millions of dollars, and which not only took over two years from original reference to award, but also provides for continuous monitoring for the future.[480]

---

476. 219 Cal. Rptr. 236 (Cal., 1985).
477. *Collins Radio Co.* v. *Ex-Cell-O-Corp.* 467 F.2d 995 (8th Cir., 1972). See also *Good (E) Business Systems Inc.* v. *Raytheon Co.* 614 F.Supp. 428 (W.D. Wis., 1985).
478. 629 F.Supp. 587 (S.D.N.Y., 1986).
479. 614 F.Supp. 428 (W.D. Wis., 1985).
480. See *International Business Machines Corp.* v. *Fujitsu Ltd.* 8 C.L.S.R. 595 (1987).

Chapter 6

Tort

A. Introduction

Tort constitutes one of the largest and most varied branches of the law. It is a fundamental part of every law course, and furnishes the basis for a multitude of claims every year in all of the common law countries, not least in the United States. Yet in 1964 a Pennsylvania lawyer confessed in an article on computers and the law of torts that, 'there are no actual cases in this area of law that have directly involved computers'.[1] While that is no longer true, it was still possible for an American author to begin an article on the subject in 1987 by stating that, 'There is little law on the questions of whether and under what circumstances suppliers of computer software may be subject to liability for unintentional torts'.[2] The former remark would remain true in the United Kingdom. There has been a trickle of litigation in the United States, but only a trickle. There has been some increase in the amount of coverage in articles, but nothing like that in other computer-related areas.[3] What is the explanation? Perhaps the most obvious point is that computers are not in themselves inherently physically dangerous machines. They do present some electrical and fire hazards, and some peripheral equipment has moving parts. Occasional cases of direct physical injury have been reported.[4] There has also been considerable controversy over the effects upon clerical workers of sitting for long periods in front of video display terminals. Research findings are far from consistent but the authoritative World Health Organisation has drawn attention to the dangers in a recent report,[5] and at least one United States legislature[6] has passed

---

1. Levin, 'Automation and the Law of Torts' *M.U.L.L.* (June 1964) 35, 36.
2. Conley, 'Tort Theories of Recovery against Vendors of Defective Software', *13 Rutgers L. & C.T.L.J.* 1 (1987).
3. The sections devoted to tort in the bibliographies published in the *Rutgers Journal of Computer Technology and Law* are invariably shorter than those devoted to other mainstream legal subjects.
4. See, for example, *Watts v. IBM* 341 F.Supp. 760 (E.D. Wis., 1972).
5. *VDUs and Workers' Health* (1988). It has also been suggested that keyboard operators may suffer stress injuries to their wrists. *Computer Weekly* 12 January 1989 p. 1.
6. Suffolk County in New York State, see *Computing* 30 June 1988.

regulative legislation. A more potent possibility of causing physical harm is where the computer operates indirectly, for example by controlling machinery,[7] or by providing information to human beings who are controlling machinery. Increasingly, computers are being built into everyday devices, and the potential for causing physical harm in this way is increasing steadily. Yet another burgeoning area of potential liability concerns the increasing use of expert systems, especially in medicine. It may thus be expected that tortious liability in respect of physical harm can only increase in importance.

Most of the reported claims have, however, concerned loss rather than damage. The computer is used most often in business, and the loss it causes is predominantly economic. In principle the law of contract is the main vehicle for the recovery of economic loss, but it is not always available, or eligible. It is not always available because sometimes economic loss is caused in the absence of a contractual relationship, or to a non-party; and it is not always eligible because there may be advantages in suing in tort rather than in contract, for example to take advantage of different rules relating to damages, procedure or limitations upon liability. It is not at all uncommon to find claims in tort appended to claims in contract, sometimes in respect of the very same obligations. A preliminary question which has attracted much recent judicial attention at the highest level both in the United Kingdom and in the United States is the extent to which such claims may be pursued. This will be the focus of the next section of this chapter. Where there is a valid cause of action in tort, distinctions must be made between liability based upon the intention of the tortfeasor, or upon his negligence, and cases where there is tortious liability without fault. Each of these will be considered in turn. Defamation is a quite separate tort, associated particularly with databases. There is also a miscellaneous collection of other torts, often inherent in the law relating to others of the topics considered elsewhere in this book, for example damages for infringement of copyright, or for misappropriation of a trade secret, or for infringement of privacy. Some of the remainder of such miscellaneous torts will be mentioned briefly in a separate section. The final section will consider the special situation of liability in respect of artificial intelligence systems, since such systems are of increasing importance, and there is special complexity in applying the relevant parts of the law of tort.

B. Overlap with contract

Although both the United Kingdom and the United States are common law countries in which the distinction between the law of tort and that of contract is well entrenched, there are significant differences of approach, partly on account of a greater readiness in the courts in the United States to abandon technical distinctions in a broad effort to do justice between the

---

7. In *Arizona State Highway Dept.* v, *Bechtold* 460 P2d 179 (Az., 1969), for example, an error caused computer-controlled traffic lights to turn green in unison, See also *Deromedi* v. *Litton Industrial Products Inc.* 636 F.Supp. 392 (W.D. Mich., 1986) (computer controlled grinder); *Scott* v. *White Trucks Inc.* 699 F.2d 714 (5th Cir., 1983) (computer -controlled braking system).

parties, and in part because of a different pattern of statutory intervention. As in so many other of the areas of the law encompassed by this work, so here also the principles to be applied in the context of computers are usually first established elsewhere, and only subsequently applied in that context. Here too the greater volume of litigation, and more especially of reported litigation, in the United States has resulted in there being a few reported cases of such application, while in the United Kingdom the commentator is largely left to extrapolate into the context of computers from the seminal cases themselves. It is, however, interesting that despite such differences there is an increasing convergence of approach in the two jurisdictions to the question of the overlap between contract and tort. As the distinction has traditionally been most marked in the United Kingdom, it is proposed to illustrate the questions that arise principally by reference to developments in that jurisdiction. In the United States the law of tort is predominantly a common law and state law subject. It does exhibit considerable differences from state to state, so the references to the law of the United States are necessarily illustrative, rather than comprehensive. In what follows, the basic distinctions will be elaborated in the first sections and, taking up from where the previous edition of this work concluded, the further development of the law into the current position will be described.

1. The basic distinction

The basic distinction, learned by every law student at the very beginning of his course, is that the law of contract is concerned to enforce promises, and the law of tort to remedy breaches of more generally applicable obligations. In contract the parties are, at least in principle, in control both of the nature of the obligations which they undertake and of the remedies which will be imposed if they are broken; in tort the general law sets the standards and defines the remedies. These conceptual differences find their expression in a number of differences of practical application, relating to standing to bring a claim, the nature of the obligation, and the procedure and remedies available in case of breach.

In the common law it is for the plaintiff to formulate his claim in terms of a breach of a legal obligation, so in the first instance it is for the plaintiff to choose whether to frame his claim in contract or in tort. The first point to make is that it is only if there is a contractual relationship between plaintiff and defendant that a claim can be made in contract.[8] This is known as the doctrine of privity of contract. However, it has never had a complete corollary in tort. It has never been the case that if there is a contractual relationship between the parties it is always, and necessarily, conclusive of the legal relations between them. For example, from the very earliest times it was thought that some services, such as those provided by carriers and inn-keepers, should be subject to minimum standards so as to avoid the abuse of a superior bargaining position. It may be a question whether the providers of computers and computing services should, in the modern world,

---

8. Though in the United States the development of the law of warranty has, to some extent, tended to fill the gap.

be subject to similar minimum standards to prevent such abuse. This will be considered below[9] in the section devoted to strict liability. Still less is it the case because one party owes a contractual obligation to another that damage occurring as a result of breach of that obligation can never give rise to a cause of action in tort to a third party. Thus if a computer supplier contracts, say to supply a system for monitoring the emissions of effluent from a factory so as to avoid pollution, and negligently provides a defective system, then he may be liable in tort to injured third parties, in addition to any contractual liability which he may owe to the factory owner.

In contract the basic principle is that the parties determine in their contract the nature of the obligations which they agree to undertake. In tort the nature of the obligation is broadly defined by the general law, and expressed by the judges in their decisions in particular cases. A common reason for preferring to sue in tort is to avoid some particular nuance of the duty as set out in the contract, or to broaden the obligation by reference to some pre-contractual representations which have been deliberately omitted from the contract, and that omission fortified by the inclusion of a clause specifically limiting the obligation to that set out in writing in the contract.

Because the law of contract is concerned with the enforcement of promises, the basic principle for assessing damages differs from that in the law of tort. In contract the basic principle is that a party should be put into the position in which he would have been had the contract been carried out according to its terms. In tort he is entitled to be put back into the position in which he would have been had the tortious act not occurred. Thus if a supplier contracts to supply a computer for £50 000 on the basis that it will perform tasks which would in fact have required a computer costing £100 000, the contractual basis for assessing damages would yield damages of £100 000[10] while the tortious basis would yield damages of £50 000, representing the return of the purchase price.[11] In practice it is very likely that the parties to a contract for the supply of a computer or computer services will have provided specifically for the principles of assessment of damages as discussed in the previous chapter, and one of the attractions of seeking to sue in tort rather than in contract is to avoid the operation of such provisions. To some extent the more favourable position of the plaintiff in contract in securing damages for loss of his bargain is offset by a more unfavourable view of the range of circumstances in respect of which damages may be awarded. In contract, damages are awarded in respect of those matters which are within the reasonable contemplation of the parties, either as arising naturally from the breach or on account of special facts known to the defendant.[12] In tort they are awarded in respect of reasonably foreseeable consequences of the breach.[13] The House of Lords has held that these tests

---

9. At 255.
10. Assuming that the computer had no value to the purchaser apart from its ability to perform the required tasks, for example because it was installed in such a way that it could not be used subsequently for any other purpose.
11. Assuming no further loss to the plaintiff.
12. *Hadley* v. *Baxendale* (1854) 9 Exch. 341, Exch.
13. *Overseas Tankship (U.K.)* v. *Morts Dock & Engineering Co. (Wagon Mound No, 1)* [1961] A.C. 388, P.C.

are not the same, and that the test in contract is narrower in being limited to cases where what was, or should have been, foreseen was a 'serious possibility' of damage occurring.[14] These latter differences are confined to the position in the United Kingdom. In the United States it is on the one hand possible to secure damages for the loss of a bargain in tort,[15] while remoteness rules are no less favourable to the plaintiff in contract than to a plaintiff in tort.[16] A potentially important difference between the position in the United States and in the United Kingdom in relation to awards of damages is that while damages are, in the United Kingdom, generally compensatory both in contract and in tort,[17] in the United States damages in tort may, much more often, be punitive. So in a case where the conditions for such an award may be justified there would be an added incentive for suing in tort rather than in contract.

A further difference between claims in contract and in tort is that in contract the basic principle is one of strict liability. If a party has agreed to do something, and has failed to perform, it is generally irrelevant, in all but extreme cases where the contract is frustrated, that he was not at fault in so failing. In tort, it is more common to require fault, and the most commonly alleged form is negligence. At common law the plaintiff's own negligence was a complete bar to bringing an action in tort, and that remains the position in various of the United States. In the United Kingdom[18] and in most jurisdictions in the United States[19] the law allows an apportionment between plaintiff and defendant based upon their relative fault.[20] It is less certain how far such a possibility of reduction applies in relation to a claim for breach of contract.[21]

There may also be differences in the time allowed before a cause of action expires, under the rules of the limitation of actions. This may occur either because the period of limitation is different,[22] although in the United Kingdom it is nominally the same,[23] or because the starting point for the

---

14. *Koufos* v. *C. Czarnikow Ltd. (Heron II)* [1969] 1 A.C. 350, H.L. Their Lordships varied in the terminology employed to describe the higher standard required in contract. It seems that the difference persists whether the damage is physical or economic, see *H. Parsons (Livestock) Ltd.* v. *Uttley Ingham & Co. Ltd.* [1978] Q.B. 791, C.A.
15. See *Glovatorium Inc.* v. *National Cash Register Corp.* 684 F.2d 658 (9th Cir., 1982) where no objection was taken to the recovery of lost profit.
16. See the range of damages allowed on a contractual basis in *Applied Data Processing Inc.* v. *Burroughs Corp.* 394 F.Supp. 504 (D.Conn., 1975).
17. Since the judgment of Lord Devlin in *Rookes* v. *Barnard* [1964] A.C. 1129, H.L. severely limiting the situations in which punitive damages could be awarded in tort.
18. As a result of the Law Reform (Contributory Negligence) Act 1945.
19. By 1983 only ten states retained the old common law position.
20. In the United Kingdom described as 'contributory' and in the United States as 'comparative' negligence.
21. See below at 237.
22. In *Triangle Underwriters Inc.* v. *Honeywell Information Systems Inc.* 604 F.2d 737 (2nd Cir., 1979) there were three different periods to be considered, four years if the case was pleaded in contract, three years if pleaded in negligence and six years if pleaded in fraud. There are often different periods in different jurisdictions in the United States, see *Office Supply Co. Inc.* v. *Basic/Four Corp.* 538 F.Supp. 776 (E.D. Wis., 1982) where California had a four-year period and Wisconsin a six-year period.
23. Six years under the Limitation Act 1980 sects. 2 (tort) and 5 (contract).

time beginning to run is different. Thus in contract it runs from the time of breach, whereas in tort it generally runs from the time when damage occurs. Thus in the example of the monitoring system described above the purchaser's cause of action would accrue as soon as the system was delivered, but time would run against the third parties affected by the pollution only from the time of so being affected. Since this must necessarily post-date the supply of the system, it follows that the defendant is exposed to liability in tort after his exposure in contract has ceased. A more common situation in relation to computer programs is that a negligently introduced defect may not be obvious, but lie deep in the program, virtually undetectable by anyone once the program has been completed. If the action is for damage to the program itself, then there is a case for postponing the time from which the period runs to that time at which the defect became discoverable. This has been accomplished in the United Kingdom by the Latent Damage Act 1986,[24] though it has been left somewhat uncertain whether its provisions apply only to claims in tort, or extend also to negligent breaches of contract. It should also be noted that in any case of fraud, time begins to run only from the time when the fraud was, or should have been, discovered.[25]

2. Erosion of the distinction

As previously noted, a rigid distinction between contractual and tortious claims has never been so pronounced in the United States as in the United Kingdom. It was established as early as 1916 that manufacturers could be held liable to third party sub-purchasers of their products.[26] Liability was then first made more strict, and akin to contractual liability.[27] Now it is prepared to impose such strict liability while dispensing with all need to rely upon some specific warranty.[28] In the United Kingdom matters moved more slowly. It was not until 1932 that the general liability of manufacturers in negligence to third party users of their products was conclusively established.[29] The next forty years or so saw a gradual expansion of the ambit of negligence, one of the main landmarks of which was its extension to negligent advice in *Hedley Byrne & Co. Ltd.* v. *Heller & Partners Ltd.*[30] It then became possible for the English courts to hold that even as between contracting parties it was possible to sue for a negligent misrepresentation which had led to the contract being agreed.[31] This is clearly of great potential application in the context of the law relating to computers. It is far from unknown for a salesman of computer-related products to make exaggerated claims which induce unwitting customers to enter into a contract to

---

24. Adding a period of three years to run from the time of relevant knowledge subject to an overriding period of fifteen years, though the latter is unlikely to apply very often in the context of computers.
25. Limitation Act 1980 sect. 32(1).
26. *MacPherson* v. *Buick Motor Co.* 111 N.E. 1050 (N.Y., 1916).
27. *Baxter* v. *Ford Motor Co.* 35 P.2d 1090 (Wa., 1934).
28. *Henningsen* v. *Bloomfield Motors* 161 A.2d 69 (N.J., 1960)
29. *Donoghue* v. *Stevenson* [1932] A.C. 562, H.L.
30. *Hedley Byrne & Co. Ltd.* v. *Heller & Partners Ltd.* [1964] A.C. 465, H.L.
31. *Esso Petroleum Co. Ltd.* v. *Mardon* [1976] Q.B. 801, C.A.

buy. Other factors were also at work to assimilate the position whether the claim be made in contract or in tort. As will be seen the primary duty in negligence is one to take reasonable care. At about this time, as noted in the previous chapter, the House of Lords was prepared to imply a term to take reasonable care, even into a commercial contract if such implication was regarded as necessary in the particular circumstances of the case.[32] However, developments were to some extent subverted in the context of representations by statutory intervention. Thus the Misrepresentation Act 1967 section 2(1) imposed tortious liability for innocent misrepresentations which induced contracts if there would have been liability in the case of a fraudulent misrepresentation, but only as between the subsequently contracting parties.

3. Direct and indirect overlapping

There are two main situations in which the possibility of overlapping liability in contract and in tort may be significant. There is, first of all and most obviously, the situation in which the plaintiff and defendant are in a contractual relationship with each other. In such circumstances three situations have been distinguished,[33] namely first those where the avoidable breach of contract did not otherwise constitute a tortious obligation, second those where the content of the contractual and tortious obligation overlapped but were not identical, and third those where they were identical in content. The third is obviously the context in which problems are most often likely to arise.

The second type of overlap is more indirect, but not at all uncommon in a commercial context. It arises in situations where a project involves a large number of parties, typically main and sub-contractors. This often arises in the case of a complicated commercial project involving the design, specification and installation of new computer systems, for example in some such operation as the automation of a stock exchange's activities. In such a situation it may well happen that even though there are no direct contractual links between the commissioning party and a particular sub-contractor, the commissioning party may have played some part in determining the content of the sub-contractor's obligations and be affected by any failure to perform. The question then arises to what extent the sub-contractor's contract with the main contractor should affect any liability to the commissioner for any foreseeable loss caused to the commissioner by the sub-contractor's careless breach of his contractual obligations to the main contractor.

There has been considerable recent development in the United Kingdom in both of these areas.

4. Junior Books v Veitchi[34]

The highwater mark of the overlap between contractual and tortious claims

---

32. *Liverpool City Council* v. *Irwin* [1977] A.C. 239, H.L.
33. By Hobhouse J. in *Forsikringsaktieselskapet Vesta* v. *Butcher* [1986] 2 All E.R. 488, Q.B. at 508, a categorisation expressly approved by Neill L.J. in the Court of Appeal, see *Forsikringsak-tieselskapet Vesta* v. *Butcher* [1988] 2 All E.R. 43, C.A. at 59.
34. [1983] A.C. 520, H.L.

in the United Kingdom came in the decision of the House of Lords in *Junior Books* where Lord Roskill remarked:

[T]oday the proper control lies not in asking whether the proper remedy should lie in contract or instead in delict or in tort, not in somewhat capricious judicial determination whether a particular case falls on one side of the line or the other, not in somewhat artificial distinctions between physical and economic or financial loss when the two sometimes go together and sometimes do not (it is sometimes overlooked that virtually all damage including physical damage is in one sense financial or economic for it is compensated by an award of damages) but in the first instance in establishing the relevant principles and then in deciding whether the particular case falls within or without those principles.

In that case a sub-contractor was held liable to the commissioner for the negligent provision of defective flooring for a new factory. Lord Roskill recognised that he was extending the law as it had existed hitherto, but felt that he was justified in so doing by the presence in the case before him of a number of crucial factors:

(1) the appellants were nominated sub-contractors;
(2) the appellants were specialists in flooring;
(3) the appellants knew what products were required by the appellants and their main contractors and specialised in the production of those products;
(4) the appellants alone were responsible for the composition and construction of the flooring;
(5) the respondents relied on the appellants' skill and experience;
(6) the appellants as nominated sub-contractors must have known that the respondents relied upon their skill and experience;
(7) the relationship between the parties was as close as it could be short of actual privity of contract;
(8) the appellants must be taken to have known that if they did the work negligently (as it must be assumed that they did) the resulting defects would at some time require remedying by the respondents expending money on the remedial measures as a consequence of which the respondents would suffer financial or economic loss.[35]

It takes little imagination to see how easily these conditions might be satisfied in the context of a large-scale business venture involving the use of computers.

The House of Lords was prepared to disregard the problem that the standard of the work required would inevitably be set by the contractual duties, in the sense, for example in the computer context that the provision of a microcomputer and standard package-based system according to a contract calling for a low price is not necessarily defective simply because it fails to incorporate refinements which would undoubtedly have been included in a mainframe custom-built system on an open-ended budget. The House of Lords was also quite prepared to minimise the problem of limitation or exclusion of liability, taking the view that this could be catered for by a creative application of the notion of reliance.

Such a view would, if unchallenged,[36] have had a profound effect in the area of computers. It would have extended the liability of suppliers of

---

35. At 752, the layout has been altered here, but not the content.
36. It attracted a powerful dissent at the time from Lord Brandon and a carefully qualified assent from Lord Keith.

programs and systems to a very considerable extent. The problem is exacerbated in the context of computers by the flexibility of computer systems, and the frequent considerable disparity between the costs of providing the systems and the value of the work carried out through them.

5. Current principle

That view has, however, not prevailed in the United Kingdom, and the modern cases show considerable reluctance to accept it. The general principle was repudiated by Lord Scarman in *Tai Hing Cotton Mill Ltd.* v. *Liu Chong Hing Bank Ltd.*:

> Their Lordships do not believe that there is anything to the advantage of the law's development in searching for a liability in tort where the parties are in a contractual relationship. This is particularly so in a commercial relationship. Though it is possible as a matter of legal semantics to conduct an analysis of the rights and duties inherent in some contractual relationships including that of banker and customer either as a matter of contract law when the question will be, what, if any, terms are to be implied or as a matter of tort law when the task will be to identify a duty arising from the proximity and character of the relationship between the parties, their Lordships believe it to be correct in principle and necessary for the avoidance of confusion in the law to adhere to the contractual analysis: on principle because it is a relationship in which the parties have, subject to a few exceptions, the right to determine their obligations to each other, and for the avoidance of confusion because different consequences do follow according to whether liability arises from contract or tort, eg in the limitation of action.[37]

Despite some suggestion that these words were tentative expressing no decided view,[38] and despite the fact that the words were uttered in a situation of direct contractual relations between the parties, it now seems that they are to be accorded wider significance, and that the broad and bold assimilation of contractual and tortious liability essayed by Lord Roskill in the passage quoted above[39] has now been rejected. In a recent decision the House of Lords delivered the final blow by stating:

> The consensus of judicial opinion, with which I concur, seems to be that the decision of the majority is so far dependent on the unique, albeit non-contractual, relationship between the pursuer and the defender in that case and the unique scope of the duty of care owed by the defender to the pursuer arising from that relationship that the decision cannot be regarded as laying down any principle of general application in the law of tort or delict. The dissenting speech of Lord Brandon on the other hand enunciates with cogency and clarity principles of fundamental importance which are clearly applicable to determine the scope of the duty of care owed by one party to another in the absence, as in the instant case, of either any contractual relationship or any such uniquely proximate relationship as that on which the decision of the majority in *Junior Books* was founded.[40]

While it may remain true that in a few well-defined cases, and especially

---

37. [1986] A.C. 519, P.C. Lord Roskill was a party to this decision.
38. See Steyn J. in *Banque Keyser Ullmann S.A.* v. *Skandia (UK) Insurance Co. Ltd.* [1987] 2 All E.R. 923, Q.B. at 950.
39. At p. 234.
40. *D & F Estates Ltd.* v. *Church Commissioners* [1988] 2 All E.R. 992, at 1003, H.L. by Lord Bridge.

those where the parties are in a close professional relationship, some overlap between contractual and tortious liability remains, it now seems that further extension of these categories, as would be necessary to embrace most contexts involving computers, is unlikely to take place.

In the United States similar sentiments have been expressed, occasionally in cases involving the supply of computer systems. Thus in *Black, Jackson, Simmonds Insurance Brokerage Ltd.* v. *IBM Corp.*[41] it was stated that,

if the courts allow parties to circumvent their contractual remedies by suing in tort the ability of contracting parties to allocate and bargain for risk of loss will be effectively destroyed and activity in commercial transactions will be radically under-mined. Tort law should thus be reserved to remedy hazards peripheral to the product's function, that is, those which were not in the forefront of the minds of the contracting parties.

This view was endorsed by the influential New York Bar Association in its report on this subject,[42] and this in turn quoted with approval in *Computerized Radiobiological Services Inc.* v. *Syntax Corp.*:

For reasons that are not entirely clear there is a perennial tendency in computer-related litigation to ignore centuries of common-law history distinguishing contract from tort theories.

In the case of commercial transactions the bargaining principle should be controlling. Since tort theories (other than traditional fraud) interfere with and upset the bargaining principle they should not be countenanced.[43]

6. Applied to direct overlapping

The circumstances in which a contracting party can elect to sue in tort rather than in contract in respect of conduct constituting breach are now very narrow both in the United Kingdom and in the United States. There are a few traditional areas such as those of the common callings, for example innkeepers and carriers, where such liability has been retained. There seems to be no inclination to extend them, so they are unlikely to become significant in the context of computer systems. There is also a narrow class of professional advisers such as doctors and lawyers where dual liability remains, and in this case extends to recovery for economic loss, but once again there has been no inclination to extend into the field of computer consultancy or programming. Thus in *Chatlos Systems Inc.* v. *NCR Corp.*[44] the equation was explicitly denied,

plaintiff equates the sale and servicing of computer systems with established theories of professional malpractice. Simply because an activity is technically complex and important to the business community does not mean that greater potential liability must attach.

Although in the United Kingdom none of the recent cases involved a computer, the trend is plain, and there is no reason to suppose that it will

41. 440 N.E. 2d 282 (Ill., 1982) at 283.
42. 'Tort Theories in Computer Litigation' *38 Record of the Association of the Bar of the City of New York* 426 (1983).
43. 595 F.Supp. 1495 (E.D.N.Y., 1984) at 1504.
44. 479 F.Supp. 738 (D.N.J.,1979) at 740, aff. 635 F.2d 1081 (3rd Cir., 1980).

not apply in that context. The extent to which things have developed is illustrated in the recent decision in *Greater Nottingham Co-operative Society Ltd.* v. *Cementation Piling and Foundations Ltd.*[45] This involved a large construction project, and the defendants were nominated sub-contractors. The factor which prevented it from falling into the next section was that there existed a limited collateral contract between the commissioner and the subcontractor. This collateral contract was not, however, directly concerned either with the content of the sub-contractor's obligations or the extent of his liability. Those matters were dealt with only in the sub-contract with the main contractor. It was argued that since the contract was silent on these matters, not only was there nothing to interfere with the general duty to take reasonable care, but that the case was stronger than *Junior Books* in that there was here actual, and not merely virtual, privity of contract. The court felt, however, that the existence of the contract worked in the other direction. It showed that the parties, when they had had the opportunity to impose contractual duties had not taken it, and that the special conditions necessary to impose tortious liability for economic loss were not present. The position was summarised by Mann L.J.,

> where there is a privity, then in my view the rights and obligations of the parties in regard to economic loss should be solely dependent upon the terms of the privity. I recognise that to breach a contract may also be a delictual act. That is a proposition quite different from asserting that there can be a duty in tort giving rise to a liability to compensate for economic loss in circumstances where the contract between the parties is silent. Contractual silence in my view is adverse to the establishment of a close relationship for the purposes of the law of torts in regard to economic loss.[46]

In most cases then where the parties are in a contractual relationship their obligations will be governed by it, whether or not it spells them out. In the few cases where it is still possible to claim in tort, recent decisions have attempted to assimilate the incidents of the two types of liability as far as possible. In the United Kingdom the general rule in the tort of negligence is that awards of damages may be reduced to take account of any contributory negligence of the plaintiff,[47] but that no such rule applies in contract. It has now been held that where in such a case the obligation is the same in contract and in tort, then the power to apportion applies, whether the case is pleaded in contract or in tort.[48] The court was not prepared to permit so important a matter to depend upon the technicalities of how the case was pleaded. This is further evidence of the increasing tendency in commercial matters not only to abide by the agreement of the parties, but to provide positive incentives for them to come to make some positive provision.

7. Applied to indirect overlapping

In this situation the parties are not in a direct contractual relationship, but the plaintiff may rely upon obligations assumed by the defendant, and suffer

---

45. [1988] 2 All E.R. 971, C.A.
46. *Greater Nottingham Co-operative Society Ltd.* v. *Cementation Piling and Foundations Ltd.* [1988] 2 All E.R. 971, C.A. at 991.
47. Law Reform (Contributory Negligence) Act 1945.
48. *Forsikringsaktieselskapet Vesta* v. *Butcher* [1988] 2 All E.R. 43, C.A.

damage when they are negligently broken by him. If such breach is the cause of the plaintiff's damage, and could reasonably have been foreseen by the defendant, it might be argued that the ingredients for a claim in negligence are present, and in the absence of direct contractual relations there is no reason not to permit recovery. These were indeed the arguments which prevailed in *Junior Books*. They have now been rejected. While it is recognised that in cases of foreseeable personal injury or physical damage there is something to be said for allowing a tortious claim, it is felt that where the cause of action is essentially for economic loss, and especially where the economic loss represents the provision of a defective item, then the remedy should be in contract so as to allow choice as to the allocation of risk.

It was first established that *Junior Books* had not subverted the general rule in tort that economic loss is not recoverable for damage to property belonging to a third party.[49] This was fortified by a subsequent decision of the House of Lords holding it to be irrelevant to that determination that the plaintiff was uniquely affected, and neither a member of the general public nor of a large class of possible plaintiffs.[50] It is then no more than a small extension of the principle to hold that in cases where the loss is caused by the defective quality of an item that again there should be no recovery apart from contract. In most cases the attempt to sue in tort is, in fact, dictated by the presence in the relevant contracts with a third party of limitation or exclusion clauses. In such cases it is thought inequitable for the plaintiff to bargain for one thing with a third party, who goes on to make a further contract with the defendant upon that basis, and then to seek to avoid the scheme set up in these contracts by suing the third party in tort.[51] These attitudes have now been endorsed by the House of Lords,[52] though with some reservation in the case of highly complex products where one component may be regarded as causing physical damage to another. It is interesting to note that in coming to this conclusion the House of Lords placed some importance upon a comparable decision of the Supreme Court of the United States.[53] In its turn that decision endorses the view of Traynor C.J. in *Seely* v. *White Motor Co.*[54] based upon the undesirability of allowing the law of tort to subvert what in the United States is the law of warranty. In that jurisdiction the rationale has been directly applied to the case of defective computer systems to preclude an attempt to enlist the law of tort to evade restrictions in utilising the law of contract or warranty.[56] Here too the reasoning has been that to do so would subvert the doctrine of freedom of contract, and particularly the option to contract out of the warranty

---

49. *Candlewood Navigation Corp. Ltd.* v. *Mitsui OSK Lines Ltd.* [1986] A.C. 1, P.C.
50. *Leigh & Sullivan Ltd.* v. *Aliakmon Shipping Co. Ltd.* [1986] A.C. 785, H.L.
51. In *Simaan General Contracting Co.* v. *Pilkington Glass Ltd (No.2)* [1988] 1 All E.R. 791, C.A. at 804, Bingham L.J. said to do so would make a mockery of contractual negotiation.
52. *D & F Estates Ltd.* v. *Church Commissioners* [1988] 2 All E.R. 992, H.L.
53. *East River Steamship Co.* v. *Transamerica Delaval Inc.* 476 U.S. 858 (1986).
54. 403 P.2d 145 (Cal., 1965).
55. See *Janskey Finance & Leasing Corp.* v. *Display Data Corp.* 564 F.Supp. 160 (E.D. Pa., 1983) and *Rio Grande Jewellers Inc.* v. *Data General Corp* 689 P.2d 1269 (N.M., 1984). But see *U.S. Welding Inc.* v. *Burroughs Corp.* 587 F.Supp. 49 (D. Col., 1984) where the local law demanded a different approach.

provisions of the Uniform Commercial Code. In *Rio Grande* it was said that to permit the claim would 'allow the contract to be re-written under the guise of an alleged action in tort'. It may, however, be as well in the computer context to bear in mind the reservation expressed in relation to complex items. In many cases a computer system may constitute merely one part of a complex business package, and defects in it could impair other parts. This was exactly the situation which the House of Lords had in mind, and which in a highly simplified and contextually different form occurred in *Aswan Engineering Establishment Co.* v. *Lupdine Ltd.*[56] There the Court of Appeal found it hard to decide whether the pails in which a substance was supplied and shipped were *other* property. Given the high degree of dependence in that case, the virtual inseparability of pail and content, and the disproportion in value between them, the indication is that a computer program, and still more a complete system, is much more likely to be regarded as *other* than the commercial system of which it forms a part.

It should finally be remarked that if there is, for some reason or another, to be liability in tort in this indirect situation, it may well be the case, at least in the United Kingdom, that the plaintiff will be held to be bound by any relevant exclusion or limitation clauses contained in the defendant's contract with the third party upon which liability to the plaintiff is predicated.[57]

8. Conclusion

The current tendency is thus clear. It is to steer into the ambit of contract all of those cases where the foundation of the obligation is contractual, whether direct or indirect, especially those where the context is commercial and the loss economic. Most cases involving computers will fall into those categories. There remain, however, a number of possible avenues to tortious liability which require to be explored.

C. Fraud

Fraud is a serious allegation, but one which is commonly made in the context of computers. In part this may be due to the high-pressure salesmanship which characterises the computer business, and in the way in which disparate knowledge can lead to disappointment and disillusion when unduly high expectations are unrealised. There can be no doubt that some fraud occurs, and that more is genuinely believed to have occurred. It must also be said that there are substantial legal advantages to be gained if fraud can be established. It was said in one computer case that 'fraud is a magic word and it is elementary that any contract can be put aside for fraud'.[58] The same is true in the United Kingdom, although there is remarkably little direct authority on the point.[59] A successful allegation of fraud not only

---

56. [1987] 1 All E.R. 135, C.A.
57. *Muirhead* v. *Industrial Tank Specialities Ltd.* [1986] Q.B. 507, C.A., *dicta* of Goff L.J.
58. *APLications Inc.* v. *Hewlett-Packard Co.* 501 F.Supp. 129 (S.D.N.Y., 1980) at 134, quoting *Horwitz* v. *Sprague* 440 F.Supp. 1346 (S.D.N.Y., 1977).
59. See 10th Report of the Law Reform Committee (Innocent Misrepresentation), Cmnd. 1782 (1962) para. 23.

enables contractual restrictions upon liability and damage to be evaded, but may also negate a contractual choice of law clause,[60] extend a limitation period,[61] and in the United States opens up the possibility of recovery of punitive damages. In the United Kingdom, common law remedies for fraud have, in the contractual context, been supplemented by a special statutory remedy under section 2(1) of the Misrepresentation Act 1967. Fraud may arise in a strictly contractual context where a fraudulent term is made part of the contract, for example where a machine is warranted to perform at a rate which the representor knows it cannot attain, or it may arise in a pre-contractual situation where the salesman orally represents that the machine can attain such a rate, and so induces its purchase, but upon a written contract which explicitly excludes any oral representations. Fraud may also arise quite outside the strictly contractual field where, for example, a computer manufacturer falsely advertises the performance of his machine with the result that it is purchased from an independent retailer.

Fraud, or deceit, is a tort at common law[62] both in the United Kingdom and in the United States, though there is some variation in its definition in different states. The elements of fraud were most fully set out in this context in *Clements Auto Company* v. *Service Bureau Corporation*,[63] though it should be noted that the mental element required there[64] was significantly different from that in most other jurisdictions. In this case the plaintiff was a wholesale supplier of motor parts, and wanted to automate its inventory. A number of suppliers was approached, but in the then state of the art[65] no suitable system could be provided. However, the defendant, a subsidiary of International Business Machines, was shortly to take delivery of a newer and more powerful machine, and upon that basis represented[66] to the plaintiff that it could supply an effective system. The Court of Appeals dissected the cause of action into eleven elements:

1. There must be representation;
2. That representation must be false;
3. It must have to do with a past or present fact;
4. That fact must be material;
5. It must be susceptible of knowledge;
6. The representor must know it to be false, or in the alternative must assert it as of his own knowledge without knowing whether it is true or false;
7. The representor must intend to have the other person induced to act, or justified in acting upon it;
8. That person must be so induced to act or so justified in acting;

---

60. See, for example, *Consolidated Data Terminals Inc.* v. *Applied Digital Data Systems Inc.* 708 F.2d 385 (9th Cir., 1983).
61. *Triangle Underwriters Inc.* v. *Honeywell Information Systems Inc.* 604 F.2d 737 (2nd Cir., 1979).
62. *Pasley* v. *Freeman* (1789) 3 Term Rep. 51, K.B.
63. 440 F.2d 169 (8th Cir., 1971).
64. Minnesota law applied only because of this broad definition of fraud which nevertheless still had the effect of negating the choice of New York law in the relevant contracts.
65. In 1961.
66. Ancillary representations found to be false were that the plaintiff's whole billing operation required to be automated, that controls in the system would reduce errors to a trivial level, that the input devices would be adequate, and that the system when operational would allow management by exception.

9. That person's action must be in reliance upon the representation;
10. That person must suffer damage;
11. That damage must be attributable to the misrepresentation, that is, the statement must be the proximate cause of the injury.[67]

The first five of these elements relate to the nature of the representation. It is generally accepted that in order to be actionable the representation should amount to a statement of existing fact. This requirement can open up difficult questions in the computer context, for example, of whether the statement could be regarded as more than mere sales talk not intended to be taken seriously, or was no more than an expression of opinion, or related only to what might be expected to transpire in the future. This is basically a question of fact, and is often related to the element of reliance which is also required of the plaintiff. The courts are reluctant to apply rules of thumb to determine whether statements fall on any particular side of the line, and will have regard to the circumstances of any representation, especially where the expertise is all on one side. Thus in *Dunn Appraisal Co.* v. *Honeywell Information Systems Inc.*[68] it was held that a representation made by a reputable computer company as to the suitability of its new systems for a relatively unskilled user, 'was a statement regarding a present fact rather than an opinion about the future, because it was a statement regarding the inherent, existing capabilities of the product'.

It seems that exactly the same view would be taken in the United Kingdom.[69] Even when there is expertise on both sides, as in an OEM[70] contract, it may nevertheless be necessary for one party to rely upon the representations of the other. In a highly complex and fast-moving technology, where competitive considerations compel secrecy, it will often be the case that there is no alternative to relying upon the statements of the manufacturer as to the capabilities of particular new pieces of equipment.[71] It is ironic that it is just in relation to the newest and least tried equipment that things are most likely to go wrong, and that sellers seeking to establish a position in the market for their product are most likely to misrepresent such matters as the amount of testing which has gone on, or the degree of market penetration already achieved. It may also be the case that failure to disclose significant circumstances may so distort the impression given by a statement as to constitute it a fraudulent misrepresentation. Thus in *Strand* v. *Librascope Inc.*[72] the contract was for reading heads to incorporate into a new computer. The plaintiff was technically sophisticated and employed testing equipment, but

---

67. At 175, following *Hanson* v. *Ford Motor Co.* 278 F.2d 586 (8th Cir., 1960).
68. 687 F.2d 877 (6th Cir., 1982) at 882.
69. In *Esso Petroleum Co. Ltd.* v. *Mardon* [1976] Q.B. 801, C.A. Lord Denning M.R. took account of the greater expertise of the representor in regarding an estimate of the probable throughput of a petrol filling station as a matter of present fact rather than opinion as to the future, distinguishing *Bissett* v. *Wilkinson* [1927] A.C. 177, P.C. where the parties had been equally capable of estimating the capacity of a farm to maintain sheep.
70. A situation in which a computer system supplier assembles component parts acquired from other suppliers.
71. See *Accusystems Inc.* v. *Honeywell Information Systems Inc.* 580 F.Supp. 474 (S.D.N.Y., 1984) at 482.
72. 197 F.Supp. 744 (E.D. Mich., 1961) at 754.

was denied information which would have affected his use of it. This created a situation of inequality, and was relevant to the status of the representations because:

> Librascope held itself out as an expert, had exclusive superior knowledge, and implied either that it knew facts to justify the opinions or knew of no facts to dispute them. Under these circumstances it was reasonable for Strand to rely upon Librascope's statements as representations of fact which were not inconsistent with the expressed opinions.

On the other hand where there is a proper opportunity for a purchaser of computer equipment for resale to test the equipment, it has been held that there could have been no justification for reliance upon generalised statements in sales brochures making exaggerated claims for a computer's performance.[73] It is also very difficult to establish reliance if the defect is actually known to the purchaser, but he is persuaded to go ahead on the basis that it will not seriously affect him.[74] In some other cases courts have also adopted a rather generous attitude to the existence of an intention to improve a system.[75]

The resolution of such difficult questions of fact is affected by the seriousness of any allegation of fraud, and the consequently strict standard of proof required. Fraud must be clearly alleged, and the burden of proving it lies upon the party who does so. Some jurisdictions in the United States require a specially high standard of clear and convincing proof of fraud,[76] while in others, as in the United Kingdom,[77] the test remains the same, but is harder to satisfy. California seems to be unique in inferring fraud from an immediate failure to perform an undertaking. Thus in *Glovatorium Inc.* v. *National Cash Register Corp.*[78] the defendants promised to supply a particular program module with the system, and fraud was inferred because the module was not then supplied and never, in fact, worked satisfactorily.

One of the most variable elements in different jurisdictions is the degree of knowledge of falsity required. Although the element is usually cast in terms of knowledge of falsity, it is rare for actual knowledge to be insisted upon, and recklessness is normally assimilated to knowledge. In the leading case in the United Kingdom on the intent required for liability in deceit it was said that the defendant would be liable if he had made the statement 'knowingly, or without belief in its truth, or recklessly, careless whether it be true or false'.[79] Such a formulation, while not going so far as to require actual

---

73. *APLications Inc.* v. *Hewlett-Packard Co.* 501 F.Supp. 129 (S.D.N.Y., 1980) where a system claimed to be capable of supporting 32 on-line terminals could in fact accommodate less than ten in any acceptable way.
74. *Fruit Industries Research Foundation* v. *National Cash Register Corp.* 406 F.2d 546 (9th Cir., 1969).
75. *Computerized Radiological Services* v. *Syntex Corp.* 595 F.Supp. 1495 (E.D.N.Y., 1984).
76. See *Riley Hill General Contractors Inc.* v. *Tandy Corp.* 737 P.2d 595 (Or., 1987) where the question is considered exhaustively in this context. It was held that it applied only to the elements of fraud, and not to its consequences in terms of the components of the claim for damages.
77. See *Bater* v. *Bater* [1951] P. 35, C.A. at 37 by Lord Denning, 'A civil court, when considering a charge of fraud, will naturally require a higher degree of probability than that which it would require when asking if negligence is established'.
78. 684 F.2d 659 (9tyh Cir., 1982) at 661.
79. *Derry* v. *Peek* (1889) App. Cas. 337, H.L. at 374.

knowledge, is still not prepared to ascribe fraud to statements made negligently or innocently. Some jursidictions in the United States do, however, go so far. The clearest example in the area of computers is provided by *Clements Auto Company* v. *Service Bureau Corporation*[80] where it was said that in Minnesota:

It is immaterial whether a statement made as of one's own knowledge is made innocently or knowingly. An intent to deceive is no longer necessary. Nor is it necessary to prove that defendants knew the representations were false . . . It is not necessary that the statement be recklessly or carelessly made. It makes no difference how it is made if it is made as an affirmation of which defendant has knowledge and is in fact untrue. The right of recovery in a case of this kind is based on the fact that such statement, being untrue in fact, relied upon by the other party in entering into the transaction, has resulted in the loss to him which he should not be required to bear.

That was a case where the parties entered into a contractual relationship upon the strength of the untrue representation. In some states that is a decisive factor.[81] In other states which apparently require either knowledge or recklessness, doubt has been induced by a parallel doctrine that an intent to induce action upon the faith of an untrue representation is sufficient.[82] The question may also arise of the extent to which the knowledge or intent of an employee is to be imputed to a corporate defendant. In the United Kingdom an employer will be vicariously liable for the fraud of his employee committed in the course of his employment.[83] The principle was explained by the House of Lords.

Such circumstances exist where the employer by words or conduct has induced the innocent party to believe that the servant was acting in the lawful course of the employer's business. They do not exist where such belief, although it is present, has been brought about through misguided reliance upon the servant himself, when the servant is not authorised to do what he is purporting to do, when what he is purporting to do is not within the class of acts that an employee in his position is usually authorised to do and when the employer has done nothing to represent that he is authorised to do it.[84]

In some jurisdictions in the United States it is necessary in order to ascribe liability to the employer to show that the employee is in a managerial position.[85] It is, however, rare for a corporate defendant to succeed on this basis, and there is frequently damning evidence of approbation. Thus in *Glovatorium* the court was able to point to the adoption of a deliberate corporate strategy of targeting naïve first-time users and of deceiving them

---

80. 440 F.2d 169 (8th Cir., 1971) at 176 quoting *Swanson* v. *Domning* 86 N.W.2d 716 (Minn., 1957) at 720.
81. In Michigan, for example, see *Strand* v. *Librascope Inc.* 197 F.Supp. 744 (E.D. Mich., 1961) at 745.
82. For example in California, see *Glovatorium Inc.* v. *National Cash Register Corp.* 684 F.2d 659 (9th Cir., 1982) at 660, and Note 'Imposing Liability on Data Processing Services – Should California Choose Fraud or Warranty?', *Santa Clara L.R.* 140 (1972).
83. Similar principles apply to agents.
84. *Armagas Ltd.* v. *Mundogas S.A. 'The Ocean Frost'* [1986] A.C. 717, H.L. at 781.
85. See *Glovatorium Inc.* v. *National Cash Register Corp.* 684 F.2d 659 (9th Cir., 1982).

by demonstrating a system capable of working very much faster than the system which was to be supplied.

Although in the United Kingdom damages are not awarded in tort for loss of a bargain, the rules of remoteness are none the less more generous in relation to fraud than they would be for mere negligence. Thus in *Doyle* v. *Olby (Ironmongers) Ltd.*[86] it was held:

> In contract, the damages are limited to what may reasonably be supposed to have been in the contemplation of the parties. In fraud, they are not so limited. The defendant is bound to make reparation for all the actual damage directly flowing from the fraudulent inducement.

It is interesting that this formulation was deliberately adopted to allow for the inclusion of consequential damages. In the United States also it seems that in cases of fraud consequential damages can be recovered. In *Clements Auto Company* v. *Service Bureau Corporation*[87] it was held:

> The measure of damages is the difference between the actual value of the property received and the price paid for it, and in addition thereto such other or special damages as were naturally and proximately caused by the fraud prior to its discovery.[88]

The contentious issue in *Clements* was how soon the plaintiff should have acted to terminate the relevant contracts, and so to curtail the loss. This creates a cruel dilemma for the plaintiff since he is invariably under strong pressure from the defendant not to terminate, and it may seem harsh to permit the defendant to benefit from an action which he has himself induced. Nevertheless the courts require the plaintiff to behave reasonably so as to mitigate his loss, and require him to withstand such pressure when necessary. It seems that damages are likely to be assessed liberally in cases of fraud and that only the most speculative claims will be disallowed. In particular it has been held to be immaterial that the claims are inexact,[89] and the jury is free to award more than has actually been claimed.[90] In the United States punitive damages may also be awarded in respect of fraud, and these may be very substantial indeed. In *Glovatorium* they exceeded compensatory damages by a factor of more than nine, but were not regarded as excessive, as having obviously been arrived at by 'passion or prejudice'. It should be noted though that in cases where no actual knowledge of falsity is required, and the fraud may be regarded as constructive, there may be more reluctance to allow an award of punitive damages.[91] In the United Kingdom the circumstances in which punitive damages can be awarded are very strictly limited,[92] and it seems very doubtful, even if fraud is among the cases where such damages can be awarded, that they ever will be.[93]

In the United Kingdom it is now necessary also to consider the special statutory liability instituted by the Misrepresentation Act 1967 section 2(1)

---

86. [1969] 2 Q.B. 158, C.A.
87. 440 F.2d 169 (8th Cir., 1971).
88. Quoting *L'Evesque* v. *Rognrud* 93 N.W.2d 672 (Minn., 1958) at 677.
89. *Clements Auto Company* v. *Service Bureau Corporation* 440 F.2d 169 (8th Cir., 1971).
90. *Glovatorium Inc.* v. *National Cash Register Corp.* 684 F.2d 659 (9th Cir., 1982).
91. *Burroughs Corp.* v. *Hall Affiliates Inc.* 423 So.2d 1349 (Ala., 1982) at 1354.
92. See *Rookes* v. *Barnard* [1964] A.C. 1129, H.L.
93. *Mafo* v. *Adams* [1970] 1 Q.B. 548, C.A.

which provides:

Where a person has entered into a contract after a misrepresentation has been made to him by another party thereto and as a result thereof he has suffered loss, then, if the person making the representation would be liable to damages in respect thereof had the misrepresentation been made fraudulently, that person shall be so liable notwithstanding that the misrepresentation was not made fraudulently, unless he proves that he had reasonable ground to believe and did believe up to the time that the contract was made that the facts represented were true.

It should be noted that this form of liability applies only to those who subsequently enter into contractual relations, but that it creates a basically tortious cause of action between them. Although there is no requirement of any intent to deceive, a very similar effect is achieved by the defence provided by the final phrase of reasonable belief in the truth of the statement. A practical advantage of this form of action is that it reverses the burden of proof, and requires the representor to show that he in fact had reasonable grounds for believing in the truth of the statement. It is still uncertain whether, despite the fiction of fraud, all of the other incidents of fraud apply to this form of action, such as the generosity of the rules as to remoteness.

D. Negligence

Negligence developed as an independent tort, rather than as a mode of committing other torts, only in the last century or so. However, it has burgeoned and now constitutes by far the largest part of the law of tort. It is also the most rapidly developing area, since as one British judge remarked, 'the categories of negligence are never closed'.[94] It is traditionally defined as damage caused to the plaintiff by breach of a duty to take care owed to him by the defendant. As noted in the second section of this chapter there has been considerable reluctance to apply the tort of negligence in a contractual situation, though there are still a few situations, especially of professional relationship, where this may be done. The main concern of this section will thus be on cases where duties are owed quite independently of contract. It is convenient to consider the three principal components of the tort, duty, breach and damage, in turn.

1. Duty

One of the reasons for the rapid growth of negligence, and for the increase in litigation in the area, is the vagueness of the criteria for imputing a duty to take care. In the seminal United Kingdom case of *Donoghue* v. *Stevenson* the array of duties then recognised was generalised for the purposes of expanding the categories:

You must take reasonable care to avoid acts or omissions which you can reasonably foresee would be likely to injure your neighbour. Who, then, in law is my neighbour? The answer seems to be – persons who are so closely and directly affected by my act that I ought reasonably to have them in contemplation as being so affected when I am directing my mind to the acts or omissions which are called in question.[95]

---

94. Lord Macmillam in *Donoghue* v. *Stevenson* [1932] A.C. 562, H.L. at 619.
95. [1932] A.C. 562, H.L. at 580 by Lord Atkin.

This vague guidance was gradually used to extend liability even into areas where it had previously been denied, and notably to impose liability for negligent mis-statement even though it caused only economic loss.[96] An attempt was then made to construct a further generalisation in the shape of a two-pronged test as propounded by Lord Wilberforce in *Anns* v. *London Borough of Merton*:

First one has to ask whether, as between the alleged wrongdoer and the person who has suffered damage there is a sufficient relationship of proximity or neighbourhood such that, in the reasonable contemplation of the former, carelessness on his part may be likely to cause damage to the latter, in which case a prima facie duty of care arises. Secondly, if the first question be answered affirmatively, it is necessary to consider whether there are any considerations which ought to negative, or to reduce or limit the scope of the duty or the class of person to whom it is owed or the damages to which breach of it may give rise . . .[97]

This test has the advantage of bringing the vital policy questions into clear view, and separating them from factual and causal questions of remoteness. Unfortunately the whole area has been returned to the melting pot by increasing judicial reluctance to endorse so overt an acceptance of the policy nature of the decision to be made. It has been replaced by the very vague requirement that in determining the scope of the duty 'it is material to take into account whether it is just and reasonable that it be so'.[98] It also seems that well-established situations in which liability has been denied, for example in respect of economic loss caused by damage to something not owned by the plaintiff, are much less likely to be overturned.[99] Since the development of the use of computers is still so recent there are neither well-established situations in which duties of care have been established or denied. The question then is how the law of negligence will adapt to the new technology. One aspect of this is the fundamental question of how far the use, or abstinence from use, of computers is itself evidence of negligence. The duty bearer must pick a delicate path between unreasonably failing to use a computer and using one unreasonably. In picking this path he can neither adhere blindly to the standards of the past nor follow unquestioningly the practices of his competitors. The problem may be illustrated by consideration of two pairs of cases, all concerned with the introduction of new technology, though in only one case was it that of computer technology. The first pair is concerned with shipping. Learned Hand J. gave the opinion of a distinguished United States court[100] in *The T.J.Hooper*.[101] Two barges were lost at sea, partly because their tugs had not been equipped by the owners with working radio receivers. Had they been so fitted, their masters would have been able to hear the weather forecasts which would, in turn, have enabled them to seek shelter from the storm. At that period only one line of ships in the relevant business did fit their vessels with radio receivers. The overwhelming majority did not. Nevertheless the court was prepared to hold

---

96. *Hedley Byrne & Co. Ltd.* v. *Heller & Partners Ltd.* [1964] A.C. 465, H.L.
97. [1978] A.C. 728, H.L. at 751.
98. *Governors of the Peabody Donation Fund* v. *Sir Lindsay Parkinson & Co. Ltd.* [1983] A.C. 201, H.L. at 206 by Lord Keith.
99. *Leigh & Sullivan Ltd.* v. *Aliakmon Shipping Co. Ltd.* [1986] A.C. 785, H.L.
100. The other members were Augustus Hand and Swan JJ.
101. 60 F.2d 737 (2nd Cir., 1932).

the owners negligent in failing to install the receivers. It was said that even if there were a general custom not to install receivers, this would still not be conclusive, since,[102] 'a whole calling may have unduly lagged in the adoption of new and available devices'. Here there was no such general practice, since one line did install receivers, so the court had even more justification for deciding that the majority practice was too slack. It should be noted that the court took notice of the relatively low cost of fitting the receivers, and that might affect the sort of computer system which might be required in applying the reasoning directly into this field. Exactly the same reasoning has been applied to software. In *Migden* v. *Chase Manhattan Bank*[103] a bank failed to stop a cheque notified to it by its customer on account of the customer having mis-stated the amount, but being correct in the other relevant details. The computer was programmed to accept only an exact match for the amount, and the court required the bank to show that suitably fuzzy matching was not at the time within the state of the art.[104] The duty is not, however, discharged merely by fitting current equipment. It must also be operated efficiently as illustrated by the United Kingdom case of *The Lady Gwendolen*.[105] There the master of a ship laden with a cargo of Guinness sailed at full speed from Dublin to Liverpool despite the onset of dense fog at the mouth of the Mersey. His ship had been fitted with radar, but he looked at the screen only occasionally, for most of the time had it set to the wrong range, and was generally found to have used it very negligently. On account of that negligence the court refused to limit the liability of the owners under the Merchant Shipping Act 1894.[106] Here the court was at pains to point out the changed dimensions of risk attendant upon the introduction of new technology, and the duty of those who innovate to instruct their workers in the nature of those risks and the best means of coping with them. Exactly the same approach is adopted in the United States, and in *Chute* v. *Bank One*[107] a bank was held liable in negligence when a teller paid on a stopped cheque without consulting the computer terminal in front of her on which details of stopped cheques could be displayed. They are also obliged to ensure that they are kept up to date,[108] so in the computer context there might be an obligation to use the latest releases of programs, or upgrades of equipment, at least in particularly sensitive environments.

The second pair of cases is drawn from the field of banking. As long ago as 1918 the technological battle between cheats and merchants of security devices was being fought in the banks. At that time the state of the art was that cheques written on standard paper in ordinary ink could be erased invisibly and altered so as to show larger amounts than those for which they had originally been drawn. But special papers and cheque writing devices had been developed which were not so readily alterable. In *Broad Street Bank* v. *National Bank of Goldsboro*[109] the president of the defendant bank had failed

---

102. At 740
103. 32 U.C.C. Rep. 937 (N.Y., 1981).
104. But see *Parr* v. *National Security Bank* 680 P.2d 648 (Ok., 1984) where a different result was reached on similar facts.
105. [1965] P. 294, C.A Sect. 503(1)(d).
107. 460 N.E.2d 720 (Oh., 1983).
108. *Grand Champion Tankers* v. *Norpipe A/S (The Marion)* [1984] A.C. 563, H.L.
109. 112 S.E. 11 (N.C., 1922).

to use any of these precautions and, in consequence, the plaintiff had lost very large sums of money. It was held that though it was the common practice, even of the defendant, to use such devices, it could not be regarded as negligent to fail to do so. Such a rule might prevent the drawing of negotiable instruments by private individuals altogether, since they would not have ready access to such devices, and even the large institutions who had could not reasonably be expected to provide reserve devices in case the regular ones should break down. Nor could they be expected to suspend their business while the devices were being repaired. The rapidity of the advance of technology was also mentioned:

And what would be the standard of excellence required in the procurement and use of these protective devices? It is submitted that the kind now in use do not afford complete protection, and it is well-known that, day by day the agents of these patent devices, enterprising and insistent, offer their wares claiming that they have the latest and only efficient protection.[110]

That strikes a familiar note to those acquainted with advances in computer technology, and could be applied without alteration in the context of data protection systems. The case may be contrasted with a more modern one concerned with the application of computer technology to banking. In *Port City State Bank* v. *American National Bank*[111] the defendant bank had installed a computer system for handling cheques. For a few months it ran side by side with the manual system. Back up facilities were also arranged at another bank, though as this was in a country district it was still a two and a half hour ride away by car. The computer system broke down on the very first day after the manual system was discontinued. At first it seemed that it could be brought back into operation quite quickly. By the time it had become clear that this was not so, it had become too late to get to the back-up computer and to process all of the work before the machine was required by its regular users. The result was that cheque deadlines could not be met, and the plaintiff bank paid on a cheque which would have been returned in the normal course of events. In its judgment the court found a way out of the difficulty which had exercised the court in the *Broad Street Bank* case. It decided that the breakdown of the computer qualified as an emergency so as to bring the relevant banking regulations into force and to allow a defence. As in the *Broad Street Bank* case, it was recognised that the defendant could not be expected to cease operations or to install its own back up device, but still it was held that the bank had shown reasonable care in its precautions and in their implementation. In this way the court was able to support the introduction of new technology. Cost trends have now moved so far that it would not be too much to expect the installation of fail-safe computers, and more rapid communications so as to avoid any damaging delay. Indeed, so vital is the use of computers in banking that it would almost certainly be regarded as negligence today not to have installed very sophisticated systems indeed. Some indication of what might be required can be gleaned from the decision in *Blake* v. *Woodford Bank & Trust*

---

110. At p. 16.
111. 486 F.2d 196 (10th Cir., 1973).

Co.[112] applying the reasoning in *Port City Bank* to the technology of the next decade.

These two pairs of cases rehearse the arguments for and against liability for use or non-use of computers in given fields. The court will generally be slow to ascribe liability for not adopting new devices as in the *Broad Street Bank* case, but will do so when it is convinced that a whole area of business is dragging its feet, as in *The T.J. Hooper*. The latter posture is most likely to be adopted when personal injury might otherwise be caused. When innovation has taken place and the new technology installed, the court will insist that it be maintained and operated with all due care, as in *The Lady Gwendolen*, but will not impose uneconomically high standards, as shown by *Port City State Bank*.

There are already a number of areas, like air traffic control, where it would be negligent not to use computers. There are many more where the use of computers is increasing, but it is more dubious whether a court would be prepared to ascribe liability for non-use. Medicine is a good example, though perhaps complicated in the United States by the greater strength in that area than in others of the presumption of due care arising from adherence to local customary practice.[113] Thus in *Prooth* v. *Wallsh*[114] a lower standard of care was accepted from a doctor in a remote community where no computerised scanner was available. Similarly, computers are becoming much more commonly used for legal information retrieval and litigation support by law firms, to the extent that the LEXIS computerised retrieval system has been described[115] as an *essential* tool of a modern efficient law office. Some firms certainly have adopted rules requiring consultation of such a system before allowing work to leave the office, at least in part to minimise the danger of a malpractice suit.[116]

In some other fields, where computer use has already become routine, the danger is rather that exemplified in *The Lady Gwendolen* namely one of irresponsible operation of, and reliance upon, the machine. Such an attitude is illustrated in two groups of reported cases. In a number of instances, computerised accounting systems have malfunctioned so as to fail to credit the client's account with payments so that it appears to be in arrears. Many of the reported cases concern hire purchase repayments for motor cars.[117] In these cases the car was typically repossessed, usually after repeated efforts by the customer to persuade the company's representative that the computer was in error. In such circumstances the courts in the United States have been ready to award punitive damages. It is interesting that in each of these cases, as in *The Lady Gwendolen*, the root of the problem was improper human

---

112. 555 S.W.2d 589 (Ky., 1977).
113. See Petras and Scarpelli, 'Computers. Medical Malpractice and the Ghost of *The T.J. Hooper*', *5 Rutg. L. & C.T.L.J.* 15 (1975). Cf. *Helling* v. *Carey* 519 P.2d 981 (Wa., 1974) and Note 'Computers in the Courtroom: Using Computer Diagnosis as Expert Opinion', *5 Comp. L.J.* 217 (1984).
114. 432 N.Y.S. 2d 668 (N.Y., 1980).
115. In *United Nuclear Corp.* v. *Cannon* 564 F.Supp. 581 (D.R.I., 1983) at 591.
116. An advertising campaign for LEXIS in the United Kingdom has also stressed the danger of professional negligence suits if the system is not used.
117. *Price* v. *Ford Motor Credit Co.* 5 C.L.S.R. 956 (Mo., 1973); *Ford Motor Credit Co.* v. *Swarens* 447 S.W.2d 533 (Ky., 1969); *Ford Motor Credit Co.* v. *Hitchcock* 158 S.E. 2d 468 (Ga., 1967).

operation of the system rather than the installation of a defective system. The second group of cases arose out of the practices of an Ohio public utility.[118] There the design of the system was itself faulty, though even then the technical components all functioned properly. Unfortunately the system had been designed in such a way that vast numbers of notices of cancellation of services were routinely sent out, though only a small, and apparently random, sample were acted upon. The result was that a number of customers suffered extreme discomfort, and even physical injury, despite having paid their bills. Apart from damages, both compensatory and punitive, the relief which was granted included an injunction, and a declaration of intention to establish a more satisfactory scheme of operation for the future. All of these cases exhibit a feature which has inflamed much of the debate about privacy, namely a tendency to exalt the dependability of computer output over the representations of human beings. This is an important problem, and by no means so simple to solve as is sometimes assumed. It has to be remembered that the whole utility of keeping records on a computer depends upon being able to assume their reliability. What appears to be needed is a deeper understanding of the computer systems themselves, not only by their operators, but also by other employees, and in particular by those who have to deal with customers. In all of these cases it ought to have been possible to spot the point at which something might have gone wrong, so as to evaluate the complaint quickly. Unfortunately the cases exhibit considerable crudity in system design, little sophistication in trouble chasing, and appreciable inflexibility in operation, making the correction of records extremely difficult. None of these defects is inherent in computer application, and all should be eradicated as systems improve. Just as with the radar system in *The Lady Gwendolen*, the optimum response is to rely upon technology not less, but more, and more intelligently.

It has already been noted that where the negligence is expressed in the defective nature of a product both in the United Kingdom and in the United States, contract is regarded as a more eligible form of action. In some circumstances strict liability may be imposed, and that will be considered in the next section. The one remaining consideration here is the possibility of finding a special duty of care in relation to making a statement which causes damage, usually financial loss, to the plaintiff. In the United Kingdom this form of liability became possible after the decision of the House of Lords in *Hedley Byrne & Co. Ltd* v. *Heller & Partners Ltd*.[119] that a bank was under a duty to be careful in preparing a financial reference which it knew was to be relied upon by a third party. In that case plaintiff and defendant were not in contractual relations, but it is well-established both in the United Kingdom[120] and in the United States[121] that in certain professional relationships there is concurrent liability in contract and in tort. In both jurisdictions liability is essentially based upon the degree of reliance which

---

118. *Palmer* v. *Taylor* 4 C.S.L.R. 761 (6th Cir., 1973) a representative action.
119. [1964] A.C. 465, H.L.
120. See the exhaustive analysis by Oliver J. in *Midland Bank Trust Co. Ltd.* v. *Hett. Stubbs & Kemp* [1979] Ch. 384, Ch.
121. Prosser, *Selected Topics in the Law of Tort* (1954|) p. 410.

the plaintiff is justified in reposing in the defendant. A special relationship of trust is required. It is often found in professional men, such as lawyers and doctors, and on occasion in business partners such as insurance brokers or bankers, but it has not, in the United Kingdom, so far been extended to persons in the computer industry, whether programmers, suppliers or consultants. It is likely that in such cases exclusive reliance upon contractual remedies will be thought more appropriate. The suggestion that a specially high standard applies in the computer industry has been rejected in the United States and will be considered further below.[122] Within the field of negligence any liability for negligent mis-statement appears to be very strictly confined to those who are in the business of supplying information, and the only possible plaintiff is the person for whose benefit the information was supplied.[123] Once again this limitation would very severely limit the application of the doctrine outside the realm of contract. It is rare for those in the business of supplying information to supply it gratuitously to all and sundry.[124]

In the United Kingdom as a result of the Unfair Contract Terms Act 1977 the extent to which liability can be reduced by reference to a contractual term has been severely constrained by section 2 which provides:

(1) A person cannot by reference to any contract term or to a notice given to persons generally or to particular persons exclude or restrict his liability for death or personal injury resulting from negligence.
(2) In the case of other loss or damage, a person cannot so exclude or restrict his liability for negligence except in so far as the term or notice satisfies the requirement of reasonableness.
(3) Where a contract term or notice purports to exclude or restrict liability for negligence a person's agreement to or awareness of it is not of itself to be taken as indicating his voluntary acceptance of any risk.

The criteria of reasonableness are exactly the same as those discussed in the previous chapter in relation to the exclusion of implied contractual terms.[125] It should also be noted that section 13 of the Act, which defines exemption clauses, also applies to negligence claims, and extends the reach of section 2 to attempts to limit the circumstances in which a duty arises, as well as those which purport to limit only the mere extent of liability.[126]

2. Breach

It is necessary for the plaintiff to prove that the defendant was in breach of his duty to take reasonable care. Such breach is judged by the standard of the reasonable man. It is no answer that a computer was involved, since computers act under the instructions of human beings:

---

122. At p. 255.
123. *Black, Jackson, Simmonds Insurance Brokerage Ltd.* v. *IBM Corp.* 440 N.E. 2d 282 (Ill., 1982).
124. A similarly restrictive approach was adopted by the majority of the Privy Council in *Mutual Life and Citizens Insurance C.* v. *Evatt* [1971] A.C. 793, P.C. (Australia), but has been rejected in subsequent United Kingdom cases, see, for example, *Esso Petroleum Co. Ltd.* v. *Mardon* [1976] Q.B. 801, C.A.
125. Above p. 203.
126. This provision appears to have been overlooked by the Court of Appeal in *Harris* v. *Wyre Forest D.C.* [1988] 1 All E.R. 691, C.A.

A computer operates only in accordance with the information and directions supplied by its human programmers. If the computer does not think like a man, it is man's fault. The fact that the actual processing of the policy was carried out by an unimaginative mechanical device can have no effect on the company's responsibility for . . . errors and oversights.[127]

It is necessary for the plaintiff to prove that negligence occurred, and that the defendant was responsible for it. In the case of a computer system, neither is easy. The working of computers is neither obvious, nor easy to understand. Systems also often represent the joint efforts of a number of different parties. The problem of proving negligence is sometimes assisted by the presumption *res ipsa loquitur*, the thing speaks for itself. This was a device introduced in the nineteenth century in the United Kingdom to assist the plaintiff to prove negligence.[128] It operates upon the satisfaction of two principal conditions, that the damage occurred in a way in which without negligence it does not normally occur and that the defendant was in control at the relevant time. Although a surprising amount of attention has been devoted to the application of this doctrine in the context of computers,[129] it is hard to see how the basic conditions can be satisfied. It is common experience that computer systems do malfunction without any negligence on anyone's part, just because they are so complicated and exhaustive testing in all possible situations in which they might be used is impossible.[130] The courts also take a rather pessimistic view of modern technology, and as late as 1955 were prepared to contemplate the mid-air explosion of an aeroplane engine as being not so abnormal as to attract the doctrine.[131] Even if this hurdle can be overcome there is still the problem of ascribing liability to any particular party when a number have contributed to the computer system which caused the damage. The general rule is that if one of the parties would be vicariously responsible for the act of the other, then the doctrine can apply. It is also the case that where the negligence of more than one party has itself caused the problem of identification, then, subject to contribution between them, either may be sued.

The basic requirement is that the defendant should exercise reasonable care. While it seems clear that no higher formulation is appropriate in the context of computers, it is still the case that those working in the field should maintain the standards appropriate to it. As one United States court said,

if machinists, electricians, blacksmiths and plumbers, are held to the ordinary standard of care in their professions, the court fails to see why personnel in the computer industry should be held to any lower standard of care.[132]

---

127. *State Farm Mutual Auto Insurance Co. Ltd.* v. *Brockhurst* 453 F.2d 533 (10th Cir., 1972) at 536.
128. *Byrne* v. *Boadle* (1863) 2 H. & C. 722, Exch. is often regarded as the seminal case.
129. See Nycum, 'Liability for Malfunction of a Computer Program', *7 Rutg. L. & C. T. L. J.* 1, 11, 12 (1979); Note 'Easing Plaintiff's Burden of Proving Negligence for Computer Malpractice', *69 Iowa L.R.* 241 (1983); and Friedman and Siegel, 'From Flour Barrel to Computer System', *14 Rutg. L. & C.T.L.J.* 283 (1988).
130. Although the malfunctioning of a computerised auto-pilot was brought within this reasoning in *Nelson* v. *American Airlines Inc.* 70 Cal Rptr 33 (Cal., 1968) this may have been on account of the specially high standards imposed upon public carriers in California.
131. *Williams* v. *United States* 218 F.2d 473 (5th Cir., 195).
132. *Invacare Corp.* v. *Sperry Corp.* 612 F.Supp 448 (D.C. Oh., 1984).

Nor is it likely to be material to the liability of contributors to a complex system that subsequent expert remedial measures would have been possible.[133] On the other hand a deliberate decision to refer a complex problem to an acknowledged expert may discharge a duty of care.[134] In complex and difficult matters such as the design and programming of a computer system there is room for a difference of opinion as to the best solution to a problem, and the court will not be so arrogant as to suppose that negligence can be inferred merely because the defendant failed to adopt the solution which, in the light of hindsight, appears to the court preferable. In the United Kingdom, it has been said that the court,

has to rely on and evaluate expert evidence, remembering that it is no part of its task of evaluation to give effect to any preference it may have for one responsible body of professional opinion over another, provided it is satisfied by the expert evidence that both qualify as reponsible bodies of medical opinion.[135]

Similarly in regard to diagnosis, it was said in another case:

Differences of opinion and practice exist, and will always exist, in the medical as in other professions. There is seldom any one answer exclusive of all others to problems of professional judgment. A court may prefer one body of opinion to the other, but that is no basis for a conclusion of negligence.[136]

It is just because of such an approach to simple negligence that there has been some attempt to impose stricter standards of liability, as will be considered in the next section of this chapter.[137]

3. Damage

The third traditional element of negligence is that the defendant's breach of the duty of care owed by him to the plaintiff has caused him damage. This raises questions of causation in the sense of the remoteness of the damage from the defendant's act, and of the types of loss which will be compensated.

There is clearly some connection between the definition of the duty owed to the plaintiff and the question of the extent of recovery. In the United Kingdom it was at one time thought that the verbal formulation of the test for the existence of a duty and of the loss for which recovery was available should be identical and, accordingly, the damage was required to have been reasonably foreseeable.[138] In the United States it is more common to describe the test in terms of proximity, but the result is much the same.[139] It is not necessarily fatal that there should have been third party intervention, if the third party behaved in a reasonable, and reasonably foreseeable way. Thus

---

133. *Ogwo* v. *Taylor* [1987] 1 All E.R. 668. C.A.
134. *Investors in Industry Commercial Properties* v. *South Bedfordshire D.C.* [1986] 1 All E.R. 787, C.A.
135. *Sidaway* v. *Governors of the Royal Bethlehem Hospital* [1985] A.C. 871, H.L. at 895. This was a medical case involving professional standards. The reasoning would apply *a fortiori* in a computer case.
136. *Maynard* v. *West Midlands Regional Health Authority* [1985] 1 All E.R. 635, H.L. at 638.
137. See p 255 below.
138. *Overseas Tankship (U.K.)* v. *Morts Dock & Engineering Co. (Wagon Mound No. 1)* [1961] A.C. 388, P.C. (Australia).
139. Prosser and Keeton, *Torts* (5th edn, 1984) para. 42.

in one case the defendant was held liable for supplying a circuit board which was inappropriate for its task, but resembled the correct board, when its installation by an employer caused a machine to injure an employee.[140] A similar result has been reached in cases where the loss was purely economic. In *Independent School District No. 454, Fairmont, Minnesota* v. *Statistical Tabulating Corp.*[141] a school district wished to value its schools for insurance purposes. Its surveyors took all the relevant measurements, and then sent them to the defendants to compute the relevant values. The computation was done negligently with the result that the schools were under-insured, and the authority suffered loss as a result when there was a fire. The defendants were held liable because they knew that their computation would be relied upon by innocent third parties, the duty was owed to a limited class, and because 'recovery by a foreseeable user will promote cautionary techniques among computer operators'.[142] This justification gives some cause for concern about extending liability in this way. It would be a great hardship for systems designers to be under potential liability to an unlimited extent for an unlimited time to an unlimited class in relation to an unlimited range of applications. Dangers are particularly severe in the case of computer systems which are highly flexible in their range of application, and at the same time capable of immense amounts of work. The volume and range far exceed that of other devices. Nor is it elsewhere so difficult to guard against error. The transposition of digits in an operating system could easily go undetected through all reasonable trials, and still in operation suddenly lead to disastrous error causing enormous expense to users. In such circumstances the conditions laid down in the *School Board* case could easily be satisfied without the result seeming to be obviously just. The problem is exacerbated by the difficulty of establishing in relation to any new system how to set an appropriate liability insurance premium. Nor is it obvious that insurance is the best way of distributing the risk. It should be noted that in this case the court was prepared to allow recovery despite all of the intervening acts between the inaccurate computation and the occurrence of loss, such as the Board's decision to act upon the valuation, and the occurrence of the fire. The explanation is that in this case these events were exactly those envisaged throughout the transaction. If the damage had been of a very different kind, say the suicide of a manager in consequence of learning of the lack of cover, it is less certain that recovery would have been permitted. Where the intervening act is criminal it is still more difficult to maintain that the chain of causation has not been broken. It has been held that in such a case actual knowledge, or good reason to anticipate, the commission of a specific crime may be required.[143]

So far as the type of damage is concerned, there is never much of a

---

140. *Deromedi* v. *Litton Industrial Products Inc.* 636 F.Supp. 392 (W.D. Mich., 1986).
141. 359 F.Supp. 1095 (N.D. Ill., 1973).
142. At p. 1098.
143. See *Atkins* v. *District of Columbia* 526 A.2d 933 (D.C., 1987) where the court rejected a claim that a violent assault was caused by negligent maintenance of the computer system, failure of which was involved in a deficiency of information provided to the judge who in its absence decided to release the assailant rather than to retain him in custody pending trial for another offence.

problem in respect of personal injury or property damage, so long at least as the property which has been damaged is severable from the computer system which has damaged it.[144] Economic loss is more contentious, and in many jurisdictions there is unlikely to be recovery outside the areas of contract and fraud. If economic loss is available for negligence then the normal measure is the amount required to put the plaintiff into the position he would have been in had the negligence not occurred.

E. Strict liability[145]

A form of strict liability has been mooted to cope with the perceived difficulty of securing recovery under theories of contract, warranty, fraud or negligence. Contract and warranty may be frustrated by contractual exclusions and are not always available to third parties, fraud is difficult to prove, and negligence is frequently pre-empted by the need to preserve freedom of contract. In the United States an attempt to fill the gap has resulted in the development of strict liability for a producer of a defective product in respect of physical injury which it causes.[146] Such liability is not restricted to the purchaser of the item in question, so a manufacturer may be liable however often the product has been sold on, and attaches irrespective of negligence in the producer. In the United Kingdom, although there was no similar development at common law, a form of strict liability has been introduced by statute in the form of the Consumer Protection Act 1987, implementing a directive of the European Economic Communities on Product Liability.[147]

The policy inspiring the imposition of such strict liability has been described as follows:

The disparity in position and bargaining power which forces the consumer to depend entirely on the manufacturer and the difficulty of requiring the injured party in consumer products cases to trace back along the channel of trade to the source of production in the search for the origin of the defect in order to prove negligence have been among the reasons for the emergence of the doctrine of strict liability in tort. An additional element has been the recognition that the mass producer of a product made for consumer use should as a matter of public policy bear the responsibility of an insurer against a defect in the product which causes harm to the consumer.[148]

It cannot be denied that these policies are quite capable of applying to the context of computers. There frequently is disparity of knowledge between producer and consumer; the consumer does depend upon the reputation of the manufacturer; the producer is in the best position to detect and to remedy defects; and the producer is likely to be the most efficient insurer. To the extent that a computer causes direct personal injury to a user as a result

---

144. See p. 239 above.
145. See, generally, Freed 'Products Liability in the Computer Age', *17 Jurimetrics J.* 270 (1979); Nycum, 'Liability for Malfunction of a Computer Program', *7 Rutg. L. & C.T.L.J.* 1 (1979); Gemignani, 'Product Liability and Software', *8 Rutg. L. & C.T.L.J.* 173 (1981); Note 'Computer Software and Strict Products Liability', *20 San Diego L.R.* 439 (1983).
146. See Restatement (Second) of Torts para. 402A (1966).
147. 85/374/EEC.
148. *La Rossa* v. *Scientific Design Co.* 402 F.2d 937 (3rd Cir., 1968) at 942.

of some defect, say in the electrical wiring, there can be no reasonable doubt that liability should attach under such a doctrine.

However, it is clear that the doctrine is subject to important restrictions and limitations which affect its utility in more complex situations involving the supply of computer systems. In some jurisdictions in the United States it is limited to defective products which cause personal injury, and in others to those causing physical damage. In very few does it extend to defects causing economic loss. Thus in *Professional Lens Plan Inc.* v. *Polaris Leasing Corp.*[149] the court remarked that:

> The computer and its component part, the hard disc, are clearly not products which are inherently dangerous. Here damages are sought only for economic loss, no personal injuries or property damage being involved. We find no public policy dictates extending implied warranties of fitness and merchantability to the non-privity manufacturers here.[150]

It is also restricted to the production of defective *products*, and is generally held not to apply to the provision of services.[151] This distinction is far from clear when applied to the area of computers. Hardware alone presents few hazards, but suppose that it becomes hazardous only because of its operating system, for example by misrepresentation on its internal registers of the peripheral devices in active use. The usual test is to ask whether the provision of product or of service predominates, but seems to advance matters little in this context. In the case of software it seems clear that consultancy services would not qualify for strict liability despite the delivery of any programs on tapes or discs, or however much accompanied by manuals of instructions or copies of the coding. It is more likely that packaged products for personal computers would be regarded as sufficiently like any other consumer product. The reasons for excluding professional services generally were elaborated immediately after the extract quoted above[152] from the *La Rossa* case:

> Professional services do not ordinarily lend themselves to the doctrine of tort liability without fault because they lack the elements which gave rise to the doctrine. There is no mass production of goods or a large body of distant consumers whom it would be unfair to require to trace the article they used along the channels of trade to the original manufacturer and there to pinpoint an act of negligence·remote from their knowledge and even from their ability to inquire. Thus, professional services form a marked contrast to consumer products cases and even in those jurisdictions which have adopted a rule of strict products liability a majority of decisions have declined to apply it to professional services.[153]

The general view is that expressed[154] by Traynor C.J. that clients of professionals purchase service, not insurance. For similar reasons, attempts

---

149. 675 P.2d 887 (Kan., 1984).
150. At p. 898.
151. The problem is similar to that of whether programs are goods for the purposes of the Uniform Commercial Code, see Note 'Computer Programs as Goods under the U.C.C.', 77 *Mich. L.R.* 1149 (1979).
152. At p. 255.
153. At 942.
154. In *Gagne* v. *Bertran* 275 P.2d 15 (Cal., 1954) at 21.

to extend a more general theory of professional malpractice to those in the computer industry on the basis of the special dependency of the user upon the supplier have been generally rejected.[155] This would have had the effect of extending the period of limitations, by delaying its start so long as a continuing professional relationship, during which any damage might be expected to be corrected, were still in existence.[156]

In the United Kingdom a new possibility of a tortious claim based on strict liability has been opened up by the passage of the Consumer Protection Act 1987. This area of the law was re-examined as a result of the thalidomide tragedy, both in the United Kingdom[157] and in Europe generally.[158] The Directive left a number of matters to national initiative, such as whether to impose any financial limit upon recovery, whether to cover damage to property as well as physical injury, and whether to allow a 'development risks' defence. The Consumer Protection Act does apply to damage to property, imposes no financial limit on recovery, but does incorporate a development risks defence.[159] It operates in addition to existing remedies.[160] The legislation applies only to *defective products*, It does not apply explicitly to information, and it may be thought that it does not apply to defective software as such. It is arguable whether it applies to software packages supplied on discs or plug-in boards. It should also be noted that a product is defective if,

the safety of the product is not such as persons generally are entitled to expect; and for those purposes 'safety', in relation to a product, shall include safety with respect to products comprised in that product and safety in the context of risks of damage to property, as well as in the context of risks of death or personal injury.[161]

It seems that where the software is actually built into the product which is supplied, and makes it operate defectively, then there will be liability on the part of the supplier as a result of the guidelines provided for the interpretation of sub-section 3(1) by the following sub-section:

In determining for the purposes of subsection (1) above what persons generally are entitled to expect in relation to a product all the circumstances shall be taken into account, including –

(a) the manner in which, and purposes for which, the product has been marketed, its get-up, the use of any mark in relation to the product and any instructions for,

---

155. See p. 236 above.
156. See *Triangle Underwriters Inc.* v. *Honeywell Information Systems Inc.* 604 F.2d 737 (2nd Cir., 1979), cf. a pre-trial ruling in *F. & M. Schaefer Corp.* v. *Electronic Data Systems Corp.* Civ. Vo. 77-3982 reported on a different point at 430 F.Supp. 988 (S.D.N.Y., 1977).
157. Leading to the Reports of the Royal Commission on Civil Liability and Compensation for Personal Injury (Cmnd. 7054) in 1976, and the Law Commission's Report 'Liability for Defective Products' (Cmnd. 6831) in 1977.
158. Council of Europe, *Strasbourg Convention on Products Liability in Regard to Personal Injury and Death* (1977) and the Product Liability Directive (85/374/EEC) from the European Economic Communities in 1985.
159. It is indeed controversial whether or not sect. 4(1)(e) which implements the defence does not go beyond what the Directive allows, see Crossrick, 'EEC News', *New Law Journal* 1 April 1988 p. 223.
160. Consumer Protection Act 1987 sect. 2(6).
161. *Ibid*. sect. 3(1).

or warnings with respect to, doing or refraining from doing anything with or in relation to the product;

(b) what might reasonably be expected to be done with or in relation to the product; and

(c) the time when the product was supplied by its producer to another;

and nothing in this section shall require a defect to be inferred from the fact alone that the safety of the product which is supplied after that time is greater than the safety of the product in question.[162]

It would be difficult to distinguish instructions to the user for the use of the program, from built-in instructions to the computer, and it would certainly make no sense to impose liability for the former, but not for the latter. If a defective program is built-in, the legislation provides machinery for imposing liability upon a third-party supplier.[163] However, the Act does not apply to pure information providers, and would thus not appear to apply to independent software houses, except perhaps, as noted above, in relation to packages sold on discs or boards by retail.

A special defence is provided for new technologies in section 4(1)(e) which applies if,

the state of scientific and technical knowledge at the relevant time was not such that a producer of products of the same description as the product in question might be expected to have discovered the defect if it had existed in his products while they were under his control;[164]

It is arguable that this erodes the strictness of liability under the Act to something akin to negligence under the old law in the cases to which it applies. It should, however, be noted that at the very least it reverses the onus of proof. It will be for the defendant to show that the defect could not have been expected to be discovered in the state of the art, and the generality of the standard will preclude any argument seeking to take into account the limited research resources of the defendant.

Another defence of special interest in the computer context is that which protects the supplier of a component in a further product, where the defect results from the design of the subsequent product, or instructions given by its producer.[165] This could be useful in the case of software written to fit in with the specifications of a manufacturer's operating system, which is subsequently changed so that the software operates defectively.

F. Defamation

This very different form of tortious liability may apply to databases. If a defamatory statement is published about an individual, he has a remedy at common law in both the United States and the United Kingdom, though the range of the tort is greater and it is less encumbered by defences in the latter. As a tort at common law it is remediable under state, as opposed to federal, law in the United States, but even at state law it has a significant

---

162. *Ibid.* sect. 3(2).
163. *Ibid.* sect. 2(3).
164. Cf. in the United States Model Uniform Liability Act sect. 106.
165 Consumer Protection Act 1987 sect. 4(1)(f).

constitutional dimension on account of the need to give effect to the First Amendment protection of freedom of speech. This is mainly manifested in the requirement of express malice before allowing a claim by a public figure.[166] Partly as a result of these constraints there are a number of alternative remedies in the United States for the publication of false statements, and these will also be mentioned in this section.

To the extent that a database contains false information about someone, there is potential liability in respect of its dissemination to third parties. Computers are becoming increasingly significant in this context, partly because the likelihood of this form of defamation is increasing as a result of increasing use of databases, and partly because there is a tendency to perceive computer held information as particularly reliable.

The leading United States case in which such a form of defamation occurred was *Dun & Bradstreet Inc.* v. *Greenmoss Builders Inc.*[167] where the issue reached the Supreme Court of the United States. The appellants maintained a computerised database of business information which they made available to subcribers to their service. One of their employees wrongly attributed information relating to an employee of the respondent to the respondent itself, and the information was circulated to five subscribers. Although when the mistake was discovered a retraction was also circulated to the five, it was in a form unsatisfactory to the respondent, and he sued for defamation. The appellant argued that it was covered by the rule requiring express malice derived from *Sullivan*. It was held by a thin majority[168] that while this defence would apply to a matter of public interest, it did not apply in a purely commercial context which was not of sufficient public concern to attract the operation of the First Amendment. The database proprietor was thus left liable for the substantial sums[169] which had been awarded by the jury in presumed compensatory and in punitive damages. It should be noted that in the United Kingdom the result would have been different since there is a general defence of qualified privilege to a claim in defamation in respect of trade inquiries.[170]

Alternative statutory remedies may sometimes be available in the United States for similar database errors. Thus in *Thompson* v. *San Antonio Retail Merchants' Association*[171] the computerised credit database in question provided for automatic updating. A subscriber would interrogate the database by providing details of a customer, and the system would provide details of records within the database which seemed to correspond to that customer. It was then for the subscriber to accept such a record as relating to the customer, whereupon any further details derived from the new transaction would be entered into the record thus identified as relating to that customer. Unfortunately a subscriber wrongly accepted a suggested record as relating

---

166. *New York Times Inc.* v. *Sullivan* 376 U.S. 254 (1964).
167. 472 U.S. 749 (1985).
168. Three judges joined in the majority opinion, two separately concurred in the result, and four dissented.
169. $50 000 in presumed compensatory damages, and $300 000 in punitive damages.
170. *London Association for the Protection of Trade* v. *Greenlands* [1916] 2 A.C. 15, H.L. Such a defence is available in most states of the United States, but not in all.
171. 682 F.2d 509 (5th Cir., 1982).

to the customer before him, with the result that the system conflated details relating to two quite separate people. One of them was subsequently denied credit on the basis of the delinquency of the other. The system remained impervious to attempts by the nondelinquent customer to have the record changed, and eventually an action was brought under the Fair Credit Reporting Act. Although that provision is more favourable to the defendant in requiring an element of fault, it was held that it was in breach of its duty to take reasonable procedures to ensure the maximum possible accuracy of the information provided. It is a measure of general dissatisfaction with the reluctance of system proprietors to provide and operate adequate facilities to correct erroneous records that the jury awarded $10 000 for the humilation and distress caused by the denial of credit, and the trial court refused to strike it down as being clearly wrong. However, an attempt to enlist negligence as a further alternative form of liability in respect of very similar muddling of identities was dismissed in *Scott* v. *District of Columbia*,[172] but perhaps only because the allegation had not been sufficiently pleaded. The frustration and anger caused by such errors is further illustrated in the award by an Alabama jury of no less than $500 000 in respect of a computer system failure leading to the initial refusal of a medical insurer to pay a claim for $120 in respect of hospital treatment.[173] The cause of action there was, however, for a bad faith refusal to pay, and since the insurer's failure had been induced by faulty operation of the system by the treating hospital the appeal was allowed, despite evidence of appalling inefficiency in the correction procedures. Similarly in *Gulf Life Ins. Co.* v. *Folsom*,[174] where the cause of action required knowledge of error, the court was not prepared to infer it merely from the use of an inappropriately programmed record-keeping system. In the stricter regime of defamation it seems likely that the system design and operation errors illustrated in these cases would have resulted in tortious liability.

G. Miscellaneous

The law of torts contains a great variety of nominate torts, many of which could involve the use of computers, but it would be fruitless merely to list here every possible tortious action, noting how it might apply in the computer context.[175] In fact many of the topics dealt with in other chapters, and especially in the chapter on criminal liability, may also give rise to causes of action in tort for such things as deceit, trespass, conversion or conspiracy, though there is no more evidence that they are used in addition to criminal penalties in connection with computers than with anything else. Presumably computer criminals are just as unlikely as any others to be worth suing. Two torts where attempts have been made to extend liability in respect of computers are breach of statutory duty and false imprisonment.

---

172. 493 A.2d 319 (D.C., 1985).
173. *Blue Cross and Blus Shield of Alabama* v. *Granger* 461 So.2d 1320 (Ala., 1984).
174. 349 S.E.2d 368 (1986).
175. Thus the operation of computers can cause nuisance by interference with television reception, see *Page County Appliance Center* v. *Honeywell Inc.* 347 N.W.2d 171 (Io., 1984) cp. *Bridlington Relay Ltd.* v. *Yorkshire Electricity Board* [1965] Ch. 436, Ch.

1. Breach of statutory duty

This is a tortious remedy which applies in cases where a statute prescribes a particular course of conduct without necessarily specifying any particular civil remedy. The mere fact that a criminal penalty is imposed is neither necessary nor sufficient to ground liability in tort. In each case the question of whether a tortious remedy is to be supplied and, if so, whether liability should be strict or based upon fault, is left for the courts to determine. The theory is that the legislature must have intended the duty breaker to compensate the party damaged by his breach of duty, even though it has not said so explicitly. Sometimes the courts will require only that the conditions set out in the statute have been satisfied, and sometimes they require in addition lack of proper care, thus in effect creating a new duty situation within which the ordinary rules as to breach and remoteness of damage can operate. An example of this is provided by *Data General Corp.* v. *Digital Computer Controls Inc.*[176] where the defendants, who had designed and marketed a computer identical to one produced by one of their competitors as a result of using information contained in that machine's maintenance manual, were found to be in breach of the relevant New Jersey trade secret legislation. The court held that this was sufficient to ground civil liability even though they felt that the situation without some such sign from the legislature would not have been appropriate for the application of the ordinary tortious remedies for misappropriation of trade secrets or for palming off. Damages were held over for trial, but the court awarded a permanent injunction immediately. Many of the examples of liability for breach of statutory duty occur in areas where the legislature has taken the view that particular forms of activity, unless controlled, are likely to produce public mischief. This accounts for development in situations involving the provision of supplies or services to the general public, such as catering and transportation. Occasionally protection is afforded to particular relationships such as that between employer and employee. Until recently the operation of a computer was not generally regarded as falling into the category of activities potentially mischievous to the general public. This may now be changing as will be seen in relation to some of the popular concerns with privacy and with the safety of terminals. Thus the regulations for VDU screens referred to above[177] could easily yield a claim for breach of statutory duty, provided that the necessary damage and causation could be proved.

2. False imprisonment

Reliance by the police on computerised databases can give rise to tortious liability for false imprisonment if a defect in the system goes wrong, and if the police are at fault in relying upon the computer output in making an arrest. This may be illustrated by contrasting two cases, involving the same District of Columbia system. In *Woodward* v. *District of Columbia*,[178] where the system was relied upon to dictate the arrest of someone more than a year

---

176. 357 A.2d 105 (Del., 1975).
177. At p. 227.
178. 387 A.2d 726 (D.C., 1978).

after the original charge had been dropped, but the decision to do so was omitted from the database, the claim succeeded because the arresting officers could see on the face of the documents that the delay had occurred, and should have realised that arrest was inappropriate. However, in *Scott* v. *District of Columbia*[179] where the error consisted of the conflation of two separate identities, the court was not prepared to allow the claim since the officers were entitled to rely upon the computer, and there was nothing to put them on notice that a mistake had occurred.

H. Artificial intelligence

This final section of the chapter differs from its predecessors in focusing not upon a cause of action, but upon a factual situation. It provides a convenient illustration of the way in which apparently simple legal issues can become complicated on account of the complexity of the underlying facts. The type of system in question will first be explained, then attention will be paid to the application of general legal principles, and finally certain special considerations applying to this particular environment will be explored.

1. Expert systems

In so new a field there is little agreement on terminology, so it is necessary to describe the sort of system to be considered. It might perhaps be categorised as an intelligent knowledge-based expert adviser. This is the sort of system which might be employed to assist with medical diagnosis. It would typically consist of the distillation of an area of medical expertise into a corpus of rules. This corpus would be susceptible of access in response to input to the system by the doctor of information about a particular case, for example the symptoms presented, in response to questions posed by the system. It would typically conclude with a suggested diagnosis which fitted the symptoms. Such a system might indicate authorities justifying the various stages of its interrogation, provisional conclusions, excluded possibilities with reasons for excluding them, and the degree of certainty with which its conclusions were presented. Some such systems incorporate a learning mechanism so that each successive application refines the operation of the system for the future. Despite such diversity, at least three types of activity seem to be essential before such a system can be implemented. The expertise must be harvested; it must be put into a form which the system can use; and a system for eliciting the information, drawing the inferences and presenting the conclusions, must be devised. These are the tasks of the knowledge supplier, the knowledge engineer and the system designer. When the system has been built it must be brought to the market, and once marketed it must be used, typically by a doctor advising a patient. If the advice is defective it may lead to adverse effects not, or not only, upon the patient so advised, but, or also, upon a third party.

The first point to note is the number of potentially different human beings involved in the process. It is almost certain that the knowledge will be

---

179. 493 A.2d 319 (D.C., 1985).

supplied from those outside the system. The idea is typically to secure access to the highest expertise available. It may be derived from available medical literature, but may ideally be supplemented by access to expertise derived from practical experience, and available only as a result of oral discussion with experienced practitioners in the relevant field. In practice the knowledge engineer and the builder of the inference engine are also likely to be different. The reason for this is that systems of this sort seek a wide sale so as to keep down costs, and the economies of scale are such that the cost of the inference engine is smallest when it is used over the greatest range of applications. This has led to the development of 'shells', that is to say empty structures into which expertise of many different sorts may be poured. These shells may then receive the relevant expertise, and often provide further facilities for modification to the needs of a particular application. It would not be uncommon for the enterprise of setting up such a system to be financed on a speculative basis, and then marketed through distributors and retailers. The system will then be in a state to be used, but in order to use it, the individual practitioner must secure the information about his patient which interactively drives the diagnosis through the system, culminating in advice or treatment.

Such fragmentation of input has two unfortunate effects. It enhances the possibility of the system being defective on account of a failure to match one human input precisely with another; and it renders more difficult the task of establishing exactly what went wrong with the system, and which of the many contributors may be responsible.

2. General principles

It is apparent from the above analysis, and especially from the large number of parties who might be involved, that the reduction of any problem into legal claims is likely to be exceedingly complex. Such complexity is one of the main reasons for difficulty. Another is the conflict of policies which so radically new an approach creates in the context of legal remedies. The matter may be illustrated by reference to an imaginary scenario. A patient feels ill, goes to his doctor for advice, and the doctor consults an expert system. The system suggests as a diagnosis a particular disease, and the doctor prescribes drugs to treat it. The diagnosis turns out to be wrong, the drugs in fact have the effect of causing the patient to become unconscious without warning, and as a result he is involved in a motor accident, injuring an innocent third party. The possible plaintiffs in any such scenario will include: the innocent third party who has not been in any contractual relationship with any of the possible defendants; the patient who may have had a contractual relationship with the doctor, but will not have had one with anyone else; the doctor, who may have suffered damage to his reputation, quite apart from any possible liability to other plaintiffs, and the parties in the distribution chain from the supplier, who may have suffered similar damage to their reputations and goodwill; and finally the system supplier against the knowledge suppliers, knowledge engineers and inference system designers. Even these ultimate suppliers may be possible plaintiffs if it is uncertain whether any of them is wholly to blame for the defect in the system. Any of these parties except the innocent third party are also liable to be possible defendants. Some of the claims will be in contract, and some in tort. It is also conceivable that such systems might in some contexts be categorised as *products* and so attract strict liability so far as they cause physical injury or damage. Some contractual claims will be for economic loss and pre-empt tortious claims. Some of the contracts are likely to contain exclusion clauses restricting liability. Some of the parties will have suffered personal injury, some damage to property, and some merely economic loss. Further complication is caused by the fact that some of these parties may be responsible not only for their own acts, but for those of others for whom they bear responsibility perhaps as employer and employee, or as principal and agent, or on a contractual basis, for example in respect of an agreement to indemnify. In such a situation it may well be impossible to attribute the fault entirely to one party. It would be possible for the knowledge to have been supplied in a defective or incomplete state, for the representation to disguise the defect, and for the inference engine to fail to process it properly. In such a situation questions will arise of the relative contributions of the different parties, both as a matter of causation for the purpose of ascribing liability to innocent third parties and so as to fix the amounts of contribution between themselves.

3. Special rules

It is not here possible to explore all of these potential paths of liability through the whole multi-dimensional maze of legal relations, so instead attention will be focused upon the special position of two of the potential parties, the supplier of expertise, and the user of the system, the doctor in the example given above. Problems may be caused because the whole aim of expert systems is to make available on a more general basis, services which have hitherto been offered only to a very few. In the past, in the case of the provision of professional services, there has been a close relationship, actually of, or at least akin to, contract, which readily creates liability through reliance, but also provides an opportunity to disclaim it. The expert system transfers the incidents of such a relationship into the very different context of a mass market where the parties are too far apart for this to be able to occur. The nature of expert systems is, in essence, that professional services are packaged and sold as consumer products. Given the wholly different legal policies which apply to the provision of professional services and of consumer products, it is not surprising that difficulty occurs.

(a) Supplier of information
In both the United Kingdom and in the United States it is possible in certain circumstances for someone who supplies information to be liable to its user. Thus in the leading United Kingdom case of *Hedley Byrne & Co. Ltd. v. Heller & Partners Ltd.*[180] it was said:

In a sphere in which a person is so placed that others could reasonably rely on his

---

180. [1964] A.C. 465, H.L. at 502.

judgment or his skill or on his ability to make careful inquiry, a person takes it on himself to give information or advice to, *or allows his information or advice to be passed on to, another person who,* as he knows or should know, will place reliance on it, then a duty of care will arise.[181]

So too in the United States even in the influential judgment rejecting strict liability for the supply of professional information, Traynor C.J. conceded liability for negligence:

The general rule is applicable that those who sell their services for the guidance of others in their economic, financial and personal affairs are not liable in the absence of negligence or intentional misconduct . . . Those who hire [experts] . . . are not justified in expecting infallibility, but can expect only reasonable care and competence.[182]

The supplier of information for an expert system must thus take reasonable care in the information which he supplies. The House of Lords has expressed approval of the remark that 'The test is the standard of the ordinary skilled man exercising or professing to have that special skill.'[183] Expertise must also be supplied in a suitable form,

advice, like any other communication, should be in terms appropriate to the comprehension and experience of the particular recipient. It is . . . clear . . . that the professional man does not necessarily discharge his duty by spelling out what is obvious. The client is entitled to expect the exercise of a reasonably professional judgment.[184]

While it may be argued that this is the function of the knowledge engineer so far as the suitability of the information for the system is concerned, it remains the case that the engineer is likely to be a layman in the particular field of expertise, and it is for the supplier to make sure that it is in a form which the engineer can understand sufficiently to work with. It seems unlikely that the supplier's duty will be in any way diminished by the prospect of its being filtered through the expertise of another,[185] though if the latter is also negligent a question of contribution between the negligent parties may arise.

A problem with this line of authority is that it does contemplate a personal relationship upon which reliance is founded. It may be contrasted with a dearth of authority for liability where the information is not provided to a particular known recipient. Thus it was said in one United States case where damages were sought for injury incurred by following a procedure published in a book that:

Plaintiffs concede that they have discovered no case in any jurisdiction which has imposed liability on a publisher for negligent misrepresentation merely because of publication of material written by a third party.[186]

---

181. Emphasis supplied.
182. *Gagne* v. *Bertran* 275 P.2d 15 (Cal., 1954) at 20, 21.
183. In *Whitehouse* v. *Jordan* [1981] 1 All E.R. 267m H.L. by Lord Edmund-Davies at 277.
184. *County Personnel Ltd.* v. *Pulver & Co.* [1987] 1 All E.R. 289, C.A. at 295 by Bingham L.J.
185. See *Ogwo* v. *Taylor* [1987] 1 All E.R. 668, C.A.
186. *Alm* v. *Van Nostrand Reinhold Co. Inc.* 480 N.E.2d 1263 (111., 1985) at 1266. Though in the bizarre case of *Herceg* v. *Hustler Magazine Inc.* 495 F.Supp. 802 (S.D. Tex., 1983) at 804 n.1 an unreported case in which a claim for $1.1 in respect of a chemistry textbook was settled was mentioned.

Nor do there appear to be any cases imposing liability upon the authors of such books. The same holds true, both for authors and publishers, in the United Kingdom. In such abhorrence is such liability regarded that the extreme case of a marine hydrographer who is negligent in drawing a map as a result of which a ship sinks is used as an exemplar of the lengths to which liability should not be stretched.[187]

This very situation has, however, provoked a converse reaction in the United States. While it is recognised that in the case of professional services, including the giving of advice, there can be no liability without the presence of both special reliance and fault, chart and map cases are regarded as being different. The charts and maps are capable of being regarded, not as services but as goods, and as being subject to strict liability. In particular this reasoning has been applied to approach charts used by pilots when coming in to land. The reasoning for this was explained in *Salomey* v. *Jeppeson & Co.*:

> Though a 'product' may not include mere provision of architectural design plans or any similar form of data supplied under individually tendered service arrangements . . . the mass production and marketing of these charts requires Jeppeson to bear the costs of accidents that are proximately covered by defects in these charts.[188]

Although all of these charts were in a conventional form, it was stressed in *Brocklesby* that the fact that the basic information was transformed into a graphic form was a contributing factor to the decision that a product was involved. It is submitted that an expert system involves a no less radical transformation of the basic information, and that it would be anomalous to distinguish between a chart in hard copy and one built into the plane's electronics. The elements of mass marketing and the fungibility of different copies of a computerised expert system suggest that there is no intrinsic reason to deny the application of product liability in this sphere. Such reasoning would not apply to a custom-built system geared to the requirements of a particular individual customer, but in such a case the law of contract should suffice.

(b) User of system
This scenario imagines a system in which a practitioner acts as an intermediary between the system and the subject, though in some areas expert systems might be designed to be consulted directly. Given the current early, and often experimental, state of expert systems it seems unlikely that a practitioner would be regarded as negligent for failing to consult an expert system.[189] Conversely it is unlikely that the mere decision to use a system would itself be regarded as evidence of negligence so long as some responsible body of opinion would regard such use as reasonable. As Lord Diplock

187. An example invented by Winfield in his *Textbook on the Law of Tort*, and endorsed even by those seeking to extend the boundaries of negligent mis-statement, see Denning L.J. in *Candler* v. *Crane, Christmas & Co.* [1951] 2 K.B. 164, C.A. at 183.

188. 707 F.2d 671 (2nd Cir., 1983) at 677. See also *Aetna Casualty and Service Co.* v. *Jeppeson & Co.* 642 F.2d 339 (9th Cir., 1981); *Brocklesby* v. *United States* 767 F.2d 1288 (9th Cir., 1985); and *Halstead* v. *United States* 535 F.Supp. 780 (D. Conn., 1982).

189. Though there is a well-established duty upon a general practitioner to refer a case which he cannot treat to a competent human specialist, see for example *Osborne* v. *Frazer* 425 S.W.2d 768 (Tenn., 1968) and Annotation 35 A.L.R.3d 349.

remarked in *Sidaway* v. *Governors of the Royal Bethlehem Hospital*:

Those members of the public who seek medical or surgical aid would be badly served by the adoption of any legal principle that would confine the doctor to some long-established well-tried method of treatment only, although its past record of success might be small, if he wanted to be confident that he would not run the risk of being held liable in negligence simply because he tried some more modern treatment, and by some unavoidable mischance it failed to heal but did some harm to the patient. This would encourage 'defensive medicine' with a vengeance.[190]

The consultation of an expert may indeed provide a defence to a claim for negligence as stated in *Investors in Industry Commercial Properties* v. *South Bedfordshire D.C.* in relation to a claim against an architect who had consulted a structural engineer:

If . . . a consultant with these qualities is appointed, the architect will normally carry no legal responsibility for the work to be done by the expert which is beyond the capability of an architect of ordinary competence; in relation to the work allotted to the expert, the architect's legal responsibility will normally be confined to directing and co-ordinating the expert's work in the whole.[191]

Expert systems may still be at too early a stage even to be regarded as a sufficiently legitimate recourse for the practitioner to avoid a claim of negligence, but such a first step towards legal recognition cannot in some areas be very far away.

In such a case the practitioner still retains some responsibility, and the Court of Appeal went on to make it more explicit:

If any danger or problem arises in connection with the work allotted to the expert, of which an architect of ordinary competence reasonably ought to be aware and reasonably could be expected to warn the client, despite the employment of the expert, and despite what the expert says or does about it, it is . . . the duty of the architect to warn the client. In such a contingency he is not entitled to rely blindly on the expert, with no mind of his own, on matters which should have been apparent to him.[192]

Such a requirement will require very sensitive application, otherwise it will place the practitioner in an intolerable position. Given that damage will have occurred as a result of the application of the system, there is a danger of the practitioner being held liable both in the situation where his over-riding of the system's suggestion causes the damage, and in the case where his refusal to act upon his own judgment by over-riding the system causes the damage.

The practitioner will also remain liable for any negligence in interpreting and entering the client's answers and responses into the system, or in explaining or acting upon the output of the system.

Since it seems that expert systems are more advanced in the field of medicine in the United States than in other fields or jurisdictions, and are correspondingly more likely to come into regular use there, it is probable that the first cases on expert systems will be decided by American juries when personal injury or death has resulted. The prospect of the requirement

---

190. [1985] A.C. 871, H.L. at 893.
191. [1986] 1 All E.R. 787, C.A. at 807.
192. At p. 808.

of the imposition of very high standards, and for widely interpreted categories of damages cannot be discounted, and could have a distorting effect on the development of this branch of the law.

Chapter 7

Crime[1]

This chapter, like its two predecessors, largely applies legal rules well established in other contexts to the special situation of computers. For the most part, these give rise to little difficulty since so many of the ordinary values of the criminal law such as respect for life and property are unaffected in their application by any relevant special features of the computer. Problems do, however, occur in relation to the ascription of some of the basic concepts of the criminal law, such as those of property or deception in the context of computers. It is partly for that reason that there has arisen an orchestrated popular clamour for legislative intervention in this area, a clamour which, much more than in the case of the liability under the civil law discussed in the two preceding chapters, has in many jurisdictions met with a ready legislative response. It is often symptomatic of such clamorous situations that there is a tendency to substitute emotion for analysis, and rhetoric for argument. Both this area, and that of privacy to be covered in the next chapter, have suffered in this respect. In neither case is it at all easy to define the field of relevant concern or, consequently, to assess the scale of the problem to be addressed. The first section of this chapter will consider the nature and dimension of the problem in more detail. Some particular areas of difficulty will then be considered. Some of these arise in relation to what may be described as the general criminal law and some to more specific statutory regimes dealing with criminal aspects of such matters as copyright, trade secrets and privacy. These will be considered in separate sections, and a final section will be devoted to the reform of this branch of the law.

A. The Problem

1. Its nature

It is common, though not uncontroverted, to characterise this area of the law

---

1. Much of the substance of this chapter appears in Tapper, 'Computer Crime: Scotch Mist?' [1987] *Crim. L.R.* 4.

as that relating to 'computer crime'. The apposition of these two nouns might be regarded as symptomatic of more fundamental confusion. Does the phrase connote crimes directed at computers, or crimes utilising computers, or merely crimes in any way at all related to computers? Some authors have deliberately avoided this apposition,[2] just because they believe that it begs the question of whether there is, or should be, a separate compartment of the criminal law reserved for crimes involving computers. This question is quite central to much of the argument in this chapter. It is largely addressed to an inquiry how far current criminal law is adequate to cope with the increasing incidence of the use of computers in modern life, and to what extent it may require to be modified or augmented, whether by the extension of definitions, the modification of conditions of liability or by the creation of wholly new offences. Debate on such matters is rife within the common law world and, indeed, outside it;[3] legislative action has been implemented in many jurisdictions, and proposed in more.[4]

It is something of a mystery why computers should have attracted such attention in the context of the criminal law. They are exceptionally simple machines, capable only of distinguishing between the digits 0 and 1, of adding and subtracting them, and of storing, moving and displaying the result. Their versatility comes from their being able to perform these feats very quickly, in a very small physical space, with the consumption of little power and, for all practical purposes, quite infallibly. They are now neither particularly expensive nor particularly rare. Most people have access to one, often in the home.[5] Children have access to them in school. Yet in the abstract they seem to inspire in otherwise rational human beings, feelings of such distrust, suspicion and awe as to subvert all sensible judgment. It is very hard to find any convincing explanation for the hypnotic fascination which they appear to exude; a fascination exploited and exacerbated by the media of communication. These teem with stories of monstrous databases relentlessly collating every detail of our private lives; of transactions being recorded, often wrongly, and being accorded a weight far beyond any that they deserve; and of their being penetrated by intruders, or otherwise subverted to sinister uses. Such stories help to create an atmosphere of terror which is then seized upon by those astute enough to exploit it commercially with offerings of security services and counselling to avert these dangers. Such exploiters, and they include those who derive remuneration from fees and royalties for their studies and reports, add to the clamour. A further element in the brew is constituted by the busy self-promotion of those with

---

2. See Brown, 'Crime and Computers', 7 *Crim. L.J.* 68 (1983).
3. See OECD Report *Computer Related Crime* (1986).
4. A brief account of some such developments appears as Appendix A to the Scottish Law Commission's Consultative Memorandum No. 68, *Computer Crime* (1986); a comprehensive list of legislation in the United States appears, despite the title, in Smith *Compilation of State and Federal Privacy Laws* (1988) pp. 8, 9.
5. 20 per cent of working households in the United Kingdom were recorded as possessing a home computer in 1987, the first year for which such a statistic was recorded, *Social Trends No. 18* Table 6.15 (1988); the estimate for the United States is that 33 per cent will have one by 1990, see Jurkat, 'Computer Crime Legislation: Survey and Analysis', *New York University Annual Survey of American Law* (1986).

pretensions to expertise in such matters, an expertise made to appear more valuable the more arcane it can be made to seem. It is not uncommon for these ingredients to coalesce into a critical mass giving rise first to the generation of pressure for action and then erupting into the production of such egregious legislation as the Data Protection Act 1984 or section 5 of the Civil Evidence Act 1968. Such a cycle has already run its course in the United States in relation to 'computer crime' and is in its early stages in this country.[6]

It is worth a glance at the example of the United States. The great majority of the states[7] and the federal administration have succumbed to the fashionable pressure, and enacted some sort of 'computer crime' legislation.[8] Despite the fact that such legislation has in some states been in force for over ten years, it is significant that there is, so far, a dearth of reported cases; a phenomenon not capable of being explained because of the crystal clarity of the drafting. It is not uncommon for such legislation to be introduced by a recital of legislative intent such as is to be found in the Florida prototype:[8]

The Legislature finds and declares that:
(1) Computer-related crime is a growing problem in government as well as in the private sector.
(2) Computer-related crime occurs at great cost to the public since losses for each incident of computer crime tend to be far greater than the losses associated with each incident of other white collar crime.
(3) The opportunities for computer-related crimes in financial institutions, government programs, government records and other business enterprises through the introduction of fraudulent records into a computer system, the unauthorised use of computer facilities, the alteration or destruction of computerized information or files, and the stealing of financial instruments, data, and other assets are great.
(4) While various forms of computer crime might possibly be the subject of criminal charges based on other provisions of law, it is appropriate and desirable that a supplemental and additional statute be provided which proscribes various forms of computer abuse.[9]

The first of these propositions is both unclear and controversial.[10] It is unclear because 'computer-related crime' is so inherently vague a concept. Take the facts of *R.* v. *Ewing*.[11] The accused altered the figures on a warrant, probably printed by a computer, and paid it into a bank for the

---

6. It has already been given preliminary consideration by the Law Commission in 'Computer Misuse' Working Paper No. 110 (1988), and has also been considered by the Scottish Law Commission 'Report on Computer Crime' S.L.C. No. 106 (1987).
7. Only Arkansas, District of Columbia, Maine, Vermont and West Virginia are shown in Smith, *Compilation of State and Federal Privacy Laws* (1988) as standing out against the trend, and of these Arkansas has now succumbed while Maine has made significant alterations to its law of theft.
8. Analysed in detail in Jurkat, 'Computer Crime Legislation: Survey and Analysis', *New York University Annual Survey of American Law* (1986).
9. Florida Statutes Annotated Vol. 22A sect. 815.02. Florida was the first state to legislate in this area under the prompting of Mr Bill Nelson who has now moved to Congress where he is a prime mover in the passage of federal legislation.
10. It has been toned down in some more recent recitals, for example in Tennessee where statute 39-3-1401 instead refers to it, rather more realistically, as being a 'potential problem in business and government'.
11. [1983] Q.B. 1039, C.A.

credit of his own account, certainly held on a computer. Should this be regarded as a computer-related crime? Definitional problems such as this are central to the whole debate about 'computer crime'. The question is often whether or not particular conduct should be criminalised at all, and sometimes whether or not it should be criminalised separately from other crimes. Such questions may be influenced by consideration of the degree of unacceptability of the motives of the actor, and of the amount of harm which his acts occasion. The involvement of a computer is unlikely to be more than peripherally related to the actor's motivation. The unacceptable drives of greed, malevolence, destructiveness and lust which motivate criminal conduct pass computers by, except as a means for their gratification. In *Ewing* the act would have been as likely to have been committed, and just as reprehensible, whether the system were computerised, or still relied upon the scratchings of clerks with quill pens.[12] It makes no sense to extract the one situation from the other, and to place it into a separate category. Nor does there seem to be any reason for treating the theft of a portable computer, the damage of an automatic telling machine, or the selection of potential victims by computer analysis of the incidence of movement in their accounts, differently from any other form of theft, criminal damage or victim selection.

2. Its dimensions

It is obvious that if there is such uncertainty about what is to count as 'computer crime', then it will be impossible to assess its incidence or its magnitude with any exactitude. If computer-related crime is to be hived off from the rest, it is, in general terms, hardly a matter of amazement to be told that it is growing. If crime is increasing, as it appears to be, and if computers are being used increasingly in society, especially for financial transactions, as they are, it would be very surprising if this were not the case. Indeed, if the cashless society ever arrives, thieves and fraudsmen will have no alternative but to commit computer-related crimes. Computers and computer-related products such as programs and data constitute an ever-increasing proportion of society's wealth, and thus increase in their likelihood as potential objects of criminal conduct. At the same time computers are being increasingly used to manage society's resources, especially in the sphere of financial and credit transactions, and so they are correspondingly more prone to be used as the means of crime. A third dimension is provided by the capacity of computers to extend the range of individual human capacity, for example to be able to calculate better or to be able to find and manipulate more information, and in these respects the enhancement applies as much to those of a criminal disposition as to those without.

Needless to say, criminal statistics do not purport to distinguish between computer-related crime and other crime. In order to assess the nature and magnitude of the problem, it is thus necessary to have recourse either to pure speculation, or to specialised surveys.

There is no shortage of speculation. Wildly contradictory estimates

---

12. In *R.* v. *Thompson* [1984] 3 All E.R. 565, C.A. at 569 the Court of Appeal's reasoning depended upon exactly such an analogy.

abound. In the United Kingdom the Confederation of British Industry estimated in 1987 that 'computer fraud' was costing British industry some thirty to forty million pounds a year, when respondents to the Audit Commission estimated the total loss at three hundred million pounds.[13] Similar discrepancy appears in relation to the problem in the United States, where the same news report[14] quoted the International Trade Commission's estimate of the losses to United States business from piracy of computer programs as amounting to over four billion dollars, while a group of lawyers and economists estimated much the same source of loss as being less than four hundred million dollars. It seems clear that little reliance can be placed upon such speculation.

Specialised surveys have also been undertaken. However, their documentation of the situation is more surprising than might have been expected. The picture of exponential growth stoked by organised criminals as painted by the media of communication is far from clear. It is necessary to distinguish between different sorts of survey however. At one extreme are those surveys which do little more than repeat and, in so doing, amplify the outbursts in the media. Much of the earliest work in the field done under the auspices of the Stanford Research Institute is of this character.[15] It tended to draw upon dubious sources, mainly newspaper reports; verification was rarely attempted; and little critical analysis was essayed. This methodology has been exposed to devastating attack.[16] Even when the survey relies upon direct responses rather than second-hand accounts, there is sometimes room for suspicion that a particular response is required. Thus in Canada a survey designed by the Ontario police, and sent to 648 corporations and institutions, asked whether the respondent had experienced a loss through unauthorised manipulation or abuse of the computer system. Although slightly suggestive, the question seems on the whole reasonable, until one finds that the only possible responses were 'yes' and 'don't know', but with no possibility of answering 'no'.[17] Interestingly enough, despite this attempt at loading, only thirteen respondents reported any such loss, about 2 per cent of the sample.[18] Nevertheless no fewer than 84 per cent of the respondents regarded computer crime as a significant problem, despite their collective dearth of actual experience of it.[19] A similar, and apparently similarly motivated, survey was carried out in 1984 by the American Bar Association's Criminal Justice Section Task Force on Computer Crime. Here the response rate was lower, but the percentage of the sample of about a thousand reporting 'a known and verifiable loss due to computer crime within the last

---

13. Audit Commission 'Survey of Computer Fraud and Abuse' (1987) p. 12.
14. In *Computerworld* 14 March 1988 pp. 79, 82.
15. A number of earlier studies for SRI were up-dated and essentially republished by Parker in *Crime by Computer* (1976).
16. By Taber, 'A Survey of Computer Crime Studies', 2 *Comp. L.J.* 275 (1980).
17. Webber, 'Computer Crime or Jay-walking on the Electronic Highway' 26 Crim L.Q. 217 (1983, 84).
18. Or just over 4 per cent of the respondents, given a less than 50 per cent response rate.
19. The motivation of the survey and its imperviousness to contradictory evidence is illustrated by the remark on page 12 of the Report that 'the fact that relatively little is known about the incidence and seriousness of computer crime is not a justification for legislative complacency'. In other words, sentence first, trial later (if at all).

twelve months' was higher at 7 per cent.[20] Here the survey also asked explicitly about opinions as well as experience, and once again the fears outstripped the facts.[21] It is interesting that when the Audit Commission in the United Kingdom invited its respondents to speculate upon the amount of computer-related crime it found that the more direct experience respondents had of computer-related crime the lower their estimate.[22]

These suspect surveys should be weighed against a number of more sober and objective exercises. The Fraud Division of the United States Department of Justice has set up a special Fraud and Corruption Tracking system to record referrals of suspected fraud against the federal government. In 1983 and the first half of 1984 there were 6700 referrals of which only 28 (0.4 per cent) were computer-related. In a survey, conducted by the American Institute of Certified Public Accountants, of 5981 banks and insurance companies, only 119 cases of computer-related fraud were recorded. In an effort to make accurate measurements a National Center for Computer Crime Data was established in Los Angeles, and in its First Annual Statistical Report published in 1985 the results of a survey of 130 prosecutors' offices in thirty-eight states for examples of computer crime, showed no more than a paltry seventy-five prosecutions.[23]

The same contrast between apprehension and actuality is to be found in this country. Studies have been carried out by a number of the large accountancy firms. Ernst and Whinney, in a survey to investigate the extent of corporate fraud, found that a third of about 400 responding firms expressed fear about computer fraud,[24] though few had done anything to prevent it.[25] This was a study of attitudes, but another study by Arthur Young based on interviews with senior executives of fifty-six companies found that only about 3 per cent were able to identify any actual example.[26] Similarly low levels have also been reported in a study by Price Waterhouse and Dr Levi of Cardiff University. Perhaps the most convincing evidence is, however, supplied by special triennial surveys of 'Computer Crime' conducted first in 1981 by the Audit Inspectorate and then in 1984 and 1987 by the Audit Commission for Local Authorities in England and Wales. The explicit aim of this exercise was to provide an authoritative survey of the extent of the problem of 'computer crime' in the United Kingdom. Their method has been to employ a very wide definition of their subject-matter as 'any fraudulent behaviour connected with computerisation by which someone intends to gain dishonest advantage'. It seems also that the width of the definition was further expanded by the respondents, since more than half of the incidents reported resulted in no financial loss to the respondents. The

---

20. About 25 per cent of the respondents.
21. For a penetrating critical assessment see Wasik, 'Surveying Computer Crime', *1 C. L. & Prac.* 110 (1985).
22. Audit Commission, *Survey of Computer Fraud and Abuse* (1987) p. 12.
23. Including as an indication of the generosity of the classification such instances as the deletion of speeding convictions from a driving record held, as it happened, on a computer.
24. Although only 3 per cent mentioned computer fraud in their initial free response, before being prompted.
25. *Attitudes of Companies in Britain to Fraud* (1986).
26. Though here too more than half were apprehensive about the possibility.

questionnaire was sent in 1987 to 1000 bodies in the public sector and 3000 in the private sector. The response rate was about 60 per cent from the former and 20 per cent from the latter. While this may not enable a very satisfactory total estimate to be made, the similarity of the methods over the three surveys does enable a reliable picture to be derived of the rate of change. Perhaps the most remarkable statistic relates to the overall trend in the incidence of offences. In 1981 the Survey found that 79 per cent of 319 respondents had suffered no computer fraud, compared to 92 per cent of 1214 respondents in 1987. It is instructive to compare these statistics with those for crime in general in the relevant areas of criminal law.[27] The Surveys do show an increase in the amount involved in the reported incidents, though comparative analysis is complicated by the fact that no allowance is made for inflation,[28] and the statistics are very heavily influenced by a very small number of particularly large incidents. Thus in the 1987 Survey two incidents, each involving more than a quarter of a million pounds, represented less than 2 per cent of the total number of incidents, but accounted for approximately 65 per cent of the total amount involved.[29]

3. Improving awareness

It is apparent from the foregoing account that it is extremely difficult to ascertain exactly what the current situation is and, until more satisfactory analysis and computation is available, any effort at reform is liable to be misguided and ineffective. It is suggested that the primary effort must be to secure a better understanding of the underlying situation. It is necessary to discover exactly what types of misuse are occurring, in what situations, by whom they are committed, and with what results. The current surveys attempt to secure some such understanding, but are widely regarded as defective. It is often suggested that crime relating to computers is deliberately under-reported so as to preserve confidence in financial institutions. Perversely some commentators argue that because the more scientific surveys reveal so much lesser an incidence of computer-related crime than speculation in the media of communication would suggest, the surveys must be under-reporting the true incidence of such crime, and that this is a particularly worrying phenomenon so far as it suggests that the incidence of such crime is not only under-reported, but also undetected. It is clearly

---

27. The comparable offences of theft and fraud reported in Tables 2.12 and 2.14 of the *Criminal Statistics* for 1987 show increases in categories 41 (theft by employees), 42 (theft from mail), 43 (abstracting electricity), 47 (theft from machines), 51 (fraud by company directors), 52 (false accounting), 53 (residual fraud) and 61 (non-drug related forgery) taken together from 166 771 in 1981, to 185 113 in 1987, an increase in 1987 on 1981 of 11 per cent.

28. Allowing for inflation, measured by the Retail Prices Index, the increase is approximately of 117 per cent over the six year period, almost certainly far less than the increase in the value of business handled by computer over that period.

29. No incidents in 1981 exceeded £250,000 in value, and if those are excluded from the calculation, 1987 shows a decline in value of the remainder on 1981, the figures then being £905 149 for 1981 and £885 381 for 1987, and all this without making any allowance whatever for inflation. If the figure for 1981 is inflated to allow for the relevant increase in the retail price index it becomes the equivalent of £1 180 062 in 1987 terms, so there is a decline in value of approximately 25 per cent in real terms.

impossible to devise any rational scheme to appease so patently irrational an argument. It should be possible, however, to improve the techniques used by such surveys, and the use of the information they contain. It has already been noted that provided the techniques remain constant the trends revealed by the surveys can be relied upon even though the absolute values reported may be suspect. A number of attempts to improve the surveys have also been reported. Some of these seem to be motivated, at least in part, by commercial concerns, such as the promotion of security systems. Thus in the United States the Stanford Research Institute has established an International Information Integrity Institute to monitor and prevent computer-related crime,[30] while in the United Kingdom a joint venture between the Post Office and a security firm has been mooted for a very similar purpose.[31] The backing of the government of the United Kingdom has also been reported for a project being set up by the Computer Industry Research Unit, an offshoot of the University of East Anglia, in conjunction with the Institute of Internal Auditors and the Confederation of British Industry.[32] Here it is hoped to provide comprehensive coverage of membership of the Confederation which would certainly represent a considerable extension of the range of any existing survey, if it could be achieved. An effort is also been made to trace otherwise unreported incidents by offering stringent conditions of confidentiality and anonymity. It remains to be seen how far such ventures prove to be successful.

There are those who feel that any voluntary effort is fated to be unsuccessful, and that commercial pressures will inhibit response. It has accordingly been proposed that a legal obligation to report computer-related crimes should be imposed. This suggestion was canvassed by the Scottish Law Commission, though with a negative recommendation.[33] It was felt that there was no special need to create such an obligation in this area when it existed in no other, and that it was impractical, since it would be very difficult to define the circumstances which would require to be reported, and that there is no reason to suppose that the detection of failure to report will be any more effective than detection of the underlying crime itself. These arguments were endorsed by the majority of respondents to the consultative memorandum, and the Commission recommended that no such offence be created in Scotland.[34]

B. General criminal law

As noted above it is proposed to distinguish between provisions of the general criminal law which apply across a whole range of activities, and those, to be considered in the next section, which are created by and limited

---

30. See *Computer Weekly* 18 December 1986 p. 1.
31. *Ibid.* 10 March 1988 p. 3.
32. *Ibid* 18 February 1988 p. 6.
33. Scottish Law Commission, *Computer Crime* consultative Memorandum No. 68 (1986) paras. 6.17–6.20.
34. Scottish Law Commission 'Report on Computer Crime', SLC No. 106 (Cm. 174, 1987) paras. 5.8–5.11 and Recommendation No. 15. The English Law Commission refused to consider this question separately in the context of computers alone, Law Commission, *Computer Misuse*, Working Paper No. 110 (1988) App. B.

to a particular area of activity, usually regulated by its own special statutory provision.

1. Classification of offences

It will come as no surprise to learn that there is no consensus between commentators, pressure groups, legislators or law reformers as to the most appropriate scheme of classification for the incidence of misconduct involving computers. The original Florida legislation divided the criminal offences it established into three broad groups, offences against intellectual property, offences against computer equipment or supplies, and offences against computer users. Each of these broad categories was further sub-divided, but on the other hand, as is apparent from the above terminology, there was considerable potential for duplication. The Federal Counterfeit Access Device and Computer Fraud and Abuse Act 1984[35] also delineates three broad areas, unauthorised computer access, obtaining private financial information, and abusing federal government computers. In the United Kingdom also one commentator has found there to be three main areas of abuse, the use of the computer for fraud, the wrongful use of computer facilities and the wrongful destruction of computers.[36] Other commentators have discerned more categories.[37] The Scottish Law Commission is among the most expansive with eight, some of these further sub-divided, but in outline as follows:

i) erasure or falsification of data or programs so as to obtain a pecuniary or other advantage;
ii) obtaining unauthorised access to a computer;
iii) eavesdropping on a computer;
iv) taking of information without physical removal;
v) unauthorised borrowing of computer discs or tapes;
vi) making unauthorised use of computer time or facilities;
vii) malicious or reckless corruption or erasure of data or programs;
viii) denial of access to authorised users.[38]

The English Law Commission has a list of five groups of criminal offences, as follows:

A. Computer fraud;
B. Obtaining Unauthorised Access to a Computer;
C. Unauthorised Alteration or Erasure of Data or Software;
D. Unauthorised Copying of Data or Software;
E. Use of Information Held under the Data Protection Act 1984.[39]

---

35. For a detailed study of this legislation see Tompkins and Mar, 'The 1984 Federal Computer Crime Statute: A Practical Answer to a Pervasive Problem', 6 *Comp. L.J.* 459 (1986).
36. Tettenborn, 'Some Legal Aspects of Computer Abuse', 2 *Company Lawyer* 147 (1981).
37. In *Crime by Computer* (1976), Parker distinguishes four, physical interference with a computer installation; abstracting or copying of data; alteration or corruption of data; and use of a computer as a tool in the commission of crime; to which Brown 'Crime and Computers', 7 *Crim. L.J.* 68, 70 adds use of computer time; and interference with communications.
38. Scottish Law Commission, *Report on Computer Crime*, SLC No. 106 (Cm. 174, 1987) para. 2.1. These categories were originally proposed in the Consultative Memorandum, and none of the responses to a direct invitation to comment on the categorisation caused the Commission to alter it.
39. Law Commission, *Computer Misuse* W.P. No. 110 (1988) Part III.

Both of these sets of classifications are based upon the categorisation of types of misuse, bearing in mind that some types may not be represented by criminal offences under current law. It is a sound and sensible policy to do as the Commissions have done, namely first to identify the types of potentially criminal misuse, and only then to examine the adequacy of different possibly applicable current criminal offences. It is also possible to take one step further back and to consider the motivation inspiring such misuse. Of the motivations mentioned earlier, only lust seems completely inapplicable, but malevolence is likely to be muted, and the most obvious candidates are greed and destructiveness, especially if the latter is extended slightly to include cases of the demonstration of the power to effect it.

The matters to be considered here will be linked to attempts to seek a direct advantage by fraud or theft, and will include the obtaining of information; to make unauthorised use of computer facilities for indirect private gain; to make unauthorised use of such resources without necessarily causing damage or loss to them, or bringing any advantage to the user apart from the satisfaction of having penetrated defences designed to exclude him; and to cause damage to the less tangible facets of a computer installation or facilities.

2. Seeking direct advantage by fraud, theft or deception

The popular misconception of a computer as being possessed of a high degree of intelligence leads to the belief that any fraud capable of defeating a computer must be one of mind-boggling complexity. This is far from the case. As noted above computers are fundamentally simple machines, and it requires little in the way of expertise to induce them to perform some unauthorised function to the benefit of the operator. Fortunately those who commit such crimes seem to take after their machines.[40] The Audit Commission in its authoritative survey found that the largest number of incidents involved the unauthorised submission and alteration of data.[41] The vast majority of these were perpetrated by employees of the firm operating the computer,[42] and very often by those in a position of trust.[43]

In many cases the fraud involved no more than entering false data so as to secure undue payments including the two most lucrative incidents reported, in one of which phantom customers were credited with over a million pounds in no more than a week's activity.[44] In all such cases the law of theft is more than adequate to furnish an appropriate offence with which to charge the accused. The 1987 Survey for the first time investigated the

---

40. It could be argued that only the most simple of crimes are discovered. Such an argument is as unprovable as it is unanswerable. All that can be said is that very few of the crimes to have been reported at all reliably do show any sophistication, that none of the serious surveys of financial institutions most at risk show computers to have been involved in substantial sophisticated fraud, and no audits of the accounts of such institutions appear to have been qualified because of large, otherwise inexplicable, deficiencies.
41. Just under 50 per cent of all cases, Table 3.
42. In nearly 70 per cent of the cases, Table 13.
43. P. 21.
44. Case No. 22.

prosecution of offenders, and found that action was taken in the vast majority of cases.[45] Where prosecutions were reported, the vast majority were indeed under the Theft Acts 1968 and 1978.[46] In some rare situations, there may be more difficulty, for example if an outsider[47] secures access to the system by entering a false password, and by so doing secures valuable services or confidential information.

The most obviously applicable offences in this area, apart from the extended conception of theft in the modern English legislation, include such peripheral offences as conspiracy to defraud, cheating at common law and false accounting. The principal possibilities will be examined in turn.

(a) Theft

In England the old law of larceny which required the physical movement of a thing was replaced in 1968 by a new offence of theft. This new offence was the result of seven years of consideration by the Criminal Law Revision Committee.[48] Although this period took in the beginning of the computer age, it is hardly explicit in the Committee's Report. Nevertheless the Theft Act 1968 which was enacted in consequence of the Report does broaden the scope of the offence. It no longer depends upon the removal of a thing, but rather upon the appropriation of property.[49] 'Appropriation' is defined widely in section 3 to amount to 'any assumption by a person of the rights of an owner', and 'property' is partially defined in section 4 to include 'money and all other property, real or personal, including things in action and other intangible property'. In the debates upon the bill in the House of Lords, Lord Wilberforce expressly referred to 'business secrets' as being within its scope.[50] Unfortunately from this point of view, however the definition retains the requirement of the old law that there be an intent to deprive the owner permanently. While this might be sufficient in cases where cash or goods are directly obtained in specie, it is unlikely to be sufficient when programs or data are merely copied from a computer storage device, or where computer facilities are used for direct gain, or even where the only result is to manipulate balances of accounts held on computers. It might have been thought that the problem of copying had been dealt with by the provisions of section 6 which address the concept of permanent deprivation. This construes permanent deprivation to extend to a situation where a thing is treated as being disposable without regard to the rights of its owner, and also where it is borrowed or lent 'for a period and in circumstances making it equivalent to an outright taking or disposal'. This provision did not appear in the draft bill, but was introduced during its passage to make it clear that a variety of otherwise dubious situations, such as using tickets, was covered.

---

45. In only six of ninety-five cases where it was disclosed was no action reported as having been taken, Table 15.
46. Only one of the twenty-four where it was disclosed was not brought under the Theft Acts, Table 16.
47. Or an insider acting in excess of his authority.
48. The matter was referred to the Committee in March 1959, and it reported in April 1966 in its Eighth report, *Theft and Related Offences* (Cmnd. 1966).
49. Sect. 1.
50. H.L. Deb. Vol 259 col. 1309.

The utility of this section to cater for the copying of intangibles in the computer context was always dubious. It is noteworthy that the section refers to a 'thing' rather than to 'property', and all of the examples used to justify its inclusion did involve tangible objects. Subsequent case law has confirmed these fears. It was held quite categorically in *Oxford* v. *Moss*[51] that intangible information did not come within the definition of property in section 4 of the Theft Act. In that case a student had seen an examination paper before the examination, thus rendering it useless, but without taking anything other than the information it contained. No point was taken on the possible application of section 6. The death knell of any such approach was sounded in England by Lord Wilberforce's judicial statement expressed in *Rank Film Distributors Ltd.* v. *Video Information Centre*[52] that 'Infringement of copyright is not theft'. In Canada it seemed at one time that information could be stolen,[53] but this decision came in for severe criticism,[54] was departed from elsewhere in Canada,[55] and has now been reversed on appeal by the Supreme Court of Canada.[56] The controversial nature of this question is illustrated by the further criticism which this retraction has received.[57]

Despite this rejection of the application of the Theft Act to intangibles it might still have been arguable that there was theft of the underlying physical entity, by use of the extended definition of permanent deprivation in section 6 of the Theft Act. Any faint hopes on that score were demolished by the decision in *R.* v. *Lloyd*[58] where a cinema projectionist lent feature films to others to copy to the detriment, and contrary to the express instructions, of the owners of the films. The Court of Appeal took a highly restrictive view of the ambit of section 6. In the Court's view section 6 should be invoked only rarely, and construed as applying only to an *outright* taking or disposal which was contrasted with a mere *diminution* in the value.[59] So conservative was the approach of the Court of Appeal that it remarked that it 'would try to interpret the section in such a way that nothing is construed as an intention permanently to deprive which would not prior to the Act of 1968 have been so construed.'[60]

These cases between them seem quite conclusive so far as intangibles or the temporary appropriation of physical entities are concerned. It nevertheless seems clear that if the system is gulled into parting with goods or money then there can be a charge of theft[61] contrary to section 1 of the Theft Act

---

51. (1978) 68 Cr. App. R. 183, C.A.
52. [1982] A.C. 380, H.L. at 443.
53. *R.* v. *Stewart* 149 D.L.R. (3d) 583 (Ont. C.A., 1983).
54. See Hammond, 'Theft of Information', *100 L.Q.R.* 252 (1984) and 'Electronic Crime in Canadian Courts', *6 O.J.L.S.* 145 (1986).
55. By the Alberta Court of Appeal in *R.* v. *Offley* 51 C.R. (3d) 378 (Alb. C.A., 1986).
56. *R.* v. *Stewart* 63 C.R. 3d 305 (S.C.C., 1988).
57. See Doherty, 'Stewart: When is a thief not a thief? When he steals the "Candy" but not the "Wrapper"' 63 C.R. 3d 322 (1988).
58. [1985] Q.B. 829, C.A.
59. For such reasons the possible enactment of a more comprehensive offence of fraud is currently under review by the Law Commission as stated in its Twentieth Report, Law Com. No. 155 para. 2.21 (1986).
60. At 836.
61. *R.* v. *Hands* (1887) 16 Cox C.C. 188, C.C.C.R. where cigarettes were obtained from a vending machine by the insertion of a brass ring instead of a coin.

1968, even if no human being is deceived. Thus such a charge succeeded in *Kennison* v. *Daire*[62] where cash was obtained from a computerised automatic bank teller by entering a false number. In such cases the law takes the view that the act is the equivalent of the application of force. Even in Scotland it seems that intangibles cannot be the subject of theft, or of similar innominate offences involving a taking.[63]

Similar difficulty to that found in England has also been experienced in the United States. In *Lund* v. *Commonwealth of Virginia*[64] it was held that a larceny statute drawn to the obtaining of goods or chattels was incapable of applying to the obtaining of services, even though they were worth a considerable sum of money.[65] In that instance the defect was specifically remedied by a statutory amendment to define property capable of being the subject-matter of larceny, embezzlement or obtaining by false pretences as including '[c]omputer time or services or data processing services or information or data stored in connection therewith',[66] and the new definition was applied in *Evans* v. *Virginia*[67] to convict of embezzlement two programmers who copied from their employer's computer a valuable list of security holders to take to a competitor whose service they were about to enter. In some states, however, the same result has been reached by construing a broad definition of property for the purposes of larceny as comprehending computer software. Thus in a civil suit for conversion of programs in *National Security Corporation* v. *Applied Systems Inc.*[68] it was argued that the claim must be allowed because it would be anomalous if criminal liability for theft should apply to such subject matter, but not a civil claim. The statute in question[69] made no more than a general reference to personal property.[70] In *U.S.* v. *Girard*[71] the Second Circuit was called upon to construe the expression 'thing of value' in the legislation making the unauthorised sale of government property a federal offence.[72] In this case the accused had conspired with one James Bond to import narcotics into the United States from Mexico. To try to preserve their operation from detection the criminals had taken steps to find out from the relevant federal agency the identities of undercover narcotics agents so as to avoid employing them inadvertently in their organisation. This information was secured by an accomplice within the

---

62. 38 S.A.S.R. 404 (S.C.F.C., 1985). For two different United States approaches to a similar situation, see *State* v. *Hamm* 569 S.W.2d 289 (Mo., 1978) said to be the first such case to have come before a United States court where the charge was of stealing by deceit, and *State* v. *Gillies* 662 P.2d 1007 (Az., 1983) where a special computer fraud statute was used.

63. *Grant* v. *Allen* 1987 S.C.C.R. 402.

64. 232 S.E. 2d 745 (Va., 1977).

65. There in excess of $26 000.

66. Va. Code 18.2-98.1, now itself replaced by Va. 18.2-152.1 *et seq.*

67. 308 S.E.2d 126 (Va., 1983).

68. 418 So.2d 847 (Ala., 1982).

69. Ala. Code sect. 13A-8-1(10).

70. Thus allowing the Supreme Court to distinguish an earlier decision in *Alabama* v. *Central Computer Services Inc.* 349 So.2d 1160 (Ala., 1977) where the reference was to *tangible* personal property.

71. 601 F.2d 69 (2nd Cir., 1978) rejecting an appeal from *U.S.* v. *Lambert* 446 F.Supp. 890 (D.D.C., 1978). See also *Sampson* v. *U.S.* 6 C.L.S.R. 879 (N.D. Cal., 1978).

72. 18 U.S. C. sect. 641.

agency who checked the identities given to him by using a computer terminal situated in his office. When the plot was discovered, the federal employees were charged with the unauthorised sale of '*things* of value' contrary to section 641 of the relevant legislation. The court decided that since the statute prohibited the unauthorised sale of a number of items obtained in a number of ways, including conversion as well as theft, there was no need to take an overly restrictive view, and that the statute was properly construed as applying to the sale of the contents of the records as well as to the medium upon which the information was stored. In this way the United States court was able to avoid the problems engendered by the notion of asportation, or removal, in the old definition of larceny, in dramatic contrast to the approach of the English courts to their new statute in *Oxford* v. *Moss*.[73]

Federal courts have also been willing to extend the scope of larceny to things other than goods or money,[74] often within the ambit of indirect federal offences such as the interstate transportation of property 'stolen, converted or taken by fraud',[75] or interstate communications by mail or wire pursuant to any scheme to 'defraud, or for obtaining money or property by means of fraudulent pretences, representations, or promises'.[76] Thus in a case dealing with the interstate transportation of infringing copies of films, the Ninth Circuit emphatically proclaimed that 'illicit copying of a copyrighted work is no less a 'theft, conversion or taking by fraud' than if the original were taken'.[77] Although this was the view of the vast majority of the courts to consider the matter, it has now been authoritatively decided by a majority in the Supreme Court that such a charge is inappropriate where materials obtained by the infringement of copyright are transported across state lines.[78] The Court seems to have been influenced by the fact that the law of copyright has always been within the federal jurisdiction and has been the subject of very cautious, and limited, criminalisation, thus dictating a restrained approach to the interpretation of section 2314 in this context. It was felt that an expansive approach would be tantamount to criminalising essentially civil wrongs, which the legislature after due consideration had itself withheld from criminalisation in its repeated reconsideration of copyright. There was also felt to be some difficulty over the valuation of the underlying intellectual property. In that case the property was copyright in sound recordings. In such a case the threshold of value may be surpassed only because of the number of infringing articles. This would often not be

---

73. (1978) 68 Cr. App. R. 183, C.A.
74. In the case of money the robust view has been expressed that if funds are transferred the means of transmission are irrelevant, *U.S.* v. *Gilboa* 684 F.2d 235 (2nd Cir., 1982) at 238.
75. 18 U.S.C. 2314.
76. 18 U.S.C. 1343. These crimes may also form the predicate for more draconian charges under the Racketeer Influenced and Corrupt Organisations legislation (RICO), 18 U.S.C. sects. 1961–1968.
77. *U.S.* v. *Drebin* 557 F.2d 1316 (9th Cir., 1977), but see the conventional and conservative view taken by the Fifth Circuit in *U.S.* v. *Smith* 686 F.2d 234 (6th Cir., 1982) where a distinction was drawn on the basis that in the latter case the copying had been from publicly available broadcasts, and not from tangible articles, though it is, in principle, unclear why this factor should have any significance.
78. *Dowling* v. *U.S.* 473 U.S. 207 (1985).

the case with computer programs or data. It is also more plausible in such a case to require some tangibility in the object of the crime since its essence is in interstate movement. This is not true of the wire fraud legislation, and a more expansive approach seems still to apply there. In *U.S.* v. *Seidlitz*[79] the accused had used the public telephone system to connect his office terminal to a large computer system, had entered someone else's password, and caused programs to be transmitted to him which he had then copied. Although there seems to have been no objection to the use of the wire fraud statute on those facts, it is somewhat odd since it seems that neither in Maryland nor in Virginia, the two states involved, was it felt possible at that time to indict the accused for any crime against the law of either state,[80] so it is not clear how the necessary criminal basis for a wire fraud prosecution was established. Nevertheless the Supreme Court has here taken a very different approach from that adopted towards section 2314.[81] It held that where a financial journalist had revealed the contents of his column in advance, in breach of his obligation of confidentiality to his employers, so as to reap the benefit of profits on share transactions facilitated by such advance knowledge that the underlying offence was sufficient to trigger the wire fraud statutes. It is possible to distinguish *Dowling*[82] on the basis that in the case of confidentiality, unlike copyright, there has been no tradition of federal legislation carrying limited criminal penalties.

(b) Fraud

The deficiencies of the law of larceny, particularly in cases where a service rather than a thing was obtained, or where a thing was not so much taken as received, led throughout the common law world to the development of offences based more upon fraud or deception. In England the Theft Act 1968 provided for offences of obtaining property by deception[83] and of obtaining a pecuniary advantage by deception.[84] The latter provision was so defective that it was partly repealed in 1978, and replaced by the Theft Act 1978 which created offences of obtaining services by deception,[85] evasion of liability by deception,[86] and making off without payment.[87] The Theft Act 1968 contains a number of other provisions involving fraud which might apply in the context of computers, such as false accounting[88] and the dishonest procurement of the execution of a valuable security.[89] Many of these offences explicitly require that they be caused by deception. Deception is defined in the Theft Act 1968 to mean,

---

79. 589 F.2d 152 (4th Cir., 1978).
80. Both subsequently remedied their definition of 'property' within the year to cover the situation, but in both states the new laws have themselves been overtaken by the current fashion for specific computer legislation which is sweeping the United States.
81. *Carpenter* v. *U.S.* 108 S.Ct.R. 316 (1987).
82. Which is not mentioned in the opinion.
83. Sect. 15.
84. Sect. 16.
85. Sect. 1.
86. Sect. 2.
87. Sect. 3.
88. Sect. 17.
89. Sect. 20(2).

any deception (whether deliberate or reckless) by words or conduct as to fact or as to law, including a deception as to the present intentions of the person using the deception or any other person.[90]

The application of these offences in the context of many situations involving computers, such as using a false password or causing false information to be entered, is handicapped by the view that the section requires a human being to have been deceived, and that it is not enough to deceive a machine.[91] This view was adopted, *obiter*, by Bridge J. in *Davies* v. *Flackett*[92] and was applied to prevent a conviction in relation to securing unwarranted repayments from the government by submitting false value added tax returns for entry into the relevant computer.[93]

This reasoning also finds strong support in the decision of the Court of Appeal in *R.* v. *Thompson*[94] where a computer operator employed in Kuwait by a bank first identified five substantial but dormant accounts in branches there, then wrote programs removing sums from those accounts to be credited to savings accounts which he had opened in his own name in the same branches. After returning to England the accused wrote to the bank in Kuwait asking for the balances which had been so credited to be transferred to various bank accounts in England. He was charged under section 15 with obtaining property from the bank by deception, in respect of the letters asking for the sums to be transferred. He argued that the English courts had no jurisdiction since the fraud had occurred in Kuwait at the time when the victim's accounts were debited and his own credited. The decision turned on the rejection of that submission. In the view of the Court of Appeal the whole transaction in Kuwait was a nullity, and the bank's position was unaltered until it acted upon his letter and transferred funds to him in England. In those circumstances it was the officers of the bank who read and acted upon the letters who were deceived, and not the computer in acting upon the instructions in the program to alter the various account balances, nor was any property appropriated by the accused before the transfer of funds to England. While it caused no problem here, it is dubious whether rigid insistence upon the unavailability of a remedy for deception is appropriate for large-scale computer systems. It will invariably be the case that human intervention could be invoked before a transaction is processed to prevent its being consummated if some fraud were detected at a sufficiently early stage. If it is the falsity of the data which prevents such human intervention from taking place, it is not obvious that there has necessarily been no deception of those human beings who would otherwise have intervened. It is somewhat ironic that the old law of obtaining by false pretences which was superseded by the Theft Act, because it concentrated on

---

90. Sect. 15(4).
91. *D.P.P.* v. *Ray* [1974] A.C. 370, H.L. at 384 per Lord Morris, and see Smith 'Some comments on deceiving a machine', *69 Law Soc. Gaz.* 576 (1972). See also supporting dicta in *Kennison* v. *Daire* 38 S.A.S.R. 404 (S.C.F.C., 1985).
92. [1973] R.T.R. 8, Q.B.D., but was subject to a forceful reservation of opinion from Ackner J.
93. *R.* v. *Moritz* (unreported Cr. Ct. case, 1981). This particular problem was solved by section 12(5) of the Finance Act 1985 which amended the relevant definition so as to read 'intend to secure that a machine will respond to the document as if it were a true document'.
94. [1984] 3 All E.R. 565, C.A.

the fraud of the perpetrator rather than the deception of the victim, would have been unlikely to have been so susceptible to such arguments. It seems that in Scotland the common law offence of fraud, which incorporates the notion of a false pretence, is regarded as adequate to deal with the deception of a computer.[95] Similarly in Canada where there is a statutory offence of fraud[96] there appears to be no problem in relation to the deception of a machine.[97]

The problem of deceiving a machine has also been raised in the United States, and on occasion received a statutory response by way of alteration of the definition of deception as, for example, in the Alaska Code which provides that:

> In . . . an offense that requires 'deception' as an element, it is not a defense that the defendant deceived or attempted to deceive a machine. For the purposes of this section, 'machine' includes a vending machine, computer, turnstile, or automated teller machine.[98]

There the provision comes as part of a general extension of the meaning of 'deception', whereas elsewhere it was only the computer that was so treated.[99]

Specific federal provision has been made for the situation by the passage in 1984 of a new provision[100] creating offences of fraud achieved by means of false access devices, a phrase deliberately left vague to allow for development in the relevant technology. In the field of federal computers there are now also further specific offences involving unauthorised use or access to such machines with intent to defraud.[101]

In many cases the problem of deceiving a machine can perhaps, in England, be avoided by charging not the substantive offence, but a common law conspiracy to defraud. It was clearly established in *Scott* v. *Commissioner of Police for the Metropolis*,[102] another film copying case, that deceit is not a necessary ingredient of a conspiracy to defraud. The law of conspiracy has however undergone a number of recent vicissitudes[103] and is still under review.[104] In some cases where unauthorised access to a system is obtained

---

95. Scottish Law Commission, *Report on Computer Crime* SLC No. 106 (1987) para 2.6.
96. Criminal Code of Canada sect. 338(1).
97. *R.* v. *Kirkwood* 148 D.L.R. (3d) 323 (Ont. C.A., 1982), *R.v. Fitzpatrick* 11 C.C.C. (3d) 46 (B.C.C.A., 1984).
98. Aka. Code 11.46.985.
99. See Utah Code Ann. section 76-6-703, now replaced by a different version.
100. 18 U.S.C. sect. 1029.
101. 18 U.S.C. sect. 1030(a)(4).
102. [1975] A.C. 819, H.L.
103. The Law Commission in its Report 'Conspiracy and Criminal Law Reform', *Law. Com.* No. 76 (1976) paras. 1.14–1.16 recommended that conspiracy to defraud should be preserved from the drastic pruning accomplished by the Criminal Law Act 1977, but that Act as interpreted in *R.* v. *Ayres* [1984] A.C. 447, H.L., and applied in this general area in *R.* v. *Lloyd* [1985] Q.B. 829, C.A., proved to be too restrictive, and the crime has now been reinstated by the Criminal Justice Act 1987 sect. 12 on the advice of the Criminal Law Revision Committee in its 18th report *Conspiracy to Defraud* (Cmnd. 9873, 1986).
104. By the Law Commission which put forward possible options in its Working Paper No. 104, *Conspiracy to Defraud* (1987), and has solicited further comment, particularly on its application in the context of computers in its Working Paper No. 110, *Computer Misuse* (1988) para. 5.5. It hopes to publish its final paper in 1989.

from outside, it results from the provision of information assisting its accomplishment derived from electronic bulletin boards. In such circumstances a conspiracy to defraud might lie against those involved in furnishing the information, although perhaps only if it can plausibly be argued that no other purpose than to defraud could be thus accomplished.[105] This might well limit the utility of any such an approach. Even if conspiracy should one day become a more satisfactory offence suitable for use in the context of computers, it will still be deficient in requiring the concerted action of more than one person and will thus fail to cater for the stereotypical programmer alone at his terminal in the middle of the night. It is also a serious offence, triable only on indictment and carrying a stiff maximum penalty, and so is inappropriate for the vast majority of trivial offences.[106]

It is perhaps worth mentioning a number of other more minor offences which might be employed in this context. Cheating was a general offence at common law, until largely superseded by the Theft Act 1968.[107] It remains an offence to cheat the public revenue, and that offence shares with conspiracy to defraud the same advantage of not necessarily requiring any element of deception. In *R. v. Mavji*[108] the Court of Appeal approved of the trial judge's view that:

Cheating can include any form of fraudulent conduct which results in diverting money from the revenue and in depriving the revenue of money to which it is entitled.

It is clear that a number of cases involving computers could, with a little imagination on the part of the Crown Prosecution Service, be brought within such a broad-meshed net.[109] Another possibility, this time statutory, is furnished by the Theft Act itself in its definition of a separate offence of false accounting.[110] While this requires the destruction, defacement, concealment or falsification of any record or document required for accounting, or the knowing use of any misleading, false or deceptive such record or document, it seems that it is usually given a generous interpretation and is not restricted to records made *exclusively* for accounting purposes.[111] It might also, in some cases, be possible to bring a charge under section 20(2) of the Theft Act 1968 of dishonestly procuring the execution of a valuable security, though, as noted above, this offence suffers from the disadvantage in the current context of requiring an element of deception.

3. Using computer facilities for indirect private gain

Although this category overlaps the one discussed above, the emphasis is upon the unauthorised use of the computer not for the sake of direct benefits,

---

105. *R. v. Hollinshead* [1985] A.C. 975, H.L.
106. The Audit Commission's survey revealed that more than 75 per cent of offences involved sums of less than £2500, see Table 2.
107. Sect. 32(1)(a).
108. [1987] 2 All E.R. 758, C.A., at 762.
109. Probably including *R. v. Moritz* (unreported Cr. Ct. case, 1981), see above p. 284.
110. Sect. 17.
111. Law Commission Working paper No. 110, *Computer Abuse* (1988) para. 3.9, quoting *R. v. Mallett* [1978] 3 All E.R. 10, C.A.

but for the opportunity it provides to support some other enterprise. The Audit Commission reported twelve such cases in 1981, eleven in 1984 and twelve in 1987.[112] The 1987 cases were almost all trivial, only one of which involved loss to the employer,[113] though as the Survey points out the cost of investigation is likely to be high, given the ease of committal and conceal-ment on high-powered modern machines with sophisticated operating sys-tems. This is not a novel problem. In *R.* v. *Cullum*[114] an employee was charged with embezzling the proceeds of unauthorised hiring of his em-ployers' barge. He was acquitted upon the basis that the proceeds had not been received on his employers' account. Although some writers seem to have thought that the situation had been ameliorated by the Theft Act 1968, sometimes praying in aid notions of constructive trust,[115] this view was conclusively rejected in *Attorney General's Reference (No 1 of 1985)*.[116] It was felt that such conduct is just too far away from the general understanding of the essence of theft, and as Lord Wilberforce once put it, 'persons in a fiduciary capacity making a secret profit at the expense of their companies [is] conduct for which there exist classical remedies in equity ... Breach of fiduciary duty ... [is] one thing; theft and fraud are others.'[117] The only possibility of charging such an offence successfully might be in a case where an employer sells computer services to the public, and an employee offers those same services, but without authority and without accounting to his employer, for his own private profit. In such a case it has been suggested[118] that he might be guilty of an offence under the Theft Act 1978 section 1, but this would once again require an element of deception, which might be very difficult to establish. This would not, however, apply to a charge of dishonestly obtaining a telecommunications service contrary to section 42 of the Telecommunications Act 1984.

It might be thought where a computer is used in this way an alternative possibility would be to charge the accused with the fraudulent abstraction of electricity,[119] but this also seems rather unsatisfactory.[120] In many cases it might be very hard to prove that the machine used more electricity running the work than it would have used in its idle state.[121] The necessary fraudulent intent might be very difficult to establish, and in any event this is not the nub of the misconduct. Certainly in *Malone* v. *Metropolitan Police Commissioner*,[122] Megarry V.C. was unwilling to engage in fine distinctions

---

112. Audit Commission, *Survey of Computer Crime and Abuse* (1987) Table 8.

113. According to Table 8, but reference to the details of case 106 reveals that the loss recorded was mainly referable to other illegal activities of the relevant employee.

114. (1873) L.R. 2 C.C.C.R 28, C.C.C.R.

115. See Williams, *Textbook of Criminal Law* (2nd edn) section 33.10.

116. [1986] Q.B. 491, C.A., endorsed by the House of Lords in *R.* v. *Cooke* [1986] A.C. 909, H.L. at 921, 922.

117. *Tarling (No. 1)* v. *Government of the Republic of Singapore* 70 Cr. App. R. 77, P.C. at 110.

118. By the Law Commission in Working Paper No. 110, *Computer Misuse* (1988) para. 3.34.

119. Theft Act 1968 sect. 13.

120. It appears to have been used successfully in at least one case of 'hacking', however, see *Computing* 29 January 1987 p. 6.

121. See *R.* v. *Siu Tak-Chee* unreported (Hong Kong, 1984), mentioned in Law Reform Commission of Tasmania Report No. 47, *Computer Misuse* (1986) para. 7(ii); see also Law Commission Working Paper No. 110, *Computer Misuse* (1988) para. 3.25 n. 31.

122. [1979] Ch. 344, Ch. at 357.

between the information being transmitted and the medium of transmission itself. In the United Kingdom the closest specific statutory provision is probably section 1(1) of the Interception of Communications Act 1985, but its ambit is limited to the *interception* of communications rather than their *initiation*, which will here be by far the more common case. British courts are also traditionally reluctant to extend the ambit of ambiguously worded statutory offences to the prejudice of the accused. This is well illustrated by the decision of the Supreme Court of Canada in *R.* v. *McLaughlin*,[123] where the accused, from a remote terminal, used the central computing facilities of a university for his own purposes without authorisation, and was charged with a special offence under section 287(1)(b) of the Criminal Code. The section had been enacted to plug a gap revealed when a group of dissidents took over a radio station to make illicit broadcasts[124] and extended the definition of theft to apply to the fraudulent use or obtaining of any telecommunication service. McLaughlin's appeal against conviction was allowed by the Alberta Court of Appeal, and that decision was upheld by the Supreme Court of Canada, on the basis that the concept of telecommunication was not obviously applicable to a person performing data processing tasks at a remote location. The whole saga illustrates, not only reluctance to extend the ambit of the criminal law, but also the disadvantages of the gap-plugging approach in a rapidly developing field. The legislator is in a dilemma. In order to secure a conviction, the offence must be drafted so as to apply to the misconduct very precisely, but if it does so, it is unlikely to apply to subsequent new forms of misconduct mandated by technological development. Nevertheless in Canada his response has been to draft a special offence to fill the further gap revealed in the law by the passage of a new section 301.2 of the Canadian Criminal Code which makes it an offence fraudulently and without colour of a claim of right to,

(a) obtain directly or indirectly any computer service; or
(b) intercept or cause to be intercepted any function of a computer system; or
(c) use or cause to be used a computer system with intent to commit an offence of wilful damage to property.

It remains to be seen how that section will be interpreted and what further gaps will be found.

Similar problems have concerned both state and federal courts in the United States. In *State* v. *McGraw*[125] the accused was a computer operator employed by the City of Indianapolis. He used his employer's facilities to administer his private business of selling a slimming product. The City dismissed him for spending his time on his private enterprise, but when the magnitude of the work left on the machine was realised he was, at first successfully, charged with theft of services under the relevant local legislation.[126] At a rehearing, however, the result was reversed upon the basis that one key element of the crime had not been satisfied, namely that there

---

123. [1980] S.C.R. 331, S.C.C.
124. *Maltais* v. *R.* [1978] 1 S.C.R. 441.
125. 459 N.E.2d 61 (Ind., 1984).
126. Ind. Code sect. 36-41-1-2 in which the definition of 'property' explicitly applied to 'services'.

should have been an intent to deprive the victim in relation to the computer system of 'any part of its value or use', and that on the admitted facts no such deprivation was intended or had occurred. It seems to have been accepted that the capacity limits of the system had not been reached. It was felt that the transgression was predominantly trespassory in nature, 'and de minimis at that'.[127] It is interesting to compare this reasoning with that in the earlier case of *People* v. *Weg*[128] where the accused, a programmer employed by the New York Board of Education, was in similar circumstances acquitted of the misdemeanour of theft of services. The New York statute[129] prohibited the unauthorised use of business, commercial or industrial equipment for gain, and the court held that as the Board of Education was not engaged in business, commerce or industry, the elements of the crime had not been established. It reached this conclusion in the absence of authority on the basis that the statute 'was not designed to make it a crime for a public or private employee to use his employer's internal office equipment without permission'. In so finding it relied upon statutory history in the form of a draftsman's note that the offence was intended to be restricted to facilities designed for the specified uses, since otherwise it would 'lead to hosts of criminal charges of a *basically civil nature*'.[130] This construction was assisted by the presence in the relevant legislation of other provisions explicitly extending the notion of a business to non-commercial activities. The problem is basically one of the proper range of criminal liability. It may be thought rather dubious whether the distinction made in *Weg* corresponds to any substantial moral distinction, and quite certain that it could lead to considerable uncertainty in application.

In the federal courts it is possible to use the broad offences of mail and wire fraud mentioned above. Thus in *U.S.* v. *Kelly*[131] where the accused had used his employer's facilities to develop a program for printing musical scores by computer, the accused was charged under the mail fraud legislation.[132] This was possible because the accused had set up a business to exploit his development and had posted brochures to advertise it. The fraud alleged in this case was the deprivation by the employees from their employer of their faithful service, though it seems that the commercial nature of the infidelity was significant, since it was used to tie in the mailings, and to distinguish the situation from those where employees simply played computer games on the facilities.[133]

There is now a federal offence of gaining unauthorised access or exceeding such access to a federal computer with intent to defraud,[134] or by doing so to prevent authorised use.[135] Some of the situations covered by this section could presumably be brought within the range of these offences.

---

127. 480 N.E. 2d 552 (Ind., 1985) at 554.
128. 450 N.Y.S.2d 957 (N.Y., 1982).
129. Penal Law sect. 165.15(8).
130. Commission Staff Notes p. 356 (emphasis supplied by the court in its quotation).
131. 507 F.Supp. 495 (E.D. Pa., 1981).
132. 18 U.S.C. sect. 1341.
133. Some of the cases recorded by the Audit Commission were as trivial as this.
134. 18 U.S.C. sect. 1030(a)(4).
135. 18 U.S.C. sect. 1030(a)(5), provided that the loss exceeds $1000.

In some ways this is the most difficult of the various situations to be considered here. It certainly left the Scottish Law Commission undecided on first impression,[136] although it finally recommended against the creation of a special offence to deal with this, on the basis that there was no justification for treating use of the employer's computer differently from the use of anything else.[137] This is also the provisional view of the English Law Commission.[138] On the one hand there is no obvious crime to charge and, on the other, it can be argued that the advent of the computer has created a special danger. In almost every other context any use of an employer's facilities to secure substantial gain for an employee would cause obvious loss to the employer, who could then implement some internal discipline and control. The problem with computers is their enormous power. Many commercial systems are under-employed, and can perform further unauthorised tasks with no perceptible degradation of the performance of their authorised functions.[139] This is widely recognised as making casual games playing misuse an inappropriate subject for criminal sanctions, yet it would be difficult to draft legislation drawing the line in precisely the appropriate place. It is also the case that almost all such misconduct is performed by employees, rather than by intruders, and this means that extra-criminal disciplinary remedies will be available in those cases, and less structured informal and internal procedures of this type may be more appropriate for providing a flexible response in a conceptually vague area.[140]

4. Securing unauthorised access to computing facilities

This further overlapping category concentrates on those cases where the aim and essence of the misconduct is to secure access to the facilities without authorisation. It is what is commonly called 'hacking'. Whereas the previous two categories of misconduct concentrate largely on the activities of employees of the facility in question, this one does not. Although the concept might be extended to include cases of employees who exceed their authorisation to use the facility, most concern seems to concentrate on those who secure unauthorised access wholly externally. In 1987 the Audit Commission included questions about 'hacking' in their survey for the first time. Thirty-five such[141] incidents were reported,[142] involving a total loss of £100 between them, but involving further costs, for example of investigating and

---

136. Scottish Law Commission, *Computer Crime*, consultative Memorandum No. 68 (1986) para. 4.26.
137. Scottish Law Commission, *Report on Computer Crime*, SLC No. 106 (Cm. 174, 1987) para. 3.13(5).
138. Law Commission, *Computer Misuse*, Working Paper No. 110 (1988) para. 3.67.
139. This point was relied upon in *McGraw*.
140. Though the ultimate control of such procedures by judicial review and unfair dismissal proceedings should not be ignored.
141. In fact of the twenty-three incidents of 'hacking', clearly enough described by the Audit Commission for attribution, only four appear to have been committed completely externally, while thirteen were cases of employees, and six of authorised users, exceeding their authorisation.
142. Audit Commission, *Survey of Computer Crime and Abuse* (1987) Table 3, apparently including three cases classified elsewhere as 'sabotage'.

correcting security procedures, of £21 950.[143] It is interesting that despite the fact that these amounted to nearly 30 per cent of the total number of incidents to be reported, the respondents, who were generally more apprehensive about misuse and fraud than the statistics warranted,[144] did not think that 'hacking' represented a significant threat.

If nothing is removed, copied, altered or destroyed, it may be asked first how the misconduct is recognised, and second whether it is worth legislating against it. Where facilities are made available to remote access, the most common form of security is to require the use of at least one password, though in sensitive areas like that of banking much more is normally required.[145] Routine precautions are sometimes installed which log and then cut off connections where a threshold of false passwords has been exceeded. So internal auditing of this nature reveals some hacking attempts. Another simple technique is to provide for the computer to dial back to anyone seeking access to it, and once again if there is a high incidence of such calls failing it may be indicative of 'hacking' attempts. In other cases the hacker is so proud of his achievement that he leaves a message boasting of it. This matter was also the subject of the latest Audit Commission survey. It found that by far the great majority of cases[146] were discovered by internal methods, though of the four clearly external cases, two were detected as a result of information received, in one case from the 'hacker' himself.

The misconduct of the hacker seems legally akin to trespass, or morally to breach of privacy. Trespass is, however, not a criminal offence in itself without some further aggravating feature, and breach of privacy is not generally protected in English law.[147] It was indeed the conclusion of the Younger Committee on Privacy that it should not be. The Law Commission found that there is, in general, no protection at present.[148] It considered the possible applicability of a number of offences, of which the most applicable in this particular category, as opposed to the others discussed here, is forgery, which has attracted a decision of the House of Lords.

In *R.* v. *Gold*[149] false identification numbers and passwords were used to secure access to databases offering a service to the general public upon payment of charges. The co-accused did not pay the charges themselves, caused others to be charged, and perused and altered information stored in the databases without authority. It seems that their object was to demonstrate the fallibility of the security of these systems, and one of the two co-accused did indeed alert the proprietor of the database to the breach of security which he had accomplished. Charges of making a false instrument were brought under section 1 of the Forgery and Counterfeiting Act 1981.

---

143. Ibid. Table 4.
144. Ibid. p. 12.
145. But not always, as the recently reported Prudential–Bache case illustrates, and a system depending upon only one password was very nearly defrauded of over five million pounds.
146. 75 per cent (24 out of 32), see Table 10.
147. See *Malone* v. *Metropolitan Police Commssioner* [1979] Ch. 344 at 358, Ch.
148. Law Commission, *Computer Misuse*, Working Paper No. 110 (1988) para. 3.65. Though the Audit Survey reveals that in at least one case of external 'hacking', Case No. 96, there was a successful prosecution under the Theft Acts.
149. [1988] 2 All E.R. 186, H.L. It is also case No. 94 in the Audit Commission's survey.

This Act is of sufficiently recent origin to have made a conscious effort to cater for modern technology. It defines an instrument to mean, among other things, 'any disc, tape, sound track or other device on or in which information is recorded or stored by mechanical, electronic or other means',[150] and in section 10 addresses the problem of communication with machines by providing,

(3) . . . in this Part of this Act references to inducing somebody to accept a false instrument as genuine . . . include references to inducing a machine to respond to the instrument . . . as if it were a genuine instrument . . .
(4) Where sub-section (3) above applies, the act or omission intended to be induced by the machine responding to the instrument . . . shall be treated as an act or omission to a person's prejudice . . .[151]

The key objection to the application of these provisions, apparently taken for the first time by the trial judge himself, was as to the identity of the relevant instrument. It was argued that it was the registers in the main computer used to verify the user's authorisation to secure access. The trial judge left the question of whether so ephemeral an electronic state could constitute a false instrument. The jury thought that it could, but the Court of Appeal took the view[152] that there were two fatal defects, first that the registers were not sufficiently permanent in their nature to qualify as false instruments within the relevant definitions, and secondly that even if they were, then it was hard to detect anything separate from them which was induced to respond. In reaching this conclusion the Court of Appeal relied upon the discussion of the problems of the application of forgery to high technology made by the Law Commission in its Report,[153] and finding that its recommendations, which the 1981 legislation embodied, had been intended to deal with more permanently stored information, deplored 'The Procrustean attempt to force these facts into the language of an Act not designed to fit them'.[154] The first of these arguments, and the general justification for that approach, was upheld, without material alteration by a unanimous House of Lords.[155] It is unfortunate that their Lordships should baulk in this way at extending the meaning of words such as 'recording' or 'storing' when used in the context of the computer. It seems immaterial whether a piece of false information requires to be stored for a short or a long period to accomplish its object. If words in common usage cannot be adapted to deal with modern technology, the terminology of the law will have to become even more cumbrous and jargon-ridden than it is at present. It is true that the Court of Appeal described the essence of the conduct in this case as 'dishonestly gaining access to the relevant Prestel databank by a trick',[156] but it is not obvious that so simple a description could not itself be opened up to the sort of pedantry which prevailed in *Gold*.

---

150. Sect. 8(1)(d).
151. Sect. 10.
152. [1987] Q.B. 1116, C.A.
153. *Forgery and Counterfeit Currency*, Law Com. No. 55 (1973).
154. At p. 1124.
155. *R.* v. *Gold* [1988] 2 All E.R. 186, H.L.
156. At 1124.

It should be noted that there is a number of variants upon the conduct normally described as 'hacking'. In its most restrictive sense it suggests the act of a totally external user, external, that is, both organisationally and physically from the computer system. It also suggests securing communication with the system in both directions, though it may not go so far as to require the ability to change the state of the system to which access is secured; it is probably enough to be able to secure the transmission of information from it. If someone is content with more passive access than this, for example, by intercepting messages to authorised users, or by eavesdropping on a terminal by electronic means, it is possible that offences under the Interception of Communications Act 1985 might be committed.[157]

It should, perhaps, be mentioned that even without 'hacking' amounting to a crime abstention from it may be still be made a condition for bail or of binding over.[158]

Most current debate in the United Kingdom is concerned with the desirability of reforming this area of the law and, in particular, of creating a new offence of securing access to a computer. The Scottish Law Commission has recommended the creation of a new offence of securing unauthorised access to programs or data stored in a computer.[159] It decided not to limit the offence, by reference to the means of access, and to include cases where it was only the extent of authorisation which was exceeded. In order to limit the width of the offence it was recommended that such access should be made either with the intent of obtaining an advantage or of damaging the interests of another. Where the damage consisted in causing an adverse effect upon the programs or data, then recklessness would also amount to a sufficient mental element.

In England the Law Commission has so far professed to have formed no final view as to the desirability of instituting such a new crime.[160] It does however put forward four possible options.[161] One of these is mainly concerned with causing damage to programs or data, and will be considered in the next section. The other three are of different scopes. The most restricted would be limited to obtaining unauthorised access to a computer so as to inspect particular types of information, especially, but not exclusively, the sort of personal data defined by the Data Protection Act 1984. The second option would extend this to all types of information. The third, and most extensive, option is to criminalise all unauthorised access to a computer. Within any such scheme the Law Commission would wish to exclude merely passive eavesdropping,[162] and quite unlike the Scottish Law Commission it is most reluctant to extend the offence to unauthorised use by authorised users. A principal argument in favour of any such offence is as a

---

157. Section 1 deals with interception and section 43 with the initiation of certain types of message.
158. See *Computer Weekly* 21 July 1988 p. 7 reporting just such a decision.
159. Scottish Law Commission, *Report on Computer Crime*, SLC No. 106 (Cm. 174, 1987) recommendations 5–14.
160. Law Commission Working Paper No. 110, *Computer Misuse* (1988) para. 6.2
161. Paras. 6.20–6.37.
162. Unlike the Scottish Law Commission it is less tolerant of catching such conduct by a sidewind.

bulwark for the more heinous offences of theft, fraud or malicious damage. However, this argument is weakened by the admission that it will most often be only by the discovery of such further offences that 'hacking' can be detected. It is, thus, unclear how it will operate as a bulwark, since the further criminal conduct being more likely to be discovered, and carrying much more serious penalties, must clearly be the principal deterrent. Given that such offences will carry with them the normal apparatus of inchoate offences, it seems that the extra assistance given by the criminalisation of 'hacking' in other circumstances is likely to be small.

It is just this sort of conduct which has been so widely publicised in the United States, and which features so often in current statutory provisions both at state and federal level.[163] These statutes are characterised by their vagueness and breadth. For example, computer is often defined so widely as to make it necessary to exclude battery powered watches and hand-held calculators by *ad hoc* exception. One state[164] even goes so far as to exclude home and dedicated computers from the ambit of the legislation.[65] Similarly 'access', often used as a verb,[166] is frequently defined to include 'approach'. These statutes seem to have been used to secure convictions in a number of states. The federal version, the Counterfeit Access Device and Computer Fraud and Abuse Act 1984,[167] was first employed to secure a conviction in a case where someone secured access to a government computer as a result of random dialling.[168] The conviction was secured by a plea bargain, but the prosecutor is reported to have been concerned that a constitutional challenge to the statute on vagueness grounds might have succeeded.[169] There certainly appears to be some foundation for such a view. Most of the legislation can be traced back to the Florida Computer Crimes Act enacted in 1978.[170] This was largely copied in Senate Bill 240 of 1979, and many of the provisions of that legislation have been copied in later bills, sometimes slightly modified.[171] Thus the egregious definition of 'access' has been modified in California by omitting 'approach',[172] and omitted altogether by the federal statute. This clearly creates some doubt about its meaning.[173]

---

163. Statutes passed before 1980 are collected and reproduced in Krieger, 'Current and Proposed Computer Crime Legislation', 2 *Comp. L.J.* 721 (1980).
164. Maryland, see Code art. 27 sect. 146.
165. See also 18 U.S.C. sect. 1030(a)(1). In England the Law Commission has suggested that it is unnecessary to define a computer, but that some such exclusions should be made explicit, Law Commission Working Paper No. 110, *Computer Misuse* (1988) para. 6.23.
166. As such, found offensive by the Scots, Scottish Law Commission, *Computer Crime*, Consultative Memorandum No. 68 (1986) para. 6.7.
167. The clumsy title reflects the tortuous process of legislation which involved tacking one pending bill on to another. In an amended form these bills are now represented by 18 U.S.C. sects. 1029 and 1030.
168. Programs can be written to enable random dialling of numbers until a data tone is encountered indicating that the number of an on-line database has been located.
169. *Computerworld* 1 July 1985 p 22.
170. Fla. Code sect. 815.01.
171. It is neither possible, nor appropriate in a work of this description, to attempt a comprehensive survey and analysis of all of the state legislation on this topic in the United States.
172. Cal. Penal Code sect. 502(a)(1).
173. For a general critique see Tompkins and Mar, 'The 1984 Federal Computer Crime Statute', 6 *Comp. L.J.* 459.

5. Causing damage to the less tangible facets of a computer system

There is clearly no difficulty in charging an offence under the Criminal Damage Act 1971 in respect of intentional or reckless damage to computer hardware. It might, however, be questioned whether the same could be said of damage to programs or data held in some erasable medium such as a disc. The Act requires damage to property, and property is defined as 'property of a tangible nature'. If erasure takes place it could be argued that since the medium in question is still as suitable for any new task as when it was originally supplied, it has not been damaged. All that has happened is that certain magnetic particles have been rearranged. It is true that the information represented by the original ordering of the particles can no longer be reproduced, but that is different from damage to the disc. This is implausible. In the context of larceny the law has long since recognised that a change of form can be equivalent to a taking.[174] Recent case law has extended similar reasoning into the field of criminal damage. In *Cox* v. *Riley*[175] the accused erased the programs on a card governing a mechanical saw, raised arguments similar to those advanced above, and had his conviction upheld, on the basis that the card was property, and had been damaged in that time and money would be needed to restore it to its previous condition. It is refreshing to find so flexible an approach here, justified as it was by reference to changed modern conditions. Exactly the same analysis would appear to apply to cases involving 'logic bombs' where the alterations to the program do not come into immediate effect, but have a delayed action. Where a threat of such action is made, a charge of blackmail would clearly be appropriate.[176] An alternative approach would be to charge the offence in relation to the computer, or other device, in which the affected program or data operated.[177] This might be advantageous in certain circumstances where there is less direct contact with a tangible object than in the case of *Cox* v. *Riley*.

The Audit Commission found little evidence of the commission of such offences and categorised only three as falling within this category, though a number of those categorised differently seem to have involved some alteration of data[178] or damage to a computer system in the form of causing some part of it to be disabled during remedial[179] or investigatory procedures.[180] The Commission found that the incidental cost of computer misuse, most of which might on the expansive reasoning in *Cox* v. *Riley* amount to criminal damage, was substantial.[181]

---

174. *R.* v. *Morfit* R.R. 307, N.P. (1816) where a groom was successfully charged with stealing beans even though he had fed them to his master's horse, who retained both the horse and the horse's excrement.
175. 83 Cr. App. R. 54, Q.B.D. (1986). See also *R.* v. *Turner* 13 C.C.C. (3d) 430 (Ont. H.C., 1984).
176. Cp. *R.* v. *Cox and Jenkins* 1 Cr. App. R. (S) 190, C.C.A. (1979).
177. As in *R.* v. *Fisher* L.R. 1 C.C.R. 7, C.C.C.R. (1865) where a steam engine was disabled.
178. Including *R.* v. *Gold* [1988] 2 All E.R. 186, H.L. where amendments were made to information within the Prestel system.
179. For example case No. 90 where all identification numbers had to be changed.
180. For example case No. 101.
181. See Audit Commission, *Survey of Computer Crime and Abuse* (1987) Table 4, £201 950 or more than 7 per cent of the total loss caused by the incidents reported.

The position is more doubtful in the United States. Much depends upon the precise terms of the local legislation, and may be affected by the attitude of the judiciary. In New York, in the first case[182] to be decided under the new specialised legislation[183] for crimes involving computers a very robust view was taken,

a hypertechnical statutory interpretation would certainly defy the statute's plain language as well as its very purpose to deter this kind of activity by employees entrusted with special computer privileges.

There the accused had shut down a computerised telephone system on two occasions by the use of commands to which he, as a programmer, had access. It was his contention that by using the commands to achieve their intended purpose he had not altered or destroyed either programs or data.[184] that met with this rebuff. Nor did his contention that the instructions were countermanded in one case by two hours' manual programming,[185] and in the other by a standard recovery routine, meet with any greater success. A very different approach was adopted in *State* v. *Olson*[186] where just such an argument as that rejected in *Versaggi* succeeded. Because the accused had authority to use the relevant police computer it was held that the fact that he was using it for an unauthorised purpose was irrelevant to a charge of intentionally accessing a computer without authority. In *Mahru* v. *Superior Court*[187] the court simply ignored the clear meaning of the local statute and interpreted it in the way it felt that the legislature would have drafted it, had it thought of the particular situation. The statute[188] prohibits malicious alteration of a computer program. The accused had altered a program, and was malicious. He was also, however, the owner of the computer in which the victim had a security interest. The accused had a contract to provide data processing services for the victim, and when it decided to change suppliers the accused instituted the malicious alteration of the programs. The court felt that this was essentially a civil dispute. It is problematic how the federal courts will react. Some indication may be derived from a recent incident in which a self-replicating program was deliberately inserted into nationwide networks with the intention that it should spread through the systems using those networks. It was a characteristic of this program that it did not destroy programs or data, but merely occupied all the vacant space on the systems. This, of course, had the effect of making them inoperable, since running any program involves the use, at least temporarily, of unoccupied memory. It was necessary for organisations to mobilise teams of programmers to cleanse their systems, often at vast expense.[189] In England it seems that the enlightened and flexible approach of the judiciary as

---

182. *People* v. *Versaggi* 518 N.Y.S.2d 553 (N.Y., 1987) at 557.
183. Penal Law sect. 156.20 which came into force in 1986.
184. As required by the relevant legislation.
185. In the light of this finding it is hard to understand the assertion that no expense was caused by the accused's actions.
186. 735 P.2d 1362 (Wash., 1987).
187. 237 Cal. Rptr. 298 (Cal., 1987).
188. Penal Code sect. 502(c).
189. See *Computerworld* 14 November 1988 pp. 1–16.

exemplified in *Cox* v. *Riley* would lead to criminal liability.[190] In the federal courts however, because a different legislative form has been adopted it seems much more dubious that a successful prosecution can be brought.[191] It need hardly be added that the reaction of some federal legislators has been to reach for their pens to add yet another segment to the crazy patchwork of criminal legislation applying to computers in the United States.[192]

C. Special Crimes

This section of the chapter will consider a few of the more prominent situations where a special legal regime has been set up to deal with a special problem related to the use of computers, or to which such use is central, part of which involves the creation of criminal offences. These will include two areas of traditional intellectual property, trade secrets and copyright, and the other is the specialised area of data protection. The general law in these areas is considered elsewhere.

1. Trade secrets

Industrial espionage seems now more prevalent, and more sophisticated, than ever before. This is largely because technology has so inevitably become the key to wealth both internationally and domestically in the modern world. It is now almost axiomatic to suppose that development must be associated with industrialisation, and riches with the consumption of power. This constant striving for technological development leads both government and industry into expensive and wide-ranging investment in research and development. At different times in history, different nations have led the way technologically; Italy, France, Great Britain, Germany, the United States and Japan have taken it in turns to lead the world, and new challenges will now be met from China, the Far East and leading Communist states. It is extremely difficult to estimate the true value of modern technology, even as regards that part in the public domain. It is still more difficult to accomplish in respect of the part that is kept secret. Not all such secrets qualify as trade secrets, of course, since that concept, while broad and nebulous is not universal in extent. It may have been this which accounted for such diverse estimates as those published by two leading United States newspapers within the space of a single month.[193] As noted above, matters seem not to have improved.[194] Despite so evident a lack of precision it is clear that trade

---

190. This is also the view of the Law Commission, see Law Commission Working Paper No. 110, *Computer Misuse* (1988) para. 3.40.
191. Because of the narrow drafting of 18 U.S.C. sect. 1030(a), of which sub-sect. (5) is the most appropriate, but it is far from clear whether recklessness is sufficient, see *Computerworld* 14 November 1988 p. 16.
192. See *Computerworld* 14 November 1988 p. 16 reporting the submission of bill H.R. 5061.
193. On 16 March 1965 the *New York Times* estimated that the value of trade secrets stolen from United States firms was running at 2 billion dollars each year, while on 8 April 1965 the *Wall Street Journal*, not to be outdone, informed its readers that 3 billion dollars' worth of trade secrets were stolen by foreigners alone in the same period.
194. See above p. 273.

secrets in the strict legal sense, and such allied information as is customarily kept secret, or disclosed only under conditions of confidentiality, constitute a valuable resource to be defended by the law.

The question arises of how far the law provides such protection at present. The civil law of trade secrets, which was considered in Chapter 3, provides some relief, principally by way of injunction or compensation. Is that enough, or should there be criminal remedies in addition? It must be remembered that the theory of the function of the civil law, and in the United Kingdom its practice also, is to reimburse the injured party rather than to punish the tortfeasor. In the United States, readier resort to punitive damages has blurred this line of distinction. Nevertheless, it may be assumed that the criminal law has a greater deterrent effect. There are a number of situations in which this may be important.[195] It can be argued that a large firm with a substantial share of a relevant market will be relatively undeterred by the prospect of incurring purely fiscal penalties which it may be able to pass on to its customers in the shape of higher prices. This will be true to the extent that demand for the firm's products is inelastic, and elasticity of demand depends not only upon market dominance, but also upon such other factors as reputation, relative price and product superiority which all contribute to brand loyalty. Such factors are often especially strong in the computer industry as users tend to become dependent upon a single supplier for a number of easily understandable reasons. The most important of these is the disruption which is likely to be caused to the firm's activities by a major change of supplier.[196] Almost inevitably programs will have to re-written and de-bugged, and consequential difficulties will occur in other linked parts of the system as the new elements are introduced. Then there is the psychological strain of having to set up personal relationships with a new set of people; a situation aggravated if only a part of the system has changed, and two different groups in competition with each other have to be encountered on the user's own premises. This strong sense of dependence puts the supplier into a very strong position so far as price is concerned, and such strength may encourage an unscrupulous attitude towards the appropriation of trade secrets. On the other hand, if the criminal law applies and senior officers are put at risk of terms of imprisonment, the effectiveness of the sanction is in no way mitigated by any amount of commercial power *vis-à-vis* third party users.

A similar argument can be pressed in the exactly converse case of the supplier who is in a weak commercial position. Weakness can also become an effective weapon. If the defendant is likely to lapse into bankruptcy when successfully sued for damages, litigation becomes a no-win strategy for a potential plaintiff. Either he wins the case and fails to recover either damages or his own expenses, or he loses the case and pays damages and at least his own expenses. He will accordingly be disinclined to sue whenever he perceives a sufficiently significant risk of such a result. The state, on the

---

195. Set out in Vandevoort, 'Trade Secrets: Protecting a Very Special Property', *26 Bus. L.* 681 (1971).
196. Such a change led to the destruction of the business in *Triangle Underwriters Inc.* v. *Honeywell Inc.* 457 F.Supp. 765 (E.D.N.Y., 1978).

other hand, does not expect to show a profit on its criminal prosecutions, and should feel no such disincentive. Thus here, too, the availability of a criminal sanction may deter abuse. A closely linked argument looks at the situation more from the position of the plaintiff. The outcome of almost all litigation is highly uncertain, and in the area of trade secrets with the vagueness of common law criteria and the difficulty of proof, it is still more uncertain than it is elsewhere. This means that with the cost of litigation being so high, all but the most affluent of plaintiffs will hesitate before embarking upon it. Once again, the state ought not to be too dependent upon such pressures and should not be so reluctant to bring a criminal prosecution. Similar considerations apply at the pre-litigation stage. Perhaps the most significant elements in the costs of trade secret litigation are those incurred long before the case comes to trial by way of preparation for it, and especially in collecting and collating evidence. No private suitor is able to command the same resources as the state for the detection of crime, and for gathering and analysing evidence.

While such arguments have a theoretical plausibility, they still lack conviction. The flaw lies in their assumption that the state will be prepared to allocate its resources for these purposes in sufficient measure. But it is unrealistic to suppose that many prosecution departments regard the mis-appropriation of trade secrets as their most serious concern, or even a particularly pressing one. Many of them legitimately and understandably take the view that their resources are better deployed in combating direct threats to the lives and liberties of their citizens than in duplicating the protection already afforded to business by the civil law. They may also seek to avoid the invidious position of appearing to interfere in competition between different firms which might have unpleasant political repercussions.

There is, nevertheless, a different argument, admittedly of a more nebulous and speculative character, by which criminal intervention in this area may be justified. This depends upon the simple moral force of criminal proscription. To stigmatise an act as criminal fortifies social pressure against its commission and has a salutary effect upon business practice. The executives of large public companies, which depend upon the trust and confidence of the people, will not wish to be seen to authorise, or even to profit from, the commission of crimes. The deliberate determination that a certain course of conduct constitutes a crime is likely to be much more effective to prevent its commission than is some consensus of belief that a practice is likely to be regarded as unethical by others. The availability of a criminal remedy may also serve to strengthen other branches of the law. The civil law of trade secrets may benefit from the ability to refer to definitions made for the purpose of the criminal law,[197] and other crimes and torts which depend upon the establishment of unlawful or improper means, such as conspiracy and intimidation, will have a more solid basis for their application. So, too, the availability of criminal remedies for violation more clearly serves to establish the proprietary cast of trade secrets, and thus in turn to strengthen the application of civil proprietary remedies,[198] and the

---

197. *Stamicarbon N.V.* v. *American Cyanamid Corp.* 506 F.2d 532 (2nd Cir., 1974).
198. As in *National Security Corporation* v. *Applied Systems Inc.* 418 So.2d 847 (Ala., 1982).

development of a more open market for the limited disclosure of secrets, which should itself tend to lessen the incidence of misappropriation.

If these arguments are accepted, it seems odd that specific criminal protection for trade secrets does not exist at all in modern United Kingdom law, and is of such recent origin in the United States.[199] An interesting explanation has been propounded,[200] to the effect that such criminal proscription is generally used by the world leader in technology in an effort to preserve its lead over the rest of the world, and that in the eighteenth century British laws to this effect became associated with the mercantilist school of thought. Such ideas were subsequently discredited in advanced circles after the publication in 1776 of *The Wealth of Nations.* Thus at the very time when the framework of American law was being laid, such ideas were in decline and never adopted, while in Britain they were gradually abolished under the pressure of *laissez-faire* ideology. It may be noted though that some other European nations, such as France and Germany, retained, and still retain, their criminal legislation against the misappropriation of trade secrets, especially when their ultimate destination is foreign.[201] It is likely that pressure for harmonisation will build up as the European Economic Community moves towards the implementation of a single market in 1992.

Criminal law has probably never lacked the power to protect the technical secrets of the government, especially in the realm of weaponry, whether reliance is to be placed upon the general law of treason or upon more specific legislation, such as the Official Secrets Act 1911 in the United Kingdom, or the Espionage Act in the United States.[202] Similarly there never seems to have been any serious doubt, even in the United States, of the government's ability to regulate trade with foreign powers, presumably in part so as to prevent the revelation of advanced technology. This power is still actively employed to prevent the export to Communist countries of the most advanced types of computer. In fact more other nations have been coerced into cooperation by refusal to supply equipment without undertakings not to re-export in defiance of United States internal rules.[203]

In the early 1960s, however, attention was particularly directed towards commercial espionage where the public welfare was less obviously affected. In a number of well-publicised cases, trade secrets were gleaned from United States companies, and then used by foreign competitors. This had the effect of undercutting the United States manufacturer who had incurred all of the research and development expenses, while the foreign competitor need have expended no more than was necessary to subvert an employee. The greatest effrontery occurred in the pharmaceutical field where in one case[204] not only

---

199. The state of New York enacted the first such statute in 1964.
200. By Fetterley, 'Historical Perspectives on Criminal Laws Relating to the Theft of Trade Secrets', *25 Bus. L.* 1535 (1970).
201. See, for example, French Penal Code art. 418; German Unfair Competition Statute sects. 17, 18 and 20.
202. 18 U.S.C. sect. 793.
203. Currently regulated by 50 U.S.C. sects. 2401 *et seq.* A very full and helpful account is to be found in Letterman, 'Exporting High Technology from the United States under the Revised Distribution Licence Procedures', *7 Comp. L.J.* 289 (1987).
204. Described in considerable, and somewhat shrill, detail by Bartenstein, 'Research Espionage: A Threat to our National Security' *17 F.D.C.L.J.* 813 (1962).

did the foreign competitor purloin the secret, but registered first in some foreign countries, and instituted suit against the United States initiator for infringement of the foreign patent.

It was widely agreed that the then existing provisions of the criminal law were ineffective, and that special criminal statutes should be drafted to provide better protection against the misappropriation of trade secrets.

It is first necessary to see exactly why existing laws should have been regarded as ineffective and then to scrutinise the new statutes which appeared in the United States in the late 1960s.[205] The law of theft provides the normal remedy against misappropriation of property. Why should it not protect trade secrets? The main problem is that the law of theft depends so heavily upon the proprietary nature of those things within its ambit, and the proprietary nature of trade secrets has been seriously controverted.[206] At common law, theft was predicated upon the asportation of tangible objects with the intent to deprive the owner of them permanently. In the case of the misappropriation of trade secrets, none of these elements need be present. The secret is itself not tangible, and thus cannot be taken away, and if it is not taken away it is hard to see how there can be any intent to deprive the owner of it permanently.

One way of avoiding this sort of difficulty might be to charge not the theft of the secret itself, but theft of some tangible object embodying the secret, such as a piece of paper upon which the secret might be written. Thus where a list of new telephone subscribers is kept secret, misappropriation of the list might be regarded as theft if a physical piece of paper on which the list is inscribed should be removed.[207] Of course, in such a case the secrecy of the material is, in principle, immaterial, since the taking, even of a blank sheet of paper, could amount to theft. Since these cases hinge neither on secrecy nor value, but instead upon purely proprietary considerations, the accused may always seek to show that he believed the object to have been abandoned,[208] or perhaps that he reasonably believed that the owner would have agreed to the taking.[209] Many states of the United States distinguish different grades of theft depending upon the value of the goods which have been taken. When this is the case, and the accused is charged with a graver offence, it is necessary to show that the value of the object stolen exceeds the threshold value for the grade. It then becomes a question of how far the value of the secret can be relied upon to increase the value of the physical object which has been taken. This was the issue in *Hancock* v. *State*[210] where a programmer made photocopies of some fifty-nine computer programs

---

205. Many of these statutes have since been amended to cope with computer technology, and in many cases have been supplemented by special statutes dealing with computers. The discussion which follows is intended to do no more than illustrate the original difficulties of interpretation.

206. In the United States by no less a figure than Justice Holmes, see above p. 92. See also Weinrib, 'Information as Property' *38 U. Tor. L.J.* 117 (1988).

207. *People* v. *Dolbeer* 214 Cal. App. 2d 619 (Cal., 1963).

208. As in *State* v. *Gage* 136 N.W.2d 662 (Minn., 1965).

209. As made explicit in the English Theft Act 1968 sect. 2(1)(b).

210. *Hancock* v. *State* 402 S.W. 2d 906 (Tex., 1966) *habeas corpus den.* 379 F.2d 552 (5th Cir., 1967).

which he attempted to sell to his employer's customers for five million dollars. It was estimated that the value of the paper on which the programs were written was thirty-five dollars, less than the fifty dollar threshold required by the relevant statute. The Texas Penal Code, under which the accused was charged, defined property as including,[211] 'all writings of every description, providing such property possesses any ascertainable value'. Such a provision is clearly apt to defeat a defence to a charge of stealing a 100-dollar bill, on the basis that the bill, as a piece of paper, did not exceed thirty-five dollars in value. Here, however, the question was more difficult, since the original was not removed as in the hypothetical case of the 100-dollar bill, but was instead copied. Nevertheless the Texas court held, and a federal court upheld, the conclusion that paper on which the programs in question were written did constitute property with a value in excess of fifty dollars. This seems correct since, unlike a forged or copied banknote, a copy of a computer program is just as effective for its purpose as the original would have been. This leaves only the question of how the value should be established. In this case there was no reasonable doubt that once the programs were valued as programs their value exceeded fifty dollars. The vice-president of the victim company whose programs had been copied, was allowed to testify as to their value, on the basis of his estimate of the price which a willing buyer would pay to a willing seller for them. In a case where the question of value was more crucial, there might be greater difficulty, especially in the area of trade secrets. The owner might never have contemplated selling, or there might be no market for the programs. In such a case the value of the programs might plausibly be regarded as equivalent, either to the commercial advantage to the victim in having them kept secret,[212] or perhaps to the cost of preparing them.

Those findings were enough to dispose of that prosecution, based as it was upon the misappropriation of tangible property, namely the piece of paper on which the programs were recorded. They would not cover the case where the employee either provided his own paper for the copier or merely memorised the programs for later transcription elsewhere[213] nor, perhaps, where the misappropriation took the form of electronic transmission from the memory of the victim's computer system to the memory of the intruder's computer.[214] It was principally to deal with such defects that the states began to enact their trade secret legislation in the 1960s.[215] Few cases have been reported on the application of these statutes to computer programs. In *Ward* v. *Superior Court of California*[216] the relevant program was held in the memory of the victim's computer, but made available for transmission over a telephone line to anyone who knew the telephone number, and could furnish a valid site and billing number. Here another competing service bureau had a customer in common with the victim. This customer insisted on having the

---

211. Sect. 1418
212. Though this might be just as difficult to quantify.
213. See *Commonwealth* v. *Engleman* 142 N.E. 2d 406 (Mass., 1957).
214. See above p. 283 *U.S.* v. *Seidlitz* 589 F.2d 152 (4th Cir., 1978).
215. This legislation was a precursor of, and has now in many cases been succeeded by, more general legislation dealing with the misuse of computers.
216. 3 C.L.S.R. 206 (Cal., 1972).

same site and billing number with both of its computer service bureaux. This became known to one of the competitor's employees. He was then able to telephone in to the victim's computer, supply a valid site and billing number, and secure transmission of the programs to his own computer's memory. Having done so, he had the program printed out in his own computer room, whence he took it to his office. Charges were laid under both the grand theft[217] and the trade secret[218] provisions of the California Penal Code which had been added in 1967. Most of the argument was directed to the latter. These provisions were keyed to the definition of an 'article' as meaning[219] 'any object, material, device or substance or copy thereof, including any writing, record, recording, drawing, sample, specimen, prototype, model, photograph, micro-organism, blueprint or map'.[220] This list conveyed the flavour of the apprehended threat. It was decided that for the purposes of section 499(c) (b)(l), which was infringed by anyone who 'steals, takes, or carries away an article representing a trade secret', the electronic representation of the program contained in the memory of the computer could not be regarded as an article within the scope of the definition. On the other hand it was felt that the conduct of the accused fell within the proscription of section 499c (b)(3) as that of one who, 'having unlawfully obtained access to an article without authority makes or causes to be made a copy of any article representing a trade secret'. It might have been possible to reconcile these findings on the basis that the 'article' for the purposes of section 499c (b)(3) to which access was had was the victim's physical core medium. Since the core medium itself was not taken from the victim's premises, there could thus be no offence in respect of that under section 499c (b)(l). Such a view was, however, confounded by the court's further holding that conviction under the grand theft provision was also justified upon the basis that section 499c had extended the ambit of personal property susceptible of theft. The court justified such an interpretation by reference to the preamble to the 1967 legislation which recited the intention of the California legislature to 'clarify and restate the law with respect to crimes involving trade secrets, and to make clear that articles representing trade secrets, *including the trade secrets represented thereby.*[221] constitute goods, chattels, materials and property, and can be the subject of criminal acts'. It is hard to see how such an interpretation of the legislation in general for the purpose of grand theft was consistent with the restrictive interpretation of 'article' for the purposes of section 499c (b)(l). Either an electronic impulse was an article, in which case it could have been stolen for the purposes of both grand theft and section 499c (b)(l); or it was not, in which case the only plausible line of reasoning would have been that suggested above to justify a conviction for copying under section 499c (b)(3). The better view, certainly the more convenient view, and the one according best with the

---

217. Sect. 487.
218. Sect. 499c.
219. Sect. 499c (a)(l).
220. To this list in 1983 were added the words 'or tangible representation of computer programs or information, including both human and computer readable information and information while in transit'.
221. Emphasis supplied.

sentiments expressed in the preamble, would have been that an electronic impulse was an article within section 499c (a)(1). It should be noted that the definition distinguished clearly between the physical storage medium[222] and a copy of its contents, the latter being cast in much broader and less physical terminology, especially in the explicit inclusion of both 'record' *and* 'recording'. The presence of the latter could have been explained only on the basis that it extended to something beyond the recording medium itself, which was sufficiently defined by the term 'record'. If such a view were to have been adopted, a potentially serious loophole in the Californian legislation would have been sealed much earlier.

There is no special federal offence directed at the misappropriation of trade secrets.[223] Nevertheless some of those responsible for taking the secrets of pharmaceutical firms in the early 1960s, the events which gave rise to the burgeoning of state legislation in this area, were successfully prosecuted under the federal legislation proscribing interstate transportation of stolen property to a value in excess of $5000.[224] The statute in question is cast in terms of 'goods, wares, merchandise, securities or money'. Questions thus arise of whether copies of computer programs can be said to have values in excess of that figure and, more fundamentally, whether transportation of such copies can be regarded as coming within the proscription of the statute at all. The former question was at first disposed of by the federal courts in the same robust and satisfactory way as taken in Texas in *Hancock*.[225] Thus in *U.S.* v. *Lester*[226] it was accepted that the idea gave its value to the paper on which the map in that case had been copied. It was argued that there was no market for such maps, but the court brushed the objection aside on the basis that 'any reasonable method may be employed to ascribe an equivalent monetary value to the items'. Since some 2000 maps were involved, and the sums being asked were far in excess of 5000 dollars, the court had no difficulty in deciding that the value exceeded the statutory threshold.[227] The further question of whether the copies could themselves be regarded as stolen 'goods, wares or merchandise' was easily resolved since the copies had in *Lester* been made on the victim's own paper.

In the subsequent case of *U.S.* v. *Bottone*[228] this question was ventilated as there the accused had copied secrets relating to pharmaceutical techniques upon their own paper, using their own copier. The court held that this was immaterial so long as the secrets were put in some tangible form. This reasoning is very difficult to follow since there could be no question but that the tangible form itself, the paper with printing on it, had not been stolen from anyone. Only the idea had been taken. But the court was not prepared

---

222. Sect. 499c (b)(4).
223. For a fuller account see Nycum, 'Criminal Law Aspects of Computer Abuse' Part 11, 'Federal Criminal Code' 5 *Rutgers C. & T. L. J.* 297 (1976).
224. 18 U.S.C. 2314 (1964). See above p. 282.
225. 402 S.W. 2d 906 (Tex., 1966) *habeas corpus den.* 379 F.2d 552 (5th Cir., 1967).
226. 282 F.2d 750 (3rd Cir., 1960).
227. This approach seems to have been rejected where the underlying offence is infringement of copyright, and it is uncertain whether the value of the copyright in any individual item exceeds the threshold, see *Dowling* v. *U.S.* 473 U.S. 207 (1985).
228. 365 F.2d 389 (2nd Cir., 1966).

to rest its decision upon the theft of an idea alone since, as it pointed out, the statute would not apply to someone who memorised a secret, took it away in his head and subsequently divulged it to a third party. The court seems itself to have had doubts of the logicality of its ambivalent position, since it took care to point out that on each count a physical object, namely a culture used in the preparation of the relevant drug, had also been transported. In some cases *Bottone* appeared to have been limited to the area of strict intellectual property as applying only to,

ideas formulated with labor and inventive genius in the use of literary works or scientific researches ... [or] where they constitute fair and effective commercial competition.[229]

The contents of private letters which had been copied were there regarded as being outside the scope of *Bottone*, while in *Re Vericker*[230] the same Second Circuit Court of Appeals held that it did not extend to secret documents kept by the Federal Bureau of Investigation. Indeed, the court seemed there inclined to limit the doctrine still further to matter which could be the subject of patent claims. A rather wider view was essayed in a later case[231] which apparently sought simply to apply criteria of commercial value, though the point seems not to have arisen directly as in that case the tangible form was taken. The weakness of the reasoning in *Bottone* has now been exposed by the decision in *Dowling* v. *U.S.*[232] which refused to apply sect. 2314 in the absence of some physical taking.

It seemed at one time as if this would spell the end of attempts to employ peripheral federal crimes in the area of trade secrets. Thus in *McNally* v. *U.S.*[233] the Supreme Court refused to apply the mail and wire fraud statutes[234] to a case where the victims had been deprived of the intangible right to good government.[235] However, such a view was rejected in *Carpenter* v. *U.S.*[236] where the Supreme Court reaffirmed the application of these sections to cases where betrayed confidential information had been the subject of the crime. It seems that the key difference from *McNally* was indeed that the underlying subject matter counted as property, even though it was intangible. Thus the position appears to be that if a trade secret is appropriated and that there is a sufficient interstate communication, then the mail and wire fraud statutes may be invoked. What is still unclear is whether they can be invoked if the misappropriation of the secret involves an infringement of copyright. It is submitted that the better view is that this should be regarded as immaterial. It is also unclear whether an offence can be charged under the stolen property statute when such a secret is misappropriated, and transported across state lines. It is tentatively suggested that the fact that the underlying offence involves more than infringement of copyright, and thus falls outside the exclusive purview of copyright

---

229. *Pearson* v. *Doss* 410 F.2d 701 (D.C.Cir., 1969) at 707.
230. 466 F.2d 244 (2nd Cir., 1971).
231. *U.S.* v. *Greenwald* 479 F.2d 320 (6th Cir., 1973).
232. 473 U.S. 207 (1985).
233. 107 S.Ct.R. 2875 (1987).
234. 18 U.S.C. 1341 and 1343. See above p. 564.
235. By a corrupt agreement involving interstate communication by telephone.
236. 108 S.Ct.R. 316 (1987).

and its limited criminalisation, means that such an offence could still be charged, provided only the problem of valuation can be surmounted, notwithstanding the decision in *Dowling*.

2. Copyright and other forms of intellectual property

It has already been noted that in the United Kingdom the courts have been reluctant to interpret the principles of the general law of theft so as to apply to the temporary borrowing of an article for the purposes of copying it.[237] In *R. v. Storrow and Poole*[238] an ingenious attempt was made to avoid this problem by making the infringing copies of a copyright film the subject matter of a conspiracy to steal, in reliance upon section 18(1) of the Copyright Act 1956[239] deeming such copies the property of the owner of the original. However, the argument was rejected upon the basis that section 18(1) applied only for the purposes of the civil law.

The copyright legislation has since 1911 included its own provisions imposing criminal liability in respect of a broad range of infringing acts. These were, however, rarely invoked.[240] It is possible that part of the reason was the heavier burden of proof applicable in criminal cases, and in particular the difficulty of proving that the accused knew that he was infringing copyright. The ineffectiveness of these provisions[241] to deal with piracy, both of sound and video recordings, and of computer programs, caused disquiet and was addressed by the Whitford Committee.[242] It recommended that possession of infringing items by way of trade be made an offence, that the scale of penalties be increased and, to facilitate proof, that the burden of proof be cast upon the accused. It declined to recommend any enhancement of the provisions for search and seizure by criminal process. The government, in its response,[243] accepted that possession in the way of trade should be made an offence and that penalties should be increased. It refused to accept the proposal to reverse the onus of proof. Pressure from the relevant industries continued, however, and in piecemeal statutory amendment in the early 1980s[244] extensions were made.[245] In the particular case of computer software the effect of these changes intended to make possession by way of trade into an offence, to increase the scale of penalties, and to provide

---

237. Above p. 280.
238. [1983] Crim. L.R. 332, C.C.C.
239. Now repealed by the Copyright, Designs and Patents Act 1988 which has adopted a different conceptual approach to this aspect of remedies.
240. In *Rank Film Distributors Ltd.* v. *Video Information Centre* [1982] A.C. 380, H.L. Lord Wilberforce noted that only one case seemed to have been reported since 1911, and none at all for more than fifty years.
241. Contained at the time in Copyright Act 1956 sect. 21.
242. *Copyright and Designs Law* (Cmnd. 6732, 1977) paras. 708–14
243. *Reform of the Law relating to Copyright, Designs and Performers' Protection* (Cmnd. 8302, 1981) Ch. 14 paras. 11–13.
244. Copyright Act 1956 (Amendment) Act 1982; Copyright (Amendment) Act 1983; and Copyright (Computer Software) Amendment Act 1985.
245. These have led to successful prosecutions, in one case resulting in the imposition of a term of imprisonment, see *Computer Weekly* 14 January 1988 p. 1; and in another resulting in a fine of more than £5000, see *Computer Weekly* 2 June 1988 p. 112.

for a criminal process of search and seizure.[246] All of these Acts have now been repealed, along with the Copyright Act 1956, by the Copyright, Designs and Patents Act 1988.[247] Section 107 provides that:

(1) A person commits an offence who, without the licence of the copyright owner –
    (a) makes for sale or hire, or
    (b) imports into the United Kingdom otherwise than for his private and domestic use, or
    (c) possesses in the course of a business with a view to committing any act infringing the copyright, or
    (d) in the course of a business –
        (i) sells or lets for hire, or
        (ii) offers or exposes for sale or hire, or
        (iii) exhibits in public, or
        (iv) distributes, or
    (e) distributes otherwise than in the course of a business to such an extent as to affect prejudicially the owner of the copyright,
an article which is, and which he knows or has reason to believe is, an infringing copy of a copyright work.
(2) A person commits an offence who –
    (a) makes an article specially designed or adapted for making copies of a particular copyright work, or
    (b) has such an article in his possession, knowing or having reason to believe that it is to be used to make infringing copies for sale or hire or for use in the course of a business.

The Act continues to refrain from casting the burden of proof upon the accused,[248] but continues the provision of enhanced penalties,[249] and of criminal process in respect of search and seizure.[250] It should also be noted that the Act confers powers to forfeit infringing copies pursuant to criminal proceedings.[251]

It is interesting to note that the legislation relating to patents and trademarks, while containing minor offences in relation to registration, does not include any comparable provision for criminal offences of infringement. However, more useful offences are to be found in legislation such as the Trade Descriptions Act 1968, as amended, and the Consumer Protection Act 1987. Under the provisions of these Acts it is a criminal offence, for example, to sell a pirated copy of a computer program on the basis that it is genuine.[252] It should be noted that the criminal proscription applies to services, as well as to goods,[253] and to false statements in advertisements.[254]

---

246. While the second and third objectives were accomplished, it is by no means clear that the form of words adopted was apt to accomplish the first.
247. Sch. 8.
248. Sect. 107(6) expressly excludes such criminal offences from the operation of presumptions as to knowledge which apply elsewhere.
249. Sect. 107(4).
250. Sect. 109.
251. Sect. 108.
252. Charges have been brought under this legislation in relation to the sale of pirated software, see *Computer Weekly* 14 January 1988 p. 1.
253. Trade Descriptions Act 1968 sect. 14.
254. *Ibid.* sect. 5.

In *Dowling* v. *U.S.* the Supreme Court of the United States rehearsed the history of the application of the criminal law to the infringement of copyright in the United States. It noted that the offence appeared in its developed form for the first time in the Copyright Act of 1909, but that it was very rarely invoked. Penalties were subsequently increased, and the ambit of the crime extended to include sound recordings. It was not, however, until 1982 that the crime became capable of being a felony. The current version provides that:

Any person who infringes a copyright willfully and for purposes of commercial advantage or private financial gain shall be punished as provided in section 2319 of title 18[256]

Section 2319, which specifically deals with penalties for copyright offences, enhances penalties in respect of 'sound recordings, motion pictures, and audio-visual[257] works', but does not otherwise[258] enhance penalties in relation to computer-related acts. It will be noted that this legislation tracks the civil law more closely than that in the United Kingdom, though criminal and civil liability are still not identical. As in the United Kingdom the burden of proof remains upon the prosecution, and there is, in addition, provision for the forfeiture of infringing articles.[259]

It is also worth mentioning that there is a special federal offence of trafficking in counterfeit goods or services,[260] which might be applicable in the case of a number of offences of piracy.

3. Data protection

Although not a form of intellectual property as such, a number of special rules have grown up to govern the handling of personal data within computer systems.[261] Most of such regulation is administrative, or involves the civil law, but there are a number of criminal offences, and some of them might be utilised in relation to the problem of unauthorised access to a computer system. In addition to such general and, in the United Kingdom at least, computer specific provisions, there are numerous[262] other statutory provisions prohibiting the disclosure of information under sanction of criminal punishment.

The statutory scheme adopted in the United Kingdom by the Data Protection Act 1984 for the protection of personal information is confined to

---

255. 473 U.S. 207 (1985) at pp. 221–6.
256. 17 U.S.C. sect. 506(a).
257. As defined in 17 U.S.C. sect. 101.
258. This definition extends to computer-based video games, see *Stern Electronics Inc.* v. *Kaufman* 669 F.2d 852 (2nd Cir., 1982).
259. 17 U.S.C. sect. 506(b).
260. 18 U.S.C. sect. 2320.
261. To be considered more fully in the next chapter.
262. In *Administrator, Federal Aviation Authority* v. *Robertson* 422 U.S. 288 (1975) it was estimated that over one hundred different statutes, or parts of them, defined such offences in the United States, while Gurry, *Breach of Confidence* (1984) listed over eighty such provisions in the United Kingdom by 1981, while acknowledging that the list was not comprehensive, see App. 1.

the regulation of circumstances in which such information is held on a computer. The Act sets out a number of principles which are to govern the acquisition, holding and use of such information. Breach of these principles is not, as such, a criminal offence. Nevertheless, at one remove they are reinforced by criminal sanctions.

It is required under the Act that anyone[263] who holds personal information for the purpose of processing it on a computer must register with the Data Protection Registrar.[264] The scheme of definitions in the Act makes it clear that personal information is that relating to a living human being who is capable of being identified in respect of it;[265] that processing on a computer means in the case of such data 'amending, augmenting, deleting or re-arranging the data, or extracting the information' by reference to its human subject;[266] but that operations conducted only for the purpose of preparing the text of documents are exempt from its provisions.[267] The Registrar is required to ensure, as a condition of registration, that applicants respect the Data Protection principles.[268] In order to do so he is specifically empowered to discover the type of data to be held, the purposes for which it is to be held, the provenance of the data, and the destination of the data, both personal and geographic. It is an offence of strict liability to hold relevant data without having been registered,[269] or knowingly or recklessly to supply false or misleading information in any application for registration.[270] After an application has been accepted, the Registrar must ensure that the Data Protection principles continue to be observed, and to that end may serve an enforcement notice requiring certain action to be taken,[271] may serve and enforce a notice of de-registration,[272] and may serve a notice prohibiting the transfer of data outside the United Kingdom.[273] Dis-regard of any such notice is a criminal offence.

From this farrago of offences it can be seen that in certain circumstances an offence is committed by 'hacking' into such a system. If such an intruder is not registered under the Act and holds the proceeds of such intrusion, being personal information, on his own computer, and there 'processes' it in the defined manner,[274] he will be guilty of an offence of holding personal information without being registered.[275] If he is registered, then he will, almost certainly, be guilty of transgressing the terms of his registration.[276]

---

263. Subject to certain exemptions.
264. Sect. 5(1).
265. Sect. 1(3).
266. Sect. 1(7).
267. Sect. 1(8).
268. Sect. 7(2).
269. Sect. 5(5).
270. Sect. 6(6).
271. Sect. 10.
272. Sect. 11.
273. Sect. 12.
274. It is arguable that the use of the term 'extract' in the definition of processing renders it enough that the intruder merely use information displayed to him at a remote location, and that he need not store the information any more permanently than is required for such a purpose.
275. Contrary to sect. 5(5).
276. Which is also made an offence by sect. 5(5).

As noted above, there are innumerable minor statutory provisions prohibiting the disclosure of information of various types. So useful is the
computer for the storage and searching of information, and so commonplace
has its use become, that in almost all of these cases there is some possibility
of the offence coming within the range of this work. In the United Kingdom
the most notorious of these was section 2 of the Official Secrets Act 1911. It
is interesting that the first Official Secrets Act, that of 1889, was enacted
simply because a prosecution under the law of larceny had failed in respect
of a secret treaty which a civil servant had memorised so as to be able to
provide its contents to a newspaper. That section came in for widespread
criticism,[277] and has at last been replaced by the Official Secrets Act 1989
which nevertheless retains a number of offences relating to the disclosure of
secret information.[278] Many of these offences relate to the non-disclosure by
official employees of information acquired either compulsorily, or quasi-
compulsorily[279] in the course of their official duties. Thus officials of the
Inland Revenue are sworn to secrecy on taking office.[280] Similar obligations
apply both in the United Kingdom[281] and in the United States to keep
census information secret.[282] Such provisions are designed to reassure
members of the public, and to encourage compliance with the duty to
provide the information. Exactly the same motivation inspires rules regulating situations of quasi-compulsion.[283] Similar provisions apply to some
private citizens employed by organisations with a strong public service
element, even though not as such emanations of the state.[284] Sometimes in
the United Kingdom offences of this nature have been included as part of a
package of privatisation.[285] Sometimes specific reference is made to information acquired in the course of data-processing services.[286] It is particularly
interesting to note the special obligations of secrecy imposed upon those
charged with preserving the secrecy of others both in the United States[287]
and in the United Kingdom.[288] Juvenal has clearly been taken seriously.[289]

The question has arisen of how far the common law recognises a crime of
tricking someone into disclosing confidential information relating to another.
In *Withers* v. *D.P.P.*[290] the accused were indicted on two counts of conspiracy

---

277. See Franks Committee, *Departmental Report on Section 2 of the Official Secrets Act 1911*, Cmnd.
5104 (1972) ch. 3.
278. Cf. 18 U.S.C. sect. 1905 for a similar provision in the United States.
279. Where it is necessary to disclose the information in order to secure some vital benefit, such
as a social security payment.
280. Cp. 26 U.S.C. sect. 7213.
281. Census Act 1920 sect. 8(2).
282. 13 U.S.C. sect. 214.
283. See, for example in the United Kingdom, Financial Services Act 1986 sect. 179, and in the
United States 42 U.S.C. sect. 1306.
284. For example, officials of the Law Society in respect of information furnished in order to
secure legal aid, Legal Aid Act 1974 sect. 22.
285. See, for example, Telecommunications Act 1984 sect. 45(2)
286. See, for example, British Telecommunications Act 1981 sect. 60.
287. Privacy Act 1974 sect. 5(h), see 5 U.S.C. sect. 552a notes.
288. Data Protection Act 1984 sect. 17(2).
289. Satires vi. 147.
290. [1975] A.C. 842, H.L.

to effect a public mischief by tricking private citizens, such as bank managers, into revealing details of personal accounts and, secondly, of similarly tricking some national and local government officials into revealing details relating to such matters as criminal records. The House of Lords quashed convictions for such offences on the basis that conspiracy to effect a public mischief was not a crime known to the common law, and that conspiracies could be charged only by reference to established categories. Thus conduct such as that in *Withers* amounted to a conspiracy only if it would have amounted to a crime if conducted by an individual acting alone, or could be subsumed under one of the limited classes of case where conspiracy can lie in the absence of such a condition, such as an agreement to pervert the course of justice. In the case of official secrets, the Official Secrets Act 1989 is so sweeping that it is hard to see there could be any defence to conspiring to commit a breach of its provisions. The information secured from private individuals in *Withers* presents more of a problem. It clearly falls outside the Official Secrets Act 1989. The Court of Appeal canvassed the application of conspiracy to defraud. It is not a conclusive objection to such a charge that the victim suffers no economic loss.[291] The House of Lords was, however, divided in *Welham* on the question of whether such defrauding was limited to persons holding public positions, thus excluding bank managers. In the later case of *Scott* v. *Commissioner of Police for the Metropolis*,[292] the speeches in which were delivered on the same day as those in *Withers*, Lord Diplock made a very clear statement on this point:

Where the intended victim of a 'conspiracy to defraud' is a private individual the purpose of the conspirators must be to cause the victim economic loss by depriving him of some property or right, corporeal or incorporeal, to which he is or would or might become entitled.[293]

However, the statement was made *obiter*, and Viscount Dilhorne, with whom the remainder of the House agreed, did not advert to the point.

Failing the certainty of any such extension of conspiracy, the question becomes one of whether or not such conduct would be criminal if perpetrated by one individual acting alone. In *Withers*, Lord Simon was quite clear that:

On [the] state of the authorities, and on principle, I think that the better view is that English law knows no offence of conduct by an individual effecting or tending to effect a public mischief.[294]

The question still remains of whether it might amount to an offence of fraud, but this seems to be governed by the considerations mentioned above.[295] These considerations led the Law Commission to propose the creation of a special offence of inducing another by deception to give information.[296] This

---

291. *Welham* v. *D.P.P.* [1961] A.C. 103, H.L.
292. [1975] A.C. 819, H.L.
293. At p. 841.
294. At p. 867.
295. See above p. 280.
296. Law Commission Working Paper No. 56, *Conspiracy to Defraud* (1974) para. 77, though no such recommendation was included in the final report of the Law Commission, see *Law Com.* 76, 'Conspiracy and Criminal Law Reform' (1976) paras. 4.8–4.12.

could be accomplished either by some such general prohibition or limited by reference to the information being such as the person deceived was under a duty not to disclose. However, as any such offence would constitute only part of a far-reaching review of all offences involving fraud, its enactment cannot be regarded as imminent. It should be noted that the general consensus of opinion, and certainly the assumption of the Younger Committee on Privacy, is that English law, as yet, knows no concept of a 'right to privacy' which could provide the basis for a right orientated definition.

D. Reform

As noted above, there has been considerable pressure for legislative reform of this part of the law relating to computers. In many jurisdictions, especially in the United States, legislatures have succumbed and enacted special criminal statutes to deal with computers. The matter is, at the time of writing, under active review in the United Kingdom. A number of questions need to be addressed. What types of abuse are being perpetrated? To what extent? How far do they fall outside the range of existing criminal laws? How far would they fall outside the criminal law, if it were amended in ways currently under consideration? Should such conduct be made criminal? If so, should it be made criminal in a way different from surrounding areas of the law? Is legislation the most appropriate response? If so, what form should it take? Should it then be kept under review? If so, by what means and by whom?

It has already been seen that there is no reliable indication of the extent of crime relating to computers. It may, however, be accepted that the range of conduct is indicated by the Audit Commission's survey. Neither the Scottish[297] nor the English Law Commission[298] has, so far, been persuaded that the existing criminal law is unable to cope with the vast majority of different types of crime related to computers. Nevertheless both Commissions felt that there were some areas where reform was necessary. It may be useful to consider first the general principles governing any attempt to reform the area, and then the more specific proposals which are currently under consideration in the United Kingdom.

1. General principles

The Law Commission helpfully drew attention[299] to guidance offered by the Home Office to govern the creation of new criminal offences suggesting that such offences should be created only if it could be established that the behaviour in question was so serious as to go beyond that for which compensation by civil means was appropriate; that other less drastic means of control would be ineffective, impracticable or insufficient; and that any new offence should be enforceable.

---

297. Scottish Law Commission, *Report on Computer Crime*, SLC No. 106 (Cm. 174, 1987) paras. 3.15–3.20.
298. Law Commission Working Paper No. 110, *Computer Misuse* (1988) para. 4.1.
299. *Ibid.* para. 1.11.

If these conditions can be satisfied, there appear to be three main possibilities. The first is for the legislature to do nothing, but instead to rely upon the judiciary to interpret the existing rules in such a way as to embrace computer-related crimes. The second is for the legislature to assist the task of the judiciary by modifying the definitions and conditions for liability of existing offences, but without enacting new ones. The third is to enact new offences specifically aimed at computer-related crime. This third alternative should perhaps be further sub-divided between new offences which are intended to supplant existing offences in the computer-related area, and those which are intended to supplement them. Choice between these various alternatives must largely be determined by some perception of the particular uses or abuses of computers which fall outside the ambit of existing offences. Some general considerations are, however apposite here.

The principal argument for the first alternative is that it is in many ways the most flexible. Development can proceed by minute steps, and those steps can often be retraced if a new perspective shows them to have started out in the wrong direction. It is also likely to be the method most congenial to the judiciary, and so most likely to be accorded a sympathetic reception by them. It is much rarer to find determined opposition, and destructive interpretation, offered to a new common law development than to a new and unwelcome statute. It has the further advantage that the pace of development automatically reflects the incidence of the relevant situation. If no cases come to court for decision, the law stands still; but if many cases come, then some development, or at least crystallisation, is inevitable. This method is also least likely to foster anomalies, either between different applications of the same offence or between different offences.

The disadvantages are in some ways the converse of the advantages. Just because the law proceeds in a flexible, and reversible, manner, it may lose some of its deterrent effect. It can be argued that in order to influence conduct, potential actors must have some clear idea of when the law is likely to intervene, and that this will be denied if each new situation gives rise to a new decision. Such an argument can be overstated, however. Criminal law is concerned with morally reprehensible conduct, and the effect of uncertainty may be to restrain potential actors from doing anything remotely reprehensible in the area. Nevertheless there remains a constraint upon the judges in this respect. They will be reluctant to depart very far from established rules. In general it is not the province of the judges to create new criminal offences, and this general policy is embodied in rules requiring all doubts to be resolved in favour of the accused, a maxim just as applicable to the establishment of rules as to the finding of facts. These considerations have been given clear expression at the highest level of the judiciary in a number of different jurisdictions.[300] It may also be thought that the process of litigation is unlikely to lead to the development of the best-informed rules. Rules of relevance confine lawyers to the proof of facts clearly and closely

---

300. For example in the United Kingdom by the House of Lords in *R.* v. *Gold* [1988] 2 All E.R. 186, H.L. at 192; in the United States by the Supreme Court in *Dowling* v. *U.S.* 473 U.S. 207 (1985) at 228; and in Canada by the Supreme Court in *R.* v. *Stewart* 63 C.R. 3d 305 (S.C.C., 1988) at 317.

applicable to the particular facts before the court, and neither counsel nor judiciary may be thought sufficiently computerate[301] to be trusted to understand the subject sufficiently to develop the best rules. It may indeed be because such feelings are shared by the judiciary itself that it has exhibited such caution in its attitude towards the creation of new offences.[302]

The third alternative lies at the opposite extreme. New legislation can be moulded to fit the precise delineation of the perceived need. It can come replete with exact definitions and explicit exceptions. The range of procedures, forms of proof and level of penalty are all capable of being adapted to the special problems of the situation. It may also be argued that it is just as, if not more, flexible than common law development, since legislation can always be amended or, if necessary, repealed and replaced. However true this may be in theory, it is, given the pressure on parliamentary time, less than practically possible.

The principal disadvantages are those of creating anomalies and, by so doing, injustice. It is unlikely to be acceptable if criminality, or even sentence or procedure, depends upon whether or not a computer happens to have been involved, in say a scheme to defraud a bank. Just such objections as these beset legislation like the Data Protection Act 1984, or section 5 of the Civil Evidence Act 1968. Nor is it clear that legislators and draftsmen are so much more conversant with the technology of computing than counsel and judges, though they do have more opportunity to seek expert advice. Even so the encapsulation of a burgeoning technology within the strait-jacket of the ordinary language and comprehensible structure ideally characterising Acts of Parliament, constitutes a formidable task. It is made more formidable still by the hinterland of presumptions, policies and principles customarily bestowed upon the construction of Acts of Parliament establishing new criminal offences, especially if recourse to anything beyond the words themselves is artificially restricted. It is significant, as noted above, that in the United States, despite the wide wording of the new federal legislation specifically aimed at computers, it has seemed less able to cope with the problem of damage to computer systems than has judicial development of an existing general offence in the United Kingdom, and has spawned pressure for still more legislation.[303]

The middle course of tailoring definitions and conditions mitigates both advantages and disadvantages of the two extremes. It is likely to reduce anomalies when compared to the creation of wholly new offences, but it can often achieve this only at the expense of some distortion of the pattern of existing offences. The principal point of engagement in the legislative process is also perhaps the most hazardous in terms of drafting, namely in the casting of definitions. It is also extremely difficult, as noted by the Scottish

---

301. If such a neologism may be permitted, cf Audit Commission, *Computer Fraud Survey* (1985) para. 110.
302. Above p. 297.
303. Nor was specific legislation able to cover the ground sufficiently in Canada either in the area of interception of communications, see *R.* v. *McLaughlin* [1980] S.C.R. 331; or in the field of obtaining information held on a computer by deception, see *R.* v. *Stewart* 63 C.R. 3d 305 (S.C.C., 1988).

Law Commission,[304] to apply this approach in the area of common law offences.

2. Specific proposals

It can be seen from this account that in the abstract there is no clear choice to be made between these different approaches. All must depend upon the array of conduct which is sought to be suppressed, and the aptitude of application of such crimes as already exist. The two main areas under current consideration in the United Kingdom are an extension of the general criminal law in England so as to encompass quite unequivocally the deception of a machine, and a proposal to create a new offence of securing unauthorised access to a computer, both in Scotland and in England.

(a) Deception of a machine
The Law Commission has recommended an extension of the definition of deception so as to make it quite clear that it includes the deception of a machine.[305] Although it is certainly arguable that any case of the deception of a machine in fact involves the deception of those who operate by means of the machine there seems to be no good objection to making this more specific. Such legislation is already in place in more limited contexts within the United Kingdom,[306] and elsewhere.[307] The Law Commission proposed as a possible form of words, 'inducing a machine to respond to false representations which the person making them knows to be false, as if they were true'.[308]

This would affect the interpretation of a number of sections of the Theft Acts 1968 and 1978.[309] Almost all of the conduct covered by the Audit Commission's survey is capable of being subsumed under section 1 of the Theft Act 1978 which provides generally for obtaining services by deception. It is limited, however, to services of a commercial nature, by requiring an understanding that they should be paid for.[310] As the Law Commission remarks, it will be necessary to make some minor revision to the wording of this sub-section, to ensure that the argument that only human beings can be deceived is extirpated completely. It should be noted that this requirement of commercial provision may be very useful in the computer context by permitting the distinction between trivial and serious offences to be drawn by the victim. If a computer user feels that his facilities are seriously at risk, for example by being used without authorisation by his employees, all he need do is to require payment for any such use by anyone, even an employee.

---

304. Scottish Law Commission, *Report on Computer Crime*, SLC No. 106 (Cm. 174, 1987) para. 3.12
305. Law Commission Working Paper No. 110, *COmputer Misuse* (1988) paras 5.1–5.5.
306. See above p. 292 (forgery) and p. 284 (taxation provisions).
307. For example in the State of Victoria, see Victoria Crimes (Computers) Act 1988 sect. 6.
308. Para. 5.3.
309. Theft Act 1968 sects. 15, 16 and 20(2); Theft Act 978 sects. 1 and 2.
310. Theft Act 1978 sect. 1(2).

(b) Securing unauthorised access to a computer

As noted above,[311] the Scottish Law Commission has recommended the creation of such an offence. Although the English Law Commission has provisionally remained neutral, pressure continues to mount to legislate in this area. It has been exacerbated by recent incidents, widely reported in the media of communication.[312] It is to be hoped that the Law Commission will adhere to the sentiments expressed in its working paper,

to justify legislative action and particularly the creation of any new criminal offence, ... it is essential to be able to identify the nature and extent of any risks involved. For this purpose it is ... insufficient to rely simply on anecdotal evidence and generalisations. What is required is a clear statement of the kinds of damage which might be caused by hacking and of the nature of any risks posed to programs and data stored in the computer and of access being obtained to data which the owner of the installation is required by law to protect. We need to know the extent to which owners are able to guard against these risks by the use of up-to-date technology and security measures.[313]

It is submitted that the clarification of the definition of deception will have the effect of reducing the problem to one which does not require the attention of the criminal law. To the extent that non-commercial use of computers poses a threat to privacy, it should be governed by data protection law, and to the extent that it is concerned with non-commercial access to other private information, it would be unwise to legislate in the area of information held upon computers alone.

Although pressure to legislate upon the basis of alarm fostered by the media of communication is already strong, it is submitted that it can, and should, be resisted. Even in North America there is a persistent under-tow of reasoned argument against the current tide.[314] In Australasia, alarm bells have also been rung.[315] It is difficult to do more than agree with the summary of a Canadian commentator that:

Legislators must not permit themselves to be awestruck by new technology and over-legislate in response, either by creating new offences that duplicate elements of existing crimes or by unjustifiably extending the criminal law beyond the types of interests currently protected.[316]

---

311. At p. 293.
312. See, for example, *Computing* 3 November 1988 p. 18.
313. Para. 6.18.
314. See, for example in the United States, Taber, 'On Computer Crime (Senate Bill S240)', *1 Comp. L.J.* 517 (1980); Wagner, 'The Challenge of Computer-Crime Legislation: How Should New York Respond?', *33 Buff. L.R.* 777 (1984); MacFarlane and Freed quoted in Wharton, 'Legislative Issues in Computer Crime', *21 Harvard J. of Leg.* 239 (1984); and in Canada, Webber, 'Computer Crime or Jay Walking on the Electronic Highway' *26 Crim. L.Q.* 217 (1983).
315. In Australia by Brown, 'Crime and Computers', *7 Crim. L.J.* 68 (1983), and in New Zealand by Dunning 'Some Aspects of Theft of Computer Software', *4 Auckland U.L.R.* 273 (1982) and Quinn, 'Computer Crime' [1983] *N.Z.L.J.* 270.
316. Piragoff, 'Bill C-19: Reforming the Criminal Law II. Computers', *16 Ottawa L.R.* 306 (1984).

Chapter 8

Privacy

The security of information held in large computerised stores was the first legal problem involving computers to receive significant attention. Some of the first monographs,[1] government reports,[2] and even legislation, both specific[3] and more general,[4] were to be found in this area. The area has continued to receive very serious attention, and has spawned more literature than any other aspect of this subject.[5] It was also the first such area to have been popularised by the media of communication. There has been an even greater volume of popular books, newspaper and magazine articles, and television programmes, often of the most breathtaking superficiality and inaccuracy. Such a process of popularisation has created a conventional analysis and a set of conventional claims. They have both obscured and rigidified the real issues, since without some such real issues such clamour could not have been sustained for so long, nor so widely.

It is useful to consider this conventional wisdom in order to expose its shortcomings in diagnosis and prescription. Remedies should be specific, otherwise they are liable to be worse than the disease. And appropriate treatment can start only after the real symptoms and their causes have been clearly perceived, distinguished and classified. The first part of this chapter will accordingly consider some of the more general considerations. It will then go on to explain how prophylactic measures can prevent some of the worst excesses from arising. Only in the third section will the current range of remedies be considered in any detail.

---

1. Such as Miller, *The Assault on Privacy* (1971); Westin, *Data Banks in a Free Society* (1972); and Sieghart, *Privacy and Computers* (1977).
2. Such as *Report of the Committee on Privacy*, Cmnd. 5012 (1972) (U.K.); House Committee on Government Operations Hearings, 89th Congress *The Computer and Invasion of Privacy* (1966) (U.S.); Departments of Justice and Communications, *Privacy and Computers* (1972) (Canada).
3. Such as Fair Credit Reporting Act 1970 (U.S.); Consumer Credit Act 1974 (U.K.).
4. Such as Land of Hessen Data Protection Act 1970; Data Law (1973) (Sweden).
5. By 1979 it was possible for Flaherty to compile a bibliography running to some 200 pages and over 1750 entries, and still dealing no more than partially with literature relating only to government data, see Flaherty *Privacy and Access to Government Data for Research* (1979).

A. The conventional wisdom

1. Shallow analysis

Conventional analysis may be expressed in five propositions. The first of these maintains that intrusions upon personal privacy are greater now than they have ever been before, that they are increasing, and that the rate of increase is itself increasing. Second, it is held that at least part of the blame for such deterioration must be ascribed to the development of modern technology, and especially to the application of computers to data processing, which permits virtually instantaneous access to enormous quantities of information. It is contended, third, that much of this information is inaccurate, goes unchecked and, worst of all, is regarded by its users as to be so far above suspicion as to be accepted as irrefutable, ineradicable and irresistible evidence of whatever it asserts or suggests. Fourth, it is feared that this information is available to anyone who seeks it whether their access is authorised or unauthorised, open or clandestine, legal or illegal. Fifth, and finally, it is argued that what legal remedies there are have been left so far behind by the speed of technological change as to have become quite incapable of protecting the subject of the information.

Those who hold such a view of the situation tend to propose a number of possible remedies for it. These range from provisions of the most minute particularity to those of the broadest generality. They encompass such suggestions as restriction upon the use of computers to process personal information, and prohibition of the interchange of personal information between its users, so that information collected for one purpose can never be used for another. Then, so as to place the subject of the information in a position to exercise his rights, they propose that he should be provided with a print-out of all the information held about him within such systems. Finally, and most comprehensively of all, it is proposed that a general legal right of privacy should be bestowed upon the subject of the information.

It is submitted that this analysis, and these solutions, are either misleading or wrong in every detail.

The question of the current extent of intrusion into personal privacy, and comparison with the situation in the past, is bedevilled, like so much else in this area, by a total failure to define the notion of privacy. Commentators are internally inconsistent, and disagree with each other, about what is connoted by the concept. The coinage of argument has become debased. A particular set of abuses is condemned on the one side, and a particular set of remedies, responsive to a totally different set of abuses, commended on the other. It is clear that the widest definitions of privacy, such as the right to be let alone,[6] are incompatible with the very idea of a society. This remains true even if the definition is restricted to the area of personal information. Human beings are both sociable and sensible. No one except an anchorite can prevent the flow of information about himself reaching the perception of others. It is not,

---

6. Cooley, *Torts* (2nd edn 1888).

however, clear that such diffusion is, in a modern urban environment, either significantly greater or more distasteful than it was in the rural village years ago. There is perhaps a greater chance of more information getting into the hands of strangers, but each one of them is likely to have little, and care less about it, than in the older situation. The kernel of truth in this proposition of the conventional wisdom is that social life is now more extensive than it used to be. More people live in conurbations, they move about further and more rapidly, they can communicate with each other at greater distances, their lives are more active, and they are governed more. The result is that human contacts are more numerous, and such contacts inevitably lead to the exchange of some personal information. However, it is not obvious that this can be equated with a decline in personal privacy. Human life lasts a finite time, if contact is made with more people during its continuance, contact with any one is more fleeting. It is indeed said that loneliness and a sense of isolation are greater among city dwellers, and the denizens of tower blocks, than among those who live in villages and cottages. People frequently complain that they are treated too impersonally, and that they have become no more than numbers. This complaint is that the system has too little personal information, not too much. Increased contact has been matched by increased anonymity; relations have become more extensive, but less intensive.

What then of the computer? Does it threaten the preservation of personal privacy? It is certainly true that modern computer systems can store more personal information in a more limited space, and can collate it more quickly and more cheaply, than was ever possible in older conventional systems, and that the aim of such systems is to make that information more readily accessible. Here again it is not obvious that this necessarily implies any reduction in personal privacy. An obvious feature of such systems is that the information which they contain must be held in a greatly compressed form, itself inaccessible to the naked eye. This reduces both the inclination and the opportunity for casual eavesdropping. Those who handle the store will know personally a much smaller percentage of the individuals to whom the information it contains relates, and will have to go to much greater trouble to secure access to the information. The change is like the replacement of a village telephone system in which all calls had to be dialled personally by the postmistress by one in which the calls are dialled directly by subscribers but pass through one large automatic exchange. Such aggregation increases rather than diminishes personal privacy.

It may still be argued that modern facilities for the collection of information stimulate the activity unnecessarily, and that the result is the accumulation of more personal information than is either necessary for any reasonable purpose, or completely safe. This argument is probably more applicable to public than to private organisations since in the latter the financial consequences of over-collection are likely to make a more immediate impact. It must further be admitted that the ever-decreasing costs and ever-increasing capabilities of physical storage tend to dilute the economic argument, and may even in some cases make it cheaper to hold information than to prune it, at least selectively. Any such arguments are, however, far removed from the simplisticity of the second proposition of the conventional wisdom as originally formulated, and suggest a correspondingly different response.

The third proposition relates to the quality of the information held in computer systems. It is argued that such information is much more likely to be inaccurate than information held in conventional systems and that, conversely and perversely, it is more likely to be accepted as being accurate. A distinction must first be made between input and output data, that is, before and after processing by the computer. So far as input is concerned, there are two stages, that before and after transcription into a computer-readable format. Before transcription there is no reason why collection of data for eventual input to a computer system should be any more likely to be inaccurate than collection of data for input to a conventional system. It is true that errors may be introduced during transcription as a new stage is added at that point, though these will be minimised in systems employing optical character recognition, check digits and other automatic verification techniques which can now virtually eliminate unconscious copying errors. Indeed, in systems where the original collection is directly keyboarded into the computer, for example in airline ticket reservation systems, the benefits of automation will accrue undiminished by further opportunities for error. There will nevertheless remain a small residue of undetected errors. These will, however, be more than compensated for by the vastly greater reliability of electronic processing which will ensure that the incidence of error in the final output data will be significantly lower in a computer-based system than in a conventional one. Despite the hoary popular accounts of astronomically large gas bills, this sort of improvement has frequently been demonstrated,[7] and is now widely accepted. Use of the computer also permits much more thorough cross-checking of data during processing. For example, a police computer in the United States which automatically checks the birth date of the accused against the date of the offence was able to reject a file apparently showing a serious crime to have been committed by someone born only two days earlier. These facilities are nowadays much enhanced by the greater use of artificial intelligence techniques, such as those used to vet share flotations for multiple applications. It is sometimes difficult to compare the performance of the computer and that of conventional systems, just because errors in the conventional system so often go undetected, whereas in a computer system the error is more likely to be obvious. One indication of the relative incidence of error is the state of manual files which is disclosed for the first time when they are prepared for entry into a newly installed computer system. A questionnaire addressed to data processing organisations in Canada revealed that no fewer than 301 out of 406 definite respondents had found errors in their manual systems at that stage, and that only 25 out of 480 definite respondents had experienced new significant problems in maintaining the accuracy of records within the computer system, and that was long before the advent of more efficient modern computer systems.[8]

---

7. See, e.g., Lord Gardiner L.C., *Hansard* H.L. (1969) Vol. 306 col. 166 reporting a controlled experiment by the General Post Office which showed that where the same data was handled by a computer and by conventional means, errors were greater by a factor of ten in the latter.
8. See Report of Departments of Justice and Communications *Privacy and Computers* (1972) App. p. 213 qu. 19A. Westin, *Data Banks in a Free Society* (1972) App. A pp. 434–6, Tables A-10, A-11 and A-12, gives similar results for a survey conducted in the United States.

It should be noted that an ostensible complaint about the inaccuracy of data often turns out instead to be a complaint about its incompleteness or that they contain a contested judgment or expression of opinion, or that they are inappropriate for their designated purpose. It is, in fact, much easier to ensure that data in a computer system are complete than it is in manual systems because automatic checks and warnings can be incorporated, and the system can be prevented from proceeding until the data are complete. There is then the further complaint that records produced by computerised systems are more likely to be accepted uncritically. This is manifested both by those who act upon the basis of the information put out by the systems and, if different, by those who operate the systems, and are legendarily reluctant to alter any information contained in them.[9] There is no reason at all why such attitudes should be adopted. Up-dating techniques are well-developed and inexpensive to operate, partly because one of the earliest uses of computers was in the area of stock control, where constant up-dating was necessary.[10]

The fourth proposition is that this concentration of personal information endangers privacy because it makes access to the information so much easier. But it is not access by those who are authorised to use the information which is usually in question. It is unauthorised, or illegal, access which causes most concern. This may be dissected into three elements, fear of unauthorised use by those to whom the information has been entrusted for some other purpose, for example medical information divulged by a husband to a hospital for the purpose of seeking treatment might be passed on to his wife's legal advisers for the purposes of instituting divorce proceedings. Even more potent is the threat of a generalised form of this, namely the compilation of a large personal dossier bringing together into one large file information from every different source which relates to a given individual. The second type of fear is that personal information may be passed on to third parties, for example where a service bureau mixes up the files of different customers, or where statistical information is released in a form from which personal information relating to individuals may be deduced. The third type of fear is that outsiders may break down the security of the computer system, either by suborning employees or, more extravagantly, by intrusion, physical or electronic. The degree of danger differs in each case, as does the remedy which is appropriate. As a general proposition it is not obvious that computerised systems are more susceptible to such misuse than are manual systems. Intrusion is indeed less likely to occur in such a system, though it might be more serious when it does, partly because of the ease of copying information held in an electronic form. Those who are unfamiliar with the operation of information retrieval systems are apt to underestimate the difficulty of extracting relevant information. It is often hard enough even when all the conditions are favourable such as complete control over and knowledge of the input routines, file structures, coding, programming and

---

9. See *Blue Cross and Blue Shield of Alabama* v. *Granger* 461 So.2d 1320 (Ala., 1984) for an indication in the jury's verdict of its resentment at such attitudes, above p. 260.
10. It is just possible that a temporary problem may be consequential upon the use of optical storage for archival information. At present such storage is not easy or cheap to up-date, but the technology is expected to improve in this respect very soon.

procedure, and where there is unlimited time and ready access to help facilities. When any of these are absent, the task is formidable. When all are absent it is virtually insuperable. As will be seen later, the development of security techniques, such as access checks and encryption of data both during storage and in communication, have added still further depth to the protection available for data in computer systems.

The final element in the conventional analysis is that there exist at present no legal remedies to protect an individual whose privacy is so threatened. It is often pointed out that the law is slow to change, and quite inadequate in an area where technical change is so rapid. To some extent such a criticism misconceives the nature of legal rules. It assumes that each new advance in computer technology requires a correspondingly specific new legal response, which must wait upon the slow shuffle of the process of creating new legal rules. If all legal rules were stated in terms of minute technical particularity, and if they could be changed only by repeal and re-enactment by the legislature, this might be true. But that is not the case. Legal rules tend to be general in form, and are constantly and instantaneously applied by judges to new situations. Where there are no rules capable of direct application, then the judges are quite prepared to extend them, or even to create new ones by analogy with the old. Similarly, the judges need not wait upon statutes to repeal obsolete rules; they can often do it for themselves.[11] The real problem is not that legal rules are totally deficient, but that they are under strain as a result of somewhat lop-sided development.

In this, as in almost all of the points raised above, the main fault lies in exaggeration and over-simplification. There are dangers in the present system, and there are abuses for which there are no adequate remedies, but they are more diffuse and more subtle than the conventional wisdom allows.

B. Fashionable solutions

Similar faults also impair the suggested remedies, perhaps to a still greater degree. It is clearly true that the infringement of personal privacy by computer systems will decline to the extent that such systems are prohibited from storing such information. But this will be of doubtful benefit if the relevant activity becomes either impossible or uneconomic as a result, or if personal privacy is instead impaired by leakage from substituted manual systems. The trouble here is not with the suggested remedy itself, but with the failure to appreciate that it should be applied selectively, and consequently with the failure to indicate the criteria upon which the basis of such selection should be made. No doubt there are some forms of handling personal data which should not be entrusted to a computer, though it will be rare in most such cases for manual systems to be preferable. Other forms should be permitted subject only to the fulfilment of certain conditions, such as the provision of guaranties of the security of the data handled by the system. These conditions will clearly vary from application to application.

---

11. The Supreme Court of the United States has always had the power to overrule its own previous decisions, and in the United Kingdom the House of Lords has had it since 1966, see Note [1966] 3 All E.R. 77.

The drawback of argument in terms of a general prohibition is that it diverts attention from the crucial issue of the content of such conditions.

The second suggested remedy, which is the prohibition of the interchange of information between different users, suffers from similar defects. Its justification is that one of the standard responses to pleas for the prohibition of the use of computer systems is that the subject has voluntarily chosen to provide the information. The concept of voluntariness is certainly disputable in this context, but even if it is conceded so far as uses of which the supplier is aware are concerned, it can clearly not be raised in respect of those uses of which he is unaware. But it is not necessarily the case that such unauthorised use would be unwelcome to the subject. For example, the information might be extremely embarrassing to its subject, but still relevant to a number of different purposes, all of which he would regard as beneficial to him. He might well prefer that the relevant information be passed on automatically rather than that each body should send round its own representative, to each one of whom the same embarrassing details must be repeated. Then there is the question of the accuracy of personal information. The subject might well be affected adversely by the use of inaccurate information which could be revealed and corrected by comparison with information held by another user. It might also be useful to the community at large if information of certain sorts were more freely transferred. In the United Kingdom there have been a number of examples of this. In one a doctor, undergoing treatment for mental illness, was appointed to a position in a hospital which was kept in ignorance of the fact, and in which he murdered a number of newborn babies. In another a man was discharged from Broadmoor, a hospital for mentally deranged criminals, and was given a job in which he took advantage of the opportunity to poison a number of his fellow employees. A third example is of a man released from a hospital to which he had been committed for ill-treating young children who was thereafter registered by a local authority as a suitable foster parent, and went on to kill a child entrusted to his care. Here too solutions must vary with different situations, and criteria and procedures developed to regulate rather than to prohibit the exchange of information between users, and to specify appropriate conditions.

A third commonly recommended panacea is that the subject of the information should be informed of all of the data held about him in computerised files. It is frequently suggested that he should be supplied with a print-out of the relevant part of his file. With fine disregard for the basic elements of grammar, this has been called a right of *habeas scriptus*. The right is rarely specified in much more detail. It is usually left unclear how often the subject is to be informed, who is to pay, or what the procedure for challenge is to be. A moment's thought reveals that the analogy with *habeas corpus* breaks down at every point. We have only one body, we, and our close friends and associates, know where it is, and it is extremely difficult for anyone to restrain it without authority and against our will without creating a tremendous commotion. In such conditions it is not unreasonable to provide a drastic and dramatic remedy deploying the full dignity of the highest echelons of the legal order. None of these conditions applies to the case of personal information. Any number of bits and pieces exist, we, and our family and friends, have no idea how many there are nor where they are, and they are consequently very easy to conceal. No clear criteria exist to determine which of them are in the public domain, and which of them it is permissible for others to have and to hold. It is sometimes suggested that the subject should be told of every transaction in relation to which some reference is made to some information relevant to him. It would clearly be impossible to enforce any such suggestion, and this is just as well since its implementation would bring the postal service to a standstill, and bankrupt the users of such information.[12] Even the more limited suggestion that the subject be informed of all possible uses of information held about them, for example in relation to mailing lists, has been said to be prohibitively expensive.[13] In common with a number of the other remedies often suggested, this one is also extremely dangerous and likely to cause more mischief than it would prevent. It premises that personal information should be held within a computer system in such a way that it can speedily be related to any given individual and supplied to him. Such file organisation also makes it easier for an intruder, or insufficiently authorised a user, to gain access to such information. Further, since a regular procedure must be created to supply this information, the danger of its being misdirected or intercepted en route to its intended recipient, of the impersonation of the intended subject, or of pressure being brought to bear on a subject to secure a print-out for the use of a third party are either created or increased.[14]

Perhaps the most vague and most pervasive of the suggested remedies is that the individual should be invested with a legal right to privacy. Such a right already exists to a greater or lesser extent in France, West Germany and the United States. Even in the United Kingdom it is arguable that adhesion to the Universal Declaration of Human Rights, to the United Nations Covenant on Civil and Political Rights, and to the European Convention for the Protection of Human Rights and Fundamental Freedoms, all of which recognise a general right of privacy, gives such a right, especially now that actions have been brought to enforce such rights in the European Court of Human Rights. Such an argument was, however, rejected in *Malone* v. *Commissioner of Police of the Metropolis (No.2)*[15] whether operating either directly as supra-national law, or indirectly by affecting the content, or even interpretation, of the law of the United Kingdom. The Younger Committee went further, and not only took the view that no such right existed, but that it should not be created either.[16] There is a number of difficulties about any such proposal. First it requires clarification to determine what remedies are

---

12. The Younger Committee on Privacy (Cmnd. 5012) 1972 para. 615 pointed out that the cost of one mailing shot each year to each of the individuals on the records of the largest credit bureau in the United Kingdom would exceed annual turnover by 25 per cent.
13. By the British Direct Marketing Association, see *Computing* 22 September 1988 p. 1.
14. The existence of such pressure has been documented in relation to files held by the Social Security Administration in the United States in Westin, *Data Banks in a Free Society* (1972) p. 40; and in the United Kingdom in relation to police records by prospective employers, see Fourth Report of the Data Protection Registrar (1988).
15. [1979] Ch. 344, Ch. at 373.
16. Cmnd. 5012 (1972) Ch. 23. Two members dissented on this point.

implied. In many states where such a general right is recognised to exist it is incorporated as part of the constitution and can be relied upon as such to stigmatise any repugnant legislation. This could clearly not be applied to a state like the United Kingdom with a strong tradition of parliamentary sovereignty. There remains a number of alternatives ranging from the treatment of the invasion of privacy as a crime to mere entitlement to personal privacy wherever there is no rule authorising infringement. It is relatively rare for it to be suggested that invasion of privacy should amount to a crime, though a crime of disclosing information does exist in certain circumstances,[17] and in others unauthorised interception of communications is an offence.[18] Such abstention is mildly surprising, since in the United Kingdom at least this would, provided that the offences were sufficiently serious, ensure that the determination of guilt would lie with a jury, and so insulate the judges from political implication in the establishment of the limits of what would inevitably be a vaguely defined offence. It is perhaps this which accounts for the rarity of the suggestion. Crimes should be defined precisely, and their definitions construed strictly in favour of the accused. It is not clear that this would be acceptable to the protagonists of a right to privacy. It is more common for them to recommend that invasion of privacy should become a tort actionable at the hands of the subject, either by way of injunction to prevent an apprehended infringement, or by the recovery of damages after such an infringement has occurred. One snag here is that in most places legal action is public, and there is something very odd about the idea of vindicating one's right to personal privacy in the bright glare of a public trial.[19] It is also arguable that privacy is far too weak and indefinite a concept to sire a justiciable issue.[20] There is no firm foundation upon which the edifice of a new tort can be raised. As Megarry V.C. explained in *Malone v. Commissioner of Police of the Metropolis (No.2)*[21] in this context,

One of the factors that must be relevant in such a case is the degree of particularity in the right that is claimed. The wider and more indefinite the right claimed, the greater the undesirability of holding that such a right exists. Wide and indefinite rights, while conferring an advantage on those who have them, may well gravely impair the position of those who are subject to the rights. To create a right for one person you have to create a duty on another. In the present case, the alleged right to hold a telephone conversation in the privacy of one's own home without molestation is wide and indefinite in its scope, and in any case does not seem to be very apt for covering the plaintiff's grievance. He was not 'molested' in holding his telephone conversations; he held them without 'molestation', but without their retaining the privacy he desired.

The common law is good at articulating the policies inherent in previous

---

17. See above p. 310.
18. Interception of Communications Act 1985 sect. 1.
19. Although a court may hold a hearing in camera just so as to prevent any such danger to the personal privacy of the litigant which the case is designed to restrain, see *X* v. *Y* [1988] 2 All E.R. 648, Q.B.
20. The strength and viability of any concept of privacy has been fiercely debated, see for example, Wacks, 'The Poverty of Privacy' *96 L.Q.R.* 73 (1980); Gavison, 'Privacy and the Limits of Law' *89 Yale L.J.* 421 (1980).
21. [1979] Ch. 344, Ch.

decisions and at extending them by analogy; it is less able to innovate and to prescribe completely new policies. It is especially inappropriate where, as here, fundamental policies are opposed and public sentiment divided.[22] The most compelling argument, however, is that privacy is far too fragmented a notion for it to be possible for any one common approach to cope with every part of it. Justice requires not only that like cases be treated alike, but also that different cases be treated differently.

This is very clear at the particular technical level, for example in considering possible defences. Consent to the use of personal information must often constitute a defence in relation to uses consented to, but need not in respect of other uses. It may be noted that the concept of consent is itself exceedingly obscure since it is often given only in the most formal sense, for example where information is provided in order to secure a credit or a tax rebate. The situation is further muddied by the concept of implied consent. It is also necessary to distinguish between consent to give information, consent to use information, and consent to publish information. All of these must themselves be distinguished from mere waiver of suit. Privilege, absolute or qualified, may in some, but not in all, cases be appropriate, as may a defence of public interest. The more each limb of privacy is examined, the clearer it becomes that it must be clothed in its own bespoke legal rules.

A final difficulty in the path of a general tortious remedy lies in the assessment of damages. In many cases the damage will reside in the injured sensibility of the plaintiff rather than in any quantifiable financial loss. This inevitably leads to wide discrepancy between different awards and to great difficulty in fixing any regular tariff. There may also be some demand for an exemplary element in the damages, an element so rebarbative to United Kingdom lawyers that it has had to be restricted most severely.[23] This particular problem would be likely to lead to a demand for jury assessment with the proliferation and prolongation of litigation bred by the increased dimension of uncertainty which that entails. It would also be likely to lead to problems in relation to the provision of legal aid in exactly the same way as defamation where there is similar emphasis on sentimental damage, and the danger of 'gold-digging' actions.

3. False assumptions

It is suggested that this conventional wisdom is so flawed that it should be abandoned. Its implicit assumptions are both extreme and self-contradictory. The assumption of the first and second analytical points is that the use of the computer has somehow converted good uses of personal information into evil uses of personal information. This is an extremely dangerous assumption. It diverts attention from the truth that the computer, being a piece of inanimate machinery, is itself a morally neutral agent. If its introduction does lead to evil results, the fault is not in the computer but in its operators. The correct response is not a blanket prohibition on the use or exchange of

---

22. Against the desire for privacy should be weighed the desirability of freedom of access to information, and the desirability of the freedom to communicate such information to others.
23. *Rookes* v. *Barnard* [1964] A.C. 1129,H.L.

personal information, but to look at each different computer application separately to determine how far the opportunities for human wrongdoing might be reduced.

A somewhat similar fallacy underlies the third and fourth points of the conventional wisdom. On the one hand are fears of the fallibility of computer systems, the million pound gas bill syndrome, while on the other there is an assumption that anyone can get any information he wants from a computer system. Here too the machine is too often made the innocent scapegoat for guilty human beings. It is very easy for those who have bungled the installation of a computer system to tell their customers or clients that the introduction of a computer has caused the unexpected difficulties, probably in the hope that ill-informed laymen will assume that some sort of mechanical error has occurred. It is time to recognise that immorality and incompetence are human vices and not mechanical failings. They are merely magnified, and more readily revealed, by the enormous power of the modern computer.

The conventional wisdom conceals another pair of contradictory assumptions. It assumes that the security of every computer system can be broken no matter how much effort has been devoted to the provision of safeguards. The experience of Project MAC at the Massachusetts Institute of Technology appears to bear out this assumption. But it is implicit in many of the remedies suggested that an aim of reform should be to make computer systems safe against any intrusion. If the first assumption is correct, such efforts are doomed to certain failure. This objection may be met by recasting the demand into one that the system be made as secure as possible. But the root of the problem, which is the formulation in absolute terms, has still not been eradicated. Can the security of the system be broken in *any* way? Have *all* possible measures been taken to guard against it? This way of thinking stems from another common assumption, that the value of the information in the hands of an intruder corresponds to the degree of injury felt by the victim as a consequence of the intrusion. In other words, the *sensitivity* of the information is equated with its worth. This may, in some cases, be true, but it is not necessarily true. In this, as in a number of other respects, resources in data banks differ from resources in money banks.[24] It is suggested that the problem is not the insoluble one of satisfying simultaneously two absolutely inconsistent demands, but rather one of adjusting and balancing against each other a set of continuous variables. An economic approach may enable this to be accomplished. A hypothetical situation will be considered in which a given service is offered to the public, the efficiency of which depends upon the accretion of sensitive personal information. It is further assumed that this information is valuable to competitors. Thus dealer A sells a service to X[25] at a given price which requires the provision of sensitive information by X about himself, and dealer B will also benefit from having that information about X. The positions of A and B will be considered. A's course of action will be determined by the elasticity of X's demand for the service in terms of

---

24. See Tapper, *Computers and the Law* (1973) pp. 47–8.
25. For the purposes of the example, X is treated as being singular, but can equally validly be considered to be the public at large.

its price and the security of the information which X divulges. The price of the service will be affected by the cost of providing security for the information. B's actions will be determined by the value to him of the personal information about X, and the cost of breaking the security of X's system to secure it. Thus A's security ceiling will be the level at which the cost of providing security increases the cost of the service to the point at which X ceases to subscribe to it. A's security floor will be that level at which X's demand for the service ceases because of the low security provided for the information which he supplies. Between these two levels, and in a situation in which B is the only competitor, A's best strategy is to spend just enough on security to ensure that the marginal cost to B of breaking the security of the system will exceed his marginal return from the use of the information relating to X.

This analysis is designed to be suggestive rather than definitive. It is designed to show that the protection of personal information is a matter of degree rather than an absolute, and that its provision will, in a commercial environment, depend upon the cost of providing it, and of breaking it.[26] It also shows that while the sensitivity of the information is a factor to be taken into account, it can be catered for in terms of the economic consequences of such sensitivity. This has the advantage of avoiding the necessity of making any arbitrary assessment, and leaves its determination to the subject in terms of his economic responses. It may, of course, be the case that in some situations economic factors should not be allowed to be decisive for social reasons, and that some especially sensitive items of personal information should not be disclosed whatever the economic behaviour of the subject. It may also be true that in circumstances where there is no direct economic benefit to the subject, for example where information is held by public bodies, it will be much harder to apply any such analysis. But in principle it should not be impossible, on the assumption that there is a social value to the community at large, in the public body having and holding that information.

The analysis is also intended to focus attention on the too often ignored factor that subjects do not divulge personal information, nor bodies seek it, simply for its own sake. The world of commerce and government is not just the world of private individuals writ large. The aim in these areas is to secure advantage of some sort, not the satisfaction of curiosity. It is pointless to prescribe a security system so expensive to implement as to frustrate the advantages which generate the whole activity. A somewhat similar argument may be made in relation to the accuracy of personal information, except that in that case there is little advantage to anyone in having inaccurate information. The interests of subject and user coincide. Both require the information to be accurate, and the system will incorporate accuracy checks at the highest levels which demand for the service will sustain.

One of the basic assumptions underlying the whole debate about privacy and the security of personal information is that invasion of privacy is a serious and widespread problem worthy of such debate, and that one of its

---

26. For further analysis see Goldstein, *The Cost of Privacy* (1975); Posner, 'The Right of Privacy', *12 Ga. L.R.* 393 (1978) and 'Privacy, Security and Reputation', *28 Buff. L.R.* 1 (1979).

aims is to secure the adoption of precautions which will reduce the incidence of such invasions. It is true that unless there were some sort of problem there would be no sustainable debate. What is more questionable is whether the problem is really one of the invasion of privacy. The media of communication are certainly full of, sometimes somewhat hysterical, foreboding. We are told, often wrongly, of the capacity of computers to correlate all sorts of personal information. We are warned, often unnecessarily, of the dangers of manipulation, oppression and extortion by tyrannical authorities or unscrupulous individuals. The interesting feature is that it is always foreboding, capacity and danger. There is a conspicuous, and widespread, failure to adduce evidence of actual examples of real abuse. Indeed, such empirical evidence as exists suggests that invasion of personal privacy in this way is extremely rare. Thus the Younger Committee in the United Kingdom found that no one in their entire sample had experienced a single invasion of personal privacy in respect of a computer or databank within the previous year, and this denial was maintained even after prompting.[27] This constituted the smallest incidence of invasion of privacy of all of the types surveyed. But it should not be deduced from this evidence that there is no problem at all, since the Committee also found that the strongest public reaction to a hypothetical invasion of privacy, and the greatest demand for prohibitive legislation, were also both felt in respect of personal information held in a central computer, and made freely available for inspection.[28] As the Committee itself recognised,[29] the value of such a response is diminished by the extreme and unrealistic nature of the hypothesis. Such a view is supported by a study conducted at Harvard University where it was found that all of those questioned withdrew their hostility to the idea of a national databank when they were allowed to prescribe conditions relating to its use and accessibility.[30] This rather vague fear also finds expression in the number of complaints made about invasion of privacy. As one might expect, the level of actual complaints lies between the high figure for concern about privacy in relation to computerised records and the low figure for experience of invasion. In the Canadian survey only four out of 998 definite respondents admitted that they had received frequent complaints about disclosure of personal information to outsiders, and only five out of 1067 about the methods used to collect the information.[31] On the other hand, occasional complaints were admitted by 121 definite respondents in the former respect and 159 in the latter.[32] Perhaps the best evidence, however, is to be culled from the incidence of requests for access to information by subjects after the institution of such rights. In the United Kingdom the Data Protection Act 1984 was passed to provide for such access, but the number of requests for

---

27. Cmnd. 5012 (1972) App. E Table F, see also para. 580; cp. in the United States, Westin, *Databanks in a Free Society* (1972) p. 477 App. B Table B-2.
28. Cmnd. 5012 (1972) App. E Table H.
29. *Ibid.* para. 576.
30. Westin, *Data Banks in a Free Society* (1972) App. B p. 471.
31. Departments of Justice and Communications, *Privacy and Computers* (1972) (Canada) qus. IIE, 13B; for similar figures in the United States, see Westin, *Data Banks in a Free Society* (1972) App. A Tables A-20, A-21 and A-22, pp. 449–51.
32. These proportions are also supported by Westin's statistics.

access has been remarkably low,[33] except for special areas where requests have come from employees.[34] Nor can this be blamed on high fees alone.[35]

It seems to follow from this analysis that greater emphasis should be placed upon the reassurance of the public than upon the prevention of abuse. These are not, of course, incompatible aims, and the greater the actual security of personal information, the less credible will be stories of its invasion. But it is important to recognise that there is a problem of trust and of communication. It must also be remarked that the exaggerated and hysterical approach of some commentators has done immense harm. By whipping up fear and suspicion of the computer they have themselves helped to create the evil which they have blamed upon the machine. This has further provoked a defensive reaction on the part of those who operate such systems which itself makes the collection of reliable information about, and control of, such activities very much more difficult.

Finally, the analysis and proposed remedies oscillate between two totally opposed ideas, that on the one hand there is a comprehensive and simple remedy for these difficulties if only people could agree to adopt it, and that on the other infractions are inevitable, that nothing can be done, and that George Orwell was right. The problems are too diffuse, too ill-defined and too various to admit of one simple solution. But for the very same reason it is far too defeatist to assume that because there are some problems which cannot be solved no problems can be solved. The clue to a successful approach lies, as it usually does, in drawing distinctions and in adopting a flexible approach which treats each different problem in the light of its own special difficulties and complexities. As perhaps the leading worker in this field has said, 'Efficient protection thus begins when the quest for abstract, generally applicable provisions is abandoned'.[36]

It will be here possible only to indicate the outline of possible solutions to some of the different problems comprehended within the generic question of the invasion of personal privacy by the computer. These solutions will be roughly divided into those which are essentially positive in that they reduce the chance of invasion of personal privacy and create a greater sense of confidence in the individual, and those which are remedial in that they offer a course of action to mitigate or compensate for the harm caused by an invasion once it has occurred. Each has been greatly facilitated by recent legislation, both in the United Kingdom[37] and in the United States.[38]

---

33. The Department of Health and Social Security expected 200 000 requests in the first six months of the operation of the access provisions, but received only 270; the Home Office expected up to 50 000 but received only 16, see *Computer Weekly* 17 March 1988 p. 4.
34. In the Attorney-General's Department, 699 out of 700 requests came from employees.
35. The Department of Health and Social Security charges no fee.
36. Professor Simitis, Data Commissioner of the Land of Hessen and architect of the pioneering West German approach, in 'Privacy and an Information Society' *135 U. Pa. L.R.* 707 (1987) at 742.
37. Principally by the Data Protection Act 1984.
38. At the federal level, principally by the Privacy Act 1974 (5 U.S.C. sect. 552a), and in regard to remedial measures by the Computer Security Act 1987 (amending 15 U.S.C. sect. 271).

B. Preventive measures

It is acknowledged on all sides that there is scope for improvement in the handling of personal information so as to preserve and enhance personal privacy. To that end a number of different approaches have been considered. Some of these are of general application, while others are more specifically linked to particular types of information or methods of handling it. The earliest legislation tended to concentrate on particular types of information, for example the legislation already mentioned[39] dealing with information about credit. Perhaps in an attempt to limit, or to redefine, the conceptual reach of reform of this area, it is interesting that the terminology of the subject so far as computers are concerned has, in the United Kingdom, shifted from 'privacy' to 'data protection'.[40] As noted above, the technical features of computers are double-edged. To the extent that they permit easier access to information, at a secondary level they also permit easier access to information about access to information. They also have facilities which can be utilised to safeguard, check and enhance information automatically. In addition, it is quite clear that the adoption of certain principles relating to the design and operation of computer systems containing personal information can improve their performance so far as the preservation of privacy is concerned. In Europe the tendency has been to impose the adoption of better practices by systems of indirect control through licensing and registration. In the United States the Privacy Act 1974 tended to require rather more detailed Codes of Practice, and this approach was also recommended in the United Kingdom.[41] However, it was not adopted, and the Data Protection Act 1984 adopts a straightforward registration approach. Too much should not, however, be made of such differences. In all jurisdictions the basic aim has been to encourage the adoption of better practices, and in those that have opted for broad principles there has been a secondary effort spelling out their implications in particular areas, while in those with detailed codes of practice there has often been an elaboration of overall principles in recitals, and in constitutional provisions.

This section will consider, first, technical security measures and, second, principles of system design and operation.

1. Technical measures

It is perhaps a misnomer to describe much of what will follow as 'technical measures'. Most are no more than the application of the most elementary canons of common sense. Such measures will be considered in relation to the collection of data, storage of data, operation of computer systems, control of access to data, and destruction of data.

---

39. Above p. 317.
40. The Younger Committee (Cmnd. 5012) reported in 1972 on Privacy, but the Lindop Committee (Cmnd. 7341) reported in 1978 on Data Protection; the first bill to be presented to Parliament was the Right of Privacy Bill 1961, but the legislation eventually enacted was the Data Protection Act 1984.
41. By the Lindop Committee on Data Protection, Cmnd. 7341 (1978) para. 19.62, though combined with registration.

At the point of collection the greatest physical danger is probably that of inaccuracy of transcription. In many cases the computer can be enlisted to improve accuracy at this stage. One simple method is to build into the data collection process an element of cross-checking so that discrepancies are readily revealed. Simple typographical mistakes can virtually be eliminated by the use of check digits. The incidence of error is diminished to the extent that the entry of data can be carried out automatically without the need for physical transcription. This has been greatly facilitated by the use of direct entry devices, either by scanning written documents or by the use of portable data entry devices. One method of eliminating embarrassing repetition of requests for information is to make increased use of the generation of records for multiple applications from a single interview. There are, however, serious dangers of the use of such methods itself constituting an invasion of privacy to the extent that the subject of the information is not apprised of the complete range of applications for which the data might be used. This danger has been addressed by some modern legislation on the design of systems and will be considered in more detail below. To the extent that automated methods cannot be employed, then it is an elementary precaution to give any human employees engaged in the garnering of personal information the clearest guidelines for working practices, and to institute techniques for auditing and enforcing compliance with such practices. Here again there may be recursive problems since it might well be regarded as an infringement of the privacy of such employees to monitor too closely either their past records or their present practice.

Once information has been collected, it needs to be stored. Here again the most simple precautions, and those likely to give the greatest return in terms of benefit, are not only simple to institute but cost very little. Physical security of the various installations and stores is the most obvious example. It is clearly sensible to restrict physical access to such sites, but in practice it is rarely done, except perhaps in relation to the computer room itself, and then usually for technical reasons alone. It is the commonest sight in the world to see unattended reels of tape and banks of discs, often identified by easily readable labels. By tightening up physical security in these respects, on-site third party intrusion could probably be reduced to a negligible level. Much more can also be done in relation to the organisation of data within the storage system, and in protection against off-site intrusion by telecommunications or electronic eavesdropping. A relatively simple, and increasingly cheap,[42] method of protection is to employ encryption techniques in relation to at least part of the data. Another technique involves the fragmentation of files separating the content of each segment from the information necessary to link it together. Here again there is a certain tension between the method of protection and the demands of those seeking to check the accuracy of records relating to their own personal information. The effect of such protective techniques is to make the assembly of personal

---

42. The encryption techniques embodied in a popular word-processing package, Word Perfect, sold cheaply over the counter in the United States were regarded by the government of the United States as so powerful that they could be of material advantage to an enemy if made available outside the United States.

information into a form in which it can be read by a human being more difficult to accomplish. This means that access by subjects is to that extent also made more costly, so an element of economic balancing is involved. The most common off-site invasion is likely to consist in an approach through the telecommunications system to a database the operation of which requires the provision of some off-site access. Most such systems require the use of passwords, but there is considerable laxity in the use of such passwords, as will be described below in relation to access control. Electronic eavesdropping is relatively uncommon since the off-site eavesdropper has no control over the information collected, at least in the absence of an on-site accomplice. In those areas where the security of information is most important, such as defence secrets, very elaborate and very expensive electronic screening is used. Personal information will rarely, if ever, require quite such stringent precautions, but cheaper products have been developed which are more suitable for the prevention of this sort of casual intrusion.[43]

So far as the operation of computer systems is concerned, the most worrying development is the advent of networking within organisations. There are many different forms of network, but they all share the aim of distributing access to central resources such as databases. If those databases contain personal information it means that they will be at risk not only in more locations, but in the course of transmission between them. The risk of impersonation, or of the subornation or carelessness of employees, is greatly magnified. The most simple answer is to secure that so far as possible the operation of computer systems is in the hands of trustworthy, and demonstrably so, individuals. No system can attract trust, or deserve it, unless the people who operate it are themselves trustworthy. However numerous and sophisticated the safeguards built into the system, they cannot be guaranteed against all the efforts of dedicated ingenuity. The problem here is that the computer industry is new and vast; it lacks an established or a self-contained structure. It has neither historical continuity nor professional cohesion. It draws entrants from a wide variety of backgrounds with a miscellany of different qualifications, and then trains them in many different ways in numerous separate skills. The organisations involved are of many different types. They are frequently small and under-capitalised. Competition is savage, and the margin between ruin and riches minute. Mobility is high both within and between organisations, nationally and internationally. None of this is conducive to effective control. Even so, and however difficult to accomplish, the creation of some sort of professional ethic would be highly desirable. It would, for example, enable entry and training to be controlled. Those with records of crime or abuse of confidence could be barred from posts involving the handling of personal information. It could be made a requirement for achieving acceptance into the profession that the candidate should have undergone adequate instruction in the need for, and methods of, ensuring the security of personal information held within computer systems. It would also be possible to establish disciplinary procedures so that those who nevertheless abused, or permitted the abuse of, such systems could be

---

43. See *Computing* 7 August 1986 p. 11.

dealt with on a professional level as seemed most appropriate. Expulsion from a professional association is often a more drastic sentence than any which an ordinary court is able to impose. The most important effect of the creation of a professional ethic would, however, be less tangible. It would lie in the development of a sense of identity and solidarity creating a spirit conducive to keeping personal information secure whatever the pressures. It is in this way that the traditional professions, clergy, doctors and lawyers, have earned the trust of the community. It should be noted that such a professional spirit imbues not only the qualified professionals themselves, but also their most humble employees. In view of the considerations mentioned earlier, it may be too much to expect the immediate creation of any all-embracing professional body, though many organisations have already made significant strides.[44] A significant push towards improving the standards of training in the United States federal government area was provided by the Computer Security Act 1987[45] which allocated to the National Bureau of Standards responsibility for,

developing technical, management, physical and administrative standards and guidelines for the cost-effective security and privacy of sensitive information in Federal computers . . . the primary purpose of which standards and guidelines shall be to control loss and unauthorized modification or disclosure of sensitive information in such systems and to prevent computer related fraud and misuse.

Although the primary aim is indeed to improve standards in the federal area, which it had been revealed had become diffused by the large number of overlapping supervisory bodies, it was a secondary aim that the expertise obtained from devising and supervising such rules would be made available to the private sector, partly through the setting up of a Computer System Security and Privacy Advisory Board within the Department of Commerce. The Act also includes provision for mandatory training programmes in computer security awareness and practice.[46]

Systems vary greatly in the extent to which access to them is necessary. Some systems which contain personal information are available to all, for example those which systematically aggregate publicly available information for dissemination to subscribers or advice bureaux. At the other end of the spectrum the information may be made available to no more than the necessary operators of the system, and a strictly limited network of users, for example information on espionage agents. In all such systems, however, some method of regulating access has to be adopted. The most commonly used method is that of a password. In a surprising number of cases no more seems to be required. Thus it transpired that one international bank relied upon a single password to authenticate the transfer of very substantial sums through a computer network. In the case of the less obviously valuable resource of personal information, it is thus hardly surprising to find that practice is lax. It is not at all uncommon to find very short passwords, easily

---

44. See, for example, the Code of Conduct proposed by the British Computer Society, reproduced in the Younger Committee·Report on Privacy, Cmnd. 5012 (1972) App. N.
45. Amending 15 U.S.C. sects. 271–8h.
46. It is estimated that this will affect some 3 million employees in 1300 government agencies, at an annual initial cost of 20 to 25 million dollars, (1987) *U.S. Code Congressional and Admin. News* p. 3196.

guessed, which are displayed on a monitor,[47] or capable of being printed out, and which remain unchanged for long periods of time. These practices can be tightened with dramatic results at virtually no cost at all. In the case of more sensitive information it may be necessary to require more than one password, or the combination of a physical device and a password.[48] In the case of remote access it is now common for the central computer to re-dial the remote terminal to prevent access from unauthorised machines, or for the automatic transmission of identifying information. Even more sophisticated systems involving the use of 'one-time' passwords, fingerprint, voiceprint or eyeball monitoring have also been mooted, but are very expensive and complicated to operate, and would seem unlikely often to be justified in relation to personal information.

Finally there is the question of how to rid a system of personal information that is no longer required. It is once again not uncommon to find print-out being disposed of without shredding, and by the use of private contractors who may be appointed by tender without adequate requirements for the security of information or, if in fact required, of proper monitoring. Here again simple precautions like insistence on shredding and the fulfilment of suitable conditions of disposal can transform the incidence of risk. There is a further risk which arises from the disposal of old equipment such as personal computers incorporating hard discs. Not all users appreciate how easy it is to recover information which has apparently been removed from the disc.[49] Ordinary deletion is not sufficient, but it is, again, very simple to cleanse such equipment before disposal without the expenditure of vast effort or expense.

2. System design and organisation

It is in this area that, especially in Europe, the main effort has been made by legislative means. The Younger Committee identified ten such principles in 1972,[50] and numerous similar sets were subsequently propounded and enacted.[51] The most important of these from the point of view of the United Kingdom were those propounded by the Council of Europe.[52] These are distilled in Part 1 of Schedule 1 to the Data Protection Act 1984:[53]
Personal data held by data users

1. The information to be contained in personal data shall be obtained, and personal data shall be processed, fairly and lawfully.

---

47. Not always electronically; it is not unknown to find passwords physically and visibly attached to terminals.
48. Like the combination of plastic card with magnetic strip, and PIN number required for cash dispenser withdrawals.
49. As in *Defiance Button Machine Co. v. C. & C. Metal Products Corp.* 759 F.2d 1053 (2nd Cir., 1985), above p. 92.
50. Cmnd. 5012 (1972) paras. 592–600.
51. For a convenint selection, see Sieghart, *Privacy and Computers* (1976) App. A.
52. See Council of Europe Resolution (73) 28 (Private Sector); Resolution (74) 29 (Public Sector); and especially the Council of Europe Convention on Data Processing to which the United Kingdom subscribed and which the Data Protection Act 1984 is designed to implement.
53. They are glossed in Part II of Schedule 1.

2. Personal data shall be held only for one or more specified and lawful purposes.

3. Personal data held for any purpose or purposes shall not be used or disclosed in any manner incompatible with that purpose or those purposes.

4. Personal data held for any purpose or purposes shall be adequate, relevant and not excessive in relation to that purpose or those purposes.

5. Personal data shall be accurate and, where necessary, kept up to date.

6. Personal data held for any purpose or purposes shall not be kept for longer than is necessary for that purpose or those purposes.

7. An individual shall be entitled

    (a) at reasonable intervals and without undue delay or expense –

        (i) to be informed by any data user whether he holds personal data of which that individual is the subject; and

        (ii) to access to any such data held by a data user; and

    (b) where appropriate, to have such data corrected or erased.

Personal data held by data users or in respect of which services are provided by persons carrying on computer bureaux

8. Appropriate security measures shall be taken against unauthorised access to, or alteration, disclosure or destruction of, personal data and against accidental loss or destruction of personal data.[53]

The Act further provides for the modification or supplementation of these principles.[54] The scheme of the Act requires that it be interpreted so as to apply those principles, and the chosen method was to make compliance with them a condition for registration under the Act,[55] or their subsequent breach for the issue of an enforcement notice,[56] deregistration notice[57] or transfer prohibition notice.[58] This represents a departure from the scheme proposed by the Lindop Committee[59] which went further in requiring not only broad principles of this type, but their implementation in legally binding statutory codes of practice for particular sectors of information. Here too the supervision of the Act is primarily delegated to a Registrar, as opposed to the Data Protection Authority recommended by the Lindop Committee. These changes were explained on the grounds of flexibility and economy. To some extent it can be argued that the interpretation of these principles in different contexts will, effectively, establish binding Codes of Practice, quite apart from the establishment of voluntary Codes of Practice which it is among the duties of the Registrar to foster.[60] However, it is submitted that such an argument overlooks the stress placed by the Lindop Committee on relevant economic considerations.[61] Although it is, as yet, too early to see how effective the Act will be in regulating particular areas, there is already some indication of insensitivity to economic calculation. One particular abuse of privacy is that in an effort to reduce cost, private data banks often choose to use data which is cheap to collect, but might give only an approximate measure of guidance. Thus in the United States it is easier to collect and use

---

54. Sect. 2(3).
55. Sect. 7(2).
56. Sect. 10(1).
57. Sect. 11(1).
58. Sect. 12(2).
59. Cmnd. 7341 (1978).
60. Sect. 36(4).
61. Cmnd. 7341 (1978) esp. para. 21.12,

unamended arrest records than to maintain a check on the progress of the charge with a view to alteration of the record when the case is disposed of. Similarly in the United Kingdom it is cheaper to organise credit information by reference to household than by reference to the name of the particular member of the household. The Registrar has recently announced his intention to require the use of names for this purpose.[62] It appears to be supposed that this will facilitate compliance with principles 4 and 5.[63] The industry reckons that the change will cost it a billion pounds in bad debts and many millions in programming costs. While such an estimate ought not to be accepted without further examination, it seems likely that such a change will lead to substantial cost. Under the Lindop formula this would trigger an enquiry into the likely effects upon the cost of credit and the treatment of marginal cases, as balanced against the incidence and seriousness of the harm caused by the present system, and consideration of other possible means of ameliorating the situation. At present it looks as if a rather more sweeping and arbitrary interpretation of the principles is being applied. It should also be noted that under the Lindop recommendations the final proposals would attract parliamentary scrutiny before coming into force, whereas under the Data Protection Act 1984 implementation is less democratic.

As its name indicates, the legislation applies only to automatic data processing, within a scheme of definitions suggested by the Council of Europe, and incorporated into section 1 of the Data Protection Act 1984.[64] Subject to that, the sweep of the Act is broad and, unlike the Privacy Protection Act 1974 in the United States, it extends[65] to all personal data subject to automatic processing in both the public and private sectors. In fact, most of the exemptions and exclusions are in the public sector, which is exactly where fears were greatest, and it is dubious whether it has satisfied the privacy lobby. It is also confined to *personal* information, and so excludes information relating to corporate bodies. The European Convention allows for its application to extend beyond human beings, but few states have so far taken advantage of this provision.[66] Such an extension is generally opposed by the business community, since it could be used to garner competitively valuable information. The inclusion of such entities would certainly raise the profile of such legislation, since they could be expected to employ it, and to employ it in extremely dubious and contentious situations.

As noted above, enforcement is primarily in the hands of the Data Protection Registrar and his small staff,[67] subject to an appeal to a special Data Protection Tribunal using part-time members, with provision for a further appeal to the ordinary courts. It is not yet clear whether or not this

---

62. See *Computer Weekly* 26 May 1988 p. 3; *ibid.* 13 October 1988 p. 10.
63. Although a naïve observer might suppose that a closer relationship between name and information actually diminished personal privacy.
64. Although the Convention does allow for application to manual systems.
65. Subject to exemptions and exclusions.
66. So far only Austria, Denmark, Iceland, Luxembourg and Norway. Switzerland is considering such a development.
67. This has already attracted some criticism, for example from the Institute of Chartered Accountants, see *Computing* 18 August 1988 p. 4.

will prove to be an adequate way of enforcing the relevant principles. In the United States there have been several shifts in the enforcement body for the application of the privacy legislation in relation to federal data banks, reflecting some discontent about the efficacy of the relevant agencies.[68] The burden of some of these criticisms is that the enforcement agency should take on something of the character of an Ombudsman. There are many variants of such an institution, but similar functions appear to be within the remit of the directors of newly privatised industries. In the private financial sphere it is also common to find 'compliance officers' charged with ensuring that the provisions of regulatory legislation are observed. It is interesting to note that just such a pattern was considered by the Younger Committee,[69] based upon the institution of the 'responsible person' under the Mines and Quarries Act 1954. Within this context he was defined as,

the person to whom the owner or user of a computerised personal information store has delegated the responsibility for ensuring that whatever principles the legislation requires him to enforce are complied with and who would be acceptable, both as regards technology and status to the registering authority.[70]

No further consideration seems to have been accorded to this suggestion, but it seems to have considerable merit. The object of any such exercise is to amplify and to apply the bland prescriptions of the data protection principles in the context of particular applications. It is necessary to condescend to greater particularity if such principles are really to have an effect upon practice with regard to personal privacy. It is interesting that the Council of Europe which first propounded the broad principles has itself considered it necessary to amplify them by reference to particular applications.[71]

In considering the security situation, and the need to adjust methods and organisation to deal with it, it is obviously desirable to detect breaches at as early a stage as possible. In the case of personal information there may well be a delay before such a breach becomes known to the subject. For example, if information leaks from a government system to a credit agency it may be some time before it is acted upon by the agency in refusing credit or declining to raise a limit. Even then the subject will not necessarily know that the reason is such a leakage of personal information. It is thus desirable to try to detect insecurity, or potential insecurity, before there is a complaint, and preferably before it occurs. Some detection measures are routine. For example, if there are repeated unsuccessful attempts to break into a telecommunications system, it is likely that measures will be taken to identify the source of the attempts. Another simple technique is to insert deliberately

---

68. See the legislative history of the Computer Security Act 1987 in (1987) United States Code, *Congressional and Administrative News* p. 3120 *et seq*. criticising in particular the performance of the Office of Management and Budget.
69. Cmnd. 5012 (1972) paras. 623–25, and App. O.
70. *Ibid.* App. O para. 1.
71. It has so far published five booklets applying the principles to, and making recommendations for the regulation of automated medical data banks (No. (81) 1); personal data used for scientific research and statistics (No. (83) 10); personal data used for purposes of direct marketing (No. (85) 20); personal data used for social security purposes (No. (86) 1); and personal data in the police sector (No. (87) 15). Further areas to be covered include employment, new technologies, and 'smart cards' and point of sale transfer of funds.

false information into the system to check whether abuse is taking place. For example, if it is suspected that there is leakage to a direct mailing organisation it is a simple matter to insert a variant spelling of a name and then to see if the same variant appears on the address of a subsequent mailing. However, it is possible to utilise modern technology to achieve a more sophisticated approach to monitoring the operation of a computer system. A model can be constructed on the computer of the normal operation of the system, and then any significant deviation from that model can be made the subject of report and investigation. It may, however, be rather sanguine to hope that such methods will be employed on a purely voluntary basis, since they involve some cost, and even after the passage of much federal legislation including the Privacy Act 1974 and its successors, it was found by the Office for Technical Administration in the United States that as late as 1986 no more than 13 per cent of Federal record systems were audited for quality, and that privacy policies were in existence for only 8 per cent of micro-based systems.[72]

C. Remedies

Prevention is certainly better than cure in the field of infringement of personal privacy. Indeed as, noted above any remedy is likely to exacerbate the loss of personal privacy. Nevertheless remedies can have a deterrent effect, and do serve to provide some counterbalancing redress for the infringement of personal privacy. Discussion of remedies is inevitably complicated. It cannot be unitary or simple because so many different interests are pressing for recognition and can be advanced in so many different ways. The advocacy of blanket solutions has already been criticised. It will be seen that, at present, no such remedies exist. A short catalogue of possible primary parties to a dispute involving privacy illustrates the complexity which any adequate scheme of remedies must display. There is first the subject of the relevant personal information, and those who claim through him; then there is the holder of the information, including those who are privy with him; there is the violator who wrongly secures access to the information; and finally there is the user, or chain of users, who ultimately benefit from the act of the violator. In a simple private situation when the parties are distinct from each other, the subject may have claims against holder, violator or user; the holder may have claims against the violator or user; and the user may have claims against the violator. In many cases the public interest in these questions may be reflected by vesting a cause of action in the state authorities. This might be exercised against holder, violator or user. The availability of any of these causes of action will itself be conditioned by such matters as the intentions or awareness of the parties, and the reasonable or unreasonable character of their actions. Finally, any mention of remedies should emphasise that not all remedies, nor even all of the most effective ones, operate by way of legal process. Sometimes private action, such as

---

72. In 1985 the General Services Administration estimated that in 1990 the Federal Government would have 17 000 large or medium-sized computer systems in operation, and 500 000 micro-based systems.

dismissal from employment, withdrawal of professional status, withholding the provision of a service, termination of a contract, or the use of the media of communication to give wide publicity to an abuse, may be much more effective. Nor is the state limited in its provision of remedies. It is a commonplace of modern public law that the provision of an administrative remedy, such as a report by an independent agency, like the Ombudsman, may be regarded as superior to any offered by the courts. If all of these permutations are then applied to each of the different types of vehicle for the disclosure of personal information such as credit reports, bank accounts, government department files, medical histories and criminal records, just to mention the most commonly discussed examples, it is readily apparent that not just one, or a few remedies, are eligible for consideration, but a vast panoply of them. Here primary emphasis will be placed upon the legal remedies available to the subject of the information, but this should in no way detract from the importance of the others. In some jurisdictions there are overriding constitutional provisions which have an effect upon legislation, and in many there is a combination of legislative remedies and the operation of the common law. Some of these have been mentioned in earlier chapters, especially the criminal remedies, but it is useful to provide a short overview here.

1. Constitutional provision

It is perhaps misleading to refer to constitutional provisions which relate to privacy as remedial, since their effect, if they have one, is usually achieved only by the more indirect route of regulating remedies of the other types. It was once axiomatic that the United Kingdom had no written constitution in any sense at all, and that its legal remedies were neither regulated, nor capable of being regulated, in any such way. Now, however, the United Kingdom is a member of a number of supranational groups and has, as such, submitted to the provisions of multifarious declarations, conventions and covenants, some of which purport to guarantee fundamental, and general, rights in the area of privacy, and one of which deals explicitly with data protection. The general provisions will be considered first.

Article 8 of the European Convention on Human Rights thus states,

(1) Everyone has the right to respect for his personal and family life, his home and his correspondence.
(2) There shall be no interference by a public authority with the exercise of this right except such as is in accordance with the law and is necessary in a democratic society in the interests of national security, public safety or the economic well-being of the country, for the prevention of disorder or crime, for the protection of health or morals, or for the protection of the rights and freedoms of others.

Article 12 of the Universal Declaration of Human Rights is on the same lines, but spells out the exceptions less explicitly; it provides:

No one shall be subject to arbitrary interference with his privacy, family, home or correspondence, nor to attacks upon his honour and reputation. Everyone has the right to the protection of the law against such interference or attacks.

Finally, article 17 of the International Covenant on Civil and Political Rights repeats the essence of article 12 of the Declaration:

(1) No one shall be subjected to arbitrary or unlawful interference with his privacy, family, home or correspondence, nor to unlawful attacks on his honour or reputation.
(2) Everyone has the right to the protection of the law. against such interference or attacks.

It should be noted that article 8 of the Convention appears to be concerned only with governmental interference. Article 12 is limited to 'arbitrary' interference, and this is hardly made any clearer by the addition in article 17 of the Covenant of 'unlawful' interference. In none of these documents is the issue of impermissible interference squarely faced. They are typically broad-brush provisions which require a considerable body of case law based interpretation to flesh them out into meaningful standards. Only the European Convention provides for a special Court, the European Court of Human Rights, to construe its provisions. The operation of this process, in the case of the United Kingdom in this context, is illustrated by litigation both in the courts of England and the European Court of Human Rights of a case involving the tapping of the telephone of a man suspected of receiving stolen property.

The case first came before the English courts as *Malone* v. *Commissioner of Police of the Metropolis (No.2).*[73] It seems that in 1977 the accused's telephone was tapped pursuant to a warrant granted by the Home Office under the procedure then in operation. At the accused's trial in the following year he claimed a declaration that such an interception of the accused's communications was in breach of article 8 of the Convention. Megarry V.C. first held that he had no power to grant such a declaration under the Rules of the Supreme Court because, notwithstanding the procedure for petition to the European Commission for Human Rights, and for subsequent litigation before the European Court for Human Rights:

The short answer ... is that declarations will be made only in respect of matters justiciable in the courts; treaties are not justiciable in this way; the convention is a treaty with nothing that takes it out of that category for this purpose; and I therefore have no power to make the declaration claimed . . ..[74]

The plaintiff relied upon two further arguments. First he argued that article 8 had in fact created a new right in English domestic law and, secondly, that, even if it had not, it should be used as an aid to the interpretation of the relevant rules of English law. The first point was rejected on the basis that the convention was addressed to the parties to it, namely governments of states, and thus it was a matter firmly within the legislative sphere, and there was no such legislation. This vacuum was also an answer to the second point. Even if the convention could suggest one interpretation in preference to another, there must first be something to interpret, and in the United Kingdom there was nothing. The judge took the view that the detailed regulation which would be necessary in such a field precluded judicial action in isolation:

---

73. [1979] Ch. 344, Ch. The previous case of this name raised a different point.
74. At p. 354.

Various institutions or offices would have to be brought into being to exercise various defined functions. The more complex and indefinite the subject-matter, the greater the difficulty in the court doing what is really appropriate, and only appropriate, for the legislature to do.[75]

In the course of his judgment he did, however, compare English law on the interception of communications most unfavourably with that of West Germany in considering a case[76] in the European Court of Human Rights in which the German provision had been narrowly upheld. However, that was not the end of the matter, for Malone secured leave from the European Commission[77] to apply for a ruling to the European Court of Human Rights which condemned the English procedure as contravening the convention.[78]

The ultimate result was the passage by the United Kingdom of the Interception of Communications Act in 1985 in order to bring practice into line with that prescribed by the Convention. This illustrates the effect that such a quasi-constitutional provision can have in English law. In the end it stirs the government into reluctant action, but it should be noted that the process is slow,[79] and of no direct benefit to the individual who suffers under the contravening practice. It cannot, unlike a true constitutional provision, directly invalidate domestic legislation. Reliance upon such general conventions, even when buttressed by some judicial support, seems unsatisfactory.

In this area, however, there is a more specific treaty, the Council of Europe Convention for the Protection of Individuals with Regard to Automatic Processing of Personal Data. The United Kingdom signed this convention in 1981 and ratified it in 1987. In this case, however, there is no provision for enforcement by judicial, or other, process. The Convention merely establishes a Consultative Committee which could consider the position of any state which did not comply with its provisions. In fact the true impetus to implementation is expected to be more economic than legal. This is made abundantly clear in the White Paper issued by the United Kingdom government in announcing its plans to legislate,

without legislation firms operating in the United Kingdom may be at a disadvantage compared with those based in countries which have data protection legislation. When the Council of Europe Data Protection Convention comes into force it will confirm the right of countries with data protection legislation to refuse to allow personal information to be sent to other countries which do not have comparable safeguards. This could threaten firms with international interests operating in this country and the activities of British computer bureaux which increasingly process data for customers in many different countries.[80]

It was in this spirit that the Data Protection Act 1984 was conceived. It is, in fact, rather dubious whether any such disadvantage would have occurred, or whether it will have been removed by the 1984 Act, since it is minimal in

---

75. At p. 380, and see above p. 325.
76. *Klass* v. *Federal Republic of Germany* 2 E.H.R.R. 214 (E.Ct.H.R., 1978).
77. 4 E.H.R.R. 330 (E.Com.H.R., 1981).
78. 7 E.H.R.R. 214 (E.Ct.H.R., 1984).
79. The Act was brought into force on 10 April 1986 (S.I. No.384 of 1986), some nine years after the incident which triggered its passage.
80. *Data Protection* Cmnd. 8539 (1982) para. 2.

extent, and under the Convention[81] any party can refuse to allow data to be processed in another jurisdiction where the safeguards, although complying with the Convention, are nevertheless less extensive than those provided by the national law of the party resisting transfer.

In the United States the situation is quite different since both the Federation and the individual states do have written constitutions to which direct effect is regularly given by the courts. The Constitution of the United States makes no explicit reference to privacy. Nevertheless in *Griswold* v. *Connecticut*[82] the Supreme Court of the United States held that the concept of personal privacy was inherent in the Bill of Rights, and in the First, Third, Fourth, Fifth, Ninth and Fourteenth Amendments to the Constitution. In *Griswold*, however, the context was very different from that of privacy in relation to computerised systems of personal information. Indeed, the case was precipitated by an attempt to make information public rather than to keep it secret.[83] The major area of private life invoked was the relationship of marriage and the preservation of the sanctity of the home, and especially of the bedroom, from invasion. Most of the American cases extending the doctrine have also been careful to limit the extension to situations of bodily or proprietary freedom.[84] However, constant attempts are made to extend the doctrine into the area of informational privacy. In *California Bankers' Association* v. *Schultz*[85] the Supreme Court of the United States repelled an attempt to invalidate, partly on privacy grounds, the Bank Secrecy Act 1970 which compels banks to keep certain records about their customers' identities and financial transactions. A feature of the opinion of the Court delivered by Justice Rehnquist was its strict limitation to consideration of the literal words of the various amendments. On the other hand, all of the dissentients[86] did rely upon broad considerations of privacy, and two other justices,[87] while concurring in the majority opinion, foresaw possible privacy problems in certain circumstances not presented by the instant case. The distinction between the impact of constitutional requirements in the area of the person on the one hand, and of personal information on the other was clearly stated in a New York case upholding a regulation requiring a pregnancy termination certificate to include a patient's name and address:

> Both petitioners and dissenters manifest a misunderstanding of the scope of the right to privacy as articulated by the United States Supreme Court ... Courts have generally not found that the privacy interest extends to situations in which the government gathers information for legitimate purposes.[88]

This view was vindicated by two further cases in the Supreme Court relating to the disclosure of information, one in relation to financial records held by a

---

81. Art. 12 para. 3(a).
82. 381 U.S. 479 (1965).
83. See Gross, 'The Concept of Privacy', *42 N.Y.U.L.R.* 34 (1967) for a devastating attack upon the concept of privacy as it appears in *Griswold*.
84. For example, *Roe* v. *Wade* 410 U.S. 113 (1973).
85. 416 U.S. 21 (1974).
86. Justices Douglas, Brennan and Marshall.
87. Justices Powell and Blackmun.
88. *Schulman* v. *New York City Health and Hospital Corporation* 342 N.E.2d 501 (N.Y., 1975) at 506; see *Roe* v. *Ingraham* 403 F.Supp. 931 (S.D.N.Y., 1975).

bank in *U.S.* v. *Miller*,[89] and the other, *Paul* v. *Davis*,[90] where the complainant's photograph had been circulated as that of an active shoplifter on the basis of his arrest for such an offence.[91] In the latter, the Court[92] stated that:

> His claim is based not upon any challenge to the State's ability to restrict his freedom of action in a sphere concluded to be 'private', but instead on a claim that the State may not publicize a record of an official act such as an arrest. None of our substantive privacy decisions hold this, or anything like this, and we decline to enlarge them in this manner.[93]

One of the few Supreme Court decisions in this area to have involved the use of a computer system was *Whalen* v. *Roe*[94] where the constitutionality of a New York statute[95] requiring medical records of the prescriptions of control-led drugs to be kept was reviewed. They were in fact kept, in practice quite securely, on a central computer. It was held that because the precautions were adequate the statute could not be regarded as unconstitutional. The Court refused to commit itself to any general opinion about the constitutionality of other situations of storage or disclosure:

> We therefore need not and do not, decide any question which might be presented by the unwarranted disclosure of accumulated private data – whether intentional or unintentional – or by a system that did not contain comparable security provisions.[96]

This caution was amplified by Justice Brennan in his concurring opinion. While accepting that the use of computer technology did not *per se* make an application unconstitutional, he nevertheless felt that:

> The central storage and easy accessibility of computerized data vastly increase the potential for abuse of that information, and I am not prepared to say that future developments will not demonstrate the necessity of some curb on such technology.[97]

The Circuit courts have been understandably divided on the question, some apparently denying a sufficient constitutional interest,[98] and others accepting it, but usually only on a basis of balancing it against a state interest justifying disclosure.[99]

One of the reasons for the United States Supreme Court's reluctance to extend constitutional protection in this direction may be the weight of considerable social pressure in the opposite direction.[100] Indeed, some such

---

89. 425 U.S. 435 (1976).
90. 424 U.S. 465 (1976); but see *Detroit Edison Co.* v. *National Labour Relations Board* 440 U.S. 301 (1979) where an employer's refusal to disclose psychological test results on his employees was upheld.
91. Of course he was subsequently acquitted.
92. In an opinion written by Justice Rehnquist.
93. At p. 713.
94. 429 U.S. 589 (1977).
95. Controlled Substances Act 1972 (New York).
96. At 605, 606.
97. At p. 609.
98. See *J.P.* v. *DeSanti* 653 F.2d 1080 (6th Cir., 1981); *Burucki* v. *Ryan* 827 F.2d 836 (Ist Cir., 1987).
99. See *Fadjo* v. *Coon* 633 F.2d 1172 (5th Cir., 1981); *U.S.* v. *Westinghouse Electric Corp.* 638 F.2d 570 (3rd Cir., 1980).
100. See Rehnquist, 'Is an Expanded Right to Privacy Consistent with Fair and Effective Law Enforcement? Or Privacy You've Come a Long Way Baby', *23 Kansas L.R.* 1 (1974).

policies may themselves claim constitutional protection.[101] Thus the right to privacy in respect of personal information might be regarded as antithetic to the right to know and to the free flow of information often claimed to be protected by the First Amendment. The difficulty with this approach is that it relies upon an implicit interpretation of the Amendment rather than upon its explicit text, and to that extent is no better established constitutionally than the right to privacy itself. It has also been frequently recognised that in a suitable case it may be overridden by a sufficiently compelling countervailing value.[102] It is further possible to mount an attack upon the constitutionality of a right to privacy upon the basis of the 'void for vagueness' doctrine.[103]

In its most recent decision on personal privacy, though in the context of sexual morality, the Supreme Court, as presently constituted, has disclosed its reluctance to expand any constitutional guarantee of privacy beyond the narrowest limits on the basis that:

The Court is at its most vulnerable and comes nearest to illegitimacy when it deals with judge-made constitutional law having little or no cognizable roots in the language or design of the Constitution . . .. There should be, therefore, great reluctance to expand the substantive reach of those clauses [5th and 14th Amendments], particularly if it requires modifying the category of rights claimed to be fundamental. Otherwise the Judiciary necessarily takes to itself further authority to govern the country without express constitutional authority.[104]

It seems that it would, for these reasons, be unlikely to be willing to create and delineate any new such fundamental right to informational privacy.

A number of states[105] have adopted explicit constitutional protection for privacy. These reveal some interesting differences of approach. Alaska provides that,[106] 'The right of the people to privacy is recognised and shall not be infringed. The legislature shall implement this section.' In Montana, on the other hand, legislative implementation is not expressly mentioned, but a showing of compelling state interest is explicitly made a defence to a claim of infringement.[107] California's right is unqualified by any explicit words, but may be thought to be diminished by its close conjunction with a similarly unqualified right to *obtain* happiness.[108] This provision has, nevertheless, been held to apply to privacy in relation to personal information,[109] by reference to the brochure for the state election at which the measure was adopted. The Court interpreted the provision as being intended to be self-executing, but as being defeated by a compelling state interest. By

---

101. See Zimmerman, 'Requiem for a Heavyweight: A Farewell to Warren and Brandeis's Privacy Tort', *68 Corn. L.Q.* 291 (1982).

102. See, for example, *Kleindienst* v. *Mandel* 408 U.S. 753 (1972).

103. See Amsterdam, 'The Void for Vagueness Doctrine in the Supreme Court', *109 U. of Pa. L.R.* 67 (1960).

104. *Bowers* v. *Hardwick* 106 S.Ct. 2841 (1986), at 2846.

105. Smith in his 1988 *Compilation of Privacy Laws* lists eight states (Alaska, Arizona, California, Hawaii, Illinois, Montana, South Carolina and Washington) where the constitutional provision is quite explicit, and others where it is implicit either in the Constitution or in some general provision of the law of the state.

106. Art. 1 sect. 22.

107. Constitution of Montana Art. 11 sect. 10.

108. Constitution of California Art. 1 sect. 1.

109. *White* v. *Davis* 120 Cal. Rptr. 94 (Cal., 1975).

reference to the same brochure, it was held that the mischiefs against which the provision was directed are:

(1) 'government snooping' and the secret gathering of personal information;
(2) the overbroad collection and retention of unnecessary personal information by government and business interests;
(3) the improper use of information properly obtained for a specific purpose, for example, the use of it for another purpose or the disclosure of it to a third party; and
(4) the lack of a reasonable check on the accuracy of existing records.

This interpretation was further supported in *Valley Bank of Nevada* v. *Superior Court of San Joaquin County*,[110] 'Although the amendment is new and its scope as yet is neither completely defined nor analysed by the courts, we may safely assume that the right of privacy extends to one's confidential financial affairs as well as to the details of one's personal life.' On the other hand it has been said that such provision is not to be regarded as effecting an instant repeal of all previous legislation relating to privacy.[111] Most recent authority confirms that the state constitutional protection extends to informational privacy, but only subject to a balancing test, so that where, for example, an arrest, the record of which ought not to have been disclosed, was followed by a conviction, then no claim could be sustained.[112]

2. Legislation

In the absence of a direct constitutional right, or perhaps in pursuance of one,[113] reliance must be placed upon specific legislative remedies. These may range from the very general, such as the Data Protection Act 1984 in the United Kingdom or the Privacy Act 1974 in the United States, to the most particular, such as the British Telecommunications Act 1981 sect. 50(1) in the United Kingdom.[114] or a New York statute prohibiting public utilities from offering or selling lists of customers.[115] In so far as such legislation imposes criminal penalties or remedies in tort for breach of statutory duty, it is covered elsewhere. In the United States there has been a deluge of legislation at both federal and state level.[116] It is clearly impossible to consider so much legislation in any detail. Instead it is proposed to compare the position in the United Kingdom with that in the United States,[117] first in relation to one specific area, credit reporting, and then in relation to privacy or data protection at its most general level.[118]

---

110. 125 Cal. Rptr. 553 (Cal., 1975).
111. *People* v. *Ayers* 124 Cal. Rptr. 283 (1975) at 287.
112. Compare *Central Valley 7th Step Foundation* v. *Younger* 157 Cal. Rptr. 117 (Cal., 1979) with *Pitman* v. *City of Oakland* 243 Cal. Rptr. 306 (Cal., 1988).
113. See, for example in the United States, Privacy Act 1974 sect.2(a)(4).
114. Which imposes a duty on employees of the Post Office to keep secret information learned from the operation of data-processing services by the Post Office.
115. N.Y. Pub. Syc. law sect. 91.
116. Smith in his 1988 *Compilation of State and Federal Privacy Laws* lists 564 separate pieces of legislation.
117. At the federal level.
118. Other jurisdictions display the same sequence, for example Canada, where the Saskatchewan Credit Reporting Agencies Act in 1972 (R.S.S. 1978 C-44) was subsequently followed by the federal Privacy Act in 1980 (R.S.C. 1985 P-21).

(a) Credit reporting
This area has been chosen since it was among the first to be governed by
legislation, to some extent inspired by fears about privacy in both jurisdictions at about the same time. It is also an area where a vast amount of
information is held by private bodies, and so provides something of a
contrast with the general legislation which, especially in the United States, is
directed more to publicly held information.

At the time of the Younger Committee Report[119] in 1972 none of the
major credit bureaux in the United Kingdom had yet changed to computerisation, but such a development was the subject of some concern[120] and was
anticipated by the Committee as likely to be adopted more widely. It felt,
however, that computerisation was immaterial and that its main recommendation that a subject refused credit on the basis of an agency report
should have a right to be told the source of the information, and to be able
to object to it, would be applicable whether or not the relevant records were
held on computer. It found little evidence of other abuses and felt that some
possible ones, such as reliance upon gossip and hearsay in compiling reports,
would be eliminated incidentally by its main recommendation. This report
was shortly followed by the enactment of the Consumer Credit Act 1974.
The Act for the first time implemented a procedure whereby the customer
could require to be told of any credit reference given in his respect, and to
secure a copy of the agency's record on him for a small prescribed fee. He
could then object to an entry he considered incorrect and ask for its removal
or amendment. If this were not done, or not done to his satisfaction, then he
could draft a short notice which the agency was bound to add to the
particulars on the file, and circulate.[121] Although the Act makes no specific
reference in this part to computers, they seem clearly to be covered since a
'file' is defined to apply to information 'regardless of how the information is
stored', and a copy 'as respects any information not in plain English, means
a transcript reduced into plain English'.[122] It should be noted that the
Younger Committee proposed a more stringent approach to data held on
computers, but only after further investigation of the problem. This matter
was then considered again by the Lindop Committee in 1978, which found
that computerisation had still not taken place to any great extent in the area
of credit reporting.[123] It felt, however, that it was imminent, and recommended the application to that field of a more testing régime, and in
particular that records should be capable of being challenged for irrelevance
as well as for inaccuracy, that methods of obtaining data should be
controlled, that customers should be informed when data about them was
being transferred, and that there should be some control on the scope of
disclosure. It further felt that the subject should be provided with a civil
remedy, and that he should be informed of his rights rather than always
having to take the initiative. In general they felt that the same sort of régime
should be applied to credit bureaux as to any other body holding data on a

---

119. Cmnd. 5012.
120. *Ibid.* para. 252.
121. Subject to a procedure for vetting.
122. Sect. 158(5).
123. Cmnd. 7341 para. 13.04. It has now; see above p. 337.

computer, and as a result of the Data Protection Act 1984 that will be seen now to be the case.

The Fair Credit Reporting Act 1970 may be regarded as the first major piece of federal legislation in the United States to have been inspired by the outcry against computerised record-keeping.[124] It is not in terms limited to computerised records, indeed the word 'computer' does not appear anywhere in the legislation. Nevertheless the size of the credit industry in the United States is such that it has become a very highly computerised operation. The industry, and the Act in regulating it, distinguishes credit reporting for such items as loans from investigative reporting for insurance or employment purposes. Both branches include very large organisations such as TRW-Credit Data Inc. in the former class, which already in 1969 was adding half a million files to its store each month,[125] and in the latter, the Retail Credit Co. which in 1974 was producing investigative reports at the rate of 15 million a year. Various complaints were made of the practices of such bureaux, including improper methods of data collection, improper selection of subject-matter, improper evaluation of data, refusal to disclose data to those affected by it, refusal to correct inaccurate data, or to complete incomplete data, and improper use, especially in disclosing the information to those for whom it was never intended, and more especially to government agencies like the Federal Bureau of Investigation and the Internal Revenue Service.[126] It has since transpired that files were also tampered with at TRW-Credit Data Inc. by corrupt employees.[127]

The proposed legislation was itself subjected to considerable attack by the credit industry, largely on grounds of the expense of compliance. In the end an attenuated version was, in desperation, tacked on to legislation providing for special record-keeping practices by banks. The broad scheme of the legislation is to inform the subject of an investigative report that one is being compiled,[128] and anyone prejudiced by a credit report of the reason.[129] The subject is then entitled to disclosure of the nature and substance of the information in the file, the names of the recipients of the report, and in the case of a consumer, but not in that of an investigative, report, the sources from which it was compiled. The subject can then demand a re-investigation of a disputed item, have it deleted if it is recognised to be inaccurate, have a brief statement included in the file in the case of an unresolved dispute, and have notice of such changes sent to recipients of the original report.[130] Further provisions require reports to be made only with the consent of the subject, in response to a court order or to those with a *bona fide* business

---

124. See McNamara, 'The Fair Credit Reporting Act: A Legislative Overview' *22 J. Pub. L.* 67 (1973).
125. Hearings before the Sub-Committee on Consumer Credit of the Senate Committee on Banking, Housing and Urban Affairs, 91st Congress 1st Session 227 (1969).
126. Hearing on Credit Reporting Abuses before the Sub-Committee on Consumer Credit of the Senate Committee on Banking, Housing and Urban Affairs, 93rd Congress 2nd Session 1 (1974),
127. *Computerworld* 13 September 1976 p.l.
128. 15 U.S.C. sect. 1681a (e).
129. *Ibid.* sect. 1681m (a).
130. *Ibid.* sect. 1681i.

need;[131] that obsolete information be excluded;[132] that adverse information be re-verified after a period of three months;[133] and in the case of public information included in an employment report either that the subject be notified or strict procedures be maintained to ensure that the information remains current.[134] Disclosure to government agencies is permitted only to the extent of identifying matter.[135] Enforcement is by a mixture of criminal[136] and civil[137] penalties reinforced administratively by the Federal Trade Commission,[138] in lieu of ordinary tortious liability which is excluded.

(b) General

There is one general piece of legislation in the United Kingdom, the Data Protection Act 1984. As mentioned above it was introduced in order to protect the data processing industry in the light of the threat supposed to be posed to it by the European Convention. It has also been noted that it seeks to improve data-processing practice through its statement of certain basic principles, and provision for their indirect enforcement through the registra- tion process. It also provides a number[139] of direct remedies which can be considered here.

The principal remedies are closely linked to the registration requirements so as to ensure that all those eligible for registration do so register, and that they keep to the conditions for such registration. This brings into play consideration of the conditions for registration, and of the scheme of exclusions and exemptions. The Act applies only to the processing of personal data. These key concepts are defined by section 1:

(2) 'Data' means information recorded in a form in which it can be processed by equipment operating automatically in response to instructions for that purpose.
(3) 'Personal data' means data consisting of information which relates to a living individual who can be identified from that information (or from that and other information in the possession of the data user), including any expression of opinion about the individual but not any indication of the intentions of the data user in respect of that individual.
(7) 'Processing', in relation to data, means amending, augmenting, deleting or re-arranging the data or extracting the information constituting the data and, in the case of personal data, means performing any of these operations by reference to the data subject.

It will be seen from this that the Act deals only with automatic, and not with manual, processing of information; that it applies only to information about human beings, and not to artificial persons such as corporate entities; that it applies to both the public and private sector; and that it applies to all information relating to an identifiable individual, whether or not it is already

---

131. *Ibid.* sect. 1681b.
132. *Ibid.* sect. 1681c.
133. *Ibid.* sect. 16811.
134. *Ibid.* sect. 1681k.
135. *Ibid.* sect. 1681f.
136. *Ibid.* sect. 1681q and 1681r.
137. *Ibid.* sect. 1681n and 1681o.
138. *Ibid.* sect. 1681s.
139. See Gulleford, *Data Protection in Practice* (1986) App. 3 which conveniently lists 15 criminal offences created by the Act, and five civil remedies.

in the public domain. Given so wide a potential range, it is hardly surprising to find that the Act exempts various types of activity from a number of its provisions. These exemptions operate in a number of different ways with somewhat divergent consequences. Three of the more important are exemption from any duty to register at all under the Act; exemption from the general right of the data subject to have access to data relating to him; and exemption from the duty not to disclose personal data otherwise than in accordance with the registration particulars without the consent of the subject.

Registration is intended to be wide,[140] but not universal, so some mundane uses of computers do not come within its provisions at all. These include personal data used only for word processing,[141] for payroll or accounting purposes,[142] for the domestic purposes of an individual,[143] or for the purposes of recording members of a club or a distribution list.[144] All of these exemptions are strictly limited by reference to their sole use for the exempted purpose.[145] These exemptions from registration are governed by considerations of their triviality, and the need to avoid unnecessary bureaucracy. It is also envisaged that some personal information may be so highly sensitive so far as national security is concerned that it too should be exempt from the need for registration.[146] Nor is registration required in cases where there is a statutory duty to publish the data.[147]

Conversely, considerations of national security may dictate that non-disclosure provisions should not apply so as to restrict disclosure of some personal data for purposes of national security.[148] Similar exemptions from the non-disclosure provisions apply in relation to personal data needed for the prevention of crime or the assessment of taxes,[149] where disclosure is required for specific legal purposes[150] or where urgently required to prevent injury or damage to health.[151]

Personal data is excepted from the provisions for access by its subject in a number of cases, including such data relating to health,[152] to social work,[153] to financial services,[154] to judicial appointments,[155] to data subject to legal

---

140. The registration fees are expected to finance the whole operation, and had to be increased when it became apparent that fewer registrations were going to be made than had originally been anticipated.
141. Sect. 1(8).
142. Sect. 32(1).
143. Sect. 33(1).
144. Sect. 33(2), though in this case only if the prior consent of subject to such data being held by the user on a computer has been obtained.
145. Or presumably a combination of them.
146. Sect. 27.
147. Sect. 34(1).
148. Sect. 27(3).
149. Sect. 28(3).
150. Sect. 34(5).
151. Sect. 34(8).
152. Sect. 29 as implemented by subsequent order, SI 1987 No. 1905 and SI 1987 No. 1906.
153. Sect. 29(2)(b), as implemented by subsequent order, SI 1987 No. 1904.
154. Sect. 30, as implemented by subsequent order, SI 1987 No. 1905.
155. Sect. 31(1).

professional privilege,[156] or that kept only for the purpose of replacing other data.[157]

The principal criminal offences under the Act are largely concerned with the obligation to register, failure to do so being an indictable offence of strict liability,[158] or of contravening the conditions under which registration was obtained although here it is required that the offence be committed knowingly or recklessly.[159] A second group of offences is committed if the regulatory efforts of the Registrar are flouted, for example by failing to comply with an enforcement[160] or transfer prohibition notice.[161] Such prosecutions may be instituted only by the Registrar or with the consent of the Director of Public Prosecutions.

So if a private individual wishes to vindicate his own rights he must employ the civil remedies provided in Part III of the Act. He may first secure orders for access to data relating to himself, though only after a request has been refused, and not if a court thinks it unreasonable.[162] He may also secure an order that inaccurate data be erased or rectified. Such an order can be obtained without the necessity of showing damage. The order may also provide for supplementation of the data.[163] The second type of recourse to the court can be to seek compensation in respect of inaccurate data which have caused him damage or distress,[164] or in respect of loss or disclosure of personal data having similar results.[165] In either case it is a defence to show that reasonable care was taken. A quirk of the wording of these provisions is that the cause of action is bestowed only upon 'an individual who is the subject of personal data held by the data user'. If a computerised credit agency provides information relating to someone other than the customer in the shop, as a result of which he suffers damage,[166] there seems to be no route to compensation under the Data Protection Act 1984 since the customer is not the subject of data held by the agency, that is indeed the nub of his complaint.

Although it was expected that the passage in the United States of the Fair Credit Reporting Act in 1970 would result in a surge of demand for copies of credit records, such expectations proved to be unfounded.[167] However, such legislation in the private area was not sufficient to stem the rising tide of feeling on the issue of privacy, much of which was focused upon the activities

---

156. Sect. 31(2).
157. Sect. 34(4).
158. Sect. 5(1). A few such prosecutions have been reported in the computer press, see *4 A.C.C.L.* No. 9 p. 7 (1988), *Computer Weekly* 15 February 1988 p. 6 and *Computing* 18 August 1988 p. 1.
159. Sect. 5(2).
160. Sect. 10(9).
161. Sect. 12(10).
162. Sect. 21(8).
163. Sect. 24.
164. Sect. 22.
165. Sect. 23.
166. Cp. the position in the United States under the provisions of the Fair Credit Reporting Act, *Thompson* v. *San Antonio Retail Merchants' Association* 682 F.2d 509 (5th Cir., 1982), above p. 520.
167. See Westin, *Data Banks in a Free Society* (1972) pp. 131–41.

of the state.[168] In the United States this demand created an exceptionally interesting situation since legislation was already in place to enforce publication of some government material.[169] It is true that this legislation specifically excepts material of a confidential nature,[170] or certain records 'disclosure of which would constitute a clearly unwarranted invasion of personal privacy'.[171] Thus manufacturers of equipment have been unable to use the legislation to secure lists of potential customers by the simple expedient of filing an application.[172] The concept of privacy is, however, under continuous review. It has been held not to be infringed when personal information is made public at the time of an event like an arrest.[173] Then, in 1974, a new Privacy Act was juxtaposed to this legislation in the United States Code to sharpen still further the contrast between the aim of open government espoused by the Freedom of Information Act and that of personal privacy which motivated the Privacy Act. The conflict is created by the fact that government in modern times requires the collection of information of a private character.[174] So strong has been the conflict between these pieces of legislation that it has been necessary to amend the Privacy Act to make it clear that any exemption under it does not in itself establish a corresponding exemption under the Freedom of Information Act.[175] It has also generated large volumes of litigation at both the federal level[176] and also within those states having both freedom of information and privacy legislation at state level.[177] The Senate Report on the Privacy Bill clearly reflected the strong influence exercised upon the framing of the measure by fear of computer technology. In describing the purpose of the bill the Report states:

It is to promote accountability, responsibility, legislative oversight, and open government with respect to the use of computer technology in the personal information systems and data banks of the Federal Government and with respect to all of its other manual or mechanised files.[178]

This objective has also won judicial recognition as exemplified in *Thomas* v. *U.S. Department of Energy*[179] where the court held that the legislative history of the Act,

indicates that Congress was concerned predominantly with the increasing use of

---

168. Similar dissatisfaction with the purely private focus of the Report of the Younger Committee (Cmnd. 5012) 1972 in the United Kingdom led to the Report of the Lindop Committee on Data Protection, Cmnd. 7341 (1978), and ultimately to the passaage of the Data Protection Act 1984 which applies, in principle, to both public and private sectors.
169. Freedom of Information Act 1967 (5 U.S.C. sect. 552). In the United Kingdom no such legislation has yet been passed, though there is an active lobby in favour of such a development.
170. 5 U.S.C. sect. 552 (b)(4).
171. *Ibid.* sect. 552 (b)(6).
172. See *Wine Hobby U.S.A. Inc.* v. *U.S. Internal Revenue Service* 502 F.2d 133 (3rd Cir., 1974).
173. See *Tennessee Newspaper Inc.* v. *Levi* 403 F.Supp. 1318 (D.C. Tenn., 1875).
174. See *Time* 6 July 1987 for an estimate that the Federal government then held 3 billion files containing personal information.
175. Central Intelligence Agency Act 1984 sect. 2(c) (5 U.S.C. sect. 552a(q)).
176. Reflected in no less than five separate annotations, 16 A.L.R. Fed. 516; 50 A.L.R. Fed. 336; 52 A.L.R. Fed. 181; 55 A.L.R. Fed. 903; and 59 A.L.R. Fed. 550.
177. See the annotation in 26 A.L.R. 4th 667.
178. Senate Report No. 93-1183.
179. 719 F.2d 342 (10th Cir., 1983) at 345.

computers and sophisticated information systems and the potential abuse of such technology.

The Act sets out to accomplish these objectives by requiring agencies to give notice of their personal data banks, information systems and computer resources.[180] It seeks to safeguard the individual by laying down minimum standards for the collection of information, including such matters as prevention of the collection of irrelevant information,[181] hearsay information,[182] and specification of the purposes for which the information is to be used.[183] It seeks to circumscribe use of the information by an agency by reference to the purpose for which it was originally provided.[184] Like the Fair Credit Reporting Act, it also establishes a procedure according to which an individual is afforded an opportunity to review and to contest his record.[185] The Act further provides for civil,[186] and for criminal,[187] remedies, though in the latter case in a more restricted form than originally envisaged. Administrative enforcement was at first entrusted to a new body set up under the Act, the Privacy Protection Commission, but was subsequently transferred to the Office for Management and Budget. Discontent with a tendency to dissipate the unity[188] of administrative control was one of the main forces dictating the passage of the Computer Security Act 1987. Discontent has also been expressed[189] in relation to a number of other defects, such as the limitation to systems of records maintained by agencies, thus denying a remedy when the disclosure, although of information contained in such a record, was otherwise obtained.[190] So too, the remedies exist only in respect of information which is retrievable by reference to the personal information.[191]

This legislation had a direct effect only upon information held by federal authorities, and as the Supreme Court has been reluctant to find a general right of informational privacy in the Constitution,[192] further federal legislation has been enacted to fill particular gaps. In 1978 the area of financial information was affected by two pieces of legislation, the Right to Financial Privacy Act[193] and the Electronic Funds Transfer Act.[194] The former was designed to protect individuals against the disclosure by financial institutions

---

180. 5 U.S.C. sect. 552a (e)(4).
181. *Ibid.* sect. 552a (e)(1).
182. *Ibid.* sect. 552a (e)(2).
183. *Ibid.* sect. 552a (e)(3).
184. *Ibid.* sect. 552a (b).
185. *Ibid.* sect. 552a (d).
186. *Ibid.* sect. 552 (g). Damages are available for distress caused by breach, and are not limited to the recovery of costs sustained, see *Johnson* v. *Internal Revenue Service* 700 F.2d 971 (5th Cir., 1983).
187. 5 U.S.C. sect. 552a (i).
188. By 1986 six separate agencies had become involved in different aspects of such control, see 1987 *U.S. Code, Congressional and Administrative News* p. 3120.
189. Initially by the Privacy Protection Study Commission in its report *Personal Privacy in an Information Society* (1977).
190. *Thomas* v. *U.S. Department of Energy* 719 F.2d 342 (10th Cir., 1983).
191. *Baker* v. *Department of the Navy* 814 F.2d 1381 (9th Cir., 1987).
192. See *U.S.* v. *Miller* 425 U.S. 435 (1976). See also above p. 343.
193. 12 U.S.C. sect. 3401 *et seq.*
194. 15 U.S.C. sect. 1693.

of the state of their customers' financial affairs. The general method is to provide for notice of any requirement of such information to be served also on the customer before its enforcement so as to give him a chance to challenge it.[195] The latter was mainly concerned to regularise the practice of operating electronic funds transfer systems, but also imposed obligations upon institutions operating such systems to provide information to customers of any disclosure of personal information to third parties.

A further and more general concern at the Federal level has been that advances in technology have so changed the situation that the 1974 Act pattern has become increasingly out of date.[196] In particular, concern was felt about the increasing use of microcomputers and the practice of cross-matching different systems. These concerns led in 1986 to the passage of the Electronic Communications Privacy Act 1986[197] which both prohibits unauthorised interception of electronic communications and limits access to stored communications.

It should be noted that a number of states have also acted in such areas. For example, eighteen states already have legislation in place on bank records, and as many as forty-five on the interception of communications.[198]

Current concern is strong in the area of control of the use of criminal records, especially those of arrests which sometimes remain unamended even after an acquittal or the charge has been dropped. Another lively area is that of cross-matching of computer records. Here again there has been legislative activity at the federal level, culminating in the regulation of the activity by the passage of the Computer Matching and Privacy Protection Bill, sent to the President for signature in 1988. This does not seek to prohibit the practice, which indeed prevents considerable amounts of fraud,[199] but rather to impose procedural safeguards to allow challenge before the results of such crossmatching can be acted upon. Some objections to the use of cross-matching techniques are based upon Fourth Amendment concerns about 'unreasonable searches and seizures'. While there is an analogy between such cross-matching and trawling for evidence, it should not be overlooked that the privacy of the individual is affected much more dramatically by a thorough search of his house or body than by a similarly thorough search of electronic files in a remote location. In particular, the innocent suffer much more from an unproductive physical search than from a similarly unproductive electronic search. In the latter case no human being will even know the identity of those whose files have been searched unsuccessfully. The computer will merely have passed very ephemerally and quite imperceptibly through their files. However, it is right to impose procedural safeguards for another reason, namely that the quality of the data checked and the

---

195. Such a procedure was already in operation in relation to financial information required from institutions by the Internal Revenue Service, see 26 U.S.C. sect. 7609.
196. See Office of Technology Assessment Report, *Federal Government Information Technology: Electronic Record Systems and Individual Privacy*, OTA-CIT-296 (1986).
197. For a full discussion of this legislation, see Burnside, 'The Electronic Communications Privacy Act 1986: The Challenge of Applying Ambiguous Statutory Language to Interstate Telecommunications Technologies' *13 Rutg. L. & C.T.L.J.* 451 (1987).
198. See Smith, *Compilation of State and Federal Privacy Laws* (1988) pp. 5, 38–9.
199. Simply removing the names of the dead from Social Security files in the United States by a computer-matching technique saved approximately 50 million dollars in 1987, see *Time* 6 July 1987 p. 37.

adequacy of the criteria selected are sometimes open to question. It would be wrong to permit people to be prejudiced without being able to challenge the accuracy of the one or the relevance of the other.

C. Common Law

It is neither uncommon, nor necessarily undesirable, to find that the common law in the United Kingdom and the United States has diverged, after starting from some common root. It is, however, rare for it to have diverged so greatly as it has in the case of the common law of privacy. The tort of invasion of privacy was first elaborately adumbrated in an academic article published by Warren and Brandeis in the United States in 1890.[200] Their analysis was largely based on a few English cases, notably *Prince Albert v. Strange*.[201] In that case the defendant was restrained from publishing, inter alia, a catalogue of certain etchings drawn by the Prince. Since the defendant had originated the catalogue there could be no claim against him for breach of copyright, and yet an injunction was granted to prevent publication. In the United States a whole new chapter of the law of tort was opened. English law has, however, resisted the temptation to develop a full-blown tort of infringement of privacy from this foundation. The situation in the United Kingdom and the United States must accordingly be treated separately.

1. United Kingdom

The existence of any general legal right of privacy in the United Kingdom was examined in some detail by the Younger Committee in 1972.[202] It concluded:

> There is no legal right to privacy as such in the law of England and Wales. There is no recorded case in Scotland to establish that the right is recognised on the basis of an action at law, though there is at least one case which suggests the opposite . . . the protection that the law in Great Britain gives is scattered throughout civil and criminal law, both common and statute.[203]

It felt that the closest parallel was to be found in the law relating to breach of confidence. Partly as a result of this view, the law relating to breach of confidence was referred to the Law Commission. In its report it was at pains to distinguish the law relating to breach of confidence from that of privacy.[204] It pointed out that privacy turns on the content of the information, whereas confidence turns on the means of its acquisition. This affects the incidence of the remedy. If private information relating to A is passed in confidence from B to C, in a cause of action based on privacy A might have an action against C, but in one based on confidence he would not. It is also pointed out that infringement of privacy might be visited by criminal sanctions, whereas breach of confidence is an exclusively civil matter.

---

200. 'The Right to Privacy', *4 Harv. L.R.* 193 (1890).
201. (1849) 2 De G. & Sm. 652, Ch.
202. Cmnd. 5012 paras. 82–91 and App. I
203. Para. 82.
204. Law Commission Report No. 110, *Breach of Confidence*, Cmnd. 8388 (1981) Part II A.

Nevertheless there may on occasion be an overlap between the two concepts, for example where private personal information is divulged in confidence or acquired by illegal means. It is worth examining the thin trickle of authority in this area. Much of the law of breach of confidence is concerned not with personal information, but rather with business information, and has already been discussed in Chapter 3. There is, however, a residue of cases where there is a confidential relationship, but the information is personal. It was said in relation to the question of there being an obligation between husband and wife to keep the communication of personal matters confidential that 'it can hardly be an objection that such communications are not limited to business matters'[205] An interesting feature of this decision was that it was enforced against a third party into whose hands the information had come improperly. At the same time it was recognised that the law on this subject was not well-settled, but the judge was not deterred, saying:

If this were a well-developed jurisdiction doubtless there would be guides and tests to aid in exercising it. But if there are communications to be protected . . . then the court is not to be deterred merely because it is not already provided with fully-developed principles, guides, tests, definitions and the full armament for judicial decision.[206]

While it cannot be maintained that so full an armament has been furnished, some further clarification has developed. It seems now clear that the confidential communication need not take place pursuant to a contract, or proprietary right. Thus in *Stephens* v. *Avery*[207] the obligation was extended to communications between sexual partners who were not married to each other. It had been said that 'equity ought not to be invoked merely to protect trivial tittle tattle, however confidential'.[208] In *Stephens* v. *Avery* this was interpreted as referring not so much to the quality which the information must possess in order to qualify for protection, as to the inherent discretion which a judge always has in determining whether to order an equitable remedy. Even if personal information is trivial, the fact that someone decides to put it into a computer databank and act upon it might well persuade a judge that the matter is not so insignificant as to prevent him from acting. *Stephens* v. *Avery* also extended the obligation upon third parties beyond situations in which the private information had come to them improperly. The Vice Chancellor held that:

The mere fact that two people know a secret does not mean that it is not confidential. If in fact the information is secret, then in my judgement it is capable of being kept secret by the imposition of a duty of confidence on any person to whom it is communicated. Information only ceases to be capable of protection as confidential when it is in fact known to a substantial number of people.[209]

It seems, however, that in the case of personal privacy at least, so long as

---

205. *Duchess of Argyll* v. *Duke of Argyll* [1967] Ch. 302, Ch., at 329.
206. At p. 330.
207. [1988] 2 All E.R. 481, Ch.
208. By Megarry J. in *Coco* v. *A.N. Clark (Engineers) Ltd.* [1969] R.P.C. 41, Ch. at 48.
209. At p. 481.

there is some further damage to be done by wider publication, then an action may lie to restrain it, and this will be the case even in the absence of any further detriment to the confider than his wish to restrain such further publication.[210] On the other hand, since this is a cause of action in breach of confidence, and not one to restrain breach of privacy as such, it is actionable only by the person to whom the confidence is owed, and not by a third party, even though he may be the subject to whom the information relates.[211]

If the confider has himself put his own personal information into the public domain, then the information is no longer confidential and he can have no claim to restrain further disclosure. This will apply both as to the personal information which has been so published,[212] and even as to other personal information which he has not published but which concerns the same subject-matter. Thus in *Woodward* v. *Hutchins*[213] the plaintiffs employed the defendant as a press agent. After leaving their employment, but arguably still under a duty of confidence, the defendant started to publish unsavoury details of the plaintiffs' private lives. It was held that:

If a group of this kind seeks publicity which is to their advantage, it seems to me that they cannot complain if a servant or employee of theirs afterwards discloses the truth about them. If the image which they fostered was not a true image, it is in the public interest that it should be corrected. In these cases of confidential information it is a question of balancing the public interest in maintaining the confidence against the public interest in knowing the truth.[214]

The question of whether or not there is a duty not to disclose, or give further publicity to, personal information which has to some extent seeped out, is an important one for the proprietors of computerised data banks. In *Schering Chemicals Ltd.* v. *Falkman Ltd.*[215] Shaw L.J. took the view that,

though facts may be widely known, they are not ever present in the minds of the public. To extend the knowledge or to revive the recollection of matters which may be detrimental or prejudicial to the interests of some person or organisation is not to be condoned because the facts are already known to some and linger in the memories of others.[216]

These issues were much discussed in the different situation of government secrets in the litigation surrounding the publication of the memoirs of a former officer in the United Kingdom security service. Unfortunately it cannot be said to have been greatly clarified by the discussion on either of the two occasions when the matter came before the House of Lords.[217] It seems, however, that in cases of private information, Lord Keith was inclined to preserve protection even in the face of limited publicity,[218] while

---

210 *Att. Gen.* v. *Guardian Newspapers Ltd. (No.2)* [1988] 3 All E.R. 545, H.L., especially Lord Keith at pp. 639–40.
211. *Fraser* v. *Evans* [1969] 1 Q.B. 349, C.A.
212. *Mustard (O) & Son* v. *S. Allcock & Co. Ltd. and Dosen* [1963] 3 All E.R. 416, H.L. (1982).
213. [1977] 2 All E.R. 751, C.A.
214. By Lord Denning M.R. at p. 754.
215. [1982] Q.B. 1, C.A.
216. At p. 28.
217. *Att.-Gen.* v. *Guardian Newspapers Ltd.* [1987] 3 All E.R. 316, H.L.; *Att.-Gen.* v. *Guardian Newspapers Ltd. (No.2)* [1988] 3 All E.R. 545, H.L.
218. *Att.-Gen.* v. *Guardian Newspapers Ltd.(No.2)* [1988] 3 All E.R. 545, H.L. at p. 643.

Lord Goff, taking a more general view,[219] was most reluctant to find any duty in respect of information which was no longer strictly confidential.[220] It may be noted that the latter was also the final view of the Law Commission.[221]

It is necessary also to note that even where an obligation of confidence would otherwise exist it cannot be used to prevent disclosure of 'iniquity'. While this qualification is old,[22] it has been subjected to continuing reinterpretation in the light of changing conditions, social and technical, and of evolving attitudes, moral and political. In more modern times this has been expressed as a defence applying whenever it is more in the public interest that the information be disclosed than that it be suppressed. This view has been espoused in relation to commercial,[223] political,[224] and personal[225] information. It does not necessarily justify completely free disclosure, however, since in many cases the public interest will be satisfied by a more limited disclosure to particular bodies best fitted to deal with them.[226]

It remains the case that the precise delineation of the law of confidence in relation to personal information is undeveloped. In a recent case[227] the Vice Chancellor admitted as much saying,

> this case undoubtedly does raise fundamental difficulties as to the relationship between on the one hand the privacy which every individual is entitled to expect, and on the other hand the freedom of information . . .. The point requires the most accurate formulation and analysis. It is not the subject matter of existing decision directly in point . . ..

The Younger Committee referred to no fewer than nine further tortious remedies in England in its investigation of privacy.[228] Few of these are of much importance, except for trespass which is quite useful in giving a remedy for unauthorised intrusion on to the premises of another for the purpose of securing information.[229] Conspiracy might also be thought eligible, if only because its inherent vagueness suggests that it might be applied in any context whatever. Yet in *Withers* v. *D.P.P.*[230] the House of Lords held the invasion of the privacy of a man's bank account not

---

219. Though he seems to equate personal and commercial information, while distinguishing both from information relating to national security, *ibid.* p. 664.
220. *Ibid.* at pp. 661–4.
221. Law Com. No. 110, *Breach of Confidence*, Cmnd. 8388 (1981) paras. 6.67–6.69, in the case of personal information departing from the provisional view expressed in its Working Paper No. 58 para. 102, but still subject to the point that information did not become public if its reassembly from publicly available sources would involve the expenditure of substantial amounts of time, money or effort.
222. It was formulated in these terms in *Gartside* v. *Outram* (1856) 26 L.J. Ch. 113,Ch.
223. *Initial Services Ltd.* v. *Putterill* [1968] 1 Q.B. 396, C.A.
224. *Fraser* v. *Evans* [1969] 1 Q.B. 349, C.A.
225. *Woodward* v. *Hutchins* [1977] 2 All E.R. 751, C.A.
226. *Francome* v. *Mirror Group Newspapers Ltd.* [1984] 2 All E.R. 408, C.A.
227. *Stephens* v. *Avery* [1988] 2 All E.R. 481, Ch. at 483.
228. Cmnd. 5012 (1972) App. I.
229. Though its limitations in the field of privacy are exposed in *Lord Bernstein of Leigh* v. *Skyviews & General Ltd.* [1978] Q.B. 479, Q.B.
230. [1975] A.C. 842, H.L.

sufficiently wrongful to ground the crime of conspiracy. It is possible that an action in tort for conspiracy might fare a little better, but no support for any such proposition can be gleaned from the speeches of their Lordships. Indeed, Lord Simon went so far as to say,

the information which they were charged with conspiracy to obtain was in varying degrees confidential – some highly confidential. The conspiracy was therefore to invade privacy. There was a time when it might have been appropriate and possible for the courts so boldly to develop the law as to give greater protection to privacy. But the matter must now be considered as within parliamentary cognisance.[231]

The most useful branch of the civil law may turn out to be that of contract. In many of the commercial situations where the risks are greatest, the best guarantee of information being kept secret is to contract explicitly that it shall not be disclosed to any third party without the written consent of the subjects. Similarly, employers and employees in computer establishments can include guarantees of the privacy of information handled by such centres in their standard contracts of employment. It is true that any such remedies will generally be restricted to the contracting parties, and may be limited by such doctrines as that invalidating agreements in restraint of trade, but notwithstanding such limitations the initial stipulation being made known to the affected party is liable to be more effective than a nebulous remedy in tort, probably unknown to and unsuspected by those who might be affected by it.

2. United States

As noted above[232] the seminal development in the United States was the article by Warren and Brandeis in 1890. It had been inspired by the then currently revolutionary technology of the flashlight photograph and the burgeoning business of cheap journalism. It is doubtful if any academic legal publication has ever been accorded such immediate, and so favourable, recognition. In the very year of publication the courts of New York enjoined a photographer from publishing a picture he had taken of an actress attired in the then highly daring costume of tights.[233] After experiencing some setbacks one variant of the tort received the accolade of the legislature of New York in 1903.[234] Its confirmation at common law followed in 1905.[235] It is now accepted in virtually all of the states in one form or another, and is firmly entrenched in the Restatement of Torts.[236] The most widely, though not universally,[237] accepted analysis of the tort is that propounded by Prosser.[238] According to his analysis there are four basic forms of the tort:

---

231. At pp. 862, 863.
232. P. 355.
233. *Manola* v. *Stevens*, *N.Y. Times* 15, 18 and 20 June 1890.
234. Session Laws ch. 132 sects. 1 and 2, now amended as New York Civil Rights Law sects. 50 and 51.
235. *Pavesich* v. *New England Life Insurance Co.* 50 S.E. 68 (Ga., 1905).
236. Restatement (2nd) of Torts sect. 652A.
237. See Bloustein, 'Privacy as an Aspect of Human Dignity', 39 *N.Y.U.L.R.* 962 (1964).
238. Prosser, 'Privacy', 48 *Cal. L.R.* 383 (1960).

unreasonable intrusion upon the seclusion of another; appropriation of another's name or likeness; unreasonable publicity given to another's private life; and publicity which places another in a false light before the public. The first of these might seem inapplicable in the computer context were it not for the fact that it has been applied in an extended sense to protect personal information about a subject. Thus banks have, on this basis, been enjoined from permitting inspection of their customers' accounts,[239] and the United States government required to compensate in respect of the Central Intelligence Agency intercepting and copying private correspondence on to its computers without any authority to do so.[240] This form of the tort would also provide protection against many of the offensive or illegal means of securing data for input to a computer system. The remaining three forms are more obviously applicable in the computer context, though all, unlike the first, require that the information so acquired be made public. This is something of a stumbling block to the utility of the tort, as invasion of privacy is most often attempted for private gain, and dissemination of the information garnered is often the very last thing intended.

Appropriation was one of the earliest forms of the tort, and formed the basis for the statutory tort in New York and elsewhere. It protects the use of a person's name or likeness, and has had little application so far in the area of computers, though it would, in principle, seem to be capable of being applied to the unauthorised use of lists of names and addresses for commercial purposes, which is one of the most common types of invasion of privacy, and one which today almost invariably involves the use of computers. The most apparently appropriate form of the tort is probably the third, namely the public disclosure of private facts. It seems that the facts must be truly private, both in the sense that they have not previously been made public and in the sense that any person of reasonable sensibility would wish that they should not be made public. Thus in *Sidis* v. *F.R. Publishing Co.*[241] it was not enough that a newspaper story revived interest in someone who had once, years before, been a child prodigy. In *Melvin* v. *Reid*,[242] however, there was a cause of action when the revelation was of the present name, address and past history of a former prostitute who had been the defendant in a famous murder case. The final form of the tort, namely the false light doctrine, while clearly responsive to many of the complaints made of computer operations, is of uncertain extent, impinges heavily on the law of defamation, and is inappropriate for discussion here.

As previously remarked the requirement of publicity in both of the most eligible forms of the tort is inimical to success in the most common categories of complaint against computer systems. So too the availability of a defence of qualified privilege by analogy with its availability in defamation is likely to quell the use of the tort of invasion of privacy in the context of credit reporting systems.[243] Indeed, the analogy between the two torts has been

---

239. *Brex* v. *Smith* 146 A. 34 (N.J., 1929).
240. *Birnbaum* v. *U.S.* 436 F.Supp. 967 (E.D.N.Y., 1977).
241. 113 F.2d 806 (2nd Cir., 1940).
242. 297 P. 91 (Cal., 1931).
243. *Shorter* v. *Retail Credit Co.* 251 F.Supp. 329 (D.S.C., 1966).

pushed so far as to give counter-balancing relief by refusing the defence in a privacy suit where it is refused in defamation.[244] Consent may also prove an obstacle to the useful development of the tort of invasion of privacy in the computer context, especially where the information has been disclosed for the purpose of seeking some advantage such as a claim for social security benefit or an application to rent property. In such cases there would appear to be room for development in the analysis of the concept of consent.

D. Conclusion

The concept of a general tortious remedy is a widely accepted aim of advocates of a 'right to privacy'. It is rarely suggested that such a remedy should extend to the criminal law, in part no doubt because it would be so difficult to define, whether the task of definition were to be essayed by the legislature or left to the courts. It seems to be generally agreed that in the United Kingdom no such right, or general tortious remedy, exists at present. Acceptance of that view was assumed by the government when it set up the Younger Committee to enquire into the desirability of establishing such a general remedy.[245] The Committee, with two dissentients,[246] rejected the idea. In *Malone* v. *Commissioner of Police of the Metropolis (No. 2)*[247] it was accepted by counsel on both sides and by the judge. Nor was the Law Commission at all favourably disposed to smuggling it in by the back door as an extension of the law relating to breach of confidence.[248] The principal concern of the Younger Committee appears to have been that the provision of such a general remedy would be fundamentally unjusticiable. It would force the judiciary to apply extremely vague standards of totally uncertain extent, while at the same time attempting to give weight to equally vague principles pressing in the opposite direction. The interplay of such forces would, however, take place in especially sensitive and controversial areas of public policy. Such considerations are almost precisely those which have impelled the Supreme Court of the United States to move so circumspectly despite its enforced and extended exposure to such exercises on account of its constitutional role. This argument is sustained by the committee's judgment that the situations left unresolved by its more particular proposals were neither especially extensive nor particularly portentous.

It is submitted that the committee was correct in its judgment, and particularly in its perception that some such vague catch-all provision might actually damage the protection of privacy in those areas of greatest risk. There can be no adequate substitute for the careful discrimination of one situation from another, and the prescription of a particular scheme of response. Failure of analysis promotes caricature over characterisation, assertion over argument, and panacea over remedy. It is no accident that the concept of privacy has never been defined at all satisfactorily. It is no more

244. *Pinkerton National Detective Agency Inc.* v. *Stevens* 132 S.E.2d 119 (Ga., 1963).
245. H.C. Deb. Vol. 794 col. 941 (23 January 1970).
246. Messrs. Lyon and Ross.
247. [1979] Ch. 344, Ch.
248. Law Com. No. 110, *Breach of Confidence*, Cmnd. 8388 (1981) Part II A.

than a name for an attitude towards a set of abuses, very weakly, if at all, associated with each other. The provision of a blanket remedy obscures this truth. It suggests that because one type of abuse should be actionable, so should another; because one remedy should apply somewhere, it should apply everywhere; and because one defence is appropriate in one situation, it should be available in all. It suggests that all different types of abuse should be treated in exactly the same way. Such an approach is unclear, impractical and unjust. The problem of privacy deserves more sophisticated treatment.

Part 3

Procedure

This third and final part of the book addresses the practical problems of proof. Because computers employ new techniques, and have themselves consequently transformed business methods, some strain has been placed upon the processes of proof, both so far as the evidence which is acceptable to a court is concerned, and so far as the means of securing it by a party is feasible and fair. The law of evidence is largely a concern of common law jurisdictions, and even in them rules have become very liberal, at least in civil cases. Rules of practice are more universal, but also more parochial. Neither chapter in this part strays far beyond the confines of common law jurisdictions, and the second, because United States procedure is so different from British, concentrates most heavily upon Commonwealth jurisdictions. As yet the greater weight of authority exists in relation to the rules of evidence, and the relevant chapter is much the longer of the two. It may be expected, however, that more stress will in future be placed upon the procedural matters discussed in the final chapter.

Chapter 9

Evidence

This chapter is concerned with the conditions under which material derived from computers can be admitted into evidence. The problem arises in this form in common law jurisdictions where the adduction of evidence is the prerogative of the parties, regulated by general rules rather than by arbitrary individual judicial decision in each specific case. Such rules have, however, in the past themselves originated in particular judicial decisions or in specific legislative acts, and thus reflect both the state of the social and business conditions and the state of the law prevailing at the time the rule was established. These factors will be considered in the first section of the chapter. If evidence derived from computers is to be adduced, conditions must define the form in which the evidence is to be tendered and how its authenticity is to be established, at least as a preliminary matter. The second section of the chapter will deal with these questions. The major question, however, relates to the extent to which such evidence can be admitted, and what it can be admitted to prove. In common law jurisdictions these questions relate to the technicalities of the rule excluding hearsay. Indeed, so technical and restrictive were those rules that in almost all jurisdictions some statutory amendment, of varying degrees of specificity, has been enacted. The third, and by far the largest, section of the chapter will consider these questions in the light of different developments in different jurisdictions.

A. Nature of the problem

The law of evidence is not the most ancient branch of English law, but it does take its origin back to the problems of differentiating the roles of jurors and witnesses in the late seventeenth century. It continued to evolve with the development of different forms of trial throughout the nineteenth century. Those times were characterised by different social and business conditions from those which prevail today. They were also served by different legal institutions. Both need to be considered if the agony of adaptation to the needs of the present day is to be understood.

1. Technical

It is necessary to remember that when the law of evidence was developed, communities and businesses tended to be smaller, more parochial and far worse funded than they are today. Labour was relatively cheap. Businesses were typically reflections of no more than a household. Most transactions were for cash and involved no need for record-keeping. Governments were little concerned with the regulation of the lives of citizens, and themselves required few records to be kept. Most trading was done with people who were personally known to each other. Education was rare, and many, if not most, people were barely literate.

These conditions gradually ceased to apply. Business expanded. Regulation increased. Education improved. Documents became increasingly necessary, and increasingly available for the conduct of business. The process of their production was greatly accelerated as typescript replaced manuscript, and duplicate replaced copy. In modern times the versatility of the computer allows the processes of document production and reproduction to take place within a single machine, by the manipulation of electronic signals. The versatility is greater still in that the computer has also taken on other rôles than merely that of an efficient recorder of information provided by human beings. It is capable of creating data for itself, and of transforming them into information by processes of collation and calculation.

The computer when first introduced to private business in the 1950s was enormously expensive to purchase, and was typically used in vast enterprises which justified its cost by the volume of material which could be processed. So fewer and fewer human beings came into contact with more and more information. The dramatic reduction in the cost per transaction of computing since then has largely been achieved by increases in speed and capacity. Such increases can be achieved only by reducing still further the intervention in such processes of human beings. Nor should it be ignored that human beings are not only slow in the performance of the routine and repetitive activities characteristic of large-scale record-keeping; they are also inaccurate. In part these factors play off each other. It is just because the machine is so fast and so cheap to run that it becomes feasible to perform multiple checks for accuracy. A further significant factor is that the machines achieve their efficiency from breaking tasks down into very simple operations, which do not correspond in detail to the more complicated functions performed by human beings in seeking to achieve similar results. Cost is a further factor influencing the way in which a task might be performed. If calculation is a much cheaper operation than storage, a computer-based system might choose to update itself, not by storage of interim results, but by recalculation from the beginning. Similarly, where many different uses can be generated from the same data, it makes sense to store it only once, but to present it in the specifically required form only when it is needed. Whole categories of intermediate records might thus become redundant.

Computing has developed so far and so fast that it is now available to all. It long ago attracted judicial comment, 'it is common knowledge, which a court need not ignore, that computerized record keeping is rapidly becoming a normal procedure in the business world.'[1] Its most common personal use is for the preparation of documents. Perhaps partly because such documents used always to be prepared by the efforts of human beings, and perhaps partly because the output from early computers was unpleasing in appearance, it became customary to seek to make such output indistinguishable in appearance from documents prepared by conventional means.

More and more information is now created and stored than ever before. It is commonplace to characterise our present condition as being 'an information society'. Businesses use computers to assist in this process because it is cheaper and more reliable for them to do so. Human beings use computers in their personal affairs because it is more convenient for them to do so. Where information is expressed in documentary form it is, in principle, quite obscure whether, or to what extent, a computer has been involved. The law of evidence has to address this changed environment.

2. Legal

Given its origins as described above, it is hardly surprising that the law of evidence was based upon an oral tradition. Witnesses were called to testify to what they knew, and their veracity was guaranteed by the terror of swearing an oath and by the prospect of being exposed to being questioned by their opponent in the presence of the jury. A pre-condition was to distinguish effectively between the rôles of juror and of witness. This was achieved by requiring witnesses to present their own perceptions to the jury, leaving it for the jury to evaluate them. This fundamental distinction gave rise to the rules excluding hearsay and opinion. It was buttressed by a different rule requiring the best evidence that the nature of the case allowed. If a piece of evidence itself suggested the existence of a better, then that should be used. This rule was sometimes invoked to exclude copies of documents.

The aim of introducing such rules was to enhance the reliability of the evidence available to the jury. The greatest virtue of any system of law lies in its provision of some foundation of certainty in undertaking transactions with implications for the future. In order to achieve such certainty, the law must be conservative. Its history is the history of tension between its need to provide facilities useful in the given state of society without destroying confidence in its endurance. The law of evidence has to provide a basis upon which people can rely in knowing what evidence to create, or to use, so as to be able to realise their expectations of future events. The conservative facet became increasingly prominent, and manifested itself in concentration upon the forms of the rules rather than upon the reasons for adopting them. The hearsay rule is a good example. It was originally designed to promote reliability by requiring, wherever possible, the evidence of the person who had perceived the relevant matters. Exceptions were, at first, created to provide for situations where there was some other guarantee of reliability, such as that a hearsay statement was contrary to the interest of its provider,

---

1. *Union Electric Co.* v. *Mansion House Center North Redevelopment Co.* 494 S.W.2d 309 (Mo., 1973) at 315.

and where there was some good reason for dispensing with its maker, such as that he was dead. Gradually, however, the form became exalted over the substance, and by the late nineteenth century the rule had crystallised to such an extent in the United Kingdom that no new common law exceptions were created, however reliable a category of statements had become in the light of changed methods, and whatever new reason there might be for dispensing with the attendance of the maker of the relevant statement.

It was all the more poignant, since this increased rigidity coincided with the decline in the use of the jury in civil cases, the very body the whole rule had been designed to protect. The decline of the jury in civil cases was not extended to serious criminal cases, nor did it occur in the United States. Criminal proceedings either took place before lay magistrates or with juries. Civil and criminal procedure were never assimilated with the result that some techniques apply differently in the two areas, and the law of evidence has been bifurcated in the United Kingdom, but to a very much lesser extent in the United States. On the other hand it is much easier to change the law of evidence by legislative action in the United Kingdom than it is in the United States.[2]

B. Means

In a sense the whole of the law of evidence is concerned with the means of proving the facts which are in issue. Within that broad sense it is nevertheless possible to distinguish between those rules which relate to the way in which the material is to be presented to the court, and those which are more concerned with its content. The latter is by far the larger category, but the former is logically prior. In a few cases it is unnecessary to produce evidence at all because the court will take judicial notice of certain matters, but where evidence is to be adduced it must first be authenticated, a task sometimes eased by the operation of a presumption. Questions may also arise as to the form in which material is to be presented, and in this context the extent to which a copy can be accepted of material either held in some other medium or, where the original is not itself adduced, traditionally considered as an aspect of the 'best evidence' rule.

1. Judicial notice

It will be rare for a court to take judicial notice of the operation of particular machines of any complexity, and computers would generally be regarded as too new and too sophisticated to attract the operation of the doctrine.[3] Thus in a recent Australian decision the court refused to take judicial notice of the operation of a computerised satellite navigation system.[4] The one exception

---

2. Because evidence is a state matter in the United States, and it is difficult to secure the agreement of all of the states on a common text. The Federal Rules of Evidence 1976 go some way towards this, but agreement was secured only for a relatively conservative draft, and there are still local variations of detail even in those states which have adopted the Rules.
3. In *Neal* v. *United States* 5 C.L.S.R. 913 (D.N.J., 1975) the court took judicial notice of a notorious error in the Revenue's computer system.
4. *Chiou Yaou Fa* v. *Morris* 46 N.T. 1 (S.C.N.T., 1987).

to this may lie in the operation of those computer records the operation of which come before the courts with great frequency, such as the output of automatic breath-testing devices.

2. Authentication

In most cases evidence derived from a computer must be authenticated in some way. A document or other thing cannot authenticate itself at common law, but must be introduced to the court by a human being whose task it is to explain its identity, its nature, its provenance and its relevance. Only if these matters are satisfactorily put before the court and found acceptable to it can such a thing be admitted in evidence. The establishment of such foundations is necessary, and the rules governing this process constitute the rules relating to the authentication of things considered in evidence.

These topics are likely to be particularly contentious and difficult in their application to evidence derived from computers. In many, if not most, cases the evidence is produced from the custody of a party to the proceedings, who will have an interest to serve and may have an inducement to tamper with the evidence. In many cases the thing produced to the court, most often a print-out, will have been printed for the purposes of the proceedings. Any alteration will have taken place not on the thing produced in court, but on the storage medium from which it has been derived. This storage medium may well itself be, or be derived in its turn from, a record on a magnetic disc. The whole point of such discs is that they should be easy to alter, and unless specific precautions are taken they normally keep no record of having been altered. This means that much less weight can be given on the question of authentication to the appearance of the thing itself, and much more must depend upon the testimony describing the operation of the computer system and the provenance of the particular things before the court. To a considerable extent these matters are canvassed in connection with the substantive conditions of admissibility,[5] such as the hearsay rule, and as such are often dealt with in the relevant legislation.

So far there are no English cases which deal directly with the problem of the authentication of evidence derived from a computer, but some guidance can be secured from cases concerned with the authentication of tape-recordings. The leading case on this point is *R. v. Maqsud Ali*.[6] It is the more significant since the tape-recording there was of a conversation in an obscure Punjabi dialect which could not itself be understood by the jurors who had to be supplied with a specially prepared English translation.[7] This situation is not so far divorced from that of a computer-readable record which can be made accessible to the jury only by the transcription of the magnetic coding on the disc into ordinary characters such as letters, numbers and punctuation, themselves presented by the application of the coding yielding such

---

5. Many of the United States decisions turn on the adequacy of the foundation testimony required to authenticate the admissibility of evidence derived from computers.

6. [1966] 1 Q.B. 688, C.C.A.

7. English law finds no problem in providing the jury with a transcript of the recording to assist interpretation of the tape, *R. v. Rampling* [1987] Crim. L.R. 823, C.A. The position is the same in Australia, see *Butera* v. *R.* (1987) 76 A.L.R. 45, H.C.A.

things as spacing, lineation and pagination. The general approach adopted by the Court of Criminal Appeal in that case is of great significance as illustrative of the wise approach generally adopted by the courts to the treatment of evidence derived from computers. It is encapsulated in the following passage,

it does appear to this court wrong to deny to the law of evidence advantages to be gained by new techniques and new devices, provided the accuracy of the recording can be proved and the voices recorded properly identified; provided also that the evidence is relevant and otherwise admissible, we are satisfied that a tape recording is admissible in evidence. Such evidence should always be regarded with some caution and assessed in the light of all the circumstances of each case.[8]

Such sentiments are equally applicable to evidence derived from computers. It will be noted that stress is placed upon proof of the accuracy of the recording and the identification of the voices. The quality of the translation was also at issue in that case, and a *voir dire* lasting more than two days was devoted to its resolution. It is at that stage that the battle over authentication will be fought. Unfortunately, in those English cases where it has been fought, the issues have been clouded by interaction with the 'best evidence' rule.[9] In *R. v. Stevenson*[10] recordings had changed possession in the two years since they had been made, and were rejected on the basis that there was an opportunity to have interfered with the original recording, and clear evidence that some interference may have taken place. The aim of this decision was to ensure that, in the future, tape-recorded evidence should be treated with care and circumspection by those who obtained it in the first place. Such a consideration is clearly applicable to evidence derived from records held on computer. Two years later in *R. v. Robson and Harris*,[11] when a similar issue came before the Court, Shaw J. decided that the proper course was for the trial judge to determine whether a *prima facie* case had been made out that the tapes were authentic. Such a case would involve evidence of the history of the tapes from the actual process of recording up to the time of their production in court. Although in the case itself, he had, in fact, gone on to consider further expert evidence tending to refute the authenticity of the tapes, and then some rebutting expert evidence in their support, and came to a decision on the balance of probabilities, he felt that this was inappropriate. The question of authenticity should be decided first by the judge on a *prima facie* basis, and could then be re-ventilated before the jury in the same way as any other question of fact to be decided at the trial. Similarly in a case involving evidence derived from computers, it might be necessary to prove the procedures for collecting the data, those governing their checking and entry into the computer, any further manipulation, checking and storage, the security of the computer from the time the data were entered until the time they were removed to secondary storage, the means and security of such storage, and the process of removal, and subsequent custody until presentation to the court.

---

8. At 701.
9. See below 372.
10. [1971] 1 All E.R. 678, Ass.
11. [1972] 2 All E.R. 699, C.C.C.

In civil proceedings, where there tend to be more effective pre-trial procedures, it is possible to prescribe fairly elaborate rules of authentication. Thus in South Africa, the Computer Evidence Act 1983, which applies only to civil proceedings, requires any evidence from a computer to be supported by an affidavit relating to the identification of the print-out, the sources of the data from which it was compiled, any necessary programming, and to certify that the computer was functioning correctly at all relevant times. A criminal penalty for default adds teeth to this requirement. Other jurisdictions are less specific. In the United States the Federal Rules of Evidence merely provide that:

> The requirement of authentication or identification as a condition precedent to admissibility is satisfied by evidence sufficient to support a finding that the matter in question is what its proponent claims.[12]

This general rule is illustrated by a number of examples of which the ninth was designed[13] to relate to computers:

> *Process or System.* Evidence describing a process or system used to produce a result and showing that the process or system produces an accurate result.[14]

Even without such legislative guidance, courts in the United States tended to take a sensibly relaxed view of such requirements,[15] on the basis that a system of record-keeping relied upon outside the court should not be regarded with such suspicion as to bar any use of it by the court, especially given the opportunity to test and evaluate it which ordinary forensic techniques supply,

> arguments for a level of authentication greater than that regularly practiced by the company in its own business activities go beyond the rule and its reasonable purpose to admit truthful evidence.[16]

Courts in the United States have taken the view that to adopt any more rigorous approach would be tantamount to the quite unacceptable presumption that records coming from a computer are *prima facie* inaccurate.[17] In Australia the converse presumption of accuracy has in some circumstances been used to overcome defects in enabling legislation,[18] and recent legislation has reduced the rigour of authentication requirements.[19] It is perhaps doubtful whether courts in England would go quite so far,[20] though in one

---

12. Rule 901(a).
13. According to the Advisory Committee's official note.
14. Federal Rules of Evidence Rule 901(b)(9).
15. *U.S* v. *Weatherspoon* 581 F.2d 595 (7th Cir., 1978); *U.S.* v. *Vela* 673 F.2d 86 (5th Cir., 1982) at 90; *U.S.* v. *Croft* 750 F.2d 1354 (7th Cir., 1985) at 1365; but contrast *U.S* v. *Scholle* 533 F.2d 1109 (8th Cir., 1977).
16. *U.S.* v. *Vela* 673 F.2d 86 at 90 (5th Cir., 1982).
17. *U.S* v. *Scholle* 533 F.2d 1109 (8th Cir., 1977) citing *U.S.* v. *Fendley* 522 F.2d 181 (5th Cir., 1975).
18. *Mehesz* v. *Redman* (1980) 26 S.A.S.R. 244, S.C.; *R.* v. *Weatherall* (1981) 27 S.A.S.R. 238; but not in New Zealand, *Holt* v. *Auckland City Council* [1980] 2 N.Z.L.R. 124, C.A.
19. Evidence Amendment Act 1985 (Cth.).
20. In *Bogdal* v. *Hall* [1987] Crim. L.R. 500, Q.B.D. the court was not prepared to presume, at least against an accused person on a central issue, that a computerised mailing sytem had worked satisfactorily.

case they appear to have rejected the qualification upon presuming the regular operation of a machine that it need be shown to be one of which it is common knowledge that more often than not it is in working order.[21]

Where the contents of a document produced by a computer are relied upon in criminal proceedings in the United Kingdom, and to be proved by the use of a microfilmed copy, the court is given an unrestricted discretion to approve any method of authentication.[22]

3. Best evidence

The best evidence rule, which had its origins in the eighteenth century, required that a party should adduce the best evidence that the nature of the case allowed. This came to be interpreted as a requirement that no evidence which on its face indicated the existence of better evidence should be admitted, at least until a satisfactory explanation of the absence of that better evidence had been given. This rule has sometimes been used to question the admissibility of evidence derived from computers, though more often in other jurisdictions than in England.[23] It might, for example, have been used to exclude the print-out of the balance of a bank account maintained on a computer until the nonproduction of paying-in slips and cheques had been accounted for. It now seems most unlikely that it could be used in England to frustrate the admissibility of a print-out in that way. In *Kajala* v. *Noble*[24] the Divisional Court regarded the rule as obsolete except in relation to conventional documents and copies. In that case the Court was quite prepared to accept a video-copy of a film shot for television when the BBC was unwilling to permit original footage to leave its premises. It should be emphasised, however, that this rejection of the rule is confined to the rule as a rule of exclusion. It may well be the case that the weight of a print-out may be diminished if serious questions are raised as to the accuracy of transcription from original records in the system in question if manual records within the control of the party adducing the print-out are not produced. In criminal cases in England, copies of documents, or parts of them, have now been made generally[25] admissible by section 27 of the Criminal Justice Act 1988. In Scotland also, the best evidence rule has been prevented from frustrating the admissibility of oral evidence of the reading of a computerised breath-testing device when the normal print-out was incapable of being used.[26] A patently defective print-out clearly is not, and was held not to be, the best evidence of the reading of a breathalyser which has generated an apparently completely normal visual display.

---

21. *Castle* v. *Cross* [1985] 1 All E.R. 87, Q.B.D.
22. Police and Criminal Evidence Act 1984 sect. 71, see also Criminal Justice Act 1988 sect. 27.
23. See, for example, *Harned* v. *Credit Bureau of Gillette* 513 P.2d 650 (Wy., 1973) where this objection succeeded.
24. (1982) 75 Cr. App. Rep. 149, Q.B.D.
25. This relaxation is not confined to documents made admissible under the Criminal Justice Act 1988.
26. *Hamlin* v. *McLeod* [1986] S.C.C.R. 219.

Although the best evidence rule has been explicitly retained in the United States by the Federal Rules of Evidence,[27] it is subject to an exception[28] where the contents of recordings cannot conveniently be examined in court, and it is dubious[29] whether it will prevail over the general business records exception to the hearsay rule,[30] most commonly relied upon to admit the evidence of records held on a computer.[31] In the United Kingdom there is also now power to make rules in criminal cases so as to allow juries to understand technical matters better by the provision of evidence in a different form, notwithstanding the existence of the original.[32]

C. Admissibility

It is necessary to distinguish between situations where the computer generates evidence, for example, by performing a calculation, and where it merely reproduces information which has been stored in it. Although, as with most such distinctions, there may be demarcation problems at the frontier, the difference between the two territories is well-established and is reflected in the operation of different rules, principally rules relating to the admissibility of real evidence in the one case, and of hearsay in the other.

1. Real evidence

Evidence derived from a computer constitutes real evidence when it is used circumstantially rather than testimonially, that is to say that the fact that it takes one form rather than another is what makes it relevant, rather than the truth of some assertion which it contains. This rule would be simple to apply were it not for its interaction with the hearsay rule which not only bars the testimonial use of an assertion, but also bars the circumstantial use of an assertion. This is necessary in order to preserve the rule from being too readily undermined. Suppose that an employer says that X is a thief. If the employer chooses not to testify, then his statement cannot be admitted to show that X is a thief. Nor is it made any more eligible if instead of being spoken the assertion is entered into a computerised database which is regularly checked for the accuracy of the statements that it contains by efficient and impartial third parties. A print-out from such a system of the statement 'X is a thief' is not even circumstantial evidence that X is a thief.

The problem occurs because some statements although in form assertive, and which would be excluded if they originated in the minds of human beings, in fact originate in some purely mechanical function of a machine,

---

27. Rule 1002.
28. Federal Rules of Evidence Rule 1006.
29. The position is very well analysed in Bender, *Computer Law* para. 5.03(2) where it is noted that the formulation of Rule 803(6) of the Federal Rules of Evidence as an *exception* to the hearsay rule rather than as an independent rule of inclusion could leave some basis for the application of the best evidence rule.
30. Federal Rules of Evidence Rule 803(6).
31. See *King* v. *State ex rel. Murdock Acceptance Corp.* 222 So. 2d 393 (Miss., 1969) at 397; *U.S* v. *De Georgia* 420 F.2d 889 (9th Cir.,1969) at 896; *Schiavone Chase Corp.* v. *U.S* 553 F.2d 658 (Ct.Cl., 1977) at 666.
32. Criminal Justice Act 1988 sect. 31.

and can be used circumstantially to prove what they appear to assert. The basis for this view was laid in a case having little to do with computers. In *The Statue of Liberty*[33] a collision occurred in the Thames estuary between two vessels, each of which blamed the other. The estuary was at the time continuously monitored by radar, and a cinematograph record of the radar traces was made wholly automatically. The admission into evidence of the film was resisted on the basis that it was hearsay. Clearly if a human being had been watching the estuary, dictating the while into a tape recorder, the recording would amount to hearsay and would be inadmissible in evidence, assuming that no exception to the hearsay rule could be invoked. It was argued that the film was susceptible to a similar objection. Simon P. wisely rejected this contention on the basis that the film constituted real evidence and not hearsay. He placed it on a par with direct oral testimony. To revert to the example of the human observer of the estuary. He may clearly testify to what he has seen, and is then present for cross-examination. It is only if he absents himself so that cross-examination is evaded that the evidence is rejected. In the case of the machine there is no human being to testify, and so no potentially damaging cross-examination is avoided. Where machines have replaced human beings, it makes no sense to insist upon rules devised to cater for human beings, but rather, as Simon P. said, '[t]he law is bound these days to take cognisance of the fact that mechanical means replace human effort.'

This useful distinction was apparently overlooked in *R. v. Pettigrew*[34] where the prosecution wished to prove that some banknotes found in the possession of the accused were part of a particular consignment despatched by the Bank of England. They adduced a print-out from the Bank's computer which listed the number of the first note in the consignment, the number of the last note in the consignment, and the numbers of any notes within the numerical sequence which had not been included in the consignment. It followed that if the numbers of the relevant notes fell between the first number and last number, and did not coincide with the numbers of those notes listed as not having been included, then they were part of the consignment. If the whole operation had been conducted by hand, and all the numbers entered by the operator, then it would be hearsay if he were not called to testify. It was a hybrid system, however. The computer performed a dual role of checking the printing of banknotes and bundling them up into appropriately sized bundles. The system seems to have operated upon the basis that the operator placed a sequence of printed notes into the machine, and entered the number of the first note, and the nominal amount to be included in the bundle. The machine then checked the printing of the notes and rejected any whose printing was imperfect. It appears that it incorporated a counter, starting from the number of the first note which had been entered by the operator. Rejection of an imperfectly printed note seems then to have triggered two further operations, calculation of the number of the

---

33. [1968] 2 All E.R. 195, P.D.A.
34. (1980) 71 Cr. App. R. 39, C.A. See also *R. v. Wiles* [1982] Crim. L.R. 669, Kingston Cr. Ct., where *Pettigrew* was applied to the reading calculated automatically by the meter on a petrol pump.

note so rejected, by reference to the automatic counter, and up-dating the count of further notes required to fill the quota. When the quota was filled, the machine then printed out two automatically compiled records, a list of the numbers of any rejected notes, and the number of the last note in the bundle. Thus while the human operator supplied the number of the first note from his personal observation of the first note in the bundle, the machine itself calculated the numbers of the last note and of the rejected notes, given that starting point. Counsel for the prosecution unfortunately argued that the print-out was admissible under the provisions of the Criminal Evidence Act 1965 as a business record. Section 1(1)(a) required that in order for such a record to be admissible as evidence of the truth of any matter dealt with in it, any requisite information should be supplied by those who have, or may reasonably be supposed to have, personal knowledge of those matters. The Court of Appeal took the view that the operator did not have personal knowledge of the numbers of the rejected notes since they were compiled completely automatically by the computer. This conclusion is quite accurate, and a perfect application of the hearsay rule. As such it was rightly fatal to the testimonial use of the print-out. What it ignored, as the commentators speedily pointed out,[35] was any consideration of the use of the print-out as real evidence.

Since the whole ratio for the decision was that no human being had personal knowledge of the relevant information, it must have been compiled automatically by the computer. If it was compiled automatically by the computer, then *The Statue of Liberty* should have been brought into play. The relevant consideration would then have been whether or not the machine was working correctly at the appropriate time. This would require foundation testimony from the makers of the machine, from those who programmed it, and those who tested it. If such testimony were satisfactory, then there could be no reason to exclude such evidence. It would fall into the same category as the film in *The Statue of Liberty*, and the photographs, barometer traces and clocking-in cards there mentioned. This seems to make very good sense. So far as the evidence depends upon the reliability of human intervention, that is, in relation to the starting point, it is provided by the testimony of the operator. So far as it depends upon the reliability of the operation of the machine, that is as to the numbers of the rejected notes as calculated automatically, it is provided by testimony as to the design and operating condition of the machine.

This analysis seems now to have been accepted as a matter of common law.[36] In *R.* v. *Wood*[37] it was necessary to identify the precise chemical composition of some ingots of metal in order to establish whether they were part of a stolen consignment. In relation to two of the metals, the initial analysis was performed respectively by an X-ray spectrometer and a neutron transmission monitor. The output of these machines can be transmuted into an assessment of the amount of those metals present in the ingots only by

35. Smith, 'The Admissibility of Statements by Computer' [1981] *Crim. L.R.* 387, and the third edition of this work at p. 226.
36. And, despite the statutory language, also under the relevant legislation, see below p. 403.
37. (1983) 76 Cr. App. Rep. 110, C.A.

extensive and laborious mathematical calculation, which it is convenient to perform upon a computer. This was done, and the computer output tendered in evidence. The defence objected to it as hearsay, and the prosecution countered by arguing that it was admissible either as real evidence or, alternatively, under the provisions of the Criminal Evidence Act 1965. The latter argument was rejected, as it had been in *R.* v. *Pettigrew.* The former argument was accepted. The court explained that here the computer was being used only as a calculator, and did not purport to reproduce any human assertion which had been entered into it. Where it was so used the court held that its output was just as admissible, and with as little reference to the hearsay rule, as any calculation performed by a witness for the purposes of giving evidence, for example using a sliderule or a weighing machine. It was pointed out that there was no more room for objecting to the output of the computer as hearsay than there was for objecting to that of the spectrometer or transmission monitor upon which the computation had been based. In this case, evidence was given of the programming of the computer by its programmer, and of its operation by its operator. It is interesting that in this case counsel for the defence conceded that his objection was purely technical and that the computer analysis was correct. It would be scandalous if the use of a computer should lead to the exclusion of such perfectly reliable evidence. So far as the output of a computer is tendered as real evidence, the court indicated that it was immaterial that more than one person might have been involved in setting up the system within which it was used:

Virtually every device will involve the person who made it, the persons who calibrated, programmed or set it up (for example with a clock the person who set it to the right time in the first place) and the person who uses or observes the device. In any particular case how many of these people it is appropriate to call must depend upon the facts of, and the issues raised and concessions made in that case.[38]

The court recognised that the dividing line between admissibility as real evidence at common law and inadmissibility as hearsay would not always be so easy to draw,

no two cases are the same and there are no doubt many intermediate stages between a simple storage and retrieval computer programme and a calculating programme.[39]

The same distinction was made, and the same result reached, in *Castle* v. *Cross.*[40] The document in question in that case was the print-out of a breath-testing machine. It was rejected by the magistrates on the basis that it was hearsay, but the Divisional Court was clear that 'the result in the form of a print-out was the product of a mechanical device which falls into the . . . category of real evidence.' It felt that references to computers, and to statutes reforming the law in admitting evidence derived from computers by way of derogation from the hearsay rule, were inappropriate in such a case and amounted to blinding the justices by science. However, it was not

---

38. At p. 27.
39. At p. 28.
40. [1985] 1 All E.R. 87, Q.B.D.

denied that in some circumstances where the memory of the computer was more directly involved there might not have been scope for some such argument. It should also be stressed that in this case no evidence was adduced that the device was in anything other than proper working order. The Court was further quite prepared for the operator to give oral evidence of the reading, again on the basis that there would be no infraction of the hearsay rule.

Courts in the United States also distinguish between print-outs of computer generated information, where the hearsay rule is not involved at all, and computer-recorded information. In the former case the evidence is admitted as real evidence, and no hearsay problem arises because there is no human maker of the statement to be called as a witness, or to be excused from testifying. Thus in *State* v. *Armstead*[41] the prosecution was allowed to prove the origin of obscene telephone calls by reference to the computer records of the operation of wholly automatic switching devices. As the court put it:

> The printout of the results of the computer's internal operations is not hearsay evidence. It does not represent the output of statements placed into the computer by out of court declarants. Nor can we say that this printout is a 'statement' constituting hearsay evidence.[42]

2. Hearsay

By far the most important rule of the law of evidence in this context is that which excludes hearsay. The hearsay rule operates to exclude assertions made by persons other than the witness who is testifying as evidence of the truth of that which was asserted. Thus if a system for recording the numbers of various components of a motor car is maintained on a computer, the print-out will amount to hearsay if proffered to prove that combination of numbered components in a given motor car.[43] In almost all jurisdictions it has been extensively modified, and excepted from, by statutory provision. In some, including the United Kingdom, different provisions apply to civil and to criminal proceedings. The most recent of these modifications often make specific provision for evidence derived from, or generated by, computers. This part of the chapter will accordingly consider first the common law, then in increasing order of specificity, first general provisions, then special provisions directed towards computers, and finally statutes dealing with particular subject matter in relation to computers.

(a) *Common law*

In principle the same rule should apply when it is sought to prove a positive or an inconsistent negative proposition, for example in *Myers* v. *D.P.P.*[44] that

---

41. 432 So. 2d 837 (La., 1983).
42. At 840.
43. Cp. *Myers* v. *D.P.P.* [1965] A.C. 1001, H.L. where in fact the records were held on microfilm, but it would have made no difference had they been held in a computer.
44. [1965] A.C. 1001.

not only did a given car possess that combination of numbered parts, but that no other car did so. It was, indeed, necessary to the decision in *Myers* that that conclusion followed. Doubt has, however, been cast upon this conclusion in the United Kingdom by two recent cases. In *R.* v. *Patel*[45] it was held that evidence of an immigration officer that he had perused Home Office records of legal immigrants without finding a given man's name was inadmissible, when tendered to show that the man was an illegal immigrant. This conclusion was rested entirely upon the fact that the witness was not responsible for keeping the records. It was expressly asserted that if the custodian were to give evidence of the non-occurrence of the name that his evidence would have been admissible. This *obiter dictum* was acted upon in *R.* v. *Shone*[46] which concerned records of motor car parts. The accused was charged with handling some parts allegedly stolen from a garage. The relevant record-keeping system happened to be manual, but it could just as easily have been held on a computer. As each part was received, a stock entry was generated indicating the serial number of the part. If the part was used in a repair or sold to a customer, the card was marked accordingly. The prosecution sought to show that the parts in question had been removed from the garage unlawfully by proving the operation of the system, and that no such marks indicating lawful removal appeared on the relevant cards. The court was referred to *Myers* and to *Patel*, but took the view that on these facts the evidence was not hearsay but direct evidence from which the jury was entitled to draw the inference that the parts had been stolen. This enabled the court to ignore the difficult question of whether the requirements of the business record exception to the hearsay rule, as established by the Criminal Evidence Act 1965, had been complied with. It is, however, very hard to distinguish the case from *Myers*. In both, records were tendered to show the truth of what they indicated. It is true that in *Myers* the reliability of the very record in question depended upon the accuracy of an absent person. It can, however, hardly make the evidence *more* eligible that it depends not upon the accuracy of one absent person, but upon inferences premised upon the accuracy of an indefinite number of absent persons. It seems that the court failed to notice that the hearsay rule bars circumstantial inference just as much as it bars direct evidence, when that inference or evidence depends upon the accuracy and reliability of absent persons.[47] As will be seen, it is quite possible that the business record exception could have been invoked without insuperable difficulty on the facts of *Shone*.

Shone also illustrates one reason why it is necessary to consider the common law relating to hearsay, despite the development of widespread statutory exceptions which will be considered in detail in the next part of this chapter. In *Shone* it was the strict interpretation of the definition of hearsay at common law which enabled the evidence to be tendered, rendering consideration of the statutory exceptions to the hearsay rule

---

45. (1981) 73 Cr. App. R. 117, C.A.
46. (1982) 76 Cr. App. R. 72, C.A.
47. See also *R.* v. *Muir* (1983) 79 Cr. App. Rep. 153, C.A., where the court appears to have evaded the operation of the rule by treating the testifying witness as an expert entitled to rely upon hearsay for part of his expertise.

unnecessary. Similarly in the cases mentioned above[48] where the computer record was accepted as real evidence, such acceptance depended upon successfully distinguishing such use from a hearsay use, given the ambit of hearsay at common law. It was also noted in that connection that the oral evidence of the operator of such a device is no more hearsay at common law than is a documentary print-out.[49]

Because the common law of hearsay was so restrictive, a number of exceptions was developed, some of which may be applicable in the context of evidence derived from computers. So far as these have been incorporated into statutory provisions, they will be considered in the next part of this section. The scheme of statutory reform of the hearsay rule differs in England and Wales as between civil and criminal cases. In relation to the former the common law has been supplanted by the new statutory régime, but in the case of the latter it has merely been supplemented. The effect of this is that strictly common law exceptions to the hearsay rule may still operate in criminal cases, in addition to the new statutory exceptions in the Police and Criminal Evidence Act 1984 and the Criminal Justice Act 1988. It should be noted, however, that it has been authoritatively determined by the House of Lords that no new common law exceptions can now be created.[50]

The first main common law exception which might apply in the context of evidence derived from computers is that for statements in public documents. In most cases there will be explicit statutory provision for the holding of a particular class of public documents on computer as will be seen in a later section. Even in the absence of such specific provision, it may however be possible to fall back upon this exception since there seems no reason to construe the concept of a document so narrowly as to exclude records derived from a computer.

The next two categories of the principal common law exceptions are premised upon the death of the maker of the statement, and comprise declarations by such a person against his interest, or those made in the course of duty. The latter has probably been eclipsed for all practical purposes by the former specific statutory exception in section 68 of the Police and Criminal Evidence Act 1984, and its successor, section 24 of the Criminal Justice Act 1988, though like all common law rules it may still have the advantage of sufficient flexibility to overcome any difficulty experienced by the court in consequence of inappropriate statutory drafting. Thus the only remaining common law exception to require some consideration is that for declarations of deceased persons made against their interest. Such statements must have been contrary to the maker's pecuniary or proprietary, but not penal, interest when made, known by the maker to be against his interest, and the maker must have had personal knowledge of the matters so stated. When these conditions have been satisfied, the statement is evidence of collateral matters, such as dates, just as much as those with which it is principally concerned.

---

48. At p. 373.
49. See *Gaimster* v. *Marlow* [1985] 1 All E.R. 82, DC; and in Scotland *Hamlin* v. *McLeod* [1986] S.C.C.R. 219.
50. *Myers* v. *D.P.P.* [1965] A.C. 1001.

The common law also provided more generally for admissions binding a party to the proceedings. Here there was no necessity for the maker to be dead, which would be a rare occurrence, and nor was the range of matters considered to constitute an admission so limited as those taken to be contrary to a deceased maker's interest. In particular, statements contrary to penal interest might well count as admissions at common law. All that seems to be necessary is that the statement should be potentially adverse to the party in legal proceedings. It is not even absolutely clear that the maker must have personal knowledge of the truth of the contents of the statement. In certain circumstances a party may be bound by statements in documents in his control, so that where the books of a society of which the party was a member referred to a purchase it was held to be evidence that the purchase was authorised.[51] There is no reason to suppose that the computerisation of such books would lead to a different result.

The situation in the United States presents the most fruitful contrast with that in the United Kingdom. The underlying structure of the law is sufficiently similar for the comparison to be meaningful, and the surface detail sufficiently different for it to be suggestive. Such a comparison has the further advantage of exploiting the earlier and more intense use of computers in business in the United States than anywhere else in the world. When the insatiable American appetite for litigation and for law reporting is taken into account, the result is by far the richest crop both of decided cases and enacted legislation to be found in any jurisdiction. Some caution is neverthe-less necessary. Differences between the approaches in the United States and in the United Kingdom are perhaps more deeply rooted here than in any other area of the law of evidence; there is great diversity both between different jurisdictions and over different periods of time; and most important of all it must not be forgotten that in the United States civil cases are still decided by juries, and that it was to protect juries from error that the hearsay rule was first devised.

While in England the development of any general hearsay exception for shopbooks was inhibited by statute in 1609, the position in the United States was more fluid. In part, this was a reflection of the different stage of economic and business development to be found there in colonial times. More transactions had to be conducted on credit, and more tradesmen worked individually without the assistance of clerks or servants. In part, it was due to the absorption in New York of the older Dutch civil law attitude to the use of documentary evidence.[52] There were, in fact, two separate models for the shopbook rule to admit a party's own books,[53] and a quite separate regular entries rule to admit the records of a third party. These were themselves distinct from the stronger development in the United States of the admission of documents prepared by a testifying witness who could vouch for their accuracy as evidence of past recollection recorded.[54] On the

---

51. *Alderson* v. *Clay* (1816) 1 Stark. 405, N.P.
52. See *Vosburgh* v. *Taylor* 12 Johns 461 (N.Y., 1815); *Conklin* v. *Stamler* 17 How. Pr. 399 (N.Y., 1859).
53. The New York and New England models, see *Radtke* v. *Taylor* 210 P. 862 (Or., 1922).
54. In this case not limited to business documents, or indeed membership of any category of regularly compiled documents, thus enabling occasional documents to be admitted.

statutory front there was similar diversity. Some statutes enacted shopbook rules, some dealt with particular areas of business or human activity, some with the best evidence rule, some with more general hearsay, and some with rules for the admissibility of past recollections. Quite apart from these there have been no fewer than five separate attempts to draft model statutes devoted to the admission of business records.[55] The most striking and encouraging feature of this mosaic lies in the willingness which has been exhibited by the judiciary to approach these rules in such a way as to ensure their sensible interpretation and smooth working in relation to evidence derived from computers, an attitude aptly summarised by the Supreme Court of Mississippi as early as 1969,:

> The rules of evidence governing the admission of business records are of common law origin and have evolved case by case, and the Court should apply these rules consistent with the realities of modern business methods. The law always seeks the best evidence and adjusts its rules to accommodate itself to the needs of the age it serves.[56]

As indicated in the quotation above, despite the fever of legislative activity in the states, even those which have not participated have found themselves able to adapt the common law so as to admit computer print-outs in evidence. *King* was one of the first such cases. A finance company sought to prove the outstanding balances owed to it on various accounts by tender of such print-outs. They showed a complete record of the relevant transactions, and were proved by the company's manager responsible for their compilation and maintenance. The system involved the remote recording in conventional form of such transactions. The paper records were then transferred to a central site where they were transcribed to punch cards,[57] and the cards read into a computer where they were processed so as to adjust the existing records, and the updated records were then dumped on to magnetic tape for permanent storage. The paper records of individual transactions were retained for two years, then microfilmed as a form of secondary storage, and the original paper records destroyed. The records in the instant case had passed through these phases, and the question was whether the print-outs were 'original records' within the Mississippi common law development of the shopbook rule. The court was prepared to follow earlier precedent[58] to hold the requirement satisfied when it would be inconvenient to call the originators of the records from which the permanent record was compiled. Nor was the court deterred from holding the print-out admissible evidence of the permanent record on the magnetic tape:

---

55. The Model Act drafted by the Commonwealth Fund Committee; the Uniform Business Records as Evidence Act drafted by the Commissioners for Uniform State Laws; sect. 541 of the Model Code of Evidence drafted by the American Law Institute; rule 63(13) of the Uniform Rules of Evidence drafted by the Commissioners for Uniform State Laws; and rule 803(6) of the Federal Rules of Evidence promulgated by the Supreme Court of the United States and approved by the Judiciary Committee of both Houses of Congress. The first four of these are compared in detail by Laughlin, 'Business Entries and the Like' *46 Iowa L.R.* 276 (1961).

56. *King* v. *State ex rel. Murdock Acceptance Corp.* 222 So. 2d 393 at 397 (Miss., 1969).

57. And at this stage verified.

58. *Grenada Cotton Compress* v. *Atkinson* 47 So. 644 (Miss., 1908).

Records stored on magnetic tape by data processing machines are unavailable and useless except by means of print-out sheets . . . .. We are not departing from the shop book rule, but only extending its application to electronic record keeping.[59]

The conditions laid down for admissibility were that:

(i) the electronic computer equipment be recognised as standard equipment;[60]
(ii) the entries be made in the normal course of business at or reasonably near the time of the event recorded; and
(iii) foundation testimony satisfy the court of the reliability of the sources of information, and the method and time of preparation.

The court explicitly recognised that the weight of the evidence was still disputable and could be attacked in exactly the same way as any other business entry. It may be noted that the evidence was eventually rejected because of the failure of the foundation testimony to show the accuracy of information. This common law approach has been applied equally liberally to admit print-outs of telephone bills as evidence for the prosecution in criminal cases, even on so serious a charge as murder, and even in the American state most remote from the common law tradition.[61] It may perhaps be a reflection of the fact that the evidence was being admitted to the prejudice of the accused that the court should have endorsed the necessity for the proponent of such evidence to proffer positive foundation testimony showing satisfaction of the relevant conditions, rather than simply place the burden of refutation upon an objector.[62]

(b) General statutes

In almost all common law jurisdictions there has been some statutory modification of the hearsay rule. These statutes take a number of different forms. Sometimes the statutory provision is of general application, and sometimes it deals with a particular technology or situation. In some jurisdictions, including the United Kingdom, different rules apply to civil and to criminal proceedings.[63] It is proposed here to deal first with general provisions, so far as possible in isolation from any special rules for evidence from computers. The next section will deal with such special provisions and their interaction with more general provisions. The final section of this part of the chapter will mention a few statutory provisions dealing with particular situations where some special recognition has been given to the application of new technology.

Civil The Evidence Act 1938 was the first statute to essay a general exception to the hearsay rule so as to admit documentary records. It was a somewhat tentative measure, and admitted documents only under rather

---

59. At 398.
60. It is interesting that as early as 1969 a Mississippi court was prepared to recognise a device as standard, albeit having heard foundation testimony to that effect.
61. *State* v. *Hodgeson* 305 So. 2d 421 (La., 1974).
62. At 478, quoting Ely J., in *U.S* v. *De Georgia* 420 F.2d 889 at 896 (9th Cir., 1969).
63. But not in the United States, perhaps in part because juries are used in both types of proceedings.

strict conditions which limited its usefulness.[64] It was accordingly replaced by the Civil Evidence Act 1968 and its main provisions repealed. The Law Reform Committee had, however, recommended that the new legislation should not apply to civil proceedings in magistrates' courts, and although provision was made for it to do so in the 1968 Act, that Act has never been implemented for proceedings in magistrates' courts. The result is that the Evidence Act 1938 continues to apply to such proceedings.[65] Since the Act antedates the use of computers and has been replaced for most proceedings by more modern provisions, its terminology is inapt for easy application to evidence derived from computers.

It applies to admit statements in documents as evidence, provided that the original document is produced, and provided also that the maker of the statement in the document had personal knowledge of the matters dealt with, or that the document is part of a continuous record made by a person with a duty to record a statement made by someone with personal knowledge, and providing that the maker is called as a witness, subject to various reasons for non-appearance. The court is empowered to dispense with the condition relating to calling the maker, and to the originality of the document produced in lieu of a certified copy, in order to avoid undue delay or expense. A still more restrictive condition, and one which the court is given no power to disregard, is that,

a statement in a document shall not be deemed to have been made by a person unless the document or the material part thereof was written, made or produced by him with his own hand, or was signed or initialled by him or otherwise recognised by him in writing as one for the accuracy of which he is responsible.[66]

The Act prohibits the use of a statement if the maker were a person interested at a time when proceedings were pending,[67] and further makes any incentive to conceal or misrepresent facts relevant to weight. In more general terms, weight is also affected by the contemporaneity of the statement with the facts to which it refers.

The principal obstacle to the application of this legislation in the computer context is first the definition of a document, as including 'books, maps, plans, drawings and photographs'.[68] While it is true that this is, in terms, not an exhaustive list, it is just the sort of list which has elsewhere been amended so as to apply more readily to computer-based records.[69] Quite apart from that, the requirements of authentication by the maker, of continuity of the record,[70] of personal knowledge at no more than one remove, and of the necessity of calling the maker if he can be identified, even though he might not be able to remember anything of the transaction, all

64. See Law Reform Committee 13th Report, *Hearsay Evidence in Civil Proceedings*, Cmnd. 2964 (1966) para. 11.
65. *R. v. Wood Green Crown Court ex parte P.* (1982) 4 F.L.R. 206, Fam. D.
66. Sect. 1(4).
67. Sect. 1(3).
68. Sect. 6(1).
69. Thus the next general Act, the Criminal Evidence Act 1965, extended the definition of document to 'any device by means of which information is recorded or stored'.
70. See the remarks of the Law Reform Committee in its 13th Report para. 16(b).

militate against the application of the Act to computer-based systems. So in addition on the question of weight does the consideration of contemporanei- ty. The Act was not designed to cater for evidence derived from computers, has not been amended to do so, and can be applied to them only with the greatest difficulty and inconvenience. Fortunately it remains applicable to a very restricted range of proceedings, and they are those in which such evidence is least likely to be required.[71]

It was largely because the law of evidence was conceived to be so defective in its application to modern business records that the Law Reform Committee was asked in 1964 to consider 'what provisions should be made for modifying rules which have ceased to be appropriate in modern condi- tions'. It chose hearsay as its first topic within the field of evidence, and taking as its starting point the 1938 legislation, found it defective in excluding 'many business records, particularly under modern systems of record-keeping'.[72] It explicitly extended its recommendations to mechanically recorded statements, so long as there was a duty to record them.[73] The Law Reform Committee made no proposal to deal separately with evidence derived from computers, but rather intended its general proposals to cater for such evidence.

In general, the scheme recommended by the Law Reform Committee was adopted by the government and enacted as the Civil Evidence Act 1968. So far as evidence derived from computers is concerned, the most significant change was the decision to incorporate a special section into the Act to regulate the admissibility of such evidence. The general scheme of the Act was first of all to provide that, in civil proceedings, hearsay should be admissible only under the provisions of Part 1 of the Act, by any other statutory provision, or by agreement of the parties.[74] It should be noted that the Act made no attempt to repeal particular pre-existing statutes, but did repeal the principal parts of the 1938 Act. It has been supplemented by a number of subsequent Acts which will be mentioned in the second section of this part of the chapter. The term 'statutory provision' is defined so as to extend to an instrument made under an Act.[75] In many cases in which hearsay is admitted without reference to the Act, it must be taken that an agreement by the parties is presumed in default of objection, given the mandatory terms in which the Act is drafted. A further effect of this approach is that all common law exceptions to the hearsay rule are abrogated to the extent that the Act applies.

Having reduced the extrinsic avenues for admissibility so drastically, the Act provides three new principal routes to admissibility for, respectively, first-hand hearsay,[76] records made by one acting under a duty,[77] and statements produced by computers.[78] The interaction of these three routes to

---

71. See Law Reform Committee 13th report para. 51.
72. Cmnd. 2964 (1966) para. 16(a).
73. Para. 19.
74. Sect. 1.
75. Sect. 1(2).
76. Sect. 2(1).
77. Sect. 4(1).
78. Sect. 5(1).

admissibility is obscure. The only explicit reference to linkage is contained in section 4(1) which provides that it is without prejudice to section 5, which is the section explicitly admitting statements produced by computers, subject to certain conditions to be discussed below. It should be noted that there is no corresponding phrase either in section 2, which admits first-hand hearsay whether oral or documentary, nor in section 5 itself in relation either to section 2 or to section 4.

The most important of these inter-relationships is that between sections 4 and 5, just because most documents produced by computers are made in the course of duty. The most plausible construction of this inter-relationship, though one untested by any judicial decision, is that statements coming within the ambit of section 5 are unaffected by anything in section 4. So far as the application of sections 4 and 5 to them are concerned, there are four categories of document: those which satisfy the conditions of both sections; those which satisfy the conditions of neither section; those which satisfy the conditions of section 4, but not those of section 5; and those which satisfy the conditions of section 5, but not those of section 4.

If a document satisfies the conditions of neither section, and comes within the ambit of the Act as a whole, it can therefore be admitted only by virtue of a statutory provision, by agreement of the parties, or under the provisions of section 2 or of section 9 of the Civil Evidence Act 1968 itself.[79] If a document is admissible under the provisions both of section 4 and of section 5, it is admissible without any need for further discussion. Some computer output may, however, satisfy the provisions of section 4 because recorded under a duty, or series of duties, stretching back to an originator with personal knowledge, but still not satisfy the requirements of section 5 because, for example, the information from which the statement was derived was not regularly supplied to the computer in the ordinary course of its business use.[80] It seems, on account of the introductory words of section 4(1), that such a document is not admissible, because to admit it would prejudice the operation of the conditions imposed upon the admissibility of such records by section 5. Similarly, if a statement derived from a computer should satisfy the conditions of section 5, but is say prepared from information supplied by someone without personal knowledge of its truth, and thus incapable of satisfying the provisions of section 4, it will nevertheless be admissible, since to hold otherwise would operate to the prejudice of the operation of the exception to the hearsay rule constituted by section 5.

Section 5 is thus paramount in civil proceedings, but is supplemented by section 2 and section 9, and may operate in tandem with section 4. If the maker of the statement in a document had personal knowledge of the truth of its contents, then the document is, in principle, admissible under section 2 of the Act, provided that direct oral evidence of those matters by the maker would have been admissible. Thus if a clerk allocates serial numbers to products, and enters the numbers so allocated into a database, the print-out

---

79. Which enacts some of the common law exceptions to the hearsay rule of which those for admissions, public documents and public records are those most likely to involve evidence derived from computers.
80. Contrary to the requirement of sect. 5(2)(b).

may be admissible under section 2 even though the conditions of section 5 have not been satisfied, say because the entry was originally made as part of an experiment which was so successful that it has now been approved as a routine procedure.

As noted above, section 4(1) is stated to be without prejudice to section 5, and need not be considered here since section 5 will prevail over it to the extent of any divergence between them. The common law exceptions preserved by section 9 for admissions, published works dealing with public matters, public documents, records, and reputation to establish good or bad character are expressly exempted from the conditions of section 5 should evidence derived from computers fall within them.[81] Any such evidence need satisfy only the relevant conditions at common law.[82]

In a number of jurisdictions the full weight of catering for evidence derived from computers has been borne by legislation concerned with business records. The United States has by far the richest jurisprudence in this area, with both the greatest variety of legislative provision of this type, and the most abundant crop of decisions. As explained above,[83] it is not possible to consider in detail all of the varieties of business record legislation. However, the generous spirit which has largely inspired the interpretation of those provisions[84] has been carried over into the interpretation of rule 803(6) of the Federal Rules of Evidence, which now dominate the statutory field.

Rule 803(6), denominated 'Records of Regularly Conducted Activity', provides that:

A memorandum, report, record, or *data compilation*, in any form, of acts, events, conditions, opinions, diagnoses, made at or near the time by, or from information transmitted by, a person with knowledge, if kept in the course of a regularly conducted business activity, and if it was the regular practice of that business activity to make the memorandum, report, record, or *data compilation* all as shown by the testimony of the custodian or other qualified witness, unless the source of information or the method or circumstances of preparation indicate lack of trustworthiness. The term 'business' as used in this paragraph includes business, institution, association, profession, occupation, and calling of every kind, whether or not conducted for profit.[85]

The rubric was chosen so as to mark the greater width of the definition than would be commonly understood by the simple use of the word 'business'. The final formulation of the rule itself deliberately increased the guarantee of reliability by requiring it to be the regular practice of the business to make the relevant record.[86] The reference to 'data compilation' is one of several references dotted throughout the rules[87] in an effort to cater

---

81. Sect. 9(5).
82. The function of sect. 9 is limited to identifying the relevant rules rather than to modifying them in any way, sect. 9(6).
83. At p. 381.
84. See, for example, *Transport Indemnity Corporation* v. *Seib* 132 N.W.2d 871 (Neb., 1965) at 875.
85. Emphasis supplied.
86. Thus attempting to preserve the bar on self-serving and presumptively less reliable statements specially prepared for the purposes of the litigation in which they are tendered, see *Palmer* v. *Hoffman* 318 U.S. 109 (1943).
87. See also Rules 803(7), 901(b)(7), 901(b)(8) and 902(4).

for modern business methods. It should also be noted that the Federal Rules contain a quite separate requirement for authentication as a condition precedent to admissibility.[88] Two of the illustrations to that rule expressly refer to 'data compilations',[89] and a third is intended also to cater for them.[90] The rules make further explicit provision for proof of summaries[91] and for negative hearsay.[92]

Despite changes in wording, this provision has been construed upon the same principles, and often by reference to the very same authorities, as its federal, or sometimes state,[93] precursor. This approach was established, very soon after rule 803(6) came into effect, in *U.S* v. *Scholle*[94] where the defendant, a lawyer accused of drug trafficking, took numerous objections under the new rules. So far as computer records were concerned, he objected to the use of print-out analysing the chemical composition of drugs seized throughout the United States arranged by date and location, which had been tendered to show the pattern of distribution of the particular batch of drugs with which he was alleged to have been concerned. The Eighth Circuit relied upon authorities construing the old rules in stressing the ambit of the discretion of the trial court.[95] It has since even been doubted whether there are any special rules for computer print-outs,[96] and in another recent case the admission of a routine print-out was upheld despite denial of access for the defendant to the relevant program.[97] It is, of course, still necessary to authenticate the printout, and in *United States* v. *Weatherspoon*[98] the proving witness testified not only to the nature of the relevant input procedure, but also to its accuracy and to the procedures for checking its accuracy.[99] Nevertheless it has been held that the authenticating witness need have no knowledge of the accuracy of any individual records nor to have prepared the print-out tendered at the trial,[100] nor is it necessary to put the program itself into evidence,[101] nor, even after the objection has been made that the accuracy of the output depends as much upon the accuracy of the program as of the input data, is it necessary to call the programmer.[102] Indeed, in one case where the raw output of one computer, automatically monitoring telephone dialling, was used as input to another, automatically generating billing data, the output of the latter was held to be authenticated even though the witness,

---

88. Rule 901(a).
89. (7) Public records or reports, and (8) Ancient documents or data compilations.
90. (9) Process or system, see Advisory Committee's note.
91. Rule 1006.
92. Rule 803(7).
93. See, e.g., *McAllen State Bank* v. *Linbeck Construction Co.* 695 S.W.2d 10 (Tex., 1985).
94. 533 F.2d 1109 (8th Cir., 1977).
95. Citing *U.S.* v. *Johnson* 516 F.2d 209 (8th Cir., 1975).
96. *U.S.* v. *Vela* 673 F.2d 86 (5th Cir., 1982) at 90 explicitly casting doubt on *Scholle*.
97. *U.S.* v. *Croft* 750 F.2d 1354 (7th Cir., 1985) at 1365.
98. 581 F.2d 595 (7th Cir., 1978).
99. In *Croft* similar matters were adumbrated, but less thoroughly.
100. *Rosenberg* v. *Collins* 624 F.2d 659 (5th Cir., 1980).
101. *U.S.* v. *Sanders* 749 F.2d 195 (5th Cir., 1984).
102. *U.S.* v. *Young Bros.* 728 F.2d 682 (5th Cir., 1984).

was unable to identify the brand, type and model of each computer, or to vouch for the working condition of the specific equipment during the billing periods covered.[103]

The basic conditions for admissibility were re-stated in *Rosenberg* v. *Collins* to be,

(i) that the records be kept pursuant to some *routine* procedure;
(ii) that they be created for motives tending to promote accuracy (and thus not extending to those prepared especially for the purposes of litigation); and
(iii) that they should not themselves be mere accumulations of hearsay or uninformed opinion.

Most objections have concentrated either upon a combination of the first and second, or upon the third of these, though rarely with very much success. It has been held here, just as under other provisions in the United States, that the test is not whether the print-out has been prepared especially for the litigation, but whether the information which it presents was being used regularly for the purposes of the business:

It is not necessary that the printout itself be ordered in the ordinary course of business, at least where the program that calls forth the data only orders it out rather than sorting, compiling or summarising the information.[104]

In that case the print-out in question made the basic information more comprehensible to the jury by expressing numeric customer codes as their ordinary English equivalents, and by re-ordering the information so as to group together records relating to the same customer. The requirement that the record should have been made at or near the time of the matter recorded is interpreted in a similar spirit, and the view has been taken that the court should distinguish for these purposes between the 'record' and the 'print-out',

the 'record' is stored in the computer in a form that is not comprehensible to human beings by sight, sound, taste, smell or touch. The printout is not the record; the printout is the means of making the record available for perusal by human beings.[105]

In *U.S.* v. *Sanders* attention was also paid to the third condition, and it was stressed that the entries in question emanated from the defendant, being claims for reimbursement under the Medicare scheme, and were effectively admissions. The intervention of a bureau to prepare these claims in machine-readable form was discounted on the basis that the bureau was acting as the agent for the defendant principal.

It seems that no further conditions will be countenanced, and in *McAllen State Bank* v. *Linbeck Construction Co.*[106] attempts to import the common law requirements of standard equipment, prepared by persons who understood it and whose duty it was to operate it, were rejected.

Although Rule 1006 regulates the proof of summaries, a computer print-out will not be regarded as a summary so long as it merely reproduces the original information, even though it might re-order it. It should also be noted that while it is a recognised condition for admissibility under Rule

---

103. *Vela* at 90. See also *State* v. *Knox* 480 N.E.2d 120 (Oh., 1984).
104. *U.S.* v. *Sanders* at 198.
105. *Brown* v. *J.C. Penney & Co.* 688 P.2d 811 (Or., 1984).
106. 695 S.W.2d 10 (Tex., 1985).

1006 that original documents be available for inspection, some summaries amount to business records in their own right, and may be proved under Rule 803(6) without reference to any such requirement.[107]

Australia, like the United States, is a federal jurisdiction, and the law of evidence is within the province of the various states. Unlike the United States, perhaps because the states are fewer in number, it has no similar tradition of uniform legislation, except that which occurs consequentially upon a common borrowing from another jurisdiction, traditionally from England. It will not be possible to deal completely with the law of each separate Australian jurisdiction in this chapter.[108]

As the courts have in England, and have done even more in the United States, the Australian courts have also shown themselves ready to adapt the common law to the reception of evidence derived from computers. In the absence of any very suitable exception to the hearsay rule at common law, the various Australian legislatures have addressed the problem of admitting hearsay in business records when the common law rules mentioned above are inapplicable because the computer is reproducing a statement originally made by a human being, or information derived from such a statement. In many Australian states a local version of the English Evidence Act 1938 was in force but, as noted elsewhere,[109] that provision is quite unhelpful in the context of the admissibility of evidence derived from computers. The inconvenience of this situation inspired the New South Wales Law Reform Commission to draft a special report in 1973, and was succinctly stated by them

considerable use is made of computers by government and business for keeping and producing records. Yet, in civil proceedings, statements in documents produced by computers cannot be admitted in evidence if objected to.[110]

The Committee was initially attracted by the approach of section 5 of the English Civil Evidence Act 1968, but rejected it on the excellent grounds that it would make a document admissible if produced by a computer, but inadmissible if produced by other reliable means.[111] The Committee accordingly recommended, and the legislature enacted,[112] a completely new business records exception to the hearsay rule, designed to cope with evidence derived from computers.[113]

In broad outline the legislation applies to the admission of business

---

107. *Id.* Where invoices summarised slips relating to the cost of labour and materials, but were themselves business records.
108. The Australian Law Reform Commission has described the existing situation as one of great disharmony throughout Australia in both civil and criminal proceedings, *Evidence* Interim Report No. 26 Vol. 1 para. 132 (1985).
109. At p. 383.
110. Report on Evidence (Business Records) L.R. 17 (1973) para. 3.
111. Para. 4.
112. Evidence (Amendment) Act 1976 incorporating a new Part IIC, Admissibility of Business Records, into the New South Wales Evidence Act 1898.
113. Similar legislation has been enacted by the Commonwealth in the Evidence Amendment Act 1978 as Part IIIA of the Evidence Act 1905 (itself further amended in 1985), and by Tasmania in the Evidence Amendment Act 1981 as Part 111, Division IIB of the Evidence Act 1910, in the case of Tasmania replacing an earlier provision modelled upon the United States business record legislation.

records in both civil and criminal proceedings; it applies to statements[114] of both fact and opinion; and it operates in derogation both of the hearsay rule and of the rules relating to secondary evidence of documents. The legislation refers explicitly to computers, which are defined to mean 'any device for storing or processing information',[115] and 'document' is defined to include 'any record of information'.[116] 'Business' is widely defined, but would presumably exclude any personal financial documents maintained by private individuals however business-like their system might be, even to the extent of running the same programs on the same computer, and in the case of a one-man business perhaps even using the same data as input. It is, however, required that the records be part of the records of a business, have been made in the course of, or for the purposes of, the business, and have been made or derived from either a 'qualified person' or be supplied by business devices themselves. These latter alternatives are worthy of further consideration. The idea was to encompass both cases where there was a human author of the statement in question, in which case hearsay problems arise, and cases where the device operates to process objective data without further human intervention, where the relevant common law rules are those relating to real evidence and scientific devices.

A 'qualified person' is defined[117] as one who is, in summary, closely engaged in or associated with the business in question, and who has, or may reasonably be supposed to have, personal knowledge of the truth of the fact stated. It is necessary for the qualified person to have produced or recognised the statement in some way. In principle, the 'qualified person' must possess personal knowledge of the fact stated, but the rigour of this requirement may be mitigated by a relaxed view of the circumstantial use of the statement of another.[118]

The other situation with which this legislation was designed to deal is that where the device itself contributes useful information, like the numbers of the rejected notes in *R.* v. *Pettigrew*.[119] This is achieved by the alternative condition in sub-section 14CE (6)(b)(ii) that the statement reproduce or be derived from,

information from one or more devices designed for, and used for the purposes of the business in or for, recording, measuring, counting or identifying information, not being information based on information supplied by any person.

This definition is further assisted by the definition in sub-section 14CD (1) of 'derived' as meaning,

---

114. It is significant that its focus is concerned with the admissibility of statements rather than of documents, concepts frequently confused in other legislation.

115. Sub-sect. 14CN (5), while this is an improbably wide definition it does no harm in this context since there are no special restrictive conditions attaching to the admissibility of records derived from computers.

116, Sub-sect. 14CD(1). It is possible that the notion of a 'record' which is not explicitly defined might cause difficulty, see *Bates* v. *Nelson* (1973) 6 S.A.S.R. 149, *O'Leary* v. *Lamb* (1973) 7 S.A.S.R. 159, and *O'Donnel* v. *Dakin*[1966] Tas. S.R. 87.

117. Sub-sect. 14CD (1)(a).

118. See *Re Marra Developments Ltd.* [1979] 2 N.S.W.L.R. 193, S.C.(Eq.,) and *Albrighton* v. *Prince Alfred Hospital and others* [1980] 2 N.S.W.L.R. 542 C.A.

119. (1980) 71 Cr.. App. Rep. 39, C.A., above 374.

derived, by the use of a computer or otherwise, by calculation, comparison, selection, sorting, consolidation or by accounting, statistical or logical procedures.

In a case like *Pettigrew* the legislation is apt to permit the operator to input the opening number from his own personal knowledge, and thus to be a 'qualified person', and then for the machine to derive the numbers of the rejected notes by a process of counting. The legislation also has a well-drawn provision to enable print-out to be adduced,

a statement in a record of information made by the use of a computer may be proved by the production of a document produced by the use of a computer containing the statement in a form which can be understood by sight.[120]

The legislation applies both to civil and to criminal proceedings, though in the case of the latter, where there is a human originator of the statement, he must either be called as a witness or be unavailable for one of a number of specified reasons.[121] Nor in such a case is a statement made in connection with the proceedings or with any investigation admissible. In civil proceedings the court may exclude otherwise admissible records if the evidence is of slight relevance, would unduly prolong the proceedings, or be unfair to any other party.[122] In criminal proceedings such a statement may also be excluded if its admission would operate unfairly against the accused.[123] An unusual discretion, bestowed by section 14CQ, permits the court to exclude a statement admissible under the Act from the jury room if it is considered that the jury might accord the statement too much weight. Although it seems not yet to have caused difficulty, it is possible that the condition in sub-section 14CF(1) which excludes statements made or obtained in contemplation of legal proceedings is too restrictive, since unlike the special provision for criminal proceedings it is not limited to hearsay, and many perfectly reliable computer print-outs are made specially for the purposes of litigation.[124] A particularly useful innovation in the legislation is to make explicit provision for the admissibility of evidence of the absence of a record among business records to show a negative.[125]

The thrust of the legislation is to liberalise the admission of business records. The weight of the evidence is left to the court to determine.[126] The evidence is not accorded the accolade of amounting to even *prima facie* proof of anything, but a number of provisions are devoted to assisting the court to assess the weight of the evidence. In particular, attention is drawn to the contemporaneity of the statement with the matters referred to in it, any motive to misrepresent either in the maker or anyone concerned with the system, and the reliability of the devices from which the information is derived, including the means of derivation.[127]

---

120. Sub-sect. 14CN 1(c).
121. Unusually for criminal proceedings, undue delay or expense may suffice to establish unavailability, sub-sect. 14CG (2)(b)(vi).
122. Sect. 14CP.
123. Sect. 14CS makes admissibility subject to this discretion which is assumed to exist already.
124. As in the English case of *R.* v. *Wood* (1983) 76 Cr. App. Rep. 110, C.A., above 376.
125. Sect. 14CH, thus dealing with the situation discussed above 378.
126. L.R.C. No.17 (1973) App. F para. 8.
127. Sects. 14CI to 14CK.

Canada, like Australia and the United States, is a federal jurisdiction. The provinces are, however, more prone than the Australian states to adopt common statutory rules, and they are now more often taken from United States than from English models. As will be seen, even the common law has tended to depart from its traditional approach to that more usual in the United States. Thus in relation to evidence derived from computers, the modern Canadian judicial approach shows a greater willingness than the English to espouse new exceptions to the hearsay rule, and the legislatures to adopt business record provisions on the United States model. In both, the tendency has been to treat evidence derived from computers in exactly the same way as any other documentary business record.

The first radical departure from the English common law approach to the admission of hearsay came in the Supreme Court of Canada's decision in *Ares* v. *Venner*.[128] In that case the Supreme Court upheld the admission of hospital records as evidence of the condition of a patient. It was a most unusual case in that the nurses who had made the records were present in Court, but were not called to give evidence. The Supreme Court was confronted by the decision of the English House of Lords in *Myers* v. *D.P.P.*[129] It deliberately chose to follow the minority view in *Myers*, and avowed the competence of the courts to create new common law exceptions to the hearsay rule, and to create them on the basis of the twin justifications of necessity and some guarantee of trustworthiness advanced by Wigmore.[130] It is not yet clear how much impact this new power will have upon the attitude of the courts to evidence derived from computers. Part of the reason for uncertainty is that the decision in *Ares* v. *Venner* came a few years after *Myers* and, as it was expected that the Canadian courts would accept that decision, a number of legislatures quickly enacted statutory provisions to admit business records. These statutes have accordingly siphoned off many situations which might otherwise have led to the development of *Ares* v. *Venner* in this context. It is sometimes the case, however, that a particular situation is overlooked in bringing the statutory position up to date. Thus in *R.* v. *Sunila and Solayman*[131] while it was felt that the use of the term 'book' in section 26[132] of the Canada Evidence Act could be extended to sheets of computer print-out only with difficulty, the common law exception could be used to remedy the deficiency.

Canadian legislatures reacted just as strongly and just as adversely to the decision in *Myers* as did the courts. The Dominion reaction, a new section 30 of the Canada Evidence Act inserted in 1970, was introduced by the Minister of Justice in terms which made its motivation quite clear:

A few years ago in England it was held [i.e. in *Myers*] that the court has no power to

---

128. [1970] S.C.R. 608.
129. [1965] A.C. 1001, H.L., above p. 377.
130. Wigmore, *Treatise on Evidence* (3rd edn) Vol. 6 para. 1707.
131. 26 C.C.C. (3d) 331 (N.S.S.C., 1986).
132. Here the Canadian Air Force was assisting the Customs Service by surveillance of a ship, and the print-out was a transcription of digitised radar traces, but sect. 30 could not be applied because of the exemption in sub-sect. 30(10)(a)(i) of exercises being part of investigations.

create or recognize further exceptions to the hearsay rule. This decision, which results in legislation in 1965 [i.e. Criminal Evidence Act 1965] in England, has been followed in at least two reported cases in Canada. It is therefore apparent that the law in this country has fallen far behind the major changes which the computer has brought to business methods.[133]

There are too many variants between the different jurisdictions, and within any one at different times for any comprehensive analysis to be attempted. Section 30 itself broadly admits evidence of business records of matters of which oral evidence would be admissible. Despite some initial uncertainty, it seems that the second of these conditions has not been interpreted so restrictively as to exclude all second-hand hearsay.[134] In the rather sketchily reported case of *R. v. Vandenberghe*,[135] section 30 was applied to computer print-outs which appear to have comprised both second-hand and negative hearsay.[136] It seems also that the Canadian courts are prepared to adopt an expansive notion of what constitutes a record,[137] no doubt assisted by the generous definition of 'record' in sub-section 30(12) as including 'any . . . other thing on or in which information is written, recorded, stored or reproduced'; and of what constitutes a 'copy', in this case in reliance upon the *Oxford English Dictionary's* inclusion of 'transcript' among the possible synonyms.[138]

In general these statutes operate in addition to ordinary common law exceptions, as noted above. They also apply both to civil and to criminal proceedings. They tend to define 'business' very broadly,[139] and to define 'record' in a sufficiently wide way as to apply to computers.[140] It is usually a further condition that the record should have been made in the ordinary course of business and within a reasonable time of the transaction recorded. It is not then a further requirement for admissibility that the maker have personal knowledge, though it is regarded as a matter going to weight. While Canadian courts have construed the conditions liberally in some respects,[141]

---

133. *Canadian Hansard* 20 January 1969 p. 4496.
134. Compare the terminology of the English Civil Evidence Act 1968 which achieves a distinction between the first-hand hearsay admitted under sub-sect. 2(1) and the more remote hearsay admitted under sub-sect. 4(1) by including the crucial requirement in the former that oral evidence *by him*, that is the maker, be admissible. These words are omitted by sect. 30, so the two interpretations harmonise.
135. 6 C.R. (3d) 222 (B.C.C.A., 1976).
136. Though it is arguable that the records were admitted not as direct evidence but as part of the expertise upon which the expert witness was relying.
137. See *R. v. Anthes Business Forms Ltd.* [1978] 1 S.C.R. 970, S.C.C.
138. *R. v. Sunila and Solayman* 26 C.C.C. (3d) 331 (N.S.S.C., 1986).
139. For example, the typical Evidence Act of Ontario defines 'business' in sect. 35 as including 'every kind of business, profession, occupation, calling, operation or activity, whether carried on for profit or otherwise'.
140. Here sect. 35 defines 'record' to include 'any information that is recorded or stored by means of any device'.
141. For example, in *Setak Computer Services Corp.* v. *Burroughs Business Machines Ltd.* 76 D.L.R. (3d) 641 (Ont. H.C., 1977), rejecting the limitation to the principal activity of the business adopted by the Supreme Court of the United States in *Palmer* v. *Hoffman* 318 U.S. 109 (1943), and in effect reading in as an extra condition the absence of motive to misrepresent.

they have been more conservative in others.[142] Some of the Canadian legislation provides specifically for proof of negatives by reference to the absence of business records, and some for notice to be given to the opposing party.[143]

An even more promising approach, and one within the United Kingdom, has been adopted in Scotland with the passage of the Civil Evidence (Scotland) Act 1988.[144] In outline this legislation allows for the liberal admission of hearsay, both positive[145] and negative.[146] The Act clearly applies to computers, defining 'document' in the same expansive way as in the Civil Evidence Act 1968 section 10, and 'record' to mean 'records in any form'.[147] It is a feature of this legislation that unlike its English counterparts it treats records produced by a computer in exactly the same way, and with no additional requirements, as those produced by any other means.

Criminal The only major common law jurisdiction to have a separate and substantially modified hearsay regime for criminal proceedings is the United Kingdom. This stemmed initially from the passage of the Criminal Evidence Act 1965 in hurried response to the decision of the House of Lords in *Myers* v. *D.P.P.*[148] Its perpetuation is a largely accidental consequence of the dual mechanism for law reform, which led to the Law Reform Committee reporting on the reform of the hearsay rule in 1966,[149] and its recommendations being acted upon in Part 1 of the Civil Evidence Act 1968.[150] The Criminal Law Revision Committee which had the evidence reference for criminal cases adopted a different strategy of reporting wholesale rather than piecemeal. This strategy was disrupted when its report on evidence[151] was not immediately implemented, for reasons largely unconnected with its proposals for the reform of the law of hearsay which were based upon those of the Law Reform Committee. Reform was delayed until the passage of the Police and Criminal Evidence Act 1984. By this time it was well appreciated that computers needed to be considered, and experience with the special provision for that purpose in the Civil Evidence Act 1968 had indicated the need to change strategy. Nevertheless both that Act, and its successor the Criminal Justice Act 1988, continue to make special provision for computers and will be considered in the next part of this section.

---

142. For example, in *Kolesar* v. *Jeffries* 68 D.L.R. (3d) 198 (Ont. H.C., 1976) refusing to accept that a medical diagnosis came within the statutory words 'act, transaction, occurrence or event', a matter on which courts in the United States have differed in the interpretation of identically worded provisions.
143. Sect. 30 of the Canada Evidence Act does both.
144. As a result of criticism of the existing law in civil cases which mirrored that in England by adopting a counterpart of sect. 5 of the Civil Evidence Act 1968, especially by the Scottish Law Commission in its Report No. 100, *Evidence* (1986) para. 3.66.
145. Sect. 2(1)(a).
146. Sect. 7(1).
147. Sect. 9.
148. [1965] A.C. 1001, H.L., see above p. 377.
149. Law Reform Committee 13th Report, *Hearsay Evidence in Civil Proceedings*, Cmnd. 2964 (1966).
150. Subsequently supplanted in respect of hearsay evidence of opinion by the Civil Evidence Act 1972.
151. Criminal Law Revision Committee 11th Report, *Evidence (General)*, Cmnd. 4991 (1972).

(c) Special computer provisions
It is unfortunate that the United Kingdom initiated the idea of providing specifically for the reception of evidence from computers. Not only was the initial attempt to do so in the Civil Evidence Act 1968 fundamentally flawed, but the very idea had little to commend it.[152] There is no intrinsic reason why different régimes should apply to different forms of record-keeping, and every reason why they should not when the different forms are not readily distinguishable upon their face. There may be no obvious difference in appearance between a document produced by the use of a computerised word-processing system and one produced by the use of a manual typewriter, nor is there the slightest justification for subjecting them to different hearsay rules. To do so creates nothing but anomaly and confusion. This seems now to be increasingly appreciated, and the more modern statutes represent a great improvement upon their predecessors, largely by assimilating the conditions of admissibility. A further problem is created by the technical interaction of the two regimes of modification, one for business documents and another for documents produced by computers. In the discussion which follows of such special provisions, that enacted in South Australia, although applying both to criminal and civil proceedings, will be considered in connection with civil proceedings since it was so clearly derived from the English Civil Evidence Act 1968 which was itself confined to civil proceedings.

Civil As noted above,[153] section 5 of the Civil Evidence Act 1968 prevails over the business record provisions of section 4, so it is desirable to examine the conditions imposed by section 5 in a little more detail. It should be noted at the outset that its construction has attracted remarkably little judicial attention, despite the increasing adduction of evidence derived from computers. This might be regarded as a striking endorsement of its effectiveness, but the opinion has been expressed that the true explanation lies in the unnecessary complexity of the relevant provisions.[154]

The general subject-matter of section 5 is described as 'a statement contained in a document produced by a computer'. 'Statement' is defined by section 10(1) as including 'any representation of fact, whether made in words or otherwise'. It should be noted that this definition is explicitly excluded from the relaxation in favour of representations of opinion made, in respect of other provisions, by the Civil Evidence Act 1972. 'Document' is defined to include *inter alia* 'any disc, tape, sound track or other device in which sounds

---

152. It is significant that the Law Reform Committee intended its general proposals to apply to 'modern systems of record-keeping', para. 16(a).
153. At p. 385.
154. See comments on the operation of sect. 5 submitted to the Australian Law Commission by the London Common Law Bar Association, reproduced in Australian Law Reform Commission Paper No. 3 p. 83; comments made by an unnamed London commercial silk quoted in Didcott, *Legislation Regulating the Admissibility of Computer Generated Evidence* (1980) para. 20; and comments by the Scottish Law Commisssion, 'Evidence', *Scot. Law Com.* No. 100 (1986) para. 3.66 on the similarly worded sect. 13 of the Law Reform (Miscellaneous Provisions) (Scotland) Act 1968.

or other data (not being visual images) are embodied so as to be capable . . . of being reproduced therefrom'. This seems sufficiently comprehensive to cater for most commonly used forms of computer storage. The exclusion of visual images in the quoted extract is not significant since there is a further provision which explicitly applies to visual images, and would be capable of applying to optical storage technologies. 'Computer' is defined as 'any device for storing and processing information'.[155] This definition seems rather expansive since neither storage nor processing is expressly required to be automatic,[156] and even if this were implied would apply to such devices as the more modern electric typewriters and hand-held calculators. It may be better to eschew altogether any attempt at a definition, and rather accept that 'computer' is now an ordinary word in the English language which a judge is perfectly capable of construing.[157] This has the distinct advantage of not confining the definition to the technology of a particular time which could create anomalies. It must, however, be conceded that even then the standard output of a word-processing package running on a small home computer would come within the complex of definitions, and so become subject to the conditions imposed by section 5. As noted above, there seems no good reason for records output by a word-processor operated by one typist in the typing pool to be made subject to a different set of conditions from those imposed by section 4 for the conventionally typed records of her neighbour.

It remains necessary for the statement to be contained in a document. It follows that section 5 has no effect at all upon the admissibility of oral evidence of the operation of a computer derived, for example, from reading the result of a calculation from a visual display device, or looking over the shoulder of a secretary working at a word-processor.

The most surprising feature of section 5 is that it makes no requirement that the originator of the information processed by the computer should have had, or even be reasonably capable of being supposed to have had, personal knowledge of the truth of that information. This seems quite extraordinarily lax, given that most computer error is either immediately detectable or results from error in the data entered into the machine. So widely has this been accepted that it has become institutionalised into the acronym 'GIGO', or 'garbage in, garbage out'. This laxity is also in stark contrast to the other principal avenues to admissibility under the Act, sections 2 and 4, which both insist upon personal knowledge in the originator of the information, as do virtually all other hearsay exceptions for evidence derived from computers throughout the common law world. There seems no good reason for section 5 to have departed from this requirement. Indeed, had it not done so there

---

155. Sect. 5(6), subject to sect. 5(3) which governs computers operating in combination.
156. This may account for the different approach adopted by the Data Protection Act 1984 which instead of referring to computers as such refers instead to 'data equipment' stressing the automatic processing of such data.
157. This has become the preferred approach, see, for example, the Police and Criminal Evidence Act 1984 and Copyright, Designs and Patents Act 1988. But the definition in Civil Evidence Act 1968 sect. 5 may, by an apparent oversight, have been imported into the Criminal Justice Act 1988 by Sch. 2 para. 5, see Birch 'The Criminal Justice Act 1988 (2) The Evidence Provisions' [1989] *Crim. L.R.* 15, at 30.

would have been no need for section 5 to have adopted the complex and widely criticised conditions relating to the operation of the computers from which the relevant evidence is derived. The whole situation illustrates the lack of wisdom in tacking special statutory provision for computers, separately devised and independently promoted by a special interest group, on to a scheme constructed as a whole after careful consideration by competent law reformers and experienced draftsmen.

The complex conditions of admissibility are specified in sub-sections 5(2) and 5(3). They were probably intended to enable a court to use the same sort of information, and the same sorts of computer operation, which would be used for making decisions in the commercial world.

The permissible information is defined by sub-sections 5(2)(b) and 5(2)(d) to require,

(b) that over that period there was regularly supplied to the computer in the ordinary course of those activities information of the kind contained in the statement or of the kind from which the information so contained is derived;

(d) that the information contained in the statement reproduces or is derived from information supplied to the computer in the ordinary course of those activities.

Such a requirement is unsuitable, being in some respects too broad and in others too narrow. It may sometimes be over-restrictive. It is quite possible that on occasion the only way of securing the output of certain reports might be by comparison of the information routinely held by the machine with other information specially input to elicit useful cross-checking.[158] Provided that this comparative information were capable of being satisfactorily proved, there seems no reason to exclude it simply because it was not used on a regular basis. Conversely the provision may also, in some circumstances, be far too expansive. Some organisations routinely and quite deliberately use computers to generate false information.[159]

Conditions relating to the operation of the computer itself are imposed by sub-sections 5(2)(a) and 5(2)(c). They require,

(a) that the document containing the statement was produced by the computer during a period over which the computer was used regularly to store or process information for the purposes of any activities regularly carried on over that period, whether for profit or not, by any body, whether corporate or not, or by any individual.

(c) that throughout the material part of that period the computer was operating properly or, if not, that any respect in which it was not operating properly or was out of operation during that part of that period was not such as to affect the production of the document or the accuracy of its contents.

---

158. In civil proceedings arising out of facts like those in *R. v. Wood* (1983) 76 Cr. App. Rep. 110, C.A., above p. 376 for example.

159. In the notorious *Equity Funding* case in the United States the computer generated false identities for the purposes of defrauding insurance underwriters on a large scale, and in England criminal convictions have been recorded for the vendors of a program designed to understate sales of video shops for the purpose of defrauding the revenue, *Times* 20 December 1986 p. 4. Nothing in sect. 5 would prevent the output from these computers being admitted to show that such fictitious persons existed or that total sales were at the fictitiously low level recorded.

'Regularly' is not defined,[160] but means more than that the computer was operating properly since that is superimposed by the later condition. Once again it is not obvious why the statute is drafted in this manner. If the computer is operating properly on appropriate information, it is unclear why the output should be inadmissible simply because it is not used to produce that sort of output on a regular basis.

Section 5(3) treats any combination of computers as if they were one computer for the purposes of the application of the conditions established by section 5(2). This presumably means that the failure of any one of those conditions in relation to any one of such multiple computers will invalidate the admissibility of any statement produced by their interaction with each other. This approach, which might well be appropriate given better drafted conditions, may yield unsatisfactory results with them drawn as they are. For example, a given system might be so vital to a given business that its functions are duplicated on a back-up machine which automatically takes over if the first machine should become faulty. If over the relevant period this occurs very infrequently, it is not obvious that the conditions could be said to be satisfied on such occasions. Thus the back-up machine will not have been used regularly, and if it has been used perhaps only the once, it is not clear that information of the relevant kind could be held to have been ordinarily supplied to it. It would be a bizarre result, however, to exclude the print-out when special precautions have been taken to guard against any inaccuracy, and appear to have operated exactly as planned.

If the maker of the statement in a document had personal knowledge of the truth of its contents, then the document is, in principle, admissible under section 2 of the Act, provided that direct oral evidence of those matters by the maker would have been admissible. Thus if a clerk allocates serial numbers to products, and enters the numbers so allocated into a database, the print-out may be admissible under section 2 even though the conditions of section 5 have not been satisfied, say because the entry was originally made as part of an experiment which was so successful that it has now been approved as a routine procedure.

South Australia has its own distinctive provisions specifically designed to admit evidence derived from computers.[161] To judge from internal evidence alone, these provisions seem to have been drafted by someone who had given careful consideration to section 5 of the English Civil Evidence Act 1968, but had decided to re-draft them so as to redress deficiencies both in relation to understanding of computer methodology and terminology, and in relation to legal adequacy. In broad outline the legislation applies to both criminal and civil proceedings, and to 'computer output'. It is important to note that since restrictive conditions are put upon the admission of such output it was thought necessary to confine the definition of a 'computer' more narrowly than in section 5. The most important difference from section 5 and its Australian progeny is that the South Australian legislation does implicitly

---

160. 'Regularly' has been judicially construed in the context of the equivalent section to 5(2)(b) in the Australian Capital Territory in *Punch* v. *John Fairfax & Co. Ltd.* (A.C.T., 1976) (unreported).
161. Part VIA of the Evidence Act 1929–83.

require personal knowledge of the data from which the print-out is derived.[162] In fact the statute lists some seven conditions of which the court must be satisfied, and although there is a provision making a certificate *prima facie* evidence of their satisfaction, this has not prevented the South Australian Supreme Court from twice[163] finding itself unable to admit print-out under the provision because of its lack of satisfaction of these matters. Since in both such cases the court was able to admit the documents as real evidence at common law, this is an ominous indictment of even the most promisingly drafted specific provisions.

South Africa, although in some respects incorporating civil law principles, has largely adopted a common law model for the admissibility of evidence, despite having no jury system. In 1961 it formally adopted the common law of England, subject only in the case of hearsay to its own subsequent statutory amendment. It is, like England, one of the rare jurisdictions where separate statutory treatment has been accorded to civil[164] and to criminal law.

In civil cases the first general legislation amending the admissibility of hearsay was based upon an English model, the Evidence Act 1938, which became section 34 of the Civil Proceedings Evidence Act 1965. The efficacy of that legislation was tested in the case of *Narlis* v. *South African Bank of Athens*[165] where the admissibility of computerised bank records was in issue. The decision was unfortunately bedevilled by the failure of counsel to appreciate the necessity of proving these records otherwise than by reference to the South African version of the English Bankers' Books Evidence Act 1879.[166] Nor was the authenticating witness able to give very convincing evidence of the the reliability of the records.[167] The Appellate Division was not persuaded that the evidence would have been admissible under common law before 1961 in South Africa, and held that it was not admitted by section 34 because it was not a statement made by a *person*,[168] and had not been signed, initialled or otherwise recognised by anyone. The Appellate Division seems also to have been influenced in its interpretation of this provision by the consideration that in England it had been thought necessary to admit hearsay by a special statutory provision, section 5 of the Civil Evidence Act 1968. This is a further baleful consequence of that provision. The court recommended that the legislature consider the possibility of providing statutory relief from the effects of the decision.

As a result of this decision the whole business community, and in particular the banking profession, given the high incidence of computer use in banking, was very reasonably disturbed by the prospect of the difficulty of pursuing perfectly sound claims. The Association of South African Clearing

---

162. Sub-sect. 59b (2)(b).
163. In *Mehesz* v. *Redman* (1980) 26 S.A.S.R. 244, S.C. and in *R.* v. *Weatherall* (1981) 27 S.A.S.R. 238, S.C.
164. And within civil proceedings to maritime claims where the court is given a very general discretion to admit hearsay, Admiralty Jurisdiction Amendment Act 1983 sect. 6(3).
165. 1976 (2) SA 573, A.D.
166. It does not apply in South Africa in cases to which the bank in question is itself a party.
167. He was, for example, unable to say whether the opening balance was accurate.
168. The court opined it to be fortunate that computers are not persons.

Banks accordingly commissioned Didcott, J., a judge of the High Court of Natal, to report and to advise the South African Law Reform Commission upon the need for legislation. Didcott, J. conducted a particularly thorough study of the position throughout the common law world.[169] He first considered the possibility of following the American model, and essentially leaving it to the judiciary to develop a suitable exception to the hearsay rule. He rejected this solution, partly because there was, in South Africa, no firmly established shopbook exception upon which to build, and partly because of the more conservative approach of the judiciary in South Africa.[170] He went on to assess the relative merits of generic and specific legislation, coming down in favour of specific legislation, largely because he took the view that a very sharp distinction existed between computer-derived records and those of different provenance.[171] He also took the view that as a result of the decision in *Narlis* it was necessary to secure as rapid a legislative response as possible, and that since the South African Law Reform Commission already had the whole of the law of evidence under review it would take far too long to recommend, agree and enact a comprehensive solution.[172] A feature of the Didcott report is the clear separation of the questions of admissibility and weight,[173] leaning towards expanding the former, and leaving the latter to the judges with as little interference from the legislature as possible.

The Computer Evidence Act 1983 was enacted in substantially the terms recommended by Didcott J., and essentially provides for the admissibility of computer output as evidence of any fact recorded in it of which direct oral evidence would be admissible, and that it should be accorded such weight as the court consider appropriate in the circumstances.[174] It is required to be supported by an authenticating affidavit, relating to the identification of the print-out, the sources of the data from which it was compiled, any necessary programming, and certifying that the computer was functioning correctly at all relevant times. A criminal penalty for default adds teeth to this requirement. This legislation has not yet been authoritatively considered by the courts, and has had a mixed reaction from commentators.[175] It is certainly arguable that by concentrating so heavily upon the supporting affidavit the legislation makes it very difficult for a party to rely upon the print-out of a computer as against the party responsible for its production.[176]

---

169. See Didcott, *Legislation Regulating the Admissibility of Computer Generated Evidence* (1980).
170. Para. 10.
171. Para. 16.
172. This situation is strongly reminiscent of the situation with regard to statutory reform of the hearsay rule in criminal proceedings in England where the decision of the House of Lords in *Myers* drew a fast legislative response in the form of the Criminal Evidence Act 1965, without waiting for the lucubrations of the Criminal Law Revision Committee to which the question of the reform of the whole of the law of evidence in criminal proceedings had been referred, see above p. 394.
173. A distinction which seems to baffle those commentators with no, or little, legal training.
174. Sect. 2.
175. See discussion in Van Der Merwe, *Computers & The Law* pp. 121–6.
176. Though it might be possible to meet this objection by sensible use of the doctrine of admissions at this early stage.

Criminal When it was eventually thought expedient to reform the law of evidence in criminal proceedings in the United Kingdom, further thought was given to the reform of the hearsay rule. This resulted in changes not only from the draft provisions proposed by the Criminal Law Revision Committee in 1973,[177] but also from those contained in the government bill which lapsed when parliament was prematurely dissolved for the purposes of a general election in 1983. The scheme differs in conception from that of the Criminal Evidence Act 1965, and is in many respects much less radical than that of the Civil Evidence Act 1968, or than that proposed by the Criminal Law Revision Committee. In outline, Part VII of the Police and Criminal Evidence Act 1984 admits documentary records made pursuant to a duty if the maker is either unavailable or not worth calling, and in the case of computer records subject to proof of the proper operation of the computer.

An important difference from the Criminal Evidence Act 1965 is that there is under the 1984 Act no limitation to business records. The Act applies to all statements in documents compiled by a person acting under a duty from information supplied by someone who had, or could reasonably be supposed to have had, personal knowledge of the matters dealt with in it. The conditions of non-availability were slightly improved and modernised. The most important difference, however, is that the special requirements for computer records are superimposed upon the general provision, so in the case of a document derived from a computer it will be admissible only if it satisfies the requirements both of section 68 *and* of section 69.[178]

In this latter respect it also differs from the Civil Evidence Act 1968. It further differs from that legislation in not seeking to replace the existing law. This meant that it was unnecessary to re-enact the existing common law exceptions as they applied to the admissibility of hearsay in criminal proceedings.[179] Standard procedure in criminal cases also made inappropriate specific provision for the admissibility of hearsay by agreement of the parties. There is no separate general provision, comparable to section 2 of the Civil Evidence Act 1968, to admit oral first-hand hearsay. The Act does, however, retain all existing exclusionary discretions.[180]

Since both sections 68 and 69 will apply to documents derived from computers, it is first necessary to consider section 68. The Criminal Evidence Act 1965 had already been applied to computers,[181] so it was not very surprising that section 68 which directly replaced those provisions, should also apply to them. It should be noted that section 68 equally requires that the document form part of a record. 'Record' is not separately defined for these purposes, and the existing law may be taken to be applicable.[182] The Police and Criminal Evidence Act 1984 specifically applies the definitions of 'copy' and 'statement' from Part 1 of the 1968 Act.[183]

---

177. See Part II of the draft bill clauses 30 to 41.
178. See *R.* v. *Minors, Times* 24 December 1988, C.A.
179. See sub-sect. 68(3).
180. Sub-sect. 72(2).
181. *R.* v. *Ewing* [1983] Q.B. 1039, C.A.
182. See *Cross on Evidence* (6th edn) at p. 494.
183. Sub-sect. 72(1).

The wording of section 68 is largely taken from section 4 of the Civil Evidence Act 1968. The most significant deviation is its omission of section 4's requirement that each intermediary between the original supplier and the ultimate compiler of the information should have been acting under a duty. In this respect it adopts the model of the Criminal Evidence Act 1965 which also omits any such requirement. The most significant adhesion to the wording of section 4 of the Civil Evidence Act 1968 is the retention of the reference to 'record'. This term also appeared in the Criminal Evidence Act 1965, and a common construction was adopted. In civil cases this is irrelevant to records derived from computers since they are, as noted above,[184] governed only by the provisions of section 5 which eschews any reference to 'records'. The scheme of the Police and Criminal Evidence Act 1984 preserves the effect of the Criminal Evidence Act 1965 in applying the restricted concept to statements in documents derived from computers.

Section 69 has the effect of adding further conditions to the admissibility of records derived from computers. While it would have been better to have reverted to the original plan of the Law Reform Committee and to have treated all documents alike whatever their provenance, it cannot be denied that section 69 of the Police and Criminal Evidence Act 1984 is a vast improvement upon section 5 of the Civil Evidence Act 1968. Like section 5 it applies to any statement contained in a document produced by computers. It makes three specific requirements,

(a) that there are no reasonable grounds for believing that the statement is inaccurate because of improper use of the computer;
(b) that at all material times the computer was operating properly, or if not, that any respect in which it was not operating properly or was out of operation was not such as to affect the production of the document or the accuracy of its contents; and
(c) that any relevant conditions specified in rules of court under subsection (2) below are satisfied.

Because of the general scheme of the Act it has the effect of remedying the chief defect of section 5 which was its abstinence from any requirement of personal knowledge in the supplier of the information. Here both section 68 and section 69 apply, so the personal knowledge requirement of section 68 takes effect. This relieves section 69 of any need to contain elaborate conditions relating to the information supplied to the computer or to its physical operation. The requirements of proper use and operation are clearly expressed, and should be capable of being applied by a jury without undue difficulty. It is also significant that the draftsman felt it unnecessary to define a computer, thus freeing himself from the difficulty of specifying a particular technology and from the constraint of being bound by it.

It has recently been decided by the Divisional Court, in a so far vestigially reported case,[185] that where a computer has been used as a tool to facilitate analysis, the conditions imposed by section 69 do not apply. It is hard to understand this proposition without access to the full facts of the case or to the arguments of the court. It must, however, be noted that such an

---

184. At p. 385.
185. *Sophocleous* v. *Ringer* [1987] Crim. L.R. 422, C.A.

interpretation appears to fly in the face of the wording of section 69 which purports to apply to 'a statement contained in a document produced by a computer'. If the computer in this case produced a document indicating the result of its calculation it is very hard to see why it is not covered. The definition of 'statement' is borrowed from section 10 of the Civil Evidence Act 1968 where it includes any representation of fact. It is not obvious why this excludes cases where there is no hearsay element, indeed the fact that it applied in the 1968 Act for the purposes of section 5 as well as sections 2 and 4 suggests that it was intended to apply to both situations. Such an interpretation is also suggested by Schedule 3 Part 11 to the Police and Criminal Evidence Act 1984 itself. In relation to the weight of a statement admitted pursuant to section 69, paragraph 12 equates cases where the supply of information is direct '(with or *without*[186] human intervention)'. If there is no human intervention, then there can be no hearsay element. It is accordingly very hard to resist the argument that section 69 *was* designed to include such cases. It is, however, possible to take a fairly relaxed view of this question since the conditions which would be required to be satisfied at common law for the admissibility of the output of a scientific device[187] are not very different from those imposed by section 69.

Before the Police and Criminal Evidence Act 1984 had even been enacted, much less brought into force, the government had referred the whole question of criminal proceedings in cases of fraud to an independent committee under the chairmanship of Lord Roskill. The Committee discovered widespread concern about the adequacy of criminal procedure in general, and the law of evidence in particular, in relation to the successful prosecution of fraud. The Committee accordingly devoted a full chapter of its report to suggestions for the reform of the law of evidence, and came to the conclusion that acceptance of its proposals in this area was essential to the success of its recommendations.[188] It appreciated that in many cases it would be anomalous to limit its suggestions to the law of evidence in fraud cases. The government was persuaded both that reform was necessary and that fraud could not, and should not, be isolated from the rest of the criminal law. Thus a further change in the admissibility of evidence derived from computers in criminal proceedings was set in train.

The broad intention of this statute, the Criminal Justice Act 1988,[189] is to liberalise still further the admissibility of hearsay, and the relevant provisions appear in Part II of the Act. It is, as its name suggests, limited to criminal proceedings, and thus has no direct effect upon the admissibility of evidence derived from computers in civil proceedings.[190] It applies to *all* criminal proceedings, including those in magistrates' courts. The first bill which

---

186. Emphasis supplied.
187. See p. 375 above.
188. *Fraud Trials Committee Report* (1986) para. 5.32.
189. See generally Birch, 'The Criminal Justice Act 1988 (2) The Evidence Provisions' [1989] *Crim. L.R.* 15.
190. It may still have an indirect impact upon the outcome of given civil proceedings to the extent that evidence of a conviction in criminal proceedings achieved by the use of such hearsay is admissible in the civil proceedings under the provisions of Part II of the Civil Evidence Act 1968.

lapsed when Parliament was prorogued in 1987 differed in some significant respects from the legislation which was finally enacted. It made no explicit provision for special conditions to be applied to evidence derived from computers, and its relation to the sections 68 and 69 of the Police and Criminal Evidence Act 1984 was left obscure. This is no longer so. The conditions imposed upon the admissibility of evidence derived from computers by section 69 of the Police and Criminal Evidence Act 1984 have been applied quite specifically to the two principal sections expanding the range of admissible hearsay.[191]

Part II of the Criminal Justice Act 1988 provides for the general admissibility of all first-hand documentary hearsay;[192] of more remote hearsay if contained in a business document;[193] but subject to a general exclusionary discretion if its admission is considered inimical to the interests of justice;[194] and to a more specific exclusionary rule if prepared for the purposes of pending or contemplated criminal proceedings or of a criminal investigation, though this in its turn is tempered by an inclusionary discretion for any such statements the admission of which are considered to be in the interests of justice.[195] Specific provision is made for the admissibility of hearsay expert reports,[196] and for a number of minor improvements in the form in which documentary evidence may be presented to the court. These provisions will now be considered in a little more detail.

Section 23 deals with first hand documentary hearsay and admits statements made by a person in a document as evidence of any fact of which oral evidence from that person would be admissible. This is capable of applying to evidence derived from a computer, if such a statement is stored on one. Thus in *R.* v. *Ewing*[197] the court considered the operator to have had personal knowledge of the information contained in the document produced by the computer, and this could clearly be the situation in many cases where small businesses or private individuals use micro-computers to conduct their administrative and clerical work. Any hearsay in principle admissible under section 23 will be subject to the exclusionary rule under the provisions of section 24 for documents prepared for the purposes of the proceedings, and to the exclusionary discretion under the provisions of section 25 for evidence the admission of which would, in the opinion of the court, be contrary to the interests of justice.

So far as more remote documentary hearsay is concerned, the pendulum has swung between conditions geared to business records as in the Criminal Evidence Act 1965, and those geared to duty as in the Civil Evidence Act 1968 and the Police and Criminal Evidence Act 1984. In section 24 of the Criminal Justice Act 1988 it has swung back again, though it may be

---

191. By sub-sects 23(1)(c) and 24(1)(c).
192. Sect. 23.
193. Sect. 24.
194. Sect. 25(1).
195. Sect. 26, a rare example of a genuinely inclusionary discretion in the law of evidence as it applies in criminal proceedings.
196. Sect. 30 which applies notwithstanding the general exclusion of documents made for the purposes of criminal proceedings or investigations.
197. [1983] Q.B. 1039, C.A., above p. 401.

significant that the reference is now not to business *records* but to business *documents*. The practical consequences of the retreat from the terminology of duty are unlikely to be very dramatic, given the definition of the scope of section 24 which, although summarised in the shoulder note as applying to business documents, provides that the section applies to cases where,

the document was created or received by a person –
(i) in the course of a trade, business, profession or other occupation; or
(ii) as the holder of a paid or unpaid office.

This definition is, in substance, identical to that of the relevant duty in section 4 of the Civil Evidence Act 1968. It differs only in being definitive instead of merely exemplary as it was there. Section 24 retains the requirement that the original supplier of the information should have had, or be reasonably supposed to have had, personal knowledge of the truth of the information supplied. Like the Civil Evidence Act 1968, the Criminal Justice Act 1988 requires any intermediate supplier to have been acting in the course of business as defined above. It is, however, more explicit than the Civil Evidence Act 1968 or the Criminal Evidence Act 1965 in applying to documents *received*, as well as those made, in the course of business. If such documents are themselves derived from computers, admissibility is made subject to the provisions of section 69 of the Police and Criminal Evidence Act 1984. It is submitted that this could cause unnecessary difficulty since the party tendering the documents will often derive them from a business which has received them, and may well have no knowledge of or access to their original means of provenance. Since computer output is no longer self-identified as such, a party may not even know whether the conditions of section 69 need to be satisfied, much less be able to prove it. This is a further example of the practical problems created by the quite irrational distinction between different documents based upon considerations of the method of producing them which is quite irrelevant to their potential reliability.

Section 25 invests the court with a broad general discretion to exclude evidence falling within the above two categories if it feels that in the interests of justice the statement ought not to be admitted. However, the generality of this discretion is supplemented by the recital of four considerations which the court is mandated to take into account. These relate to the apparent authenticity of the document, its importance to the litigation, its relevance, and its controvertibility. To some extent these considerations point in opposite directions. Thus the more necessary a document is as the *only* evidence of a particular point, so likewise it may become more difficult to controvert. Many of these matters may also affect the weight of a document and will, as such, be considered in the next part of this chapter. The consideration most likely to be given increased significance in the computer context is the first which requires the court to have regard to,

the nature and source of the document containing the statement and to whether or not, having regard to its nature and source and to any other circumstances that appear to the court to be relevant, it is likely that the document is authentic.

It should be noted that this provision relates only to *authenticity*, and not at all to accuracy or reliability, so it does not appear to import the requirements of section 69 of the Police and Criminal Evidence Act 1984 that the computer be used and operating properly. A computer print-out may be perfectly authentic, in the sense of being what it purports to be, without being in the least accurate or reliable. On the question of controvertibility, it should be noted that the Act specifically provides for the use of previous inconsistent statements to discredit the supplier of the information.[198] No restrictive conditions seem to be attached to the proof of such statements, so they may themselves be statements derived from computers. Such statements are, however, not made evidence of the truth of what they state. Their sole function is to contradict, and so to weaken, the weight to be attached to the statement of the maker thus impugned.

In an attempt to minimise the dangers of the fabrication of false documents the Act specifically excludes statements in documents prepared for the purposes of contemplated proceedings or of criminal investigations.[199] There are, however, two very significant qualifications to the generality of this exclusionary rule.

It would *prima facie* exclude documents of the sort tendered in *R.* v. *Wood*[200] showing the analysis of metal ingots for the purpose of demonstrating in court the identity of two samples.[201] In fact, this consequence is averted since the exclusionary rule applies only to documents prepared otherwise than under certain later sections of the Act. In the case of documents of the sort mentioned above, it is likely that they would be tendered by expert witnesses as 'expert reports' under the provisions of section 30, one of the specifically excepted such sections. As expert reports they would be admissible as evidence of any fact or opinion of which the person making (or expressing) it could have given oral evidence. There is in section 30 no reference to section 69 of the Police and Criminal Evidence Act 1984. Given the references in the earlier sections, it is thus arguable that it is not here necessary to show satisfaction of any such conditions.[202] This seems unsatisfactory. There is here no further guarantee of the reliability of such a document than the fact that it is tendered by an expert. Since everything will in such a case depend upon the proper use and operation of the computer used to prepare the document, it is submitted that the conditions of section 69 should be proved to have been complied with, especially as there may be no human witness present to cross-examine.

This exclusionary rule is also made subject to an inclusionary discretion on the basis of the satisfaction of the interests of justice. The effect of this is to make documents prepared for the purposes of criminal proceedings or investigations potentially *more* admissible than other documents. In the case of a record, prepared for the purposes of the proceedings and held on a

---

198. Sched. 2 para. 1(c).
199. The extension to criminal investigations has no precedent even in the broadly similar provision in the draft bill appended to the 11th Report of the Criminal Law Revision Committee, Cmnd. 4991 (1972) cl. 32(3).
200. (1982) 76 Cr. App. Rep. 23, C.A., above p. 376.
201. Another example would be the computer analysis of the control group of documents used for purposes of comparison with the disputed statements as described in Niblett and Boreham, 'Cluster Analysis in Court' [1976] *Crim. L.R.* 175.
202. This seems to accord with the previous position, see *Sophocleous* v. *Ringer* [1987] Crim. L.R. 422, C.A. above p. 402.

computer for example, if it cannot be demonstrated that the supplier of the information contained in it either had, or might reasonably be supposed to have had, personal knowledge of its truth, then the record would be inadmissible under section 26. It might nevertheless be admitted under section 26 if the court felt that it was, even so, in the interests of justice that it be admitted. In making this determination, the court is bound to have regard to the contents of the statement, to the likelihood of prejudice to the accused if the maker does not attend to give oral evidence, and to any other circumstances which appear to be relevant.

The Act follows the recommendation of the Roskill Committee in providing for the admissibility of expert opinion by hearsay, subject only to the leave of the court in a case where the maker does not propose to attend to give oral evidence. No guidance is explicitly offered in this case to guide the exercise of the discretion. The only condition is that the report should deal wholly or mainly with matters, whether of fact or opinion, of which its maker could have given expert evidence.

The Act also liberalises a number of the restrictive rules relating to the means of tendering different types of evidence. It thus provides that a copy of a document is as admissible as an original, notwithstanding the existence of the original, and no matter how many removes there are between the original and the copy; that documents and copies can be authenticated in any manner approved by the Court;[203] that Crown Court rules may provide for the furnishing of evidence in any form notwithstanding the existence of admissible material from which it might be derived, for the purpose of helping jurors to understand complicated issues of fact or technical terms;[204] and that Crown Court Rules, Criminal Appeal Rules and Rules made under section 144 of the Magistrates' Courts Act 1980 can generally be made to implement the purposes of the Act.[205]

(d) Particular statutes

Every jurisdiction has its own special provisions dealing with particular matters of evidence. It is possible here to do no more than indicate in the case of the United Kingdom the range of such provisions, which will be illustrative of the range of choice for all jurisdictions.

Bankers' Books Evidence Act 1879 One of the first statutes to make inroads into the exclusionary rules of the common law of evidence in favour of the smooth operation of commercial practice was the Bankers' Books Evidence Act 1879. Its primary purpose was to ensure that the business of banking was not disrupted by the need to produce the bank's original records in court. In permitting the use of copies it also made a dent in the hearsay rule in providing[206] for the entry to amount to *prima facie* evidence of the matters recorded in it.

Although the definition in the original legislation referred exclusively to

---

203. Sect. 27.
204. Sect. 31.
205. Sched. 2 para. 4.
206. Sect. 3.

'books' of various descriptions,[207] a robust construction was applied so as to encompass more modern methods:

The Bankers' Books Evidence Act 1879 was enacted with the practice of bankers in 1879 in mind. It must be construed in 1980 in relation to the practice of bankers as we now understand it. So construing the definition of 'bankers' books' and the phrase 'an entry in a banker's book', it seems to me that clearly both phrases are apt to include any form of permanent record kept by the bank of transactions relating to the bank's business, made by any of the methods which modern technology makes available, including, in particular, microfilm.[208]

This extract gives the lie to a certain fashionable distrust of the inclination and abilities of the judiciary to mould existing rules to cater for the computer. Such judicial flexibility is all the more commendable since here it was a statutory, rather than common law, rule which was so adapted.

The original definition was replaced by a new section 9(2) as a result of the enactment of Schedule 6 of the Banking Act 1979, and now reads as follows:

Expressions in this Act relating to 'bankers' books' include ledgers, day books, cash books, account books and other records used in the ordinary business of the bank whether those records are in written form or are kept on microfilm, magnetic tape or any other form of mechanical or electronic data retrieval mechanism.

It can hardly be doubted that as optical storage techniques become increasingly used, a similarly robust interpretation will be used to still any pedantic quibbles about the applicability of this definition.

It should be noted that in order to be admissible the record must be one made in the ordinary course of the business of the bank, it must have been under the bank's control,[209] and it must be further proved that the copy adduced in court has been examined against the original entry and is correct.[210] It is not completely clear how these provisions will be applied in the case of computers, though they seem to have caused no difficulty in *R. v. Ewing*[211] and their satisfaction will perhaps be challenged only rarely.

These provisions should not, in general, be applied to foreign banks in order to secure the production in the United Kingdom of the books of a foreign bank, and certainly not without notice to the bank.[212]

Data Protection Act 1984 It will be recalled that this Act deals exclusively with information which is processed automatically, invariably in a computer. It provides for an elaborate scheme of registration, imposes duties on data handlers and confers rights upon data subjects. These provisions may have an adverse impact upon some commercial enterprises, and are designed to

---

207. Sect. 9.
208. *Barker* v. *Wilson* [1980] 2 All E.R. 81 at 83, Q.B.D, per Bridge L.J.
209. Sect. 4.
210. Sect. 5.
211. [1983] Q.B. 1039, C.A.
212. *Mackinnon* v. *Donaldson, Lufkin and Jenrette Securities Corp.* [1986] 1 All E.R. 653, Ch., following *R. v. Grossman* (1981) 73 Cr.. App. R. 302, C.A.

provide redress for grievances harboured by data subjects. The Act accordingly sets up a special tribunal to deal with appeals against the determinations of the Registrar, and allows access to the ordinary courts for the redress of grievances, for example to secure compensation where damage has been caused by the use of inaccurate data. It might thus have been expected that the Act would incorporate special provision for the admissibility of evidence derived from computers, as most of the evidence will be in this context. In fact the Act contains no such provision relating to the admissibility of evidence. It seems to assume that the ordinary rules can cope with such evidence without difficulty. Thus in the guidelines set out for establishing rules of procedure to be followed by the Tribunal in hearing appeals, reference is made to securing 'data material' as well as documents, presumably on the basis that it will be admissible in evidence, but without even there any explicit provision for such admissibility.[213]

Companies Act 1985 s. 723 This is included here as an exemplar of the sort of provision which may be adopted to facilitate the use of modern business methods. It is necessary to provide that institutions soliciting funds should keep adequate records as a check against fraud. Thus provision has always been made for keeping and publishing the accounts of public companies. Such records are increasingly held on computers, and this has required explicit authorisation. Section 723 of the Companies Act 1985 accordingly bestows power to keep such records 'otherwise than in a legible form', but only so long as 'the recording is capable of being reproduced in a legible form'. The Act then simply transfers access provisions to the legible form.

Others The most common form of explicit statutory reference is an authorisation to hold a particular form of register on a computer, sometimes, but not always, accompanied by an expanded definition of a 'record' or a 'copy'.

Among the registers and lists explicitly authorised to be maintained by computer in addition to the company records mentioned above are those of the roll of solicitors,[214] of local land charges,[215] of titles to land,[216] of members of trade unions,[217] of trade marks, designs and patents,[218] the land registration day list,[219] and of burials.[220]

Some legislation explicitly refers to the possibility of taking into account 'computer or non-documentary' records.[221] It is sometimes recognised that this will involve consequential changes in the application of other rules, thus

---

213. Despite explicit mention being made of such mundane matters as the summoning of witnesses and the administration of oaths, and by contrast with the much more specific provision made for the consideration of computer records in the Insolvency Practitioners Tribunal (Conduct of Investigations) Rules 1986 SI 1986 No 952 s. 7(b).
214. Solicitors Act 1974 sect. 6(2).
215. Local Government (Miscellaneous Provisions) Act 1982 sect. 34.
216. Administration of Justice Act 1982 sect. 66.
217. Trade Union Act 1984 sect. 4(2).
218. Patents, Designs and Marks Act 1986 sect. 1.
219. Land Registration Rules 1925, S.R. & O. 1925 No. 1093 sect. 7A.
220. Local Authorities' Cemeteries Order 1977 S.l. 1977 No. 204 sect. 11(1).
221. Insolvency Practitioners Tribunal (Conduct of Investigations) Rules 1986 S.l. 1986 No. 952 sect. 7.

in the case of customs entries, which need to be precisely timed, special provision is made for fixing the time as that at which an entry is accepted by the computer.[222] Similarly, modifications had to be made for the rules relating to the registration of share transfers in authorising the use of computers for that purpose.[223] It is useful in such cases to specify with some particularity the means of authentication of the certified copy of a record held on a computer. One of the best examples is to be found in section 11A of the Local Authorities Cemeteries Order 1977 which requires a responsible person to identify the relevant document and its means of production, and to give particulars of any ancillary device used in conjunction with the computer to produce the document.

D. Miscellaneous points of evidence

The law of evidence, while mainly concerned with the admissibility of evidence, also contains other sorts of rules, among them rules about the qualifications and privileges of witnesses. Two linked topics which may be of some interest in the area of the law relating to computers are those which concern the use of experts, and the privileges which experts and indeed other witnesses in litigation relating to computers may enjoy.

A. Expert witnesses

Given the nature of the computer and the general unfamiliarity of the Courts with the principles of their operation, it will often be necessary to adduce expert evidence on these matters. There are two main avenues in the United Kingdom by which this may be accomplished, one much broader and more frequented than the other.[224] The more popular option is for a party to call his own expert; the less popular is for a party to apply to the court under the provisions of Order 40 for it to appoint its own 'court expert'.

The rules relating to calling expert evidence were substantially amended in the United Kingdom by the Civil Evidence Act 1972, and the rules made under it, which implemented the recommendations of the Law Reform Committee in its report on the matter.[225] The general intention of these proposals was to reduce reliance upon and conflict between oral expert evidence adduced by the parties at the trial. To this end it was proposed to extend the relaxation of the hearsay rule to evidence of opinion as noted above,[226] though as there pointed out the relaxation does not apply to statements produced by computers. In further pursuit of the same general end it was hoped to encourage agreement between experts and settlement, by restricting the amount of expert evidence which could be called at the trial and by making its use conditional upon its having been disclosed in advance

---

222. Customs and Excise Management Act 1979 sect. 43(4).
223. Stock Transfer Act 1982 sect. 1.
224. The same two avenues are available in the United States under Federal Rules of Evidence rule 702 (expert called by party) and rule 706 (expert called by court).
225. 17th Report of the Law Reform Committee (Evidence of Opinion and Ex pert Evidence) Cmnd. 4489 (1970).
226. P. 395 above.

of the trial, especially in those cases where there was no real dispute about the facts upon which the expert opinion was based. Provision was accordingly made in section 2 of the Civil Evidence Act 1972 for rules of court to be made to implement these policies. The result is that a party may not call expert evidence[227] at the trial unless he has sought a direction relating to disclosure to his opponent,[228] and such an order will ordinarily be made unless the facts are in dispute, or unascertainable by the expert and not within his professional expertise. It is also possible for such evidence to be given in the form of a written statement notwithstanding the general prohibition in the Civil Evidence Act 1968 upon putting in the statement of a witness whom it is proposed to call.

The Law Reform Committee was not much disposed to recommend any radical extension of the power of the court to call an expert witness itself,[229] taking the view that there were problems in the selection of such an expert, in deciding in advance upon the view of the facts which his report should assume, and in the status to be accorded to his conclusions. Nevertheless the power to call such a witness existed at common law, whether or not the parties agreed, and formal provision was made for the procedure in 1934 and is now contained in Order 40 of the Rules of the Supreme Court. Such an expert is given explicit power to conduct an experiment or 'test of any kind (other than one of a trifling character)', and if a party objects the court has power to require that the test be permitted. Such a power would appear to be adequate to authorise such an expert to run computer programs and to report upon their results. Although some judges[230] have expressed enthusiasm for this procedure, they seem to be in a small minority. Parties generally prefer to control their own destinies and to provide their own evidence for themselves.

The general rules relating to the evidence of experts naturally apply to those whose expertise relates to computers in the same way as to any others. Computing has not yet acquired a professional status in the same way as other areas of expertise, such as medicine or foreign law, and there is less of a history of academic qualifications. It is thus hardly surprising to find experts more often qualified by reference to their working experience.[231] An expert on computers may rely upon what he has learned from books and other second-hand sources of expertise even though these are not put in evidence. He should not, however, rely upon material which has not acquired authoritative status. The line between these categories can be very fine, and might cause difficulty if an expert on computers testified on the basis of a program which he had once seen demonstrated in public, for example.[232]

---

227. Either direct or hearsay.
228. Or unless all parties agree, Order 38 rule 36(1).
229. Cmnd. 4489 para. 14.
230. Notably Lord MacNaghtan in *Coles* v. *Home and Colonial Stores Ltd.* [1904] A.C. 179, H.L. at 182, and Lord Denning M.R. in *Re Saxton* [1962] 3 All E.R. 92, C.A. (where the expert would have conducted scientific tests upon a disputed document).
231. See, e.g., *Texas Warehouse Co. of Dallas Inc.* v. *Spring Mills Inc.* 511 S.W.2d 735 (Tex. Civ. App., 1974).
232. See *H.* v. *Schering Chemicals* [1983] 1 All E.R. 849, C.A. and *R.* v. *Abadom* [1983] 1 All E.R. 364, C.A.

In criminal proceedings the Criminal Justice Act 1988 has made special provision for the furnishing of expert reports by hearsay, although if the maker is not to be called it is necessary to enlist the leave of the court.[233] It is noteworthy that this provision, unlike the Civil Evidence Act 1972, makes no attempt to exclude evidence derived from computers.

2. Privilege

Privileges in the law of evidence entitle their holders to refrain from producing or testifying about certain matters, or to restrain others from doing so. Since they operate not to authorise, but to prevent, the use of potentially relevant material, they require a strong social basis, and are construed rigorously. Traditionally such rules fall into two categories, those where there is a directly applicable public interest and those where the public interest is expressed indirectly by the endorsement of a category of private interest. In the United Kingdom this distinction is now[234] marked by a difference in terminology, the former categorised as a species of immunity on the basis of public policy, and the latter as a species of privilege.[235]

The difference is mainly apparent in the fact that in the case of the immunity the objection must be taken by the court if not raised by a party, cannot be waived, and cannot be circumvented by the production of secondary evidence of the immune material.[236] By contrast, in the case of private privilege only a party may take the objection, it may be waived by its holder, and secondary evidence is generally admissible. It is convenient to consider these two areas separately.

(a) Public policy immunity

The only significance for the law relating to computers in this branch of the law of evidence is that it may be expected to be invoked abnormally often, since computers are used disproportionately by the government in its most secret and advanced operations. Thus weapon systems, diplomatic communications and governmental financial transactions are among the operations most likely to involve computers in simulation, cryptography and calculation. In the United Kingdom,[237] but not apparently in the United States,[238] it is, in the last resort, possible for a judge to inspect the relevant document in order to determine whether the claim to such immunity should prevail over the opposing public interest in the administration of justice requiring all relevant material to be accessible to the court. If the evidence is held only on a computer, this power would be nugatory unless supported by a power to require the document to be made accessible in an intelligible

---

233. Sub-sect. 30(2).
234. See *Duncan* v. *Camell Laird & Co. Ltd.* [1942] A.C. 624, H.L. at 641, recently re-affirmed in *Air Canada* v. *Secretary of State for Trade (No.2)* [1983] 2 A.C. 394, H.L. at 436.
235. No similar terminological distinction is made in the United States, see e.g. *U.S.* v. *Reynolds* 345 U.S. 1 (1953).
236. Though in some cases where it is the means of proof rather than the subject-matter itself which is immune, other evidence of the subject-matter may be adduced.
237. *Air Canada* v. *Secretary of State for Trade (No.2)* [1983] 2 A.C. 394, H.L.
238. *Environmental Protection Agency* v. *Mink* 410 U.S. 73 (1973).

form, by output in the form of printing or visual display, and perhaps supplemented by some explanation of coding. It should be noted that the courts will be most reluctant to permit this immunity to be claimed to the disadvantage of the accused in a criminal prosecution.

(b) *Private privilege*

The tendency, especially in the United Kingdom, has been to reduce to a minimum the categories of private privilege. It has effectively been reduced to the privilege against self-incrimination, legal professional privilege, and privilege for statements made without prejudice in the course of attempting to settle a dispute. In the United States a significant addition to this list is a privilege in respect of confidential trade secrets.

The privilege against self-incrimination is, in the United States, invested with constitutional strength,[239] and in the British Commonwealth it is well-entrenched as a matter of common law. Thus in *Rank Film Distributors Ltd.* v. *Video Information Centre*[240] the House of Lords was prepared to apply the privilege so as to defeat the whole rationale of the judicially created adjunct to discovery known as the *Anton Piller* order.[241] So, too, it has been suggested that it can be invoked, not only in relation to legal proceedings, but also in respect of proceedings for penalties under administrative process.[242] However, in those jurisdictions where it does not enjoy a formal constitutional status, it is possible for the legislature to intervene to abridge the privilege, as it did in the United Kingdom in intellectual property cases with the passage of section 72 of the Supreme Court of Judicature Act 1981. In such cases it is common for the legislation to confer in return some inhibition upon the use of the incriminating material, and even in the United States it is not necessarily unconstitutional for such a position to be reached. It should also be noted that in the United Kingdom, and in most Commonwealth jurisdictions, the privilege inheres in corporate bodies as it does in individual human beings, though this is not so in the United States.[243]

The other main branch of private privilege is concerned to secure the relationship of lawyer and client. This privilege may be somewhat weaker than that against self-incrimination, but is nevertheless of universal application in the common law.[244] Now that lawyers are using computers to an ever-increasing extent there is an increasing likelihood that the privilege may have to be invoked in respect of communications held in computer-readable form.[245] It should be stressed, however, that the privilege applies only to

---

239. By the fifth amendment to the Constitution. It has also achieved formal constitutional status in Canada.
240. [1982] A.C. 380, H.L.
241. Discussed more fully in the next chapter.
242. *Rio Tinto Zinc Corp.* v. *Westinghouse Electric Corp.* [1978] A.C. 547, H.L.
243. Compare *Triplex Safety Glass Co.* v. *Lancegay Safety Glass (1934) Ltd.* [1939] 2 K.B. 395, C.A. with *Hale* v. *Henkel* 201 U.S. 43 at 74 (1906).
244. And even outside it, see *A.M. & S. Europe* v. *E.C. Commission* [1983] Q.B. 878, E.C.
245. Despite some academic anxiety, see Marcellino, 'Expert Witnesses in Software Copyright Infringement Actions', *6 Comp. L. J.* 35 (1985), there seems to be as yet no evidence of abuse of discovery processes to secure computer-readable materials properly subject to the privilege.

communications made for the purpose of securing legal advice, and does not extend to documents coming into existence before the establishment of the relevant relationship. Here too it seems that the privilege may extend beyond the realm of litigation into that of administrative inquiry.[246] Recent legislation seems here to have been more prone to recognise and to respect the existence of the privilege.[247] Even where the privilege is recognised to exist, it may still be waived, though in one case involving computers there was some dispute whether such waiver occurred when information subject to the privilege was revealed in error to an opponent, and the question arose of whether privilege could be claimed by the party who had erred in subsequent litigation against a third party.[248]

In the United States a further arguable head of privilege protects trade secrets.[249] The argument is whether this should truly be regarded as a privilege since it is generally accepted that the courts must apply a balancing analysis, and can adopt a number of expedients so as to permit justice to be done without encroaching too far upon the trading position of the disclosing party.[250] In the United Kingdom there is no doubt that there is no such privilege, but much the same effect is achieved by the application of the law of confidence, and in particular by seeking injunctive relief preventing the use of confidential material, even at the hands of innocent recipients.[251] This area is potentially of some significance in relation to computers since an increasing proportion of trade secrets directly concern them, or are capable of being revealed by evidence derived from them. So far, however, there seems to have been no full discussion of the issues.[252] Given that the area is in both jurisdictions discretionary, it is probably safe to assume that any such claim will rarely, if ever, be upheld against an accused person in a criminal case.

---

246. More certainly in Commonwealth jurisdictions than in the United Kingdom; compare, for example, *I.R.C.* v. *West-Walker* [1954] N.Z.L.R. 191, C.A. and *Baker* v. *Campbell* 49 A.L.R. 385 (H.C.A., 1983) with *Parry-Jones* v. *Law Society* [1969] 1 Ch. 1, C.A. But see also *A.M. & S.Europe* v. *E.C. Commission* [1983] Q.B. 878, E.C.
247. See, e.g., Police and Criminal Evidence Act 1984 sect. 10.
248. *U.S.* v. *International Business Machines Inc.* 3 C.L.S.R. 811 (S.D.N.Y., 1972).
249. Such categorisation was proposed as Rule 508 in the Federal Rules of Evidence, but like other detailed rules relating to privileges was not enacted.
250. For example, by limiting disclosure to legal advisers.
251. See *Lord Ashburton* v. *Pape* [1913] 2 Ch 469, C.A.
252. Though in *Perma Research & Development Co.* v. *Singer Co.* 542 F.2d 111 (2nd Cir., 1976) the Court does seem to have upheld such a claim absolutely despite opposing counsel's undertaking to keep the computer output confidential.

Chapter 10

Practice

As shown in the previous chapter, courts generally take a liberal view of the theoretical admissibility of evidence derived from computers. There may, however, still be practical problems to be overcome, and some of these are addressed in this chapter. They may be divided very roughly into those which arise before the trial has started and those that arise once it has begun. The former are mainly problems concerned with securing the evidence, and the latter with its assessment by the trier of fact.

A. Pre-trial

Common law civil procedure depends upon the parties being able to compel their adversary to discover information in his possession bearing upon the issues set out in the statement of claim. In the case of information held in a computer, but where no print-out has yet been made, there may be special problems. It will be necessary to consider how far the ordinary processes of discovery are sufficient. If the ordinary processes of discovery are unavailable, as in criminal proceedings, or liable to be frustrated by the actions of the other party in civil proceedings, some more summary or faster procedure for securing access to relevant information may be desirable, and in this connection attention will be paid to the use of search warrants in the former case, and of *Anton Piller* orders in the latter. Sometimes computers can be used to create relevant evidence in advance of the trial, and such creation may require access to an opponent's programs or data. It is necessary to consider how far the rules are adequate to cope with this situation. Finally, because modern business, and especially that on a scale likely to involve the use of computers is frequently international, some mention must be made of the means of securing evidence from other jurisdictions, and for providing it to them.

1. Discovery[1]

The process of discovery originated in the Courts of Chancery, and the position was concisely summarised in *Flight* v. *Robinson*:

> The general rule is, that a defendant is bound to discover all the facts within his knowledge, and to produce all documents in his possession, which are material to the case of the plaintiff.[2]

The modern position in the United Kingdom[3] is governed by the Rules of the Supreme Court of Judicature, Order 24, as follows:

> After the close of pleadings in an action begun by writ there shall, subject to and in accordance with the provisions of this Order, be discovery by the parties to the action of the documents which are or have been in their possession, custody or power relating to matters in question in the action.[4]

It will be noted that since there is no explicit reference to computers or print-outs, everything must depend upon the construction of the word 'documents'. When this question arose before the Australian courts in *Cassidy* v. *Engwirda Construction Co.*[5] in relation to its application to a tape-recording, Hoare J. adopted a liberal interpretation upon the basis that:

> Nothing is more likely to destroy the effectiveness of the law and our legal system than a timid, restrictive, interpretation of procedural provisions.[6]

Exactly the same view, and result, was reached when the same question was ventilated in England in *Grant* v. *Southwestern and County Properties Ltd.*[7] where it was held to be a sufficient identifying characteristic of a document that it teach something, and that it is immaterial whether it deliver its learning to ear, nose or 'any other sense'. Nor is it material that the information be held in an unintelligible form:

> It is . . . quite clear that the mere interposition of necessity of an instrument for deciphering the information cannot make any difference in principle. A litigant who keeps all his documents in microdot form could not avoid discovery because in order to read the information extremely powerful microscopes or other sophisticated instruments would be required.[8]

Or, one might add, if they were held in an electronic form in a computer from which they could be rendered intelligible only by the application of a program calling up a display or commanding a print-out. *Grant* has itself

---

1. This section deals with the normal case where discovery is sought as part of the process of trying some other dispute, but it should be noted that it is in exceptional circumstances possible to bring an action for discovery itself, if the party against whom it is brought has 'become mixed up in the tortious acts of others so as to facilitate their wrongdoing', per Lord Reid in *Norwich Pharmacal Co.* v. *Commissioners for Customs and Excise* [1974] A.C. 133, H.L. at 175.
2. (1844) 8 Beav. 22, Ch.
3. No attempt has been made here to explain in detail the very different and more expansive procedural rules which apply in the United States.
4. Rule 1(1).
5. [1967] Q.W.N. No. 16, S.C.. See also *Hyslop* v. *Australian Paper Manufacturers Ltd. (No.2)* [1987] V.R. 309, S.C.
6. At 31.
7. [1975] Ch. 185, Ch.
8. At 198.

now been approved in *obiter dicta* by the High Court of Australia,[9] and by a direct decision of O'Bryan J. in the State of Victoria where he remarked that,

new technology – and I include a tape recording as being within that description – should not be allowed to limit the obvious purposes of Order 31. The word 'document' in rule 12 should be construed to include any material contained in a permanent form whether in writing or otherwise which can be released for inspection by some appropriate equipment.[10]

It should be noted that not only do these rules provide for discovery in the sense of the revelation of the existence of relevant documents, but also for their inspection and copying,[11] and if necessary for their production for this purpose at such time and place as the court think fit.[12] In the modern law, service of lists of documents on discovery replaces the need to serve specific notices to produce, and also helps save unnecessary cost in establishing authenticity.[13] The major constraint on these powers is that a party is not obliged to permit inspection of any document for which a valid claim of privilege may be maintained. In this context the privilege against self-incrimination may sometimes be invoked, though as will be seen below this has now been excluded by statute in intellectual property cases.[14] In the United States some concern has been expressed in extra-judicial commentary about the impact upon legal professional or work product privilege when a computerised litigation support system has been employed. It is, however, unnecessary to consider this question in detail here as it has not yet bothered the courts in the United States despite the greater width of discovery there, and the vastly greater use made of such litigation support systems.

Quite apart from these rules the court has power to order the inspection of any property which is the subject-matter of any cause of action and which is in the possession of a party.[15] This power can be exercised at any time after acknowledgement of the service of the writ. This might be useful in a case relating to, say, the efficiency of the operation of a computer-controlled machine installed upon the premises of one of the parties.

In the United States discovery is much more extensive than in the United Kingdom, and more of the special problems peculiar to computers have emerged. A party who has few details of his opponent's record-keeping activities is always in a difficult situation. If he asks for records according to too precise a specification he may receive a truthfully negative answer; if he asks according to too broad a specification he may be deluged with more information than he can manage. This can be particularly serious in the computer context where the seas of material susceptible of being discovered are often both fathomless and uncharted. In *Greyhound Computer Co.* v. *International Business Machines Corp.*[16] the defendant made available thousands

---

9. *Australian National Airlines Commission* v. *Commonwealth of Australia* (1975) 132 C.L.R. 582 at 594.
10. *Overlander Australia Ltd.* v. *Commercial Union of Australia* (unreported) S.C. Victoria 11 March 1982.
11. Order 24 rule 9.
12. Order 24 rule 11(1).
13. See Order 27 rules 4 and 5.
14. P. 421 below,
15. Order 29 rule 2.
16. 3 C.L.S.R. 138 (D. Minn., 1971).

of documents in four different locations, as well as six reels of magnetic tape, the total corpus being both unmanageable and incomprehensible. To make matters worse, no facilities were made available to explain even the formatting of the documents. Yet this was still held to be sufficient. It is likely that a different view would be taken today.

Rule 34 of the Federal Rules of Civil Procedure entitles a party to discover all documents relevant to his case in an appropriate form.[17] The annotation to this rule by the Advisory Committee makes it quite clear that in the computer context this may be interpreted as provision in a usable form which may be legible print-out, but which may also be required to be machine-readable. Thus in the *Greyhound* case the print-out was, in some sense, legible but without being usable. It has now been decided that where discovery is ordered the seeker is *prima facie* entitled to have the information in the form most useful to him.[18] Matters are in some areas assisted by specific statutory provision. Thus the Internal Revenue Code in the United States provides[19] that taxpayers should keep records of their business, and by regulation[20] machine-sensible data are explicitly subsumed under this obligation. In *U.S.* v. *Davey*[21] it was accepted at all levels that this was desirable:

In this era of developing information-storage technology there is no conceivable reason to adopt a construction that would immunise companies with computer-based record-keeping systems from IRS scrutiny.

Thus the tender of hard copy print-out was held to have been rightly rejected.[22] The only real question was whether the Internal Revenue Service was entitled to use the original copies of the defendant's tapes and, if not, whether it had to pay the cost of duplication. Here the only reason for keeping the tapes was the statutory obligation to do so, thus the argument that production of them would be unduly onerous could hardly be sustained. An attempt to make the Internal Revenue Service pay the cost of duplication failed for the same reason.

In order for discovery to be ordered it is, of course, first necessary to establish that the records exist in the form required. This was much debated in the pre-trial stages of *U.S.* v. *International Business Machines Corp.*[23] There the court made a preservation order enjoining both parties from destroying any documents related to electronic data processing. But subsequent to the order, and in pursuance of a settlement in other litigation, the defendant secured the destruction of a computer-readable database in this very area which would have been of the greatest use to the government in the preparation of its case. The government's claim that the defendant should bear the cost of reconstituting the database in machine-readable form complete with index was disallowed, but the court still regarded the defendant's conduct as a violation of the preservation order, even though the

---

17. See further below p. 426.
18. *Adams* v. *Dan River Mills* 40 F.R.D. 220 (W.D.Va., 1972).
19. 26 U.S.C. sect. 6001.
20. Revenue ruling 71-20, 1970-1 Com. Bull. 392.
21. 543 F.2d 996 (2nd Cir., 1976) at 999.
22. Cf. *Luther* v. *Jackson* 6 C.L.S.R. 362 (Ark., 1976).
23. 58 F.R.D. 556 (S.D.N.Y., 1973).

settlement had been phrased in terms of the destruction of material covered by the 'work product' rule. Under that rule, protection is often allowed to material which represents the efforts of counsel on one side. Here, however, the court was aggrieved because it had had no chance either to see the documents so as to decide for itself whether or not to exercise its discretion to order discovery even though the material could be said to fall within the rule.

If the material has once been established to exist, and has been preserved in machine-readable form, the defendant may still raise any number of objections to its production. He may first of all claim that he will be involved in serious expense. It is necessary to be clear exactly what the claimant is seeking. Does he merely want the holder to produce the data, or does he also require the holder to provide machine time for processing, or does he go further still and seek data, time and relevant programming? An impasse may occasionally arise where the claimant wants to use the holder's machine, but is reluctant to trust the holder's staff to do the programming, while the holder is reluctant to allow the claimant to program the holder's machine.[24] In such a case the only solution is to order production of the data and to let the claimant make what arrangements he can for outside processing. In any case the claimant must be prepared to pay any costs incurred by the holder on this account. If the holder is unable to complete the work required on his own equipment he should seek an extension of time, or even employ outside assistance. It is not enough to perform in part, especially where, as in *Local 743, IAM* v. *United Aircraft Corp.*,[25] the unhelpful result of such part performance is to supply the claimant with 120 000 pieces of paper to sort out and analyse. In all of these cases the court has,

to strike a balance between requiring a party defendant to make compilation and tabulation and to expensive research to make answers and exhibits for his opponents, and to deliberate employment of delaying tactics on the part of a defendant designed to impede the progress of discovery.[26]

The principle remains valid even though its application on the facts of the case now seems highly questionable. The claimant will, in most cases, require, in addition to copies of the raw data, as much supporting documentation on such things as character codes and input formats as it is possible to supply. He needs everything which may be necessary for him to be able to use the data productively. Thus the holder will have to produce a program as well as the data if he proposes to adduce evidence of exhibits so created. Effective cross-examination of his witnesses would otherwise be impossible.[27]

Here the claimant may run into more formidable objections than those based on time, trouble and expense, all of which can be mitigated, if not completely cured, by an appropriate order as to costs. The holder may claim that to reveal data, formats and programming may infringe rules restricting

---

24. As in *U.S.* v. *Davey, Secretary of Continental Corp.* 543 F.2d 996 (2nd Cir., 1976).
25. 3 L.R.R.M. 2904 (D. Conn., 1963).
26. *Greyhound Computer Co.* v. *International Business Machines Corp.* 3 C.L.S.R. 138 (D. Minn., 1971).
27. *U.S.* v. *Dioguardi* 428 F.2d 1033 (2nd Cir., 1970).

the disclosure of trade secrets, confidential information or attorney's work product.

So far as the objection is based on the revelation of trade secrets, computer programs seem no different from any other secret information, and the court has power to order production subject to protection pursuant to Rule 26(b) of the Federal Rules of Civil Procedure[28] which prohibits any unauthorised use or further disclosure. Confidential information poses more problems. The courts are, of course, bound by the terms of any non-disclosure statutes,[29] though these invariably make an exception for documents disclosed pursuant to an order for production made by a court. Nevertheless the court will be anxious to protect confidentiality as far as possible, and may go to great lengths to offer acceptable alternatives. In *U.S.* v. *Liebart*[30] and a number of similar cases the defendants, accused of failing to file tax returns, sought to discover lists of other nonfilers, ostensibly to check the procedures which had been used. The court held that the proper course for the government was to offer all other possible assistance to the claimant to check the procedures used, and even to provide time for experiment on the government's computer. It was felt that such facilities should be adequate for the claimed purpose and yet not infringe the privacy of any taxpayer.

A final, and particularly difficult, objection is one based upon attorney's work product. It is clear from *U.S.* v. *International Business Machines Corp.*[31] that the decision whether documents so qualify is one for the court, and not one for the parties to determine for themselves. It has become increasingly difficult to determine as parties move more and more to litigation support systems which marshal documents ready for trial. Such systems may be expensive to run and complicated to devise. The main problem, however, is that the principle of their organisation may provide a very clear clue to the theory of the case adopted by the holder. For this reason it has been held[32] that only the documents held in the system, and not the system itself, are required to be disclosed. This seems fair though it imposes upon the holder the burden of stripping out any revealing codes, and perhaps even of re-ordering the information so as to prevent reverse system design. In some cases it may be difficult to distinguish between original documents and work product. Thus in *U.S.* v. *International Business Machines Corp.*[33] the database destroyed pursuant to the settlement had been heavily annotated and it is not clear that the government would have been satisfied with a bland, unannotated, version. It should be remembered that the privilege for work product is itself liable to be disregarded if in the opinion of the court the claimant can show substantial need, and the inability to satisfy it in any other way.

---

28. As was done in *Adams* v. *Dan River Mills* 40 F.R.D. 220 (W.D. Va., 1972) and *U.S.* v. *International Business Machines Corp.* 58 F.R.D. 556 (S.D.N.Y., 1973).
29. See above p. 310.
30. 519 F.2d 542 (3rd Cir., 1975).
31. 58 F.R.D. 556 (S.D.N.Y., 1973).
32. *International Business Machines Inc. Peripherals* 5 C.L.S.R. 878 (N.D. Cal., 1973).
33. 58 F.R.D. 556 (S.D.N.Y., 1973).

These orders which were designed to buttress the ordinary processes of discovery, especially in cases involving intellectual property have already been described, (see above pp 71, 72).

3. Search warrants

Discovery is peculiar to civil proceedings, as is the extraordinary *Anton Piller* procedure. If evidence is to be secured for the purposes of criminal proceedings, it must be obtained by way of a search warrant. The law relating to the searching of premises and seizure of property was codified in Part II of the Police and Criminal Evidence Act 1984, and guidelines for its exercise were set out in the Code of Practice issued pursuant to section 66 of the Act. A magistrate may issue such a warrant upon being satisfied that there are reasonable grounds to believe that a serious arrestable offence has been committed, that material valuable to its investigation is on the premises in question, that the material is likely to be relevant evidence, and that unless the warrant is issued the material is unlikely to be forthcoming.[34] The Code of Practice deals specifically with material held in a computer and provides:

Where an officer considers that a computer may contain information that could be used in evidence, he may require the information to be produced in a form that can be taken away and in which it is visible and legible.[35]

This provision does not in terms cater for the situation where the officer wishes to take away a copy in machine-readable form, but that would be catered for by the power to photograph or copy any document or other article.[36]

The Police and Criminal Evidence Act 1984 is not, however, an exclusive and exhaustive code for search and seizure, and different powers exist under other provisions. Thus the subsequently enacted Financial Services Act 1986 contains further provisions allowing warrants to be issued in respect of a number of offences of fraud and insider trading, where computer evidence might well be necessary to authorise those named,

(a) to enter the premises specified in the information, using such force as is reasonably necessary for the purpose;
(b) to search the premises and take possession of any documents . . . or to take, in relation to any such documents, any other steps which may appear to be necessary for preserving them or preventing interference with them;
(c) to take copies of any such documents; and
(d) to require any person named in the warrant to provide an explanation of them or to state where they may be found.[37]

---

34. Police and Criminal Evidence Act 1984 sect. 8. The evidence should be admissible in criminal proceedings, and not fall within stated categories of excluded material, that is of a privileged, confidential or journalistic nature.
35. Code of Practice for the Searching of Premises by Police Officers and the Seizure of Property found by Police Officers on Persons or Premises (1985) para. 6.5.
36. Para. 6.4.
37. Sect. 199(3).

As might be expected in legislation intended to apply to modern business dealings, there is an explicitly extended definition of the documents to which it relates to include,

information recorded in any form, and in relation to information recorded otherwise than in legible form, references to its production include references to producing a copy of the information in legible form.[38]

Since this is an inclusive definition it would appear equally possible to secure a machine-readable copy if necessary. It might also be possible to construe the provision for explanation in sub-section 199(3)(b) so as to require an explanation of the format and coding of information held in such a form. It is, however, more dubious that the holder of such data could be forced to recreate a program to process them if it had disappeared.

Quite apart from these general provisions, specific powers authorise magistrates to issue warrants in intellectual property cases. Section 21 of the Copyright Act 1956 created certain criminal offences in relation to copyright, and the provisions of section 21 were amplified and extended by the Copyright (Amendment) Act 1983 and the Copyright (Computer Software) Amendment Act 1985. The former amplified the power to issue search warrants in the case of films and sound recordings, while the latter extended the amplified powers to infringing copies of computer programs whether they consist of 'a disc, tape or chip or of any other device which embodies signals serving for the importation of the program or part of it'.[39] This legislation, which has now been incorporated into the Copyright, Designs and Patents Act 1988, apes the *Anton Piller* procedure in permitting the authorisation of other persons to accompany the constable executing the warrant,[40] but the wording does not seem apt to permit such person to participate in the conduct of the search, nor does it seem that it may be *his* reasonable belief that any material is evidence of the commission of an offence under the Act which justifies its seizure, though there is no reason to suppose that his view might not be influential in assisting the constable to form such a view as is required by the legislation.[41]

It is interesting to note that in the United States, where no similar civil jurisdiction to the *Anton Piller* tactic has developed, there have been cases where much the same effect has been achieved by the use of search warrants. Thus in *Farro Precision Inc.* v. *International Business Machines Corp.*[42] the defendants were able to provide the police with sufficient information to justify the serving of a search warrant pursuant to Californian trade secret legislation, and their employees were permitted to accompany the police when the warrant was executed, so as to help identify any incriminating material.

---

38. Sect. 199(9).
39. Copyright (Computer Software) Amendment Act 1985 sect. 3.
40. Copyright, Designs and Patents Act 1988 sect. 109(3)(a).
41. *Ibid.* sect. 109(4).
42. 673 F.2d 1045 (9th Cir., 1982).

4. Simulations

Thus far attention has been concentrated on securing access to evidence the creation of which has antedated the matters in dispute, though as noted it might sometimes be necessary to perform a further machine operation to secure adequate access to it. This section will instead concentrate upon those situations where the operation of the computer postdates the occurrence of the matters in dispute, but may nevertheless provide evidence material to its resolution. Perhaps the most common situations are those where a device incorporating a computer is used to measure or to calculate, as in modern breath-testing,[43] or assaying[44] devices.

More sophisticated and problematic situations may be envisaged. Suppose in a discrimination dispute a complainant wishes to analyse the defendant's personnel records held on a computer database to determine the distribution of employees of the relevant category in different jobs and grades, or to compare it with the distribution of the category in the local population.[45] The most directly applicable rule appears to be Order 29 rule 3(1):

Where it considers it necessary or expedient for the purpose of obtaining full information or evidence in any cause or matter, the Court may, on the application of a party to the cause or matter, and on such terms, if any, as it thinks just, by order authorise or require any sample to be taken of any property which is the subject matter of the cause or matter or as to which any question may arise therein, any observation to be made on such property or any experiment to be tried on or with such property.[46]

This seems on its face to give the court adequate power, at least where the information is in the possession of a party. It is, however, likely that the court would also regard such a course as being within its own inherent authority.[47] It is nevertheless possible that the court might take a restrictive view of the applicability of the rule to computer programs since its predecessor had been held[48] to apply only to physical things, and not to processes, though in that case Scrutton L.J. was clearly influenced by his view of the application as being of a 'fishing' character and, even if executed, of dubious relevance to the issues to be tried.

An interesting example of the use of the computer to prepare evidence especially for a criminal trial occurred in 1975[49] when the court had to determine the authenticity of a confession which the accused denied had been made by him. The accused was permitted to tender a special computer

---

43. Such as in *Castle* v. *Cross* [1985] 1 All E.R. 87, Q.B.D. above p. 377.
44. Such as in *R.* v. *Wood* (1983) 76 Cr. App. R. 110, C.A., above p. 376.
45. Cp. *Adams* v. *Dan River Mills* 40 F.R.D. 220 (W.D. Va., 1972).
46. In patent cases Order 104 rule 10 would also be available.
47. In *Lewis* v. *Earl of Londesborough* [1893] 2 Q.B. 191, Q.B.D., the court exercised the predecessor of this rule to authorise the photography of a document in the possession of a party, but intimated that even apart from any such rule the court could have acted under its inherent powers.
48. In *Tudor Accumulator Co.* v. *China Mutual Steam Navigation Ltd.* [1930] W.N. 200, C.A. In *Unilever P.L.C.* v. *Pearce* [1985] F.S.R. 475, Pat., Falconer J. refused to hold that the change in wording between the old and the new rules had rendered the *Tudor* case impotent, and preferred to leave such a decision to the Court of Appeal.
49. Described in Niblett and Boreham, 'Cluster Analysis in Court' [1976] Crim. L.R. 175.

analysis of the disputed document for comparison with a similar analysis of another of undisputed authorship. The technique was new and unfamiliar to the court, and to support its reliability the defence was permitted to exhibit the results of the application of the same tests to two other pairs of documents.[50]

The use of computer simulation techniques has been further developed in the United States than here, and there the relevant procedural rule[51] has been specifically adapted to cater for computer technology, and now applies, *inter alia*, to,

any designated documents (including . . . data compilations from which information can be obtained, translated, if necessary, by the respondent through detection devices into reasonably usable form).[52]

The purpose of this 1970 amendment was explained in the official notes as follows:

The inclusive description of 'documents' is revised to accord with changing techno-logy . . .. In many instances, this means that respondent will have to supply a print-out of computer data . . . the courts have ample power under Rule 26(c) to protect respondent against undue burden or expense, either by restricting discovery or requiring that the discovering party pay costs. Similarly, if the discovering party needs to check the electronic source itself, the court may protect respondent with respect to preservation of his records, confidentiality of non-discoverable matters, and costs.

These rules have permitted the American courts to require the supply of full details of a computer simulation program and of the data used to make an econometric model of the market for beer in Texas,[53] and input data for a payroll system.[54]

Experiments and simulations of this sort may be very complicated and difficult for the court to cope with unless they are properly tested. For this reason, notice of intention to rely upon simulation evidence must in the United States always be given to the opposing party, so as to enable him to mount a challenge to the eventual admissibility of the results of the experiment. For similar reasons in one case where a sophisticated simulation of a motor car accident was contemplated, the court required the technique to be one as to which there is wide acceptance among experts, and opined that:

Our concern is not with the precision of electronic calculations, but with the accuracy and completeness of the initial data and equations which are used as ingredients of the computer program.[55]

---

50. Showing that the two confessions were more alike than the novels of Damon Runyon and the Book of Common Prayer, but less alike than the sonnets of Shakespeare and Wordsworth!
51. Itself originally based on a predecessor of Order 29.
52. Federal Rules of Civil Procedure, Rule 34(a).
53. *Pearl Brewing Co.* v. *Jos. Schlitz Brewing Co.* 415 F. Supp. 1122 (S.D. Tex., 1976); but not details of discarded programs upon which it was not proposed to rely.
54. *Adams* v. *Dan River Mills* 40 F.R.D. 220 (W.D. Va., 1972).
55. *Schaeffer* v. *General Motors Inc.* 368 N.E.2d 1062 (Mass., 1976).

So too in *Renfro Hosiery Mills Co.* v. *National Cash Register Co.*[56] an attempt to adduce test results in evidence failed because it had not been demonstrated that the test, in laboratory conditions, really simulated the situation which the component in question had encountered in practical operation.

Difficult questions may arise in relation to the application of discovery rules to simulations, to some extent spilling over into the field of evidence at trial.[57] Thus in *Perma Research & Development Co.* v. *Singer*[58] the court permitted evidence to be adduced despite refusal to divulge the computer programs used to model the braking performance of a car as being the work product of the relevant expert. But in a powerful dissent, Van Graafeiland Cir. J. said,

a court should not permit a witness to state the results of a computer's operations without having the program available for the scrutiny of opposing counsel and his use in cross-examination.

That view was accepted in *Pearl Brewing Co.* v. *Jos. Schlitz Brewing Co.*[59] where the court decided that not only were the respondents bound to provide programs in the shape of listings, but that they were also bound to supply all the documentation necessary to explain them, and even to depose as witnesses the employees who had been hired to do the programming.[60]

5. Evidence from other jurisdictions

Because so much business is now international in character, and with overseas travel having become so common, it may often be necessary to secure access to evidence which is held in a computer situated abroad. In many cases it will be possible to supply such evidence to an English court in the form of a print-out, or by some other secondary means.[61] However, occasionally it will be necessary to consider whether some more compulsory process is available at the pre-trial stage. The most common procedure for doing so appears to be that provided by Order 39. It has been recently extended so as to apply explicitly to the production of documents as well as to the deposition of testimony.[62] A letter of request may be issued by the court in its discretion to the judicial authorities of the relevant jurisdiction providing for the evidence to be taken before a special examiner, or by some other appropriate process.[63] It should be stressed that this procedure largely operates upon a discretionary basis and that the court is likely to lean against the taking of evidence overseas, and is unlikely to order it without

---

56. 552 F.2d 1061 (4th Cir., 1977).
57. See Aldous, 'Disclosure of Expert Computer Simulations' *8 Comp. L. J.* 51 (1987).
58. 542 F.2d 111 (2nd Cir., 1976).
59. 415 F. Supp. 1122 (S.D. Tex., 1976).
60. It was not regarded as sufficient to tender the system designer when he was remote from the day-to-day programming.
61. Perhaps by an affidavit.
62. Rule 2(2) as amended by R.S.C. (Amendment) 1984 (S.I. 1984 No. 1051).
63. Details vary according to whether the foreign state within which the jurisdiction is situated is, or is not, a party to the Hague Convention on the Taking of Evidence Abroad in Civil and Commercial Matters (1970) which came into force in the United Kingdom in 1976. Bilateral conventions exist with a number of other states.

being satisfied that there is no reasonable alternative. If the cause of action is one for discovery it seems that the court will be most reluctant to order production of documents from a foreign jurisdiction,[64] though it might so do in the most extreme circumstances of crime and fraud to prevent the fruits of the crime being spirited away.[65]

A further possibility which may be noted here is that since each party is, in principle, responsible for obtaining its own evidence, it may seek to institute proceedings in a foreign jurisdiction which allows it to do so, for the purpose of securing evidence, including evidence derived from foreign computers, which is relevant and which it wishes to use in English proceedings.[66] This may be particularly useful if the foreign rules of discovery are wider than those in England.[67] Such an application might be refused by the courts of a foreign jurisdiction if it felt that its invocation was intended only to subvert the procedural rules of the other jurisdiction, and so to encroach upon its sovereignty.[68] That is, however, a matter for the foreign court, and not one for the English courts to determine, and they will not necessarily enjoin a party from instituting or prosecuting any such proceedings in a foreign tribunal for this reason.[69] It now seems that such an injunction can be obtained only if the foreign proceedings can be regarded as a real attempt to oust the jurisdiction of the English courts, or to overturn its important public policies.[70]

The rules in criminal proceedings which relied exclusively on letters of request were criticised as inadequate by the Roskill Committee,[71] and have now been simplified by the passage of section 27 of the Criminal Justice Act 1988. This section envisages *ex parte* application for a letter of request to a court or tribunal or other appropriate authority in the foreign jurisdiction concerned, and applies whether proceedings have been instituted or are to be instituted. Any such application must be supported by an affidavit from the Director of Public Prosecutions or like officer in the case of an application by the prosecution; or by the accused in the case of an application by the defence.

---

64. *MacKinnon* v. *Donaldson, Lufkin & Jenrette Securities Corp.* [1986] 1 All E.R. 653, Ch.
65. See *London and Counties Securities* v. *Caplan* (26 May 1978, unreported), Ch.
66. Though the converse situation will rarely arise openly in an English court since in English procedure documents obtained on discovery may not be used for the purposes of other proceedings, and a court would give short shrift to any litigant proclaiming any such purpose, see *Riddick* v. *Thames Board Mills Ltd.* [1977] Q.B. 881, C.A.; *Home Office* v. *Harman* [1983] A.C. 280, H.L.; and the leave of the court is required even in the very extraordinary situations in which this might be permitted, *Sybron Corp.* v. *Barclays Bank P.L.C.* [1985] Ch. 299, C.A.
67. As, for example, in the United States where sect. 1782 of the Federal Rules of Civil Procedure expressly permits evidence and documents to be secured for use in foreign proceedings from those not party to such proceedings.
68. See, for example, *John Deere Ltd. and Deere & Co.* v. *Sperry Corporation* 754 F.2d 132 at 135 (3rd Cir., 1985).
69. *South Carolina Insurance Co.* v. *Assurantie Maatschappij 'De Zeven Provincien' N.V.* [1986] 3 All E.R. 487, H.L.
70. This represents a change from the views expressed by Lord Scarman in *Castanho* v. *Brown & Root (U.K.) Ltd* [1981] A.C. 557, H.L. which were doubted by Lord Goff in *South Carolina Insurance* for the reasons first enunciated by him in *Bank of Tokyo Ltd.* v. *Karoon* [1986] 3 All E.R. 468, C.A. (decided in 1984).
71. Para. 5.20.

6. Evidence for other jurisdictions

The converse situation occurs where evidence from a computer situated in England is required for proceedings in some other jurisdiction. The law in this area was thoroughly revised by the Evidence (Proceedings in Other Jurisdictions) Act 1975. This Act governs the situation in relation to both civil and criminal proceedings. It allows for the satisfaction of a foreign request by making provision:[72]

a) for the examination of witnesses, either orally or in writing;
b) for the production of documents;
c) for the inspection, photographing, preservation, custody or detention of any property;
d) for the taking of samples of any property and the carrying out of any experiments on or with any property

What it does not permit is a general 'fishing' inquiry to force a party to state the documents held by him, or to produce any but specified documents.[73] Nor does it permit any process which would not be allowed under ordinary English rules,[74] and this provision was inserted into the legislation just so as to preserve the sharp distinction in English law between pre-trial and trial procedure. The court must be satisfied that the evidence is required for the purpose of proceedings already started or imminently pending in the foreign court. These rules extend with minor variations of detail to evidence which is required for foreign criminal proceedings. Any request under these provisions will be defeated by a valid claim to privilege under the law either of the United Kingdom or of the requesting jurisdiction.[75] This would include evidence barred under considerations of public policy according to the ordinary English rules, and in addition any evidence the furnishing of which 'would be prejudicial to the security of the United Kingdom'.[76] These restrictions have been further fortified by the Protection of Trading Interests Act 1980 which provides first in the case where a request is made under some relevant foreign power that the Secretary of State can prohibit compliance if in his opinion:

(a) . . . it infringes the jurisdiction of the United Kingdom or is otherwise prejudicial to the sovereignty of the United Kingdom; or
(b) if compliance with the requirement would be prejudicial to the security of the United Kingdom or to the relations of the United Kingdom with the government of any other country.[77]

Similarly if the application is made under the Evidence (Proceedings in Other Jurisdictions) Act 1975 then the position is governed by section 4 of the Protection of Trading Interests Act to the effect that:

A court in the United Kingdom shall not make an order under section 2 of the Evidence (Proceedings in Other Jurisdictions) Act 1975 for giving effect to a request

---

72. Sub-sect. 2(2).
73. Sub-sect. 2(4).
74. Sub-sect. 2(3).
75. Sub-sect. 3(1); and see *Re Westinghouse Uranium Contract* [1978] A.C. 547, H.L.
76. Sub-sect. 3(1).
77. Sub-sect. 2(2).

issued by or on behalf of a court or tribunal of an overseas country if it is shown that the request infringes the jurisdiction of the United Kingdom or is otherwise prejudicial to the sovereignty of the United Kingdom; and a certificate signed by or on behalf of the Secretary of State to the effect that it infringes that jurisdiction or is so prejudicial shall be conclusive evidence of that fact.

The inability to challenge a certificate under the latter provision removes much significance from the differences in the wording of the relevant conditions in the two Acts. It should also be noted that the 1980 Act goes further than the 1975 Act in extending the ban on commercial documents to any case where proceedings are merely imminent. It requires them already to have been instituted.[78]

The Act clearly contemplates its application to evidence derived from computers by defining 'document' to include 'any record or device by means of which material is recorded or stored'.[79] If evidence is requested in any particular form then the request may be acceded to so long as it is not repugnant to English procedure. Thus in *J. Barber & Sons* v. *Lloyd's Underwriters*[80] it was held that evidence could be required to be video-taped. On the same basis it seems clear that it could be required in a computer-readable form, if that were desired, subject always to reimbursement of any extra expense which might be occasioned.

B. Trial

Evidence at a trial may be testimonial, documentary or real. Thus evidence derived from a computer can be presented to the court by the testimony of its operator, by the production of a print-out, or by the spectacle of its operation. Each of these presents somewhat different procedural problems so far as the presentation of the evidence to the court is concerned. Short sections will consider the application to evidence derived from computers of the rules relating to a view which regulate the computer's operation as a species of real evidence; to foundation testimony which is required for the admission of documentary evidence in the shape of a print-out; and subpoenas which may be used to secure the attendance of a witness to testify and to bring documents with him. Once the evidence has been got before the court it is necessary to consider its weight, and this is likely to be influenced by the possibility of cross-examination.

1. Views

Small moveable objects can be presented to the court as exhibits, but some are too large or too immobile to be brought into the courtroom, and accordingly Order 35 rule 8 confers power upon the judge to inspect any such thing outside the courtroom:

(1) The judge by whom any cause or matter is tried may inspect any place or thing with respect to which any question arises in the cause or matter.

---

78. Sub-sect. 2(3)(a).
79. Sub-sect. 2(6).
80. [1986] 2 All E.R. 845, Q.B.

(2) Where a cause or matter is tried with a jury and the judge inspects any place or thing under paragraph (1) he may authorise the jury to inspect it also.

While it may sometimes be sufficient to inspect a static object, it is more likely in the case of a computer for it to be helpful to see the machine in operation. There is no intrinsic objection to this,[81] but care must be taken to ensure that the evidence so gleaned is really relevant. For example, if the appearance of a display is in dispute, say in a copyright dispute,[82] the operation of the relevant program must be shown to be the same at the time of the view as at the time of the alleged infringement. There seems to have been no reported English case involving a view of the operation of a computer, but it does not seem to differ in principle from playing a record on a gramophone or showing a film through a projector.[83] Although it is necessary for both parties to have an opportunity to attend the view, this has not prevented views from taking place out of the jurisdiction.[84]

The Roskill Committee was very concerned about the difficulties experienced by juries in assimilating complicated information in the form in which it has traditionally been presented to them. It considered a number of ways in which this could be improved, including the use of computer terminals.[85] The Criminal Justice Act 1988 accordingly provides in section 31 for evidence to be furnished to the court in any form for the purpose of helping juries to understand, *inter alia*, complicated issues of fact. The wording has been deliberately drafted in a form sufficiently wide to permit the possibility of using such terminals to display information in a more graphic form. It is interesting to note that even before the passage of this legislation some courts were already using computer terminals to assist with the presentation of evidence.[86]

2. Foundation testimony

The previous chapter has already shown how relaxed a view English common law takes of the necessary foundation required for the admissibility of evidence derived from computers. This relaxation has been echoed in recent statutory provision. In civil proceedings, computer output is made admissible by section 5 of the Civil Evidence Act 1968,[87] while section 8 provides for relevant rules of court to be made to achieve this purpose. The scheme of the Act is such that a party proposing to tender such evidence must notify his opponent of his intention to tender the evidence,[88] in order to give him an opportunity to serve a counter-notice[89] to require the attendance

---

81. *Buckingham* v. *Daily News Ltd.* [1956] 2 Q.B. 534, C.A.
82. Cp. *Whelan* v. *Jaslow* 797 F.2d 1222 (3rd Cir., 1986).
83. As in *R.* v. *Quinn and Bloom* [1962] 2 Q.B. 245, C.A. where only the relevancy issue prevented the film from being shown.
84. As in *Tito* v. *Waddell* [1975] 3 All E.R. 997, Ch.
85. Report of Fraud Trials Committee (1986) para. 9.24.
86. The civil courts in part of the litigation involving the International Tin Council, and the criminal courts in some of the litigation resulting from the Brinks Matt bullion robbery.
87. See pp. 395 to 398 above.
88. Order 38 rule 21.
89. Under Order 38 rule 26.

of the maker of the statement.[90] A party proposing to tender a statement derived from a computer must certify that the conditions imposed by section 5 have been satisfied,[91] and his initial notice must contain particulars of:

(a) a person who occupied a responsible position in relation to the management of the relevant activities for the purposes of which the computer was used regularly during the material period to store or process information;
(b) a person who at the material time occupied such a position in relation to the supply of information to the computer, being information which is reproduced in the statement or information from which the information contained in the statement is derived;
(c) a person who occupied such a position in relation to the operation of the computer during the material period;
and where there are two or more persons who fall within any of the foregoing subparagraphs and some only of those persons are at the date of service of the notice capable of being called as witnesses at the trial or hearing, the person particulars of whom are to be contained in the notice must be such one of those persons as is at that date so capable.
(2) The notice must also state whether the computer was operating properly throughout the material period and, if not, whether any respect in which it was not operating properly or was out of operation during any part of that period was such as to affect the production of the document in which the statement is contained or the accuracy of its contents.[92]

This rather elaborate procedure of notice and counter-notice was thought inappropriate for criminal proceedings, but provision is made by the Police and Criminal Evidence Act 1984 in Schedule 3 Part II paragraph 8 for a certificate to be tendered together with the statement adduced pursuant to section 69:

(a) identifying the document containing the statement and describing the manner in which it was produced;
(b) giving such particulars of any device involved in the production of that document as may be appropriate for the purpose of showing that the document was produced by a computer;
(c) dealing with any of the matters mentioned in subsection (1) of section 69 above; and
(d) purporting to be signed by a person occupying a responsible position in relation to the operation of the computer.[93]

Here it is the court which is given the power to require oral evidence to be given of any matters capable of being included in such a certificate,[94] but it is just as much a criminal offence to tender a certificate known to be false or not believed to be true.[95] It is further provided that a document made admissible under these provisions may be proved:

---

90. Unless the initial notice has contained a statement specifying one of the reasons set out in Order 38 rule 25 for not calling such person, Order 38 rule 24(3).
91. Sub-sect. 5(4). It is a criminal offence to make a false statement, or one not believed to be true, in such a certificate, sub-sect. 6(5).
92. Order 38 rule 24.
93. See pp. 402 to 403 above.
94. Sched. 3 Part II para. 9.
95. Para. 10.

(a) by the production of that document; or

(b) (whether or not that document is still in existence) by the production of a copy of that document, or of the material part of it, authenticated in such manner as the court may approve.[96]

It will be noted that the court is here given a general discretion as to the means of authentication. The Act also bestows general rule-making powers,[97] which appear not yet to have been exercised. The new Criminal Justice Act 1988 has in section 27 adopted the words quoted above.

3. Subpoena duces tecum

It will be noted that discovery is a procedure designed for securing access to material held by a party to civil proceedings. If relevant material exists in the hands, or computer, of a third party, the appropriate procedure would be to serve its holder or owner with a *subpoena duces tecum* requiring him to attend to testify, and to produce the document or print-out to the court. It has been held[98] that since the procedure is normally initiated at a lower level than is discovery, and because in the case of tape recordings or other 'modern inventions which require special equipment to make them speak or be seen', this procedure should not apply to documents held only in such less conventional forms. Nonetheless a similar spirit of improvisation is to apply:

These new inventions are capable of providing the most valuable evidence and the court should have the means of making them available. We are the masters of our own procedure and have authority to adapt it to meet the needs of the time. In my opinion the High Court has an inherent jurisdiction to make orders for the production and showing of cinematograph film ... A witness may be required to provide not only tape recordings and films, but also the apparatus that is required to operate it.... The application should be made by notice to the witness so that he can raise any point that he desires. On such an application the judge should have discretion to make such order as he thinks fit. He can order the witness to produce the tape recording or the film, and also the necessary apparatus, and order it to be played over or shown at such place as may be most convenient. And, of course, all expenses must be paid. But the judge may refuse to make an order if he thinks it would be oppressive or unreasonable or otherwise not proper to be ordered.

The provision for notice, in effect, gives the witness the same protection as is enjoyed by a party through the formal mechanics of the process of discovery. The flexibility of possible response is also noteworthy in allowing the court either to order the production of a print-out, or the generation of a visual display on a screen on the witness's premises, or presumably it might even be convenient to install a terminal in the courtroom connected by ordinary communication facilities to the relevant computer.[99] It should be noted that these processes are available in criminal as well as in civil proceedings.

---

96. Para. 11.
97. Sub-sect. 69(2) and Sched. 3 Part III para. 15.
98. In *Senior* v. *Holdsworth* [1976] Q.B. 23, CA.
99. Such facilities are likely to be more widely available in courtrooms now that the provisions of sect. 32 of the Criminal Justice Act 1988 have been brought into force.

4. Cross-examination

Because computers represent a new, sophisticated and somewhat arcane technology, courts will understandably, and rightly, be reluctant to accept evidence from them without permitting adequate opportunity for it to be challenged. Since, as noted in the previous chapter, the admissibility of such evidence is widely permitted in derogation of the hearsay rule, the question arises of how far cross-examination can be used to mount such a challenge. The general scheme of the Civil Evidence Act 1968 is to rely upon a special notice procedure to secure, if possible and practicable, the attendance before the court of the appropriate witnesses when required. The notice procedure in relation to section 5, which explicitly deals with statements contained in documents produced by computers, provides an opportunity for the opponent of such evidence to secure the attendance of persons occupying responsible positions in relation to the management of the computer. Such a person can then be cross-examined in the usual way. However, as section 5 makes no requirement of personal knowledge in any supplier of information contained in the statement, there is no provision for securing the attendance of such a supplier in relation to a statement admitted under section 5. If, however, such a statement is tendered not as statement from a computer pursuant to section 5, but as first-hand hearsay pursuant to section 2 or as a statement made under a duty pursuant to section 4, then the attendance of the supplier can be required by notice for cross-examination.[100]

An additional safeguard is furnished by section 7 of the Civil Evidence Act 1968 in any case when the relevant person is unable to attend for whatever reason by providing for the admissibility of 'any evidence which, if that person had been so called, would be admissible for the purpose of destroying or supporting his credibility', though subject to the proviso that no evidence could be given under that section which could not have been used to rebut a denial to a suggestion made in cross-examination.

In criminal proceedings the Police and Criminal Evidence Act 1984 Schedule 3 Part II paragraph 9 enables the court to require oral evidence of any matter as to which a certificate might be adduced in evidence as noted above.[101] This too would have the effect of bringing the relevant manager before the court for cross-examination. It may be recalled that the principal advance in the drafting of the provisions applicable to criminal proceedings is that, in any case involving the use of evidence derived from computers in derogation of the rule against hearsay, the ordinary requirement of personal knowledge of the truth of the matters there stated has also to be satisfied. In that respect, Schedule 3 Part I paragraph 3 provides that:

Where in any proceedings a statement based on information supplied by any person is given in evidence by virtue of section 68. . .–
(a) any evidence which, if that person had been called as a witness, would have been admissible as relevant to his credibility as a witness shall be admissible for the purpose in those proceedings;
(b) evidence may, with the leave of the court, be given of any matter which, if that

---

100. Order 38 rules 22(1)(b) and 23(1)(a)(ii) in conjunction with rule 26.
101. The requirements imposed by sect. 69, see p. 402 above.

person had been called as a witness, could have been put to him in cross-examination as relevant to his credibility as a witness but of which evidence could not have been adduced by the cross-examining party;

These same provisions have now reappeared as sub-paragraphs 1(a) and (b) of Schedule 2 to the Criminal Justice Act 1988.

5. Weight of evidence

It is particularly important in the context of evidence derived from computers to distinguish between the question of the admissibility of such evidence and of its weight, once admitted. Admissibility is a matter for the judge as arbiter of law, but weight is for the jury in criminal proceedings, or in civil almost invariably for the judge as trier of fact. While the weight of any evidence must ultimately be a complex matter of subjective judgment involving assessment of such factors as the credibility of witnesses, the legitimacy of inferences and the materiality of what is so established to the issues in dispute, it has nevertheless become fashionable to provide statutory guidelines to assist in the making of such judgments. In the case of a trial by judge alone, such guidelines do little more than operate as an *aide-mémoire*, but in the case of trial by jury they may dictate the form of summing up by the judge.

In the Civil Evidence Act 1968, sub-section 6(3) which sets out such guidelines in the case of evidence admitted pursuant to the Act concentrates upon the contemporaneity of the statement with the others to which it relates, and to the existence of any motive to conceal or to misrepresent. In relation to first-hand hearsay admitted pursuant to section 2, the relevant motive is that of the maker of the reported statement; in the case of records admitted pursuant to section 4, it is the motive either of the maker of the statement or of the compiler or keeper of the record; in the case of evidence derived from a computer, the Act provides for attention,

(c) in the case of a statement falling under section 5(1) of this Act, to the question whether or not the information which the information contained in the statement reproduces or is derived from was supplied to the relevant computer, or recorded for the purpose of being supplied thereto, contemporaneously with the occurrence or existence of the facts dealt with in that information, and to the question whether or not any person concerned with the supply of information to that computer, or with the operation of that computer or any equipment by means of which the document containing the statement was produced by it, had any motive to conceal or misrepresent the facts.

It is sensible to distinguish in the first part of this provision between 'supply' and 'recording for the purpose of supply' since it is clear that once recorded in a permanent form the mere passage of time before processing is not sufficiently material to justify being singled out in any special way. The more interesting point is that no explicit mention is made of the motives of the originator of the information contained in the statement. It might be argued that such a person comes within the reference to 'any person concerned with the supply of that information', but this phrase seems better construed to be limited to those wittingly participating in the involvement of the computer.

It should be noted that consistently with this view sub-section 6(4) which provides, it is submitted unnecessarily,[102] that a statement admitted as hearsay under the Act cannot corroborate its maker, does not contain any provision similarly preventing a statement contained in a document produced by a computer from corroborating the evidence of the originator of such information. It is ironic that this omission is harmless in relation to evidence admitted under section 5 only upon the supposition advanced above that the rest of the provision relating to sections 2 and 4 is redundant.

As noted above,[103] the special merit of the organisation of the provisions of the Police and Criminal Evidence Act 1984 is that in the case of evidence derived from a computer which is admitted in derogation of the hearsay rule it is necessary to satisfy the provisions both of section 68 and of section 69. The general provisions as to weight appear in Schedule 3 Part 1 paragraph 7 in relation to section 68, and in Part II paragraph 11 in relation to section 69. They are closely modelled upon the provisions of the Civil Evidence Act 1968 and cover the same ground of contemporaneity and motive to conceal or to misrepresent. The terminology of the 'supply' of information is repeated, and paragraph 12 elaborates its meaning in providing[104] that,

... information shall be taken to be supplied to a computer whether it is supplied directly or (with or without human intervention) by means of any appropriate equipment.

This seems to offer some support for the contention advanced above that the scope of the notion of 'supply' is limited to witting supply since here the notion of an indirect supply is given so limited an ambit.

The Criminal Justice Act 1988 is less expansive in its guidelines as to the weight of the hearsay admitted under it, and provides only in Schedule 2 that:

In estimating the weight, if any, to be attached to such a statement regard shall be had to all the circumstances from which any inference can reasonably be drawn as to its accuracy or otherwise.[105]

There is also provision[106] for the supplementation of the Act by conferring powers to make Crown Court Rules or rules under section 144 of the Magistrates' Court Act 1980. It will be noted that there is here no reference to contemporaneity or to motives, but rather all is left in the melting pot. Although the guidance is too vague to be positively helpful, its very breadth does at least bring within its potential range considerations relating to the reliability of the originator of the information.[107]

---

102. Because it is a basic condition of corroborative material that it emanate from an independent source.
103. P. 402.
104. Cp. Civil Evidence Act 1968 sub-sect. 5(5)(a).
105. Para. 3.
106. Sched. 2 para. 4.
107. It should be observed that sub-sect. 24(1)(c)(ii) distinguishes sharply between the supplier of information contained in a document and the maker of a statement contained in it.

Selected bibliography

A complete bibliography of this subject would be a work in its own right, or perhaps even a series. The works listed below are biased towards those to which reference is made in the body of the text. Some works which have been well received by knowledgeable judges, but which have not been available to the author, have also been included. The bibliography has been classified primarily by general subject, following the scheme of the division adopted here into three parts, though there is an initial and additional general part. Within each part of the bibliography a division is made between the form of the work listed, whether a bibliography, book, journal or article. Within each sub-division the order roughly corresponds to the order of topics in the book, but sometimes alphabetic listing is adopted to avoid difficulty or inconvenience.

General

Books

Bender, *Computer Law* (periodically updated)
Bernacchi, *On Computer Law* (1986)
Millard, *Legal Protection of Computer Programs and Data* (1985)
Nimmer, *The Law of Computer Technology* (1985)
Scott, *Computer Law* (1984)
Soma, *Computer Techology and the Law* (periodically updated)
Sookman, *Computer Law* (1989)
Van Der Merwe, *Computers and the Law* (1986)

Journals

Applied Computer and Communications (UK)
Computer Law and Practice (UK)
Computer Law and Security Report (UK)
Computer Law Journal (US)

International Computer Law Adviser (US)
Journal of Law and Information Science (Australia)
Jurimetrics Journal (US)
Rutgers Journal of Computer Technology and the Law (US)
Santa Clare Computer and High-Technology Law Journal (US)
The Computer Lawyer (US)

Much invaluable older material, including much otherwise unobtainable, is to be found in Bigelow (ed.), *Computer Law Service* which discontinued publication in 1981. One of its features was a special Reporter Service for cases in this area and, at least to that extent, it has been resurrected in Volume 3 of Bigelow, *Computer Contracts Negotiating and Drafting Aids*

Part 1. Property

Books

Borking, *Third Party Protection of Software and Firmware* (1985)
Brett and Perry (eds.). *The Legal Protection of Computer Software* (1981)
Carr, *Computer Software: Legal Protection in the United Kingdom* (1987)
Gervaise, *Software Protection: Practical and Legal Steps to Protect and Market Computer Programs* (1985)
Hanneman, *The Patentability of Computer Software: An International Guide to the Protection of Computer-Related Inventions* (1985)
Hoffman, *The Software Legal Book* (1986)
Huband and Shelton, *Protection of Computer Systems and Software* (1986)
Lautsch, *American Standard Handbook of Software Business Law* (1985)
Niblett, *Legal Protection of Computer Programs* (1980)
Practising Law Institute, *Computer Software and Chips* (1986)
Stern, *Semiconductor Chip Protection* (1986)

Journals

European Intellectual Property Review (non-specialised but many contributions to the topic)
Software Law Journal

Articles

Gall, 'European Patent Office Guidelines 1985 on the protection of inventions relating to computer programs', *2 C.L. &Prac.* 2 (1985)
Breyer, 'The Uneasy Case for Copyright: A Study of Copyright in Books, Photocopies, and Computer Programs', *84 Harvard L.R.* 281 (1970)
CONTU Final Report (1979)
Goldstein, 'Infringement of Copyright in Computer Programs', *47 U. Pitt. L.R.* 1119 (1986)
Raskind, 'The Uncertain Case for Special Legislation Protecting Computer Software', *47 U. Pitt. L.R.* 1131 (1986)

Samuelson, 'CONTU Revisited: The Case Against Copyright Protection for Computer Programs in Machine-Readable Form', *1984 Duke L.J.* 663

Karjala, 'The First Case on Protection of Operating Systems and Reverse Engineering of Programs in Japan' [1988] *6 E.I.P.R.* 172

Note 'Copyright Protection of Computer Program Object Code' *96 Harv. L.R.* 1723 (1983)

Laurie and Everett, 'The Copyrightability of Microcode: Is it Software or Hardware or Both?' *The Computer Lawyer* March 1985 p. 1

Sandison, 'NEC Corp. v. Intel Corp.' [1987] *1 E.I.P.R.* 25

Sternberg, 'NEC v INTEL: The Battle over Copyright Protection for Microcode' *27 Jur. Jo.* 173 (1987)

Stern, 'Computer Software Protection after the 1984 Copyright Statutory Amendments', *60 A.L.J.* 333 (1986)

Hart, 'Semiconductor topography: Protection in the UK contrasted with the US Semiconductor Chip Protection Act and the EEC Directive on Topographies', *4 C, L. & Prac.* 151 (1988)

Jehoram, 'The European Commission Pressurized into a 'Dis-harmonising Directive on Chip Protection' [1987] *E.I.P.R.* 35

Kastenmeier and Remington, 'The Semiconductor Chip Protection Act of 1984: A Swamp or Firm Ground?' *70 Minn. L.R.* 417 (1985)

Oxman, 'Intellectual Property Protection and Integrated Circuit Masks' *20 Jur. J.* 405 (1980)

Raskind, 'Reverse engineering, unfair competition and fair use under the Semiconductor Chip Protection Act 1984', *70 Minn. L.R.* 385 (1985)

Stern, 'Determining Liability for Infringement of Mask Work Rights Under the Semiconductor Chip Protection Act 1984', *70 Minn. L.R.* 271, at 317–22 (1985)

Law Commission No. 110, *Breach of Confidence*, Cmnd. 8388 (1981)

Bender, 'Protection of Computer Programs: The Copyright/Trade Secret Interface', *47 U. Pitt. L.R.* 907 (1986)

Burns, 'Litigating Computer Trade Secrets in California' *6 Comp. L.J. 485* (1986) Gilburne and Johnstone 'Trade Secret Protection for Software Generally and in the Mass Market' *3 Comp. L.J.* 211 (1982)

Solomon, 'The Copyrightability of Computer Software Containing Trade Secrets', *63 U. Wash. L.Q.* 131 (1985)

Bender, 'Protection of Computer Programs: The Copyright/Trade Secret Interface', *47 U. Pitt. L.R.* 907 (1986)

Bender, 'Trade Secret Protection of Software', *38 Geo. Washington L.R.* 909 (1970)

Burns, 'Litigating Computer Trade Secrets in California', *6 Comp. L.J.* 485 (1986)

Gilburne and Johnstone 'Trade Secret Protection for Software Generally and in the Mass Market', *3 Comp. L.J.* 211 (1982)

McNeil, ' Trade Secret Protection for Mass Market Software', *51 Alb. L.R.* 293 (1987)

Mooers, 'Accommodating Standards and Identification of Programming Languages', *4 C.L.S.* sect. 4–5

Vines, 'Consumer meets Computer: An Argument for Liberal Trademark Protection of Computer Hardware Configurations under Section 43(a) of the Lanham Trademark Act', *44 Wash. & Lee L.R.* 283 (1987)

Frazer, 'Competition law: mapping the minefield', *3 C.L. & Prac.* 199 (1987)

Helein, 'Software Lock-in and Antitrust Tying Arrangements; The Lessons of Data General', *5 Comp. L.J.* 329 (1985)

Lavey, 'Antitrust Issues Critical to Structuring Vertical Channels of Distribution for Computer Businesses', *4 Comp. L.J.* 525 (1984)

Menell, 'Tailoring Legal Protection for Computer Software', *39 Stan. L.R.* 1329 (1987)

Higashima and Ushiku, 'A New Means of International Protection of Computer Programs Through the Paris Convention – A New Concept of Utility Model', *7 Comp. L.J.* 1 (1986)

Samuelson, 'Creating a New Kind of Intellectual Property: Applying the Lessons of the Chip Law to Computer Programs', *70 Minn. L.R.* 471 (1985)

Davidson, 'Protecting Computer Software: A Comprehensive Analysis', *23 Jur. Jo.* 337 (1983)

Galbi, 'Proposal for New Legislation to Protect Computer Programming', *17 Bull. Copyright Soc.* 280 (1970)

Comment, 'Softright: A Legislative Solution to the Problem of Users' and Producers' Rights in Computer Software', *44 Loyola L.R.* 1413 (1984);

Karjala, 'Lessons from the Computer Software Debate in Japan', *1984 Ariz. St. L.J.* 53

Brown, 'Eligibility for Software Protection: A Search for Principled Standards', *70 Minn. L.R.* 579 (1985)

Kidwell, 'Software and Semi-Conductors: Why Are We Confused?', *70 Minn. L.R.* 533 (1985)

Kline, 'Requiring an Election of Protection for Patentable/Copyrightable Computer Programs', *6 Comp. L.J.* 607 (1986)

Stern, 'The Bundle of Rights Suited to New Technology', *47 U. of Pitt. L.R.* 1229 (1986)

Part 2. Liability

Common law

Books

Bigelow, *Computer Contracts Negotiating and Drafting Aids* (Matthew Bender, 1987)

Davidson and Davidson, *Advanced Legal Strategies for Buying and Selling Computers and Software* (John Wiley, 1986)

Edwards, *Understanding Computer Contracts* (Waterlow, 1983)

Gordon, *Computer Software: Contracting for Development and Distribution* (1986)

Morgan and Stedman, *Computer Contracts* (Longman, 2nd edn 1984)

Pearson, *Computer Contracts* (Financial Training Publications, 1984)

Raysman and Brown, *Computer Law: Drafting and Negotiating Forms and Agreements* (1987)

Articles

Douglas, 'Some Ideas on the Computer and the Law', *2 Tex. S.U.L.R.* 20 (1973)

Harris, 'Complex Contract Issues in the Acquisition of Hardware and Software', *4 Comp. L. J.* 77 (1983)

Fakes, 'Mainframe Computer Conversions: Buyer and Seller Beware', *6 Comp. L. J.* 469 (1985)

Hemnes and Montgomery, 'The Bankruptcy Code, The Copyright Act and Transactions in Computer Software', *7 Comp. L. J.* 327 (1987)

Nycum, Kenfield and Keenan, 'Debugging Software Escrow: Will It Work When You Need It', *4 Comp. L. J.* 441 (1984)

Martin and Deasy, 'Licensing of Intellectual Property Rights Needed for Software Support: A Life Cycle Approach', *28 Jur. J.* 223 (1988)

Wheeler, 'Trade Secrets and the Skilled Employee in the Computer Industry', *61 U. Wash.* 823 (1983)

Lickson, 'Protection of the Privacy of Data Communications by Contract', *23 Bus. L.* 971 (1968)

Annotation *37 A.L.R.* 4th 110 (1985)

Burke, 'Third party leasing from a User's Viewpoint' *Datamation* November 1969

Birnbaum, 'Lease Financing for Fledgling Manufacturers of Computer Peripheral Equipment', *29 Business L.* 477 (1974)

Note 'Computer Programs as Goods under the U.C.C.', *77 Mich. L.R.* 1149 (1979)

Note 'Computer Software as a Good under the Uniform Commercial Code; Taking a Byte out of the Intangibility Myth', *65 Boston U.L.R.* 129 (1985)

Rodau, 'Computer Software: Does Article 2 of the Uniform Commercial Code Apply?', *35 Emory L.J.* 853 (1986)

Himelson, 'Frankly Incredible: Unconscionability in Computer Contracts', *4 Comp. L.J.* 695 (1984)

Note 'Unconscionability and the Fundamental Breach Doctrine in Computer Contracts', *57 Notre Dame L.R.* 547 (1982)

Chretien-Dar, 'Uniform Commercial Code – Disclaiming the Express Warranty in Computer Contracts – Taking the Byte out of the Uniform Commercial Code', *40 Ok. L.R.* 471 (1987)

Levin, 'Automation and the Law of Torts', *M.U.L.L.* (June 1964) 35, 36

Conley, 'Tort Theories of Recovery against Vendors of Defective Software', *13 Rutg. L. & C. T. L. J.* 1 (1987)

'Tort Theories in Computer Litigation', *38 Record of the Association of the Bar of the City of New York* 426 (1983)

Fossett, 'The Development of Negligence in Computer Law', *14 Northern Kentucky Law Review* 289 (1987)

Petras and Scarpelli, 'Computers, Medical Malpractice and the Ghost of *The T.J. Hooper*', *5 Rutg. L. & C. T. L. J.* 15 (1975)

Note 'Computers in the Courtroom: Using Computer Diagnosis as Expert Opinion', *5 Comp. L. J.* 217 (1984)

Note 'Easing Plaintiff's Burden of Proving Negligence for Computer Malpractice', *69 Iowa L.R.* 241 (1983)

Nycum, 'Liability for Malfunction of a Computer Program', *7 Rutg. L. & C.T.L.J.* 1, 11, 12 (1979)

Friedman and Siegel, 'From Flour Barrel to Computer System' *14 Rutg. L. & C.T.L.J.* 283 (1988)

Note 'Computer Software and Strict Products Liability', *20 San Diego L.R.* 439 (1983)

Nycum, 'Liability for Malfunction of a Computer Program', *7 Rutg. L. & C.T.L.J.* 1 (1979)

Gemignani, 'Product Liability and Software', *8 Rutg. L. & C.T.L.J.* 173 (1981)

Freed, 'Products Liability in the Computer Age', *17 Jurimetrics J.* 270 (1979)

Note 'Computer Programs as Goods under the U.C.C.', *77 Mich. L.R.* 1149 (1979)

Crime

Books

Bequai, *Technocrimes* (1987)

Everson, *Computer Crime* (1987)

Law Commission, *Computer Misuse* W.P. No. 110 (1988)

Parker, *Crime by Computer* (1976)

Scottish Law Commission, *Report on Computer Crime* S.L.C. No. 106 (1987)

Sieber, *The International Handbook on Computer Crime* (1986)

Articles

Jurkat, 'Computer Crime Legislation: Survey and Analysis', *New York University Annual Survey of American Law* (1986)

Brown, 'Crime and Computers' (1983) *7 Crim. L.Q.* 68

Taber, 'A Survey of Computer Crime Studies' *2 Comp. L.J.* 275 (1980)

Tapper, 'Computer Crime: Scotch Mist?' [1987] *Crim. L.R.* 4

Wasik, 'Surveying Computer Crime', *1 C. L. & Prac.* 110 (1985)

Webber, 'Computer Crime or Jay-walking on the Electronic Highway' *26 Crim L.Q.* 217 (1983, 84)

Doherty, 'Stewart: When is a thief not a thief? When he steals the "Candy" but not the "Wrapper"', *63 C.R. 3d* 322 (1988)

Tettenborn, 'Some Legal Aspects of Computer Abuse', *2 Company Lawyer* 147 (1981)

Tompkins and Mar, 'The 1984 Federal Computer Crime Statute: A Practical Answer to a Pervasive Problem', *6 Comp. L.J.* 459 (1986)

Hammond, 'Electronic Crime in Canadian Courts', *6 O.J.L.S.* 145 (1986)

Smith, 'Some comments on deceiving a machine', *69 Law Soc. Gaz.* 576 (1972)

Krieger, 'Current and Proposed Computer Crime Legislation', *2 Comp. L.J.* 721 (1980)

Fetterley, 'Historical Perspectives on Criminal Laws Relating to the Theft of Trade Secrets', *25 Bus. L.* 1535 (1970)

Letterman, 'Exporting High Technology from the United States under the Revised Distribution Licence Procedures', *7 Comp. L.J.* 289 (1987)

Nycum, 'Criminal Law Aspects of Computer Abuse', Part II, 'Federal Criminal Code', *5 Rutgers J. of Comp. L.* 297 (1976)

Vandevoort, 'Trade Secrets: Protecting a Very Special Property', *26 Bus. L.* 681 (1971)

Weinrib, 'Information as Property', *38 U. Tor. L.J.* 117 (1988)

Dunning, 'Some Aspects of Theft of Computer Software', *4 Auckland U.L.R.* 273 (1982)

Piragoff, 'Bill C-19: Reforming the Criminal Law 11. Computers' *16 Ottawa L.R.* 306 (1984)

Quinn, 'Computer Crime' [1983] *N.Z.L.J.* 270.

Taber, 'On Computer Crime (Senate Bill S240)', *1 Comp. L.J.* 517 (1980)

Wagner, 'The Challenge of Computer-Crime Legislation: How Should New York Respond?', *33 Buff. L.R.* 777 (1984)

Wharton, 'Legislative Issues in Computer Crime', *21 Harvard J. of Leg.* 239 (1984)

Privacy

Bibliographies

Flaherty, Hanis and Mitchell, *Privacy and Access to Government Data for Research* (1979)

Smith, *Compilation of State and Federal Privacy Laws* (1988)

Books

Goldstein, *The Cost of Privacy* (1975)

Gulleford, *Data Protection in Practice* (1986)

Lindop Committee, *Report on Data Protection*, Cmnd. 7341 (1978) (United Kingdom)

Miller, *The Assault on Privacy* (1971)

Sieghart, *Privacy and Computers* (1977)

Tapper, *Computers and the Law* (1973) ch. 2

Wacks, *The Protection of Privacy* (1980) ch. 4

Westin, *Data Banks In a Free Society* (1972)

Younger Committee, *Report on Privacy*, Cmnd. 5012 (1972) (United Kingdom)

Journals

Privacy Journal

Articles

Gavison, 'Privacy and the Limits of Law', *89 Yale L.J.* 421 (1980)

Posner, 'The Right of Privacy', *12 Ga. L.R.* 393 (1978)

Posner, 'Privacy, Security and Reputation', *28 Buff. L.R.* 1 (1979)

Simitis 'Privacy and an Information Society' 135 U. Pa. L.R. 707 (1987)

Wacks, 'The Poverty of Privacy', *96 L.Q.R.* 73 (1980)

Gross, 'The Concept of Privacy', *42 N.Y.U.L.R.* 34 (1967)

Rehnquist, 'Is an Expanded Right to Privacy Consistent with Fair and Effective Law Enforcement? Or Privacy You've Come a Long Way Baby', *23 Kansas L.R.* 1 (1974)

Zimmerman, 'Requiem for a Heavyweight: A Farewell to Warren and Brandeis's Privacy Tort', *68 Corn. L.Q.* 291 (1982)

Burnside, 'The Electronic Communications Privacy Act 1986: The Challenge of Applying Ambiguous Statutory Language to Interstate Telecommunications Technologies', *13 Rutg. L. & C.T.L.J.* 451 (1987)

McNamara, 'The Fair Credit Reporting Act: A Legislative Overview', *22 J. Pub. L.* 67 (1973)

Bloustein, 'Privacy as an Aspect of Human Dignity', *39 N.Y.U.L.R.* 962 (1964)

Prosser, 'Privacy', *48 Cal. L.R.* 383 (1960)

Warren and Brandeis, 'The Right to Privacy', *4 Harv. L.R.* 193 (1890)

Part 3. Procedure

Books

Bender, *Computer Law* (regularly updated) chs. 5–10

Articles

Ann., 'Admissibility of Computerized Private Business Records', *7 A.L.R.* 4th 8 (1981)

Bender, 'Computer Evidence Law: Scope and Structure', *1 Comp. L.J.* 699 (1979)

Brown, 'Computer-Produced Evidence in Australia *8 Univ. of Tas. L.R.* 46 (1984)

Laughlin 'Business Entries and the Like', *46 Iowa L.R.* 276 (1961)

McNiff, 'Computer Documentation as Evidence', *1 J.L.I.S.* 45 (1981)

Peritz, 'Computer Data and Reliability: A Call for Authentication of Business Records under the Federal Rules of Evidence', *80 N.S.W.U.L.R.* 956 (1986)

Roberts, 'Practitioners' Primer on Computer-Generated Evidence', *41 Un. of Chi. L.R.* 254 (1974)

Smith, 'The Admissibility of Statements by Computer', [1981] *Crim. L.R.* 387

Aldous, 'Disclosure of Expert Computer Simulations', *8 Comp. L.J.* 51 (1987)

Fromholz, 'Discovery, Evidence, Confidentiality and Security Problems Associated with the Use of Computer-Based Litigation Support Systems', (1977) *Wash. U.L.Q.* 445

Index of Names

Index of Concepts